THE LAW OF INTERNATIONAL
HUMAN RIGHTS PROTECTION

The Law of International Human Rights Protection

WALTER KÄLIN

Professor of Constitutional and International Law, Faculty of Law,
University of Bern and former Dean of the Faculty and
Head of Legal Department

JÖRG KÜNZLI

Associate Professor of Public International and
Constitutional Law, Faculty of Law, University of Bern

OXFORD
UNIVERSITY PRESS

OXFORD
UNIVERSITY PRESS

Great Clarendon Street, Oxford OX2 6DP

Oxford University Press is a department of the University of Oxford.
It furthers the University's objective of excellence in research, scholarship,
and education by publishing worldwide in

Oxford New York

Auckland Cape Town Dar es Salaam Hong Kong Karachi
Kuala Lumpur Madrid Melbourne Mexico City Nairobi
New Delhi Shanghai Taipei Toronto

With offices in

Argentina Austria Brazil Chile Czech Republic France Greece
Guatemala Hungary Italy Japan Poland Portugal Singapore
South Korea Switzerland Thailand Turkey Ukraine Vietnam

Oxford is a registered trade mark of Oxford University Press
in the UK and in certain other countries

Published in the United States
by Oxford University Press Inc., New York

© Walter Kälin and Jörg Künzli 2009

The moral rights of the authors have been asserted

Crown copyright material is reproduced under Class Licence
Number C01P0000148 with the permission of OPSI
and the Queen's Printer for Scotland

Database right Oxford University Press (maker)

First published 2009

British Library Cataloguing in Publication Data

Data available

Library of Congress Cataloging-in-Publication Data

Kälin, Walter.
The law of international human rights protection / Walter Kälin, Jörg
Künzli.
    p. cm.
Includes bibliographical references and index.
ISBN 978–0–19–956520–7 (alk. paper)
1. Human rights. I. Künzli, Jörg. II. Title.
K3240.K35 2009
341.4'8—dc22   2009020964

Typeset by Newgen Imaging Systems (P) Ltd., Chennai, India
Printed in Great Britain
on acid-free paper by
CPI Antony Rowe, Chippenham, Wiltshire

ISBN 978–0–19–956520–7

1 3 5 7 9 10 8 6 4 2

Acknowledgements

This book is the fruit of research undertaken at the Institute of Public Law of the University of Bern in the area of international human rights protection over the course of several years. It is based on and expands our book *Universeller Menschenrechtsschutz* (2nd edition, 2008) published by Helbing & Lichtenhahn (Basel) and Nomos (Baden-Baden). We sincerely thank our publishers for granting the rights for this English edition.

The book could not have been published without the important support and assistance by many and we would like to gratefully acknowledge their contributions. The Political Division IV of the Swiss Federal Department of Foreign Affairs provided a grant supporting part of the work. Patricia Deane translated an initial draft from German into English and Brendan Naef edited the final version. Our staff at the Institute, in particular Nina Schrepfer, Annina Schneider, Sabiha Akagündüz, Monika Wyss and Erland Möckli, helped with preliminary research as well as the completion of the manuscript and the preparation of tables and bibliographies.

Walter Kälin
Jörg Künzli

Bern
27 February 2009

Contents—Summary

Contents

III. SUBSTANTIVE GUARANTEES

Table of Cases

AFRICAN COMMISSION ON HUMAN AND PEOPLES' RIGHTS (ACmHPR)

COMMITTEE AGAINST TORTURE

COMMITTEE ON THE ELIMINATION OF DISCRIMINATION AGAINST WOMEN (CtteeEDAW)

COMMITTEE ON THE ELIMINATION OF RACIAL DISCRIMINATION (CtteeERD)

EUROPEAN COMMISSION OF HUMAN RIGHTS (ECmHR)

EUROPEAN COMMITTEE OF SOCIAL RIGHTS (ECtteeSR)

EUROPEAN COURT OF FIRST INSTANCE

EUROPEAN COURT OF HUMAN RIGHTS

EUROPEAN COURT OF JUSTICE

HUMAN RIGHTS COMMITTEE (HRCttee)

INTER-AMERICAN COMMISSION OF HUMAN RIGHTS (IACmHR)

INTER-AMERICAN COURT OF HUMAN RIGHTS (IACtHR)

INTERNATIONAL COURT OF JUSTICE (ICJ)

INTERNATIONAL CRIMINAL TRIBUNAL FOR RWANDA (ICTR)

INTERNATIONAL CRIMINAL TRIBUNAL FOR
THE FORMER YUGOSLAVIA (ICTY)

IRAN-UNITED STATES CLAIMS TRIBUNAL

NATIONAL COURTS

Israel

United Kingdom

Table of Other Materials

COMMITTEE AGAINST TORTURE

COMMITTEE ON ECONOMIC, SOCIAL AND CULTURAL RIGHTS

COMMITTEE ON THE ELIMINATION OF DISCRIMINATION AGAINST WOMEN

General Comments

Issues in Focus and Examples

List of Tables

List of Abbreviations

ACHPR	African Charter on Human and Peoples' Rights (Banjul Charter) of 27 June 1981; 1520 UNTS 217, OAU Doc CAB/LEG/67/3 rev. 5
ACHR	(Inter-) American Convention on Human Rights of 22 November 1969; 1144 UNTS 123, OAS TS No 36
ACmHPR	African Commission on Human and Peoples' Rights
ACmHR	American Commission of Human Rights
ACRWC	African Charter on the Rights and Welfare of the Child of 11 July 1990; OAU Doc CAB/LEG/24.9/49 (1990)
AJIL	*American Journal of International Law*
AP	Additional Protocol
AP I	Protocol Additional to the Geneva Conventions of 12 August 1949, and relating to the Protection of Victims of International Armed Conflicts (Protocol I) of 8 June 1977; 1125 UNTS 3
AP II	Protocol Additional to the Geneva Conventions of 12 August 1949, and relating to the Protection of Victims of Non-International Armed Conflicts (Protocol II) of 8 June 1977; 1125 UNTS 609
ArCHR	Arab Charter on Human Rights of 22 May 2004; *reprinted in* 12 *International Human Rights Reports* 893 (2005)
ASEAN	Association of Southeast Asian Nations
AU	African Union
BJIL	*Berkeley Journal of International Law*
CAT	Convention against Torture and Other Cruel, Inhuman or Degrading Treatment or Punishment of 10 December 1984, 1465 UNTS 85
CCW	Convention on Prohibitions or Restrictions on the Use of Certain Conventional Weapons which May be Deemed to be Excessively Injurious or to Have Indiscriminate Effects of 10 October 1980; 1342 UNTS 137
CEDAW	Convention on the Elimination of All Forms of Discrimination against Women of 18 December 1979; 1249 UNTS 13
CERD	International Convention on the Elimination of All Forms of Racial Discrimination 7 March 1966, 660 UNTS 195
CHR	(former) Commission on Human Rights
CPAPED	Convention for the Protection of All Persons from Enforced Disappearance of 20 December 2006; UN General Assembly Resolution A/61/177 (2006)
CPPCG	Convention on the Prevention and Punishment of the Crime of Genocide of 9 December 1948; 78 UNTS 277
CRC	Convention on the Rights of the Child of 20 November 1989, 1577 UNTS 3
CRPD	Convention on the Rights of Persons with Disabilities of 13 December 2006; UN General Assembly Resolution 61/106 (2006)
CSCE	Conference on Security and Co-operation in Europe

CSR	Convention relating to the Status of Refugees of 28 July 1951; 189 UNTS 137
CSSP	Convention relating to the Status of Stateless Persons of 28 September 1954; 360 UNTS 117
CtteeAT	Committee against Torture
CtteeEDAW	Committee on the Elimination of Discrimination against Women
CtteeERD	Committee on the Elimination of Racial Discrimination
CtteeESCR	Committee on Economic, Social and Cultural Rights
CtteeRC	Committee on the Rights of the Child
DR	Decisions and Reports
EC	European Community
ECHR	European Convention on Human Rights of 4 November 1950; 213 UNTS 221, ETS No 5
ECHRB	European Convention for the Protection of Human Rights and Dignity of the Human Being with regard to the Application of Biology and Medicine (Convention on Human Rights and Biomedicine) of 4 April 1997; ETS No 164
ECJ	European Court of Justice
ECmHR	(former) European Commission of Human Rights
ECML	European Charter for Regional or Minority Languages of 5 November 1992; ETS No 148
ECOSOC	Economic and Social Council
ECPC	European Convention on Protection of Children against Sexual Exploitation and Sexual Abuse of 25 October 2007; ETS No 201
ECPT	European Convention for the Prevention of Torture and Inhuman or Degrading Treatment or Punishment of 26 November 1987; ETS No 126
ECSR	European Committee of Social Rights
ECTHB	European Convention on Action against Trafficking in Human Beings of 16 May 2005; ETS No 197
ECtHR	European Court of Human Rights
EJIL	*European Journal of International Law*
EPIL	*Max Planck Encyclopedia of Public International Law*
ESC	European Social Charter of 18 October 1961; 529 UNTS 89; ETS No 35
ESCrev	European Social Charter revised of 3 May 1996; ETS No 163
ETS	European Treaty Series
EU	European Union
EuGRZ	*Europäische Grundrechte Zeitschrift*
FAO	Food and Agriculture Organization of the United Nations
FCPNM	Framework Convention for the Protection of National Minorities of 1 February 1995; ETS No 157
GC I	Geneva Convention for the Amelioration of the Condition of the Wounded and Sick in Armed Forces in the Field of 12 August 1949; 75 UNTS 31
GC II	Geneva Convention for the Amelioration of the Condition of Wounded, Sick and Shipwrecked Members of Armed Forces at Sea of 12 August 1949; 75 UNTS 85

GC III	Geneva Convention relative to the Treatment of Prisoners of War of 12 August 1949; 75 UNTS 135
GC IV	Geneva Convention relative to the Protection of Civilian Persons in Time of War of 12 August 1949; 75 UNTS 287
GYIL	*German Yearbook of International Law*
HRC	Human Rights Council
HRCttee	Human Rights Committee
HRQ	*Human Rights Quarterly*
IACAT	Inter-American Convention to Prevent and Punish Torture of 9 December 1985; OAS TS No 67
IACDAPD	Inter-American Convention on the Elimination of All Forms of Discrimination against Persons with Disabilities of 7 June 1999; AG/RES 1608 (XXIX-O/99)
IACFD	Inter-American Convention on the Forced Disappearance of Persons of 9 June 1994; OAS Doc OEA/Ser.P/AG/Doc 3114/94
IACmHR	Inter-American Commission on Human Rights
IACtHR	Inter-American Court of Human Rights
IACVAW	Inter-American Convention on the Prevention, Punishment and Eradication of Violence against Women (Convention of Belem do Para) of 9 June 1994
ICC	International Criminal Court
ICCPR	International Covenant on Civil and Political Rights of 16 December 1966; 999 UNTS 171
ICCPR-OP1	Optional Protocol to the International Covenant on Civil and Political Rights of 16 December 1966; 999 UNTS 302
ICCPR-OP2	Second Optional Protocol to the International Covenant on Civil and Political Rights, aiming at the abolition of the death penalty of 15 December 1989; 1642 UNTS 414
ICESCR	International Covenant on Economic, Social and Cultural Rights of 16 December 1966; 993 UNTS 3
ICESCR-OP	Optional Protocol to the International Covenant on Economic, Social and Cultural Rights of 10 December 2008; UN General Assembly Resolution A/63/435 (2008)
ICJ	International Court of Justice
ICRC	International Committee of the Red Cross
ICRMW	International Convention on the Protection of the Rights of All Migrant Workers and Members of Their Families of 18 December 1990; 2220 UNTS 93
ICTR	International Criminal Tribunal for Rwanda
ICTY	International Criminal Tribunal for the Former Yugoslavia
ILC	International Law Commission
ILO	International Labour Organization
IntCompLawQ	*International and Comparative Law Quarterly*
IPEC	International Programme on the Elimination of Child Labour
IRRC	*International Review of the Red Cross*
LJIL	*Leiden Journal of International Law*

LoNTS	League of Nations Treaty Series
Max Planck YUNL	*Max Planck Yearbook of United Nations Law*
NATO	North Atlantic Treaty Organization
NGO	Non-governmental organization
NILR	*Netherland International Law Review*
NQHR	*Netherlands Quarterly of Human Rights*
OAS	Organization of American States
OAU	(former) Organization of African Unity
OP	Optional Protocol
OPCAT	Optional Protocol to the Convention against Torture and Other Cruel, Inhuman or Degrading Treatment or Punishment of 18 December 2002; UN General Assembly Resolution A/RES/57/199 (2002)
OP-CEDAW	Optional Protocol to the Convention on the Elimination of Discrimination against Women of 6 October 1999; 2131 UNTS 83
OP-CRC-AC	Optional protocol to the Convention on the Rights of the Child on the involvement of children in armed conflict of 25 May 2000; UN General Assembly Resolution A/RES/54/263 (2000)
OP-CRC-SC	Optional protocol to the Convention on the Rights of the Child on the sale of children, child prostitution and child pornography of 25 May 2000; UN General Assembly Resolution A/RES/54/263 (2000)
OP CRPD	Optional Protocol to the Convention on the Rights of Persons with Disabilities of 13 December 2006; UN General Assembly Resolution A/RES/61/106 (2006)
OSCE	Organization for Security and Co-operation in Europe
P 1/ACHPR	Protocol to the African Charter on Human and People's Rights on the Establishment of an African Court on Human and People's Rights of 9 June 1998, AU Doc OAU/LEG/EXP/AFCHPR/PROT (III)
P 2/ACHPR	Protocol to the African Charter on Human and Peoples' Rights on the Rights of Women in Africa of 13 September 2000; OAU Doc CAB/LEG/66.6
P 1/ACHR	Additional Protocol to the American Convention on Human Rights in the Area of Economic, Social and Cultural Rights (Protocol of San Salvador) of 17 November 1988; OAS TS No 69
P 2/ACHR	Protocol to the American Convention on Human Rights to Abolish the Death Penalty of 8 June 1990; OAS TS No 73
P 1/ECHR	Protocol to the Convention for the Protection of Human Rights and Fundamental Freedoms of 20 March 1952; 213 UNTS 262, ETS No 9
P 4/ECHR	Protocol No 4 to the Convention for the Protection of Human Rights and Fundamental Freedoms, securing certain rights and freedoms other than those already included in the Convention and in the first Protocol thereto of 16 September 1963; 1469 UNTS 263, ETS No 46

P 6/ECHR	Protocol No 6 to the Convention for the Protection of Human Rights and Fundamental Freedoms concerning the abolition of the death penalty of 28 April 1983; ETS No 114
P 7/ECHR	Protocol No 7 to the Convention for the Protection of Human Rights and Fundamental Freedoms of 22 November 1984; 1525 UNTS 195, ETS No 117
P 9/ECHR	Protocol No 9 to the Convention for the Protection of Human Rights and Fundamental Freedoms of 6 June 1990; ETS No 140
P 11/ECHR	Protocol No 11 to the Convention for the Protection of Human Rights and Fundamental Freedoms of 11 May 1994; ETS No 155
P 12/ECHR	Protocol No 12 to the Convention for the Protection of Human Rights and Fundamental Freedoms of 4 November 2000; ETS No 177
P 13/ECHR	Protocol No 13 to the Convention for the Protection of Human Rights and Fundamental Freedoms, concerning the abolition of the death penalty in all circumstances of 3 May 2002; ETS No 187
P 14/ECHR	Protocol No 14 to the Convention for the Protection of Human Rights and Fundamental Freedoms, amending the control system of the Convention of 13 May 2004; ETS No 194
P 1/ECHRB	Additional Protocol on the Prohibition of Cloning Human Beings of 12 January 1998; ETS No 168
P 2/ECHRB	Additional Protocol on Transplantation of Organs and Tissues of Human Origin of 24 January 2002; ETS No 186
P 3/ECHRB	Additional Protocol concerning Biomedical Research of 25 January 2005; ETS No 195
P 1/ECPT	Protocol No 1 to the European Convention for the Prevention of Torture and Inhuman or Degrading Treatment or Punishment of 4 November 1993; ETS No 151
P 2/ECPT	Protocol No 2 to the European Convention for the Prevention of Torture and Inhuman or Degrading Treatment or Punishment of 4 November 1993; ETS No 152
RICR	*Revue Internationale de la Croix-Rouge*
Rome Statute	Rome Statute of the International Criminal Court of 17 July 1998; 2187 UNTS 90
RTDH	*Revue trimestrielle des droits de l'homme*
SAARC	South Asian Association for Regional Cooperation
SICTR	Statute of the International Criminal Tribunal for Rwanda of 8 November 1994; UN Security Council Resolution 955 (1994)
SICTY	Statute of the International Criminal Tribunal for the Former Yugoslavia of 25 May 1993; UN Security Council Resolution 827 (1993)
Slavery Convention	Convention to Suppress the Slave Trade and Slavery of 25 September 1926; 60 LoNTS 253, Registered No 1414
TS	Treaty Series
UDHR	Universal Declaration of Human Rights of 10 December 1948; UN General Assembly Resolution 217 A(III)

UN	United Nations
UN Charter	Charter of the United Nations of 26 June 1945; 1 UNTS XVI
UNCC	United Nations Compensation Commission
UNHCR	Office of the United Nations High Commissioner for Refugees
UNTS	United Nations Treaty Series
VCLT	Vienna Convention on the Law of Treaties of 23 May 1969; 1155 UNTS 331
WHO	World Health Organization
ZaöRV	*Zeitschrift für ausländisches öffentliches Recht und Völkerrecht*

PART I

THE FOUNDATIONS OF INTERNATIONAL HUMAN RIGHTS LAW

1

Origins and Universality

'What does it mean to be a human being and what are we entitled to?'—a question societies have asked themselves for centuries—was not seriously addressed at the international level until after the Second World War. The Universal Declaration of Human Rights (UDHR), solemnly proclaimed by the United Nations General Assembly on 10 December 1948 'as a common standard of achievement for all peoples and all nations', provided a clear answer: 'All human beings are born free and equal in dignity and rights. They are endowed with reason and conscience and should act towards one another in a spirit of brotherhood' (Article 1). Everyone is therefore 'entitled to all the rights and freedoms set forth in this Declaration, without distinction of any kind, such as race, colour, sex, language, religion, political or other opinion, national or social origin, property, birth or other status' (Article 2).

The human rights listed in the Declaration encompass a wide range of categories of entitlements. Among the basic rights relevant to the protection of life and limb are the right to life, the prohibitions of torture or arbitrary detention and the right to a fair trial including the right of access to an independent and impartial tribunal or the right to a defence. Civil liberties such as freedom of opinion, freedom of assembly, freedom of religion and the right to marry are covered along with a series of economic, social and cultural rights, including the right to work, the right 'to a standard of living adequate for the health and well-being of himself and of his family, including food, clothing, housing and medical care and necessary social services,' and the right to education. In drawing up this list, states agreed on and defined, for the first time in world history at the international level, the core guarantees that human beings regardless of their nationality need for effective protection of their dignity as persons. Although the Universal Declaration of Human Rights was meant to be merely an outline for a 'human rights project' and not a legal instrument, it nonetheless became the starting point for contemporary human rights protection, now firmly established in a wide range of legally binding conventions. Adopted in reaction to the horrors of the Second World War, the Declaration is based on the conviction that 'recognition of the inherent dignity and of the equal and inalienable rights of all members of the human family is the foundation of freedom, justice and peace in the world' and that it is therefore essential 'that human rights should be protected by the rule of law' at the supranational level.[1]

As a result, it became possible to transcend, at least at the level of political declarations, the traditional principle that a state's treatment of its own citizens is exclusively an internal affair. This change of paradigm paved the way for the establishment in the second half of the twentieth century of a comprehensive system of universally recognized human rights guarantees. This development, however, consisted of a step-by-step process, and the path was not always smooth. In 1953, for instance, the United States made it clear that it would have nothing to do with any human rights treaty elaborated by the United Nations.[2] Other states were also reluctant. The conflict between East and West during the Cold War over whether civil liberties or social rights qualified as true human rights delayed completion of the two UN International Covenants on Civil and Political Rights and on Economic, Social and Cultural Rights until 1966. In the closing decades of the twentieth century, tensions between the industrialized North and the developing South over the universality[3] of human rights made it difficult to reach agreement on new rules and their enforcement.

I. The National Origins of Human Rights

The question of the nature of the human person and the resulting basic entitlements has been addressed in the Euro-American tradition since the Enlightenment by reference to the inherent freedom and intrinsic rights of the individual.[4]

The first human rights declaration of modern times, the Virginia Declaration of Rights (1776), states: 'That all men are by nature equally free and independent, and have certain inherent rights...' (Article 1). Other American rights declarations[5] and the 1776 Declaration of Independence of the United States employ similar language. The term 'all men' in these documents does not, however, mean every individual irrespective of origin, race and sex. Black slaves, Native American Indians, and women in general did not benefit from

---

[1] UDHR, first and third preambular paras.

[2] Philip Alston, 'The UN's Human Rights Record: From San Francisco to Vienna and Beyond' (1994) *HRQ* 376.

[3] See below, section V.

[4] In the Magna Carta Libertatum (1215), the Habeas Corpus Act (1679), and the Bill of Rights (1689), English kings had already granted rights such as the right to punishment commensurate with the crime and to timely review of detention, the right of petition and the prohibition of cruel and unusual punishment. While these documents are of great importance for the development of human rights, the guarantees they contain are not human rights in the modern sense of the term since they were confined to specific social groups (aristocrats and free men).

[5] The Declaration of Rights of the State of Virginia of 12 June 1776 was followed on 4 July of the same year by the American Declaration of Independence drafted by Thomas Jefferson. It inspired the Bill of Rights: the ten amendments to the 1787 United States Constitution adopted in 1789 and ratified in 1791.

fundamental freedoms. In other words, free and equal applied to those white men who no longer wanted to be subjects of the British Crown but to live as free citizens in the newly founded United States of America. The universalist language of natural rights was not primarily intended to serve as the basis for a fundamental reform of social conditions but rather to provide moral justification for the struggle of the English colonies on the North American continent for independence from the English Crown and for the establishment of a new state by its free citizens.

Issue in focus: The Declaration of Independence of
the United States of America of 4 July 1776

'We hold these truths to be self-evident, that all men are created equal, that they are endowed by their Creator with certain unalienable Rights, that among these are Life, Liberty and the pursuit of Happiness.—That to secure these rights, Governments are instituted among Men, deriving their just powers from the consent of the governed,— That whenever any Form of Government becomes destructive of these ends, it is the Right of the People to alter or to abolish it, and to institute new Government, laying its foundation on such principles and organizing its powers in such form, as to them shall seem most likely to effect their Safety and Happiness.'

The tension between universalism at the level of language and an underlying tendency to link human rights to the concept of citizenship is also apparent in the French Declaration of the Rights of Man and of the Citizen (1789). On the one hand, the 1789 Declaration enshrined the idea of the inherent freedom and intrinsic rights of the human person in Article 1. Moreover, it stated in Article 2 that '[t]he aim of every political association is the preservation of the natural and imprescriptible rights of man', including, first and foremost, 'freedom, property, security and resistance to oppression'. Based on these promises, the French Revolution and Napoleon's subsequent expansionary endeavours purported to liberate citizens even beyond the frontiers of France from the chains of tyranny imposed by rigid social orders based on the privileges of the clergy and the nobility. On the other hand, these universalist ideals were tempered by Article 3 of the 1789 Declaration stressing that 'sovereignty resides essentially in the nation'. Citizenship thus became the distinguishing characteristic of membership to a nation and *human* rights were essentially understood as *citizens'* rights.[6] This is borne out by Article 1 of the French Constitutional Charter of 4 June 1814, which guarantees equality before the law (only) to 'the French'[7]—there is no longer any

---

[6] Felix Ermacora, *Menschenrechte in der sich wandelnden Welt* (Österreichische Akademie der Wissenschaften: Vienna, 1974) vol I, 115.

[7] Constitutional Charter of 4 June 1814: '*Les Français sont égaux devant la loi, quels que soient d'ailleurs leurs titres et leur rangs.*' The Constitutional Charter of 14 August 1830 reproduces this wording.

mention of the 'natural, inalienable and sacred rights of man' referred to in the 1789 Declaration of the Rights of Man and of the Citizen.

The French and American models had a formative influence on the liberal nation states of the nineteenth and early twentieth century. A constitution was deemed to be an essential attribute of the modern nation, and it was not only in the United States and France that such documents incorporated a bill of rights. The Belgian Constitution of 1831 became a model of its kind, influencing such diverse instruments as the (failed) draft German Imperial Constitution of 1848 and the Turkish Constitution of 1876.[8] In the USA and Switzerland, the highest courts began at an early stage to bridge gaps in the constitution through creative case law in the area of fundamental rights. A common characteristic of all these constitutions was their marked *inwardly oriented* perception of fundamental rights. Rights were granted primarily to a state's own citizens,[9] and even where aliens could exceptionally invoke such rights on a state's territory, the rights had their origin in the state's own sovereignty.

Human rights had very little influence on *international* relations in the eighteenth and nineteenth centuries except in rules of international law regarding the protection of foreigners (see section II.1 below). During this period, the principle of absolute state sovereignty was paramount in international law. Not only could states wage war at their own discretion (*jus ad bellum*) but they were also left entirely free to treat their citizens as they saw fit. Criticism of human rights violations was therefore viewed, not only in political but also in legal terms, as unacceptable interference in domestic affairs, and the protection of human rights through international instruments was virtually inconceivable.

II. Precursors of International Human Rights Protection

1. International minimum standard of treatment of aliens

Despite the emphasis on national constitutions as the source of human rights, states had to acknowledge in the eighteenth and nineteenth century that massive human rights violations could have negative repercussions on their international relations. Various steps were taken even at this early stage to address this problem by internationalizing human rights protection.

Before the twentieth century, international law was applicable only to relations between states. The result was that only the relevant municipal law determined whether and to what extent private actors were protected by fundamental rights in the country concerned. This caused tensions where citizens of a state were mistreated by the authorities of another state. Here, links between

---

[8] For an overview, see Ermacora (n 6), 116 and 132.
[9] Thus, eg, the Swiss Federal Constitutions of 1848 (Art 4) and 1874 (Art 4) limited the guarantee of equality and the procedural guarantees derived from it to 'all Swiss citizens'.

international law and the individual could be forged only indirectly and under specific circumstances by creating the legal fiction that a state whose citizens were ill-treated by the authorities of another country was violated in its own rights (so-called 'mediatization' of individuals). This was the logical course to take in the nineteenth century as emigration from an overpopulated Europe and closer international economic relations led to an increasing number of cases in which people whose basic rights were protected at home fell victim to ill-treatment and violations of their rights by states abroad. In such cases, the state of origin was entitled, under the rules of international law governing aliens, to exercise so-called 'diplomatic protection' on behalf of its nationals. The state of origin could therefore make representations to the violating state, demanding that the violation be halted and, where appropriate, that reparations be made. This institution made it necessary to define international minimum standards of treatment that were to be respected *vis-à-vis* all foreign nationals. The outcome was a list of guarantees for private actors that included the right of access to the courts in the state of residence, the right to a legal hearing, the right to protection against unjustified killing and ill-treatment, and the right to protection of private property from expropriation without full, prompt and effective compensation.

While this minimum standard of treatment of aliens strongly influenced the content of twentieth century human rights treaties, it did not qualify as human rights for two reasons. First, the state of origin enforced its own rights and not those of the victim, and, second, the minimum standard of treatment of aliens afforded protection only to foreigners but not to citizens in their own country. In other words, it was quite conceivable, in states without a modern constitution, that a government would be compelled to grant foreigners rights that it refused to extend to its own citizens.

The institution of diplomatic protection still exists today. Nowadays, however, it not only applies to the international minimum standard of treatment of aliens but all rules of international law that a foreign state is required to respect in its dealings with nationals of a specific state by virtue of customary or treaty law, including human rights.[10]

2. Selective international law protection in the nineteenth and early twentieth centuries

Although no concept of *international* human rights protection was developed in the course of the nineteenth century, states would have been able even then to take action to protect victims of human rights violations abroad, provided the requisite consensus among states existed.

---

[10] See, for instance, 'Report of the International Law Commission, Fifty-fourth session' (2002), paras 104 ff, UN Doc A/57/10, *Official Records of the General Assembly, Supplement No 10*.

As early as 1815, the Congress of Vienna imposed on a number of states the obligation to afford equal protection to all religious denominations and to guarantee non-discrimination on grounds of belief in access to public office.[11] The Congress was also a milestone in the international fight against the slave trade. On 8 February 1815 it adopted a Declaration on the slave trade that called for its abolition on the grounds that slavery was incompatible with the principles of humanity and universal morality. This objective was subsequently included in a number of bilateral treaties and on 3 July 1842 was embodied in the Quintuple Treaty involving a total of 26 European and Latin American states.[12] These efforts culminated in the Berlin Congo Act of 26 February 1885 and in the more detailed provisions of the General Act of the Brussels Conference of 1890 on the Suppression of Slavery. Yet all such agreements and decisions were conceived as purely interstate obligations, and the individual beneficiaries were not accorded any individual rights. This continued to be the case even in the Slavery Convention of 25 September 1926, which committed the parties to suppression of the slave trade and the abolition of slavery.[13]

The so-called 'humanitarian interventions' by European powers on behalf of persecuted Christians in the territories of the Ottoman Empire were a highly problematic but nonetheless important chapter in the history of international human rights protection.[14] While such interventions were often motivated by power politics and carried out by military means, they nevertheless did help in some cases to improve the plight of those suffering persecution. At any rate, they enhanced awareness of the fact that the community of states could not remain indifferent, at least in the case of serious human rights violations, to the manner in which a government treated its subjects.[15] Accordingly, the Treaties of San Stefano and of Berlin of 1878 on the independence of Bulgaria, Romania, Serbia and Montenegro provided for the recognition of religious rights.[16]

A further step was taken after the First World War with the establishment of a system for the protection for minorities under international law. The League of Nations, founded in 1918 in the wake of the Great War and inspired by the slogan 'No more war!' was unable to bring itself to enshrine the idea of human

---

[11] Art 8 of the Treaty of Union between Belgium and Holland of 31 May 1815. Art 16 of the records pertaining to the the Final Act of the Vienna Congress stipulated in Art 3 of Protocol 12 (of 29 March 1815) that freedom of the Catholic religion was guaranteed in the territories ceded by Sardinia to Geneva. For references see André N Mandelstam, 'Der internationale Schutz der Menschenrechte und die New-Yorker Erklärung des Instituts für Völkerrecht' (1931) *ZaöRV*, vol II, Part 1, 341.

[12] For a detailed account of the fight against slavery, see Ermacora (n 6), 235 ff.

[13] On the prohibition of slavery, see Chapter 14.

[14] For example, the interventions in 1828 on behalf of the Greeks, in 1875 in Bosnia, in 1877 in Bulgaria, and in 1887 in Macedonia.

[15] Mandelstam (n 11) 344 ff.   [16] Ermacora (n 6) 238 f.

rights in its Covenant. President Wilson of the United States proposed that explicit provisions be made for the preservation of religious freedom and for non-discrimination against national and religious minorities, but withdrew his proposal when Japan demanded that this be extended to include the protection of racial minorities.[17] On the other hand, a regime of international law that afforded protection to minorities was imposed upon the new Central and Eastern European states established after the collapse of the Ottoman and Austro-Hungarian Empires.[18] The peace treaties with Austria, Bulgaria, Hungary, and Turkey, the special agreements with Czechoslovakia, Greece, Poland, Romania, and Yugoslavia, and the unilateral declarations of Albania, Finland, and the Baltic states all contained human rights guarantees on behalf of specific minorities. These states committed themselves to ensure full protection of life and person, freedom of religious worship, certain linguistic rights, and to prohibit discrimination. Thus, pursuant to Article 63 of the Treaty of St. Germain-en-Laye of 10 September 1919, Austria undertook 'to assure full and complete protection of life and liberty to all inhabitants of Austria without distinction of birth, nationality, language, race or religion', and to recognize that all inhabitants were 'entitled to the free exercise, whether public or private, of any creed, religion or belief, whose practices are not inconsistent with public order or public morals'.[19]

These provisions were not, however, genuine human right guarantees. First, they did not establish any individual rights, only state obligations *vis-à-vis* the League of Nations. Moreover, the obligations were not owed to individuals but to minorities as collective entities. This conceptual shortcoming was nevertheless mitigated by the fact that the individuals concerned were entitled to submit petitions to the League of Nations. Second, anyone who did not belong to an explicitly protected minority was left without any form of protection. Thus, in the case of Franz Bernheim, the League of Nations was obliged to accept the German Reich's claim that the application of Germany's anti-Jewish racial laws in Upper Silesia was an 'internal affair' and hence beyond the scope of international criticism.[20] Lastly, these obligations were not universal, since they were binding only on the states concerned and not on the victors of the First World War. This one-sided arrangement was justified by reference to the fact that the new states established in the wake of the First World War could be recognized as such only if they renounced internal oppression of minorities as it was feared that without such guarantees peace would not be secured.

---

[17] Jan H Burgers, 'The Road to San Francisco: The Revival of the Human Rights Idea in the Twentieth Century' (1992) *HRQ* 449.

[18] On this subject, see Ermacora (n 6) 353 ff; Burgers (n 17) 449 ff; Mandelstam (n 11) 346 ff.

[19] Staatsgesetzblatt für die Republik Österreich No 303/1920. English version available at <http://www.austlii.edu.au/au/other/dfat/treaties/1920/3.html> (accessed 18 January 2009).

[20] Ermacora (n 6) 238 f.

3. The emergence of international humanitarian law

International humanitarian law provides for the protection of victims of armed conflict and determines which means and methods of warfare are prohibited.[21]

What is now perceived as a *lex specialis*, ie as the law governing human rights in armed conflicts, is in many respects both a precursor of and trailblazer for international human rights protection. The endeavour to protect people from the impact of brute force in war gradually gave rise to more extensive protection of rights, albeit still within the context of armed conflicts. Until the Second World War, however, these rules were based on the principle of reciprocity and limited to the relationship between a belligerent and combatants fighting for the adverse party. In conceptual terms, they thus constituted something resembling a minimum standard of treatment of aliens in wartime. Notwithstanding this limitation, they paved the way for an understanding that individuals might have rights under international law *vis-à-vis* states.

The foundations of international humanitarian law in its current form were laid in the nineteenth century, having built on models from the more distant past. The realization that the physical destruction of enemy soldiers could only be a means but never the object of war was a breakthrough in this regard. Rousseau, eg, argued that war 'is a relation, not between man and man, but between state and state, and individuals are enemies only accidentally, not as men, nor even as citizens, but as soldiers; not as members of their country, but as its defenders'. He accepted that the object of war is to destroy the enemy state, a goal that necessitates the 'right to kill its defenders, while they are bearing arms'. At the same time, he stressed that as soon as soldiers lay down their arms 'and surrender, they cease to be enemies or instruments of the enemy, and become once more merely men, whose life no one has any right to take'.[22]

Two basic postulates were deduced from this premise: that persons who are not (or are no longer) taking an active part in the hostilities should be protected and that restrictions should be placed on the means of warfare used. These two requirements correspond to the two main branches of international humanitarian law, the Law of Geneva (Geneva Law) and the Law of The Hague (Hague Law). Notwithstanding the two branches developed separately over time, they belong together in terms of content.

The development of the Geneva Law, ie a body of law conceived from the perspective of victims of hostilities who have fallen into the hands of the enemy, is closely associated with Henry Dunant. In his book *A Memory of Solferino*, Dunant proposed measures for the protection of war victims that provided the impetus for the founding of the International Committee of the Red Cross and

---

[21] On the concept of international humanitarian law, see Chapter 5.

[22] Jean-Jacques Rousseau, *The Social Contract (Du contrat social)*, Book I, Chapter 4, [translation by GDH Cole, available at <http://www.constitution.org/jjr/socon.htm>, accessed 3 February 2009].

the drafting of the Geneva Convention 'for the Amelioration of the Condition of the Wounded and Sick in Armed Forces in the Field' (1864).

Issue in focus: Henry Dunant—A Memory of Solferino, 1859[23]

There were poor fellows who had not only been hit by bullets or knocked down by shell splinters, but whose arms and legs had been broken by artillery wheels passing over them. The impact of a cylindrical bullet shatters bones into a thousand pieces, and wounds of this kind are always very serious. Shell-splinters and conical bullets also cause agonizingly painful fractures, and often frightful internal injuries. All kinds of splinters, pieces of bone, scraps of clothing, equipment or footgear, dirt or pieces of lead, often aggravate the severity of a wound and double the suffering that must be borne...

But why have I told of all these scenes of pain and distress, and perhaps aroused painful emotions in my readers? Why have I lingered with seeming complacency over lamentable pictures, tracing their details with what may appear desperate fidelity?

It is a natural question. Perhaps I might answer it by another: Would it not be possible, in time of peace and quiet, to form relief societies for the purpose of having care given to the wounded in wartime by zealous, devoted and thoroughly qualified volunteers?...

Societies of this kind, once formed and their permanent existence assured, would naturally remain inactive in peacetime. But they would be always organized and ready for the possibility of war. They would have not only to secure the goodwill of the authorities of the countries in which they had been formed, but also, in case of war, to solicit from the rulers of the belligerent states authorization and facilities enabling them to do effective work. The societies, therefore, should include, in each country, as members of their governing board, men enjoying the most honourable reputation and the highest esteem. The committees would appeal to everybody who, for sincerely philanthropic motives, would undertake to devote himself for the time to this charitable work. The work itself would consist in bringing aid and relief (in agreement with the military commissaries, *ie*, when necessary with their support and under their instructions) onto the battlefield whenever battle was joined, and subsequently to continue to care for the wounded in the hospitals until their convalescence was complete...

The 'Instructions for the Government of Armies of the United States in the Field' issued by President Lincoln in 1863 for the American Civil War (named the Lieber Code after its author) was an early example of the development of law regulating the means of warfare. The first result of this development in terms of international law was the prohibition of explosive projectiles weighing less than 400 grams in the St Petersburg Declaration of 1868. This agreement came about in response to an initiative by Tsar Alexander II, which he took when he realized that English troops in Afghanistan had firearms with explosive projectiles. He wanted to prohibit his own troops from using this particularly cruel type of ammunition, but only on condition that the other European powers followed suit. The agreement is noteworthy primarily for the statement in the first line of its Preamble that 'the only legitimate object which States should endeavour to accomplish during war is to weaken the military

---

[23] Henry Dunant, *A Memory of Solferino* (International Committee of the Red Cross, 1986), online version at: <http://www.icrc.org/WEB/ENG/siteeng0.nsf/htmlall/ p0361?OpenDocument&style=Custo_Final.4&View=defaultBody2> (accessed 18 January 2009).

forces of the enemy', ie that unnecessary suffering must be avoided in pursuing that aim. The Hague Conventions of 1907 were of fundamental importance, especially Convention IV respecting the Laws and Customs of War on Land with the annexed Hague Regulations governing land war, which comprehensively codified the law of war. The Preamble to this Convention contains the important 'Martens Clause', according to which, in the absence of a specific legal rule applicable to a case, 'the inhabitants and the belligerents remain under the protection and the rule of the principles of the law of nations, as they result from the usages established among civilized peoples, from the laws of humanity, and the dictates of the public conscience'.

Both the Hague and the Geneva branches of international humanitarian law were revised and further developed in the twentieth century under the influence of the two World Wars. The main impetus for the development of Geneva Law came from the atrocities of the Second World War, which highlighted the need to enhance the protection given to the civilian population. Today the four Geneva Conventions of 1949 and the two Additional Protocols of 1977 are the core components of the Geneva branch of international humanitarian law.[24]

4. Protection of the working population

The 'social question', ie the question of how to handle the consequences of the impoverishment and 'proletarianization' of large sectors of the population in the context of European industrialization was a core nineteenth century concern. Efforts to protect the working population led to recognition in the Versailles Peace Treaty of 28 June 1919 of the fact that world peace 'can be established only if it is based upon social justice'. An improvement in working conditions was therefore 'urgently required'. With that end in view, the Treaty provided for the establishment of the International Labour Organization (ILO), which formed part of the League of Nations and would be transferred to the United Nations after the Second World War as a specialized agency. The tripartite composition of the International Labour Conference and the Governing Body, which comprise representatives of governments, employers and employees of the states parties, remains a unique feature of the ILO.

Issue in focus: Versailles Peace Treaty of 1919—The foundation of the International Labour Organization[25]

Article 427

Among these methods and principles, the following seem...to be of special and urgent importance:

First. The guiding principle above enunciated that labour should not be regarded merely as a commodity or article of commerce.

---

[24] See Chapter 2, section II.4.
[25] The Peace Treaty of Versailles of 28 June 1919 between Germany and the Allied and Associated Powers, Part XIII, Labour.

Second. The right of association for all lawful purposes by the employed as well as by the employers.

Third. The payment to the employed of a wage adequate to maintain a reasonable standard of life as this is understood in their time and country.

Fourth. The adoption of an eight hours day or a forty-eight hours week as the standard to be aimed at where it has not already been attained.

Fifth. The adoption of a weekly rest of at least twenty-four hours, which should include Sunday wherever practicable.

Sixth. The abolition of child labour and the imposition of such limitations on the labour of young persons as shall permit the continuation of their education and assure their proper physical development.

Seventh. The principle that men and women should receive equal remuneration for work of equal value.

Eighth. The standard set by law in each country with respect to the conditions of labour should have due regard to the equitable economic treatment of all workers lawfully resident therein.

Ninth. Each State should make provision for a system of inspection in which women should take part, in order to ensure the enforcement of the laws and regulations for the protection of the employed.

An important development from the standpoint of human rights is the fact that Article 427 of the Versailles Peace Treaty lists labour-related human rights, including freedom of association, ie the 'right of association for all lawful purposes by the employed as well as by the employers', the abolition of child labour and the 'principle that men and women should receive equal remuneration for work of equal value'. These were not, however, rights creating entitlements for individuals, but merely 'guiding principles' for the ILO's work that became binding only when converted into specific treaties. The ILO succeeded rapidly in securing agreement on important issues such as the eight-hour day (Convention No 1 of 1919), maternity protection (Convention No 3 of 1919), night work by young people (Convention No 6 of 1919), and forced labour (Convention No 29 of 1930).[26]

It is also important to note that the ILO succeeded as early as 1926 in setting up a monitoring regime. A Committee of Experts composed of representatives of governments, employers and employees could examine reports from states on their efforts to implement ILO conventions and recommendations and report to the International Labour Conference on their findings.

III. The Breakthrough: the UN Charter and the Universal Declaration of Human Rights

The terror unleashed by the National Socialist regime and the horrors of the Second World War gave rise to a debate on the need to limit the sovereign

---

[26] On contemporary ILO conventions, see Chapter 2, section II.2.c.

power of states to treat their citizens as they see fit and to make protection of the individual a task to be addressed by the international community. In the Atlantic Charter of 24 September 1941, the Allied Powers committed themselves to the idea 'that all the men in all the lands may live out their lives in freedom from fear and want'. This reflected the idea of the four freedoms—freedom of expression, freedom of religion, freedom from want and freedom from fear—that United States President Roosevelt had proclaimed in January of that year as the basis of a new world order.[27] A number of intellectuals and non-governmental organizations began to discuss the idea of international human rights protection, formulating concepts or even drafting texts on the subject.[28]

In 1945 the concept of human rights *for all* was enshrined in the Charter of the United Nations. Article 1 mentions 'international co-operation...in promoting and encouraging respect for human rights and for fundamental freedoms for all without distinction as to race, sex, language, or religion' as one of the main purposes of the United Nations. Article 56, in conjunction with Article 55, commits member states to cooperating with the UN in promoting 'universal respect for, and observance of, human rights and fundamental freedoms for all without distinction as to race, sex, language, or religion'. The time was ripe for such provisions, and the deliberations were accordingly fairly brief. Apart from the principle of non-discrimination, however, the content of these human rights remained unspecified and the extent to which they were directly binding under international law was not made clear in the Charter.

As mentioned above, the real breakthrough for international human rights protection came with the Universal Declaration of Human Rights of 10 December 1948. It was not, however, a legally binding instrument. States proclaimed their willingness to adopt the Declaration 'as a common standard of achievement for all peoples and all nations' to be reached 'by progressive measures, national and international'. The United Nations therefore started gradually to translate the content of the Declaration into binding treaty law. This process took longer than anticipated. While it was possible to quickly adopt the Convention on the Prevention and Punishment of the Crime of Genocide of 9 December 1948 and the 1951 Convention relating to the Status of Refugees, the Cold War tensions between East and West delayed the adoption of two Human Rights Covenants until 1966. It would then take a further ten years until the required 35 ratifications had come together and the Covenants could enter into force in 1976. At the regional level, only the Council of Europe succeeded in adopting the European Convention on Human Rights as early as 1950.

---

[27] Franklin Roosevelt, 'The Annual Message to the Congress', Monday, 6 January 1941, available at: <http://www.feri.org/common/news/details.cfm?QID=2089&clientid=11005> (accessed 18 January 2009). On these developments see Burgers (n 17) 486 ff.

[28] For an overview, see Burgers (n 17) 471 ff.

IV. Internationalizing Human Rights: the Consequences

1. Recognition of the individual as a subject of international law

From the perspective of individuals, the most important outcome of the internationalization of human rights is the fact that human persons now enjoy individual rights under international law and have therefore become partial subjects of this branch of law. Thus, the traditional theory according to which international law by definition is limited to the legal status of states and international organizations has finally been overcome.

While this theory had long prevented any serious discussion of the question of the recognition of human rights in international law, a radical reassessment occurred when the victorious powers of the Second World War decided to try German and Japanese war criminals before the Nuremberg and Tokyo tribunals, holding them individually accountable for crimes against peace, war crimes, and crimes against humanity. Their prosecution by an international tribunal made it necessary to assume that individuals may possess direct obligations under international law. From this acknowledgement, it was a small and logical step to the recognition of the concept of internationally guaranteed individual rights.

Even today, however, the recognition of individual, legally binding, and hence enforceable human rights has been achieved only in principle. While states have created procedures for the submission of individual complaints to international bodies under several treaties, allowing victims of human rights violations to defend themselves at the interstate level against interference by their own state,[29] this protection is still deficient in at least three respects. First, the option of submitting an individual complaint exists only where the state concerned has undertaken to submit to such a monitoring regime by ratifying the relevant treaty or by making a corresponding declaration. In other words, individual complaint procedures are, as a rule, merely optional and do not exist at all when it comes to enforcing rights under customary international law. Second, while the decisions of the treaty bodies that rule on individual complaints enjoy considerable authority and are in practice frequently respected, they are not legally binding, with the exception of judgments of the European and Inter-American Courts of Human Rights. Lastly, individual rights under international law exist only at the supranational level. The question as to whether international human rights can be invoked directly by victims before domestic authorities depends on how the respective constitution regulates the relationship between international and municipal law.[30]

---

[29] For more on the enforcement of human rights, see Chapters 6–8.

[30] Thus, for a long time it was impossible to invoke the ECHR at the domestic level in the United Kingdom and Sweden. It was only with the enactment of the Human Rights Act 1998 (United Kingdom) and an amendment to one of three laws with constitutional status, the Instrument of

2. Impact on the concept of state sovereignty

In spite of these shortcomings, the creation of individual rights under international law had far-reaching implications for the concept of state sovereignty. If the individual, as Partsch[31] correctly noted as early as 1948, is to be able to assert certain rights under international law *vis-à-vis* his or her own state, the international legal order must hierarchically rank above the domestic legal order and take precedence over it.

The state thus loses its traditional right to treat its citizens as it sees fit. In principle, pressure from states parties or treaty bodies on a state that fails to abide by its human rights obligations no longer constitutes interference in its internal affairs. Moreover, state sovereignty may now be limited not only from above but also to some extent from below: the authority of a state is restricted wherever victims of human rights violations bring complaints to international organs created for that purpose. This means that individuals are now in a position to challenge the state where its authorities abuse their rights, a significant development that has arguably transformed the state's traditional purpose of maintaining the independence of the sovereign nation into, as Hersch Lauterpacht highlighted in 1947, that of 'protect[ing] the interests of the individual and . . . assist[ing] in developing, through freedom, the capacities of man'.[32]

3. Human rights as a factor shaping international relations

The weakening of state sovereignty has made it possible for human rights to become an important factor in international relations. The Second World War demonstrated beyond doubt the extent to which regimes that are repressive at home can also prove aggressive abroad. Equally, human rights violations today are not merely a concomitant of armed conflicts but often turn out to be one of the root causes of insurrections and violent clashes.

Human rights are more than subjective rights that private actors can assert *vis-à-vis* the state. They additionally serve to protect fundamental interests of the international community, thereby establishing what may be described as an objective order or an international *ordre public*.[33] As such they influence

---

Government (Sweden), that the ECHR was incorporated in domestic legislation. In the Federal Republic of Germany, while the ECHR can be directly invoked, the Convention basically enjoys only statute-law rank under German law. In Switzerland, on the other hand, the Federal Court accords the ECHR precedence even over federal laws. A number of new constitutions in Central and Eastern Europe have also adopted the principle of granting precedence to international human rights treaties (eg Art 20 of the Romanian Constitution of 8 December 1991 and Art 4 of the Constitution of the Republic of Moldova of 29 July 1994).

[31] Karl J Partsch, 'Internationale Menschenrechte?' (1948) 74 *Archiv für öffentliches Recht* 160.

[32] Hersch Lauterpacht, 'The International Protection of Human Rights' (1947) 70 *Recueil des Cours* 9.

[33] See Walter Kälin, 'Menschenrechte als Gewährleistung einer objektiven Ordnung' (1994) 33 *Berichte der Deutschen Gesellschaft für Völkerrecht* 9 ff.

the formation of interstate relations. In Europe this became clear soon after the Second World War. The Council of Europe was founded, for example, with the aim of restoring democracy, the rule of law and human rights protection in Europe.[34] Accordingly, only states that respected human rights were entitled to become members.[35] In relations between Eastern and Western Europe, the primary significance of human rights for international relations was recognized by both sides when states endeavoured from the mid-1970s to work towards overcoming the legacy of the Cold War through the Conference for Security and Co-operation in Europe (CSCE). Principle VII of the CSCE Helsinki Final Act of 1 August 1975 states that respect for human rights 'is an essential factor for the peace, justice and wellbeing necessary to ensure the development of friendly relations' among states. This Act, together with subsequent instruments, served to legitimize the demands made by civil rights movements in former East Bloc states in their struggle for greater freedom. Respect for human rights has also become an important criterion in practice for the admission of new members to the European Union. Greece and Spain, for example, were permitted to join the European Community only after the demise of their former dictatorships, and eastward expansion was contemplated only when the Central European states had made an acceptable degree of progress towards consolidating the rule of law. In this context, it is not the protection of particular individuals that is of key importance but rather recognition that the success of all forms of European integration depends ultimately on the existence of a community of shared values.

At the universal level, human rights took far longer to achieve this role because of the Cold War. The United Nations admitted all applicant states as members, regardless of their position on human rights, in order to achieve universality. The fact that human rights protection was an urgent and legitimate concern of the international community and that criticism of other states could not be deemed to constitute interference in their internal affairs was not recognized by the UN until 1967. At this time, the Economic and Social Council adopted Resolution 1235(XLII) allowing the former Commission on Human Rights to examine information revealing a consistent pattern of human rights violations in a particular state.[36] The United Nations Security Council started to play an important role in the area of human rights after the fall of the Berlin Wall, recognizing in its practice that systematic and grave violations of human rights represent a threat to international peace and security that may warrant the adoption of coercive economic or military measures.[37] A view that has been rapidly gaining ground in recent years is that the concept of state security policy must be supplemented by a policy of 'human security' that focuses on the need to protect people from the multiple threats to which they are exposed in the modern world—ranging

---

[34] Preamble to the Statute of the Council of Europe of 5 May 1949 and Art 1(b).
[35] Arts 3 and 4 of the Statute.　　[36] See Chapter 8, section II.1.
[37] For example, UN Security Council Resolutions 688 (1991) (Iraq), 794 (1992) (Somalia), and 940 (1994) (Haiti). See also Chapter 8, section III.

from war, displacement and forced migration, to poverty and HIV/AIDS—and to empower them to deal with and overcome these threats.[38] A further important step was the recognition of a 'responsibility to protect', if necessary with coercive means, victims of the most serious forms of human rights abuses. In this sense, the 2005 World Summit recognized that '[t]he international community, through the United Nations, ... has the responsibility to use appropriate diplomatic, humanitarian and other peaceful means, in accordance with Chapters VI and VIII of the Charter, to help to protect populations from genocide, war crimes, ethnic cleansing and crimes against humanity' as well as 'to take collective action, in a timely and decisive manner, through the Security Council, in accordance with the Charter, including Chapter VII, on a case-by-case basis and in cooperation with relevant regional organizations as appropriate, should peaceful means be inadequate and national authorities are manifestly failing to protect their populations from genocide, war crimes, ethnic cleansing and crimes against humanity'.[39]

Today, human rights may also serve as a criterion for the establishment or severance of bilateral relations in the area of interstate cooperation. States have repeatedly boycotted economic partners as a means of registering protest in the wake of particularly shocking human rights violations. Some states and regional organizations have incorporated human rights clauses in their legislation on arms exports in order to prevent sales of weapons to countries that are gross violators of human rights.[40] In the area of economic cooperation, human rights have been an important decision-making criterion for some time. Donor states may suspend assistance in response to a dramatic deterioration of the human rights situation in a recipient country, and efforts have been made, under the heading of 'good governance', to employ the resources of economic cooperation to strengthen the role of human rights.[41] In the case of the former Yugoslavia, the question of respect for human rights even became a criterion for the recognition of new states.[42]

In such cases, human rights take precedence over cooperation-related interests, in particular where a state declines to fulfil treaty-based undertakings because of an impending human rights violation, a development that has been carried

---

[38] Commission on Human Security, 'Human Security Now', New York 2003. The Commission was established on a Japanese initiative and was supported by the United Nations. Its report develops the concept of 'human security' as a necessary counterpart to 'state security', analyses the various threats to human security and puts forward proposals for translating the concept into practice under the headings 'protection' and 'empowerment'. The concept as such originated with the UNDP, *Human Development Report 1993* and *Human Development Report 1994*. The UN General Assembly decided to define the notion of 'human security' in resolution A/RES/60/1 (2005).

[39] 2005 World Summit Outcome, General Assembly Resolution A/RES/60/1, para 139.

[40] See, for example, Criterion Two of the European Union Code of Conduct for Arms Exports of 8 June 1998.

[41] For a detailed discussion see Erika Schläppi and Walter Kälin, *Schweizerische Aussenwirtschaftshilfe und Menschenrechtspolitik—Konflikte und Konvergenzen* (Verlag Rüegger: Zurich, 2001).

[42] Declaration of European Community Ministers (in the framework of European Political Cooperation) on 'Guidelines on the Recognition of New States in Eastern Europe and in the Soviet Union' of 16 December 1991 (reproduced in (1993) *EJIL* 72).

furthest in the area of extradition law. It is now accepted that a treaty-based obligation to extradite persons liable to prosecution must give way to the requirement of human rights protection if the person concerned is in danger of being subjected to torture, inhuman treatment or any other serious human rights violation in the requesting state.[43]

4. Recognition of the role of non-governmental organizations

A further important outcome of the internationalization of human rights protection is the specific role of non-governmental organizations (NGOs) in promoting human rights and in monitoring their application. These activities draw legitimacy from the Preamble to the Universal Declaration of Human Rights, namely the proclamation that 'every individual and every organ of society, keeping this Declaration constantly in mind, shall strive through teaching and education to promote respect' for human rights and take the necessary measures to secure their 'universal and effective recognition and observance'. This provides a solid frame of reference for international as well as national NGOs when criticizing states for human rights violations and justifies their demands for observer status at the sessions of the UN Human Rights Council and inclusion into the activities of other human rights bodies.

The role assigned by the Universal Declaration of Human Rights to private actors highlights the fact that the international system is more than a regime of self-government of sovereign states. The international community is also dependent on an international civil society.[44] The community of states will stagnate and lose its legitimacy if private actors fail to champion basic values of the kind reflected in human rights, to assume responsibility for their realization and to taking the requisite action.

V. Are Human Rights a Universal Concept?

1. Stating the question

Are human rights really universal? Given the global prevalence of massive human rights violations, a negative answer seems to be warranted. However, the issue of the universality of human rights relates not to what 'is' but to what 'ought to be', the validity of the claim that such violations can be legitimately assessed in the light of international human rights standards.

Notwithstanding the global success of the concept of human rights since the adoption of the Universal Declaration of Human Rights in 1948, the claim that

---

[43] See Chapters 10 and 17.
[44] Dianne Otto, 'Nongovernmental Organizations in the United Nations System: The Emerging Role of International Civil Society' (1996) *HRQ* 107 ff.

human rights are universally applicable and valid is still a matter of dispute. While states recognize in principle, since the 1993 World Conference on Human Rights in Vienna, that all human rights 'derive from the dignity and worth inherent in the human person' and that they are therefore 'universal' and 'indivisible', those who criticize human rights for being essentially a product of Western culture have not fallen silent.

Issue in focus: Vienna Declaration and Programme of Action, 1993[45]

The World Conference on Human Rights...

Recognizing and affirming that all human rights derive from the dignity and worth inherent in the human person, and that the human person is the central subject of human rights and fundamental freedoms, and consequently should be the principal beneficiary and should participate actively in the realization of these rights and freedoms;...

Emphasizing that the Universal Declaration of Human Rights, which constitutes a common standard of achievement for all peoples and all nations, is the source of inspiration and has been the basis for the United Nations in making advances in standard setting as contained in the existing international human rights instruments, in particular the International Covenant on Civil and Political Rights and the International Covenant on Economic, Social and Cultural Rights;...

Solemnly adopts the Vienna Declaration and Programme of Action...

1. The World Conference on Human Rights reaffirms the solemn commitment of all States to fulfil their obligations to promote universal respect for, and observance and protection of, all human rights and fundamental freedoms for all in accordance with the Charter of the United Nations, other instruments relating to human rights, and international law. The universal nature of these rights and freedoms is beyond question. In this framework, enhancement of international cooperation in the field of human rights is essential for the full achievement of the purposes of the United Nations. Human rights and fundamental freedoms are the birthright of all human beings; their protection and promotion is the first responsibility of Governments...

5. All human rights are universal, indivisible and interdependent and interrelated. The international community must treat human rights globally in a fair and equal manner, on the same footing, and with the same emphasis. While the significance of national and regional particularities and various historical, cultural and religious backgrounds must be borne in mind, it is the duty of States, regardless of their political, economic and cultural systems, to promote and protect all human rights and fundamental freedoms.

Today, governments no longer question the validity of human rights as such, and public discourse in terms of human rights has become universal. Thus, religious fundamentalists invoke the right to practise their faith freely, and insurgents

---

[45] UN Doc A/CONF.157/23, 12 July 1993, World Conference on Human Rights in Vienna, 14–25 June 1993.

throughout the world justify their struggle, *inter alia,* on the grounds that their human rights have been violated. Yet the question of the universal recognition of human rights arises time and again in practice where states are unable to agree on the specific *content* of a right (eg Does the non-discrimination principle also protect same-sex relations? Does religiously prescribed corporal punishment constitute torture?), on the *restrictions* on human rights (eg Should the expression of opinions that challenge the basic values of a particular community be prohibited? Should persons who have breached fundamental obligations to society also be entitled to benefit from human rights protection?) and on the *relative status of different rights* (eg Do economic and social rights qualify as genuine human rights? Are they more important than civil and political rights?). Lastly, some specific rights such as the equality of men and women or the freedom to renounce one's religion are contested by reference to religious edicts or cultural traditions.

Most positions adopted in such discussions can be traced back to the theoretical concepts of 'universalism' (section 2 below) or 'relativism' (section 3). In recent years, positions trying to approximate between these two (section 4) are becoming increasingly common.

2. Universalist theories

(a) Legal positivism

From the standpoint of legal positivism, the universal recognition of human rights rests on the fact that virtually all states in the world are members of the United Nations and have therefore assumed the obligation under Articles 55 and 56 of the UN Charter to cooperate with each other in order to promote 'universal respect for, and observance of, human rights and fundamental freedoms for all without distinction…'. In addition, every state in the world has ratified at least one of the UN Human Rights Covenants, thereby explicitly recognizing the rights they contain. Furthermore, as Kühnhardt highlights, 'the overwhelming majority of the world's independent states…irrespective of political, ideological, economic and cultural differences, have incorporated human rights declarations in their national constitutions; there has never been such universality of verbal commitment to human rights as at present'.[46]

This reasoning appears convincing on the grounds that the principle of '*pacta sunt servanda*' (ie treaties must be performed in good faith) constitutes the basis of international law and as such requires no further justification. However, positivist arguments are insufficient in cases where there is no consensus on the precise content of particular rights, on the scope of the restrictions to which they may be subjected or on their relative status. It is equally insufficient in cases where the validity of a right is disputed because of the need to protect cultural traditions

---

[46] Ludger Kühnhardt, *Die Universalität der Menschenrechte* (Olzog–Aktuell: Munich, 1987), 37 f [translated for this publication from German].

or even by reference to a higher—divine—law. Finally, the reasoning also suffers from the inherent weakness that, hypothetically, simply changing the law can abolish human rights.

(b) Natural law

Historically, legal positivism played virtually no role in substantiating the universal recognition of human rights, precisely because human rights were usually invoked as an argument against positive legal systems, which were blamed for restricting liberty and treating human beings with contempt. Reasoning based on natural law, on the other hand, offered and continues to offer solid arguments to the effect that human rights are valid for all, irrespective of the legal order concerned, and place limits on unlawful claims to power.

It would exceed the scope of this section to review the extremely rich and complex Western tradition of natural-law arguments in support of human rights. A few brief references must therefore suffice.

Notions of an ideal world community of *a priori* justice (natural law) and of *equal* dignity of all humans, according to which the human person is by nature a free and rational being, already existed in Stoic philosophy (Chrysippus, Zeno, Herodotus, Seneca, and Cicero). With logical consistency, Roman jurists held that a slave was not deprived of freedom on account of divine law but on account of *jus gentium*, human-made law.[47] The basic notion of dignity as an inherent characteristic of being human was seeded by Christianity, a religion influenced by Stoicism which became the state religion of the Roman Empire in 381 AD.[48] Christianity emphasizes that every human being is created in the image of God, irrespective of race, sex, origin and status (Genesis 1:26 f), thus recognizing the special worth of the human person. Similar ideas are found in Islam. For instance, Surah 17, Verse 70, of the Quran reads: 'Verily we have honoured the children of Adam.' Recognition of human dignity and honour and of freedoms derived from them also form part of many important non-European cultural traditions:

> In Indian thought (Manu and Buddha), ten human freedoms and virtues are mentioned, namely, five social freedoms (freedom from violence, want, exploitation, dishonour, early death and disease) and five virtues (tolerance, fellow feeling, knowledge, freedom of conscience and thought, and freedom from fear). These fundamental ideas are the source of natural human demands as to how communities should be formed.[49]

Recognition of human dignity is not in itself a sufficient basis for the concept of human rights as someone may possess dignity but not be entitled to confront

---

[47] Norman Weiss, 'Die Entwicklung der Menschenrechtsidee, Heutige Ausformung der Menschenrechte und Fragen ihrer universellen Geltung', in Jana Hasse, Erwin Müller and Patricia Schneider (eds), *Menschenrechte* (Nomos: Baden-Baden, 2002), 40 f.

[48] Weiss (n 47) 41.

[49] Wolfgang Heidelmeyer (ed), *Die Menschenrechte* (4th edn, UTB: Paderborn, 1997), 11 [translated for this publication from German].

oppressors who disregard this dignity. Here, the idea of the *autonomous* individual becomes a necessary addition. This concept originated with scholasticism during the High Middle Ages and the Renaissance. According to Thomas Aquinas (1225–1274), human dignity derives from the fact that man is naturally free and exists for himself.[50] The basis for civil liberties lay in the fact that human reason partakes of divine law. Renaissance thinkers went a step further. Pico della Mirandola (1463–1494), for instance, set the individual 'in the middle of the world', a creature impeded by no restrictions and set apart from nature by free will.[51] In this he anticipated modern individualism.

By the sixteenth century, the idea that human beings possessed inalienable rights, irrespective of the realm or religion to which they belonged, had gained ground to such an extent that it determined the outcome of the discussion on the legal relationship between Christian conquerors and non-Christian peoples in the Portuguese and Spanish colonies. Bartolomé de las Casas (1474–1566) of the Salamanca school of legal thought championed the view that Indians and other peoples of different faith were human beings on a par with Christians and therefore also possessed certain inalienable rights. The papal bull *Sublimis Deus* of 1537 accordingly recognized that Indians enjoyed the right to life, security, freedom, and property.[52]

The transition from a theocentric to an anthropocentric world began in the seventeenth century with the Enlightenment, which also led to the demise of the conviction that the ruler's authority stems directly from God. At the same time, more emphasis was laid on the question of the precise nature of human beings. A common characteristic of natural law philosophers[53] is their perception of suprapositive *natural law* as a restraint on the absolute power of the ruler, precisely because of its existence prior to established law. The constituent elements of these innate and inalienable natural rights differ from author to author but revolve essentially around the basic ethical values of freedom and justice. Besides natural-law thinkers of the sixteenth and seventeenth centuries such as Grotius, Pufendorf, and Bodin, philosophers Thomas Hobbes and John Locke

---

[50] Walter Kasper, 'Die theologische Begründung der Menschenrechte', in *Staat, Kirche, Wissenschaft in einer pluralistischen Gesellschaft, Festschrift zum 65. Geburtstag von Paul Mikat* (Duncker & Humblot: Berlin, 1989), 105, with reference to Thomas Aquinas, *Summa Theologica*, II/II q.64 a.2 ad. 3.

[51] Pico della Mirandola, *Oratio de dignitatis homini*, § 15, verse 18–22; original Latin text and English translation at <http://www.brown.edu/Departments/Italian_Studies/pico/text/bori/frame.html> (accessed 6 January 2009).

[52] Wolfgang Schmale, 'Grund- und Menschenrechte in vormodernen und modernen Gesellschaften Europas', in Margarete Gradner, Wolfgang Schmale and Michael Weinzierl (eds), *Grund- und Menschenrechte, Historische Perspektiven—Aktuelle Probleme* (Böhlau: Wien and Munich, 2002), 32.

[53] The following overview is based to a large extent on Thomas Göller, 'Die Philosophie der Menschenrechte in der europäischen Aufklärung—Locke, Rousseau, Kant', in Thomas Göller (ed), *Philosophie der Menschenrechte: Methodologie, Geschichte, kultureller Kontext* (Cuvillier: Göttingen, 1999), 151 ff.

are of particular importance to the history of human rights. Thomas Hobbes (1588–1679; *De cive*, 1641; *The Leviathan*, 1651) presented a negative view of human nature. Hobbes professed that human beings possess both free will and the right to exercise it independently in pursuit of their own interests. In nature, this leads to a war of all against all. The will of self-preservation therefore makes it necessary to agree on a social contract entailing submission to the (absolute) authority of the state, which is alone capable of guaranteeing survival through security and which is thus granted a monopoly on the use of force. It follows that the purpose of the state is to guarantee individual security for all. John Locke (1632–1704; *Two Treatises of Government*, 1690) also took as his premise the autonomous individual. Everyone is the absolute lord and owner of his own person, and of life, liberty and of essential material possessions. Political authority is based on a social contract for the creation of a state whose purpose is to ensure respect for and protection of life, liberty and property. In this context, citizens surrender only some of their natural rights to the authority of the state, which has no right to enslave or annihilate its subjects, but must exercise its authority on trust. Where a state fails to meet its obligations, 'natural' rights (life, liberty, religious choice and property) can be asserted against it and the contract is invalidated. In order to avoid such situations, the state needs institutional arrangements to prevent rulers from abusing their monopoly on the use of force. This led Locke to put forward the idea of separation of powers, which Montesquieu (1689–1755; *De l'Esprit des Lois [The Spirit of Laws]*, 1748) subsequently developed and refined.

Jean-Jacques Rousseau (1712–1778; *Du Contrat Social [The Social Contract]*, 1762) presented a decidedly optimistic view of human nature. All human beings are free and equal from birth, and they are good and noble in the state of nature. Authority to govern is entrusted not to a ruler but to the citizens themselves who entrust the government with the task of ensuring the protection of their person and property. Individual action in this context must be oriented towards promoting the welfare of the community. While natural freedom constitutes unlimited freedom, the freedom of a citizen is shaped by the community, which operates on the basis of the general will (*volonté générale*), resulting in freedom to abide by self-made laws.

Immanuel Kant (1724–1804; *Grundlegung zur Metaphysik der Sitten [Foundations of the Metaphysics of Morals]*, 1797) based his position on the premise that humans, as autonomous and rational beings, possess freedom as a fundamental attribute. All individuals are entitled to freedom, and this constitutes the basis of their equality. The interests of autonomous individuals are reconciled where each individual acts according to a maxim that he or she wants to become a universal law (categorical imperative). The legal order that ensues guarantees equal freedom for all. This natural law performs a normative rather than a descriptive function. That is, it cannot be inferred from human nature but is a rational law made by human beings. It nevertheless has to be distinguished from established law enacted by the legislature, which—in contrast to *a priori* law—is subject to social and historical change, and is thus relative. The state's most important function consists in protecting citizens' freedom by means of laws. Kant took the principle of equal freedom for all seriously, calling for a cosmopolitan society of nations subject to the rule of law, since he recognized that the idea of freedom transcends the bounds of individual states.

To sum up, the 'Western' understanding of human rights that has evolved over the course of history may be said to rest on two premises: First, regarding *human nature*, all human beings are equally endowed as individuals with reason; thus, they possess the same free will and hence equal worth. It follows that by virtue of their nature human beings are entitled to respect and protection of their individual dignity and autonomy. Second, *the state is understood as being an institution that* serves primarily to ensure and protect the security and freedom of individuals. Human rights are asserted as entitlements to defend against and to protect from the state, which has a monopoly on the use of force and derives its power from this monopoly.

3. Relativist theories

The theory of the universality of human rights is challenged by several varieties of relativist critique. Like universalism, these critiques revolve around the categories of human nature and the purpose of the state.

(1) *The historical critique* argues that the human-rights-oriented purpose of the state is a product of history. The advance of human rights, according to this view, was achieved only gradually, even in Western states, as specific social, political, and economic conditions evolved, and they cannot be applied indiscriminately to states in which those conditions have not (yet) been put in place. Karl Marx, for example, held that human rights served to protect the interests of *bourgeois* society at a particular stage of historical development, and that the right to private property is therefore simply 'the right to enjoy one's property and to dispose of it at one's discretion (*à son gré*), without regard to other men, independently of society, the right of self-interest'.[54] In a similar vain, the Chinese delegation to the 1993 World Conference on Human Rights in Vienna maintained that '[t]he concept of human rights is a product of historical development. It is closely associated with specific social, political and economic conditions and the specific history, culture and values of a particular country. Different historical stages have different human rights requirements. Countries at different development stages or with different historical traditions and cultural backgrounds also have different understanding and practice of human rights. Thus, one should not

---

[54] Karl Marx, 'Zur Judenfrage' [On the Jewish Question] (1843), in *Marx-Engels-Werke* (Dietzverlag: Berlin, 1972) vol 1, 365 [English translation at: <http://www.marxists.org/archive/marx/works/1844/jewish-question> (accessed 18 January 2009)].

and cannot think [of] the human rights standard and model of certain countries as the only proper ones and demand all other countries to comply with
them.'[55] Contemporary authors stress that while normative systems also in
non-Western cultures are designed to secure human well-being and dignity,
thus imposing constraints on the state and on rulers, the Western human
rights tradition, in addition, grants people subjective rights, which can be
asserted as entitlements to defence and protection against the state if the public authorities fail to meet their obligations to the people.[56]

(2) *The cultural critique* challenges the Western image of the human being as an
autonomous individual, arguing that, by contrast, many non-European traditions perceive human beings as primarily members of their family, clan or
ethnic group. According to the *critique*, as social beings, humans have duties
first and foremost to the community, which is required to provide them with
protection and support. In societies based on these traditions, the human
being is not an individual set apart from society but a person whose identity
is shaped by the wide range of social relations in which he or she is involved.
To be part of and cared for by one's own community to which, in turn, one
owes certain obligations is still a reality for much of the world's population, a
fact that casts doubt on the universal validity of individual human rights.

Panikkar, for example, argues that human rights are not a universal concept
because they rest on a notion of the human person that is not universal. He
underlines the importance of the dignity of the human person but stresses
that 'the person should be distinguished from the individual. The individual
is just an abstraction, ie a selection of a few aspects of the person for practical
purposes. My person, on the other hand, is also in "my" parents, children,
friends, foes, ancestors, and successors. "My" person is also in "my" ideas and
feelings and in "my" belongings. If you hurt "me", you are damaging the whole
clan, and possibly yourself as well. Rights cannot be individualized in this
way....An individual is an isolated knot; a person is the entire fabric around
that knot, woven from the total fabric of the real. The limits to a person are
not fixed; they depend utterly on his or her personality. Certainly without the
knots the net would collapse; but without the net, the knots would not even
exist.'[57] Thus, human rights are not individual rights only.[58]

(3) The *cognitive critique* questions whether universal standards can be invoked to
determine precisely what constitutes human dignity and answers this question

---

[55] Speech of Liu Huaqiu, head of the Chinese delegation, Vienna 15 June 1993, cited in Pieter
van Dijk, 'A Common Standard of Achievement' (1995) *NQHR* 105, and Kevin Boyle, 'Stock-
taking on Human Rights: The World Conference on Human Rights, Vienna 1993' (1995) XLIII
Political Studies 86.

[56] Charles Taylor, 'Human Rights: The Legal Culture', in Paul Ricoeur (ed), *Philosophical
Foundations of Human Rights* (UNESCO: Paris, 1986), 49.

[57] R. Panikkar, 'Is the Notion of Human Rights a Western Concept?' (1982) 120 *Diogenes* 90.

[58] Ibid, 97.

in the negative. For instance, the American Anthropological Association, which was asked prior to the drafting of the Universal Declaration of Human Rights to state its position on the question of the universality of human rights, argued that we are all culturally conditioned by our environment. Accordingly, no scientific method can exist that would allow an objective assessment to be made of the value of specific cultural traditions from a supra-cultural standpoint. It follows that cultures must always be explained in their own terms and that cultural differences must be respected. What one culture categorizes as a human right may be perceived by another culture as asocial. As all standards and values are culturally specific, the postulates and values of *one* culture can never be applied to the whole of humankind.[59]

4. Intermediary positions: towards universality of human rights

The relativist critique of the universality of human rights is built on strong arguments. The arguments cannot, however, support a conclusion that human rights are something that only people belonging to western cultures are entitled to and that persons born with dark skin cannot assert any claim to protection when faced with the arbitrary exercise of state power. Radical relativism can thus easily turn to cynicism. At the same time, the arguments invoked by the relativist critique highlight the need for vigilance and suggest that the universality of human rights should not be taken for granted. Rather, universality must be forged through a process of consensus-building.

How this can be done without requiring cultures to give up their unique character is demonstrated by John Rawls's theory of the 'overlapping consensus'. In response to the question as to how a well-ordered society can form a unit not-withstanding the existence of a plurality of values, he argues that a minimum consensus is sufficient, with individual doctrines affirming a specific political conception from their own perspective.[60] In terms of this approach, all that can realistically be demanded is that specific cultural traditions are capable of endorsing specific human rights norms from their perspective, whatever the grounds may be. Different scenarios are conceivable in this regard. The most favourable would involve different traditions endorsing a particular norm for the same reason. However, it is also sufficient if a norm that is identical in terms of content finds support for different reasons (the word of God, human nature, a historically deep-rooted cultural practice, etc). The consensus is more fragile but still sufficiently robust where a particular human rights guarantee has no roots in a particular cultural tradition but is not incompatible with its values and rules. It is only where the particular tradition's values and precepts or prohibitions

---

[59] American Anthropological Association, 'Statement on Human Rights by the Executive Board' (1947) 49 *American Anthropologist* 543 ff.
[60] John Rawls, *Political Liberalism* (Columbia University Press: New York, 1996), 133.

clash with those of a specific human right that the claim of universal validity is undermined. Although such clashes may be of some consequence, they usually affect only a relatively small proportion of the whole range of human rights guarantees. Even traditionalist Islam recognizes the rights to be protected from genocide or torture, a Muslim's freedom to practice his or her own religion, and a person's entitlement to adequate food and housing. Conflicts arise primarily with regard to religiously prescribed corporal punishment, the freedom of a Muslim to change his or her religion, certain due process rights and how to ensure that a woman's dignity is guaranteed and protected in society.

In other words, the question as to the universality of 'the' human rights is intrinsically flawed; it is more appropriate to ask to what extent a specific right can claim to be universally acceptable.

There are real prospects for a growing global consensus on human rights issues. Bases for consensus-building include, as the following texts show, people's shared basic needs, similar experiences of injustice, related cultural concepts, the globalization of the modernization process, and the shared (long-term) interests of states and of the international community itself, which can range from securing peace to seeking stability as a prerequisite for economic investment.

Issue in focus: Bases for a universal consensus on human rights issues

---

(1) *Shared basic human needs*: 'In spite of cultural diversity and differences in customs and mores, it should not be forgotten that cultures are also bound together by shared attributes. There are countless different kinds of social systems, but this very diversity is counterbalanced by *unchanging points of reference*. These points of reference are reflected in the social, biological and psychological nature of the "individual" as subsystem, in the external circumstances in which individuals live and act, in the nature of such action and also in the need for coordination in social systems. Many unalterable facts of human life are thus universally valid. Human anatomy and physiology are broadly identical throughout the world. Every society must provide its individual members with time-honoured and socially approved patterns of behaviour and guidelines to enable them to cope with these universal circumstances (for example, the existence of two sexes, the helplessness of children, the need to satisfy elementary biological needs such as food, warmth and sex, the existence of individuals of different ages) ... The fact is that the fundamental similarities of human existence throughout the world are far more numerous than the differences. Some aspects of culture appear, in terms of the specific forms they assume, to be the outcome of historical chance, while others seem to be the result of universal forces. The crucial point to note is that biologically, psychologically and socially universal phenomena offer the possibility of finding a common denominator for all cultures.'[61]

---

[61] Tushar Kanti Barua, 'Humanität zwischen Universalität und Regionalität', in Stefan Batzli, Fridolin Kissling and Rudolf Zihlmann, *Menschenbilder—Menschenrechte* (Unionsverlag: Zurich, 1994), 26 [translated for this publication from German].

'...One might perhaps accept the idea that certain areas are viewed as globally apportioned plots that are ploughed, cultivated and demarcated by individual cultures in different ways. A few empirical observations may, however, bring to light certain basic parameters, needs and requirements that influence all humans as social beings. This perspective enables us to adapt universal human rights to the principle of cultural relativism without denying the multiplicity of cultures and the complexity of social life.'[62]

(2) *Empirically ascertainable universal norms and values*: 'Even though relativists have tended to focus on the differences among peoples, it is important to realize that *there may be cross-cultural universals which empirical research might uncover*. By seeking our specific moral principles held in common by all societies, one might be able to validate universal moral standards.'

'...where it is possible to demonstrate acceptance of a moral principle or value by all cultures, it will be feasible to erect human rights standards. The reality of universality depends on marshalling cross-cultural data.

The question remains as to which specific human rights can be derived from the apparently universal principle of retribution. If the present interpretation of the principle is accepted, namely that cultures are committed to limits on arbitrary killing and violence, then what are the practical implications for universal human rights standards? It is not claimed that the principle will clarify all moral debates about killings. For instance, it will not resolve the arguments about infanticide and abortion, for some societies view these acts as arbitrary, unjustified killings while others will take the opposite view.

Nevertheless, the demonstration of a principle is not an empty gesture. Worldwide support for the principle indicates that were we to hold a global referendum on international human rights, all societies, if they were to vote according to their own ideals, would unanimously favor certain standards. In particular, they would endorse the principle that "No one shall be arbitrarily deprived of his life" (Article 6/1, International Covenant on Civil and Political Rights)...It would follow that they would also agree with Article 6(3) of the Covenant and the Convention on the Prevention and Punishment of the Crime of Genocide, both of which condemn the arbitrary deprivation of life that is genocide...No society beliefs in the *ideal* of genocide.'[63]

(3) *Universality as the result of cross-cultural and intra-cultural learning processes*: '[C]rossing the borders of a culture involves in practice a detour entailing a comparison with other cultures...When compared with democratic values, totalitarian practices exhibit their amoral character; when compared with positive law, which strikes a balance between "civil liberties" and "rights to assert claims", traditional law displays its shortcomings...'[64]

---

[62] Ibid, 33.

[63] Alison Dundes Renteln, *International Human Rights: Universalism Versus Relativism* (Sage Publications: Newbury Park etc, 1990).

[64] Selim Abou, *Menschenrechte und Kulturen* (Winkler: Bochum, 1994), 88 [translated for this publication from German].

'...I propose to broaden and deepen universal consensus on the formation and implementation of human rights through internal reinterpretation of, and cross-cultural dialogue about, the meaning and implications of basic human values and norms. This approach is based on the belief that, despite their apparent peculiarities and diversity, human beings and societies share certain fundamental interests, concerns, qualities, traits and values that can be identified and articulated as a framework for a common "culture" of universal human rights.'[65]

Finally, it is also important to bear in mind that the notion of human rights is closely and directly linked to that of the modern nation state. As already mentioned, a characteristic feature of this type of state is the prohibition of violent self-help by private actors and the state's monopoly on the use of force through the army, the police, and judicial coercion. Human rights are perceived in this context as a necessary counterweight to the state's monopoly on the use of force which, though it may ensure private security, easily runs the risk of entailing abuse of authority. Hence the need to apply restraints to the state in the form of fundamental individual entitlements. Human rights can claim universal validity today because the nation-state model has spread throughout the world. A government that depends on the machinery of a modern state, backed by a panoply of security forces, cannot credibly defend the originally Western concept of a strong nation state while at the same time categorically rejecting human rights on cultural grounds.

[65] Abdullahi An-Na'im, *Human Rights in Cross-Cultural Perspectives* (University of Pennsylvania Press: Philadelphia, 1992), 21.

2

Notions and Sources

I. Definitions

1. Human rights

What are human rights? The conceptual foundations of international human rights protection have been described in Chapter 1. The next step is to clarify the concept of human rights in legal terms.[1] There is no legal definition that would clearly distinguish human rights from other guarantees and entitlements deriving from international law. However, the characteristic traits of human rights may be described as follows:

(1) Human rights create *entitlements*. As such, they are fundamentally different from rights established solely as state obligations that cannot be claimed by the beneficiaries.

(2) The beneficiaries of these entitlements are *individuals*.[2] As individual rights, human rights differ from collective entitlements of the kind that may be asserted by, for example, minorities or, in the case of the right of self-determination, 'peoples'.

(3) These rights can be asserted, in principle, only *vis-à-vis states or quasi-state entities* but, in principle, not private actors.[3]

(4) They are applicable, as a matter of principle, in *peacetime and in times of armed conflict*, but they may in certain circumstances be temporarily suspended during such times by virtue of the application of derogation clauses.[4]

(5) They are *internationally guaranteed*. It is this basis in international law and not their content or function that differentiates human rights from the fundamental rights set forth in national constitutions. The fact that these rights are guaranteed internationally means that international law prescribes to

---

[1] On the historical and philosophical foundations of human rights, see Chapter 1, sections I, II, and V.

[2] On the holders of human rights entitlements, see Chapter 3, section II.

[3] On state obligations flowing from human rights, see Chapter 3, section III. On the question of whether non-state actors are bound by human rights obligations, see Chapter 3, section I.2.

[4] On derogations from human rights, see Chapter 4, section IV.2.

what extent rights holders may assert and enforce their entitlements both domestically and at the international level.[5]

(6) This international entrenchment of human rights is rooted in the acknowledgment by states that the entitlements in question are *necessary to safeguard human dignity and the development of the human person* and must therefore be deemed fundamental.

Human rights may accordingly be defined as internationally guaranteed legal entitlements of individuals *vis-à-vis* the state, which serve to protect fundamental characteristics of the human person and his or her dignity in peacetime and in times of armed conflict.

The rights set out in the Universal Declaration of Human Rights and subsequent treaties represent two categories of human rights which, by reference to the time of their emergence in state constitutions, are frequently characterized as two generations of human rights. For some time, a third generation has been proposed as well. Each generation is distinguished by distinct characteristics:

(1) *First generation rights:* Human rights protecting civil liberties, now usually referred to as *civil and political rights,* include, *inter alia,* the right to life, liberty and security of person, rights in legal proceedings, freedom of religion, freedom of speech and freedom to exercise political rights. They are rooted in the late eighteenth-century American and French declarations of human rights and are intended primarily to serve as means for individuals to defend themselves against state interference (defensive rights).

(2) *Second generation rights:* The origins of *economic, social and cultural rights* can be traced to nineteenth-century measures taken to address the major social problems caused by the impoverishment and economic exploitation of important parts of the population in the wake of industrialization in Europe. Alongside rights aimed at securing human subsistence (eg the rights to food, shelter and health), they include rights in the area of employment (eg the right to decent working conditions, trade union rights, etc) and social security, and the right to education. They aim at allowing individuals to have access to specific resources, goods and services and partake in them and require states to take steps with a view to progressively achieving their full realization. In addition, they contain immediately applicable defensive components, such as the right to be protected against state interference with free access to available employment, education or food, as well as against discrimination with respect to access to state services and benefits.

(3) *Third generation rights: Solidarity or group rights* include the rights to development, peace and a clean and healthy environment. They were conceived in the second half of the twentieth century as collective rights, but have only just

---

[5] On international monitoring and enforcement of human rights, see Chapters 6–8.

begun to be incorporated in international law—eg in the African Charter on Human and Peoples' Rights.[6] Their legal content (ie Who is a rights holder? Who has obligations?) is as yet to a large extent unclear, and they face opposition, especially from industrialized states.

This categorization highlights the historical roots of distinctions between different categories of human rights, which still prevail despite the indivisibility of human rights, but does not suggest or justify any hierarchical order of rights.

From a purely legal perspective, international human rights may essentially be characterized, according to Nowak's definition, as the 'sum of civil, political, economic, social, cultural and collective rights laid down in international and regional human rights instruments [or in customary law]'.[7] This concept has the advantage of emphasizing the *indivisibility and interdependence* of human rights, ie of recognizing that the different categories belong together and that real freedom without a minimum of social security is just as inconceivable as social justice without freedom and protection of physical integrity. Thus, the Vienna Declaration of the 1993 World Conference on Human Rights states that: 'All human rights are universal, indivisible and interdependent and interrelated'.[8]

2. International humanitarian law

International humanitarian law lays down rules to protect people in situations of armed conflict. This *lex specialis* may be defined, according to Gasser, as the totality of 'international rules, established by treaty or custom, which are specifically intended to solve humanitarian problems directly arising from international or non-international armed conflicts and which, for humanitarian reasons, limit the right of the parties to a conflict to use methods and means of warfare of their choice or protect persons and property that are, or may be, affected by the conflict'.[9]

This definition covers the two traditional branches of international humanitarian law: the Law of The Hague (Hague Law) and the Law of Geneva (Geneva Law).[10] Hague Law, which is dealt with in this book only where it is of direct relevance to human rights protection,[11] restricts the manner in which war is waged

---

[6] ACHPR, Arts 22–24. Art 22, for instance, stipulates: 'All peoples shall have the right to their economic, social and cultural development.'

[7] Manfred Nowak, *Introduction to the International Human Rights Regime* (Martinus Nijhoff Publishers/Brill Academic: Leiden/Boston, 2003), 1.

[8] World Conference on Human Rights in Vienna, 25 June 1993, Declaration and Programme of Action, para 5.

[9] Definition according to Hans-Peter Gasser, 'International Humanitarian Law', in Hans Haug (ed), *Humanity for All, The International Red Cross and Red Crescent Movement* (Paul Haupt: Bern, 1993), 504 .

[10] See Chapter 1, section II.3 with reference to the historical development.

[11] See, for example, Chapter 9, section II.2.d. (right to life in situations of armed conflict).

by prohibiting particularly cruel or unfair means and methods of warfare (eg poison gas and the wearing of enemy uniforms respectively). Geneva Law is designed to protect persons who are *hors de combat*, ie those who are not, or are no longer, taking an active part in the hostilities, in particular the wounded and sick members of armed forces, prisoners of war or the civilian population. Membership in a particular category of protected persons depends on the core distinction that international humanitarian law makes between combatants and civilians in the context of international conflicts.[12]

As *jus in bello* (law in war), international humanitarian law takes no position as to the legality of the conflict itself. In other words, it is neutral with respect to *jus ad bellum* (legality of the use of force) and remains equally applicable to both belligerents, the aggressor and the defender. International humanitarian law is therefore based on a vision of history that accepts the existence of war and looks no further. It also accepts the fact that armed conflicts inevitably involve violence and the destruction and killing of the enemy. Its aim, however, is 'to protect the human being and to safeguard the dignity of men in the extreme situation of war'.[13] In the violent context of armed conflict, this can only mean setting limits on the state's use of force where its employment is not militarily justifiable and accordingly arbitrary. International humanitarian law seeks therefore to strike a balance between military necessities and the optimum protection of individuals, who are not, or are no longer, taking part in the armed conflict, and to develop corresponding norms:

> The conflicting interests of military necessity and humanitarian considerations can be dealt with in rules which limit the use of force in war but do not prohibit it when such use is legitimate. In other words, the rules should protect the individual but not aim at an absolute protection form the effects of warfare, which would in any case be impossible. International humanitarian law can only do the best possible.[14]

This realistic approach constitutes both the strength and the weakness of international humanitarian law. Its credibility and acceptance depend, from the standpoint of the belligerents, on their being able to plan and carry out their operations in accordance with military logic without constantly coming into conflict with the law. At the same time, international humanitarian law often accepts damage to the life and person of innocent people on a scale that can only be considered shocking from the standpoint of international law applicable to times of peace. This is due primarily to the vagueness of the concept of military necessity. Moreover, the dividing line between permissible military conduct and conduct that exceeds the bounds of acceptability is often so fine that standard-setting necessitates an extraordinarily high degree of detail, which frequently renders international humanitarian law rather complicated.

---

[12] On these concepts, see Chapter 5, section III.1.   [13] Gasser (n 9), 504.
[14] Hans-Peter Gasser, *Einführung in das humanitäre Völkerrecht* (Paul Haupt: Bern, 1995), 22 f.

A comparison between international humanitarian law and the characteristic traits of international human rights law yields the following results:

(1) International humanitarian law embodies no entitlements as such[15] but primarily *obligations* of the belligerent parties and members of their forces.

(2) These obligations are owed to the following *specific groups* during times of armed conflict:

   (a) Protected persons in international armed conflicts (wounded and sick combatants, prisoners of war, a foreign civilian population in enemy hands) in accordance with the four Geneva Conventions of 1949 (GC I–IV) and persons in the power of a party to the conflict in accordance with the first Protocol Additional to the Geneva Conventions of 1977;

   (b) Persons who are *hors de combat* in armed conflicts not of an international character (ie persons not involved or no longer involved in hostilities) in accordance with Article 3 common to the Geneva Conventions;

   (c) Persons affected by armed conflicts not of an international character in accordance with the second Protocol Additional to the Geneva Conventions of 1977.

(3) These obligations are binding upon states, as well as, in internal armed conflict, upon insurgents, and upon individuals to the extent that they commit grave breaches of international humanitarian law punishable under domestic or international criminal law.

(4) They are applicable *only during times of armed conflict* and, in view of their status as *lex specialis* governing extreme circumstances, they can never be derogated from, not even temporarily.

(5) Like human rights, international humanitarian law provisions aimed at protecting individuals are *internationally guaranteed*. However, unlike international human rights law, this body of law hardly addresses its enforcement, except through international criminal law.

(6) This international entrenchment is rooted in states' recognition of the need to set limits on enemy action in order to protect their own interests and those of their population, which is why they are prepared to abide by the same rules *vis-à-vis* the adversary.

3. International criminal law

International criminal law sanctions particularly serious human rights violations under the heading of crimes against humanity and genocide. The category of war crimes, on the other hand, establishes individual criminal responsibility under international law for breaches of core provisions of international humanitarian law. The crime of aggression, ie the planning and execution of a war of aggression

---

[15] On the question of the extent to which individuals have entitlements under international humanitarian law, see Chapter 5, section II.2.a.

involving a breach of the prohibition of the use of force, is also, in principle, an international crime. However, owing to a lack of consensus among states on the elements of aggression as criminal act, this crime has been left, for the time being, in abeyance.[16]

Since the most serious breaches of provisions of international law protecting the individual usually occur largely during armed conflicts or in the context of so-called 'failed states', international criminal law supplements both human rights and international humanitarian law in important ways.

While obligations flowing from human rights law are applicable, in principle, only to states, individuals not acting as state agents can also be held criminally accountable by international criminal law. This is particularly important in the case of members of insurgent and other armed non-governmental groups, as it is far from clear to what extent such entities are directly bound by obligations under international human rights.[17]

Furthermore, international criminal law makes it possible to hold public officials directly accountable for human rights violations. These officials can thus no longer hide behind state sovereignty and take advantage of immunity from prosecution or the unwillingness of their own state to prosecute such violations.

Lastly, outside the context of armed conflict, international criminal law provides a means of addressing human rights abuses associated with private actors accumulating and potentially abusing power in their hands. Thus, international criminal law provisions may be invoked against violations of core human rights values by, for instance, multinational corporations or private security firms.

International criminal law defines specific crimes at the international level and paves the way for prosecution of individual perpetrators before international courts, ie holding perpetrators directly accountable under international law. It differs therefore from international obligations to prosecute imposed on states under, for example, international humanitarian law and some human rights treaties, pursuant to which states are required to incorporate corresponding criminal offences in their domestic legislation and to bring the perpetrators to justice before their own courts.

Compared with human rights and international humanitarian law, the characteristics of international criminal law may be described as follows:

(1) International criminal law does not address obligations of states but establishes individual criminal responsibility for violations of core provisions of human rights and international humanitarian law.

---

[16] Art 5, in conjunction with Arts 121 and 123, of the Rome Statute of the International Criminal Court of 17 July 1998 stipulates that seven years after the entry into force of the Statute (specifically in 2009), an attempt should be made to define the elements of the crime of aggression.
[17] See Chapter 3, section I.2.

(2) Individuals are liable to criminal sanctions irrespective of whether or not they act as state agents.

(3) International criminal law makes it possible to hold the responsible persons directly accountable at the international level without recourse to domestic criminal law.

(4) The direct embodiment of core crimes in international criminal law resulted from the recognition that, where heinous violations of human rights are perpetrated, the preventive and punitive role of international law cannot consist solely in holding the state accountable. For state and non-state actors alike, history has repeatedly shown the inadequacy of leaving criminal prosecution to states that are unable or unwilling to act. Rather, there is a common interest of humanity in ensuring that perpetrators are prosecuted regardless of their status.

II. Treaty Law as the Main Source of Human Rights Guarantees

Where are international human rights and international humanitarian law guarantees enshrined and how? This question concerns the sources of law from which international human rights protection is derived.[18]

In the area of human rights and international humanitarian law, treaty law at the universal level (sections 2 and 4 below) has become the most important source of law. In the case of human rights, regional treaties play a role of varying importance depending on the region concerned (section 3). Treaty law is also the most important basis for international criminal law today (section 5). Treaty law applies to all states that have ratified the corresponding treaties, although the parties to a treaty can release themselves from specific obligations by entering admissible and valid reservations to a provision.[19] Customary law (section III below) plays a subsidiary role in all cases where the protection of the individual is at stake; for instance, where a state has not accepted a particular human rights guarantee by treaty or has denounced the treaty concerned. So-called 'soft law' in the form of declarations and recommendations by international organizations is also important for human rights as a legally non-binding but nonetheless authoritative source of guidance for national lawmakers and for the interpretation of written law (section IV).

---

[18] The most important sources of international law are, according to Art 38 of the ICJ Statute, international conventions, ie treaty law, 'establishing rules expressly recognized by . . . states'; customary law 'as evidence of a general practice accepted as law' by states; and general principles of law that may be inferred from the world's domestic legal systems and transposed to the international level.

[19] For a more detailed analysis, see Chapter 4, section II.2.

Issue in focus: The interpretation of human rights treaties

Broadly speaking, the general rules of interpretation are also applicable to human rights treaties.[20] According to Article 31(1) of the Vienna Convention on the Law of Treaties (VCLT), '[a] treaty shall be interpreted in good faith in accordance with the ordinary meaning to be given to the terms of the treaty in their context and in the light of its object and purpose', and according to Article 31(3)(b) 'any subsequent practice in the application of the treaty which establishes the agreement of the parties regarding its interpretation' is of relevance. On the other hand, the historical method of interpretation plays only a subsidiary role (Article 32 VCLT).

At the same time, the interpretation of human rights treaties differs from that of other treaties in terms of its dynamic approach. As the European Court of Human Rights is emphasizing in its jurisprudence since the *Tyrer* case, the ECHR is 'a living instrument which must be interpreted in the light of present-day conditions'.[21] It follows that the drafters' original intention is of less importance in the case of human rights treaties than for other treaties. There are four reasons for this. First, human rights are usually not formulated as norms but as open principles which, like fundamental rights, need to be given concrete content before they can be applied.[22] Second, this must be done in the light of the object and purpose of the treaty (VCLT, Article 31(1)), which is, as a rule, to ensure optimum protection for rights holders. Third, the principle of effectiveness (*effet utile*) must be respected, ie among the various conceivable interpretations, that which best serves to advance the object and purpose of the treaty should be selected. Finally, limitation clauses must be narrowly construed—again in the light of the object and purpose.

1. The Charter of the United Nations

Reacting to the sufferings caused by the Second World War and recognizing from experience that regimes which abuse human rights are frequently also aggressive beyond their borders, the founders of the United Nations agreed that unconditional respect for human rights is a prerequisite for securing and maintaining a just peace that allows nations and peoples to develop and prosper. As the former UN Secretary General put it, 'we will not enjoy development without security, we will not enjoy security without development, and we will not enjoy either without respect for human rights'.[23]

Article 1 of the UN Charter of 26 June 1945 therefore mentions 'international co-operation . . . in promoting and encouraging respect for human rights and for

[20] See, for instance, ECtHR, *Banković and Others v Belgium, the Czech Republic, Denmark, France, Germany, Greece, Hungary, Iceland, Italy, Luxembourg, the Netherlands, Norway, Poland, Portugal, Spain, Turkey and the United Kingdom*, Reports 2001-XII, paras 55–6.

[21] ECtHR, *Tyrer v The United Kingdom*, Series A, No 26 (1978), reaffirmed by, *inter alia, Banković* (n 20), para 64, with numerous references to the jurisprudence of the ECtHR.

[22] On the distinction between principles and norms see Ronald Dworkin, *Taking Rights Seriously* (Harvard University Press: Cambridge, 1978), 22 and 81.

[23] 'In Larger Freedom: towards development, security and human rights for all', UN Doc A/59/2005, para 17.

fundamental freedoms for all without distinction as to race, sex, language, or religion' as one of the main purposes of the United Nations. Article 56, read in conjunction with Article 55, requires member states to cooperate with the United Nations in promoting 'universal respect for, and observance of, human rights and fundamental freedoms for all without distinction as to race, sex, language, or religion'.[24]

The Charter goes some way towards translating this belief in the importance of human rights into practical action by empowering the General Assembly (Article 13(1)(b)) and the Economic and Social Council (Article 62(2)) to make recommendations on the realization of human rights.[25]

In view of the fact that virtually all states are now members of the United Nations, the Charter may be taken as the legal foundation of the universality of human rights.[26] Although it neither spells out the content of human rights nor accords legal entitlements to individuals, its provisions are important because the member states have agreed, by ratifying the Charter, that human rights are an international issue. States around the world are thus deprived of the possibility of invoking the principle of non-interference in internal affairs in order to treat their citizens as they see fit, and are placed under an obligation to treat all individuals in a manner consistent with human rights. This has practical consequences. In 1980, for instance, the International Court of Justice upheld the United States complaint against Iran regarding the taking of hostages by Islamic revolutionaries in the American Embassy in Tehran, *inter alia* on the ground that '[w]rongfully to deprive human beings of their freedom and to subject them to physical constraint in conditions of hardship is in itself manifestly incompatible with the principles of the Charter of the United Nations, as well as with the fundamental principles enunciated in the Universal Declaration of Human Rights'.[27]

2. Universal human rights treaties

(a) General human rights treaties: UN Human Rights Covenants of 1966

After 18 years of preparatory work, the UN General Assembly adopted the International Covenant on Economic, Social and Cultural Rights (ICESCR) and the International Covenant on Civil and Political Rights (ICCPR) on 16 December 1966. It took a further ten years, until 1976, to obtain the thirty-five ratifications needed for their entry into force. Even in 1990, just over ninety states,

---

[24] Basing itself on this provision, the Commission on Human Rights adopted the Universal Declaration of Human Rights in 1948.

[25] The Economic and Social Council is also entitled to set up the commissions needed for the promotion of human rights (Art 68), a task that it fulfilled primarily by establishing the UN Commission on Human Rights, which was replaced in 2006 by the Human Rights Council, a subsidiary organ of the General Assembly. For more detail, see Chapter 8.

[26] On the issue of the cultural foundations of universality, see Chapter 1, section V.

[27] ICJ, *Case concerning United States Diplomatic and Consular Staff in Tehran (United States of America v Iran)*, ICJ Reports 1980, para 91.

ie somewhat more than half of all countries, had ratified the Covenants. It is only now, with 160 (ICESCR) and 164 (ICCPR) states parties, that the Covenants may be said to have achieved global support and validity.

The delay in drafting and entry into force was due to ideological differences between East and West at the time of the Cold War. Western states, taking the European Convention on Human Rights as their model, aimed at limiting the scope of the Covenant to directly applicable rights allowing individuals to defend themselves against state interference and entrusting the enforcement of applicable rights to a court of law. The Eastern bloc pushed for a treaty protecting economic, social and cultural rights, but held that responsibility for enforcement of those rights would rest exclusively with states exercising their sovereign authority.

Together with the Universal Declaration of Human Rights, the two Covenants constitute the 'International Bill of Human Rights', the list of basic rights recognized by the international community of states. The significance of the Covenants lies in the fact that they convert the human rights outlined in utopian form in the Universal Declaration of Human Rights into a comprehensive set of legally binding rights. This provides individuals with guarantees embodied in international law and ensures compliance, at least to some extent, through the institution of a monitoring system. To enforce their human rights guarantees, the Covenants created the first ever treaty mechanism at the universal level.[28]

(i) International Covenant on Economic, Social and Cultural Rights (ICESCR)

The ICESCR is the most comprehensive codification of economic, social and cultural rights at the universal level. These rights are set out partly as individual entitlements, partly in the form of state obligations to act and partly as objectives to be achieved incrementally. Part I guarantees the right of peoples to self-determination (Article 1), a right that cannot, however, be asserted as an individual human right.[29] Part II lays down the obligations of states under the treaty (Articles 2–5).

Part III contains the substantive guarantees. *Economic* rights (Articles 6–8) comprise the right to work, the right to fair conditions of work and trade union rights. The rights to social security; to protection of the family, mothers, children, and young persons; to an adequate standard of living, including in particular the rights to food, clothing, and housing; and the right to health constitute the group of *social* rights (Articles 9–12). The right to education and free primary schooling, and the right to take part in cultural life and to enjoy the benefits of scientific progress are *cultural* rights (Articles 13–15).

Part IV deals with the implementation of the Covenant. It requires states to submit periodic reports 'on the measures which they have adopted and the

---

[28] For more detail, see Chapter 7, section III.1.
[29] See the position of the Human Rights Committee on the corresponding guarantee in ICCPR, Art 1 (n 31 below).

progress made in achieving the observance of the rights recognized' in the Covenant (Article 16). According to the Covenant, the UN Economic and Social Council (ECOSOC) is responsible for the state reporting procedure (Articles 16–24); however, ECOSOC has delegated this task to the Committee on Economic, Social and Cultural Rights. The Covenant does not provide individuals with the possibility to submit to the Committee claims that their rights are violated. However, an Optional Protocol (ICESCR-OP), which not only allows for an individual complaints procedure, but also for interstate and investigation procedures, was elaborated by the Human Rights Council and adopted by the UN General Assembly on 10 December 2008.[30]

(ii) International Covenant on Civil and Political Rights (ICCPR)

The ICCPR is the most comprehensive codification of civil and political rights at the universal level. Like the ICESCR, it sets out the right of peoples to self-determination (Article 1)[31] and states' obligations under the Covenant (Articles 2–5) in Parts I and II respectively.

Part III contains substantive rights. The provisions concerning protection of life and security of person (Articles 6–11) comprise the right to life; the prohibition of torture and cruel, inhuman, or degrading treatment or punishment; the prohibition of slavery and forced labour; the right to liberty and security of person, including the prohibition of arbitrary arrest or detention; the rights of detainees; and the prohibition of imprisonment merely on the ground of inability to fulfil a contractual obligation. Procedural guarantees are embodied in the provisions concerning protection in deportation proceedings and in the adjudication of criminal charges and civil claims (Articles 13 and 14). The prohibition of retroactive criminal legislation and the right to recognition as a person before the law are of core importance in this regard (Articles 15 and 16).

Civil liberties and related rights are set out in the guarantee of liberty of movement and freedom to choose one's residence (Article 12), the provisions protecting privacy, family, home, correspondence and honour, and those concerning freedom of thought, conscience and religion, freedom of opinion, freedom of assembly and association, marital freedom, and the prohibition of propaganda for war and incitement to racial hatred (Articles 17–23). This part closes with the rights of the child, political rights, the principles of equality before the law and non-discrimination, and the protection of minorities (Articles 24–27).

Part IV sets up the Human Rights Committee and regulates its composition and tasks (Articles 28–45). These include the consideration of state reports

---

[30] 'Optional Protocol to the International Covenant on Economic, Social and Cultural Rights of 10 December 2008', UN Doc A/63/435.

[31] ICCPR, Art 1 does not enshrine an individual right and, therefore, cannot be invoked: HRCttee, *Chief Bernard Ominayak and the Lubicon Lake Band v Canada*, Communication No 167/1984 (1990), para 32.1.

(Article 40) and, where the states concerned have made a declaration under Article 41, of interstate complaints (Articles 41 and 42).

On 19 December 1966, the General Assembly adopted an Optional Protocol (ICCPR-OP) together with the Covenant, which establishes a complaints procedure before the Human Rights Committee, allowing individuals claiming to have been victims of a violation of the Covenant by a state party to submit so-called 'communications' to the Committee for examination.[32] The Second Optional Protocol to the International Covenant on Civil and Political Rights, aiming at the abolition of the death penalty (ICCPR-OP2), dates from 15 December 1989 and requires its states parties to abolish the death penalty completely both in peacetime and, unless a corresponding reservation is made at the time of ratification, in wartime.[33]

(b) Special human rights treaties

(i) Treaties to protect specific human rights

In addition to the Human Rights Covenants, which afford comprehensive human rights protection, the UN has elaborated a number of conventions aimed at protecting specific human rights.

The oldest of these is the Convention on the Prevention and Punishment of the Crime of Genocide of 9 December 1948 (CPPCG). This treaty is primarily a criminal law treaty, which does not expressly mention an individual right to be protected against genocide.[34] The Convention declares that genocide is an international crime that the contracting parties must prevent and punish (Articles I and V), and defines the objective and subjective elements of the crime (Articles II and III). Perpetrators who belong to a government or act on its behalf cannot invoke immunity (Article IV). The contracting parties are under an obligation either to try those responsible domestically, to extradite them, or to have them tried by any international tribunal expressly established for the purpose (Articles V–VII).

The International Convention on the Elimination of All Forms of Racial Discrimination of 21 December 1965 (CERD)[35] defines the concept of racial discrimination in Article 1. It requires states not only to refrain from such discrimination themselves but also to pursue 'a policy of eliminating racial discrimination in all its forms and promoting understanding among all races' (Article 2) and, to that end, to make the expression of racist ideas and their dissemination a punishable offence (Article 4). Furthermore, states must treat all persons equally before the law and ensure that their rights are respected 'without distinction as to race, colour, or national or ethnic origin' (Article 5). In the event of a violation, the person concerned must have access to an effective remedy (Article 6). The

---

[32] See Chapter 7, section III.1.   [33] On the death penalty, see Chapter 9, section II.2.c.
[34] See more details at Chapter 9, section II.5.
[35] For more detail, see Chapter 11, section IV.

Convention establishes a monitoring body with a compulsory state reporting procedure and an optional individual complaints procedure before the Committee on the Elimination of Racial Discrimination (Articles 8–14).

The Convention against Torture and Other Cruel, Inhuman or Degrading Treatment or Punishment of 10 December 1984 (CAT)[36] combines human rights provisions with clauses pertaining to criminal, extradition and administrative law. The Convention provides a detailed definition of the concept of torture (Article 1), prohibits *refoulement* (forcible return) to states where the returnee is at risk of torture (Article 3), and sets out detailed provisions regarding the prosecution or extradition of torturers (Articles 4–9). Other provisions deal with the prevention and investigation of acts of torture (Articles 10–13), the rehabilitation of victims (Article 14) and the prohibition of the use of statements obtained by torture in criminal proceedings (Article 15). The Convention against Torture, too, has a monitoring body with a compulsory state reporting procedure and an optional individual complaints procedure before the Committee against Torture (Articles 17–22). On 18 December 2002, the UN General Assembly adopted an Optional Protocol to the Convention, which provides for a preventive system of visits to places of detention of all kinds as a contribution to the prevention of torture. A Subcommittee for the Prevention of Torture has been entrusted with this task on an international level.

On 20 December 2006, the General Assembly adopted the Convention for the Protection of All Persons from Enforced Disappearance.[37] The Convention states that 'no one shall be subjected to enforced disappearance' (Article 1). The notion is defined as 'the arrest, detention, abduction or any other form of deprivation of liberty by agents of the State or by persons or groups of persons acting with the authorization, support or acquiescence of the State, followed by a refusal to acknowledge the deprivation of liberty or by concealment of the fate or whereabouts of the disappeared person, which places such a person outside the protection of the law' (Article 2). States are required to take measures to make such acts punishable under their domestic criminal law and must investigate, prosecute and punish them or extradite the offender (Articles 3–14, 25). Victims should be assisted and have a right to reparation (Articles 15, 24). To 'expel, return ("refouler"), surrender or extradite a person to another State where there are substantial grounds for believing that he or she would be in danger of being subjected to enforced disappearance' is strictly prohibited (Article 16). Furthermore, states have to take specific legal and administrative measures (eg keeping registers of detainees, respecting the right to information) to ensure nobody can be held in secret detention (Article 17–23). The respect of these duties is monitored by the Committee for the Protection of All Persons from Enforced Disappearance, which has the following competences: to examine state reports, when commanded by urgency to demand that a state reveal information on the

---

[36] See Chapter 10, section II.5.   [37] See also Chapter 10, section III.3.

place of residence of a missing person and—if the state recognizes the respective competence of the Committee—to examine complaints made by individuals or a state and investigate where appropriate, if grave breaches of this treaty are suspected (Articles 26–36).

The implementation of the Convention will be monitored by the Committee on Enforced Disappearances, which will examine state reports and will take urgent action to request that a disappeared person be sought and found. Also, to the extent that states parties recognize the competence of the Committee, it will examine individual communications and, if the state party concerned agrees, carry out a visit to a particular country (Articles 26–36).

(ii) Treaties to protect specific categories of persons

Some human rights treaties are designed to protect particular categories of persons such as refugees, women, children, migrants, and persons with disabilities. These treaties can either regulate the legal status of these persons comprehensively or focus on individual guarantees such as the principle of non-discrimination. They sometimes deal with policy and regulatory issues going beyond human rights guarantees as such.

The Convention relating to the Status of Refugees (CSR) of 28 July 1951 is the oldest treaty aimed at protecting a specific category of persons. Although the Convention is not a classic human rights treaty, it is of the utmost importance for its beneficiaries inasmuch as it creates subsidiary international protection for persons who have lost the protection of their state of origin. While the Convention does not recognize a right of refugees to be granted asylum and is silent on the question of asylum procedures, the prohibition on returning refugees to the persecuting state (*non-refoulement*, Article 33) ensures that persecuted persons remain beyond the reach of the said state. The country of refuge thus remains responsible for refugees while they remain within its territory, even though it is not obliged to accept such persons permanently. The core of the Convention addresses questions of equal treatment of refugees and non-discrimination. It describes in detail (Articles 12–24) the rights that refugees who have found refuge in a state should enjoy in areas such as employment, welfare, education, protection of property, and freedom of association. Depending on the area, it guarantees equal treatment as that granted to foreigners in similar circumstances (eg regarding employment) or with nationals of the state (eg in the area of welfare and social security).

The Convention on the Elimination of All Forms of Discrimination against Women of 18 December 1979 (CEDAW) seeks to outlaw discrimination against women in many different spheres. It requires states to refrain from engaging in discrimination as defined in Article 1 and, in addition, to pursue 'a policy of eliminating discrimination against women'. To that end, states must take a number of concrete measures, including, for instance, embodying the principle of equality in their constitutions (Article 2). They must also take concrete measures to promote equality (Articles 3 and 5), which may include temporary special measures (including quotas), provided that they are not maintained for longer than necessary (Article 4). The Convention furthermore guarantees women the same rights as men in the areas of political rights and access to public office, in the acquisition of nationality, in education, in health care, in employment, and other areas of economic and social life (Articles 7–14). In addition, women may not be discriminated against in civil matters in general and in marriage and family law in particular (Articles 15 and 16). The Convention establishes a state reporting procedure (Article 18). Under the Optional Protocol to the Convention on the Elimination of All Forms of Discrimination against Women of 10 December 1999 (OP-CEDAW), individual complaints may now be submitted to the Committee on the Elimination of Discrimination against Women.

The human rights of children and young people below the age of 18 years are comprehensively recognized in the Convention on the Rights of the Child (CRC) of 20 November 1989. They include not only the prohibition of discrimination (Article 2) and the classic civil liberties and due process rights (eg Articles 13–16, 37, and 40), but also economic, social and cultural rights (especially Articles 24–29 and 32). Child-specific rights such as the right to registration immediately after birth (Article 7) and to a separate identity (Article 8) are of special importance. The Convention affords protection in the event of separation from parents (Article 9), and protection against illicit transfer abroad (Article 11), sexual exploitation (Article 34), and child trafficking (Article 35). It gives children the right to be heard in any judicial and administrative proceedings affecting them (Article 12(2)). The Convention further contains human rights guarantees for specific categories of children needing special protection such as the children of migrants who are separated from their family, adopted children, refugee children, children with disabilities and children in wartime (Articles 10, 21–23, and 38). The leading principles of the Convention require that all actions concerning children have the child's best interests as the primary consideration (Article 3(1)) and that the state (subject to the best interests of the child) must respect parental rights relating to the upbringing of the child (Article 5). The Committee on the Rights of the Child is responsible for monitoring implementation of the treaty via a state reporting procedure (Articles 42–44). On 25 May 2000 the Convention was supplemented by two protocols. The Optional Protocol to the Convention on the Rights of the Child on the involvement of children in armed conflict raises the age at which it is permissible to recruit children for active service in armed conflict to 18 years, and the Optional Protocol to the Convention on the Rights of the Child on the sale of children, child prostitution and child pornography enhances the protection of children and minors against sexual exploitation.[38]

The Convention on the Protection of the Rights of All Migrant Workers and Members of Their Families of 18 December 1990 (ICRMW)

---

[38] On the protection of children against exploitation, see Chapter 14, section I.3.

prohibits discrimination against persons employed in countries other than their own (Article 7). It describes in detail the rights that all migrant workers should enjoy, including those who are undocumented or in an irregular position in the country of employment (Articles 8–35). The rights include protection of life, protection against torture or slavery, freedom of belief and freedom of opinion, protection of the family and of property, protection in the event of arrest or detention, and due process guarantees. Article 22 details migrant workers' rights in connection with expulsion and Article 25 guarantees conditions of employment and remuneration on a par with nationals of the state concerned. States are required to respect their cultural identity (Article 31). Migrants who are documented or in a regular situation in the state of employment have additional rights (Articles 36–56). They include, for example, freedom of residence, trade union rights, the right to take part in the political life of their state of origin, especially in elections, the right of equal access with nationals of the state of employment to educational, social, and health services, and the right of access to a particular remunerated activity. Other provisions deal with the rights of special categories of migrant workers (Articles 57–63), eg frontier or seasonal workers. The Convention provides for a Committee on the Protection of the Rights of All Migrant Workers and Members of Their Families to monitor states parties. The Committee considers compulsory state reports and can examine individual complaints where the state concerned has made a corresponding declaration (Articles 72–78). The fact that the Convention, in particular, recognizes extensive rights for illegal residents delayed achievement of the twenty ratifications required for entry into force until 2003 and may explain why, to date, no country with a tradition or policy of employing foreign workers has ratified the Convention.

On 13 December 2006 the General Assembly adopted the Convention on the Rights of Persons with Disabilities (CRPD). It obliges states parties and regional integration organizations which have ratified it,[39] to take specific legislative and administrative measures 'to ensure and promote the full realization of all human rights and fundamental freedoms for all persons with disabilities without discrimination of any kind on the basis of disability' (Article 4), and this, with particular regard for the vulnerabilities of women and children (Articles 6–7). States parties are obliged to raise awareness throughout society regarding persons with disabilities, to ensure their access to transport, information and communication (Article 8–9) and to respect and protect human rights of particular relevance for such persons (Article 10–30). A Committee on the Rights of Persons with Disabilities will examine country reports (Article 34–39) and, to the extent that a state party has ratified the Optional Protocol to the Convention on the Rights of Persons with Disabilities, individual complaints.

---

[39] According to Arts 42 and 44 not only states but also regional integration organizations can become parties to the Convention.

(c) Human rights protection by the International Labour Organization

The International Labour Organization (ILO),[40] with its 188 binding conventions and 199 recommendations,[41] has undertaken an extensive codification of labour law with a pronounced human rights dimension, eg the conventions on the abolition of forced labour, on freedom of association and on discrimination in employment. Conventions of special importance for human rights include the Convention concerning Equal Remuneration for Men and Women Workers for Work of Equal Value of 29 June 1951 (Equal Remuneration Convention) (No 100), the Convention concerning Indigenous and Tribal Peoples in Independent Countries of 27 June 1989 (Indigenous and Tribal Peoples Convention) (No 169) and the Convention concerning the Prohibition and Immediate Action for the Elimination of the Worst Forms of Child Labour of 17 June 1999 (Worst Forms of Child Labour Convention) (No 182). These conventions usually contain no individual rights but obligations to enact certain legal provisions. A summary of the universal human rights treaties is provided in Table 2.1.

3. Regional human rights treaties

The role played by regional treaties varies from continent to continent. The European Convention on Human Rights is of such overriding importance in European countries that in practical terms it has relegated the universal treaties to second place. The Inter-American Convention on Human Rights is highly influential in the countries of Latin America. The African Charter on Human and Peoples' Rights, on the other hand, is still relatively weak, in the Middle East the Arab Charter on Human Rights has just recently come into force and in Asia as well as in the Pacific regional treaties are virtually non existent.

(a) Africa

The African Charter on Human and Peoples' Rights (the Banjul Charter) (ACHPR) was adopted on 26 June 1981 by the Organization of African Unity (OAU) (since 9 July 2002: the African Union (AU)). In addition to a list of civil and political rights and of economic, social and cultural rights for individuals, the Charter also contains collective rights, that is to say the rights of peoples to equality, self-determination, development, peace, and a satisfactory environment (Articles 22–24). The scope of these 'solidarity rights' has thus far remained rather unclear. The Charter further emphasizes the duties that every individual has 'towards his family and society, the State and other legally recognized communities and the international community' (Article 27(1)). It underlines the fact that enjoyment of the guaranteed rights is limited by the duty to exercise them 'with due regard to the rights of others, to collective security, and to morality and common interest'.

---

[40] On its establishment, see Chapter 1, section II.4.   [41] Status as of December 2008.

Table 2.1. Universal human rights treaties (status as of December 2008)

	Ratifications
International Covenant on Economic, Social and Cultural Rights of 16 December 1966 (ICESCR)	160
— Optional Protocol to the International Covenant on Economic, Social and Cultural Rights of 10 December 2008 (ICESCR-OP)	0
International Covenant on Civil and Political Rights of 16 December 1966 (ICCPR)	164
— First Optional Protocol to the International Covenant on Civil and Political Rights of 19 December 1966 (ICCPR-OP1)	111
— Second Optional Protocol to the International Covenant on Civil and Political Rights of 15 December 1989 (ICCPR-OP2)	70
Convention on the Prevention and Punishment of the Crime of Genocide of 9 December 1948 (CPPCG)	140
International Convention on the Elimination of All Forms of Racial Discrimination of 21 December 1965 (CERD)	173
Convention against Torture and Other Cruel, Inhuman or Degrading Treatment or Punishment of 10 December 1984 (Convention against Torture/CAT)	146
— Optional Protocol to the Convention against Torture and Other Cruel, Inhuman or Degrading Treatment or Punishment of 18 December 2002 (OPCAT)	41
Convention on the Elimination of All Forms of Discrimination against Women of 18 December 1979 (CEDAW)	185
— Optional Protocol to the Convention on the Elimination of All Forms of Discrimination against Women of 6 October 1999 (OP-CEDAW)	96
Convention on the Rights of the Child of 20 November 1989 (CRC)	193
— Optional Protocol to the Convention on the Rights of the Child on the involvement of children in armed conflict of 25 May 2000 (OP-CRC-AC)	126
— Optional Protocol to the Convention on the Rights of the Child on the sale of children, child prostitution and child pornography of 25 May 2000 (OP-CRC-SC)	130
International Convention on the Protection of the Rights of All Migrant Workers and Members of Their Families of 18 December 1990 (ICRMW)	40
Convention for the Protection of All Persons from Enforced Disappearance of 20 December 2006 (CPAPED)	7
Convention on the Rights of Persons with Disabilities of 13 December 2006 (CRPD)	45
— Optional Protocol to Convention on the Rights of Persons with Disabilities of 13 December 2006 (OP CRPD).	27
Convention relating to the Status of Refugees of 28 July 1951 (CSR)	144

The task of monitoring this treaty is entrusted to the African Commission for Human and Peoples' Rights, to which victims of human rights violations but also non-governmental organizations (NGOs) and other persons may submit complaints. However, no entitlement to consideration of such complaints exists, ie the Commission itself decides which cases to investigate. A Protocol adopted

Table 2.2. African human rights treaties (status as of December 2008)

	Ratifications
African Charter on Human and Peoples' Rights (Banjul Charter) (ACHPR)	53
— Protocol to the African Charter on Human and Peoples' Rights on the Rights of Women in Africa of 11 July 2003 (P 2/ACHPR)	25
African Charter on the Rights and Welfare of the Child of 11 July 1990 (ACRWC)	44

in 1998[42] on the establishment of an African Court entered into force in 2004 upon securing its fifteenth ratification. To date the African Court on Human and Peoples' Rights has been unable to start its activities.

Other African Conventions include the African Charter on the Rights and Welfare of the Child of July 1990 and the Protocol Additional to the Banjul Charter on the Rights of Women in Africa of 11 July 2003. A summary of the current African human rights treaties can be found in Table 2.2.

(b) The Americas

The American Convention on Human Rights of 22 November 1969 (ACHR), which has not been ratified by the United States, Canada, and a number of Caribbean states, plays a major role in the Americas as violations of its guarantees can be made the subject of individual complaints to the Inter-American Commission on Human Rights and the Inter-American Court of Human Rights. As the system is somewhat complicated, the Court has so far handed down just over 100 substantive judgments. The ACHR, which the Organization of American States (OAS) adopted more than two decades after the American Declaration of the Rights and Duties of Man of 2 May 1948, is largely identical to the ECHR in terms of content but contains some additional rights. These include the right to recognition as a person before the law (Article 3), nationality rights (Article 20), rights of participation in public affairs (Article 23), and minimum social rights (Article 26). The Additional Protocol in the Area of Economic, Social and Cultural Rights (Protocol of San Salvador) of 17 November 1988 contains many guarantees that are also embodied in the ICESCR, such as the right to work (Article 6) and the right to education (Article 13). The Protocol to Abolish the Death Penalty of 8 June 1990 prohibits the death penalty in peacetime and also, as a rule, in wartime. In the latter case, however, a state may enter a reservation in respect of extremely serious crimes (Article 2).

Four instruments deal with specific categories of human rights. The Inter-American Convention to Prevent and Punish Torture of 9 December 1985 contains provisions regarding the definition of torture, the obligation of states parties to prevent and punish torture and to compensate victims, and a list of

---

[42] Protocol to the African Charter on Human and Peoples' Rights on the Establishment of an African Court on Human and Peoples' Rights, 10 June 1998.

circumstances that may not be invoked as 'justification'. The Inter-American
Convention on the Forced Disappearance of Persons of 9 June 1994 obliges states
to prevent the practice of forced disappearance and to punish perpetrators. The
Inter-American Convention on the Prevention, Punishment and Eradication of
Violence against Women of 9 June 1994 prohibits physical, sexual, and psychological violence against women on account of their gender and requires the states
parties to take measures to prevent such violence in both the public and private
spheres and to prosecute the perpetrators. The Inter-American Convention on
the Elimination of All Forms of Discrimination against Persons with Disabilities
of 7 June 1999 obliges in very general terms states parties to take measures to
prevent and eradicate discrimination against persons suffering from disabilities.
A summary of the current Inter-American human rights treaties is provided at
Table 2.3.

(c) Europe

The most important Convention in Europe is the European Convention on
Human Rights (ECHR), which was adopted by the Council of Europe on
4 November 1950. It embodies the following rights in Section I (Articles 2–14):
the right to life; the prohibition of torture and inhuman or degrading treatment or
punishment; the prohibition of slavery and forced labour; the right to liberty and
security of person; due process rights; the prohibition of retroactive criminal legislation; the right to respect for private and family life, home and correspondence;
freedom of thought, conscience, and religion; freedom of expression; freedom of
assembly and association; the right to marry; the right to an effective remedy; and

Table 2.3. Inter-American human rights treaties (status as at December 2008)

	Ratifications
American Convention on Human Rights of 22 November 1969 (ACHR)	25
— Additional Protocol to the American Convention on Human Rights in the Area of Economic, Social and Cultural Rights of 17 November 1988 (P 1/ACHR; Protocol of San Salvador)	14
— Additional Protocol to the American Convention on Human Rights to Abolish the Death Penalty of 8 June 1990 (P 2/ACHR)	9
Inter-American Convention to Prevent and Punish Torture of 9 December 1985 (IACAT)	17
Inter-American Convention on the Forced Disappearance of Persons of 9 June 1994 (IACFD)	13
Inter-American Convention on the Prevention, Punishment and Eradication of Violence against Women of 9 June 1994 (IACVAW; Convention of Belem do Para)	32
Inter-American Convention on the Elimination of All Forms of Discrimination against Persons with Disabilities of 7 June 1999 (IACDAPD)	17

the right to non-discrimination. Sections II and III regulate the individual complaints procedure[43] before the European Court of Human Rights (ECtHR).

The range of guaranteed rights has been expanded by a number of additional protocols to the ECHR. Protocol No 1 of 20 March 1952 guarantees in Articles 1–3 the protection of property, the right to education and the right to free elections. Protocol No 4 of 16 September 1963 prohibits deprivation of liberty on account of debt, the expulsion of a state's own nationals and the collective expulsion of aliens, and guarantees freedom of movement, including the right to move freely in one's country of residence and to leave it (Articles 1–4). Protocol No 6 of 28 April 1983 abolishes the death penalty in peacetime and Protocol No 13 of 2 May 2002 abolishes it in wartime. In its first five articles Protocol No 7 of 22 November 1984 guarantees procedural protection to aliens threatened with expulsion, the possibility of at least one appeal to a higher court in criminal proceedings, the right to compensation for miscarriages of justice, the principle of *ne bis in idem,* and equal rights for spouses. Lastly, Protocol No 12 of June 27 2000 provides for a general and free-standing prohibition of discrimination that has a far wider scope of application than the 'merely' accessory non-discrimination clause of Article 14 ECHR.[44]

Issue in focus: The relationship between the ICCPR and ECHR guarantees

---

The ICCPR guarantees are comparable but not identical to those of the ECHR. The ECHR provides greater protection both for the right to property (Article 1 P 1/ECHR), a right not mentioned in the ICCPR (or the ICESCR), and through its explicit enumeration of the permissible grounds for limitations on the right to life (Article 2). The ICCPR goes further in terms of its guarantee of the right of peoples to self-determination (Article 1); the guarantee of equality before courts and tribunals (Article 14(1)); the right to be recognized as a person before the law (Article 16); the prohibition of propaganda for war (Article 20); the rights of the child (Article 24); the right to have access to public service (Article 25); and the rights of minorities (Article 27). Others rights, such as the right of prisoners to humane treatment (Article 10) and the right to form trade unions (Article 22) are contained only implicitly in the ECHR. The comprehensive prohibition of discrimination in Article 26 and the categorical prohibition of the death penalty in the Second Optional Protocol to the ICCPR had no counterpart in ECHR law prior to the adoption of Protocols Nos 12 and 13.

The ECHR is not the only European human rights convention. The European Social Charter (ESC) of 18 October 1961 embodies a number of economic, social and cultural rights similar to those set out in the ICESCR. A revised version of the Charter is applicable to states that have ratified the new text adopted on 3 May 1996. The 31 Charter rights are extremely varied. Contracting parties must commit

---

[43] For more detail, see Chapter 7, section III.2.
[44] On these distinctions see Chapter 11, section II.1.

themselves to be bound by at least six of the following nine rights: the right to work (Article 1); freedom of assembly, the right to bargain collectively, and the right to strike (Articles 5 and 6); protection of young people in employment (Article 7); the right to social security (Article 12); the right to social and medical assistance (Article 13); the right of families to protection (Article 16); the right of migrant workers and their families to protection (Article 19); and the right to equality of opportunity and equal treatment in employment and occupation without discrimination on grounds of sex (Article 20). States may select further obligations freely from the remaining list of rights. An Additional Protocol of 5 September 1995[45] provides for a collective complaint procedure for trade unions, employers' organizations, and international non-governmental organizations to a Committee of Independent Experts, which then prepares a report for the Committee of Ministers of the Council of Europe on whether the Convention has been violated. This procedure has thus created for the first time at the international level a body of at least quasi-judicial jurisprudence on economic and social human rights.

Individual clusters of human rights are also protected by special conventions at the regional level. For instance, the prohibition of torture is addressed in the European Convention for the Prevention of Torture and Inhuman or Degrading Treatment or Punishment of 26 November 1987 and in the two Additional Protocols of 4 November 1994. The Convention has established a system of preventive visits that enables the European Committee for the Prevention of Torture to inspect places where persons are deprived of their liberty at any time and, as a rule, without prior notification, and to make recommendations to the government of the country concerned regarding measures aimed at preventing future cases of torture or ill-treatment.

In the 1990's, the Council of Europe concerned itself with the protection of minorities.[46] The Framework Convention for the Protection of National Minorities of 1 February 1995 deals only, as its title indicates, with 'national minorities', ie minorities who are nationals of the state concerned and traditionally reside in its territory, and addresses, in particular, their linguistic and educational rights. The European Charter for Regional or Minority Languages of 5 November 1992 regulates in detail the measures that contracting states must take to promote the use of regional or minority languages in public affairs.

Further recent additions to European human rights protection include Conventions for the Protection of Human Rights and Dignity of the Human Being with regard to the Application of Biology and Medicine of 4 April 1997 (the Convention on Human Rights and Biomedicine) and its Additional Protocols on the Prohibition of Cloning Human Beings of 12 January 1998; on the Transplantation of Organs and Tissues of Human Origin of 24 January

---

[45] Additional Protocol to the European Social Charter Providing for a System of Collective Complaints of 5 September 1995, ETS No 158.
[46] On the topic of minority protection, see Chapter 11, section V.

2002; and on Biomedical Research of 25 January 2005. The Council of Europe also adopted Conventions on Action against Trafficking in Human Beings of 16 May 2005; on the Avoidance of Statelessness in Relation to State Succession of 19 May 2006; and on the Protection of Children against Sexual Exploitation and Sexual Abuse of 25 October 2007. A summary of the current European human rights treaties is shown at Table 2.4.

(d) Middle East

In the Middle East, the Council of the League of Arab States adopted the Arab Charter on Human Rights of 15 September 1994. Its provisions largely corresponded to those of the Universal Declaration of Human Rights and the two

Table 2.4. European human rights treaties (status as of December 2008)

	Ratifications
European Convention on Human Rights of 4 November 1950 (ECHR)	47
— Protocol No 1 of 20 March 1952 (P 1/ECHR)	45
— Protocol No 4 of 16 September 1963 (P 4/ECHR)	42
— Protocol No 6 of 28 April 1983 (P 6/ECHR)	46
— Protocol No 7 of 22 November 1984 (P 7/ECHR)	41
— Protocol No 12 of 4 November 2000 (P 12/ECHR)	17
— Protocol No 13 of 3 May 2002 (P 13/ECHR)	40
European Social Charter of 18 October 1961 (ESC)	27
European Social Charter (revised) of 3 May 1996 (ESCrev)	25
European Convention for the Prevention of Torture and Inhuman or Degrading Treatment or Punishment of 26 November 1987 (ECPT)	47
— Protocol No 1 of 4 November 1993 (P 1/ECPT)	47
— Protocol No 2 of 4 November 1993 (P 2/ECPT)	47
Framework Convention for the Protection of National Minorities of 1 February 1995 (FCPNM)	39
European Charter for Regional or Minority Languages of 5 November 1992 (ECML)	23
European Convention for the Protection of Human Rights and Dignity of the Human Being with regard to the Application of Biology and Medicine (ECHRB, Convention on Human Rights and Biomedicine) of 4 April 1997	22
— Additional Protocol on the Prohibition of Cloning Human Beings of 12 January 1998 (P 1/ECHRB)	17
— Additional Protocol on Transplantation of Organs and Tissues of Human Origin of 24 January 2002 (P 2/ECHRB)	8
— Additional Protocol concerning Biomedical Research of 25 January 2005 (P 2/ECHRB)	5
European Convention on Action against Trafficking in Human Beings of 16 May 2005 (ECTHB)	20
European Convention on the Avoidance of Statelessness in Relation to State Succession of 19 May 2006	3
European Convention on Protection of Children against Sexual Exploitation and Sexual Abuse of 25 October 2007 (ECPC; not yet into force)	0

Human Rights Covenants of 1966. As this instrument was not ratified by any state, a revised version of the Arab Charter on Human Rights was adopted on 22 May 2004. After the seventh ratification, the Charter entered into force on 15 March 2008.

Besides the right of peoples to self-determination and an explicit right to resistance in case of foreign occupation (Article 2), the Charter includes basic human rights guarantees: the right to life (Articles 5–7); the prohibition of torture and inhumane or degrading treatment (Articles 8 and 9); the prohibition of slavery and forced labour (Article 10); a general guarantee of equality before the law (Article 11); procedural guarantees (Article 12–19); rights of citizenship (Article 24); and civil rights such as the right to privacy and freedom of religion and opinion (Articles 21 and 30–31). The charter also lays down a catalogue of economic, social and cultural rights, including the right to an adequate standard of living (Article 38); the right to work (Article 34); the right to health (Article 39); as well as the right to education (Article 41). It also recognizes specific minority rights (Article 25) and the rights of persons with a disability (Article 40).

The Charter is monitored by the Arab Human Rights Committee, which is made up of seven independent personalities. This body only possesses the competence to review state reports and cannot therefore deal with individual complaints.

The Arab Human Rights Charter protects most human rights in a way comparable to that adopted by the other universal and regional conventions. It has been criticized for equalizing racism and Zionism (Article 2(3)), guaranteeing equality of men and women 'within the framework of the positive discrimination established in favour of women by the Islamic Shariah, other divine laws and by applicable laws and legal instruments' (Article 3(3)), and not fully outlawing the execution of persons who committed a crime under the age of 18 (Article 7). On the other hand, with its long list of non-derogable rights (Article 4(2)), the Charter goes beyond the protection afforded by other conventions.

(e) Other regions

South and South-East Asia have no regional human rights convention. The two regional organizations SAARC (South Asian Association for Regional Cooperation) and ASEAN (Association of Southeast Asian Nations) see themselves as bodies concerned strictly with interstate issues. Thus, ASEAN deals primarily with questions of peace and stability in South-East Asia as well as with regional economic issues and has, until recently, viewed human rights as forming part of the internal affairs of member states. However, on 20 November 2007, the South-East Asian Heads of State adopted a new ASEAN Charter which, while not containing a human rights catalogue, establishes an ASEAN human rights body to review human rights among the members of the organization.[47]

---

[47] ASEAN Charter, Art 14.

The SAARC is traditionally somewhat more open to human rights. While the Association's Charter does not include human rights among its objectives, the SAARC was nonetheless established, *inter alia*, to provide all individuals with the opportunity to live in dignity.[48] On 5 January 2002 in Kathmandu, the SAARC took important steps to translate this goal into practice by adopting its fifth and sixth Conventions since its foundation in 1985, dealing respectively with the protection of children[49] and the fight against trafficking in women and children.[50] While the latter obliges states primarily to take measures under criminal law and to cooperate in the area of judicial assistance and extradition, the Child Welfare Convention concerns itself directly with states' obligations to reaffirm children's rights and to implement under the UN Convention on the Rights of the Child at the domestic level.[51] The duty to ensure that national laws protect children from discrimination, abuse, neglect, exploitation, torture or degrading treatment, trafficking and violence, and to administer juvenile justice in a manner consistent with the promotion of the child's sense of dignity and worth, are ranked among the priorities of states parties in this sphere.[52] Although the Child Welfare Convention contains few new rights, it marks the first instance in which Asia has set treaty-based standards for at least one category of human rights, strengthening the basis for their enforcement at the national level. On 4 January 2004, the SAARC leaders adopted a Social Charter which, while not enshrining individual rights, obliges States to take specific measures in the areas covered by economic, social and cultural rights. Table 2.5 provides a summary of the current human rights treaties in the Middle East and Asia.

4. Humanitarian law: the Geneva Conventions and their Additional Protocols

(a) International armed conflicts

The law on the protection of human beings in times of international armed conflicts is exhaustively regulated in the virtually universally ratified four Geneva Conventions of 1949 (ratified as of December 2008 in each case by 194 states) and in Additional Protocols I and II of 1977 (ratified as of December 2008 by 168 and 164 states respectively).

---

[48] Charter of the South Asian Association for Regional Cooperation of 8 December 1985, Art 1: '... (b) to accelerate economic growth, social progress and cultural development in the region and to provide all individuals the opportunity to live in dignity and to realize their full potential'.

[49] SAARC Convention on Regional Arrangements for the Promotion of Child Welfare in South Asia, 5 January 2002.

[50] SAARC Convention on Preventing and Combating Trafficking in Women and Children for Prostitution, 5 January 2002.

[51] Art III(2) and (3).   [52] Art IV(3).

Table 2.5. Other regional human rights treaties—Middle East and Asia (status as of December 2008)

	Ratifications
Arab Charter on Human Rights of 22 May 2004 (ArCHR)	7
SAARC Convention on Regional Arrangements for the Promotion of Child Welfare in South Asia of 25 January 2002	Signed by all SAARC member states
SAARC Convention on Preventing and Combating Trafficking in Women and Children for Prostitution of 25 January 2002	Signed by all SAARC member states
SAARC Social Charter of 4 January 2004	Signed by all SAARC member states

The Geneva Convention for the Amelioration of the Condition of the Wounded and Sick in Armed Forces in the Field (I Geneva Convention (GC I)), which is based on the original 1864 Geneva Convention for the Amelioration of the Condition of the Wounded in Armies in the Field, further develops the founding tenet of the Red Cross that wounded and sick soldiers need protection,[53] adjusting it to the changed circumstances of twentieth century warfare.[54] It continues to adhere to the principle that soldiers who are wounded and sick and hence defenceless should be protected, even when they fall into enemy hands, and describes in detail who can benefit from such protection and how. The Convention also elaborates on the rights of medical personnel. The Geneva Convention for the Amelioration of the Condition of Wounded, Sick and Shipwrecked Members of Armed Forces at Sea (II Geneva Convention (GC II)) addresses the same subjects on behalf of members of naval armed forces and extends protection for the wounded and sick to the shipwrecked, towards whom belligerent parties have the obligation of taking all possible measures to rescue after each engagement.

The Geneva Convention relative to the Treatment of Prisoners of War (III Geneva Convention (GC III)) elaborates on the provisions of the Hague Convention of 1899 and the Hague Convention X of 1907 concerning prisoners of war. The Convention is based on the principle that members of regular armed forces and other combatants of similar status (Article 4) may not be punished for taking part in armed conflict and that their imprisonment does not constitute a sanction but merely serves to neutralize their capacity to fight. According to the basic principle laid down in Article 13, '[p]risoners of war must at all times be humanely treated. Any unlawful act or omission by the Detaining Power causing death or seriously endangering the health of a prisoner of war in its custody is prohibited...'. The Convention sets out in detail what is meant by humane treatment, for instance in respect of captivity (Articles 17–20); internment (Articles 21–24); quarters, food and clothing (Articles 25–28); hygiene and medical

---

[53] See Chapter 1, section II.3.
[54] The 1864 Convention had already been amended in 1906 and 1929.

attention (Articles 29–32); labour (Articles 49–57); and treatment in the event of disciplinary or criminal offences (Articles 82–108). Lastly, the Convention deals with the release and repatriation of prisoners of war (Articles 109–119).

The Geneva Convention relative to the Protection of Civilian Persons in Time of War (IV Geneva Convention (GC IV)) has the most direct bearing on human rights inasmuch as its provisions regarding the protection of life and person, the prohibition of discrimination and the due process rights of accused civilians embody, to some extent, rights that are also contained in the ICCPR. As only a few provisions of the Hague Convention IV of 1907 dealt with the protection of the civilian population, this Convention constitutes the first comprehensive codification of the protection of civilians in times of armed conflict. In addition to norms relating to the general protection of the civilian population (Articles 13–26), it contains key provisions concerning occupied territories (Articles 47–78) and the internment of civilians (Articles 79–135). Article 4, which spells out who is protected by the Convention, is particularly important. The article defines 'protected persons' as those 'who, at a given moment and in any manner whatsoever, find themselves, in case of a conflict or occupation, in the hands of a Party to the conflict or Occupying Power of which they are not nationals'. In other words, the IV Convention does not protect a country's own civilian population, differing in this regard fundamentally from human rights instruments.

This shortcoming is addressed by the Protocol Additional to the Geneva Conventions of 12 August 1949, and relating to the Protection of Victims of International Armed Conflicts of 8 June 1977 (Additional Protocol I (AP I)), which covers 'all persons who are civilians' (Article 50(2)). It thus overcomes the principle of reciprocity, according to which nationals of the enemy state are spared only because the latter has the same obligation *vis-à-vis* members of a country's own armed forces and civilian population, so that both belligerents benefit from 'humane conduct'. This step brings humanitarian law closer to human rights. The Protocol also offsets to some extent the exclusion of non-international conflicts from the protection of international humanitarian law by equating wars of liberation, especially against colonial domination, with international conflicts (Article 1(4)).

Compared with the IV Convention, Additional Protocol I also broadens the scope of protection afforded to the civilian population in terms of content (Articles 48–79) by incorporating elements of Hague Law on warfare and linking them to the protection of victims of armed conflicts. Of special importance are the prohibitions of military attacks on the civilian population and indiscriminate attacks, ie attacks such as carpet bombing, which 'are of a nature to strike military objectives and civilians or civilian objects without distinction' (Article 51). This means that the belligerents are under an obligation to distinguish at all times between the civilian population and combatants as well as between civilian and military objectives. These and other provisions (eg Articles 57 and 58 concerning precautionary measures on behalf of the civilian population in the context

of military attacks) give clear shape to the right to life in armed conflicts.[55]
Additional Protocol I also addresses social rights, for instance by categorically
prohibiting the starvation of civilians as a method of warfare (Article 54).

Additional Protocol I also relates to the other Geneva Conventions. Articles
8–34 update and clarify questions relating to the protection of the wounded,
sick and shipwrecked, and Articles 44–46 define who has prisoner-of-war
status and how persons who have not acquired such status are to be treated.
The basic rules of the law of warfare laid down in Articles 35–42 also have an
important bearing on the protection of life and person. Article 35, fundamental in this regard, stipulates that '[i]n any armed conflict, the right of the Parties
to the conflict to choose methods or means of warfare is not unlimited' and
that it is prohibited, in particular, 'to employ weapons, projectiles and material
and methods of warfare of a nature to cause superfluous injury or unnecessary
suffering'.

The guarantees set out in Article 75 are applicable to all persons who are in the
power of a party to the conflict, regardless of their status. The article contains
what resembles a bill of human rights for the special circumstances of armed conflict. It obliges parties to the conflict to treat members of the opposing side who
fall into their hands in a humane way and prohibits discrimination. Paragraph 2
contains comprehensive guarantees of protection of life and person; paragraph 3
sets out the minimum rights of detainees; paragraph 4 describes in detail fair trial
rights; while, paragraph 5 deals with the protection of women.

(b) Internal armed conflicts

One of the main challenges confronting international humanitarian law is the
fact that nowadays the vast majority of armed conflicts are not fought between
states but are wholly or primarily[56] conflicts of a non-international character (ie
civil wars).[57] The body of norms constituting international humanitarian law only
partially reflects the fact that internal conflicts have become the rule rather than
the exception. This shortcoming is mainly due to the fact that states have long
regarded such conflicts as their internal affair and are still unwilling to accept
constraints on action against insurgents and secessionist movements considered
by them to be unduly restrictive.

States that have ratified only the four Geneva Conventions are bound in this
regard by just one provision of treaty law. Article 3, which is common to all the
Conventions and was drafted in 1949 in the light of experiences from the Spanish
Civil War, lays down minimum rules to be observed in non-international armed

---

[55] See Chapter 9, section II.2.d.

[56] On the complex issue of so-called mixed conflicts, see Chapter 5, section I.4.

[57] The SPIRI Yearbook 2007 (Stockholm 2007, 80) counts three important international
conflict and 31 important internal conflicts in the years 1997–2006. An 'important' conflict has
been defined as one causing at least one thousand deaths (SIPRI: Stockholm International Peace
Research Institute <http://www.sipri.org/> (accessed 9 February 2009)).

conflicts[58] by all parties to the conflict, ie including insurgents. Article 3(1) stipulates:

1. Persons taking no active part in the hostilities, including members of armed forces who have laid down their arms and those placed *hors de combat* by sickness, wounds, detention, or any other cause, shall in all circumstances be treated humanely, without any adverse distinction founded on race, colour, religion or faith, sex, birth or wealth, or any other similar criteria. To this end the following acts are and shall remain prohibited at any time and in any place whatsoever with respect to the above-mentioned persons:

> (a) Violence to life and person, in particular murder of all kinds, mutilation, cruel treatment and torture;
> (b) Taking of hostages;
> (c) Outrages upon personal dignity, in particular humiliating and degrading treatment;
> (d) The passing of sentences and the carrying out of executions without previous judgment pronounced by a regularly constituted court, affording all the judicial guarantees which are recognized as indispensable by civilized peoples.

According to paragraph 2, the wounded and sick are to be collected and cared for, and the International Committee of the Red Cross may offer its services to the parties to the conflict without this being an interference in the internal affairs of the country concerned.

The Protocol Additional to the Geneva Conventions of 12 August 1949, and Relating to the Protection of Victims of Non-International Armed Conflicts of 8 June 1977 (Additional Protocol II (AP II)) regulates in detail the protection to be afforded to individuals and the constraints applicable to warfare. Although it does not recognize insurgents as combatants and no prisoner-of-war status can therefore exist in such circumstances, its guarantees are nonetheless applicable without discrimination to 'all persons affected by' a non-international armed conflict[59] (Article 2(1)), ie both to fighters and civilians backing the state and to those supporting the insurgents. Additional Protocol II is binding not only on the state but also on non-state parties to the conflict.

Articles 4–6 codify in detail the human rights to be respected in wartime, in particular fundamental guarantees of protection of life and person, of children, of persons deprived of their liberty, and of persons charged with a crime. Further provisions are aimed at protecting the wounded, sick and shipwrecked (Articles 7–12) and the civilian population (Articles 13–18). Of particular importance in this regard are the prohibitions on making the civilian population the object of attack and on spreading terror among the civilian population through acts of violence (Article 13), on using starvation as a method of combat (Article 14), and on

---

[58] On the distinction between an armed conflict and tensions and disturbances not covered by international humanitarian law, see Chapter 5, section I.3.

[59] On the distinction between conflicts within the meaning of common Art 3 of the Geneva Conventions and of Additional Protocol II, see Chapter 5, section I.3.

the forced displacement of civilians from their homes absent the need to provide them with security or imperative military reasons (Article 17).

Although Additional Protocol II confines itself to the most important aspects of protection of people affected by internal armed conflict, it has been ratified to date by 'only' 164 states. This reflects some states' misgivings *vis-à-vis* the Protocol, which in their view confers certain legitimacy on insurgents, if not *de jure* at least *de facto*.

5. International criminal law

(a) *The Rome Statute*

After the Second World War, the international military tribunals of Nuremberg and Tokyo, basing themselves directly on the London Agreement of 8 August 1945 between France, the United Kingdom, the Soviet Union, and the United States, convicted senior German and Japanese military and governmental figures and business leaders of crimes against the peace, war crimes and crimes against humanity. Attempts by the International Law Commission (ILC) to codify these crimes failed on account of Cold War tensions. International Criminal Tribunals for the former Yugoslavia and Rwanda were set up in the early 1990s on the basis of Security Council resolutions. The criminal provisions they applied were based on customary law.

Today, international criminal law is codified in the Rome Statute of the International Criminal Court of 17 July 1998, which entered into force on 1 July 2002 and was ratified by 108 states as of December 2008. This treaty, which was negotiated in Rome by a United Nations diplomatic conference of plenipotentiaries following lengthy preparatory work, embodies the elements of international crimes, sets out the prerequisites for individual criminal responsibility and establishes the legal foundations of the International Criminal Court.[60] The Statute thus implements the customary law principle[61] that individuals are internationally responsible, in substantive and procedural terms, for certain extremely serious breaches of international law.

Direct international liability to prosecution under the Statute is limited 'to the most serious crimes of concern to the international community as a whole' and these four categories of crimes are listed as follows: the crime of genocide, crimes against humanity, war crimes and the crime of aggression (Article 5(1) of the Statute).[62] However, as the Rome Conference was unable to define the elements

---

[60] On the jurisdiction of the International Criminal Court and the corresponding procedures, see Chapter 6, section IV.

[61] On the customary rules of international criminal law, see Jean-Marie Henckaerts and Louise Doswald-Beck, *Customary International Humanitarian Law*, 3 vols (Cambridge University Press: Cambridge, 2005), vol I: Rules, 551 ff.

[62] The individual elements of these crimes are set out in Arts 6–8 of the Statute and are characterized in greater detail, in accordance with Art 9 of the Statute, in the so-called 'Elements of Crimes', UN Doc ICC-ASP/1/3, 108 ff.

of the crime of aggression, the Statute stipulates that the Secretary-General of the United Nations shall convene a review conference seven years after its entry into force (ie 2009) to discuss this issue. Until consensus has been found on the elements of the crime of aggression it cannot be prosecuted.[63]

(b) The crime of genocide

The crime of genocide is recognized as the most serious of all crimes. The concept originated with the Polish jurist Raphael Lemkin, who coined the term genocide after the Second World War to designate the mass annihilation of people of Jewish or Polish origin. He defined genocide as the 'crime of destroying national, religious or ethnic groups'. Lemkin demanded that genocide be recognized as an international crime because 'this crime has shocked the conscience of humankind and by its very nature it is committed by the state and powerful groups which have the backing of the state', and under these circumstances, the responsible state could not be counted on to institute criminal proceedings against its own organs.[64]

The crime of genocide was legally defined in the 1948 Genocide Convention. Article II defines genocide as any of the following: killing members of a national, ethnic, racial or religious group; causing serious bodily or mental harm to members of the group; deliberately inflicting on the group conditions of life calculated to bring about its physical destruction in whole or in part; imposing measures intended to prevent births within the group; or forcibly transferring children of the group to another group. All these acts may be characterized as genocide only if the perpetrator commits them with intent 'to destroy, in whole or in part, a national, ethnical, racial or religious group'. Article 6 of the Rome Statute incorporates this definition of the elements of the crime unchanged. Genocide can be committed in peacetime or in times of armed conflict, and it is irrelevant whether the perpetrators are state agents, members of the armed forces, or private actors.[65]

(c) Crimes against humanity

Crimes against humanity, exhaustively enumerated in Article 7(1) of the Rome Statute, are extremely serious human rights violations such as deliberate murder; extermination; enslavement; deportation or forcible transfer of population; deprivation of liberty in violation of fundamental rules of international law; torture; rape, sexual slavery, enforced prostitution, forced pregnancy, enforced sterilization, and other forms of sexual violence; political, racial, national, ethnic, cultural, religious, or gender-related persecution; enforced disappearance of persons; the crime of apartheid; and other inhumane acts of a similar character intentionally causing great suffering, or serious injury to body or to mental or physical health. However,

---

[63] Art 5 in conjunction with Arts 121 and 123 of the Rome Statute.
[64] Raphael Lemkin, 'Genocide' (1946) 15(2) *American Scholar* 227.
[65] For more detail, see Chapter 9, section II.5.

these offences constitute crimes against humanity only 'when committed as part of a widespread or systematic attack directed against any civilian population, with knowledge of the attack' (Article 7(1)). An 'attack directed against any civilian population' means 'a course of conduct involving the multiple commission of acts referred to in paragraph 1 against any civilian population, pursuant to or in furtherance of a State or organizational policy to commit such attack' (Article 7(2)).

The defining element that differentiates crimes against humanity from ordinary crimes is their systematic character and the fact that they target the civilian population. They need not involve a military attack or an attack carried out in the course of an armed conflict; targeted acts of violence in peacetime also qualify. Unlike the crimes against humanity that led to convictions at the Nuremberg and Tokyo war crimes trials, crimes against humanity today can also be perpetrated outside of armed conflict situations.

Crimes against humanity are often committed by state agents, eg in states where torture is systematic or in the context of a civil war in which the armed forces of the state are guilty of mounting systematic attacks against a part of the civilian population. Organizations that plan attacks on the civilian population can, however, also be militias, insurgents, terrorist groups, or arguably also groups involved in organized crime. Responsible individuals can thus be held to account irrespective of whether they belong to, or act on behalf of, a military organization, a government or public administration, a *de facto* government or a private organization.

At the subjective level (*mens rea*), it is sufficient to be aware that the act forms part of a planned attack on the civilian population. A crime against humanity thus also occurs where the perpetrator does not share the group's objective but acts out of self-interest.

Issue in focus: The terrorist acts of 11 September 2001 as crimes against humanity

---

The then High Commissioner for Human Rights, Mary Robinson, described the attacks of 11 September 2001 on the World Trade Center in New York, in which almost 3,000 people lost their lives, as follows:

The September 11 attacks were mainly aimed at civilians. They were ruthlessly planned, and their execution timed to achieve the greatest loss of life. Their scale and systematic nature qualify them as crimes against humanity within existing international jurisprudence. There is a duty on all states to find and punish those who plan and facilitate such crimes.

The coming into force of the International Criminal Court, the first instrument to codify the elements of a crime against humanity, establishes individual responsibility for such crimes, whether these are state-sanctioned or the act of groups.[66]

---

[66] Mary Robinson, 'Human Rights are as Important as Ever', *International Herald Tribune* (21 June 2002).

(d) War crimes

War crimes are serious breaches of international humanitarian law that are perpetrated in the context of either an international or an internal armed conflict. No war crimes can be committed in peacetime or in the course of disturbances and tensions which, in terms of scale, fall short of the threshold of an armed conflict.[67] As there is no international complaint procedure against belligerent parties who violate international humanitarian law, individual liability to prosecution for war crimes constitutes the main instrument for the enforcement of this branch of law.

War crimes can be committed by members of armed forces regardless of their rank, by members of non-state parties to a conflict and by civilians who collaborate closely with the parties to the conflict, but not by civilians who do not form part of the war machinery.

Not all breaches of international humanitarian law are punishable, only those which are deemed to be particularly serious and are therefore included in Article 8 of the Rome Statute. This article defines in detail what constitutes a war crime and it is beyond the scope of this overview to enumerate all the elements. However, Article 8 divides war crimes into four main categories.

(1) *Grave breaches of the four Geneva Conventions* of 12 August 1949 against persons or property protected by those Conventions in an international armed conflict (Article 8(2)(a)(i)–(viii)). This category is linked with the provisions of the four Geneva Conventions that characterize particular violations as grave breaches and require states to prosecute the perpetrators.[68] They include, for example, wilful killing; torture and inhuman treatment; wilfully causing great suffering or serious injury to body or health; extensive destruction and appropriation of property, not justified by military necessity and carried out unlawfully and wantonly; compelling a prisoner of war or other protected person to serve in the forces of a hostile power; wilfully depriving a prisoner of war or other protected person of the rights of fair and regular trial; unlawful deportation or transfer or unlawful confinement; and taking of hostages. In all these cases, the act must have been committed against persons (sick and wounded members of armed forces on land and at sea, prisoners of war, members of the civilian population) or property (eg relief consignments, medical supplies) that are described by the Conventions as protected.

(2) *Serious violations of the law of war in an international armed conflict* (Article 8(2)(b)(i)–(xxvi)), ie the use of prohibited means and methods of warfare, such as intentionally directing attacks against the civilian population or civilian objects; intentionally launching an attack in the knowledge that such

---

[67] On this distinction, see Chapter 5, section I.3.
[68] GC I, Arts 49 and 50; GC II, Arts 50 and 51; GC III, Arts 129 and 130; GC IV, Arts 146 and 147; AP I, Art 85.

attack will cause incidental loss of life or injury to civilians or damage to civilian objects or widespread, long-term, and severe damage to the natural environment which would be clearly excessive in relation to the concrete and direct overall military advantage anticipated; the transfer, directly or indirectly, by the occupying power of parts of its own civilian population into the territory it occupies, or the deportation or transfer of all or parts of the population of the occupied territory within or outside this territory; employing weapons, projectiles and materials and methods of warfare which are of a nature to cause superfluous injury or unnecessary suffering or which are inherently indiscriminate in violation of the international law of armed conflict, provided that such weapons, projectiles, and material and methods of warfare are the subject of a comprehensive prohibition; committing outrages upon personal dignity, in particular humiliating and degrading treatment; committing rape, sexual slavery, enforced prostitution, forced pregnancy; or intentionally using starvation of civilians as a method of warfare by depriving them of objects indispensable to their survival, including wilfully impeding relief supplies as provided for under the Geneva Conventions.

(3) *Serious violations of article 3* common to the four Geneva Conventions in armed conflicts not of an international character.[69] These include violence to life and person, in particular murder of all kinds, mutilation, cruel treatment, and torture; committing outrages upon personal dignity, in particular humiliating and degrading treatment; taking of hostages; and the passing of sentences and the carrying out of executions without previous judgment pronounced by a regularly constituted court, affording all judicial guarantees which are generally recognized as indispensable, where these acts are committed 'against persons taking no active part in the hostilities, including members of armed forces who have laid down their arms and those placed *hors de combat* by sickness, wounds, detention or any other cause' (Article 8(2)(c)(i)–(iv)).

(4) *Serious violations of international humanitarian law* in armed conflicts not of an international character 'in the territory of a State when there is protracted armed conflict between governmental authorities and organized armed groups or between such groups' (Article 8 (2)(e)(i)–(xii) and (f)). Under this heading, the primary aim is to ensure the criminal enforcement of particularly important provisions of Additional Protocol II. Punishable acts include, for example, attacks against the civilian population; pillaging; rape, sexual slavery, enforced prostitution, and forced pregnancy; displacement of the civilian population unless the security of the civilians involved or imperative military reasons so demand; or destroying or seizing the property of an adversary unless such destruction or seizure is imperatively demanded by the necessities of the conflict.

---

[69] On common Art 3, see section II.4.b.

Issue in focus: the Darfur conflict and war crimes

The International Commission of Inquiry on Darfur, established by the United Nations Security Council in autumn 2004,[70] suspected the Government of Sudan and the Janjaweed horse-borne militia of having committed war crimes and crimes against humanity. However, in the Commission's view, the rebels had also committed such crimes. The five-member body of experts wrote in its report:

It is apparent from the Commission's factual findings that in many instances Government forces and militias under their control attacked civilians and destroyed and burned down villages in Darfur contrary to the relevant principles and rules of international humanitarian law. Even assuming that in all the villages they attacked there were rebels present or at least some rebels were hiding there, or that there were persons supporting rebels—an assertion that finds little support from the material and information collected by the Commission—the attackers did not take the necessary precautions to enable civilians to leave the villages or to otherwise be shielded from attack. The impact of the attacks shows that the military force used was manifestly disproportionate to any threat posed by the rebels. In fact, attacks were most often intentionally directed against civilians and civilian objects. Moreover, the manner in which many attacks were conducted (at dawn, preceded by the sudden hovering of helicopter gun ships and often bombing) demonstrates that such attacks were also intended to spread terror among civilians so as to compel them to flee the villages. In a majority of cases, victims of the attacks belonged to African tribes, in particular the Fur, Masaalit and Zaghawa tribes. From the viewpoint of international criminal law these violations of international humanitarian law no doubt constitute large-scale war crimes.[71]

On 31 March 2005, the United Nations Security Council referred the Darfur situation to the Prosecutor of the International Criminal Court (SC Res 1593).

On 27 February 2007, the Prosecution of the ICC, after having conducted an investigation on relevant crimes allegedly committed in Darfur, applied, pursuant to Article 58(7) of the Rome Statute, to Pre-Trial Chamber I for the issuance of summonses to appear ('the Application') against Ahmad Muhammad Harun, former Minister of State for the Interior of the Government of the Sudan, and Ali Muhammad Ali Abd-Al-Rahman (better-known in West Darfur as Ali Kushayb), a Militia/Janjaweed leader. The Prosecution concluded there are reasonable grounds to believe that these individuals 'bear criminal responsibility in relation to 51 counts of alleged crimes against humanity and war crimes, including persecution, torture, murder and rape committed in Darfur in 2003 and 2004'.[72] On 27 April 2007, the Pre-Trial Chamber of the Court decided to issue warrants of arrest for these two individuals for their alleged responsibility for crimes against humanity and/or war crimes.

On 14 July 2008, the Prosecution presented an Application to the Pre-Trial Chamber for a warrant of arrest for Sudanese President, Omar Hassan Ahmad Al

---

[70] UN Security Council Resolution 1564 (2004).
[71] 'Report of the International Commission of Inquiry on Darfur to the United Nations Secretary-General', Geneva, 25 January 2005, para 267.
[72] ICC-02/05, Situation in Darfur, the Sudan; 'Prosecutor's Application under Article 58(7), available at <http://www.icc-cpi.int/iccdocs/doc/doc259838.PDF> (accessed 26 February 2009).

Bashir for his alleged role in the crimes of genocide, crimes against humanity and war crimes in Darfur.[73]

On 20 November 2008, the Prosecutor made a request to Pre-Trial Chamber I for the issuance of a warrant of arrest for three rebel commanders, for war crimes against African Union peacekeepers who were killed in Haskanita, Darfur on 29 September 2007.[74]

On 3 March 2009 the Pre-Trial Chamber I issued a warrant of arrest for the Sudanese President.[75]

(e) Individual responsibility

The core principle of criminal law that only persons who are themselves guilty of an offence should be punished is embodied in Article 25 of the Rome Statute. According to that article, not only is the person who commits or attempts to commit a crime, either alone or jointly with others, liable for punishment, but also the person who orders, solicits or induces the commission of such a crime that in fact occurs or is attempted. Also liable is the person who, for the purpose of facilitating the commission of such a crime, aids, abets, or otherwise contributes to the commission or attempted commission of such a crime by a group of persons acting with a common purpose.

According to Article 33(1), the fact that a crime was ordered by a superior does not relieve a person of criminal responsibility unless: '(a) the person was under a legal obligation to obey orders of the Government or the superior in question; (b) the person did not know that the order was unlawful; and (c) the order was not manifestly unlawful'.[76]

Paragraph 2 states that orders to commit genocide or crimes against humanity are manifestly unlawful. However, even in such cases perpetrators may claim that they had to act in order to avoid 'a threat of imminent death or of continuing or imminent serious bodily harm against [themselves] or another person' (Article 31(1)(d)).

Military commanders and other superiors bear special criminal responsibility. They incur liability for punishment not only where they commit or order the commission of relevant crimes but also through what is known as 'command responsibility', ie in cases where they should have known that crimes were being committed by subordinates and failed to take all measures within their power to prevent their commission (Article 28).

---

[73] ICC-02/05, 'Situation in Darfur, the Sudan; Prosecutor's Application for Warrant of Arrest under Article 58 Against Omar Hassan Ahmed Al Bashir, Summary', available at <http://www.icc-cpi.int/iccdocs/doc/doc529671.pdf> (accessed 26 February 2009).

[74] ICC-02/05, Situation in Darfur, the Sudan; 'Prosecutor's Application under Article 58, available at: <http://www.icc-cpi.int/iccdocs/doc/doc589950.pdf> (accessed 26 February 2009). At the time of writing (26 February 2009), the Pre-Trial Chamber had not yet taken a decision on the Application.

[75] ICC-02/05 at <http://www.icc-cpi.int/iccdocs/doc/doc639078.pdf> (accessed 2 April 2009).

[76] These requirements must be fulfilled cumulatively.

III. Customary Law

1. Concept and relevance

Under international law, legal norms are deemed to form part of customary law where they constitute 'evidence of a general practice accepted as law'.[77] Customary international law is accordingly based on two elements: (1) a general practice (state practice); and (2) the conviction that this practice is legally required (*opinio juris*).

To qualify as customary law, it is, as the International Court of Justice (ICJ) emphasized in the *Nicaragua v the United States of America* case, 'sufficient that the conduct of States should, in general, be consistent with such rules, and that instances of State conduct inconsistent with a given rule should generally be treated as breaches of that rule, not as indications of the recognition of a new rule'.[78] Thus, deviations from a practice cannot be deemed to undermine its validity, but rather imply a breach of the customary rule, provided that other states oppose it and characterize the criticized conduct as a violation of international law. Thus, customary law does not depend solely on the conduct of the state that is directly responsible but also on the conduct of other states which react to the breach.

As regards the element of *opinio juris,* the ICJ stressed in the same case that resolutions adopted by the UN General Assembly and other international bodies are significant indicators of the existence of a relevant conviction if they are adopted unanimously or by a representative majority and their content consists of statements that are *de lege lata* rather than *de lege ferenda*.[79]

The relationship between the two constituent elements—state practice (ie what is) and *opinio iuris* (ie what should be)—is complex.[80] In simplified terms, the more uniform state practice is, the weaker *opinio juris* can be in terms of clarity and frequency, the reason being that in such circumstances states can be confident that the consistent practice of other states to date reflects their conviction that they wish to continue behaving this way in the future, even without their actually saying so.[81] Conversely, greater demands are made on *opinio juris* where there is no discernible consistent practice, ie where breaches of the rule frequently occur. The crucial test in such circumstances is whether other states treat the violating state as such and what kind of arguments the latter uses to justify its conduct.

The question of the customary law status of international human rights has become considerably less significant since the number of treaty ratifications

---

[77] Art 38(1)(b) of the ICJ Statute.

[78] ICJ, *Case concerning Military and Paramilitary Activities in and against Nicaragua (Nicaragua v The United States of America)*, ICJ Reports 1986, para 186.

[79] Ibid, para 188.

[80] For a seminal contribution to this discussion, see Anthea E Roberts, 'Traditional and Modern Approaches to Customary International Law: A Reconciliation' (2001) 95 *AJIL* 757–91.

[81] Jörg Paul Müller, *Vertrauensschutz im Völkerrecht* (Heymanns: Cologne, 1971), 84 f.

attained its present level, such that there are no longer any states without treaty-based obligations. However, aside from the question as to which human rights guarantees are in any case binding on these states, the debate on the customary law status of human rights is relevant in a number of other areas. It sheds light on the issue of which reservations to human rights treaties are inadmissible on the grounds that the obligation concerned is applicable in any event because of its customary law status, and also confirms that a state that denounces a treaty may under certain circumstances remain bound by some of the treaty's provisions.

The question of the applicability of customary law can also arise at the domestic level. In the Federal Republic of Germany, human rights with customary law status take precedence over other laws pursuant to Article 25 of the Constitution.[82] In Switzerland, human rights with customary law status that form part of *jus cogens* (peremptory international law) constitute a barrier to amendment of the Constitution.[83] In the United States, persons who have suffered serious human rights violations abroad at the hands of a foreign state can bring a civil action for damages before an American court on the basis of the 'Alien Tort Claims Act', provided that the right in question has customary law status. Such status has been recognized in the cases of torture and genocide.[84]

2. Human rights with customary law status

The International Court of Justice (ICJ) has repeatedly emphasized that at least some of the human rights guarantees enshrined in international human rights and humanitarian law have customary law status. As early as 1949, it held in the *Corfu Channel Case*[85] that states are bound under customary law to act on the basis of 'elementary considerations of humanity'. In its Advisory Opinion on the *Reservations to the Convention on the Prevention and Punishment of the Crime of Genocide*,[86] the Court characterized the principles underlying the Convention as binding on states even without any conventional obligations. In the *Barcelona Traction Case*, the Court held that under international law, states have certain obligations 'towards the international community as a whole' and stressed that such obligations, by their very nature 'are the concern of all States'; as a consequence and in 'view of the importance of the rights involved, all States can be held to have a legal interest in their protection; they are obligations *erga omnes*'.

---

[82] Pursuant to Art 59 of the Constitution, on the other hand, human right treaties are only on a par with the country's laws.

[83] Federal Constitution, Art 139(3). In 1996, a popular initiative to amend the constitution was declared invalid because it demanded the return of all asylum seekers who had entered the country illegally, without any examination of the risk they faced, ie even if they were at risk of torture.

[84] See Chapter 3, section I.2.c.

[85] ICJ, *Case of the Corfu Channel (United Kingdom v Albania)*, ICJ Reports 1949, 22.

[86] ICJ, *Reservations to the Convention on the Prevention and Punishment of the Crime of Genocide* (Advisory Opinion), ICJ Reports 1951, 23.

The Court recognized that such *erga omnes* customary law obligations could be derived 'from the outlawing of acts of aggression, and of genocide, as also from the principles and rules concerning the basic rights of the human person'.[87]

Issue in focus: Human rights as part of *jus cogens*

The human rights guarantees that form part of *jus cogens* constitute the hard core of human rights. According to Article 53 of the Vienna Convention on the Law of Treaties (VCLT), an international norm is peremptory and hence forms part of so-called *jus cogens* when it is 'accepted and recognized by the international community of States as a whole as a norm from which no derogation is permitted and which can be modified only by a subsequent norm of general international law having the same character'.

While it is generally recognized that certain human rights meet these requirements, the question of which rights possess the requisite legal status is still a matter of dispute. A point that has now been settled, however, is that the core content of human rights with customary law status forms part of peremptory international law, prohibiting for example, genocide,[88] slavery, torture,[89] systematic racial discrimination,[90] and arbitrary killing. It follows that, for instance, a bilateral extradition treaty would be null and void if it imposed an unconditional obligation to extradite, ie even where the person to be extradited would be tortured in the state of destination.

Since the VCLT codification in 1969, the broadening of the legal concept of *jus cogens* in terms of customary law has had important implications for human rights. Thus, it is now widely accepted that *jus cogens* provisions not only render conflicting treaty law null and void but also serve as an absolute barrier against incompatible unilateral acts such as reservations to treaties, denunciations of treaties, emergency measures,[91] or counter-measures and sanctions.

While it is now largely undisputed that human rights guarantees may have customary law status,[92] it is as yet unclear exactly which rights come within the scope of customary law. According to the Restatement of the Foreign Relations

---

[87] ICJ, *Case of Barcelona Traction, Light and Power Company, Limited (Belgium v Spain)*, ICJ Reports 1970, paras 33–4.

[88] Eg, ICJ, *Case concerning the Application of the Convention on the Prevention and Punishment of the Crime of Genocide (Bosnia-Herzegovina v Serbia and Montenegro)*, ICJ Reports 2007, para 161.

[89] See, eg, ECtHR, *Al-Adsani v The United Kingdom*, *Reports* 2001-XI, paras 60 ff, and IACtHR, *Maritza Urrutia v Guatemala*, Series C, No 103 (2003), para 92.

[90] The IACtHR actually considers that the non-discrimination principle as a whole forms part of *jus cogens*; *Juridical Condition and Rights of Undocumented Migrants* (Advisory Opinion), Series A, No 18 (2003), paras 97 ff.

[91] On so-called derogations from human rights during states of emergency, see Chapter 4, section IV.2.

[92] Few authors dispute the existence of customary law in the area of international human rights and humanitarian law. One example is Arthur M Weisburd, 'The Significance and Determination of Customary International Human Rights Law: The Effect of Treaties and Other Formal International Acts on the Customary Law of Human Rights' (1996) *25 Georgia Journal of International and Comparative Law* 99.

Law of the United States,[93] a private codification of international customary law by leading American international law experts, the following human rights violations are prohibited by customary law when practised, encouraged, or condoned as a matter of state policy: '(a) genocide, (b) slavery or slave trade, (c) the murder or causing the disappearance of individuals, (d) torture or other cruel, inhuman or degrading treatment or punishment, (e) prolonged arbitrary detention, (f) systematic racial discrimination, or (g) a consistent pattern of gross violations of internationally recognized human rights.' A noteworthy point, however, is that no economic, social or cultural rights are included in the list, reflecting the fact that some Western states still take a sceptical view of this concept.

This list arguably reflects the current status of international law correctly, at least at the universal level. The ICJ has explicitly recognized the customary law status of the prohibition of genocide[94] and the prohibition of 'violence to life and person, in particular murder of all kinds, mutilation, cruel treatment and torture' as well as the prohibition of humiliating and degrading treatment as embodied in Article 3 common to the Geneva Conventions. It has emphasized that the customary scope of these prohibitions is not confined to internal armed conflicts but is applicable to all armed conflicts.[95] A fortiori they must be strictly respected in peacetime. Hostage-taking, which was characterized by the ICJ as a violation of the Charter and of the Universal Declaration of Human Rights,[96] is an example of arbitrary deprivation of liberty. The customary status of the prohibition of state-permitted or state-condoned slavery and of systematic apartheid-style racial discrimination is also beyond doubt. Such practices have now virtually disappeared. Although cases of torture and disappearances are frequent, states responsible for such violations usually try to hide and deny their actions, and criticism of such practices by other states is regular. It is less clear, however, whether the prohibition of serious and systematic violations of other human rights has acquired customary law status. At any rate, it is apparent from the practice of the former UN Commission on Human Rights and its successor, the Human Rights Council, that the international community's ability to hold to account and to pressure states guilty of serious and systematic violations is also undisputed in the case of countries that have not assumed any treaty-based obligations in the area concerned and, therefore, arguably, must be bound by customary law, at least in the case of flagrant human rights violations.

---

[93] *Restatement of the Foreign Relations Law of the United States*, 1986, adopted and promulgated by the American Law Institute, 14 May 1986 (American Law Institute Publishers, Washington 1987), para 702, 161–75.

[94] ICJ, *Reservations to the Convention on the Prevention and Punishment of the Crime of Genocide* (Advisory Opinion), ICJ Reports 1951, 23.

[95] ICJ, *Case concerning Military and Paramilitary Activities in and against Nicaragua (Nicaragua v The United States of America)*, ICJ Reports 1986, para 220.

[96] ICJ, *Case concerning United States Diplomatic and Consular Staff in Tehran (United States v Iran)*, ICJ Reports 1980, para 91.

Apart from these cases, there is little agreement on what else may be deemed to form part of customary law. The Committee on Human Rights, which monitors implementation of the International Covenant on Civil and Political Rights, has extended the list to include the following prohibitions: 'to deny freedom of thought, conscience and religion, to presume a person guilty unless he proves his innocence, to execute pregnant women or children, to permit the advocacy of national, racial or religious hatred, to deny to persons of marriageable age the right to marry, or to deny to minorities the right to enjoy their own culture, profess their own religion, or use their own language'.[97] The fact that states do not defend themselves against criticism by asserting a sovereign right to infringe these guarantees may be cited in support of viewing these rights as part of customary law. It would probably be going too far, on the other hand, to claim that the entire Universal Declaration of Human Rights constitutes customary law.[98]

Issue in focus: Human rights as general principles of law

In addition to international treaty law and customary law, the sources of international law include 'the general principles of law recognized by civilized nations' (ICJ Statute, Art 38(1)(c)). Some legal scholars[99] have suggested abandoning the project of establishing the customary law character of human rights guarantees and proposed instead to construe unwritten human rights as general principles of law within the meaning of Article 38. This idea is strongly supported by the fact that almost all of the world's written constitutions now contain detailed lists of basic rights and human rights.

General principles of law are used to fill gaps in international law. Where neither treaties nor customary law provide an answer, international courts can develop an international rule by invoking principles of law that exist in the domestic legal order of all major legal systems and applying them *mutatis mutandis* in the context of international law. The characterization of human rights as general principles of law has the advantage of dispensing with the need to identify explicit expressions of an

---

[97] HRCttee, General Comment No 24 (1994).

[98] This is a position held, in particular, by some US legal scholars. See Humphrey Waldock, 'Human Rights in Contemporary International Law and the Significance of the European Convention', in 'The European Convention on Human Rights' (1965) *International and Comparative Law Quarterly*, Supplement No 11; John P. Humphrey, 'The International Bill of Rights: Scope and Implementation' (1976) *William and Mary Law Review* 527; Louis B Sohn, 'The Human Rights Law of the Charter' (1977) *Texas International Law Journal* 133; Myres S McDougal, Harold Lasswell, and Lung-chu Chen, *Human Rights and World Public Order* (Yale University Press: New Haven, 1980), 272; John G Merrills and Arthur H Robertson, *Human Rights in the World, An Introduction to the Study of the International Protection of Human Rights* (4th edn, Manchester University Press: Manchester, 2001) 29. For a detailed, differentiated study that sheds light on the complex ways in which the Universal Declaration of Human Rights affects national legal regimes and international law, see Hurst Hannum, 'The Status and Future of International Law of Human Rights: The Status of the Universal Declaration of Human Rights in National and International Law' (1995–96) 25 *Georgia Journal of International and Comparative Law* 287 ff.

[99] Bruno Simma and Philip Alston, 'The Sources of Human Rights Law: Custom, Jus Cogens and General Principles', *Australian Yearbook of International Law 1992*, 105 f.

opinio juris of states, since it is assumed that states will not oppose the transposition of core principles of their own legal order into the context of interstate relations. One possible objection to this suggestion, however, is that states not bound by treaty law will object to being bound by norms they have not accepted as being applicable on the international level.

3. International humanitarian law rules with customary status

The existence of customary law in the area of international humanitarian law is undisputed. In 1986 the ICJ recognized in the *Nicaragua* case[100] that the guarantees of Article 3 common to the four 1949 Geneva Conventions form part of customary law and are binding on all states. In 1996, in its Advisory Opinion on the legality of the threat or use of nuclear weapons, it accorded that status to 'a great many' of the provisions of the Geneva Conventions.[101] In the latter Advisory Opinion,[102] the ICJ also referred to the so-called 'Martens Clause' named after the Russian publicist Fyodor Fyodorovitch Martens. In its original wording, it states that, even where no specific rule of law applicable to the circumstances exists, 'the inhabitants and the belligerents remain under the protection and the rule of the principles of the law of nations, as they result from the usages established among civilized peoples, from the laws of humanity, and the dictates of the public conscience'.[103] The customary status of this clause is recognized in the 1949 Geneva Conventions and the Additional Protocols. Thus, the fourth paragraph of Article 158 of the Geneva Convention IV stipulates that a renunciation of the Convention 'shall in no way impair the obligations which the Parties to the conflict shall remain bound to fulfil by virtue of the principles of the law of nations, as they result from the usages established among civilized peoples, from the laws of humanity and the dictates of the public conscience'.

Issue in focus: The ICJ's statements on the customary status of international humanitarian law

In its Advisory Opinion on the *Legality of the Threat or Use of Nuclear Weapons*, the International Court of Justice (ICJ) stated the following with regard to the existence of customary law in the area of international humanitarian law:

78. The cardinal principles contained in the texts constituting the fabric of humanitarian law are the following. The first is aimed at the protection of the civilian population and civilian objects and establishes the distinction between combatants and non-combatants; States must

---

[100] ICJ, *Case concerning Military and Paramilitary Activities in and against Nicaragua (Nicaragua v The United States of America)*, ICJ Reports 1986, para 220.
[101] ICJ, *Legality of the Threat or Use of Nuclear Weapons* (Advisory Opinion), ICJ Reports 1996, paras 79 and 82. For a similar conclusion see ACmHPR, *Democratic Republic of Congo v Burundi, Rwanda and Uganda*, Communication No 227/1999 (2004), para 70.
[102] Ibid, para 78.
[103] Preamble to Hague Convention IV of 1907 respecting the Law and Customs of War on Land.

never make civilians the object of attack and must consequently never use weapons that are incapable of distinguishing between civilian and military targets. According to the second principle, it is prohibited to cause unnecessary suffering to combatants: it is accordingly prohibited to use weapons causing them such harm or uselessly aggravating their suffering. In application of that second principle, States do not have unlimited freedom of choice of means in the weapons they use …

In conformity with the aforementioned principles, humanitarian law, at a very early stage, prohibited certain types of weapons either because of their indiscriminate effect on combatants and civilians or because of the unnecessary suffering caused to combatants, that is to say, a harm greater than that unavoidable to achieve legitimate military objectives. If an envisaged use of weapons would not meet the requirements of humanitarian law, a threat to engage in such use would also be contrary to that law.

79. It is undoubtedly because a great many rules of humanitarian law applicable in armed conflict are so fundamental to the respect of the human person and 'elementary considerations of humanity' as the Court put it in its Judgment of 9 April 1949 in the *Corfu Channel* case *(I.C.J. Reports 1949*, p 22), that the Hague and Geneva Conventions have enjoyed a broad accession. Further these fundamental rules are to be observed by all States whether or not they have ratified the conventions that contain them, because they constitute intransgressible principles of international customary law …

82. The extensive codification of humanitarian law and the extent of the accession to the resultant treaties, as well as the fact that the denunciation clauses that existed in the codification instruments have never been used, have provided the international community with a corpus of treaty rules the great majority of which had already become customary and which reflected the most universally recognized humanitarian principles. These rules indicate the normal conduct and behaviour expected of States.

The Court came to the controversial and much debated conclusion that, in light of state practice and the fact that the deployment of low-yield nuclear weapons for strictly tactical purposes in a manner that does not affect combatants and civilians indiscriminately could not be ruled out, it was not possible to conclude that nuclear weapons were prohibited by customary law.

In 2005 the International Committee of the Red Cross (ICRC) published an extensive expert study on rules of customary international humanitarian law.[104] On the basis of a detailed analysis of treaty law, international 'soft law', national legislation, military manuals, and international and domestic case law, 161 rules of customary law were identified under six main headings (principle of distinction; attacks against specifically protected persons and objects; specific methods of warfare; weapons; protection of civilians and persons *hors de combat*; implementation of international humanitarian law). Roughly half of these rules deal with the conduct of hostilities, ie they follow the tradition of Hague Law, yet their scope of application in most cases is not limited to international armed conflicts but also extends to non-international armed conflicts. About a third of the

---

[104] Henckaerts and Doswald-Beck (n 61); a list of the 161 identified rules of customary law and comments on the basic elements of the study and its background may be found in Jean-Marie Henckaerts, 'Study on customary international humanitarian law: A contribution to the understanding and respect for the rule of law in armed conflict' (2005) *IRRC* 175 ff, esp 198 ff.

identified rules deal with Geneva Law issues, and the remainder address the question of enforcement and the prosecution of war criminals.[105]

4. International crimes having customary status

Recent developments in international criminal law are also important for determining customary rules, particularly in the area of international humanitarian law. In 1993, the United Nations Security Council established an International Criminal Tribunal for Prosecution of Persons Responsible for Serious Violations of International Humanitarian Law Committed in the Territory of the Former Yugoslavia since 1991 (the International Criminal Tribunal for the Former Yugoslavia (ICTY)).[106] The principle of *nullum crimen sine lege* demanded that the Tribunal should convict accused persons only on the basis of rules that were already in existence at the time an act was perpetrated. In the absence of a generally recognized and universally applicable international criminal code, it was imperative that the applicable law should, beyond any doubt, form part of customary law. The list of crimes set out in the Statute of the Yugoslavia Tribunal thus reflects guarantees of both human rights law and international humanitarian law that have customary status. They include genocide, a detailed list of grave breaches of international humanitarian law, and crimes against humanity, all of which relate primarily to bodily harm. This list was confirmed in 1994, in the Statute of the International Criminal Tribunal for the Prosecution of Persons Responsible for Genocide and Other Serious Violations of International Humanitarian Law Committed in the Territory of Rwanda, and Rwandan citizens responsible for genocide and other such violations committed in the territory of neighbouring states between 1 January 1994 and 31 December 1994 (the International Criminal Tribunal for Rwanda (ICTR)).[107]

IV. Resolutions and Declarations

While resolutions and declarations adopted by international organizations are not legally binding, they nevertheless play a very important role in practice as 'soft law', since they reflect a consensus among states regarding what is required

---

[105] The study was criticized in a letter of 3 November 2006 addressed to the President of the International Committee of the Red Cross and signed by the Legal Advisor of the US Department of State and the General Counsel of the Department of Defense; see (2007) IRRC 443ff.

[106] UN Security Council Resolution 827 (1993), Statute of the ICTY, UN Doc S/25704; reproduced in (1993) ILM 1192 ff.

[107] UN Security Council Resolution 955 (1994), Statute of the ICTR. In addition to the crimes mentioned in the Statute of the Yugoslavia Tribunal, the ICTR Statute also declares violations of Art 3 common to the Geneva Conventions of 1949 and of Art 4 of Additional Protocol II of 1977 to be punishable.

in the area of human rights—if not legally, at least morally. They have two basic functions in this regard. First, such instruments frequently pave the way for the development of binding law. In addition to the Universal Declaration of Human Rights, the United Nations General Assembly has adopted a number of other declarations aimed at promoting the protection of specific human rights. They include the Declaration of the Rights of the Child of 20 November 1959, the United Nations Declaration on the Elimination of All Forms of Racial Discrimination of 20 November 1963, the Declaration on the Elimination of Discrimination against Women of 7 November 1967, the Declaration on the Protection of All Persons from Being Subjected to Torture and Other Cruel, Inhuman or Degrading Treatment or Punishment of 9 December 1975, the Declaration on the Rights of Disabled Persons of 9 December 1975, and the Declaration on the Protection of all Persons from Enforced Disappearance of 18 December 1992. Although all of these were preliminary steps towards adoption of the corresponding conventions and albeit their status—unless they reflect customary law—is only equivalent to that of recommendations, they remain important in their own right in non-states parties. Further declarations, such as the Declaration on the Right and Responsibility of Individuals, Groups and Organs of Society to Promote and Protect Universally Recognized Human Rights and Fundamental Freedoms of 9 December 1998, the Declaration on the Elimination of Violence against Women of 20 December 1993, and the Declaration on the Rights of Indigenous Peoples of 13 September 2007 have not yet been converted into treaty law, but nonetheless formed the basis for thematic mandates created by the former UN Commission on Human Rights and maintained by the Human Rights Council.

Second, such declarations can help to clarify the specific content of treaty-based human rights guarantees. Particularly detailed instruments exist in the area of administration of justice. Of special importance are the Standard Minimum Rules for the Treatment of Prisoners, endorsed by the Economic and Social Council resolutions of 31 July 1957 and 13 May 1977, the Basic Principles for the Treatment of Prisoners adopted by the General Assembly on 14 December 1990 and the Body of Principles for the Protection of All Persons under Any Form of Detention or Imprisonment adopted by the General Assembly on 9 December 1988. The Swiss Federal Court has stated in a judgment—albeit with reference to the Council of Europe rather than UN recommendations—that while such minimum rules do not create legally enforceable rights, the fact that they reflect 'the legal conviction of the member states of the relevant organisation' means that judges should take them into account when interpreting and giving substance to corresponding constitutional rights and those contained in human rights treaties.[108] The Court thus encapsulated the effect that declarations and resolutions have as 'soft law' in the area of human rights. Similarly, such declarations play

---

[108] Decision of the Swiss Federal Court 118 Ia 70.

an increasingly important role in the jurisprudence of international monitoring bodies.[109]

Regional organizations also adopt resolutions that have a bearing on human rights. Those of the Council of Europe, drawn up by the Parliamentary Assembly and adopted by the Committee of Ministers in the form of recommendations to governments, are an important example.[110] On the basis of Article 15 of the Statute of the Council of Europe, for instance, the Council's Committee of Ministers adopted Standard Minimum Rules for the Treatment of Prisoners, on 19 January 1973 (last updated on 11 of January 2006)[111] and Guidelines on Human Rights and the Fight against Terrorism on 11 July 2002.

---

[109] See for example, HRCttee, *Rouse v The Philippines*, Communication No 1089/2002 (2005), para 7.8, and ECtHR, *Dybeku v Albania*, Application No 41153/06 (2007), para 48.

[110] Statute of the Council of Europe of 5 May 1949, Art 15.

[111] Committee of Ministers of the European Council, Rec 2006(2).

3

The Legal Nature of
Human Rights Obligations

How are human rights obligations fulfilled? This complex question can be addressed either from the perspective of the duty bearers, ie those bound by human rights obligations, or from the perspective of rights holders. The two approaches are combined, in this chapter and the next, in an exposition of three different facets of the question:

- Who owes obligations to whom? The purpose of this question is to identify, on the one hand, human rights *duty bearers* (section I below) and, on the other, human rights *holders* (section II).
- What is the content and scope of these obligations? This raises the issue of the different *categories of human rights obligations* and the directly related issue of the extent to which rights may be restricted (section III).
- Who has a right to what, where and when? This question addresses the *scope of application* of human rights in personal, substantive, territorial, and temporal terms. It is discussed in the next chapter (Chapter 4).

The answers to these questions can then be used to describe what constitutes a human rights violation in legal terms and how to proceed when investigating whether such a violation has occurred (Chapter 4, section V).

I. Who is Bound by Human Rights Obligations?

The question of who has obligations to whom and how is answered in each of the core human rights treaties in a general provision placed at the beginning of the text. ECHR, Article 1 is particularly concise, stipulating that the contracting parties must secure the rights and freedoms defined in the Convention 'to everyone within their jurisdiction'. Similarly, ICCPR, Article 2(1), requires each state party 'to respect and to ensure to all individuals within its territory and subject to its jurisdiction the rights recognized in the present Covenant without distinction of any kind'. According to ICESCR, Article 2(1), each state party must 'take steps, individually and through international assistance and co-operation, especially economic and technical, to the maximum of its available resources, with a view to achieving progressively the full realization of the rights recognized in the present Covenant by all appropriate means, including particularly the adoption of legislative measures'.

1. Basic rule: states as duty bearers

Human rights are enforceable primarily towards the state. They are a counterweight to the state's monopoly on the use of force, imposing restrictions on the activities of its organs and thereby reducing the threat posed, at least potentially, to private persons or entities by the sovereign exercise of state power. Human rights violations, as the abuse of such power, constitute particularly serious infringements of the law and are fundamentally different from breaches of criminal or civil law by private actors, although such acts may also seriously impair the victims.

It follows that responsibility for fulfilling the obligations arising from human rights treaties lies with states and state agents. Human rights treaties make this quite clear by consistently imposing obligations on 'states parties', 'contracting parties', or 'high contracting parties'.[1]

Who forms part of the 'state' in its capacity as duty bearer? While most human rights treaties fail to address this question, or address it only in cursory terms, the issue is dealt with by general international law. The types of human rights violations attributable to the state may be inferred from the rules of international law governing *state responsibility*. These rules are now laid down in the draft Articles on state responsibility adopted by the International Law Commission (ILC) in 2001[2] (hereinafter referred to as the ILC draft Articles). While the draft Articles are not legally binding, they represent an authoritative codification of customary international law in this regard and establish, in particular, the following principles:

(1) The state is accountable for the conduct of *all its organs*, irrespective of the higher or subordinate status of the organ concerned or of whether it exercises legislative, executive, or judicial functions.[3] This means that, for instance, no state can justify a human rights violation by invoking the independence of the judiciary or by asserting that the courts are bound by decisions of the legislature.[4] The 'state' also comprises municipal and other local authorities

---

[1] For example ICESCR, Art 2; ICCPR, Art 2; CRC, Art 2; CCPCG, Art 1; ECHR, Art 1.

[2] ILC, draft Articles on Responsibility of States for Internationally Wrongful Acts (Draft Articles on State Responsibility), 'Report of the ILC on its fifty-third session' (2001), UN Doc A/56/10, Supplement No 10 (*Official Records of the General Assembly*).

[3] ILC draft Articles on State Responsibility, Art 4(1); HRCttee, General Comment No 31 (2004), para 4, and IACtHR, *Neptune v Haiti*, C/180 (2008), paras 40 ff.

[4] Thus, the Swiss Federal Court acknowledges that Art 191 of the Federal Constitution, according to which federal enactments are authoritative for all courts, ie they must be applied even where

as well as state authorities in countries with a federal structure.[5] This general rule is explicitly stated in the two International Human Rights Covenants of 1966, which stipulate that their provisions extend 'to all parts of federal States without any limitations or exceptions'.[6]

(2) Human rights violations are perpetrated by individuals and it is conceivable that, in doing so, they are not implementing state policy but are rather *exceeding their official authority*. Their actions in such circumstances are nevertheless attributable to the state where the perpetrators are acting in an official capacity[7] or where they pretend to do so. The Inter-American Court of Human Rights emphasized in this regard, in a case involving the abduction and torture of a political opponent by members of the security forces, that the conclusion that human rights had been violated was 'independent of whether the organ or official ha[d] contravened provisions of internal law or overstepped the limits of his authority'.[8] This ruling is valid not only where individuals acting in an official capacity overstep their authority, but also where local authorities or even the entire administrative apparatus of a constituent state violate human rights while disregarding the central government's orders.[9] It follows that a state cannot evade its human rights obligations on the grounds that agents of decentralized units are no longer (fully) under its control. A state's responsibility is no longer engaged, on the other hand, where secessionist local authorities break away from the centre and form an insurgent group to achieve their aim.[10] In these circumstances, such *de facto* authorities are no longer acting in an official capacity and their conduct can no longer be attributed to the state from which they wish to secede.

(3) Private persons or entities also form part of the 'state' if they are empowered to perform public functions. Where they violate human rights in the process of exercising such authority, the state is held accountable for the violation[11] since 'the State cannot absolve itself of responsibility by delegating its obligations to private bodies or individuals'.[12] It follows that, for example, the ill-treatment of a prisoner also constitutes a violation of human rights

---

unconstitutional, is not applicable to international human rights provisions and that the ECHR therefore takes precedence over a federal enactment that is contrary to human rights. See judgment BGE 122 II 485 of the Swiss Federal Court.

⁵ ILC draft Articles on State Responsibility, Art 4(1) (second part of the sentence).

⁶ ICESCR, Art 28 and ICCPR, Art 50. CSR, Art 41 is less comprehensive in this regard.

⁷ ILC draft Articles on State Responsibility, Art 7. Compare with ECtHR (Grand Chamber), *Ramanauskas v Lithuania*, Application No 74420/01 (2008), para 63.

⁸ IACtHR, *Velásquez-Rodríguez v Honduras*, Series C, No 4 (1988), para 170.

⁹ ECtHR (Grand Chamber), *Assanidze v Georgia*, *Reports* 2004-II, paras 144 ff.

¹⁰ ECtHR (Grand Chamber), *Ilaşcu and Others v Moldova and Russia*, *Reports* 2004-VII, para 333.

¹¹ ILC draft Articles on State Responsibility, Art 5: 'Conduct of persons or entities exercising elements of governmental authority'.

¹² ECtHR, *Costello-Roberts v The United Kingdom*, Series A, No 247-C (1993), para 27, concerning corporal punishment of a child attending a private school.

attributable to the state where it is inflicted by employees of a private security firm contracted by the state to run a prison,[13] and a bar council must abide by human rights norms when it disciplines its members on behalf of the state.[14]

(4) The state is also accountable for the actions of so-called *de facto* agents, ie private persons who are not formally entrusted with the discharge of public functions but who act on the instructions of, or under the direction or control of, the state concerned.[15] This category may include, for example, paramilitary units or vigilante or terrorist groups,[16] irrespective of whether they operate within the country or abroad.[17]

(5) A particularly large number of human rights violations, many of which being serious in nature, are nowadays perpetrated by non-state groups in civil wars and similar circumstances. As such groups are generally in revolt against the state and commit human rights violations against the wishes of the official authorities, the state will not, as a rule, be held accountable for their actions. However, there are three exceptions. First, it is conceivable that such groups are under the direction or control of a foreign state to such an extent that they may be regarded as its *de facto* agents resulting in their conduct being attributable to the foreign state.[18] Second, during an international armed conflict, a civil war or a revolution the authority of the state may collapse completely and in the resulting vacuum private groups without formal authority begin to discharge state functions, such as laying the foundations for a rudimentary police force and judicial authority or collecting taxes. If, in such circumstances, private actors violate human rights while exercising *de facto* governmental authority, the violations are attributable to the state concerned. The authorities of said state, however, must genuinely be incapable of functioning in the area in

---

[13] Explicitly stated in para 2 of the ILC's commentary to Art 5 (Commentary—Draft Articles on responsibility of States for internationally wrongful acts, adopted by the International Law Commission (2001), UN Doc A/56/10, Supplement No 10 (*Official Records of the General Assembly*)). The commentary mentions as a further example the case of an airline company that performs certain functions on behalf of the state in the area of immigration control. The same conclusion may be drawn with regard to private security firms that discharge *de facto* police or military functions on behalf of a state.

[14] ECtHR, *Casado Coca v Spain*, Series A, No 285-A (1994).

[15] ILC draft Articles on State Responsibility, Art 8.

[16] See, for example, ECtHR, *Acar and Others v Turkey*, Applications Nos 36088/97 and 38417/97 (2005), paras 83 ff, and particularly pointedly IACtHR, *Case of the Mapiripán Massacre v Colombia*, C/134 (2005), paras 110 ff.

[17] See also Chapter 4, section III.

[18] Thus, the International Criminal Tribunal for the former Yugoslavia held in the *Tadić* case, albeit in connection with international humanitarian law, that the former Yugoslavia (Serbia and Montenegro) was responsible for ethnic cleansing by irregular Serbian troops in Bosnia and Herzegovina: ICTY (Appeals Chamber), *The Prosecutor v Tadić*, Case No IT-94-1-A (1999), especially paras 117 ff. The ICJ confirmed the principle of attribution but did not concur with this opinion, however, inasmuch as the state of Serbia exercised insufficient control over the conduct of the troops involved; ICJ, *Application of the Convention on the Prevention and Punishment of the Crime of Genocide (Bosnia and Herzegovina v Serbia and Montenegro)*, ICJ Reports 2007, paras 402 ff.

question and the assumption of *de facto* governmental authority must appear to be necessary in the circumstances.[19] For instance, the Islamic Republic of Iran was held accountable for the actions of the Revolutionary Guards who took over border control functions at Tehran airport immediately after the outbreak of the Islamic revolution in 1979, holding a United States citizen in custody for several days and expelling him from the country in a manner that breached international law.[20] Third, it is quite common for insurrectionary movements to prevail, either assuming governmental authority in the country or establishing a new state. In such circumstances, the country concerned or the newly emerging state is held accountable retrospectively for acts carried out by the insurgents before they assumed power.[21]

(6) The conduct of private actors is attributable to a state if and to the extent that the state subsequently acknowledges and accepts the conduct in question as its own.[22] For instance, the ICJ recognized the responsibility of the Islamic Republic of Iran for the hostage-taking of United States diplomats by students at the United States Embassy in Tehran, because the Iranian leadership subsequently expressed explicit approval of the students' conduct and maintained the illegal situation.[23]

(7) Lastly, the state can become accountable for actions carried out by rebel groups if the latter take over the control of the country or create a new state after a successful secession.[24]

(8) The state is *not* accountable for strictly private actions, ie infringements by private persons or entities that do not fall into any of the above-mentioned categories. This also applies, in particular, to belligerents in a civil war and insurgents who are not directed or controlled by another state, who cannot be characterized as legitimate *de facto* governments and who are defeated in the conflict, ie do not assume state power when the conflict is over. In this instance, the question of the state's responsibility for neglecting to protect victims against private actors when human rights would have demanded that they do so may arise.[25]

2. Exception: private actors as duty bearers?

As a rule, individuals are not human rights duty bearers unless, as just described, they exercise *de facto* governmental authority on behalf of a state in circumstances

---

[19] ILC draft Articles on State Responsibility, Art 9.
[20] Iran–United States Claims Tribunal, *Yeager v Iran*, 17 *Reports* 92, para 43.
[21] ILC draft Articles on State Responsibility, Art 10(1) and (2).
[22] ILC draft Articles on State Responsibility, Art 11.
[23] ICJ, *United States Diplomatic and Consular Staff in Tehran, United States of America v Iran*, ICJ Reports 1980, paras 63 ff.
[24] ILC draft Articles on State Responsibility, Art 10.
[25] On the duty to protect as one of the key human rights obligations see below section III.3.

involving the collapse of state power, or if they subsequently become the lawful government or they establish a new state. This does not mean, however, that private individuals or groups are permitted to disregard and violate the protected rights of other private persons. There is accordingly a growing demand for human rights obligations to be extended to private actors. This debate focuses on such diverse issues as the accountability of terrorists or of rebels and irregular troops in civil wars, the human rights obligations of multinational corporations and the question of rights-based approaches to domestic violence.

The fact is that insurrectionary and terrorist groups or transnational criminal organizations today often pose no less serious a threat to persons' lives, physical integrity, or general security than the abuse of state power. Moreover, interests protected by human rights norms can also be adversely affected by the *de facto* power of large corporations. While traditional remedies under domestic criminal and private law are the primary means of recourse against private violations, they often prove inadequate in cases involving private entities operating on a transnational or even global scale. To address this shortcoming, international law provides a range of instruments that may be used to impose human rights obligations, directly or indirectly, on private actors.

(a) Direct obligations originating in international law

The very few cases in which international human rights instruments impose direct obligations on private actors by prescribing specific duties for individuals are laid out in general terms and lack precise normative content. For instance, Article 29 of the Universal Declaration of Human Rights stipulates that everyone has 'duties to the community in which alone the free and full development of his personality is possible', but it fails to specify the content of those duties.

The idea is echoed in Article 27 of the African Charter on Human and Peoples' Rights, which states that '[e]very individual shall have duties towards his family and society, the State and other legally recognized communities and the international community.' Here again, the content of the duties remains unspecified. Article 28 of the Charter, however, does stipulate that '[e]very individual shall have the duty to respect and consider his fellow beings without discrimination, and to maintain relations aimed at promoting, safeguarding and reinforcing mutual respect and tolerance'. Yet provision is made in the African Charter only for complaints directed against states,[26] so that there is no mechanism available to enforce Article 28.

International criminal law,[27] by virtue of the statutory definitions of genocide, crimes against humanity and war crimes, compels private persons and entities to refrain from acts that constitute particularly serious violations of human rights. It imposes direct, binding and legally enforceable obligations on individuals and punishes particularly serious violations of core human rights. The further

---

[26] ACHPR, Arts 47 ff and 55 ff.   [27] See Chapter 2, section II.5.

development of international criminal law after 1990 was motivated, at least to some extent, by the need to proceed more vigorously against private offenders and to have more effective mechanism for dealing with cases in which there is no state that can be held accountable.

(b) Indirect obligations originating in international law

Private actors also have indirect but equally binding obligations under international law by virtue of provisions of domestic criminal law enacted by states to fulfil a corresponding obligation to legislate. The obligation to punish certain offences under domestic criminal law is set out, for instance, in the International Convention on the Elimination of All Forms of Racial Discrimination (Article 4), the Convention on the Prevention and Punishment of the Crime of Genocide (Article V in conjunction with Articles II and III), the Convention against Torture (Article 4)[28] and the International Convention for the Protection of All Persons from Enforced Disappearance (Article 4). In contrast to international criminal law, the obligations applicable in such cases to the individual do not stem directly from international law but from domestic law, even though the relevant provisions are enacted to give effect to an obligation under international law.

Indirect obligations applicable to private actors under international law also arise where a state, giving effect to its obligation to protect, proceeds under criminal, civil or administrative law against the perpetrator so as to protect people against infringements by other non-state actors. Although in such cases, it is not the responsibility of private actors that is engaged under human rights law but that of the state, private actors are compelled to respect other people's human rights as a result.

(c) Other obligations of private actors

A country may conceivably make its private-law liability regime and courts available for legal proceedings aimed at compelling perpetrators to provide compensation to the victims of certain human rights violations.

Issue in focus: Compensation for human rights violations—The United States Alien Tort Claims Act

Under § 1350 of the Alien Tort Claims Act of 1789,[29] courts in the United States have jurisdiction to hear claims by foreign nationals for compensation for harm suffered

---

[28] It should be noted, however, that, according to the definition of torture in CAT, Art 1 the Convention deals essentially with torture practised by the state. Art 1 is nevertheless also applicable to cases in which the state incites the commission of private acts of torture or overtly or tacitly condones such acts.

[29] § 1350 of the Alien Tort Claims Act of 1879 stipulates: 'The district courts shall have original jurisdiction of any civil action by an alien for a tort only, committed in violation of the law of nations or a treaty of the United States.'

outside the United States in breach of customary international law, involving primarily cases of torture and violations of the right to life. In 1980, this provision was, for the first time, applied to a human rights case: in *Filartiga,* the court found that torture constituted a violation of customary international law, allowing Filartiga to sue a member of the Paraguayan security forces, whom he had met by chance in the United States, for compensatory damages for torture suffered in Paraguay.[30] In other cases, the leader of the Bosnian Serbs in the war in Bosnia, Radovan Karadzic,[31] and Indonesian General Panjaitan,[32] who was responsible for crimes against humanity in East Timor, were ordered to pay large sums in compensatory damages. In 2004, the US Supreme Court restricted the scope of application of § 1350 when it decided in *Sosa v Alvarez-Machain* that in light of its history this provision should be read in a narrow sense, providing jurisdiction only in traditional law of nations cases such as violations of safe conducts, murder and robbery punishable as piracy if committed on high sea, assaults on ambassadors and its modern equivalents such as torture and arbitrary deprivation of life, but not cases of arbitrary arrest.[33]

Such judgments are important even though they are often unenforceable. Victims' prospects of obtaining the money awarded to them are better in cases where a multinational corporation is sued. For instance, a federal court in the United States held in 2002 that a suit filed by victims of forced labour in Myanmar (formerly Burma) against Unocal was admissible because the company's management had been guilty of complicity with the Burmese military regime when it mobilized forced labour for the construction of an oil pipeline.[34] The proceedings ended with a settlement whereby the corporation stated its readiness to pay the plaintiffs an unnamed sum for development projects in the pipeline region.[35]

The question as to whether similar suits could be filed in Europe remains open. In principle, it should be possible to invoke liability for damages for breach of contract since the requisite unlawfulness could be inferred from international law (particularly international criminal law). Problems would arise, however, in the establishment of jurisdiction of domestic courts if the case had no domestic connection, ie if neither the perpetrators nor the victims were nationals of the forum state. Most states are not prepared to invest their courts with jurisdiction for such cases.

Codes of conduct play an important role in attempts to extend human rights obligations to the private sphere. Attention has focused in recent years on rules of conduct for business firms. In 1999, the UN Secretary-General Kofi Annan launched the 'Global Compact' initiative, which seeks to promote business self-regulation by persuading corporations to comply with human rights principles.

---

[30] *Filartiga v Peña-Irala*, United States Court of Appeals for the Second Circuit, 1980, 630 F.2d 876.

[31] *Kadic v Karadzic*, United States Court of Appeals for the Second Circuit, 1995, 70 F.3d 232.

[32] *Todd v Panjaitan*, No 92-12255, 1994 WL 827111 (D Mass 26 October 1994).

[33] *Sosa v Alvarez-Machain,* United States Supreme Court, 542 US 692 (2004).

[34] *Doe I v Unocal Corp.*, United States Court of Appeals for the Ninth Circuit, 2001, 248 F.3d 915.

[35] See American Society of International Law, *International Law in Brief,* 28 January 2005. For information and documents on the proceedings, see <http://www.asil.org/ilib050128.cfm#b1> (accessed 7 January 2009).

Businesses operating on a global scale can voluntarily undertake to espouse and advocate nine out of ten general Global Compact principles in the areas of human rights, labour standards and the environment. The success of these efforts is debatable; to date (2008) more than 4,000 firms have subscribed to the initiative. The draft norms on the human rights responsibilities of trans-national corporations[36] elaborated in 2003 by the former Sub-Commission for the Promotion and Protection of Human Rights of the former United Nations Commission on Human Rights are more detailed in terms of content and more firmly rooted in legal principles. The draft, which failed to secure the support of the Commission on Human Rights and whose fate remains uncertain,[37] declares that corporations have a general obligation to promote, protect and secure the fulfilment of human rights within their spheres of activity and influence. It furthermore describes in detail exactly what these obligations entail in the areas of non-discrimination, security of the human person, rights of workers, prohibition of corruption, consumer protection and environmental protection.

Issue in focus: The human rights-related principles of the Global Compact

---

Businesses should:

1. Support and respect the protection of internationally proclaimed human rights;
2. Ensure they are not complicit in human rights abuses;
3. Uphold the freedom of association and the effective recognition of the right to collective bargaining;
4. Eliminate of all forms of forced and compulsory labour;
5. Effectively abolish child labour; and
6. Eliminate discrimination with respect to employment and occupation.

---

3. Do international organizations have human rights obligations?

(a) Direct obligation of international organizations to respect human rights?

Do international organizations have human rights obligations? The argument that they do not because human rights treaties are binding only on states has become problematic in light of the fact that human rights are increasingly exposed to violations by persons acting on behalf of international organizations. The risk

---

[36] 'Norms on the Responsibilities of Transnational Corporations and Other Business Enterprises with regard to Human Rights', UN Doc E/CN.4/Sub.2/2003/12/Rev.2 (2003).

[37] In 2005 the Commission on Human Rights created the mandate of a 'Special Representative of the Secretary-General on human rights and transnational corporations and other business enterprises' to pursue work on the subject of human rights standards for corporations. In 2008, the Human Rights Council renewed the mandate.

of such violations is due to two developments. First, there is a growing tendency for states to transfer powers to organizations with supranational decision-making authority such as the EU or the UN which under certain circumstances may take binding decisions. Second, international organizations may conceivably provide support, financial or otherwise, for projects that are contrary to human rights[38] or agents of an organization may act *ultra vires* in a manner that violates human rights.[39] In some instances (as in Kosovo and East-Timor), the UN may even be entrusted with responsibility for the administration of territories thereby effectively acquiring a monopoly on the use of force. Lastly, member states of international organizations are sometimes faced with the dilemma of having to implement binding decisions adopted by such organizations although they are incompatible with human rights.

In Europe, the member states of the Council of Europe responded in Protocol No 14 to the ECHR, with the possibility of ratification of the ECHR by the European Union.[40] The Protocol would enable private persons to file complaints in Strasbourg against decisions by EU bodies. However, EU ratification of the ECHR is unlikely within the near future. At the universal level, the Convention on the Rights of Persons with Disabilities of 2006 followed this approach by allowing 'regional integration organizations' to become a party to the treaty (Articles 42–43).

Most human rights treaties contain no such provision for the accession of international organizations. That states are bound under customary law by core human rights does not necessarily mean that other subjects of international law are bound in the same way.[41] Human rights provisions in founding charters or statutes fall well short of what is required to demonstrate the existence of human rights obligations for international organizations since they consist, for the most part, of general statements of goals.[42] In principle, internal decisions, rules and regulations of organizations cannot be invoked as the source of a general obligation to respect human rights.[43] The contrary is only true where the Security

---

[38] For instance, big infrastructure causing forced evictions and displacements incompatible with human rights.

[39] Such cases may include sexual exploitation of women by members of UN field missions or discrimination against staff members of international organizations.

[40] ECHR, Art 59(2) as amended by P 14/ECHR.

[41] This conclusion is not applicable to the EU, since the European Court of Justice ruled (as early as 1984 in *Regina v Kirk*, Case 63/83) that ECHR guarantees, as principles shared by all legal systems of member states, constitute general legal principles that the ECJ has a duty to safeguard. Individuals can therefore file complaints with the Court regarding contraventions of these legal principles, allowing them to indirectly claim breaches of ECHR standards by EU bodies.

[42] See, for example, Arts 1(3) and 55 of the UN Charter.

[43] For instance, the UN Secretary-General's Bulletin on Observance by United Nations Forces of International Humanitarian Law (UN Doc ST/SGB/1999/13, excerpts cited in Chapter 5, section II.1.d) requires troops under UN command to respect core principles of international humanitarian law. It is clear, however, from the Bulletin's cautious wording that it was not meant as accepting that the UN is fully bound by international humanitarian law, which is often ill-equipped to deal with the special characteristics of peacekeeping and peace enforcement missions.

Council, in a binding resolution, declares explicitly that, eg, a UN mission is bound by human rights norms. This step was taken when it established the UN mission in Kosovo (UNMIK[44]).

International organizations are, however, prohibited from violating peremptory human rights norms. This is derived from the legal character of *jus cogens*: given that a treaty becomes void under VCLT, Article 53 if it is in conflict with peremptory norms of international law, the charter of an international organization cannot under any circumstances explicitly or implicitly permit its organs or agents to disregard peremptory human rights obligations.[45]

If it can therefore be assumed that international organizations are, after all, bound to respect human rights with *jus cogens* status, the question arises as to under which conditions such organizations, as subjects of law, can be held responsible for conduct that is incompatible with human rights. A preliminary answer may be found in the ILC draft Articles on Responsibility of International Organizations and their Member States,[46] which have not yet been finalized. According to this draft, an international organization incurs responsibility for conduct by its organs or agents that breaches the organization's obligations under international law.[47] Furthermore, according to the draft, an international organization also breaches international law if it adopts decisions that bind member states to commit an act that would be internationally wrongful if committed by the international organization.[48] In other words, supranational organizations

It should be noted, however, that, according to Section 4 of the Bulletin, members of the military personnel of a United Nations force are subject to prosecution in their national courts in cases of violations of international humanitarian law.

[44] Security Council Resolution 1244, para 11(j) (1999) mentions 'protecting and promoting human rights' as one of the main responsibilities of the international civilian presence of the United Nations Mission in Kosovo (UNMIK). UNMIK Regulation 1999/24, which was promulgated on the basis of that resolution, stipulates that '[i]n exercising their functions, all persons undertaking public duties or holding public office in Kosovo shall observe internationally recognized human rights standards' as reflected, in particular, in the core UN treaties and the ECHR. Acting on these principles, the Human Rights Committee's requested UNMIK to submit a report on implementation of ICCPR guarantees in the context of its review of the Serbian state report in accordance with Article 40 ICCPR: see the Concluding Observations of the HRCttee, CCPR/C/UNK/CO/1 (2006). This example cannot be generalized as UNMIK exercised governmental authority in Kosovo and therefore had to ensure that the treaties ratified by Serbia continued to be implemented on this territory.

[45] For resolutions of the UN Security Council, see also the European Court of Justice, Court of First Instance, Case T-315/01 *Kadi v Council and Commission* (2005), para 230, and Case T-306/01 *Yusuf und Al Barakaat International Foundation v Council and Commission* (2005), para 281.

[46] Draft Articles on Responsibility of International Organizations. For the most recent (2008) version see ILC, 'Report on the work of its sixtieth session' (2008), UN Doc A/603/10, 262 ff. The ILC has so far adopted 53 draft Articles at first reading.

[47] Rules on responsibility set out in ILC draft Articles on Responsibility of International Organizations, Arts 4–7. They closely parallel the corresponding rules in the ILC draft Articles on State Responsibility.

[48] ILC draft Articles on Responsibility of International Organizations, Art 15(1). According to para 2, an international organization also incurs responsibility under these circumstances if it authorizes member states to commit an act and a member state subsequently commits the act in reliance on that authorization.

are prohibited to adopt decisions that bind their member states which, if implemented, would breach peremptory human rights norms.

To date, however, with the exception of the EU, no international organization has set up internal oversight bodies with jurisdiction to hear complaints from individuals of human rights violations by organs or agents of the organization. Moreover, victims are also barred from suing international organizations before domestic courts, since such organizations currently enjoy absolute immunity under international law from state jurisdiction. Even the most rudimentary obligations flowing from *jus cogens* are thus suspended in a vacuum. The fact that international law fails to offer any legal protection against human rights violations that may occur in the context of coercive military measures, economic sanctions, measures against terrorism, the establishment of international criminal tribunals, or indeed the administration of a territory by the United Nations, may affect the credibility of the UN and of international human rights protection in the long run.

(b) Human rights obligations of the member states of international organizations?

Does this mean that individuals are largely defenceless in the face of decisions of international organizations or acts by their organs or agents that are contrary to human rights? While the manifest current shortfall in legal protection cannot be remedied, it may at least be mitigated if states, in their capacity as members of the organization, can be held to account under such circumstances. Specifically, the question arises whether member states can be held responsible and whether legal action can be taken by the victims:

- when they implement, through their own organs or agents, binding decisions issued by an international organization that are contrary to human rights (section (i));
- when they transfer powers to the organization or adopt measures as a member that are contrary to their own human rights obligations (section (ii)); or
- when personnel that they make available to international organizations for peace-keeping and other similar missions (eg military forces and police officers), violate human rights while operating on behalf of the organization (section (iii)).

(i) Responsibility of member states for the implementation of decisions of international organizations

How should the responsibility of member states be characterized when they implement recommendations or decisions issued by the organization that are contrary to human rights? Can an aggrieved person take legal action in such cases against the member state instead of the organization? In practice, there are no obvious reasons why a different approach should be adopted in assessing a state's responsibility where its failure to respect the human rights of persons within its territory is not based on independent decisions but on the implementation of decisions taken by international organizations. In principle, therefore, a reference to the possibly binding character of an international organization's decision cannot absolve its member states of responsibility for compliance with their human rights obligations.

Example: The ECtHR judgment in *Bosphorus Airways v Ireland*[49]

In this judgment, handed down in 2005, the ECtHR undertook an in-depth analysis of the responsibility of member states of an international organization with supranational powers to respect ECHR guarantees when implementing decisions of the organization. Specifically, the Court had to determine whether Ireland breached the ECHR guarantee of the right to property by implementing an EU regulation requiring Ireland to seize an aircraft owned by a Yugoslav airline company (but leased to a Turkish company) in order to comply with a binding UN Security Council resolution on sanctions imposed against the Federal Republic of Yugoslavia. The Court reached the following conclusions of a general nature:

152. The Convention does not, on the one hand, prohibit Contracting Parties from transferring sovereign power to an international (including a supranational) organisation in order to pursue co-operation in certain fields of activity...

153. On the other hand, it has also been accepted that a Contracting Party is responsible under Article 1 of the Convention for all acts and omissions of its organs regardless of whether the act or omission in question was a consequence of domestic law or of the necessity to comply with international legal obligations...

154. In reconciling both these positions and thereby establishing the extent to which State action can be justified by its compliance with obligations flowing from its membership of an international organisation to which it has transferred part of its sovereignty, the Court has recognised that absolving Contracting States completely from their Convention responsibility in the areas covered by such a transfer would be incompatible with the purpose and object of the Convention: the guarantees of the Convention could be limited or excluded at will thereby depriving it of its peremptory character and undermining the practical and effective nature of its safeguards ... The State is considered to retain Convention liability in respect of treaty commitments subsequent to the entry into force of the Convention ...

155. In the Court's view, State action taken in compliance with such legal obligations is justified as long as the relevant organisation is considered to protect fundamental rights, as regards both the substantive guarantees offered and the mechanisms controlling their observance, in a manner which can be considered at least equivalent to that for which the Convention provides ... However, any such finding of equivalence could not be final and would be susceptible to review in the light of any relevant change in fundamental rights protection.

156. If such equivalent protection is considered to be provided by the organisation, the presumption will be that a State has not departed from the requirements of the Convention when it does no more than implement legal obligations flowing from its membership of the

---

[49] ECtHR (Grand Chamber), *Bosphorus Hava Yolları Turizm ve Ticaret Anonim Şirketi v Ireland*, Reports 2005-VI.

organisation. However, any such presumption can be rebutted if, in the circumstances of a particular case, it is considered that the protection of Convention rights was manifestly deficient. In such cases, the interest of international co-operation would be outweighed by the Convention's role as a 'constitutional instrument of European public order' in the field of human rights....

157. It remains the case that a State would be fully responsible under the Convention for all acts falling outside its strict international legal obligations.

158. Since the impugned act constituted solely compliance by Ireland with its legal obligations flowing from membership of the EC..., the Court will now examine whether a presumption arises that Ireland complied with its Convention requirements in fulfilling such obligations and whether any such presumption has been rebutted in the circumstances of the present case.

The Court concluded that human rights protection within the EU could be presumed equivalent to the protection afforded by the ECHR, and that, in the case before it, this presumption had not been rebutted given the public interest of the sanction imposed. The complaint was therefore dismissed. However, the Court failed to deliver an opinion on the highly relevant issue of whether the UN, which originally ordered the measures, also protects human rights in accordance with ECHR norms. It was thus spared the need to state its position on how a conflict between the implementation of binding resolutions of the UN Security Council and human rights treaty obligations should be resolved.

Special problems arise, however, in the case of the UN when states have to implement Security Council resolutions, since pursuant to Article 103 of the UN Charter, such binding provisions prevail over other international legal obligations of member states. States are thus obliged to implement Security Council decisions even when they violate human rights. The relevance of this issue is apparent, for instance, in the case of sanctions[50] that require member states to freeze the assets of specific persons included on a list. As the freezing of bank accounts and other sources of funds cannot be challenged, it is difficult to reconcile mandatory national implementation measures with the right to access to a court in civil matters.[51] Both the Human Rights Committee[52] and the European Court of Human Rights[53] have therefore taken up complaints alleging human rights violations in connection with the national implementation of UN sanctions. At a minimum, the obligations to protect[54] flowing from the relevant human rights guarantees oblige the implementing states to intervene *vis-à-vis* the Security Council and its subsidiary bodies responsible for the implementation of sanctions[55] on behalf of

---

[50] See, in particular, UN Security Council Resolution 1267 (1999).

[51] ICCPR, Art 14(1) and ECHR, Art 6(1).

[52] HRCttee, *Sayadi and Vinck v Belgium*, Communication No 1472/2006 (2008).

[53] ECtHR (Grand Chamber), *Bosphorus Hava Yolları Turizm ve Ticaret Anonim Şirketi v Ireland*, Reports 2005-VI.

[54] See below section III.3.

[55] The implementation of UN Security Council sanctions is regularly reviewed by Sanctions Committees.

private parties who, in their view, have been unjustly affected by a measure.[56] In concrete terms, human rights obligations would require a state to take steps, for instance, to ensure that an individual of proven innocence was deleted from the list of persons suspected of terrorism and that the person's assets were released. As the European Court of First Instance[57] has stressed, there is in any case no obligation to implement Security Council decisions that are contrary to human rights in cases where the Council exceeds its authority, ie where it compels member states to take measures that breach human rights norms with *jus cogens* status; it follows that such decisions have no binding effect on member states.

In two recent decisions the European Court of Justice (ECJ) and the Human Rights Committee went a step further. The ECJ held that 'the lawfulness of any legislation adopted by the Community institutions, including an act intended to give effect to a resolution of the Security Council remains subject, by virtue of Community law, to full review by the Court'.[58] It stressed that the European Community is based on the rule of law, 'inasmuch as neither its Member States nor its institutions can avoid review of the conformity of their acts with the basic constitutional charter, the EC Treaty'; that another international agreement cannot affect the allocation of powers fixed by the EC Treaty; and that fundamental rights form an integral part of the community law. Based on these considerations it concluded that 'the obligations imposed by an international agreement cannot have the effect of prejudicing the constitutional principles of the EC Treaty, which include the principle that all Community acts must respect fundamental rights …'.[59] Based on the further consideration that the 'international legal order under the United Nations' does not exclude the judicial review of the permissibility of the internal implementation of a resolution adopted under Chapter VII by the Security Council[60] the ECJ annulled a Council Regulation incorporating a Security Council resolution into community law which violated fundamental freedoms not having the character of *jus cogens*. With a similar reasoning the Human Rights Committee in a decision of November 2008 came to the conclusion that Belgium, by implementing Security Council resolutions requesting member states of the UN to issue a travel ban on and freezing the assets of specifically listed individuals, violated the right to privacy and the freedom of movement *vis-à-vis* the authors of the communications.[61]

---

[56] See the analogous jurisprudence of the European Court of Human Rights, ECtHR (Grand Chamber), *Ilaşcu and Others v Moldova and Russia, Reports* 2004-VII, para 333.

[57] European Court, Court of first instance, Case T-315/01 *Kadi v Council and Commission* (2005), para 230 and Case T-306/01 *Yusuf and Al Barakaat International Foundation v Council and Commission* (2005), para 281. See also Case T-253/02 *Ayadi v Council* (2006) and Case T-49/04 *Hassan v Council and Commission* (2006).

[58] ECJ (Grand Chamber), Joined Cases C-402/05 P and C-415/05 P *Kadi v Council and Commission and Al Barakaat International Foundation v Council and Commission* (2008), para 278.

[59] Ibid, paras 281–5.   [60] Ibid, paras 288 ff.

[61] HRCttee, *Sayadi and Vinck v Belgium*, Communication No 1472/2006 (2008).

(ii) Responsibility of member states for conduct by organs or agents of international organizations that violate human rights

Can member states also be held responsible for conduct by organs or agents of an international organization on the basis that they ceded their authority to it by virtue of their membership and hence delegated powers with which they were previously vested? As noted above,[62] a state cannot shirk its human rights obligations by entrusting private actors with state functions. This principle also applies where state functions are delegated to international organizations. The European Court of Human Rights has for some time emphasized that states parties to the ECHR cannot evade their obligation to respect Convention guarantees by transferring their powers to international organizations. It held, for example, that the United Kingdom had violated the political rights of an inhabitant of Gibraltar who was unable under EU law to participate in elections to the European Parliament.[63] On the basis of this jurisprudence, the International Law Commission incorporated a general rule in its draft Articles on the Responsibility of International Organizations, according to which a member state 'of an international organization incurs responsibility if it circumvents one of its international obligations by providing the organization with competence in relation to that obligation, and the organization commits an act that, if committed by that State, would have constituted a breach of that obligation'.[64] Hence, if they wish to avoid running the risk of being held accountable themselves for human rights violations of the organization, member states must assert their influence in order to ensure that its conduct is compatible with human rights obligations.

(iii) Responsibility of member states for the conduct of their nationals during peacekeeping missions

Lastly, does a state incur responsibility when human rights violations are perpetrated by state agents whom it has placed at the disposal of an international organization? This question arose in recent proceedings before the European Court of Human Rights.[65] The issue to be addressed was whether troop-contributing states incurred responsibility for their own nationals serving with the Kosovo Forces (KFOR), a NATO military presence, and the United Nations Mission in Kosovo (UNMIK). As both the KFOR and UNMIK missions are based on binding Security Council resolutions, the Court had to decide whether the conduct of the persons concerned was attributable to the UN or to the troop-contributing states. The Court relied on the ILC draft Articles on the Responsibility of International Organizations, according to which organs or

---

[62] See above, section I.1.

[63] ECtHR (Grand Chamber), *Matthews v The United Kingdom*, Reports 1999-I, paras 32, 64 and 65.

[64] ILC draft Articles on Responsibility of International Organizations, Art 28.

[65] ECtHR (Grand Chamber), *Behrami v France and Saramati v France, Germany and Norway* (Admissibility Decision), Applications Nos 71412/01 and 78166/01 (2007).

agents placed by a state at the disposal of an international organization are to be considered organs or agents of the organization if the latter exercises effective control over their conduct.[66] If, on the other hand, the troop-contributing state, in accordance with standard practice during peacekeeping missions, continues to exercise a certain control, for instance in the area of disciplinary law, attribution of responsibility for the conduct to the troop-contributing state cannot be ruled out. The key question before the Court was whether it was the international organization or the troop-contributing state that actually exercised control or should have exercised control over conduct in question. Having framed the issue in those terms, the Court concluded that the conduct of the KFOR troops and that of the UNMIK staff was attributable to the UN.[67] In view of the UN's lack of standing, however, it declared the complaint inadmissible.[68] This reasoning is correct to the extent that it is based on the control criterion, but it fails to solve the problem of protection loopholes in the case of UN peacekeeping missions. Thus, it remains to be seen whether and how the case law of international organs on this issue will further develop.

II. To Whom are Obligations Owed?

Human rights treaties are always multilateral. It follows that universal human rights treaties can be ratified by all states and that regional treaties can be ratified by all member countries of relevant regional organizations. In the case of multilateral treaties and universal or regional customary law, which by their nature are binding on a large number of states, a question that invariably arises is on whose behalf the obligations stemming from international law are to be fulfilled. The answer to this question is of decisive importance when it comes to deciding who, in the event of a violation, can take action against the violating state, demanding that it respect the rights concerned and, where harm has been suffered, demand compensation.[69]

There are essentially three conceivable scenarios in which states are required to fulfil obligations under general international law. (1) The obligations are discharged bilaterally, ie fulfilled mutually between pairs of two states. This

---

[66] ILC draft Articles on Responsibility of International Organizations, Art 5.

[67] According to the Court, the conduct of KFOR is attributable to the UN, while UNMIK is characterized as a subsidiary organ of the UN; ECtHR (Grand Chamber), *Behrami v France* and *Saramati v France, Germany and Norway* (admissibility decision), Applications Nos 71412/01 and 78166/01 (2007), paras 141 and 143.

[68] Ibid, paras 144 ff. For a similar constellation see ECtHR, *Berić and Others v Bosnia and Herzegovina*, Application No 36357/04 etc (2007), paras 26 ff.

[69] A distinction should be made between the existence, in principle, of this entitlement and the question of the procedures that are available to exercise it. As a rule, outside the sphere of human rights, private actors have no access to interstate and supranational procedures and can assert their rights under international law only before domestic courts, provided such rights have been incorporated into domestic law or are directly applicable at the domestic level.

applies primarily to rules requiring reciprocal performance (eg the extradition of offenders). (2) The obligations are discharged domestically *vis-à-vis* private actors. This applies to rules that protect the interests of private actors or that accord them particular rights (such as an agreement on customs facilities for importers or states' obligation under customary law to provide appropriate compensation to foreign companies in the event of expropriation). (3) The obligations are fulfilled simultaneously and indivisibly *vis-à-vis* all states, inasmuch as a breach of such obligations—for instance breaching the ban on nuclear testing in the atmosphere—necessarily affects everyone simultaneously. An obligation under customary law that can only be performed simultaneously and indivisibly *vis-à-vis* all parties is referred to in legal parlance as an *erga omnes* obligation; where such an obligation is owed solely to the parties to an international treaty, it is referred to as an obligation *erga omnes partes*.

All these dimensions of obligations are present in human rights:

First and foremost comes the obligation owed to private persons to respect and protect their human rights as guaranteed by applicable treaty or customary law, and such persons can assert such rights domestically[70] and (by means of individual complaints to regional courts or the United Nations treaty monitoring bodies) to some extent also internationally.

Bilateral human rights obligations to other states are a consequence of, and inextricably bound up with, obligations to private actors. In bilateral relations, a third state may exercise diplomatic protection[71] where the human rights of its own nationals are violated abroad, making representations to the violating state and demanding that it respect the rights concerned.[72] However, this is only possible if the rights in question apply in both states by virtue of treaty or international customary law.

A state's obligations under human rights treaties are applicable simultaneously and indivisibly to all states parties in the sense that the other states parties, irrespective of whether their interests are directly affected by a violation, are entitled to call on the violating state to comply with its treaty obligations and may, if necessary, apply forms of pressure permitted under international law (complaints to international tribunals, reprisals, economic sanctions, etc).[73] This *erga omnes*

---

[70] Human rights treaties frequently require parties to provide effective domestic remedies; see Chapter 6, section II.2.a.

[71] On this concept see Chapter 1, section II.1.

[72] For instance, Liechtenstein filed a complaint with the International Court of Justice against the Federal Republic of Germany in connection with the seizure of property from the Princely House during the Second World War, alleging that the German courts had prevented the Prince, acting in his private capacity, from exercising due process rights and had violated his property rights (ICJ, *Case concerning Certain Property (Liechtenstein v Germany)*, ICJ Reports 2005). The Court declared the case inadmissible *ratione temporis*.

[73] HRCttee, General Comment No 31 (2004), para 2. On the means of exerting pressure available to states, see Chapter 6, section III.1.

partes effect stems from the fact that such treaties are not concluded with individuals but with states, which undertake mutually to fulfil human rights obligations to private actors. Such obligations are given a procedural dimension in treaties that permit interstate complaints;[74] they also exist, however, in treaties that make no provision for such a procedure.

Erga omnes obligations also exist under customary law. They oblige states simultaneously and indivisibly towards all other states in the world, ie *vis-à-vis* the community of states. As a consequence, a state whose rights and interests are not directly affected may also take action in such cases against the violating state, using forms of pressure permitted under international law. The ICJ laid the basis for such action in the Barcelona Traction case, in which it recognized the special significance of 'obligations of a State towards the international community as a whole' which '[b]y their very nature...are the concern of all States. In view of the importance of the rights involved, all States can be held to have a legal interest in their protection; they are obligations *erga omnes*'.[75] It mentioned as examples of such obligations the prohibition of genocide and 'the principles and rules governing the basic rights of the human person, including protection from slavery and racial discrimination'[76] ie fundamental human rights. The international community as a whole is clearly affected in such cases inasmuch as its basic values are undermined by systematic or, in individual cases, particularly serious violations of core human rights guarantees under customary law.[77]

---

[74] The interstate complaint procedure allows a state to bring a claim against another state party for breach of a treaty obligation without having itself suffered direct harm; see Chapter 7, section IV.1.

[75] ICJ, *Case concerning the Barcelona Traction, Light and Power Company, Limited (Belgium v Spain)*, ICJ Reports 1970, para 33; reaffirmed, eg, in ICJ, *Legal Consequences of the Construction of a Wall in the Occupied Palestinian Territory* (Advisory Opinion), ICJ Reports 2004, para 155.

[76] Ibid, para 34. In its Advisory Opinion on the *Legality of the Threat or Use of Nuclear Weapons*, the ICJ stated that a great many rules of international humanitarian law were so fundamental to the respect of the human person that they enjoyed customary law status and hence created *erga omnes* obligations (ICJ, *Legality of the Threat or Use of Nuclear Weapons* (Advisory Opinion), ICJ Reports 1996, especially para 79).

[77] See Art 2(3) of the resolution of the International Law Institute, 'The Protection of Human Rights and the Principle of Non-Intervention in Internal Affairs of States' (1989) 63 *Institut de Droit International Annuaire* 338. In such cases states are arguably entitled to resort to countermeasures, eg in the form of economic sanctions, against the violating state. Article 54 of the ILC draft Articles on State Responsibility fails to provide a clear answer to this question, since—in order not to endanger the adoption of the draft articles—it was drafted as saving clause, stipulating that the draft articles do not prejudice the right of states affected by a violation of human rights creating obligation *erga omnes* to take lawful measures against the state responsible for that conduct. State practice, however, indicates that such so-called collective countermeasures are in principle permissible; Jörg Künzli, *Vom Umgang des Rechtsstaats mit Unrechtsregimes—Völker- und landesrechtliche Grenzen des Verhaltensspielraums der schweizerischen Aussenpolitik gegenüber Völkerrecht missachtenden Staaten* (Bern: Stämpfli Verlag, 2008) 41 ff.

III. Categories and Scope of Obligations
Arising from Human Rights

1. Overview: positive and negative obligations

As mentioned at the beginning of this chapter, the most important human rights treaties contain Articles setting forth general obligations, ie Articles describing the categories of obligations that states have assumed upon ratification of the treaty in question. Regardless of these descriptions, it is broadly acknowledged today in both doctrine and jurisprudence that human rights guarantees, whether classified in legal terms as civil and political rights or economic, social and cultural rights, entail both negative obligations (to refrain from interfering with the enjoyment of rights) and positive obligations (to take action).[78] Three categories of obligations may be identified in this regard (as illustrated in Table 3.1).

(1) *Obligations to respect*: All human rights can be effectively protected at a basic level through lack of state interference in their enjoyment. This gives rise to the obligation to respect. From the point of view of rights holders, this obligation entails a corresponding right to be let alone *vis-à-vis* the state. Obligations to respect flow automatically from human rights, ie without further prerequisites. They are thus characterized as *negative* obligations.

(2) *Obligations to protect*: At a second level, states have positive human rights obligations to protect interests safeguarded under human rights law from threats emanating, in particular, from breaches by third parties, but also from threats emanating from natural or human-made risks. In practice, this involves, for the most part, ensuring that the relevant human rights guarantees are also enforced in relations between private actors,[79] but also *vis-à-vis* state agents acting *ultra vires* or agents of third states.[80] Rights holders in this context have a claim to protection by the state, meaning that the human rights obligations of the state and not those of third parties are at issue. The obligation to protect arises only insofar as the state is aware, or could have been aware, if sufficient caution had been exercised, of the violation or threat thereof and has the practical and legal means to prevent it. It is a preventive obligation where action is needed to avert an impending violation and it is remedial where the state comes to the aid of victims during or after the fact. Protection can either be immediate and operational,

---

[78] Described in particularly clear terms in ACmHPR, *Social and Economic Rights Action Centre and the Centre for Economic and Social Rights v Nigeria*, Communication No 155/96 (2001), paras 44 ff.

[79] HRCttee, General Comment No 31 (2004), para 8.

[80] See for example ECtHR (Grand Chamber), *Makaratzis v Greece*, *Reports* 2004-XI, paras 56 ff.

Table 3.1. Obligations arising from human rights

Obligations arising from human rights			
negative	to respect		
positive	to protect	preventive	operational and immediate (eg police)
			through legislation (eg prohibitions)
		remedial	operational and immediate (eg rehabilitation)
			through legislation (eg legal remedies)
	to fulfil	legislative, institutional and procedural facilities to ensure full realization of the right	
		benefits in the narrow sense (money, goods, services)	

eg taking the form of police intervention or precautionary measures by a court, or it may take the form of legislative enactments such as statutory prohibitions and penalties.

(3) *Obligations to fulfil*: At a third level, states are required to fulfil human rights, ie to ensure that they are realized in practice as comprehensively as possible. This may, in some circumstances, call for the adoption of wide-ranging legislative or administrative measures in order to establish the legal, institutional and procedural basis for full realization of the right concerned. Thus, the prohibition of inhumane conditions of detention remains an empty promise even in the absence of breaches by state agents if no action is taken to build prisons with sufficient space and facilities to ensure the humane execution of custodial sentences. Sometimes a right can only be fully enjoyed by an individual if the state provides certain benefits in the form of money, goods (eg food) or services (eg medical care, basic education or free interpretation services in criminal proceedings).[81] Rights holders in this context are entitled to receive such benefits to the extent that the state is able to provide them. State obligations in such cases thus depend essentially on its capacity to ensure fulfilment, ie on the availability of resources.

The prohibition of discrimination on the basis of race, sex, language, religion, political or other opinion, national or social origin, property, birth or other status must be respected at all levels. Thus, it is inadmissible to impose limitations, which as such would be permissible, on persons with one of these characteristics (eg women or members of a religious minority) without serious and objective grounds, or to withhold protection or a particular benefit from them which they are entitled to as a human right.[82]

---

[81] HRCttee, General Comment No 31 (2004), para 7.
[82] This so-called *accessory* status of the prohibition of discrimination should be distinguished from non-discrimination as an *autonomous* human right. On this distinction see Chapter 11, section II.1.

Example: Obligations resulting from the right to life and the right to education

---

The right to life, at the first level (duty to respect), constitutes a prohibition of deprivation of life by the state; at the second level (duty to protect), it calls for the adoption of reasonable precautionary measures by the state to protect the lives of individuals from threats emanating from third parties; and at the third level (duty to fulfil), it requires the state, for example, to take steps to control life-threatening infectious diseases or to reduce infant mortality.[83]

The obligation to respect the right to education means, for instance, that the state may not prohibit a person who has been admitted to an educational establishment from completing a course of studies or that it must respect parents' right to enrol their children in a private rather than public school. To protect this right, it may occasionally be necessary to take action against parents who deny their children access to any form of education, even though they are eligible for admission to educational establishments. The obligation to fulfil requires, for example, states to set up a primary school system accessible to all children free of charge.

In the case of both rights, the authorities at all levels must take care to ensure that their conduct does not adversely affect particular persons, unilaterally and without legitimate grounds, on account of their race, sex, language, religion, political or other opinion, national or social origin, property, birth or other status.

The issue of the nature of human rights obligations and that of their 'justiciability', ie their suitability for adjudication by a court must be distinguished. As the case law of international courts and treaty bodies shows, obligations to respect and to protect and the discrimination prohibition are, in principle always justiciable. The duty to fulfil eg the obligation to take measures aimed at full and productive employment (ICESCR, Article 6) may be mainly addressed to the legislator and the executive. However, if such obligations as, for instance, the right to free assistance of an interpreter in criminal proceedings (Article 14(3)(f)) are specific enough for application to an individual case they can be invoked before a court.[84]

2. The obligation to respect human rights

(a) Basic principle

The obligation to 'respect' human rights is negative and means that states parties must refrain from interfering with guaranteed rights. Persons derive from this obligation an entitlement to freedom from state interference in their rights. As the obligation to respect does not require any positive action by the state, it is discharged by remaining passive. Freedom of the press is respected where the state remains passive

---

[83] HRCttee, General Comment No 6 (1982), para 5.
[84] For more details see below, section III.6.

and refrains from controlling or censoring the press; the prohibition of torture is respected where the state abstains from ill-treating detainees; and this dimension of the right to education consisting of the liberty to choose an education is deemed to be secured where the state does not interfere with the decision of students and their parents to take up specific studies at a particular university.

(b) Limitations on human rights

The obligation to respect human rights and the related right to freedom from state interference form the core of the human rights concept. At the same time, the state must fulfil public functions and tasks entrusted to it by its constitution and its laws that serve the public interest as well as ensure the respect of the rights of third parties. Both of these duties may necessitate the imposition of limitations on human rights. With few exceptions, therefore, human rights guarantees are not absolute but are subject to limitations on specific grounds. The extent to which rights may be restricted cannot be determined in general terms but has to be ascertained for each right individually. It is nevertheless possible to identify in general a number of models and scenarios for human rights limitations.

(i) Scenario 1: absolute obligation

Relatively few human rights guarantees can never be restricted and thus entail absolute obligations. Examples are the prohibition of genocide, the prohibition of torture and inhuman treatment or punishment, the prohibition of slavery and the principle that none shall be held guilty of any criminal offence on account of behaviour that was not prohibited at the time when it was committed. Rights with an absolute character are always non-derogable.[85]

Thus, in the *Soering* case, the European Court of Human Rights stated with respect to ECHR, Article 3 according to which '[n]o one shall be subjected to torture or to inhuman or degrading treatment or punishment', that this Article 'makes no provision for exceptions and no derogation from it is permissible under Article 15 (…) in time of war or other national emergency. This absolute prohibition of torture and of inhuman or degrading treatment or punishment under the terms of the Convention shows that Article 3 (…) enshrines one of the fundamental values of the democratic societies making up the Council of Europe.'[86]

(ii) Scenario 2: narrow substantive scope of application with provision for exceptions

Some rights are characterized by the fact that, although they entail in principle absolute obligations, there are special cases in which an interference with the

---

[85] On derogations from human rights, see Chapter 4, section IV.2.

[86] ECtHR, *Soering v The United Kingdom*, Series A, No 161 (1989), para 88. This opinion was confirmed in ECtHR (Grand Chamber), *Saadi v Italy*, Application No 37201/06 (2008), paras 137 ff, where the court rejected Italy's argument that in the case of dangerous terrorists a balancing of interests must be allowed.

right in question manifestly does not constitute a violation. Thus, although the state is prohibited in principle from taking life, members of the armed forces are, as a rule, permitted to kill in wartime. In such cases, human rights treaties define the intangible content of the right and add a list of interferences which are not deemed to constitute violations, ie declare exceptions from the prohibition to be permissible. In cases not covered by an exception, any interference with the right automatically constitutes a human rights violation. For instance, while ICCPR, Article 8(3)(a) strictly prohibits forced and compulsory labour, subparagraph (b) characterizes 'imprisonment with hard labour' as a permissible punishment for a crime and subparagraph (c) lists a series of circumstances—such as military service, services compelled in cases of emergency or calamity, and the perform-ance of normal civil obligations—as not constituting forced labour. Similarly, although ICCPR, Article 6 prohibits violations of the right to life (paragraph 1), it allows states that have not yet abolished the death penalty to impose capital punishment under strictly defined conditions (paragraphs 2, 4 and 5).[87] Where all these conditions are fulfilled the right to life is deemed respected even if the person is executed. If, however, one requirement is disregarded, the right to life is violated.

(iii) Scenario 3: broad substantive scope of application subject to limitations

In the case of traditional civil rights protecting the sphere of social auton-omy from state intervention (eg right to private and family life, freedom of expression, and the freedom of religion), human rights treaties usually stipu-late that, while a specific area is safeguarded, state interference is permissible under certain conditions. For instance, ECHR, Article 9 states that everyone has the right to freedom of thought, conscience and religion and is free to manifest his or her religion or belief. The article goes on to add, however, that those freedoms may be subject to 'such limitations as are prescribed by law and are necessary in a democratic society in the interests of public safety, for the protection of public order, health or morals, or the protection of the rights and freedoms of others'. Similar provisions are contained, for example, in the ICCPR.[88] This scenario allows for interfering with freedoms and liberties if limitations are provided for by law, serve a legitimate public interest or protect the rights of others and are proportional, ie do not go further than is necessary to achieve such goal.

Economic, social and cultural rights are also subject to limitations. For instance, ICESCR, Article 4 stipulates that the state may subject these rights 'only to such limitations as are determined by law only in so far as this may be compatible with the nature of these rights and solely for the purpose of promot-ing the general welfare in a democratic society'. However, the complex nature of

---

[87] See Chapter 9, section II.2.c.   [88] For example, ICCPR, Arts 18, 19, 21, 22.

the obligations derived from these rights endows them with distinctive features that render the scope of this provision subject to qualification.[89]

Issue in focus: Permissible limitations of civil rights

Several freedoms and liberties of the ICCPR[90] and regional conventions[91] are typically endowed with limitation clauses according to which state measures, which infringe upon the guarantee, do not violate that human right if (1) they are based on the law, (2) serve a legitimate goal and (3) are necessary in a democratic society.

Interferences with freedoms and liberties occur in the form of individual acts or orders, often pronounced at the outcome of a formal procedure, ie orders of an administrative authority or court judgments. Exceptionally, a decree, ie a general abstract rule, already infringes upon such civil rights, for instance where a prohibition in a law and the threat of sanctions have a chilling effect on the exercise of a right. For this reason, the European Court of Human Rights held that a law which penalized adult homosexual relations violated the right to privacy, even though it was never enforced *vis-à-vis* the complainant.[92] The Human Rights Committee has not yet had the occasion to determine whether the existence of a law is sufficient as such to infringe upon the civil rights of the ICCPR. However, in its concluding observations on state reports, it criticized repeatedly domestic legal provisions for lack of compatibility with the Covenant.[93]

As regards the three elements necessary for permissible limitations, the following remarks can be made:

(1) Limitations of freedoms and liberties are sufficiently *provided by law* if domestic legislation in the form of an act of parliament or a constitutionally valid executive decree explicitly authorizes them.[94] Such legislation must be accessible, ie duly published. Furthermore it must, as the European Court on Human Rights stressed in the *Hertel v Switzerland* case, be 'formulated with sufficient precision to enable the citizen to regulate his conduct; he must be able—if need be with appropriate advice—to foresee, to a degree that is reasonable in the circumstances, the consequences which a given action may entail. Those consequences need not be foreseeable with absolute certainty' as it may be necessary to keep a certain flexibility by using open legal terms; in such cases it is sufficient that the meaning of the law can be determined by resorting to its interpretation and application in practice.[95] Finally, the law's content must not contradict human rights principles,

---

[89] On the structure of the ICESCR in terms of obligations, see section III.6.

[90] ICCPR, Arts 12(3), 18(3), 19(3), 22(2).

[91] ACHR, Arts 12(3), 13(2), 15, 16(2), 22(2); ACHPR, Arts 11, 12(2); ArCHR, Arts 30(2), 32(2), 35(2); P 4/ECHR, Arts 9(2), 10(2), 11(2) ECHR; Art 2 (3).

[92] ECtHR, *Modinos v Cyprus*, Series A, No 259 (1993), paras 17 ff. Similarly ECtHR, *Wolfmeyer v Austria*, Application No 5263/03 (2005), paras 36 ff.

[93] See for example, HRCttee, Concluding Observations Vietnam (2002), para 18, and Republic of Korea (2006), para 18.

[94] See for example, ECtHR, *Kruslin v France*, Series A, No 176-A (1990), para 29, and *Groppera Radio AG and Others v Switzerland*, Series A, No 173 (1990), paras 65 ff. Similarly HRCttee, *Suárez de Guerrero v Colombia*, Communication No 45/1979 (1982), paras 12.2 ff.

[95] ECtHR, *Hertel v Switzerland*, *Reports* 1998-VI, para 35.

ie it must embody certain ideals of democracy and justice, thus protecting against arbitrary action taken by the authorities.

(2) Limitations must pursue a legitimate aim as defined in the limitation clauses, such as the protection of national security, of public order and safety, public health or morals, or the protection of the rights of others. As these aims are defined in broad terms, this requirement is usually deemed to be fulfilled in the case law of international human rights courts and treaty bodies.

(3) Limitations must be necessary in a democratic society to achieve the aim invoked in a specific case and thus respond to a pressing social need.[96] Thus, they 'must conform to the principle of proportionality; they must be appropriate to achieve their protective function; they must be the least intrusive instrument amongst those which might achieve the desired result; and they must be proportionate to the interest to be protected'.[97] The last element is not present where the private interest to be protected against state interference outweighs the public interest to limit the exercise of the right in question. Such balancing of interests must be undertaken in light of 'of that pluralism, tolerance and broadmindedness without which there is no "democratic society"....'[98]

(iv) Scenario 4: prohibition of arbitrary interference

The ICCPR prohibits 'arbitrary' interference with rights in a number of articles. Pursuant to Articles 6 and 9, for example, no one may be 'arbitrarily deprived of his life' or 'subjected to arbitrary arrest or detention'. Article 12(4) prohibits arbitrary deprivation of the right to enter one's own country and Article 17(1) provides protection against 'arbitrary or unlawful interference' with private and family life. In this scenario, arbitrary interference automatically amounts to a violation. An analysis of the case law of the Human Rights Committee shows that, in practical terms, this scenario has a great deal in common with the limitations scenario (scenario 3). Thus, the Committee treats as 'arbitrary' all cases of interference with a right that are not reasonable or proportionate in the circumstances[99] or, in other words, that are not proportional to the end sought and are not necessary in the circumstances of a given case.[100] Deprivation of liberty, for example, is deemed arbitrary within the meaning of ICCPR, Article 9 where it is not warranted by the facts, appears to be unjust or cannot be considered necessary in the circumstances of the case.[101]

---

[96] ECtHR, *Handyside v The United Kingdom*, Series A, No 24 (1976), paras 48–50.

[97] HRCttee, General Comment No 27 (1999), para 14; similarly General Comment No 22 (1993), para 8.

[98] See on this point for example ECtHR, *Zana v Turkey*, Reports 1997-VII, para 51.

[99] For example, HRCttee, *Suárez de Guerrero v Colombia*, Communication No 45/1979 (1982), para 13.3, and Sarah Joseph, Jenny Schultz, and Melissa Castan, *The International Covenant on Civil and Political Rights* (2nd edn, Oxford University Press: Oxford, 2004), 156 with respect to the right to life.

[100] HRCttee, *Toonen v Australia*, Communication No 488/1992 (1994), para 8.3: 'The Committee interprets the requirement of reasonableness to imply that any interference with privacy [Art. 17] must be proportional to the end sought and be necessary in the circumstances of any given case.'

[101] For example, HRCttee, *A v Australia*, Communication No 560/1993 (1997), para 9.2: '... the Committee recalls that the notion of "arbitrariness" must not be equated with "against the

It follows that interference with these rights is permissible only where it serves a legitimate purpose and where the interference is proportionate.[102] The requirement of a legal basis authorizing the interference flows from the requirements in ICCPR, Article 6(1) that the law must protect life, in Article 9(1) that the deprivation of freedom must be lawful, ie compatible with national law, and in Article 17(1) which prohibits unlawful interferences with private and family life.[103]

3. The obligation to protect human rights

(a) Basic principle

The treaty monitoring bodies now recognize that human rights can be threatened not only by the state but also by private actors or particular situations (eg natural disasters). In such cases respect alone is inadequate to ensure the enjoyment of human rights. Indeed, States must be compelled to protect private actors from violations of their human rights in such cases. The general obligations 'to respect and to ensure to all individuals'[104] their human rights, or 'to secure to everyone'[105] such rights under the core human rights treaties[106] cannot be fulfilled if the rights of private actors are not protected against breaches by third parties.

Example: The IACtHR judgment in *Velásquez-Rodríguez v Honduras*

The Inter-American Court of Human Rights stressed, in the *Velásquez-Rodríguez v Honduras* case, that the obligation of states parties under ACHR, Article 1(1) to guarantee rights holders 'the free and full exercise' of the rights recognized by the American Convention implies in the case of human rights violations by third parties 'the duty of States Parties to organize the governmental apparatus and, in general, all the structures through which public power is exercised, so that they are capable of juridically ensuring the free and full enjoyment of human rights. As a consequence of this obligation, the States must prevent, investigate and punish any violation of the rights recognized by the Convention and, moreover, if possible attempt to restore the right violated and provide compensation as warranted for damages resulting from the violation.'[107]

---

law" but be interpreted more broadly to include such elements as inappropriateness and injustice. Furthermore, remand in custody could be considered arbitrary if it is not necessary in all the circumstances of the case, for example to prevent flight or interference with evidence; the element of proportionality becomes relevant in this context.'

[102] Thus, arbitrariness within the meaning of the ICCPR is quite different from the concept of arbitrariness under constitutional law, which covers only what is blatantly wrong, unjust and indefensible.

[103] ICCPR, Art 12(4) does not contain any reference to the law but a non-arbitrary case of prohibiting someone to return to his or her country cannot be imagined without the law providing for such a possibility.

[104] ICCPR, Art 2(1); similarly CRC, Art 2(1) and ACHR, Art 1.   [105] ECHR, Art 1.

[106] See also ACHPR, Art 1 ('recognize the rights'), ArCHR, Art 3 ('ensure to all individuals... the right to enjoy the rights and freedoms').

[107] IACtHR, *Velásquez-Rodríguez v Honduras*, Series C, No 4 (1988), para 166.

Obligations to protect extend beyond injurious acts committed by private actors. The following are deemed to be equivalent to actual or imminent violations by private persons:

(1) Actual or imminent conduct in violation of human rights by state agents who are operating *ultra vires*.[108]

(2) Actual or imminent conduct in violation of human rights by foreign state agents either within a state's territory,[109] for instance in the event of the (planned) abduction of a person in violation of international law, or abroad, for instance in extradition proceedings where there is an imminent risk of execution of a death penalty by the requesting state.[110]

(3) Actual or imminent, direct or indirect, violations of human rights of individuals under the jurisdiction of a state as a consequence of binding decisions of international organizations.[111]

(4) Actual or imminent violations of human rights due to natural hazards or technical installations. Thus, the European Court of Human Rights recognized that a violation of the right to life had occurred where municipal authorities had knowingly failed to take steps to prevent a methane gas explosion at a landfill, as a result of which a number of people lost their lives[112] or because the authorities had neglected to raise protective dams or to set up an alert system against landslides, which had been threatening a town for years, and also neglected to prevent evacuated inhabitants from returning to their homes before the danger had ceased.[113]

Example: The ECtHR judgments in *Öneryildiz v Turkey* and *Budayeva v Russia*[114]

Threats to human rights due to natural disasters or technical installations are increasing. The European Court of Human Rights examined the duty to protect in several cases:

In the case of *Öneryildiz v Turkey*, a methane explosion occurred in a rubbish tip in Ümraniye (Istanbul) at 11 am on 28 April 1993. Ten slum dwellings in the immediate vicinity of the tip were engulfed by the refuse and 39 people died, including nine relatives of the complainant. Some two years prior, a report by experts had warned of the risk of such an explosion but the authorities had taken no steps either to arrange for the supervised burning of amassed gases or to evacuate neighbouring

---

[108] See for example, IACtHR, *Escué-Zapata v Colombia*, Series C, No 165 (2007), para 40.
[109] ECtHR (Grand Chamber), *Ilaşcu and Others v Moldova and Russia*, Reports 2004-VII, para 333.
[110] For further details see Chapter 9, section II.2.   [111] See section I.3.
[112] ECtHR (Grand Chamber), *Öneryildiz v Turkey*, Reports 2004-XII.
[113] ECtHR, *Budayeva and Others v Russia*, Applications Nos 15339/02, 21166/02, 20058/02, 11673/02 and 15343/02 (2008).
[114] ECtHR (Grand Chamber), *Öneryildiz v Turkey*, Reports 2004-XII, paras 89 ff, ECtHR, *Budayeva and Others v Russia*, Applications Nos 15339/02, 21166/02, 20058/02, 11673/02 and 15343/02 (2008).

houses and shelters. The Grand Chamber of the Court held that Turkey had violated the right to life under Article 2 of the ECHR. It reasoned that the positive obligation to take all appropriate measures to protect that right entailed above all a primary duty of the state to establish a legislative and administrative framework designed to provide effective protection against threats to the right to life. In the context of dangerous activities, this entailed, *inter alia*, an obligation to establish effective regulations and procedures governing the licensing, operation and supervision of such activities. Where lives were lost and injuries sustained, the state had a duty to ensure that breaches were repressed and punished. The Court concluded that Turkey had breached its obligation to protect under Article 2 because the responsible municipal authorities, though aware of the danger, had failed to take the necessary safety measures (installation of a system to burn off the gases) and furthermore had permitted dwellings to be built in the danger zone. The right to life had also been breached by virtue of the fact that the mayors of the municipalities responsible for the rubbish tip had not been charged with endangerment of life but only with negligence in the performance of their duties and had been sentenced to a fine equivalent to less than 10 Euros.

In *Budayeva v Russia,* the small town of Tyrnauz in the northern Caucasus was struck by landslides in July 2000. The danger of landslides for Tyrnauz was well known and a basin for collecting the sliding mud and a protective dam had been built. These were however badly damaged in 1999. Despite repeated warnings by the competent authorities and the knowledge of the general risk in the area, the authorities took no measures to repair the damage and did not procure the necessary means for anyone to do so. The Court confirmed the existence of such a duty to protect life against the consequences of disasters by reiterating that the right to life 'does not solely concern deaths resulting from the use of force by agents of the State but also...lays down a positive obligation on States to take appropriate steps to safeguard the lives of those within their jurisdiction' and stressing that '[t]his positive obligation entails above all a primary duty on the State to put in place a legislative and administrative framework designed to provide effective deterrence against threats to the right to life' (paras 128–9). While states, when implementing this obligation, have a large liberty in choosing measures, setting priorities and allocating resources, in particular 'in the sphere of emergency relief in relation to a meteorological event, which is as such beyond human control' (para 135), they have a duty 'to take practical measures to ensure the effective protection of citizens whose lives might be endangered by the inherent risks' and to 'provide for appropriate procedures, taking into account the technical aspects of the activity in question, for identifying shortcomings in the processes concerned and any errors committed by those responsible at different levels' (para 132). This applies not only in the context of risks created by industrial and other 'dangerous activities' such as the operation of waste collection sites, but also regarding foreseeable natural disasters. Furthermore, the Court stressed that it is was not sufficient to enact necessary laws and take appropriate administrative measures; rather, there is also an obligation of the authorities 'to adequately inform the public about any life-threatening emergency, and to ensure that any occasion of the deaths caused thereby would be followed by a judicial enquiry' (para 131, referring to the *Öneryildiz* case, paras 89–118).

(b) Relevant rights

The question of which rights give rise to a claim for protection and to what extent has not yet been conclusively resolved. Clearly, some rights are more apt than others to give rise to obligations to protect against breaches by third parties. For instance, the right to an effective legal remedy, the prohibition of retroactive criminal laws and most due process rights are directed exclusively against the state, and private actors (unlike international organizations[115]) can scarcely ever be deemed to violate them. By contrast, guarantees aimed at the protection of physical integrity, such as the prohibition of torture or inhuman treatment under the ICCPR and regional human rights treaties,[116] and many classic civil rights such as freedom of assembly or freedom of religion, are just as vulnerable to violation by private actors as by the state.

The obligation to protect is in some cases explicitly set out in the text of human rights treaties. Article 6(1) of the ICCPR, for example, stipulates that the right to life 'shall be protected by law'. Similar obligations are established by ECHR, Article 2(1), ACHR, Article 4(1), and ArCHR, Article 5(1). This duty to protect is violated, for instance, where the law fails to sanction certain forms of homicide or where the state fails to provide police protection for private persons whose lives have been threatened.[117]

The obligation to protect the right to private life is also explicitly recognized. Article 17(2) of the ICCPR confers on everyone 'the right to protection of the law' against 'arbitrary or unlawful interference with his privacy, family, home or correspondence' and against 'unlawful attacks on his honour and reputation'. Article 23(1) of the Covenant, for its part, recognizes the family's 'entitlement to protection by society and the State'. As emphasized by the Human Rights Committee, such protection must be afforded regardless of whether the interferences emanate 'from State authorities or from natural or legal persons'.[118] While this protection relates primarily to the family's relations with the outside world, the requirement that marriage can be entered into only with the free and full consent of the intending spouses[119] entails obligations pertaining to relations within the family. Thus, forced marriages should not be recognized and children should be protected in such cases from interference by their

---

[115] See section I.3.

[116] Although the definition of torture in CAT, Art 1 does not cover strictly private cases of torture, it nevertheless contains a rudimentary obligation to protect, inasmuch as private torture committed with the 'acquiescence' of the state is attributable to the state. This condition is, in our view, fulfilled where a state withholds protection from the victim although it is aware of the danger and has the ability to intervene. On the wider notion of torture in the ICCPR, regional conventions and international criminal law covering torture by non-state actors see Chapter 10, section II.1.a.

[117] ECtHR (Grand Chamber), *Osman v The United Kingdom*, *Reports* 1998-VIII, para 115.

[118] HRCttee, General Comment No 16 (1988), para 1. Art 23(1) confirms that the family 'is entitled to protection from society and the state', it being understood, however, that such protection pertains to the family's relations with the outside world.

[119] ICCPR, Art 23(3).

parents.[120] The European Court of Human Rights has recognized since the *Marckx* case[121] that a duty to protect exists with respect to the right to private and family life under ECHR, Article 8. In the *Airey* judgment,[122] for instance, the Court held that states have an obligation to make an appropriate remedy available to women who wish to live separately from their spouses. In so doing, the Court, for all intents and purposes, recognized a right of escape (albeit not an unlimited one) from oppressive private circumstances and imposed an obligation on states to make corresponding procedures available. This aspect is also contained in ArCHR, Article 34(3), which gives children a right to protection from economic exploitation.

The International Convention on the Elimination of All Forms of Racial Discrimination and the Convention on the Elimination of All Forms of Discrimination against Women prescribe the type of action that states must take to protect rights holders against discrimination in the private sphere.[123] Article 19 of the Convention on the Rights of the Child imposes on states a comprehensive obligation to take 'all appropriate legislative, administrative, social and educational measures' to protect children in the care of parents or other persons responsible for their upbringing from abuse, ill-treatment and neglect. Lastly, the Convention on the Rights of Persons with Disabilities obliges states parties to 'guarantee to persons with disabilities equal and effective legal protection against discrimination on all grounds' (Article 2(2)) and to take measures 'to protect persons with disabilities, both within and outside the home, from all forms of exploitation, violence and abuse, including their gender-based aspects' (Article 16(1)).

The treaty monitoring bodies recognize that even human rights guarantees containing no explicit reference to a duty to protect may nevertheless entail such an obligation. For instance, the European Court of Human Rights has recognized a right of participants in public demonstrations to protection from a violent counter-demonstration.[124] Further cases relate, *inter alia*, to protection against violations by third parties of the physical integrity of individuals, including the prohibition of torture and inhuman treatment.[125] Article 9(1) of the ICCPR

---

[120] Manfred Nowak, *UN Covenant on Civil and Political Rights*, CCPR Commentary (2nd edn, Engel: Kehl, 2005), 534 f.

[121] ECtHR, *Marckx v Belgium*, Series A, No 31 (1979), para 31.

[122] ECtHR, *Airey v Ireland*, Series A, No 32 (1979), paras 32–3: 'The Court does not consider that Ireland can be said to have "interfered" with Mrs. Airey's private or family life: the substance of her complaint is not that the State has acted but that it has failed to act. However, although the object of Article 8 is essentially that of protecting the individual against arbitrary interference by the public authorities, it does not merely compel the State to abstain from such interference: in addition to this primarily negative undertaking, there may be positive obligations inherent in an effective respect for private or family life...'.

[123] See, for example, CEDAW, Art 2(e) and CERD, Art 2(1)(d).

[124] ECtHR, *Plattform 'Ärzte für das Leben' v Austria*, Series A, No 139 (1988).

[125] The ArCHR explicitly obliges the states parties to protect individuals against torture and inhuman treatment (ArCHR, Art 8(2)).

and the corresponding articles of the regional conventions,[126] which ensure the right to security, are particularly important in this regard. The Human Rights Committee has expressly recognized that this right also implies an entitlement to protection of a person's security, ie protection of physical integrity, against attacks by private actors. Thus, it concluded that Colombia had violated Article 9(1) for failing to protect a teacher of religion from death threats made against him for having criticized the ecclesiastical authorities.[127] At the regional level, the European Court of Human Rights recognized a duty to protect the right to property.[128]

Issue in focus: The obligation to protect in the case of violence against minors

---

The *X and Y v the Netherlands* case at the European Court of Human Rights[129] concerned a 16-year-old girl with a mental disability who had been sexually abused. Her father instituted criminal proceedings but the public prosecutor's office discontinued the procedure. The father thereupon took the case to a court of appeal, but the appeal was dismissed because only the victim of an offence was legally entitled to challenge the discontinuation of proceedings and the young woman was unable to do so owing to her disability. The European Court of Human Rights held that there had been a violation of ECHR, Article 8 since the state failed to provide protection to victims under such circumstances. The Court reasoned that the ECHR imposed an obligation on the state to take positive measures to secure respect for personal integrity and that this also applied in relations between private persons.[130]

A v the United Kingdom[131] dealt with domestic violence. At the age of nine, the complainant was severely, and repeatedly, beaten with a cane by his stepfather, to the point that he suffered visible injuries. Although a report by the child's teacher triggered criminal charges, the defendant was found not guilty because domestic law allowed him to argue that his conduct was justified as a 'reasonable chastisement' of a child. The Court held that the beatings, having overstepped permissible limits, constituted inhuman treatment and that the obligation to secure human rights under ECHR, Article 1 read in conjunction with ECHR, Article 3 imposed on the state a duty to protect. The Court stressed that children and other vulnerable persons were entitled to protection against such serious breaches of their personal integrity[132] and

---

[126] ECHR, Art 5(1); ACHR, Art 7(1); ACHPR, Art 6; and ArCHR, Art 14(1).

[127] HRCttee, *Delgado Paéz v Colombia*, Communication No 195/1985 (1990), paras 5.5 f and 6.

[128] For example, ECtHR, *Budayeva and Others v Russia*, Application Nos 15339/02, 21166/02, 20058/02, 11673/02 and 15343/02 (2008), para 172 with references.

[129] ECtHR, *X and Y v The Netherlands*, Series A, No 91 (1985).   [130] Ibid, para 23.

[131] ECtHR, *A v the United Kingdom*, Reports 1998-VI.

[132] Ibid, para 22: 'The Court considers that the obligation on the High Contracting Parties under Article 1 of the Convention to secure to everyone within their jurisdiction the rights and freedoms defined in the Convention, taken together with Article 3, requires States to take measures designed to ensure that individuals within their jurisdiction are not subjected to torture or inhuman or degrading treatment or punishment, including such ill-treatment administered by private individuals (see, mutatis mutandis, the *HLR v France* judgment (ECtHR, Grand Chamber), *Reports* 1997-III, para 40). Children and other vulnerable individuals, in particular, are entitled

concluded that there had been a violation of Article 3 because domestic criminal law failed to afford adequate protection to children who were victims of bodily harm inflicted by those responsible for their care.[133]

✳(c) Categories and scale of obligations to protect

Obligations to protect can be either *preventive* or *remedial*.[134] They are preventive where the object is to prevent violations of human rights by third parties, by natural hazards or dangers emanating from technical installations, and remedial where the consequences of a violation are redressed or, where redress is not feasible, the victim receives compensation and the perpetrators are punished. Both categories of obligations can be satisfied both through the enactment of appropriate legislation and its enforcement by the courts and through the *ad hoc* adoption of operational measures such as the provision of police protection or the evacuation from areas at risk from natural disasters. Measures on both levels are often required to provide private persons with effective protection against rights-related infringements by third parties.

✳The question of the circumstances entailing obligations to protect and the scale of the obligations is a complex one. A state's obligation to afford human rights protection to private persons against breaches by third parties can never be absolute. On the one hand, the state does not possess unlimited resources that would enable it to take preventive action everywhere and at all times; it is constrained by the means at its disposal and their consistency. On the other hand, a duty to provide comprehensive protection would result in blanket state control over the private sphere as authorities can only intervene in cases they know about. Obviously, the scope of the obligation to protect should not be expanded to such an extent that the state effectively infiltrates the private domain in the name of human rights and extends its control to the point where the whole idea of human rights is undermined.

The European Court of Human Rights addressed these issues in the *Osman* case.[135] The facts underlying the Court's judgment were as follows. In 1988, Ahmet Osman was seriously injured and his father shot dead by Ahmet's former teacher. The crime followed repeated serious threats to the Osman's family by the mentally ill perpetrator, as a result of which the family had requested police protection as a preventive measure. Ahmet's mother claimed that on the day in question she alerted the police but they did not responded, thus violating the right to protection of life under ECHR, Article 2. The Court held that the state's

to State protection, in the form of effective deterrence, against such serious breaches of personal integrity (see, mutatis mutandis, ECtHR, *X and Y v The Netherlands*, Series A, No 91 (1985), paras 21 ff; *Stubbings and Others v The United Kingdom*, *Reports* 1996-IV, paras 62–4; and also Arts 19 and 37 CRC).'

[133] ECtHR, *A v The United Kingdom*, *Reports* 1998-VI, paras 23–5.
[134] IACtHR, *Velásquez-Rodríguez v Honduras* (see n 107).
[135] ECtHR (Grand Chamber), *Osman v The United Kingdom*, *Reports* 1998-VIII.

obligation to protect life under Article 2 'extends beyond its primary duty to secure the right to life by putting in place effective criminal-law provisions to deter the commission of offences against the person backed up by law-enforcement machinery for the prevention, suppression and sanctioning of breaches of such provisions' and stressed that this obligation may, in certain circumstances, entail 'a positive obligation on the authorities to take preventive operational measures to protect an individual whose life is at risk from the criminal acts of another individual'.[136] As regards the scope of this obligation, the Court noted that 'such an obligation must be interpreted in a way which does not impose an impossible or disproportionate burden on the authorities. Accordingly, not every claimed risk to life can entail for the authorities a Convention requirement to take operational measures to prevent that risk from materializing. Another relevant consideration is the need to ensure that the police exercise their powers to control and prevent crime in a manner which fully respects the due process and other guarantees which legitimately place restraints on the scope of their action to investigate crime and bring offenders to justice, including the guarantees contained in Articles 5 and 8 of the Convention.'[137] Based on this considerations, the Court defined the applicable test as follows: '[W]here there is an allegation that the authorities have violated their positive obligation to protect the right to life in the context of their... duty to prevent and suppress offences against the person..., it must be established to its satisfaction that the authorities *knew or ought to have known at the time of the existence of a real and immediate risk to the life of an identified individual* or individuals from the criminal acts of a third party and that they failed *to take measures within the scope of their powers which, judged reasonably, might have been expected to avoid that risk*.'[138] Thus, the criterion of 'reasonable and appropriate measures' recognized earlier by the Court in connection with the duty to protect[139] is applicable to the right to life. In the case in point, the Court held that there had been no violation of the duty to protect on account of the circumstances at the time of the crime.

These principles may be couched in general terms as follows: human rights give rise to obligations to protect where:

(1) the authorities *know* of an actual or imminent danger from third parties or from circumstances brought about by natural or human agents, or they ought to have known, ie they would have known had they exercised due diligence and obtained information while respecting the limits imposed by human rights norms;

---

[136] Ibid, para 115. In this case, the question was answered in the negative.

[137] Ibid, para 116.

[138] Ibid, para 116 (emphasis added). Confirmed in *Gongadze v Ukraine*, Reports 2005-XI, paras 164–5.

[139] ECtHR, *Plattform 'Ärzte für das Leben' v Austria*, Series A, No 139 (1988), para 34. In this judgment the Court held that states had an obligation under ECHR, Art 11 to protect demonstrations by means of 'reasonable and appropriate [police] measures' against private disruptors.

(2) notwithstanding their knowledge, they fail to take such protective measures as *could have been taken with available resources* and might reasonably have been expected to avert the danger or they fail to redress the damage that occurred; and

(3) such available and appropriate *measures are consistent with human rights*, ie would not violate the rights of the perpetrators or other third parties.[140]

The criteria of knowledge and of reasonable and appropriate measures are subject to stricter rules under existing jurisprudence if the person at risk of violations by private actors is in state custody, eg in detention, or if the risk of an infringement lies in the conduct of state agents operating *ultra vires*.[141] More stringent standards are likewise applicable in assessing the adequacy of state measures if the individuals at risk are deemed to require special protection on account of, for example, their age or a disability.

On the other hand, in cases where the right to be protected in a given case may be limited the application of the limitation clauses is less stringent. In such cases, according to the European Court of Human Rights, 'a *fair balance*...has to be struck between the competing interests of the individual and of the community as a whole' and in doing so, the aims mentioned in the limitation clauses 'may be of a certain relevance'.[142] Thus, for example, house owners may have to accept a certain level of noise from an airport whose expansion is in the public interest.[143] In a similar vain, the Court has come to the conclusion that—as opposed to the protection of the right to life—the duty to protect the right to property is less stringent where property is lost not as a result of events occurring under the responsibility of the public authorities but destroyed by a natural disaster.[144]

Although the European Court of Human Rights has developed these principles with reference to protective measures of an *ad hoc* operational character, they are also applicable to the obligation to take legislative measures. As demonstrated by the above-mentioned *X and Y v the Netherlands* and *A v the United Kingdom* cases, there is automatically a violation of the duty to protect where there are lacunae in criminal or civil legislation that permit immunity for foreseeable private interference in areas protected by human rights norms.

---

[140] ECtHR (Grand Chamber), *Osman v The United Kingdom*, Reports 1998-VIII, para 116.

[141] See ECtHR, *Paul and Audrey Edwards v The United Kingdom*, Reports 2002-II, and *Anguelova v Bulgaria*, Reports 2002-IV. HRCttee, *Dermit Barbato and Dermit Barbato v Uruguay*, Communication No 84/1981 (1982), *Terán Jijón v Ecuador*, Communication No 277/1988 (1992).

[142] Eg, ECtHR (Grand Chamber), *Hatton and Others v the United Kingdom*, Reports 2003-VIII, para 98 (emphasis added).

[143] Ibid, paras 119–30.

[144] ECtHR, *Budayeva and Others v Russia*, Applications Nos 15339/02, 21166/02, 20058/02, 11673/02 and 15343/02 (2008), paras 173–4.

4. The obligation to fulfil human rights

Positive obligations to fulfil human rights go beyond the obligation to afford protection against violations by private actors or risks emanating from natural forces. Broadly speaking, they require the state to create the legal, institutional, and procedural conditions that rights holders need in order to realize and enjoy their rights in full. This may call for action on a variety of levels.

A number of human rights cannot be exercised without prior enactment of specific laws and the related establishment of competent state bodies. For instance, the existence of matrimonial law and the right to contract marriage before state authorities, or at least to have the union registered, are prerequisites for the realization of the right to marry. The right to property, for its part, is only meaningful where the concept of private property is embodied in domestic law. In the area of social rights, the establishment of social insurance or similar institutional schemes is a precondition for realizing the right to social security. Beyond legislation, the elaboration and implementation of policies and action plans can play an important role. In the absence of anti-discrimination, educational, labour, or media policies, none of the associated human rights can be fully realized.

On the institutional level, the establishment of administrative bodies and tribunals providing legal protection and the provision of effective remedies to such organs, is particularly important. According to ICCPR, Article 2(3)(a) the state's duty to ensure 'that any person whose rights or freedoms as herein recognized are violated shall have an effective remedy' is one of the basic general human rights obligations[145] that states can only fulfil once they have organized and developed a normative and institutional framework for legal protection. Provisions such as the guarantees of due process in civil and criminal proceedings set out in ICCPR, Article 14 and equivalent provisions in regional conventions depend on the existence of a properly functioning judicial system, which the state must establish before it can respect the rights of accused persons and litigants.

Material benefits, such as money, goods, or services provided by the state, are necessary where a right such as the entitlement to legal assistance in criminal proceedings[146] or the right to free basic education[147] is explicitly provided for, or where a right would be devoid of substance in the absence of such a benefit. This applies in particular to the right to food, shelter and basic health care where people are in immediate need of assistance or, as in the case of institutionalized individuals, prisoners, and soldiers, are under direct state control and hence unable to attend to their own subsistence needs.[148] However, obligations to fulfil also play a significant role with respect to, for instance, freedom of expression and assembly. The core content of these rights is jeopardized where the state

---

[145] For more details see Chapter 6, section II.2.a.
[146] ICCPR, Art 14(3)(d); ECHR, Art 6(3)(c).   [147] ICESCR, Art 13(2)(a).
[148] On the legal nature of obligations to fulfil stemming from economic, social, and cultural rights, see below section 6.

categorically refuses to make public streets and squares available for political demonstrations.

The extent to which such entitlements exist in practice and are enforceable depends on the human rights guarantee in question. As a general rule, the extent of the state's obligation depends on its capacity, ie the resources available to devote to the performance of the duties concerned.

5. The obligation to respect human rights without discrimination

Human rights treaties impose a duty on states to respect, protect and fulfil human rights without discrimination. This duty implies that when states impose permissible restrictions on human rights, deny victims of violations protection on permissible grounds or, without breaching legal obligations, withhold benefits from persons who are basically entitled to them, they must do so in a manner that does not adversely affect the persons concerned on grounds pertaining solely to 'sex, race, colour, language, religion, political or other opinion, national or social origin, association with a national minority, property, birth or other status'.[149] It follows that the non-discrimination principle rules out limitations that would otherwise be permissible if they were formulated in a discriminatory manner.

This 'accessory' prohibition of discrimination should be differentiated from the prohibition of discrimination as an autonomous human right.[150] The prohibition of discrimination is an integral component of states' fundamental human rights obligations, as clearly demonstrated by its inclusion in ICESCR, Article 2(2), ICCPR, Article 2(1), ACHR, Article 1(1), and ArCHR, Article 3(1). The prohibition is ultimately grounded in Article 1(3) of the UN Charter, which includes among the main purposes of the United Nations international cooperation 'in promoting and encouraging respect for human rights and for fundamental freedoms for all without distinction as to race, sex, language, or religion'. On the other hand, the approach adopted by the drafters of the ECHR and the ACHPR, namely embodying the prohibition of accessory discrimination in a separate provision (ECHR, Article 14; ACHR, Article 2) instead of including it in the general obligations under Article 1 of the two treaties obscures the prohibition's crosscutting character.

6. The structure of obligations under economic, social, and cultural rights

(a) Overview

The obligations to respect, protect and fulfil are, albeit to different extents, relevant for all categories of rights. However, the obligation clause of ICESCR,

---

[149] The wording of ECHR, Art 14.   [150] See Chapter 11, section II.

Article 2 urging each state party 'to take steps, . . . to the maximum of its available resources, with a view to achieving progressively the full realization of the rights recognized in this Covenant by all appropriate means' was long cited as proof that economic, social and cultural rights are fundamentally different from civil and political rights. Nevertheless, it has become clear that these rights, just like civil and political rights, entail an obligation to respect, protect and fulfil, and that they differ from other human rights not in terms of principle but in terms of degree inasmuch as they place greater weight on the fulfilment components.

(b) Obligations to respect and protect: economic, social and cultural rights as freedoms and liberties

The obligations to respect and protect remain nonetheless crucially important in the case of economic, social and cultural rights. These rights protect access to, and enjoyment of, certain goods and services such as jobs and other forms of livelihood, social security, food, housing, health services and education. Such goods and services are provided not by the state but by the private sector (as is the case in certain countries even for education) unless the state defines itself as the primary provider or sees its role as complementary (as is often the case in the area of health services where at least some hospitals are run by public authorities). In both cases, people must be able freely to choose which goods and services they want to acquire or use. In this sense, Article 6 of the ICESCR on the right to work explicitly guarantees 'the right of everyone to the opportunity to gain his living by work which he *freely chooses* or accepts', Article 8 recognizes '[t]he right of everyone to form trade unions and join the trade union *of his choice*', and Article 13(3) and (4) obliges states to respect 'the liberty of parents . . . *to choose* for their children schools' as well as 'the *liberty* of individuals and bodies to establish and direct educational institutions'.[151]

Such freedoms and liberties are at the core of each economic, social and cultural right and must be respected as well as protected by state authorities. The state, for example, has the obligation to respect the right of individuals to buy or rent an accommodation or to consult a doctor of their choice, and must provide protection when third parties seek to prevent them from doing so. Arguably, the most common and serious violations of economic, social, and cultural rights consist of denial by the state of access to available goods and services protected by these rights or the refusal to provide protection against such infringements by third parties. Very often, such violations target specific groups of people (women, members of particular minorities, persons with disabilities, etc) and are based on discriminatory intent.

The freedoms enshrined in economic, social and cultural rights are not absolute. They can be limited in the cases set out in ICESCR, Article 4, ie they may be subjected to such limitations 'as are determined by law only in so far as this

---

[151] Emphases added.

may be compatible with the nature of these rights and solely for the purpose of promoting the general welfare in a democratic society'. Thus, such limitations are only permissible to the extent that they are necessary to achieve the stated goal, ie the limits must be proportionate to the promotion of general welfare.

As regards the obligation to protect, the requirements of knowledge, capacity, consistency with human rights and fair balance as described above[152] also apply to economic, social and cultural rights.

Issue in focus: The interdependence of the different categories of rights

Some civil and political rights not only overlap with economic, social and cultural rights insofar as they contain similar guarantees. In other cases, the two categories of rights are interdependent in practice. An illustrative case is the impact of infringements of freedom of movement on the enjoyment of the right to food and other social rights by the so-called security 'wall' separating Israel and the Occupied Palestinian Territory. In its advisory opinion[153] on this issue, the ICJ stated:

133. That construction, the establishment of a closed area between the Green Line and the wall itself and the creation of enclaves have moreover imposed substantial restrictions on the freedom of movement of the inhabitants of the Occupied Palestinian Territory (with the exception of Israeli citizens and those assimilated thereto)...They are aggravated by the fact that the access gates are few in number in certain sectors and opening hours appear to be restricted and unpredictably applied. For example, according to the Special Rapporteur of the Commission on Human Rights on the situation of human rights in the Palestinian territories occupied by Israel since 1967, 'Qalqiliya, a city with a population of 40,000, is completely surrounded by the Wall and residents can only enter and leave through a single military checkpoint open from 7 a.m. to 7 p.m.'...There have also been serious repercussions for agricultural production, as is attested by a number of sources...

[T]the Special Rapporteur on the situation of human rights in the Palestinian territories occupied by Israel since 1967 states that 'Much of the Palestinian land on the Israeli side of the Wall consists of fertile agricultural land and some of the most important water wells in the region' and adds that 'Many fruit and olive trees had been destroyed in the course of building the barrier.'...The special Rapporteur on the Right to Food of the United Nations Commission on Human Rights states that construction of the wall 'cuts off Palestinians from their agricultural lands, wells and means of subsistence'...

It has further led to increasing difficulties for the population concerned regarding access to health services, educational establishments and primary sources of water...

134. To sum up, the Court is of the opinion that the construction of the wall and its associated régime impede the liberty of movement of the inhabitants of the Occupied Palestinian Territory (with the exception of Israeli citizens and those assimilated thereto) as guaranteed under Article 12, paragraph 1, of the International Covenant on Civil and Political Rights. They also impede the exercise by the persons concerned of the right to work, to health, to

---

[152] See section III.3.c.
[153] ICJ, *Legal Consequences of the Construction of a Wall in the Occupied Palestinian Territory* (Advisory Opinion), ICJ Reports 2004.

education and to an adequate standard of living as proclaimed in the International Covenant on Economic, Social and Cultural Rights and in the United Nations Convention on the Rights of the Child...

136....The Court would further observe that the restrictions on the enjoyment by the Palestinians living in the territory occupied by Israel of their economic, social and cultural rights, resulting from Israel's construction of the wall, fail to meet a condition laid down by Article 4 of the International Covenant on Economic, Social and Cultural Rights, that is to say that their implementation must be 'solely for the purpose of promoting the general welfare in a democratic society'.

(c) Obligations to fulfil

The obligation to fulfil is in the forefront of discussions on the legal character of economic, social and cultural rights. The duty to fulfil only becomes relevant if people are unable to satisfy their needs on their own. Such situations may be caused by reasons as diverse as emergencies, market failures or the fact that the persons concerned are in the custody of the State. In that sense, obligations to fulfil economic, social and cultural rights are of a subsidiary nature.

Furthermore, such obligations are characterized primarily by the need to deploy scarce resources which are available in unequal measure to individual states, meaning that not all states can be required to fulfil such obligations irrespective of their economic potential. Therefore, the general obligation clause of ICESCR, Article 2 urges states parties progressively to achieve 'the full realization of the rights recognized in the present Covenant by all appropriate means'. It follows, in principle, that the obligation to fulfil under this Covenant does not have to be met immediately but rather progressively, depending on the amount of state resources available. While this means that states parties have greater latitude in terms of the choice and scale of the means deployed to achieve the aim of full realization of Covenant rights, the modalities of such actions are not left entirely to the discretion of states. Rather, ICESCR, Article 2 lays down the following binding parameters:

- states parties must, *immediately* after ratifying the ICESCR,
- to the *maximum of their available resources*, ie drawing as a matter of priority on their available resources,
- and *by all appropriate means*, including through international assistance,
- take steps towards the full realization of the Covenant rights.

Issue in focus: The legal nature of obligations to fulfil under the European Social Charter

The provision on 'Undertakings'[154] of the obligation clause of ESC, Article 20 is less generous in making allowance for circumstances that might minimize its obligations in

---

[154] ESC, Art 20; ESCrev, Part III, Art A.

the implementation of the rights it guarantees. While all rights set forth in the Charter are to be viewed, in principle, as objectives to be achieved progressively, states are required, in addition, to select certain rights from a list which become fully and immediately binding as core obligations from the time of ratification. At the same time, the wording of the individual rights mitigates to some extent the initial impression of rigidly defined obligations. For instance, language to the effect that the contracting parties undertake in respect of the right to work 'to accept as one of their primary aims and responsibilities the achievement and maintenance of as high and stable a level of employment as possible, with a view to the attainment of full employment'[155] makes it clear that the contracting states are being called upon to achieve only what is materially feasible. Viewed in this light, ESC obligations to fulfil closely resemble those of the ICESCR.

It is sometimes claimed that economic, social and cultural rights are not real human rights because they are not justiciable. However, the Committee on Economic, Social and Cultural Rights has stressed that among the 'appropriate means' to achieve full realization of the rights contained in the ICESCR, states may consider 'the provision of judicial remedies with respect to rights which may, in accordance with the national legal system, be considered justiciable'.[156] The Committee further identified specific rights that may entail such immediate applicability; it stressed that 'there are a number of other provisions in the International Covenant on Economic, Social and Cultural Rights, including Articles 3, 7(a)(i), 8, 10(3), 13(2)(a), (3), and (4), and 15(3) which would seem to be capable of immediate application by judicial and other organs in many national legal systems. Any suggestion that the provisions indicated are inherently non-self-executing would seem to be difficult to sustain.'[157] With the adoption of the Optional Protocol to the International Covenant on Economic, Social and Cultural Rights on 10 December 2008 that provides victims of alleged violations of the Covenant with the possibility to submit individual communications States have accepted this understanding. That certain elements of economic, social and cultural rights are directly applicable and justiciable is also recognized in Article 4(2) of the Convention on the Rights of Persons with Disabilities which states that the obligation progressively to achieve the full realization of such rights is 'without prejudice to those obligations contained in the present Convention that are immediately applicable according to international law.'

Issue in focus: Enforcement of economic, social and cultural rights at the domestic level

Whether individuals at the domestic level can invoke economic, social and cultural rights that, in principle, are directly applicable and justiciable depends on two conditions. First, countries following the monist approach to the relationship between

---

[155] ESC, Art 1; ESCrev, Art 1.
[156] CtteeESCR, General Comment No 3 (1990), para 5.   [157] Ibid.

international and domestic law must accept the self-executing character of such rights and countries adhering to dualism have to incorporate the full content of the Covenant into their domestic law. Second, domestic law must provide individuals with an effective remedy. With regard to the second element, the Committee on Economic, Social and Cultural Rights stated the following:

9. The right to an effective remedy need not be interpreted as always requiring a judicial remedy. Administrative remedies will, in many cases, be adequate and those living within the jurisdiction of a State party have a legitimate expectation, based on the principle of good faith, that all administrative authorities will take account of the requirements of the Covenant in their decision-making. Any such administrative remedies should be accessible, affordable, timely and effective....

10. In relation to civil and political rights, it is generally taken for granted that judicial remedies for violations are essential. Regrettably, the contrary assumption is too often made in relation to economic, social and cultural rights. This discrepancy is not warranted either by the nature of the rights or by the relevant Covenant provisions. The Committee has already made clear that it considers many of the provisions in the Covenant to be capable of immediate implementation... It is important in this regard to distinguish between justiciability (which refers to those matters which are appropriately resolved by the courts) and norms which are self-executing (capable of being applied by courts without further elaboration). While the general approach of each legal system needs to be taken into account, there is no Covenant right which could not, in the great majority of systems, be considered to possess at least some significant justiciable dimensions. It is sometimes suggested that matters involving the allocation of resources should be left to the political authorities rather than the courts. While the respective competences of the various branches of government must be respected, it is appropriate to acknowledge that courts are generally already involved in a considerable range of matters which have important resource implications. The adoption of a rigid classification of economic, social and cultural rights which puts them, by definition, beyond the reach of the courts would thus be arbitrary and incompatible with the principle that the two sets of human rights are indivisible and interdependent. It would also drastically curtail the capacity of the courts to protect the rights of the most vulnerable and disadvantaged groups in society.[158]

The following areas of social rights fall within the category of obligations to fulfil[159] that can be considered justiciable:

(1) *Minimum requirements*: The Committee on Economic, Social and Cultural Rights acknowledges that the Covenant contains a 'core' of rights in the sense of minimum requirements which, if left unsatisfied, would deprive the right concerned of its *raison d'être* and render it meaningless. It has determined that every state party has a core obligation to ensure the satisfaction of minimum essential levels of each right. A state party in which, for instance, a significant number of individuals are deprived of essential foodstuffs, essential primary

---

[158] CtteeESCR, General Comment No 9 (1998), para 10.

[159] As just outlined (above, subsection b), economic, social and cultural rights contain obligations to protect and fulfil which are fully justiciable according to the standards set at section III.1 and 2.

health care, or basic housing or education is, *prima facie*, failing to discharge its obligations under the ICESCR.[160] The Committee on Economic, Social and Cultural Rights thus takes the view that non-fulfilment in these areas creates a presumption that a state has breached its international legal obligations. This presumption is difficult to rebut, particularly for industrialized states. The requirement to guarantee survival in an emergency is therefore, at least for industrialized states, a minimum requirement that must be fulfilled immediately. Other states that fail to fulfil this obligation may, however, defend themselves against the charge of having committed a violation by demonstrating that, despite using available resources to the maximum and taking advantage of any support from the international community, they were unable to achieve the required results. Such deficient performance must, however, be attributable to the objective inability of the state party and not to its unwillingness.[161]

(2) *Obligations to fulfil in circumstances of full state control over an individual*: Additionally, states have immediately binding obligations *vis-à-vis* persons who are no longer in a position to meet their own subsistence needs because they are in the custody or otherwise under the full control of authorities. Such persons are entitled to be provided with a degree of relevant goods and services that goes beyond the minimum core. Thus, for example, prisoners, patients undergoing compulsory psychiatric treatment, asylum-seekers housed in a reception center and prohibited to work, soldiers during their military service or persons whose evacuation or relocation from a war or disaster zone was ordered by public authorities are entitled to adequate food, housing, clothing, and medical attention. The extent of a state's obligation to fulfil in such circumstances depends on the degree of a person's inability to attend to his or her own subsistence needs. This structure of obligations is also persuasively illustrated by international humanitarian law. Thus, GC III, Article 15 imposes on states a binding duty of care with respect to prisoners of war.[162] On the other hand, states' duty of care under GC IV, Article 55 with respect to the population of occupied territories is only subsidiary—since the population bears primary responsibility for attending to its own needs.

(3) Are individuals entitled to be against *retrogressive steps from an attained level of realization* of a specific right? On the one hand, the obligation of progressive realization under ICESCR, Article 2(1) renders the permissibility of such backsliding questionable with paragraph 2 of the article making it clear that moves to dismantle what has been achieved may never be discriminatory.

---

[160] CtteeESCR, General Comment No 3 (1990), para 10.
[161] CtteeESCR, General Comment No 12 (1999), para 17.
[162] If it proves impossible to provide adequate care, prisoners of war must be released on that ground. See for example Jean S Pictet (ed), *Commentary on the Geneva Conventions of 12 August 1949*, vol I–IV (International Committee of the Red Cross: Geneva, 1952–1959), vol III, 153.

On the other hand, the fact that states are not required to use more than the 'appropriate means' renders their obligation to fulfil largely dependent on the scale of the resources readily available. The Committee on Economic, Social and Cultural Rights has held that, in principle, retrogressive steps from an attained level of realization are not absolutely prohibited, but stressed that 'any deliberately retrogressive measures in that regard would require the most careful consideration and would need to be fully justified by reference to the totality of the rights provided for in the Covenant and in the context of the full use of the maximum available resources'.[163] In other words, states must either compensate for the ensuing disadvantages in some other way or prove that the retrogressive steps 'have been introduced after the most careful consideration of all alternatives'[164] and, notwithstanding the use of all available resources, are therefore unavoidable.

---

[163] CtteeESCR, General Comment No 3 (1990), para 9. Similar, General Comment No 13 (1999), para 45, and General Comment No 15 (2002), para 19.
[164] CtteeESCR, General Comment No 13 (1999) para 45 (right to education).

4

Scope of Application of Human Rights

While the previous chapter approached human rights from the standpoint of duty bearers, the perspective changes in this chapter, which asks the following: *who* has human rights entitlements, to what *extent, where,* and *when*? This question addresses the scope of application of human rights in personal terms (section I), substantive terms (section II), territorial terms (section III), and temporal terms (section IV).

I. Personal Scope of Application

1. Human rights, rights of citizens, rights of aliens

Guarantees in human rights treaties are for the most part universal in terms of personal scope, ie they are applicable to all persons regardless of nationality. However, the political rights recognized in ICCPR, Article 25, ACHR, Article 23, ACHPR, Article 13, and ArCHR, Article 24 can only be invoked by citizens of the country concerned.[1] Article 16 of the ECHR, for its part, permits limitations on the personal scope of certain rights by stating that the prohibition of discrimination and the guarantees of freedom of expression, assembly and association do not prevent states parties from 'imposing restrictions on the political activity of aliens'.[2] Article 24 of the ArCHR limits the protection of political expressions and assemblies to citizens. On the other hand, procedural guarantees in expulsion proceedings[3] protect non-citizens only.

2. Natural persons and legal persons

The natural law tradition, which influenced the language used in the Universal Declaration of Human Rights and the preambles to many human rights

---

[1] P 1/ECHR, Art 1 has a more open wording that would allow foreigners to invoke the guarantee of free elections at regular intervals if domestic law would allow them to participate in elections, eg at the local level.

[2] The personal scope of application of the right to freedom of movement and right to choose one's residence under ICCPR, Art 12 and P 4/ECHR, Art 2 is not related to the criterion of citizenship but to lawfulness of residence in a state party.

[3] ICCPR, Art 13; ACHR, Art 22(6), (8) and (9); ACHPR, Art 12(4) and (5); ArCHR, Art 26(2); P 4/ECHR, Art 4; P 7/ECHR, Art 1.

treaties, considers human rights as innate entitlements of the human person. This implies that only natural persons should be recognized as human rights holders. Accordingly, ICCPR, Article 2(1) requires states parties to ensure Covenant rights to all individuals. Article 2 of the ICCPR-OP1 is consistent with this provision, restricting to 'individuals' the capacity to file individual communications[4] and thereby barring legal persons from approaching the Human Rights Committee with complaints of violations of the Covenant.[5] By contrast, with the exception of the Arab Convention on Human Rights,[6] the regional human rights treaties[7] and some universal conventions[8] expressly state that other groups of persons, ie legal persons, may also assert their rights in the event of violations. Continental European constitutional traditions, which have always accorded fundamental rights to legal persons, probably played an important role in this regard, particularly in the case of the ECHR and the ACHR.

The foregoing clearly shows that the question of the personal scope of application of human rights is more complex than it appears at first glance. The following categories may be identified:

(1) Many human rights, such as the right to life, matrimonial freedom, freedom of conscience, the protection of detained persons or the prohibition of torture are applicable as a matter of course *only to natural persons*. Treaties aimed at protecting specific categories of individuals, such as the Convention on the Elimination of All Forms of Discrimination against Women or the Convention on the Rights of the Child, are applicable only to particular categories of natural persons.

(2) Some rights, such as the right of trade unions to function freely (ICESCR, Article 8(1)(c)) or the right of organizations to establish and administer private schools (ICESCR, Article 13(4)), can be invoked *exclusively by legal persons*.[9]

(3) In between these two categories fall rights, such as due process rights in civil proceedings or freedom of the press, which are suitable for invocation by both *natural and legal persons*. In such cases, the treaty concerned determines whether (as in the case of the ICCPR) only individuals or (as in the case of most regional treaties) both individuals and legal persons are protected.

---

[4] On this procedure, see Chapter 7, section III.1.b.

[5] However, the provision does not bar individuals acting on behalf of legal persons from access to the Committee (eg a manager on behalf of his or her business firm, a religious leader on behalf of a religious community with legal personality), provided that they are also affected by the alleged human rights violation. See generally Manfred Nowak, *UN Covenant on Civil and Political Rights, CCPR Commentary* (2nd edn, Engel: Kehl, 2005), 829 ff. See also HRCttee, *Wallmann et al v Austria*, Communication No 1002/2001 (2004), paras 8.9–8.12.

[6] ArCHR, Art 3(1) uses the term 'individuals' in the English translation.

[7] ECHR, Art 25; ACHR, Art 44; ACHPR, Art 55.   [8] CERD, Art 14.

[9] Other elements of these provisions also protect individuals.

3. Individual rights and collective rights

Human rights are traditionally conceived as individual rights, ie as rights enjoyed by individual (natural or legal) persons. They thus differ fundamentally from collective rights, which can be asserted only by a group and not by its members.

The individual nature of human rights, however, does not mean that they are invariably and exclusively considered as entitlements of isolated individuals without any social reference. Many classic human rights that identify the individual as the rights holder are exercised in community with other individuals and thus clearly involve a collective dimension. By definition, families are collective entities and associations with only one member and assemblies with only one participant do not exist; trade unions presuppose membership of a number of workers; religions are practised in the context of religious communities of various sizes; and freedom of speech is a right invoked only by someone who wants to communicate with others. While in all these cases individuals act as holders of their own rights, the rights in question relate to the group or community to which they belong. In other words, although they are not rights belonging to collective entities, they are nonetheless exercised in a collective context.

This collective dimension of human rights is even more evident in the context of the protection of minority rights. As a rule, however, such rights are recognized as belonging to *members* of minorities and not to the minority in collective terms. Article 27 of the ICCPR makes this particularly clear when it expressly prohibits states parties from withholding cultural, religious and language-related freedoms from 'persons belonging to such minorities'. The Human Rights Committee has furthermore made it clear that only individuals have the right to invoke Article 27;[10] consequently, population groups and other minorities are not entitled as such to lodge complaints with the Committee.[11]

So-called 'third generation' human rights are intended to constitute collective rights in the true sense of the term. There are difficult and largely unresolved doctrinal issues surrounding the personal scope of application of the right of peoples to self-determination under common Article 1 of the two Covenants, as well as the rights to development, to peace and security, to a healthy environment and to sovereignty over natural resources, all of which are recognized to some extent in the African Charter on Human and Peoples' Rights. Clearly, individuals cannot invoke the right of self-determination under common Article 1 of the two Covenants, inasmuch as this right is explicitly addressed to 'peoples'.[12] It

---

[10] HRCttee, General Comment No 23 (1994).

[11] See HRCttee, *Ominayak and the Lubicon Lake Band v Canada*, Communication No 167/1984 (1990), para 32.1.

[12] It is therefore the established practice of the HRCttee to declare individual complaints of violations of ICCPR, Art 1 inadmissible. The ACmHPR, on the other hand, hears complaints of violations of genuine collective rights: see ACmHPR, *Malawi African Association and Others v*

is still unclear, however, whether this concept refers to all peoples within a state, individual ethnic groups, the population of a state[13] or peoples under alien rule. The Arab Charter on Human Rights is more forthright on this point: on the one hand, it gives peoples the right to decide about their own development as part of their right to self-determination (Article 2(1)), and, on the other hand, it grants citizens, ie individuals, the right to participate in the development efforts of the government (Article 37).

Example: Collective rights in the African Charter on Human and Peoples' Rights

---

Article 19
All peoples shall be equal; they shall enjoy the same respect and shall have the same rights. Nothing shall justify the domination of a people by another.

Article 21
1. All peoples shall freely dispose of their wealth and natural resources. This right shall be exercised in the exclusive interest of the people. In no case shall a people be deprived of it.
2. In case of spoliation the dispossessed people shall have the right to the lawful recovery of its property as well as to an adequate compensation.
3. The free disposal of wealth and natural resources shall be exercised without prejudice to the obligation of promoting international economic cooperation based on mutual respect, equitable exchange and the principles of international law. . . .

Article 22
1. All peoples shall have the right to their economic, social and cultural development with due regard to their freedom and identity and in the equal enjoyment of the common heritage of mankind.
2. States shall have the duty, individually or collectively, to ensure the exercise of the right to development

Article 23
1. All peoples shall have the right to national and international peace and security. The principles of solidarity and friendly relations implicitly affirmed by the Charter of the United Nations and reaffirmed by that of the Organization of African Unity shall govern relations between States. . . .

Article 24
All peoples shall have the right to a general satisfactory environment favourable to their development.

Mauritania, Communications Nos 54/1991, 61/1991, 98/1993, 164–196/1997 and 210/1998 (2000), paras 139 ff.

[13] See ACmHPR, *Democratic Republic of Congo v Burundi, Rwanda and Uganda*, Communication No 227/1999 (2004), paras 93 ff.

II. Substantive Scope of Application

1. Scope of protection (overview)

The specific entitlements and circumstances that enjoy substantive protection under human rights treaties cannot be characterized in general terms but may be inferred from the rights set out in each treaty. They will be described in detail in Part III (Chapters 9–17) of this book.

Human rights treaties afford far-reaching but not comprehensive protection of individual needs, interests, and expectancies. Even at the domestic level, constitutional protection of basic rights is selective. Under international law, protection of the legal circumstances and interests of individuals contains even more loopholes, since human rights treaties normally codify only minimum guarantees—ie the most basic legal entitlements and circumstances. At the same time, the proliferation of human rights conventions in recent decades has resulted in a situation where only few areas of human activity remain completely untouched by human rights.

2. Reservations

(a) Admissibility

The substantive scope of application of a specific human rights treaty in a given country not only depends on its content but also on whether and to what extent the state party concerned has modified it by formulating reservations when signing, ratifying, accepting, approving or acceding to a treaty. By entering a reservation, a state can ensure that individual provisions of a treaty are not applicable to it or are applicable only to a limited extent.[14] According to Article 19 of the Vienna Convention on the Law of Treaties (VCLT), reservations are admissible unless (1) the treaty wholly or partially prohibits the reservation, or (2) the reservation in question is incompatible with the object and purpose of the treaty.[15]

In conformity with this provision, a number of treaties, including CEDAW, CERD, CRC, and CRPD,[16] expressly permit reservations that are not incompatible with the object and purpose of the treaty.

Treaties that permit certain reservations and prohibit others include the second Optional Protocol to the ICCPR, Article 2 of which permits only a reservation

---

[14] For the definition of a reservation, see Art 2(1)(d) of the VCLT.

[15] See also draft guidelines 3.1 ff of the ILC's draft guidelines on reservations to treaties: UN Doc A/62/10.

[16] CEDAW, Art 28(1) and (2); CRC, Art 51(1) and (2); CRPD, Art 46. CERD, Art 20 prohibits not only reservations incompatible with the object and purpose of the Convention but also reservations 'the effect of which would inhibit the operation of any of the bodies established by this Convention' or to which at least two thirds of the states parties object.

'that provides for the application of the death penalty in time of war pursuant to a conviction for a most serious crime of a military nature committed during wartime'. Article 57 of the ECHR permits reservations in principle but prohibits those 'of a general character', ie reservations that 'do not make it possible for the scope of the undertaking by [the state party] to be ascertained exactly', and reservations that do not 'contain a brief statement of the law concerned'.[17]

Absolute prohibitions of reservations are unusual. Such provisions are to be found in Protocol No 13 to the ECHR of 3 May 2002 (prohibition of the death penalty even in time of war) and in the Optional Protocol to the Convention against Torture (OPCAT) of 2002 setting up a system of preventive visits to places of detention (Article 30).

The two human rights Covenants belong to the category of treaties that contain no provision regarding reservations. In its General Comment No 24, however, the Human Rights Committee emphasized that, as stipulated by VCLT, Article 19, only reservations that are compatible with the object and purpose of the ICCPR are admissible, adding that its object and purpose are 'to create legally binding standards for human rights by defining certain civil and political rights and placing them in a framework of obligations which are legally binding for those States which ratify; and to provide an efficacious supervisory machinery for the obligations undertaken'.[18] According to the International Law Commission (ILC), elements to be taken into account when assessing the compatibility of a reservation with the object and purpose of a human rights convention include 'the indivisibility, interdependence and interrelatedness of the rights set out in the treaty as well as the importance that the right or provision which is the subject of the reservation has within the general thrust of the treaty, and the gravity of the impact the reservation has upon it'.[19]

The Committee characterizes as inadmissible reservations to provisions of the Covenant that form part of customary international law[20] and *a fortiori* those that constitute peremptory norms of international law (*jus cogens*).[21] As further examples of inadmissible reservations it mentions 'a reservation to the obligation

---

[17] See ECtHR, *Belilos v Switzerland*, Series A, No 132 (1988), para 55.

[18] HRCttee, General Comment No 24 (1994), para 7.

[19] Draft guideline 3.1.12 of the ILC's draft guidelines on reservations to treaties (UN Doc A/62/10).

[20] According to the ILC's draft guideline 3.1.8 of the draft guidelines on reservations to treaties (n 19), such reservations are not intrinsically invalid; however, inconsistency with customary law constitutes a rebuttable presumption of incompatibility with the object and purpose of the treaty. According to draft guideline 3.1.10, reservations to treaty provisions relating to non-derogable rights are also presumably incompatible with the object and purpose of a treaty.

[21] According to draft guideline 3.1.9 of the draft guidelines on reservations to treaties (n 19), a reservation to a peremptory norm of international law cannot exclude its legal effect for the reserving state; however, according to the ILC's commentary to this guideline, reservations to such guarantees are not excluded in principle so long as the state's purpose is not to challenge the norm but, for instance, simply to avoid being monitored by an international body (ILC Report, 59th session, UN Doc A/62/10, 99 ff).

to respect and ensure human rights, and to do so on a non-discriminatory basis (Article 2(1))' and a statement whereby a state reserves the right 'not to take the necessary steps at the domestic level to give effect to the rights of the Covenant (Article 2(2))'.[22]

(b) Procedure for dealing with inadmissible reservations

According to VCLT, Article 20, a reservation is considered to have been accepted if no state raises an objection to it within 12 months. Objecting states officially have the option of excluding the applicability of the provision that has been made subject to a reservation or of the treaty as a whole in relation to the reserving state. These rules reflect the principle under treaty law that a reservation amounts in effect to a modification of the treaty and that this requires the acceptance of the other states parties. The question arises, however, as to whether and to what extent such rules are applicable in the case of human rights treaties.

In its General Comment No 24, the Human Rights Committee expressly states that these rules are not applicable, emphasizing that human rights instruments 'are not a web of inter-State exchanges of mutual obligations' but that they concern 'the endowment of individuals with rights', to which the principle of interstate reciprocity is inapplicable. For this reason, 'States have often not seen any legal interest in or need to object to reservations'. Hence '[t]he absence of protest by states cannot imply that a reservation is either compatible or incompatible with the object and purpose of the Covenant'.[23] The Committee therefore claims for itself the competence to declare a reservation inadmissible and consequently to apply the relevant provision of the Covenant in full to the state concerned.[24]

At the regional level, it is the settled jurisprudence of the European Court of Human Rights that it has jurisdiction to examine the validity of reservations. It attributes this capacity to its competence to rule on all questions pertaining to the interpretation and application of the ECHR, including that of its own jurisdiction (ECHR, Article 32).[25] The Inter-American Court of Human Rights uses similar reasoning to assert its competence to address reservation issues.[26]

In particular the views of the Human Rights Committee have met with opposition from some states[27] and from the Special Rapporteur of the ILC on reservations to treaties. He pointed out that the VCLT rules are applicable universally

---

[22] HRCttee, General Comment No 24 (1994), paras 8 and 9.

[23] HRCttee, General Comment No 24 (1994), para 17.

[24] Ibid, paras 16–18. See also HRCttee, *Kennedy v Trinidad and Tobago*, Communication No 845/1998 (1999), para 6.

[25] ECtHR *Belilos v Switzerland*, Series A, No 132 (1988), para 50, with reference to ECHR, Arts 45 and 49 which were then applicable (now ECHR, Art 32(1) and (2)).

[26] IACtHR, *Effect of Reservations on the Entry into Force of the American Convention on Human Rights (Arts 74 and 75)* (Advisory Opinion), Series A, No 2 (1982), para 13.

[27] France, the United States of America and the United Kingdom. See Sarah Joseph, Jenny Schultz and Melissa Castan, *The International Covenant on Civil and Political Rights* (2nd edn, OUP: Oxford, 2004), 798 and 802 ff.

and without exception, a fact uncontested by the treaty bodies or by the practice of states.[28] In opposition to the Committee's view, the Special Rapporteur argued that, while treaty bodies can assess whether a reservation is valid, they are not entitled—except perhaps in the case of the ECHR—to draw the consequence from an assessment that the state is fully bound by the treaty. This is so because the conclusion of a treaty depends wholly on the will of the state concerned. It follows that the state must have the right to decide itself what consequences it wishes to draw from a determination of the inadmissibility of a reservation.[29]

This view is unduly restrictive and fails to take account of the special characteristics of a treaty equipped with a monitoring mechanism.[30] In the context of individual complaint procedures, the Human Rights Committee, the other treaty bodies as well as the regional human rights courts are required to determine whether they have jurisdiction to consider a complaint. This necessarily involves an examination of whether the complainant can invoke a provision affording protection under the treaty notwithstanding a reservation by the state party thereto. If the treaty bodies, when faced with an invalid reservation under international law, refrained from examining the complaint or rejected it citing their lack of competence to address the issue, their action would amount to a denial of justice or possibly even to the sanctioning of a human rights violation. Thus, the treaty bodies' jurisdiction to examine individual complaints necessarily entails a responsibility to examine the admissibility of reservations. However, in view of the fact that—unlike the decisions of the regional human rights courts—treaty body decisions are not binding,[31] it is anyway for the state party to decide what consequences it wishes to draw from the finding that its reservation is incompatible with the object and purpose of the human rights treaty in question.

---

[28] *ILC Report*, A/52/10, 1997, Chapter V, para 76.

[29] Ibid, paras 80–86. The ILC has not yet taken a position on this issue in the draft guidelines on reservations to treaties (UN Doc A/62/10).

[30] It also disregards the fact that, according to the Vienna Convention on the Law of Treaties, human rights treaties have characteristics that rule out the mechanical application of provisions which, like VCLT, Art 60 are based on the principle of reciprocity. According to Art 60(5) the right of the affected state to terminate or suspend a treaty in the event of a material breach does not apply to 'provisions relating to the protection of the human person contained in treaties of a humanitarian character'. The situation in which a state objects to an inadmissible reservation is structurally similar, inasmuch as, pursuant to VCLT, Art 20, the state in question is entitled in principle, as in the case of Art 60, to terminate the operation of the treaty between itself and the reserving state. In the case of reservations to human rights undertakings, the Art 60(5) prohibition must therefore be equally applicable. The German objections to the United States reservation in respect of the execution of offenders who were minors at the time of commission of the crime (ICCPR, Art 6(5) (objection of 29 September 1993, available at <http://www2.ohchr.org/english/bodies/ratification/docs/ObjectionsICCPR.pdf> (accessed 30 December 2008)) clearly did not give Germany the right on that ground to begin executing such persons itself. It follows that the 'sanction' contemplated in VCLT, Art 20 of non-applicability of the provision concerned with respect to the objecting state cannot be applied in the case of inadmissible reservations to human rights guarantees; this demonstrates that the applicability of this provision to human rights treaties must be restricted.

[31] See Chapter 7, section III.1.

III. Territorial Scope of Application

1. The issue

States are bound as a matter of principle to respect, protect and fulfil human rights within their territory. But is a state also accountable under international law in cases where its agents commit human rights violations on foreign territory, or where their laws and their application give rise to human rights violations abroad? Do such extraterritorial obligations arise only where a state exercises full control over foreign territory—for instance under circumstances of occupation—or do they apply also when, for example, its agents apprehend fugitive offenders or political opponents on foreign territory through commando raids or kill them by means of air strikes? Conversely, should a state be held accountable for human rights violations where a foreign army occupies parts of its territory or where agents of a foreign state commit acts that breach human rights norms on its territory, with or without its knowledge?

These questions raise issues pertaining to the territorial scope of human rights. The principal questions to be answered are whether a state is accountable for human rights violations that are: (1) perpetrated on its territory beyond its control by agents of foreign states or by insurrectionary groups; or (2) committed by its own agents outside its territory.

2. Basic principles

Where human rights treaties refer to their territorial application,[32] they usually take criteria of jurisdiction and national territory as their frame of reference. According to ECHR, Article 1 and ACHR, Article 1, states parties are required to secure the convention guarantees to all persons subject to their jurisdiction; Article 2 of the CRC likewise requires states to ensure rights 'to each child within their jurisdiction'. On the other hand, ICCPR, Article 2(1) combines the two criteria, requiring each state party to respect and ensure Covenant rights 'to all individuals within its territory and subject to its jurisdiction'. Article 2(1) of the CAT takes a slightly different approach, making it the duty of each state party to prevent torture 'in any territory under its jurisdiction'.

All these treaties focus on the criterion of *jurisdiction* and none of them mentions national territory as the sole frame of reference. However, as states, as an attribute of their sovereignty, exercise jurisdiction on their own territory, the territorial scope of treaties coincides as a rule for each state party with its *own national territory*. This gives rise to the following principles:

(1) In its national territory, a state exercises *de jure* jurisdiction by virtue of its territorial sovereignty over all persons within its frontiers. This also applies

---

[32] No references to territorial scope are made, for example, in ICESCR, CERD, CEDAW, and CRPD.

in principle to its conduct with respect to persons in parts of its territory over which it has lost *de facto* control (see below, section 3).

(2) Outside its national territory, on the other hand, a state is bound by a treaty only where there is a specific *de facto* or *de jure* connection between the conduct of its agents and the human rights violation. Thus, jurisdiction is triggered where (1) state agents operate on the foreign territory or (2) conduct within the state's national territory has a direct impact on a person abroad (see, below, section 4). Whether the presence of state agents on foreign territory or conduct with extraterritorial impact[33] is permissible under international law is immaterial for the issue of jurisdiction.

3. State obligation in the event of loss of sovereignty over parts of its national territory

A state may lose control over parts of its national territory, eg because another state is occupying the territory, or because insurgents have obtained full control over part of the country. According to the general rules of state responsibility,[34] human rights violations by the occupying state or the insurgents cannot be attributed to the state party in such cases. In other words, it is not responsible for human rights violations committed by these actors, which are not its own state agents.

To cope with such circumstances, the drafters of the ICCPR decided to combine the originally proposed criterion of national territory with the limiting criterion of jurisdiction exercised over that territory.[35] If persons or groups of persons who are not its agents or who are not acting on its orders or under its control violate human rights, their conduct cannot be attributed to the state concerned and it does not incur responsibility for such infringements.

By contrast, a state remains responsible for human rights violations perpetrated by governments of its constituent states when they operate *ultra vires*, since in such circumstances they are still held to be its organs or agents even though the national government may be too weak to assert itself against sub-national authorities.[36]

According to the European Court of Human Rights and in line with these principles, a state party to the ECHR is not responsible for human rights violations

---

[33] Under general international law, states may exercise jurisdiction on foreign territory only with the consent of the state concerned or on the basis of empowerment by the United Nations Security Council under Chapter VII of the UN Charter. Acts of state (individual laws and regulations) that have extraterritorial scope are permissible under customary law provided that, *inter alia*, they do not breach a specific international legal prohibition and a legitimate and sufficient jurisdictional basis for such acts exists (eg active or passive personality principle).

[34] See Chapter 3, section I.1.

[35] See Nowak (n 5) 43 ff and HRCttee, *López Burgos v Uruguay*, Communication No 52/1979 (1981), Tomuschat concurring opinion, Appendix.

[36] See above, Chapter 3, section I.1.

perpetrated by foreign armies occupying parts of its territory[37] or by insurgents who control part of the territory and enjoy the support of a foreign state.[38] On the other hand, the Court does attribute responsibility to a weak central government unable to enforce its will against local authorities. For instance, it held Georgia responsible for the continued detention, in breach of the ECHR, of the former mayor of the capital of the Autonomous Republic of Ajaria by the local authorities even though the Supreme Court of Georgia had ordered his release and the Georgian President had sought in vain to enforce the ruling. The Court reasoned that Ajaria was an integral part of the national territory of Georgia and that a violation of the ECHR by a local authority engaged the responsibility of the contracting party even if the central authorities were opposed to the violation.[39] By contrast, in the case of Transdniestria, which has completely divested itself of Moldovan governmental control with Russia's assistance[40] and is pursuing a separatist agenda, the Court recognized that Moldova has not been responsible for human rights violations by the secessionist movement since the withdrawal of its troops and the truce agreed on in 1992.[41]

The Court did not base these conclusions on the attribution rules embedded in the law of state responsibility. Instead it reasoned that a state party generally lost its jurisdiction over its national territory and hence its responsibility for the human rights situation there when the territory was controlled by foreign troops or a secessionist movement. This is, in our view, problematic. Although a state cannot be held accountable for the conduct of entities that are not its agents, it still exercises at least *de jure* sovereignty over its entire national territory as is evidenced, for instance, by its power to enact legislation (eg on the (non-)recognition of acts set by the *de facto* authorities) addressing the situation on the part of its territory it no longer controls or to prosecute, on the basis of its own laws, persons suspected of having committed a crime on that part of its territory. This explains why (1) a state remains responsible for human rights violations when its agents conduct a commando operation in territory that is otherwise beyond its control and why (2) it is still bound, within the limits of its remaining authority, to protect inhabitants of the territory concerned from human rights violations. Thus, the European Court of Human Rights emphasized in the case of a Moldovan citizens under the control of Transdniestria that loss of control over certain parts of the national territory did not release the Moldovan authorities from their obligation to protect, ie from the duty to take diplomatic, economic, judicial, and other

---

[37] This may be inferred *a contrario* from ECtHR (Grand Chamber), *Loizidou v Turkey*, Series A, No 310 (1995).

[38] ECtHR (Grand Chamber), *Ilaşcu and Others v Moldova and Russia*, Reports 2004-VII, para 312.

[39] ECtHR (Grand Chamber), *Assanidze v Georgia*, Reports 2004-II, paras 137 ff.

[40] As a result, agents of the 'government' of that territory are no longer, under international law, agents of Moldova, ie can no longer render that state accountable for their acts.

[41] ECtHR (Grand Chamber), *Ilaşcu and Others v Moldova and Russia*, Reports 2004-VII, paras 320 ff.

measures to secure the rights of the complainants, who had been ill-treated by the Transdniestrian authorities and detained in breach of human rights norms.[42]

Lastly, it is uncontested that a state which, as a result of a human rights violation by a third state on its national territory—such as an abduction or a killing—loses *de facto* control over a particular person or situation, is not directly accountable for that conduct. On the other hand, the obligation to protect stemming from, for instance, the right to life or the right to freedom and security requires it to endeavour to protect the persons concerned against such violations by third states to the extent that its resources permit and with the due diligence required of a state.[43]

4. Extraterritorial obligations

(a) Applicability of treaties beyond national territory

As regards the principle of extraterritorial scope of application, treaties such as the CRC, the ECHR, and the ArCHR, which require contracting parties to secure guarantees 'to everyone within their jurisdiction', pose no great difficulties. As a state can clearly act as such outside its own national territory, ie *de facto* exercise jurisdiction, these treaties clearly apply in such situations. The problem here, then, is not territorial scope but rather the question as to when and how behaviour qualifies as 'jurisdiction' in such circumstances (see (b) below).

The issue of whether extraterritorial applicability can be claimed for ICCPR guarantees is another complicated one to resolve. According to Article 2, each state party is required to ensure Covenant rights 'to all individuals within its territory and subject to its jurisdiction'. The wording is ambiguous inasmuch as the 'and' can be construed as a cumulative requirement (those parts of the national territory that are subject to the jurisdiction of the state concerned) or as an 'and/ or' alternative (individuals within a state's territory and subject to its jurisdiction and, in addition, individuals who are subject to the jurisdiction of the said state only, ie without a direct link to its territory). The Human Rights Committee has long espoused the second interpretation. Two complaints to the Committee in 1977 concerned Uruguay's responsibility for the torture and killing of opponents of the regime who had been tracked down and arrested abroad by the country's intelligence services. The Committee held that the Covenant had extraterritorial

---

[42] ECtHR (Grand Chamber), *Ilaşcu and Others v Moldova and Russia*, *Reports* 2004-VII, para 331. The Court concluded that although Moldova had initially taken action in support of the complainants, from 2001 onwards it had stopped to take further steps and, in particular, had failed to raise the question of their fate in the context of negotiations with Russia (paras 336 ff). The HRCttee had not yet had the possibility to examine an equivalent situation in light of ICCPR, Art 2.

[43] This principle is stated in particularly clear terms in: European Commission for Democracy through Law (Venice Commission), 'Opinion on the international legal obligations of Council of Europe member States in respect of secret detention facilities and inter-State transport of prisoners', Opinion 363/2005 (2006), para 66. On the obligation to protect, see Chapter 3, section III.3.

scope, arguing that a literal interpretation of Article 2 would lead to the absurd conclusion that states parties could perpetrate with impunity abroad human rights violations that were prohibited within their own frontiers. It stressed that the wording of Article 2 was not intended to apply to such cases but to special circumstances in which the state was faced with material problems in exercising its jurisdiction in part of the national territory.[44]

General Comment No 31 of the Human Rights Committee emphasizes that the Covenant protects anyone within the power or effective control of a state party; this principle also applies where military forces exercise such control abroad, as in the context of international peacekeeping or peace-enforcement operations, for example.[45] As the Committee has made clear,[46] the general rules of state responsibility in such circumstances determine the acts for which a state whose forces are operating in foreign territory is to be held accountable.

In its Advisory Opinion on the wall in the Occupied Palestinian Territory, the ICJ endorsed the Committee's interpretation. It referred to the ambiguity of the word 'and', held that in light of its object and purpose the ICCPR has to be interpreted as being applicable when a state is exercising jurisdiction outside its territory, and underlined that such interpretation is consistent with the drafting history because the drafters of the treaty had not intended the wording of Article 2 to allow states to shirk their obligations when they exercised jurisdiction abroad.[47]

The ICJ confirmed at the same time that the ICESCR and the CRC also have extraterritorial scope, stressing, however, that ICESCR rights, by their nature, are essentially territorial, so that a state is bound by obligations outside its territory only if it exercises effective jurisdiction as in the case of occupation.[48]

The Convention against Torture requires the closest territorial link, since it speaks of torture in all areas under the power of a particular state party (CAT, Article 2(1)). So the relevant criterion here is the power over a certain territory not over a person, although torture cannot be inflicted in the absence of such power over the victim. According to the Committee against Torture the concept of 'any territory under its jurisdiction' 'includes all areas where the State Party exercises, directly or indirectly, in whole or in part, *de jure* or *de facto*

---

[44] HRCttee, *López Burgos v Uruguay*, Communication No 52/1979 (1981), para 12.3; *Celiberti de Casariego v Uruguay*, Communication No 56/1979 (1981), para 10.3.

[45] HRCttee, General Comment No 31 (2004), para 10. The US rejected this view with the argument that the American delegation insisted on the territoriality of its application already when the Covenant was negotiated. See Comments by the Government of the United States of America on the Concluding Observations of the HRCttee, UN Doc CCPR/C/USA/CO/3/Rev. 1/Add. 1 (2008), 2 f.

[46] HRCttee, Concluding Observations Israel (2003), para 11.

[47] ICJ, *Legal Consequences of the Construction of a Wall in the Occupied Palestinian Territory* (Advisory Opinion), ICJ Reports 2004, paras 109 and 111.

[48] Ibid, para 112 (on the ICESCR, which has no general scope of application clause) and para 113 (on CRC, Art 2 which mentions only the jurisdiction aspect). This does not mean that a state has no duty to allow humanitarian access to territories not under its jurisdiction.

effective control',[49] including military bases and places of detention run by it on foreign soil.[50]

(b) Exercise of 'jurisdiction' outside a state's national territory

Jurisdiction in the sense of the ICCPR, the CRC, the ECHR, and the ACHR exists outside a state's territory when its agents exercise *control* over a particular area or over a particular situation or individual. The Human Rights Committee made it clear in its General Comment No 31 that a state must respect and ensure the rights laid down in the Covenant to anyone within its 'power or effective control', even outside its national territory.[51] It follows that the decisive factor for determining whether jurisdiction is exercised on foreign territory is a state's actual ability to exercise extraterritorial power or control over persons and not whether such action is legal.[52] Only the direct impact of such control can be characterized as the exercise of jurisdiction, however, and the borderline between direct impact and mere side-effects for people is not always clear. In practice, it is determined on a case-by-case basis (see (c) below).

Issue in focus: By what treaties is a state bound in cases of extraterritorial jurisdiction?

Is a state with agents operating abroad bound only by the human rights treaties it has ratified, or must it also respect the human rights conventions that bind the foreign state on whose territory it is operating? There is no case law on this issue.[53] However, it would seem reasonable to conclude that a state is bound to respect not only its own treaties but also those of the foreign state on whose territory its authorities are operating. If that were not the case, the inhabitants of, for instance, an occupied territory would have to endure a significant weakening of their legal protection during the period of occupation—normally a critical situation for human rights—if the occupying power was not a party to certain human rights treaties ratified by the occupied state.

Article 43 of the Hague Regulations respecting the Laws and Customs of War on Land offers a solution for cases of occupation, according to which the occupying power, once the authority of the legitimate power has passed into its hands, must take all measures to restore public order and safety, 'while *respecting*, unless absolutely prevented, *the laws in force in the country*'.[54] The 'laws in force in the country' should

---

[49] CtteeAT, General Comment No 2 (2007), para 7.
[50] Ibid, para 16.   [51] HRCttee, General Comment No 31 (2004), para 10.
[52] A different approach was adopted only by the ECtHR in *Banković and Others v Belgium, the Czech Republic, Denmark, France, Germany, Greece, Hungary, Iceland, Italy, Luxembourg, the Netherlands, Norway, Poland, Portugal, Spain, Turkey and the United Kingdom, Reports* 2001-XII, paras 59 ff.
[53] As the treaty monitoring bodies can only apply their 'own' treaty and complaints can be filed only against states parties, this question cannot be addressed in individual complaint proceedings.
[54] Regulations respecting the Laws and Customs of War on Land, Annex to the Convention respecting the Laws and Customs of War on Land of 18 October 1907 (emphasis added).

be construed as comprising all legal norms in force in the state concerned, including human rights guarantees.

Moreover, the Human Rights Committee's General Comment No 26 offers support for the view expressed above that states operating extraterritorially are bound to respect human rights guarantees already in force in the territory concerned. In this comment, drafted in response to the denunciation of the ICCPR by North Korea, the Committee reinforced its view that the ICCPR is not subject to termination with the argument, *inter alia*, that '[t]he rights enshrined in the Covenant belong to the people living in the territory of the State party. The Human Rights Committee has consistently taken the view, as evidenced by its long-standing practice, that once the people are accorded the protection of the rights under the Covenant, such protection devolves with territory and continues to belong to them, notwithstanding change in government of the State party, including dismemberment in more than one State or State succession or any subsequent action of the State party designed to divest them of the rights guaranteed by the Covenant.'[55] The Committee thus considers that human rights constitute a so-called 'territorial regime', ie that such rights belong to a territory's inhabitants regardless of who exercises jurisdiction over the territory. For example, the ICCPR continued to be applicable to Hong Kong when the United Kingdom, as the state party to the Covenant, returned the territory in 1997 to China, which had not ratified the instrument at the time.[56] Similarly, the Security Council recognized that the human rights treaties ratified by Serbia remained in force in Kosovo under UN administration,[57] and the UN mission in Kosovo (UNMIK) responded to the Human Rights Committee's request for submission of a report on the implementation of the ICCPR in Kosovo in the context of its review of Serbia and Montenegro's state report.[58]

(c) Relevant precedents

What is the practice of the monitoring bodies with respect to typical circumstances involving exterritorial conduct by a state? The following categories of cases may be distinguished:

(i) Exercise of state jurisdiction through diplomatic missions abroad

The fact that human rights obligations are applicable to acts and omissions of diplomatic and consular missions abroad is undisputed. Thus, the Human Rights Committee held that an embassy's refusal to issue a passport to a national living abroad was a violation of the right to freedom of movement under ICCPR, Article 12.[59]

---

[55] HRCttee, General Comment No 26 (1997), para 4.

[56] See, for example, HRCttee, Concluding Observations Hong Kong Special Administrative Region (2006).

[57] UN Security Council Resolution 1244 (1999).

[58] See HRCttee, Concluding Observations Serbia and Montenegro (2004), para 3, and Concluding Observations Kosovo (2006).

[59] HRCttee, *El Ghar v Libyan Arab Jamahiriya*, Communication No 1107/2002 (2004), paras 7.1 ff.

(ii) Occupation of the territory of a foreign state or comparable control over foreign territory

The extraterritorial application of human rights obligations is also largely acknowledged in such circumstances. The ICJ explicitly recognized the application of human rights conventions in this matter with respect to the Occupied Palestinian Territory[60] and the occupation of parts of Congo by Ugandan troops.[61] The European Court of Human Rights made a similar ruling in the *Loizidou v Turkey* case. In this judgment the Court further held that a state is responsible not only for the conduct of its occupying forces, but also for the conduct of the local administration if it exercises at least a general and altogether 'effective overall control' over the later,[62] ie if they can be characterized as *de facto* agents. It concluded that this condition was fulfilled in the case of the administration of the 'Republic of Northern Cyprus', which is not internationally recognized and is largely controlled by Turkey. In its judgment in the *Ilaşcu and Others v Moldova and Russia* case, the Court went a step further, holding that a state party to the ECHR exercises extraterritorial jurisdiction and is therefore responsible for human rights violations by another state or an insurgent movement if it ensures its survival by virtue of military, economic, or political support.[63] The Court may have gone too far in this case. Considered in the context of state responsibility, support alone does not constitute the exercise of jurisdiction on foreign territory and does not automatically entail responsibility.[64] The Court's finding in this case would have unforeseeable consequences for the foreign policy of contracting parties to the ECHR.

The Human Rights Committee also proceeds on the assumption that the ICCPR is applicable in cases of military presence on foreign territory. In 1991 it rejected Iraq's argument, following that country's invasion of Kuwait, that Kuwait formed part of its national territory, but it nonetheless affirmed the applicability of the ICCPR, which Iraq had ratified, in Iraqi-occupied Kuwait.[65] The Committee has affirmed that the Covenant is applicable not only in the territories occupied by Israel[66] but also to military and security operations of the

---

[60] ICJ, *Legal Consequences of the Construction of a Wall in the Occupied Palestinian Territory* (Advisory Opinion), ICJ Reports 2004, paras 107–13.

[61] ICJ, *Case concerning Armed Activities on the Territory of the Congo, Democratic Republic of the Congo v Uganda*, ICJ Reports 2005, paras 179 f.

[62] ECtHR (Grand Chamber), *Loizidou v Turkey*, Series A, No 310 (1995).

[63] ECtHR (Grand Chamber), *Ilaşcu and Others v Moldova and Russia*, Reports 2004-V, para 392.

[64] Because the provision of support, however substantial it may be, does not normally give rise to the degree of control required to achieve the status of a *de facto* agent. See Chapter 3, section I.1. On the responsibility for support in committing a violation of public international law, see Art 16 of the ILC draft articles on state responsibility, 'Report of the ILC on its fifty-third session' (2001), UN Doc A/56/10, Supplement No 10 (*Official Records of the General Assembly*).

[65] HRCttee, Concluding Observations Iraq (1991), para 652. The Special Rapporteur of the UN Commission on Human Rights on the situation of human rights in Kuwait under Iraqi occupation expressed the same view (UN Doc E/CN.4/1992/26).

[66] HRCttee, Concluding Observations Israel (2003), para 11.

United States[67] and peacekeeping missions by forces of European nations operating in third states.[68]

The Inter-American Commission on Human Rights has developed similar jurisprudence, reaffirming, for instance, the accountability of the United States for human rights violations during the invasions of Grenada and Panama and in Guantanamo Bay, Cuba.[69]

If a state exercises effective territorial jurisdiction over a foreign territory, ie if its *de jure* or *de facto* agents administer such a territory in a manner comparable to that of a government, the state is bound by human rights obligations to the same extent as in its own territory. In such cases, agents must not only refrain from inadmissible interference with rights but must also protect private persons from infringements by third parties and ensure that human rights are fulfilled.[70]

Example: The ECtHR judgments in *Loizidou v Turkey* and *Issa v Turkey*

In these proceedings, a Greek Cypriot woman who had to leave her property in order to flee to the south of the island after Turkish forces invaded northern Cyprus in 1974, argued that the refusal of the competent authorities to grant her access to property that she owned in northern Cyprus constituted a violation of her right to property for which Turkey, as the occupying power, was responsible. In response, Turkey asserted that the presence of Turkish forces in northern Cyprus did not mean that Turkey exercised jurisdiction within the meaning of ECHR, Article 1 in what Turkey viewed as the sovereign state of the 'Turkish Republic of Northern Cyprus'. The Court countered this argument by holding that a state's responsibility under the ECHR could be engaged where, as a consequence of lawful or unlawful military action, it exercised effective control of an area outside its national territory. The obligation to secure, in such an area, the guarantees set out in the Convention derived from the fact that it exercised control, irrespective of whether it was exercised directly, through its armed forces, or through a subordinate local administration. In the case in point, the complainant's loss of access to her property stemmed directly from Turkish troops and the Turkish military occupation of northern Cyprus.[71]

In its judgment in the *Issa and Others v Turkey* case, regarding the killing of Iraqi shepherds allegedly by Turkish troops during a military operation of some

---

[67] HRCttee, Concluding Observations USA (2006), para 10.

[68] HRCttee, Concluding Observations Germany (2004), para 11; Concluding Observations Belgium (2004), para 6; Concluding Observations Italy (2006), para 3; Concluding Observations Norway (2006), para 6.

[69] IACmHR, *Coard et al v The United States of America*, Report No 109/99, Case 10.951 (1999); *Salas and Others v the United States of America*, Report No 31/93, Case 10.573 (1993), and 'Request for precautionary measures in respect of detainees in Guantanamo Bay, Cuba', reprinted in ILM 2002, 532.

[70] HRCttee, Concluding Observations Israel (2003), para 11; House of Lords judgment, *Al-Skeini and Others v Secretary of State for Defence*, Consolidated Appeals [2007] UKHL 26, 13 June 2007.

[71] ECtHR (Grand Chamber), *Loizidou v Turkey*, Series A, No 310 (1995), paras 62 f. Reaffirmed in ECtHR (Grand Chamber), *Ilaşcu and Others v Moldova and Russia*, Reports 2004-VII, para 314.

four weeks in northern Iraq, the European Court of Human Rights reaffirmed that 'a State may also be held accountable for violation of the Convention rights and freedoms of persons who are in the territory of another State but who are found to be under the former State's authority and control through its agents operating—whether lawfully or unlawfully—in the latter State...Accountability in such situations stems from the fact that Article 1 of the Convention cannot be interpreted so as to allow a State party to perpetrate violations of the Convention on the territory of another State, which it could not perpetrate on its own territory.'[72] It did 'not exclude the possibility that, as a consequence of this military action, the respondent State could be considered to have exercised, temporarily, effective overall control of a particular portion of the territory of northern Iraq. Accordingly, if there is a sufficient factual basis for holding that, at the relevant time, the victims were within that specific area, it would follow logically that they were within the jurisdiction of Turkey...'.[73]

(iii) Violations perpetrated against persons on foreign territory in the absence of control over the territory

The same conclusion, ie an extension of the territorial scope of application of human rights treaties, may be drawn from international jurisprudence in respect of human rights violations by agents of a state party on foreign territory without controlling the territory concerned.[74] In accordance with attribution rules of the law of state responsibility the existence of jurisdiction may also stem from the fact that state agents exercise control over a particular individual or situation on foreign territory. In such circumstances, the state on behalf of which the agents are operating is therefore accountable under international law and not the state within whose territory the violation occurs—unless it consented thereto.[75] Thus, Russia was held responsible in the *Ilaşcu* case for a violation of ECHR, Article 3 because Russian soldiers had arrested the complainants on Transdniestrian territory and handed them over to the Transdniestrian authorities with the knowledge that they would be tortured.[76] The Human Rights Committee likewise recognized Uruguay's

---

[72] ECtHR, *Issa and Others v Turkey*, Application No 31821/96 (2004), para 71.

[73] Ibid, para 74. The Court concluded that it was not established that Turkey conducted a military operation at the time and location where the victims were killed and therefore concluded that Turkey did not exercise jurisdiction in the specific case (paras 75–82).

[74] Explicitly affirmed by the ECmHR in *Stocké v Germany*, Application No 11755/85 (1989), reprinted in Series A, No 199 (1991), para 166. In 2003 a Chamber of the ECtHR recognized the existence of extraterritorial Turkish jurisdiction in Kenya after the Kenyan authorities handed over the former leader of the PKK to Turkish agents at Nairobi airport; ECtHR, *Öcalan v Turkey*, Application No 46221/99 (2003), para 93, endorsed by the judgment of the Grand Chamber, *Reports* 2005-IV, para 91.

[75] Should the territorial state consent to acts constituting human rights violations by a third state, both states incur responsibility; Art 47 of the draft articles on state responsibility (n 64).

[76] ECtHR (Grand Chamber), *Ilaşcu and Others v Moldova and Russia*, *Reports* 2004-VII, paras 376 ff.

responsibility for the ill-treatment of opponents of the military regime abducted by Uruguayan agents abroad.[77]

Problems arise, however, when determining whether the killing of a person on foreign territory who is not in the hands of the country concerned—eg the targeted killing of opponents of a regime or alleged terrorists by means of air strikes or commando raids—triggers extraterritorial application of human rights law. It is clear from the views of the Human Rights Committee in the Uruguay cases that even an isolated act is sufficient to meet this condition if it occurs in the context of a police raid or any other activity typically resorted to by a state in the exercise of jurisdiction. The Inter-American Commission on Human Rights declared admissible a complaint alleging that Cuba had violated the right to life under the American Declaration of the Rights and Duties of Man by shooting down two small aircraft in international airspace carrying four persons fleeing the country.[78] The question as to whether an extraterritorial human rights violation occurred as part of a fully fledged military operation or in the context of a simple police raid seems to be irrelevant in this regard.[79]

The European Court of Human Rights decided otherwise, however, in the *Banković* judgment.[80] On 23 April 1999, during the Kosovo crisis, a NATO missile struck the building that housed Serbian radio and television channels in Belgrade. The relatives of victims alleged that this act violated the right to life under ECHR, Article 2. The Court declared the complaint inadmissible, *inter alia*, on the ground that the ECHR was not extraterritorially applicable in such circumstances and that the states parties to the ECHR involved in the NATO operation could therefore not be held accountable.

Issue in focus: The ECtHR decision in *Banković v Belgium and 16 Other Contracting States*[81]

The ECtHR ruling that the victims of the NATO strike on the Serbian radio and television building in Belgrade did not come within the jurisdiction of the states involved was founded essentially on the argument that jurisdiction under ECHR, Article 1 is limited to a state's jurisdiction over its own territory and persons who are in that territory.[82] The Court reasoned that a state's jurisdiction extends in exceptional

---

[77] HRCttee, *López Burgos v Uruguay*, Communication No 52/1979 (1981), para 12.3; *Celiberti de Casariego v Uruguay*, Communication No 56/1979 (1981), para 10.3.

[78] IACmHR, *Alejandre Jr et al v Cuba*, Report No 86/99, Case 11.589 (1999). The Commission, in para 53, held Cuba responsible for a violation of the right to life.

[79] ICJ, *Legal consequences of the Construction of a Wall in the Occupied Palestinian Territory* (Advisory Opinion), ICJ Reports 2004, para 111.

[80] ECtHR (Grand Chamber), *Banković and Others v Belgium, the Czech Republic, Denmark, France, Germany, Greece, Hungary, Iceland, Italy, Luxembourg, the Netherlands, Norway, Poland, Portugal, Spain, Turkey and the United Kingdom*, Reports 2001-XII. The Court addressed the issue initially as a question of personal scope of application (persons 'within their jurisdiction') but examined it in the decision itself clearly as an issue of territorial jurisdiction.

[81] Ibid.   [82] Ibid, paras 59–66.

cases to foreign territory, for instance when, as a result of military occupation, it exercises effective control over a particular territory and its inhabitants, or when, through the consent, invitation or acquiescence of the foreign government, it exercises public powers normally performed by the government concerned.[83] According to the Court, military air strikes on a hostile country in which the respondent states exercised no control over the population and in whose territory they do not exercise public powers cannot be subsumed under the concept of jurisdiction within the meaning of Article 1.[84] The Court noted that it should further be borne in mind that the ECHR is a regional instrument that has created a European 'legal space' and is not designed to be applied to the conduct of contracting states throughout the world.[85]

This judgment raises a number of questions inasmuch as the European Court of Human Rights construed the term jurisdiction for the first time in a way different from the rules of attribution in the law of state responsibility.[86] In so doing, the Court accepted the existence of a (human) rights vacuum, since the possibility of attributing responsibility to the territorial state (in this case Serbia) in the event of an air strike by a foreign state was excluded from the outset. Air strikes or other forms of extrajudicial killing are not in themselves acts of state, but a state exercises its sovereign power to the full when it decides to go to war against another state or to authorize the targeted killing of an individual. Furthermore, the fact that a third state can kill a targeted person demonstrates that this person is within reach of the attacker even in the absence of territorial jurisdiction as such. The applicability of the ECHR in such cases may also be inferred from a teleological interpretation. It is unacceptable to hold that a state which abducts a person abroad incurs responsibility for the act on human rights grounds, but that another state which—wishing to avoid an abduction that would entail legal proceedings—kills a person abroad by means of an air strike cannot be held accountable.

The Court's view that the ECHR is applicable to acts that amount to the exercise of jurisdiction on foreign territory only if the contracting party exercises such powers through the consent, invitation or acquiescence of the foreign government is also unacceptable.[87] It is difficult to see how human rights violations would not be covered by the ECHR where a state exercised jurisdiction in breach of its obligations under international law in a foreign state without the latter's consent. Lastly, the argument that the ECHR is intended to apply only to European legal space and not to contracting states' conduct throughout the world is problematic;[88] it could be read as implying in the final analysis that European states are not required to respect human rights norms outside Europe, a conclusion that would clearly be incompatible with the principle of the indivisibility of human rights and constitute, in effect, a reversion to the nineteenth century concept of the international law of 'civilized nations'.[89]

---

[83] Ibid, para 71.   [84] Ibid, paras 74 ff.   [85] See, ibid, para 80.
[86] ILC, Arts 4 ff of the draft articles on state responsibility (n 64).
[87] See *Banković* (n 80).   [88] Ibid, para 80.
[89] For a detailed critique of this decision, see Rick Lawson, 'Life after Banković', in Fons Coomans and Menno Kamminga (eds), *Extraterritorial Application of Human Rights Treaties* (Intersentia Publishers: Antwerp, 2004), 83 ff.

(iv) Direct human rights violations through internal exercise of jurisdiction with extraterritorial effects

A state is not only responsible for its agents when they operate in the territory of another state but also when legislative or administrative acts undertaken on its territory directly violate human rights of a person who is abroad—provided that person is under *de jure* or *de facto* control of the acting state.[90] It follows that human rights are binding in the case of:

- formal action (administrative decision, court judgment) by a state within its national territory that has a direct impact on persons abroad owing to the existence of a legal connection between the state and the person to whom the action is addressed. Thus, the Human Rights Committee held that France had jurisdiction in a case involving the withholding of certain benefits from a social welfare recipient who resided abroad;[91]
- *de facto* action by a state within its national territory that has an immediate impact on the rights of persons abroad. This includes, for example, the targeted shooting by a police officer of a person fleeing across a state boundary, but also a full-scale trade embargo or blockade of foreign territory that makes it objectively impossible for a third state to supply its population with basic health care facilities or food.

In such cases the state always acts on its territory, so that no problems of extraterritoriality arise. The question that remains is: How far does its duty go *vis-à-vis* people on foreign territory who carry the consequences of its actions? It is clear that the state remains bound to respect human rights and to refrain from committing human rights violations in all these cases. On the other hand, states are not, in our view, under an obligation to protect and fulfil human rights on behalf of people abroad, even where action by a state within its national territory would serve to protect or fulfil the rights of such persons. This is so because the condition of direct control over a person or factual situation is not fulfilled. For instance, the prohibition of torture does not require, as a matter of law,[92] a state to take action, using every means at its disposal, against a state that systematically tortures detainees and the right to life does not imply an obligation to prevent the export of weaponry by non-state actors even if there is a certain likelihood that these products will be used in violation of humanitarian international law in the importing state. Similarly, the right to food is not violated if states are not ready to provide food aid when famine-like conditions prevail in a third state—so long

---

[90] The ECtHR also adopts this approach when it states in an *obiter dictum* that 'acts of Contracting States performed outside their territory, or which produce effects there, may amount to exercise by them of their jurisdiction within the meaning of Article 1 of the Convention'; ECtHR (Grand Chamber), *Ilaşcu and Others v Moldova and Russia*, Reports 2004-IV, para 314.

[91] HRCttee, *Gueye et al v France*, Communication No 196/1985 (1989), para 9.3.

[92] See, however, Chapter 6, section III.1 regarding the possibilities for bilateral action in such situations.

as their conduct is not to blame for the food shortage.[93] In these instances, the immediate *de facto* or *de jure* link that must exist between a state's conduct and the victims of a human rights violation in a third state in order to establish an extraterritorial obligation emanating from human rights is lacking. Although measures that can help to protect or fulfil the human rights of persons living abroad are not required by human rights law, they may constitute a desirable element of a state's human rights policy that can contribute to the worldwide respect of human rights.

IV. Temporal Scope of Application

1. Denunciation

Guarantees embodied in human rights treaties are effective as a rule from the time of ratification[94] of a treaty until its denunciation by the state concerned. A number of treaties permit such denunciation provided that various conditions are fulfilled (eg notice or date of denunciation, or expiry of a minimum period from the date of entry into force).[95]

In the event that treaties contain no provisions regarding denunciation, as is the case with the two Covenants, the applicable provision is VCLT, Article 56(1). In such cases, the treaty is not subject to denunciation or withdrawal unless: (a) it is established that the parties intended to admit the possibility of denunciation or withdrawal; or (b) a right of denunciation or withdrawal may be implied from the nature of the treaty.

The Human Rights Committee explicitly invoked this provision while examining whether denunciation of the ICCPR was permissible after North Korea gave notice of termination in 1997.[96] In its General Comment on the issue of denunciation, the Committee concluded[97] that there was clearly no tacit agreement among the parties to admit the possibility of denunciation. The fact that acceptance of the Committee's competence to examine interstate complaints under ICCPR, Article 42(2) could be withdrawn by the state party itself and that the first Optional Protocol, which was negotiated concurrently with the Covenant, contained a denunciation clause made it clear that the drafters had deliberately intended to omit a general denunciation clause from the Covenant. Furthermore, the Covenant was not the type of treaty which, by its nature, implied a right of denunciation. Together with the ICESCR, it codified the rights enshrined in the

---

[93] In such situations, states may, however, have obligations to cooperate under Art 56 of the UN Charter.

[94] Or after expiry of a particular period from that date; see, eg, ICCPR, Art 49(2).

[95] See, for example, ICCPR-OP1, Art 12, ECHR, Art 58, ESC, Art 37, ACHR, Art 78.

[96] See the 1998 annual report of the HRCttee, 'Report of the Human Rights Committee', vol I, *General Assembly Official Records, Supplement No 40* (UN Doc A/53/40), para 413.

[97] HRCttee, General Comment No 26 (1997), paras 2 and 3.

Universal Declaration of Human Rights and therefore did not have the temporary character typical of treaties that could be denounced at any time.[98]

2. Derogation

Human rights treaties are applicable, as a matter of principle, both in peacetime and in times of war[99] and national emergency. However, subject to certain conditions, the rights they guarantee may be temporarily set aside during states of emergency, ie they can be derogated from.

(a) Legal basis

In genuine emergencies, especially during wartime, states are often not in a position to comply fully with their human rights obligations. This problem is addressed in human rights treaties through derogation clauses. Thus, ICCPR, Article 4(1) stipulates that:

In time of public emergency which threatens the life of the nation and the existence of which is officially proclaimed, the States Parties to the present Covenant may take measures derogating from their obligations under the present Covenant to the extent strictly required by the exigencies of the situation, provided that such measures are not inconsistent with their other obligations under international law and do not involve discrimination solely on the ground of race, colour, sex, language, religion or social origin.

Similarly, ECHR, Article 15 permits derogations '[i]n time of war or other public emergency threatening the life of the nation'. Equivalent provisions are contained in ESC, Article 30, ACHR, Article 27, and ArCHR, Article 4.

There are no derogation clauses in the other treaties. Under certain circumstances, however, the states parties may invoke necessity as a ground precluding wrongfulness under international law.[100] It should also be noted that human rights guarantees that are not absolute may be substantially limited in states of

---

[98] State practice supports this view. For example, Switzerland explicitly recognized upon ratifying the ICCPR that it was not subject to denunciation: Message from the Federal Council on the occasion of Switzerland's accession to the UN human rights Covenants, *Bundesblatt (BBl)* 1991 I 1208.

[99] HRCttee, General Comment No 31 (2004), para 11. The ICJ also explicitly stated this view in its Advisory Opinion on the *Legality of the Threat or Use of Nuclear Weapons*, ICJ Reports 1996-I, para 25; reaffirmed in the Advisory Opinion on the *Legal Consequences of the Construction of a Wall in the Occupied Palestinian Territory*, ICJ Reports 2004, para 106. On the relationship between human rights and international humanitarian law in times of armed conflict, see Chapter 5, section V.

[100] Art 25(1) of the ILC's draft Articles on State Responsibility (n 64) reads: 'Necessity may not be invoked by a State as a ground for precluding the wrongfulness of an act not in conformity with an international obligation of that State unless the act: (a) Is the only way for the State to safeguard an essential interest against a grave and imminent peril; and (b) Does not seriously impair an essential interest of the State or States towards which the obligation exists, or of the international community as a whole.' While the ACmHPR in its earlier jurisprudence proceeded on the assumption that no derogation from the ACHPR was permissible in the absence of a derogation clause (see, eg, ACmHPR, *Commission Nationale des Droits de l'Homme et des Libertés v Chad*, Communication No 74/1992 [1995], para 21), in its more recent jurisprudence it seems to have moved closer to the

emergency where particularly important public interests are at stake. According to ICESCR, Article 4 this also applies to economic, social, and cultural rights. However, the Committee on Economic, Social and Cultural Rights has stressed that states parties have to meet minimum core obligations 'to ensure the satisfaction of, at the very least, minimum essential levels of each of the rights' and are not allowed to remain passive if a 'significant number of individuals is deprived of essential foodstuffs, of essential primary health care, of basic shelter and housing, or of the most basic forms of education' unless they can 'demonstrate that every effort has been made to use all resources that are at its disposition in an effort to satisfy, as a matter of priority, those minimum obligations'.[101] These principles are also applicable in times of armed conflict.[102]

(b) Preconditions

Derogation measures, ie the temporary repeal of particular human rights guarantees, are permissible upon the fulfilment of six conditions:

(1) *Existence of a state of emergency:* There can be no question of derogating from human rights guarantees unless a genuine state of emergency exists. To qualify as a state of emergency, the situation must: (a) be actual or at least imminent; (b) affect the whole population or at least part of the territory of the state; (c) threaten the physical integrity of the population, the political independence or territorial integrity of the state, or the basic functioning of state institutions; and (e) be of an exceptional nature.[103] The Human Rights Committee has stressed that '[n]ot every disturbance or catastrophe qualifies as a public emergency which threatens the life of the nation' and 'that even during an armed conflict measures derogating from the Covenant are allowed only if and to the extent that the situation constitutes a threat to the life of the nation'.[104]

(2) *Respect for the principle of proportionality:* Provided a state of emergency exists, the suspension of human rights is permissible only to the extent 'strictly required by the exigencies of the situation' (ICCPR, Article 4(1); ECHR, Article 15). Derogation measures must therefore be 'of an exceptional and temporary nature',[105] ie may only last as long as the threat to the life of the

position under general international law (ACmHPR, *Amnesty International and Others v Sudan*, Communications Nos 48/1990, 50/1991, 52/1990, 89/1993 (1999), paras 42 and 79 ff).

[101] CtteeESCR, General Comment No 3 (1990), para 10.

[102] See the report of the Special Rapporteur of the UN Commission on Human Rights on the situation of human rights in Kuwait under Iraqi occupation, UN Doc E/CN.4/1992/26, para 52.

[103] See the 'Siracusa Principles on the Limitation and Derogation Provisions in the International Covenant on Civil and Political Rights' adopted by a meeting of experts (1985) 7 HRQ 3, para 39, and ECtHR (Grand Chamber), *A and Others v The United Kingdom*, Application No 3455/05 (2009), para 175.

[104] HRCttee, General Comment No 29 (2001), para 3.

[105] HRCttee, General Comment No 29 (2001), para 2. However, in *A and Others v The United Kingdom*, Application No 3455/05 (2009), para 178, the Grand Chamber of the ECtHR held that

nation persists. It follows that such measures must be scrutinized separately for each right and are acceptable only if permissible limitations on human rights are no longer sufficient to bring the situation under control.[106]

(3) *Respect for the principle of non-discrimination:* As emphasized in ICCPR, Article 4(1) and ArCHR, Article 4(1), derogation measures may not be applied in a discriminatory manner, for instance, solely to members of a particular race, religion or ethnic group or to only one sex.[107] This is a corollary of states' general obligation to apply human rights in a non-discriminatory manner.

(4) *No derogation from non-derogable rights:* As a rule, derogation clauses identify certain rights as non-derogable. The individual treaties adopt different approaches. Thus, ECHR, Article 15 lists the right to life, freedom from torture, freedom from slavery and the *nulla poena sine lege* principle as non-derogable. Protocol No 7 to the ECHR adds the *ne bis in idem* rule to the list, and Protocols Nos 6 and 13 add the prohibition of the death penalty. Under the Covenant, ICCPR, Article 4(2) further extends the list of non-derogable rights to include the prohibition of retroactive laws, the prohibition of imprisonment for debt, the right to recognition as person before the law and freedom of thought, conscience and religion. Article 27 of the ACHR is even more extensive and includes matrimonial freedom, the rights of the child, the right to nationality, democratic rights, and the judicial guarantees essential for the protection of such rights. Article 4(2) of the ArCHR in turn adds the right to access to an independent court, judiciary control of detention measures, human treatment of prisoners, the right to leave and return to one's country, the right to seek asylum abroad, and the right to nationality as non-derogable rights. Whether fair trial guarantees should also be generally non-derogable is a moot question. In any case, it is not permissible to derogate from procedural guarantees—such as procedural requirements for the imposition of the death penalty[108]—that safeguard non-derogable rights.[109]

(5) *Consistency of derogation measures with the state party's other obligations under international law:* This restriction on permissible derogation measures can entail either an extension of non-derogable rights in a particular case beyond the treaty invoked by a given state or create additional formal prerequisites for derogation. With regard to additional formal requirements, the

---

'the Court's case law has never, to date, explicitly incorporated the requirement that the emergency be temporary, although the question of the proportionality of the response may be linked to the duration of the emergency'.

[106] Siracusa Principles (n 103), paras 15 f.

[107] Similarly, ECtHR (Grand Chamber), *A and Others v The United Kingdom*, Application No 3455/05 (2009), paras 187 ff.

[108] See Chapter 9, section II.2.c.

[109] HRCttee, General Comments Nos 29 (2001), para 15, and 32 (2007), para 6; Art 4(1) ArCHR.

European Court of Human Rights examined, for instance, in the *Brannigan and McBride* case whether the emergency measures introduced in Northern Ireland under ECHR, Article 15 were also consistent with the additional requirement set out in ICCPR, Article 4 to proclaim officially the existence of a state of emergency.[110] Other international law obligations that must not be undermined by the derogation include the following:

(a) *human rights under customary international law* with *jus cogens* status;

(b) *other human rights treaties* that do not permit a particular derogation: this indirect extension of non-derogable rights can be particularly relevant in the relationship between universal and regional treaties. Thus, as mentioned above, the ICCPR, eg, in contrast to the ECHR, lists the prohibition of retroactive legislation, the prohibition of imprisonment for debt, the right to recognition as a person before the law, and freedom of thought, conscience and religion as non-derogable rights. A number of ILO conventions that render various trade union and employee rights non-derogable are also important in this connection;

(c) *international humanitarian law:* derogations under human rights treaties cannot be invoked as a ground for failing to respect humanitarian law, which was established precisely with such circumstances in mind. In practice, the lists of human rights contained in Article 75 of Additional Protocol I to the Geneva Conventions and in Article 4 of Additional Protocol II to the Geneva Conventions are particularly relevant.

(6) *Proclamation and notification*: Emergency measures must be officially proclaimed within the country concerned in accordance with the relevant treaty provisions[111] and notification of the derogation must be given to the international body specified in the treaty.

Issue in focus: Human rights and terrorism[112]

The fight against international terrorism presents a special challenge for human rights. On the one hand, states are bound by human rights obligations to afford protection to victims of violations by private actors, including terrorist acts, and to

---

[110] ECtHR, *Brannigan and McBride v The United Kingdom*, Series A, No 258-B (1993), para 67.
[111] ICCPR, Art 4(1). Art 15 of the ECHR does not require an official proclamation of the state of emergency.
[112] See OHCHR, 'Digest of Jurisprudence of the UN and Regional Organizations on the Protection of Human Rights while Countering Terrorism', available at <http://www.unhchr.ch/html/menu6/2/digest.doc> (accessed 31 December 2008); Inter-American Commission on Human Rights, 'Report on Terrorism and Human Rights', 22 October 2002, OEA/Ser.L/V/II.166 Doc 5 rev. 1 corr.; International Commission of Jurists, *Terrorism and Human Rights No 1*, 14 June 2002, *Terrorism and Human Rights No 2: New Challenges and Old Dangers*, March 2003; *Guidelines on Human Rights and the Fight against Terrorism*, adopted by the Committee of Ministers of the Council of Europe on 11 July 2002. See also the reports of the Special Rapporteur on the promotion and protection of human rights while countering terrorism, available at: <http://www2.ohchr.org/english/issues/terrorism/rapporteur/reports.htm> (accessed 31 December 2008).

take action against the perpetrators. On the other hand, counter-terrorism measures must be consistent with human rights,[113] which implies, as a matter of principle, that persons should not be deprived of their fundamental rights because they are suspected of having committed terrorist acts.

In such circumstances of heightened tension, human rights limitations or even derogations are often unavoidable. The same principles are nonetheless applicable as in other circumstances involving a serious threat to public security and order. It follows that derogations are permissible only under the conditions listed above and that absolute guarantees such as the prohibition of torture and the right to life may not be violated even in the fight against terrorism.[114]

As demonstrated by the experience of the Human Rights Committee, states often tend in such circumstances to exceed the bounds of what is really necessary for effective counter-terrorist action. The following measures are particularly questionable.

Detention without judicial authorization and without entitlement to judicial review: For example, the Committee criticized an anti-terrorist statute in Colombia that authorized the armed forces to detain persons suspected of having committed terrorist acts without a judicial order and without providing any judicial remedies.[115] The Committee criticized a statute in Sri Lanka that allowed the Ministry of Defence to keep suspects in administrative detention for up to 18 months.[116] Criticism was directed towards the USA for keeping suspected terrorists in detention for months and years without any judicial protection.[117]

Removal of foreign suspects to states where they may be subject to torture: The Committee criticized Lithuanian legislation that permitted the removal of foreigners suspected of terrorist acts to states where they were in danger of being tortured.[118] Sweden was reproached for returning two Egyptian terror suspects to their home country, where they clearly risked ill-treatment, due to the Swedish embassy's failure to undertake agreed prison visits in due time.[119] The USA was criticized for rendering people arrested outside of its territory to countries where they risk torture.[120]

Vague and unduly broad definitions of terrorist offences that make it impossible to determine the precise nature of terrorist acts are a common problem[121] and have particularly serious implications since they are prone to abuse, including invocation of such definitions to deny the legitimate expression of rights established in the Covenant.[122]

---

[113] Requirement explicitly stated in UN General Assembly resolution 57/219 (2002).

[114] See, for example, Art IV of the *Guidelines on Human Rights and the Fight against Terrorism* (n 112).

[115] HRCttee, Concluding Observations Colombia (2004), para 9.

[116] HRCttee, Concluding Observations Sri Lanka (2003), para 13.

[117] HRCttee, Concluding Observations USA (2006), para 12.

[118] HRCttee, Concluding Observations Lithuania (2004), para 7.

[119] HRCttee, Concluding Observations Sweden (2002), para 12.

[120] HRCttee, Concluding Observations USA (2006), para 16.

[121] HRCttee, Concluding Observations Israel (2003), para 14; the Philippines (2003), para 9; Uganda (2004), para 8; Estonia (2003), para 8; New Zealand (2002), para 11; Norway (2006), para 9; Canada (2006), para 12; Chile (2007), para 7; Zambia (2007), para 16.

[122] HRCttee, Concluding Observations Algeria (2007), para 17; Tunisia (2008), para 15.

Killing instead of arrest: In the case of Israel, while the Committee did not rule out the possibility that, pursuant to the rules of international humanitarian law, targeted killings were compatible in some circumstances with international law, it stressed that the principle of proportionality must be respected even in response to terrorist threats and that targeted killings were therefore inadmissible where steps could be taken to apprehend persons suspected of terrorism. Killings or house demolitions as punitive measures were also deemed inadmissible.[123]

Impunity: In the case of Russia, the Committee criticized the provision in Russian counter-terrorist legislation that exempted law-enforcement and military personnel from liability for harm caused to private persons during counter-terrorist operations, and expressed concern at the failure to investigate deaths that occurred during such operations.[124]

The rigidity of the conditions governing permissible derogation measures is tempered in practice by the fact that treaty monitoring bodies usually allow states parties a wide margin of appreciation in determining whether an emergency exists and whether the measures taken to deal with it may be characterized as proportionate. In the *Brannigan and McBride* case,[125] for instance, the European Court of Human Rights noted that national authorities were in a better position than an international court to assess the scale of the danger and the type of derogation measures needed to avert it. On the other hand, the Court noted that an international body was particularly well qualified to assess the proportionality of the measures taken.[126]

V. The Elements of a Human Rights Violation

What constitutes a human rights violation in legal terms and how can it be identified? The answers can be deduced from the elements of human rights obligations described in this chapter. The key questions relate to the scope of application, the different categories of obligations and the limitations on human rights.

When seeking to determine whether a state has violated the human rights of a private actor in a particular case, a systematic approach such as the checklist in Table 4.1 may be helpful.

---

[123] HRCttee, Concluding Observations Israel (2003), paras 15 f.
[124] HRCttee, Concluding Observations Russian Federation (2003), paras 13 f.
[125] ECtHR, *Brannigan and McBride v The United Kingdom*, A/258-B (1993).
[126] Ibid, para 43. See also *A and Others v The United Kingdom* (Grand Chamber), Application No 3455/05 (2009), paras 180 and 184.

Table 4.1. The constitutive elements of a human rights violation

Element	Question		Outcome
1. Victim status	Has personal harm been suffered?	No: ⇨ Yes: ⇩	No violation
2. Scope of application	Is the victim genuinely protected by a human rights guarantee?	No: ⇨ Yes: ⇩	No violation
(a) Substantive	(a) Does the harm affect a protected area? Has the state refrained from entering a reservation in respect of this area?	No: ⇨ Yes: ⇩	No violation
(b) Personal	(b) Does the human rights guarantee protect the category of persons to whom the victim belongs?	No: ⇨ Yes: ⇩	No violation
(c) Territorial	(c) Is the person within the jurisdiction of the state concerned?	No: ⇨ Yes: ⇩	No violation
(d) Temporal	(d) (i) Is the human rights guarantee in question in force for the state concerned?	No: ⇨ Yes: ⇩	No violation
	(ii) Has it been lawfully derogated from?	Yes: ⇨ No: ⇩	No violation
3. Category of obligation	Has the state breached an obligation (a) to respect? (b) to protect? (c) to fulfil? or (d) to act without discrimination?	No:⇨ Yes: ⇩	No violation
4. Limitations	(a) Is the human rights guarantee in question absolute, ie does the violation of the right concerned always constitute prohibited conduct?	Yes: ⇨ No: ⇩	**Violation**
	(b) Can the violation be legally justified?	Yes: ⇨ No: ⇨	No violation **Violation**

5

Basic Concepts of International
Humanitarian Law

What are the obligations of states and other duty bearers under international humanitarian law? As in the case of human rights obligations, it is useful to distinguish between the nature and scope of obligations under international humanitarian law (section II) and the different aspects of the scope of application (section III). A model can then be developed for examining violations of international humanitarian law (section IV). However, before discussing these aspects, we must first consider the important principle that humanitarian law, as *lex specialis*, is applicable only during times of armed conflict (section I). The chapter focuses on those among the provisions of the Geneva Conventions and their Additional Protocols that have a bearing on human rights.[1]

I. International Humanitarian Law as *Lex Specialis*

1. Armed conflict as a precondition for the application of international humanitarian law

The purpose of international humanitarian law is to protect individuals from the specific risks associated with war. Given that its provisions apply only during armed conflict and never in peacetime, it is therefore considered *lex specialis*. Moreover, the kind of protection it provides differs substantially according to whether the conflict is of an international or, as in the case of a civil war or a military revolt, a non-international character. International humanitarian law is not applicable where the use of force remains within the bounds of internal tensions and disturbances falling short of an armed conflict. This prerequisite for the application of humanitarian law makes it fundamentally different from international human rights law, which is applicable both in war and in peacetime, subject to permissible derogations[2] in exceptional cases.

---

[1] The Law of The Hague, ie the law regulating the conduct of warfare, is addressed only in passing.

[2] See Chapter 4, section IV.2.

The distinction between international and non-international armed conflicts is of fundamental relevance. The international or internal character of a conflict determines whether, on the one hand, the four Geneva Conventions plus Additional Protocol I are applicable or, on the other, only Article 3 common to the four Conventions and Additional Protocol II will apply.[3] In practical terms, this means, for example, that members of armed forces who fall into enemy hands in the course of an international conflict must be treated as prisoners of war, while there is no provision for such status in the law of non-international (internal) armed conflict. Similarly, the extensive provisions on treatment of the civilian population in occupied territories and on the obligations of the occupying power are applicable only during international armed conflicts.

The distinction is also important on account of differences in the conceptual background to the two sets of rules. Rules governing international armed conflicts play a dual role: 'They protect the individual as a human being and also as a member of a collective political entity operating with military means. If an individual is treated in a manner that contravenes a rule of international humanitarian law, it is not only the individual but also the collective to which he or she belongs whose rights have been violated.'[4] This collective dimension is lacking in the law of non-international armed conflict, since out of respect for state sovereignty there can be no question of recognizing insurgents as a collective entity possessing equal rights with states.

In spite of these differences, the law of international armed conflict and that of non-international armed conflict are becoming increasingly similar because the customary rules of international humanitarian law[5] are applicable, by and large, to both categories of conflict.

2. International armed conflict

International armed conflicts within the meaning of the Geneva Conventions are conflicts between two or more contracting parties, ie *inter-state* conflicts.[6] Article 2 common to the Geneva Conventions divides such conflicts into three categories: (1) declared wars;[7] (2) 'any other armed conflict which may arise between two or more of the High Contracting Parties, even if the state of war is not recognized by one of them'; and (3) 'cases of partial or total occupation of the territory of a High Contracting Party, even if the said occupation meets with no armed resistance'.

---

[3] On these instruments, see Chapter 2, section II.4.

[4] Martin Hess, *Die Anwendbarkeit des humanitären Völkerrechts, insbesondere in gemischten Konflikten* (Schulthess: Zurich, 1985), 121 f [translated for this publication from German].

[5] See above, Chapter 2, section III.3.

[6] It follows that armed conflicts between a state and insurgents or other non-state groups do not fall within the scope of the definition of an international armed conflict even if they are fought outside the territory of the state concerned.

[7] Wars started through a formal declaration of war are virtually unheard of nowadays owing to the prohibition of the use of force in Art 2(4) of the UN Charter.

Article 1(4) of Additional Protocol I places so-called wars of liberation on the same footing as international armed conflicts. The article deems such wars as 'armed conflicts in which peoples are fighting against colonial domination and alien occupation and against racist regimes in the exercise of their right of self-determination'. The article demonstrates that objective criteria, and not the assessment of the parties to the conflict, determine whether a specific situation requires the application of international humanitarian law.

3. Non-international armed conflict

International humanitarian law does not establish a uniform category of non-international conflict but differentiates between three situations: (1) *internal disturbances and tensions*, ie violent clashes which, though involving the use of weapons, are not of a military character and do not reach the threshold of armed conflict; therefore, international humanitarian law is *not* applicable to them;[8] (2) non-international conflicts that fall within the scope of *Article 3 common to the Geneva Conventions*; and (3) non-international conflicts within the meaning of *Additional Protocol II*. The qualification of the situation in a particular case is not left to the parties to the conflict but must be determined on the basis of objective criteria laid down in the Conventions and their Additional Protocol II.[9]

These conflicts are non-international because they are not conducted between states but between different parts of the armed forces of state, a state and a non-state adversary that opposes the government by force of arms, or between non-state actors.

(a) Non-international armed conflicts pursuant to common Article 3 GC

During armed conflicts that are 'not of an international character occurring on the territory of one of the High Contracting Parties', Article 3 common to the four Geneva Conventions (hereinafter common Article 3) is applicable always and without exception. This article establishes a set of minimum guarantees aimed primarily at protecting physical integrity for persons 'taking no active part in the hostilities, including members of armed forces who have laid down their arms and those placed *hors de combat* by sickness, wounds, detention, or any other cause'. Thus, it categorically prohibits:

(a) Violence to life and person, in particular murder of all kinds, mutilation, cruel treatment and torture; (b) Taking of hostages; (c) Outrages upon personal dignity, in particular, humiliating and degrading treatment; (d) The passing of sentences and the carrying out of executions without previous judgment pronounced by a regularly constituted court affording all the judicial guarantees which are recognized as indispensable by civilized peoples.

---

[8] Protection in this context is provided (only) by human rights.
[9] ICTR, *The Prosecutor v Akayesu*, Case No ICTR-96-4-T (1998), para 603.

A question that often arises in practice is at what point a situation escalates beyond mere disturbances and tensions, to which international humanitarian law does not apply, and becomes an armed conflict within the meaning of Article 3. Article 1(2) of Additional Protocol II mentions 'riots, isolated and sporadic acts of violence and other acts of a similar nature' as examples of situations not amounting to an armed conflict. A useful criterion in establishing the dividing line is whether *both sides* have resorted to military means, ie whether the conflict is of a military character.[10] This happens, for example, where the government must deploy the regular armed forces to deal with insurgents who have organized themselves along military lines and at least temporarily control parts of the country (eg some rural areas). This is especially true in the following situations: (1) where insurgents exercise *de facto* government authority over the population in part of the territory,[11] (2) where the insurgents have actually created a quasi-state entity, and (3) where a conflict between insurgents and a government is intensive enough to be recognized by the UN Security Council as being a threat to international peace pursuant to Article 39 of the UN Charter. However, participation of governmental forces is not necessary: a non-international armed conflict pursuant to common Article 3 exists also where two sufficiently well-organized non-state groups engage in military hostilities on the territory of a state party.

Issue in focus: The notion of non-international armed conflicts in the case-law of the ICTY

War crimes can only be committed during armed conflicts. Therefore, criminal courts must in such cases first determine the existence of such a conflict. In this context, the ICTY has developed criteria to determine the existence of a non-international armed conflict pursuant to common Article 3.

In the *Tadić* case, the Appeals Chamber of the ICTY held that an armed conflict exists 'whenever there is a resort to armed force between States or protracted armed violence between governmental authorities and organized armed groups or between such groups within a State'.[12]

For non-international armed conflicts in the sense of common Article 3, the Tribunal identified the two relevant criteria of the existence of a 'protracted armed conflict' and the participation of an 'organized armed group' in the military operations. In a more recent judgment from 2008, the ICTY had to decide whether members of the 'Kosova Liberation Army/KLA' had committed war crimes.[13] There was dispute concerning whether the altercations between the Serbian army and the

---

[10] Thus, for example, the deployment of government troops against violent demonstrators does not render common Art 3 applicable.

[11] Jean S Pictet (ed), *Commentary on the Geneva Conventions of 12 August 1949*, vols I–IV (Geneva: International Committee of the Red Cross, 1952–1959), vol IV 35 f.

[12] ICTY (Appeals Chamber), *The Prosecutor v Tadić*, Decision on the Defence Motion for Interlocutory Appeal on Jurisdiction, Case No IT-94-1 (1995), para 70.

[13] ICTY, *The Prosecutor v Haradinaj et al*, Case No IT-04-84-T (2008).

KLA could qualify as armed conflicts according to common Article 3. To clarify this question, the Tribunal carefully examined the two elements constitutive of the notion of armed conflict.

Based on a thorough analysis of its previous jurisprudence, the ICTY concluded the following with regard to the element of 'protracted armed violence':

> The criterion of protracted armed violence has therefore been interpreted in practice, including by the Tadic Trial Chamber itself, as referring more to the intensity of the armed violence than to its duration. Trial Chambers have relied on indicative factors relevant for assessing the 'intensity' criterion, none of which are, in themselves, essential to establish that the criterion is satisfied. These indicative factors include the number, duration and intensity of individual confrontations; the type of weapons and other military equipment used; the number and calibre of munitions fired; the number of persons and type of forces partaking in the fighting; the number of casualties; the extent of material destruction; and the number of civilians fleeing combat zones. The involvement of the UN Security Council may also be a reflection of the intensity of a conflict.[14]

On the necessity of the armed group being 'organized' the Tribunal recalled that its jurisprudence emphasizes that:

> an armed conflict can exist only between parties that are sufficiently organized to confront each other with military means. State governmental authorities have been presumed to dispose of armed forces that satisfy this criterion. As for armed groups, Trial Chambers have relied on several indicative factors, none of which are, in themselves, essential to establish whether the 'organization' criterion is fulfilled. Such indicative factors include the existence of a command structure and disciplinary rules and mechanisms within the group; the existence of a headquarters; the fact that the group controls a certain territory; the ability of the group to gain access to weapons, other military equipment, recruits and military training; its ability to plan, coordinate and carry out military operations, including troop movements and logistics; its ability to define a unified military strategy and use military tactics; and its ability to speak with one voice and negotiate and conclude agreements such as cease-fire or peace accords.[15]

(b) Non-international armed conflicts pursuant to Additional Protocol II

For Additional Protocol II to be applicable, the armed conflict in question must, according to its Article 1, take place in the territory of a 'Contracting Party between its armed forces and dissident armed forces or other organized armed groups which, under responsible command, exercise such control over a part of its territory as to enable them to carry out sustained and concerted military operations and to implement this Protocol'. During such conflicts, the detailed provisions of Additional Protocol II concerning the protection of persons affected by armed conflicts are applicable in addition to common Article 3.

The criteria of sustained and concerted military operations and the ability to implement the Protocol[16] make it clear that the applicability threshold for Additional Protocol II is higher than for common Article 3, which is also

---

[14] Ibid, para 49.   [15] Ibid, para 60.

[16] For a detailed discussion of this, see Yves Sandoz, Christophe Swinarski and Bruno Zimmermann (eds), *Commentary on the Additional Protocols of 8 June 1977 to the Geneva Conventions of 12 August 1949* (Martinus Nijhoff: Geneva, 1987), 1347 ff.

applicable to isolated military operations. Additional Protocol II is thus intended to be applied primarily to fully fledged civil wars and its area of applicability excludes conflicts between non-state groups. Military operations are 'sustained' and 'concerted' when they are not merely sporadic but take place over an extended period as part of a planned military strategy. Moreover, to be able to implement the Additional Protocol, insurgents must be highly organized, since it imposes obligations such as running schools for children (AP II, Article 4(3)(a)), establishing an efficient criminal justice system (AP II, Article 6), and providing medical care for the wounded and sick (AP II, Article 7). Furthermore, the leadership of the non-state group must be capable of imposing a certain measure of discipline and of carrying out sustained and concerted military operations.

4. Mixed armed conflict

Particular problems arise where a foreign state intervenes in a non-international armed conflict or where a civil war breaks out concurrently within an international armed conflict. The term *mixed conflict* is used to refer to such cases.[17]

What kind of law governs such conflicts? According to the so-called 'components theory', the conflict must be broken down into international and internal components to determine which law is applicable, ie for each situation one has to ascertain who is fighting against whom. Where, for instance, both a foreign state and insurgents are fighting against a government an international and a non-international armed conflict are taking place concurrently and each component is governed by the corresponding law.[18] This also applies where the foreign power and the insurgents coordinate their military operations or fight together. Where the foreign state is helping the government, on the other hand, there is no international armed conflict and the foreign forces are taking part on the side of the government in what is, legally speaking, a purely non-international conflict.

In the *Nicaragua* case, the International Court of Justice invoked the components theory, thereby implicitly recognizing it as legally valid. It held that the conflict between the armed group known as the Contras and the Sandinista Government in Nicaragua was to be characterized as a non-international armed conflict, while the alleged military actions of the United States in and against Nicaragua fell under the legal rules relating to international conflicts.[19]

---

[17] Example: A number of foreign states took part in the armed conflict in the Democratic Republic of Congo between various rebel groups and the government after the fall of the dictator Mobutu in 1997. Beginning 2 August 1998, troops from Rwanda, Uganda (on its role see ICJ, *Case concerning Armed Activities on the Territory of the Congo (Democratic Republic of Congo v Uganda)*, ICJ Reports 2005) and Burundi fought alongside the rebels. This prompted Angola, Zimbabwe and Namibia to provide military support to the former Congolese Government.

[18] Accordingly, the ICJ concluded in *Democratic Republic of Congo v Uganda* that Uganda had violated Geneva Convention IV when it occupied parts of Congo; id, at para 219.

[19] ICJ, *Case concerning Military and Paramilitary Activities in and against Nicaragua, (Nicaragua v The United States of America)*, ICJ Reports 1986, para 219.

The components theory creates difficulties where different conflicts are inter-twined in complex ways, making it difficult to identify each of the components. Furthermore, it leads to problematic results where in the context of the same con-flict one victim of violence is left unprotected because of the absence of a protect-ive rule in the law on internal armed conflict and the fact that the perpetrator is not involved in the international component of the conflict, while another vic-tim can enjoy the higher level of protection afforded by the law governing inter-national conflicts, just because the perpetrator happens to be acting on behalf of a foreign state. Some legal commentators have advocated making the law of inter-national armed conflict applicable across the board in the case of complex mixed conflicts.[20] This approach has not found favour,[21] however, *inter alia* because governments rejected a similar proposal by the ICRC during the drafting of the Additional Protocols.[22]

Faced with these difficulties, treaty law and jurisprudence have found ways to extend the scope of the law of international armed conflict to cover such mixed conflicts, despite the continued applicability in principle of the components theory.

(1) *Additional Protocol I, Article 1(4)* which now plays only a minor role, extends the law of international armed conflicts to wars of liberation 'in which peoples are fighting against colonial domination and alien occupation and against racist regimes in the exercise of their right of self-determination, as enshrined in the Charter of the United Nations and the Declaration on Principles of International Law concerning Friendly Relations and Co-operation among States in accordance with the Charter of the United Nations'.

(2) *The case law of the ICJ and the ICTY* recognize that non-international armed conflicts acquire an international character, and hence fall under the inter-national conflict regime, if the non-state group is so closely controlled by another state that it can be classified as a *de facto* organ of that state.

Issue in focus: Non-state groups as *de facto* organs of a foreign state

---

Non-state groups in mixed conflicts can be brought within the scope of the law of international armed conflict by attributing their actions to a foreign state. This approach is supported by GC III, Article 4(A)(2), which states that not only mem-bers of the regular forces of a party to the conflict who fall into enemy hands are

---

[20] For instance Theodor Meron, 'Normative Impact of the Hague Tribunal', in *War Crimes Come of Age, Essays* (Clarendon Press: Oxford, 1998), 213 f: '... any attempt to apply the Nicaragua court's decision to the conflict in Yugoslavia would result in Byzantine complexity, making pros-ecutions difficult and often impossible'.

[21] See, for example, ICTY (Appeals Chamber), *The Prosecutor v Tadić*, Case No IT-94-1-A (1999), in which the Tribunal ruled against such an extension of the law of international armed conflict to the former Yugoslavia.

[22] Hess (n 4), at 153.

prisoners of war but also '[m]embers of other militias and members of other volunteer corps, including those of organized resistance movements, *belonging to a Party to the conflict and operating in or outside their own territory*, even if this territory is occupied...'.[23] The principle enshrined in the law of state responsibility according to which a state is responsible for the conduct of persons or groups who act on its instructions or under its direction or control is also relevant.[24]

The ICJ recognized in the *Nicaragua* case that violations of humanitarian law by insurgents can be attributed to a state if the perpetrators operate under its effective control. In the particular case before it, however, it held that American control over the rebellious *contras* was not effective enough for such a conclusion to be drawn.[25] The Court confirmed the effective control-standard in the *Genocide* case, emphasizing that '[i]t must...be shown that this "effective control" was exercised...in respect of each operation in which the alleged violations occurred, not generally in respect of the overall actions taken by the persons or groups of persons having committed the violations'.[26]

By contrast, in the *Tadić* case, the ICTY held that the law of international armed conflict was applicable to the acts of Serb groups because the former Federal Republic of Yugoslavia (Serbia and Montenegro) had 'overall control' of their activities. The infringements committed against Bosniac (Muslim) and Croatian citizens of the state of Bosnia and Herzegovina were therefore to be judged in the light of the law of international armed conflict despite the fact that the Federal Republic of Yugoslavia did not direct or control each individual operation at issue.[27] The basis of this determination was the above-mentioned GC III, Article 4, from which the Tribunal deduced that an armed conflict becomes international where non-state units in a civil war 'belong' to another state, ie where they are in a relationship of dependence and allegiance *vis-à-vis* the state and hence come under its overall control.[28] The Tribunal ruled that a conflict is of international character if the state, in addition to financing, equipping and training such groups, has 'overall control', meaning that it plays a general role in the organization, coordination and planning of their military operations.[29]

The '*control theory*' has thus established itself in the case law as a means of determining when the conduct of a non-state group is attributable *de facto* to

---

[23] GC III, Art 4(A)(2). Emphasis added.

[24] ILC draft Articles on State Responsibility, Art 8 'Report of the ILC on its fifty-third session' (2001), UN Doc A/56/10, Supplement No 10 (*Official Records of the General Assembly*); see Chapter 3, section I.1.

[25] ICJ, *Case concerning Military and Paramilitary Activities in and against Nicaragua*, (*Nicaragua v The United States of America*), ICJ Reports 1986, paras 115 and 116.

[26] ICJ, *Application of the Convention on the Prevention and Punishment of the Crime of Genocide* (*Bosnia and Herzegovina v Serbia and Montenegro*), ICJ Reports 2007, para 400.

[27] ICTY (Appeals Chamber), *The Prosecutor v Tadić*, Case No IT-94-1-A (1999), paras 88 ff. The (first-instance) Trial Chamber, citing the *Nicaragua* case, had required 'effective' control ('effective control test') and had concluded that such control did not exist in the case before it. See ICTY (Trial Chamber), *The Prosecutor v Tadić*, Case No IT-94-1 (1997), paras 584 ff.

[28] ICTY (Appeals Chamber), *The Prosecutor v Tadić*, Case No IT-94-1-A (1999), paras 94 f.

[29] Ibid, para 138.

a foreign state.[30] While it is now largely undisputed that the acts of a party to a civil war may be attributed to a foreign state where corresponding control exists, thereby internationalizing the conflict, there are still differences of opinion as to how close and specific this control must be. The ICTY 'overall control' approach better reflects the actual circumstances of present-day warfare and is therefore, in our view, more fitting than the ICJ's 'effective control' test to determine the applicable law. A state is the adversary of a foreign government not only when it intervenes militarily itself or directs irregular troops on the state's territory 'by remote control', but also when it equips such forces and indicates the overall strategic path to follow, allowing them a free hand in implementing the strategy in their day-to-day combat operations. This conclusion is not necessarily at odds with the ICJ's opinion. Although the Court rejected the 'overall control' test for determining state responsibility, it left open the question as to whether this test is fitting for determining the international character of an armed conflict[31] and acknowledged that 'the degree and nature of a State's involvement in an armed conflict can very well, and without logical inconsistency, differ from the degree and nature of involvement required to give rise to that State's responsibility for a specific act committed in the course of the conflict'.[32]

(3) It has become increasingly clear that many rules of international humanitarian law that originally formed part of the conventions on the law of international armed conflict have over time also become applicable as *customary law* to non-international armed conflicts. Thus, the ICTY made it clear in the *Tadić* case that the strict dividing line between the law of international conflict and the law of non-international conflict has evaporated because fundamental treaty law norms have since acquired customary status.[33] This has recently been confirmed by the ICRC expert study on customary international humanitarian law.[34] Most of the rules identified in the study are binding for all kinds of conflicts, including mixed conflicts.

[30] The theory is supported in general international law by Art 8 of the ILC draft Articles on State Responsibility (n 24), according to which a state is responsible for the conduct of persons or groups acting on its instructions or under its direction or control.

[31] The ICJ, in the *Case concerning the Application of the Convention on the Prevention and Punishment of the Crime of Genocide (Bosnia and Herzegovina v Serbia and Montenegro)*, ICJ Reports 2007, paras 404 f, recognized that 'the degree and nature of a State's involvement in an armed conflict on another State's territory which is required for the conflict to be characterized as international, can very well, and without logical inconsistency, differ from the degree and nature of involvement required to give rise to that State's responsibility for a specific act committed in the course of the conflict.

[32] Ibid, at para 405.

[33] See ICTY (Appeals Chamber), *The Prosecutor v Tadić*, Case No IT-94-1-A (1999), paras 96 ff. The Tribunal characterized as rules of customary law, applicable to all kinds of conflicts, the protection of the civilian population from indiscriminate attack, the protection of certain civilian objects, particularly a country's cultural heritage, and the prohibition of certain methods of conflict; ibid, para 127.

[34] Jean-Marie Henckaerts and Louise Doswald-Beck, *Customary International Humanitarian Law*, 3 vols (Cambridge University Press: Cambridge, 2005); on this study, see Chapter 2, section III.3.

Table 5.1. Conditions governing the applicability of international humanitarian law

Situation	Classification Criterion	Applicable Law
Disturbances and tensions	Non-military acts of violence	human rights
Non-international armed conflict pursuant to common Art 3	Engagements of a military character, also on the part of insurgents	Common Art 3; human rights
Non-international armed conflict pursuant to AP II	Insurgents under responsible leadership exercise such a degree of control over parts of the state's territory that they can carry out sustained and coordinated military operations and can implement the Protocol	Common Art 3 and AP II; human rights
Mixed conflict	Non-international armed conflict involving military intervention against the government by another state	Depending on the component: GCs I–IV & AP I/ Common Art 3/AP II; human rights
International armed conflict	Military conflict between states; occupation of foreign territory	GCs I–IV; AP I; human rights

5. Summary

Table 5.1 provides an overview of the conditions governing the applicability of international humanitarian law.

II. Obligations Under Humanitarian Law[35]

1. Who is bound?

(a) States

Under Article 1 common to the four Geneva Conventions and Article 1 of Additional Protocol I, the 'High Contracting Parties' undertake to respect and to ensure respect for the treaties. Clearly, it is primarily *states* that are bound by the rules of international humanitarian law. The principles already enunciated in the context of human rights obligations are also valid when it comes to determining which acts are imputable to states.[36]

States must respect international humanitarian law guarantees irrespective of whether the adverse party abides by its obligations. Although the idea of

---

[35] This section deals only with obligations under international humanitarian law that are of direct relevance to the protection of the human person in an armed conflict. It does not refer, for instance, to the obligation to appoint a protecting power in wartime (GC I–III, Art 8; GC IV, Art 9).

[36] See Chapter 3, section I.1.

reciprocity is one of the historical foundations of international humanitarian law,[37] mutuality of law-abiding conduct is not a prerequisite for being bound by its rules. In this context, VCLT, Article 60(5)[38] is particularly relevant. It expressly stipulates that, contrary to the general rule of international public law, a state that has been the victim of a material breach of a treaty may not suspend or terminate the operation of the treaty in its relations with the defaulting state in the case of 'provisions relating to the protection of the human person contained in treaties of a humanitarian character'.

(b) Insurgent groups

Article 3 common to the four Geneva Conventions as well as Additional Protocol II regulate the conduct of parties to an armed conflict within a particular country, ie in the context of insurrections, civil wars, and similar non-international conflicts. In such cases, obligations *vis-à-vis* the civilian population and members of government forces who are no longer taking an active part in the hostilities (eg because of injury or sickness) are imposed not only on the state and its armed forces, but also on insurgent groups. The wording of common Article 3 makes this quite clear, binding '*each* Party to the conflict' to observe certain minimum guarantees.[39] This binding obligation exists regardless of whether the adverse party also complies. Although insurgents are not, as a rule, subjects of international law[40] in the strict sense of the term, they can nevertheless enjoy certain rights and incur certain obligations under an international treaty just like other private actors.[41] However, the fact that insurgents are bound by certain provisions of international humanitarian law does not affect their legal status (common Article 3(2), last sentence) and, in particular, does not lead to any kind of recognition.

(c) Individuals

In practice, violations of international humanitarian law are always committed by specific individuals such as military commanders or ordinary soldiers in the field. Therefore, obligations under this body of law have to be observed by anyone who belongs to a party to the conflict, including all members of the armed forces,[42]

---

[37] See Chapter 1, section II.3.

[38] Vienna Convention on the Law of Treaties of 23 May 1969.

[39] GC III, Arts 17 and 122 and GC IV, Art 136 contain similar wording.

[40] The UN has granted some measure of international legal personality in the past to certain liberation movements such as the PLO and—before the regime change in South Africa—the ANC and SWAPO.

[41] The question of the precise legal nature of insurgents' obligations under international humanitarian law and the basis for such obligations is a matter of dispute among legal writers. For a detailed discussion see Jörg Künzli, *Zwischen Rigidität und Flexibilität—Der Verpflichtungsgrad internationaler Menschenrechte* (Duncker & Humblot: Berlin, 2001), 174–87.

[42] According to AP I, Art 43 members of the armed forces 'consist of all organized armed forces, groups and units which are under a command responsible to that Party for the conduct of its subordinates, even if that Party is represented by a government or an authority not recognized by an adverse Party.'

'members of militias or volunteer corps forming part of such armed forces' or otherwise belonging to such party, provided they are organized in a military manner;[43] '[p]ersons who accompany the armed forces without actually being members thereof, such as civilian members of military aircraft crews, war correspondents, supply contractors, members of labour units or of services responsible for the welfare of the armed forces'; as well as '[i]nhabitants of a non-occupied territory, who on the approach of the enemy spontaneously take up arms to resist the invading forces, without having had time to form themselves into regular armed units, provided they carry arms openly and respect the laws and customs of war'.[44] Violations of the rules of international humanitarian law do not only incur the responsibility of the party to the conflict, but also the criminal responsibility of the individual who committed such actions.

Given the inherent difficulties in halting or reversing the consequences of unlawful acts committed in war situations, international humanitarian law pierces the veil of state authority to get at the actual perpetrators, at least for the most serious violations, requiring states to enact legislation aimed at prosecuting what are known in the Conventions and Additional Protocol I as 'grave breaches' of international humanitarian law.[45] These provisions, together with the war crimes defined in the Statutes of the International Criminal Tribunals and the International Criminal Court, entail obligations for individuals.

(d) Obligations of international forces with a UN mandate?

The question of whether and to what extent forces deployed under a UN Security Council mandate or with the Council's authorization are bound by international humanitarian law is complex. Consider the following scenarios:

(1) The Security Council, acting under Chapter VII of the UN Charter,[46] empowers states, alone or with others, to take military action against a state whose conduct threatens or has already breached international peace.[47] In such cases, notwithstanding the relevant Security Council resolution, the

---

[43] See the elements mentioned in GC III, Art 4(2) and comprising the following requirements: '(a) that of being commanded by a person responsible for his subordinates; (b) that of having a fixed distinctive sign recognizable at a distance; (c) that of carrying arms openly; (d) that of conducting their operations in accordance with the laws and customs of war.'

[44] These are the main categories of those listed in GC III, Art 4 as persons entitled to prisoner of war status.

[45] GC I, Arts 49–50; GC II, Arts 50–51; GC III, Arts 129–130; GC IV, Arts 146–147; AP I, Art 85.

[46] Under Chapter VII of the UN Charter concerning action with respect to threats to peace, breaches of the peace, and acts of aggression (Arts 39–51), the Security Council can decide on binding non-military coercive measures (such as economic sanctions) or on military measures where such action is necessary to restore peace.

[47] This was the scenario, for example, when the Security Council authorized a coalition of states led by the United States to attack Iraq and Iraqi-occupied Kuwait in 1991 following Iraq's invasion of Kuwait in 1990; UN Security Council Resolution 678 (1990).

authorized states are parties to an armed conflict and as such are fully bound by the applicable provisions of international humanitarian law.

(2) Once a military operation authorized by the Security Council has been completed and a new sovereign government takes up office or, as in the case of Afghanistan in 2002 or Iraq in 2004, an agreement is found allowing foreign troops to remain after a new government has taken office, the legal situation undergoes a fundamental change. When international forces remain in the country after the transfer of sovereignty, with the agreement of the new government, they are no longer fighting against the forces of another state but may now support the government against insurgent groups. At that point the occupation ends, hence the applicability of the law of *international* armed conflict ends as well. According to the components theory,[48] international coalitions are bound in such circumstances by common Article 3 and, where applicable, Additional Protocol II if their activities reach the threshold of an armed conflict. If there are no longer any military hostilities as such, and the international troop presence is required solely for policing duties, this set of obligations is also rendered inapplicable. The civilian population cannot therefore invoke international humanitarian law against the international forces in such cases.[49]

(3) The Security Council decides to deploy peacekeeping troops, who are mandated by the UN to assist in upholding peace agreements or restoring peace. Such decisions can be made with the consent of the state concerned under Chapter VI of the Charter[50] or as coercive measures under Chapter VII. The troops are composed of contingents provided by UN member states. These international units (sometimes referred to as 'blue helmets') are under the strategic command of the UN. As they are not a party to a conflict but have more of a policing role, and as the UN is not a party to the Geneva Conventions and their Additional Protocols, the extent to which they are bound by international humanitarian law is disputed.

The view that UN troops are under an obligation to respect international humanitarian law is supported by two main lines of reasoning.[51] The contracting parties to the Conventions and Additional Protocols are not released from their obligations under humanitarian law when they make parts of their forces available to

---

[48] See section I.4 above.

[49] It remains possible, however, to invoke the applicable human rights guarantees. See Chapter 4, section III on the extraterritorial scope of application of human rights conventions.

[50] Chapter VI of the UN Charter on the peaceful settlement of disputes (Arts 33–38) empowers the Security Council to make recommendations to the parties, albeit on a non-binding basis, for the settlement of a dispute and to take concrete measures with their consent.

[51] Robert Kolb, *Droit humanitaire et opérations de paix internationales: les modalités d'application du droit international humanitaire dans les opérations de maintien ou de rétablissement de la paix auxquelles concourt une organisation internationale (en particulier les Nations Unies)* (2nd edn, Helbing & Lichtenhahn and Bruylant: Basle and Brussels, 2006), 50 ff, with references to legal opinion.

the United Nations, placing them under the supreme command of the UN.[52] Moreover, the human rights objective set forth in Article 1(3) of the UN Charter encompasses the protection of human beings in wartime, so that the UN itself is required to respect humanitarian law. However, both arguments overlook the fact that such troops are not a party to the conflict as defined by humanitarian law. Furthermore, large portions of the Geneva Conventions and the Additional Protocols, such as those relating to occupied territories, are simply not appropriate where UN troops are concerned.[53]

In practice, the UN and states accept as a matter of principle that they are bound by international humanitarian law, while leaving open the exact extent of this obligation. Thus, agreements between the United Nations and states that provide troops have long stated that these contingents must respect 'the principles and spirit of international humanitarian law'. In 1999 the UN Secretary-General issued a directive for United Nations troops, according to which such troops must respect the fundamental principles and rules of international humanitarian law.[54] The directive states, *inter alia*, that states which provide troops are responsible for the criminal prosecution of serious violations of humanitarian law. In addition, it codifies the most important humanitarian law principles, such as those regarding permissible means and methods of combat as well as the treatment of the civilian population, persons not or no longer taking part in the fighting (persons *hors de combat*), wounded and sick persons, and medical personnel.

Issue in focus: Observance by United Nations forces of international humanitarian law—Secretary-General's Bulletin of 6 August 1999 (excerpts)

Section 1—Field of application

1.1 The fundamental principles and rules of international humanitarian law set out in the present bulletin are applicable to United Nations forces when in situations of armed conflict they are actively engaged therein as combatants, to the extent and for the duration of their engagement. They are accordingly applicable in enforcement actions, or in peacekeeping operations when the use of force is permitted in self-defence.

...

Section 5—Protection of the civilian population

5.1 The United Nations force shall make a clear distinction at all times between civilians and combatants and between civilian objects and military objectives. Military operations shall be directed only against combatants and military objectives. Attacks on civilians or civilian objects are prohibited.

---

[52] See Chapter 3, section I.3.b.iii.

[53] A detailed overview of provisions that are applicable to UN troops, applicable only to a limited extent, and not applicable at all may be found in Kolb (n 51), 60 ff.

[54] United Nations, 'Observance by United Nations forces of international humanitarian law, Secretary-General's Bulletin', UN Doc ST/SGB/1999/13, 6 August 1999, reproduced in IRRC 812–817.

5.2 Civilians shall enjoy the protection afforded by this section, unless and for such time as they take a direct part in hostilities.

5.3 The United Nations force shall take all feasible precautions to avoid, and in any event to minimize, incidental loss of civilian life, injury to civilians or damage to civilian property.

5.4 In its area of operation, the United Nations force shall avoid, to the extent feasible, locating military objectives within or near densely populated areas, and take all necessary precautions to protect the civilian population, individual civilians and civilian objects against the dangers resulting from military operations. Military installations and equipment of peacekeeping operations, as such, shall not be considered military objectives.

5.5 The United Nations force is prohibited from launching operations of a nature likely to strike military objectives and civilians in an indiscriminate manner, as well as operations that may be expected to cause incidental loss of life among the civilian population or damage to civilian objects that would be excessive in relation to the concrete and direct military advantage anticipated.

5.6 The United Nations force shall not engage in reprisals against civilians or civilian objects.

2. To whom are obligations owed?

(a) In an international armed conflict

The history of international humanitarian law shows that the original purpose of the law of war was to establish the obligations that belligerents owed to one another in terms of protection of their forces and their civilian populations. These bilateral responsibilities remain of core importance, representing the *primary obligations* arising from humanitarian law.

Unlike human rights, humanitarian law guarantees are not formulated as subjective rights of individuals but as *objective obligations* of the parties to a conflict. Thus, there are no international procedures enabling individuals to enforce their claims. At least this has traditionally been the basic assumption. A shift of perspective is nevertheless already discernible in the Geneva Conventions and even more so in the Additional Protocols. For instance, GC III, Article 7 and GC IV, Article 8 stipulate that *prisoners of war* and *protected civilians* 'may in no circumstances renounce in part or in entirety the rights secured to them' by the Conventions. These two articles, which were drafted under the influence of work on the Universal Declaration of Human Rights, were deliberately chosen to impart a personal dimension to the guarantees in the Conventions that would enable addressees to invoke them irrespective of the attitude adopted by their state of origin in respect of a detaining or foreign power.[55] Similarly, GC IV, Article 27 states that protected persons 'are *entitled*, in all circumstances, to respect for their persons, their honour, their family rights, their religious convictions and practices, and their manners and customs', and that they are to be 'treated with the same consideration by the Party to the conflict in whose power they are, without any

---

[55] Pictet (n 11), vol III, 87 ff on GC III, Art 7 and vol IV 72 ff on GC I, Art 8 V.

adverse distinction based, in particular, on race, religion or political opinion'.[56] Article 75 of Additional Protocol I even contains an extensive list of obligations to refrain from actions against persons in the power of a party to a conflict that are also prohibited under human rights law. However, as the contracting parties are not required to provide individuals with procedures to enforce these guarantees at the domestic level and as no international enforcement machinery exists, these provisions fall short of fully-fledged individual legal entitlements.

The scope of individual obligations under humanitarian law is broader than that of individual rights. Pursuant to GC III, Article 129 and GC IV, Article 146, contracting parties, as outlined above, are bound to prosecute certain acts characterized as grave breaches of the Conventions,[57] entailing the individual criminal responsibility of persons taking part in the conflict.

Finally, international humanitarian law, like human rights law,[58] contains *erga omnes* obligations, ie obligations of concern to all states, including non-state parties.[59] As regards obligations *erga omnes partes* Article 1 common to the four Geneva Conventions provides that states parties not only have 'to respect' but also 'to ensure respect' for the Conventions under all circumstances.

(b) In a non-international armed conflict

In a non-international armed conflict not only states but also non-state parties to the conflict are bound by obligations *vis-à-vis* individuals who are not (or are no longer) taking part in the conflict (common Article 3) and who are in the power of the enemy (Additional Protocol II).

The Law of Geneva contains no provision concerning the criminal responsibility of persons taking part in a non-international armed conflict. However, this lacuna has been remedied by the Rome Statute of the International Criminal Court. Article 8(2)(c) of the Statute makes violations of common Article 3 punishable and Article 8(2)(e) lists a number of violations of Additional Protocol II as criminal acts, the prosecution of which contracting parties bear prime responsibility.

---

[56] GC IV, Art 27(1) and (3). Emphasis added.

[57] GC III, Art 130 and GC IV, Art 143.   [58] See above, Chapter 3, section II.

[59] As virtually all states have ratified the four Geneva conventions, the difference between *erga omnes partes* and *erga omnes* is relevant where the two Additional Protocols contain obligations that have not acquired customary law status. The *erga omnes* status of most provisions of international humanitarian law has been recognized by the ICJ in its Advisory Opinion on the legal consequences of the Israeli separation barrier in the Palestinian territories; ICJ, *Legal Consequences of the Construction of a Wall in the Occupied Palestinian Territory* (Advisory Opinion), ICJ Reports 2004, para 157: '157. With regard to international humanitarian law, the Court recalls that in its Advisory Opinion on the *Legality of the Threat or Use of Nuclear Weapons*, it stated that 'a great many rules of humanitarian law applicable in armed conflict are so fundamental to the respect of the human person and "elementary considerations of humanity"...', that they are 'to be observed by all States whether or not they have ratified the conventions that contain them, because they constitute intransgressible principles of international customary law' (ICJ Reports 1996 (I), 257, para 79). In the Court's view, these rules incorporate obligations which are essentially of an *erga omnes* character.'

Like in the case of obligations in situations of international armed conflict, provisions applicable in non-international armed conflicts contain obligations *erga omnes* and *erga omnes* partes.

3. Categories of obligations[60]

Under Article 1 common to the four Geneva Conventions and Article 1 of Additional Protocol I, the 'High Contracting Parties' undertake to 'respect and to ensure respect for [the treaties] under all circumstances'.

(a) *The obligation to respect international humanitarian law*

Similar to obligations under human rights law, those under international humanitarian law may be divided essentially into obligations to respect, protect and fulfil without discrimination. As the Geneva Conventions and their Additional Protocols are far more detailed than human rights treaties, all three layers of obligation may not be discernible for each guarantee. Rather, many provisions address just one dimension, so that the precise obligations flowing from each provision must be determined on a case-by-case basis.

Obligations to respect are embodied for the most part in provisions that protect people's lives along with their physical and mental integrity in wartime. They include, for example, the prohibition on exercising physical or moral coercion against the civilian population in occupied territories (GC IV, Article 31), the prohibition of murder, torture, corporal punishment, mutilation, and medical experiments (GC IV, Article 32), the prohibition of measures aimed at terrorizing the civilian population (GC IV, Article 33), the prohibition of hostage-taking (GC IV, Article 34), the prohibition of attacks on the civilian population and civilian objects (AP I, Articles 51 and 52),[61] and the prohibition on attacking, destroying, removing or rendering useless 'objects indispensable to the survival of the civilian population, such as food-stuffs, agricultural areas for the production of food-stuffs, crops, livestock, drinking water installations and supplies and irrigation works' (AP I, Article 54(2)).

Obligations to protect arise primarily in connection with particularly vulnerable groups. Pursuant to GC IV, Article 16 '[t]he wounded and sick, as well as the infirm, and expectant mothers, shall be the object of particular protection and respect' and, '[a]s far as military considerations allow,' the parties to the conflict 'shall facilitate the steps taken to search for the killed and wounded, to assist the shipwrecked and other persons exposed to grave danger, and to protect them

---

[60] In this passage, only those obligations under international humanitarian law that have a direct relevance for the protection of the human being in armed conflict situations will be presented. For example, the obligation of designating a protecting power in case of war (GC I–III, Art 8; GC IV, Art 9) will not be dealt with here.

[61] For more detail, see Chapter 9, section II.2.d.

against pillage and ill-treatment'. Women must be given special protection, for instance against rape and forced prostitution (GC IV, Article 27(2) and AP I, Article 76(1)), and the parties to the conflict are required to hold interned women in separate quarters from men and to place them solely under the supervision of female staff (GC IV, Article 76(4) and AP I, Article 75(5)). Prisoners of war must also be protected from abuse, 'particularly against acts of violence or intimidation and against insults and public curiosity' (GC III, Article 13(2)), and they must be evacuated as soon as possible to camps 'situated in an area far enough from the combat zone for them to be out of danger' (GC III, Article 19).

International humanitarian law imposes *obligations to fulfil* in circumstances in which prisoners of war, interned civilians or the population of occupied territories are under the direct control of a party to the conflict, making it difficult or impossible for them to meet their subsistence needs on their own. These obligations include, in the case of prisoners of war for example, the obligation 'to provide free of charge for their maintenance and for the medical attention required by their state of health' (GC III, Article 15). The parties to the conflict must provide children 'with the care and aid they require, whether because of their age or for any other reason' (AP I, Article 77). In occupied territories the occupying power must 'make arrangements for the maintenance and education . . . of children who are orphaned or separated from their parents as a result of the war'. Pursuant to GC IV, Article 55 the occupying power has the duty '[t]o the fullest extent of the means available to it, . . . of ensuring the food and medical supplies of the population; it should, in particular, bring in the necessary foodstuffs, medical stores and other articles if the resources of the occupied territory are inadequate', and it also has the duty '[t]o the fullest extent of the means available to it, . . . of ensuring and maintaining . . . the medical and hospital establishments and services, public health and hygiene in the occupied territory' (GC IV, Article 56(1)). As may be gathered from these examples, many of the obligations are in fact analogous to obligations under economic, social and cultural human rights.

(b) *The obligation to implement international humanitarian law*

The obligation to enforce international humanitarian law differs in important respects from the obligation to enforce human rights. It exists on three levels.

First, common Article 1 and AP I, Article 1, by stipulating that the parties must not only 'respect' the obligations laid down in those instruments 'in all circumstances' but also 'ensure respect' for them, requires the states concerned to ensure that their forces comply with the treaties fully and absolutely[62] while on duty and during their free time.

---

[62] Frits Kalshoven, 'The Undertaking to Respect and Ensure Respect in All Circumstances: From Tiny Seed to Ripening Fruit' (1999) 2 Yearbook of International Humanitarian Law 60, and ICJ, *Legal Consequences of the Construction of a Wall in the Occupied Palestinian Territory* (Advisory Opinion), ICJ Reports 2004, Separate Opinion of Judge Higgins, para 14.

Second, the provisions of international humanitarian law contained in common Article 1 and AP I, Article 1(1) establish not only obligations *erga omnes*, thereby *entitling all states* to take action against breaches by other states, but also establish an *obligation on all states* to ensure that contracting states respect international humanitarian law. Although this view has not gone undisputed,[63] it was recently endorsed by the ICJ.[64] Geneva Law does not, however, specify either the circumstances in which contracting parties should take action *against violating states* or the methods they should use, an omission that has contributed to encouraging states to adopt a discretionary approach to this obligation. Possible means of action include bilateral diplomatic interventions, public criticism of individual states, non-military pressure through regional organizations, denunciation by UN bodies such as the Human Rights Council or the General Assembly, and Security Council recommendations or coercive measures under Chapter VII of the Charter. UN competence in this regard is recognized, *inter alia*, in AP I, Article 89, according to which states undertake, in the event of serious violations of humanitarian law, 'to act jointly or individually, in co-operation with the United Nations and in conformity with the United Nations Charter'.

Example: UN measures to enforce international humanitarian law in Iraqi-occupied Kuwait in 1990/91

The reactions of different UN bodies to the occupation of Kuwait by Iraqi forces from 2 August 1990 to 26 February 1991 illustrate both the potential and limits of United Nations activities aimed at enforcing international humanitarian law.

The *Security Council* reaffirmed in Resolution 670 (1990) of 25 September 1990, acting under Chapter VII of the Charter, that GC IV was applicable to the occupation of Kuwait and that Iraq was fully bound by its terms. The Council further stressed that Iraq would be liable for grave breaches of the Convention, as would be individuals who committed or ordered the commission of such breaches (paragraph 13).

The former *Commission on Human Rights*, in Resolution 1991/67 of 6 March 1991, condemned the failure of Iraq to treat prisoners of war and detained civilians in accordance with international humanitarian law and insisted that Iraq refrain from subjecting them to ill-treatment, torture, and summary executions (paragraph 5). The Commission further demanded the immediate release of all prisoners (paragraph 6) and condemned Iraq's failure to treat the civilian population in accordance with international humanitarian law and to allow the ICRC to provide them with humanitarian assistance.

The *General Assembly*, in Resolution 46/135 of 17 December 1991 adopted after the conflict, requested Iraq to provide information on all Kuwaitis who had been

---

[63] Frits Kalshoven, (n 62) 55 ff, and the ICJ, *Legal Consequences of the Construction of a Wall in the Occupied Palestinian Territory* (Advisory Opinion), ICJ Reports 2004, Separate Opinion of Judge Kooijmans paras 46 ff, and Separate Opinion of Judge Higgins, para 39.

[64] ICJ, *Legal Consequences of the Construction of a Wall in the Occupied Palestinian Territory* (Advisory Opinion), ICJ Reports 2004, paras 158 f.

deported between 2 August 1990 and 26 February 1991 and had not yet returned; to release all such persons in accordance with its obligations under GC III, Article 118 and GC IV, Article 134; and to provide information on any such persons who had died while in detention in accordance with its obligations under GC III, Articles 120 and 127 and 129 and GC IV, 130.

The *Security Council* decided by Resolution 687/1991 of 3 April 1991 to create a fund that would be financed from the proceeds of Iraqi oil exports in order to compensate for damages arising from Iraq's occupation of Kuwait. The UN Compensation Commission (UNCC), which was established to assess claims for damages, paid compensation, *inter alia*, to victims of grave breaches of international humanitarian law.

Third, contracting states are required to prosecute war criminals. As already mentioned, the four Geneva Conventions and Additional Protocol I define what constitutes grave breaches of humanitarian law and impose an obligation on contracting states to punish such breaches as war crimes.[65] Pursuant to these provisions, contracting states are under an obligation to search for persons, regardless of their nationality, who are suspected of having committed war crimes and, where appropriate, to commit them for trial before their own courts or to extradite them to another contracting state (*aut dedere aut judicare* principle). The contracting parties are furthermore required 'to afford one another the greatest measure of assistance in connection with criminal proceedings brought in respect of grave breaches' of international humanitarian law.[66]

Lastly, other violations of international humanitarian law, which are not characterized as war crimes under international law, must be made punishable offences.

Additional Protocol II contains no obligation to prosecute breaches of international humanitarian law in a non-international armed conflict. However, the Rome Statute now enumerates a series of war crimes that can be committed in such circumstances.[67]

4. Limits on obligations

Unlike human rights law,[68] humanitarian law embodies not general approaches to limitations that would be applicable to all or at least to a large proportion of its guarantees, the main reason being that in most cases the provisions of the four Geneva Conventions and the two Additional Protocols determine the content of the rules and any exceptions in great detail. Nevertheless, international humanitarian law guarantees can be classified according to whether they are subject to

---

[65] GC I, Arts 49 and 59; GC II, Arts 50 and 51; GC III, Arts 129 and 130; GC IV, Arts 146 and 147; AP I, Arts 85 and 86.

[66] AP I, Art 88.   [67] Art 8(2) (c) and (e) of the Rome Statute.

[68] See Chapter 3, section III.2.b.

the following degrees of limitations: (1) guarantees that are absolute; (2) guarantees that are not subject to limitations but whose substantive scope of application is narrow with specific exceptions; and (3) guarantees that may be limited where this is deemed necessary to safeguard important and legitimate interests.

Examples of *absolute* guarantees are the common Article 3 prohibitions, which must be respected as minimum safeguards 'at any time and in any place whatsoever', in particular in non-international armed conflicts.[69] Other absolute guarantees include the prohibitions of collective punishment, terrorizing civilians and pillage (GC IV, Article 33); the prohibition of starvation of civilians as a method of warfare (AP I, Article 54(1) and AP II, Article 14); and the prohibition on punishing a person, 'for having carried out medical activities compatible with medical ethics, regardless of the person benefiting therefrom' (AP II, Article 10(1)). It is also absolutely prohibited, for example, to include regulations in the disciplinary regimes governing civilian internees that impose forms of 'physical exertion dangerous to their health or involving physical or moral victimisation' and to subject internees to 'punishment drill, military drill and manoeuvres, or the reduction of food rations' (GC IV, Article 100).

An example of a guarantee that is *not subject to limitation but has a narrow objective scope of application* is that contained in GC IV, Article 68(2); while this provision does not prohibit the death penalty for civilians in occupied territories, it limits capital punishment to an exhaustive list of carefully defined offences, permitting it only if 'such offences were punishable by death under the law of the occupied territory in force before the occupation began'. Also, Article 51 of Additional Protocol I is particularly important, since it defines in detail the kinds of attacks on civilians that are inadmissible, thus, at least implicitly, defining permissible attacks under humanitarian law.

Many guarantees are *subject to limitations* under the specific conditions defined in the relevant articles. For instance, GC IV, Article 23 requires states parties to allow the free passage of certain kinds of humanitarian relief for civilians but permits the refusal of authorization under certain exhaustively defined conditions, such as where the enemy could derive military advantage from the consignments. The deportation of civilians in occupied territories is prohibited unless 'the security of the population or imperative military reasons so demand' (GC IV, Article 49(1) and (2); likewise AP II, Article 17). It is prohibited to deprive civilians of foodstuffs necessary for their survival unless the foodstuffs 'are used by an adverse Party ... as sustenance solely for the members of its armed forces' (AP I, Article 54). Provisions of this kind generally stipulate that deviations from a prohibition or obligation are permissible where they are necessary

---

[69] The text of common Art 3 limits its scope of application to non-international armed conflicts but, as the ICJ has held in the case of *Military and Paramilitary Activities in and against Nicaragua (Nicaragua v The United States of America)*, ICJ Reports 1986, its obligations must, by virtue of international customary law, also be respected in situations of international armed conflict.

to safeguard or to realize an explicitly mentioned interest that is specifically characterized as legitimate.[70]

A legitimate interest, mentioned in many articles,[71] is that of 'military necessity' or 'imperative military requirements'. A measure is deemed to be militarily necessary if it must be undertaken in order to achieve a strategic advantage or even victory. This is a wide open concept with extremely vague contours and is therefore difficult to apply. There can obviously be no question of military necessity where a measure is motivated by political, racial, religious or other inadmissible ends, ie where the measure is taken on non-military grounds. For example, the forced evacuation of the civilian population from a particular area is prohibited if its purpose is ethnic cleansing or to make it easier to control an unpopular ethnic group.[72] Conversely, forced evacuation is allowed if the evacuating military power is planning to mount a major attack on the enemy that cannot be carried out without exposing the civilian population to great dangers, or 'if an area is liable to be subjected to intense bombing' justified by 'overriding military considerations'.[73] Another situation in which military necessity cannot be invoked is where a measure is militarily motivated but unnecessary to achieve the military aim; for example, the evacuation of civilians is prohibited where a limited military action can be conducted without major endangerment of civilians.[74] In all cases the specific circumstances must be assessed with the greatest possible care before the existence of military necessity can be confirmed.[75]

III. Scope of Application

1. Personal scope of application

The Geneva Conventions and their Additional Protocols regulate their personal scope of application in greater detail than human rights treaties. International humanitarian law recognizes three categories of persons who can invoke its guarantees to varying degrees. These categories are the following: (a) so-called 'protected persons' in international armed conflicts, who enjoy a high level of protection; (b) persons in the power of a party to an international armed conflict, who enjoy minimum guarantees; and (c) persons in the power of a party to a non-international armed conflict and who are not (or are no longer) taking part

---

[70] They thus resemble to some extent, in terms of structure, the conditions for encroaching on civil liberties, which can be restricted on grounds of public interest and subject to proportionality (see Chapter 3, section III.2.a.iii). Given the nature of armed conflicts, international humanitarian law, unlike international human rights law, does not require a basis in law for permissible limitations on guarantees.

[71] GC III, Arts 8, 75, 76, 126; GC IV, Arts 9, 16, 18, 30, 49, 53, 55, 57, 60, 108, 111, 112, 143, 147; AP II, Arts 54, 62, 67, 71 AP I; Art 17.

[72] Sandoz, Swinarski, and Zimmermann (n 16) 1742, para 4854, on AP II, Art 17.

[73] Pictet (n 11), vol IV, 279 ff on GC IV, Art 49.   [74] See, eg, Pictet (n 11), vol IV, 279.

[75] Sandoz, Swinarski, and Zimmermann (n 16), 1742, paras 4853 on AP II, Art 17.

in hostilities, who enjoy the minimum guarantees of common Article 3 and the more extensive guarantees of Additional Protocol II.

(a) Protected persons in an international armed conflict

International humanitarian law differentiates between two categories of protected persons: combatants and members of the civilian population. The two categories must be kept strictly separate and each is subject to its own legal regime.

(i) Combatants who have fallen into the hands of the adverse party

Combatants are persons who are taking an active part in hostilities. As the Inter-American Commission on Human Rights has stated, they have 'a license to kill or wound enemy combatants and destroy other enemy military objectives'.[76] They may not be punished for taking part in hostilities unless they commit war crimes or crimes against humanity. Conversely, they must consent to be the legitimate target of acts of violence by their military adversary that may prove fatal.

According to Geneva Conventions I–III, the term 'combatants' refers to all members of the armed forces of a party to the conflict, ie not only members of the regular armed forces but also members of militias and volunteer corps belonging to the party.[77] 'Members of other militias and members of other volunteer corps, including those of organized resistance movements, belonging to a Party to the conflict and operating in or outside their own territory, even if this territory is occupied', may claim the status of combatant if they fulfil the following conditions: '(a) that of being commanded by a person responsible for his subordinates; (b) that of having a fixed distinctive sign recognizable at a distance; (c) that of carrying arms openly; [and] (d) that of conducting their operations in accordance with the laws and customs of war'.[78]

Additional Protocol I dispenses with the distinction between armed forces and other groups fighting for the party to a conflict. Its Article 43(1) states in general terms that:

The armed forces of a Party to a conflict consist of all organized armed forces, groups and units which are under a command responsible to that Party for the conduct of its subordinates, even if that Party is represented by a government or an authority not recognized by an adverse Party. Such armed forces shall be subject to an internal disciplinary system which, inter alia, shall enforce compliance with the rules of international law applicable in armed conflict.

Pursuant to Article 44(3) of Additional Protocol I, anyone who does not carry his or her arms openly during a military operation forfeits combatant status.

---

[76] IACmHR, 'Report on Terrorism and Human Rights', OEA/Ser.L/-V/II.116 Doc 5 rev. 1 corr. 22, October 2002, para 68.
[77] GC I and II, Art 13(1); GC III, Art 4(A)(1).
[78] GC I and II, Art 13(2); GC III, Art 4(A)(2).

Combatants enjoy special protection:

- as wounded and sick members of armed forces in the field (GC I);
- as wounded, sick and shipwrecked members of armed forces at sea (GC II); or
- as prisoners of war (GC III);

when they have fallen into the hands of the adverse party.[79]

Issue in focus: Unlawful combatants?

Is a person who is participating in or affected by an international armed conflict—aside from mercenaries or spies who constitute explicit exceptions—in all cases either a combatant, a prisoner of war, or a civilian? Is the system of international humanitarian law closed or are there gaps insofar as persons who cannot be assigned to any of these categories are unable to invoke the protection under this body of law?

The ICRC takes the former view. In support of its position, it can cite, in particular, Article 50 of Additional Protocol I stating that any person who is not a combatant is a civilian and that in case of doubt a person must be considered to be a civilian. In the light of this classification, a person who is taken prisoner by the adverse party enjoys protection either as a prisoner of war under GC III or as a civilian internee under the special regime set out in GC IV, Articles 79ff. The ICTY is of the same opinion.[80]

The opposing view, held in particular by the United States, is based primarily on the argument that these two special regimes are inadequate in cases where terrorists, such as members of Al-Qaida in Afghanistan, are taken captive. Such persons are thus declared 'unlawful combatants' and are denied any claim to protection under international humanitarian law. This argument was used to deprive detainees in Guantánamo initially of all legal protection.

In this regard, two questions arise which must be kept separate: (1) Do prisoners such as those in Guantánamo have the right to claim treatment as prisoners of war? (2) Must they automatically be treated either as prisoners of war or as civilians, or does a third category of 'unlawful combatants' exist?

The first question is easy to answer: 'Should any doubt arise as to whether persons, having committed a belligerent act and having fallen into the hands of the enemy' are prisoners of war, they should, according to GC III, Article 5(2), enjoy the protection of that Convention, at least 'until such time as their status has been determined by a competent tribunal'. In other words, all persons who fell into American hands during the hostilities in Afghanistan are entitled to have their status examined. The prisoners in Guantánamo were long denied that right, until, on 29 June 2004, the United States Supreme Court ruled that prisoners

---

[79] On the content of these Conventions, see Chapter 2, section II.4.

[80] In the case *The Prosecutor v Delalic et al*, Case No IT-96-21-T (1998), the Trial Chamber of the ICTY invoked the commentary of the ICRC and concluded: '271. It is important, however, to note that this finding is predicated on the view that there is no gap between the Third and the Fourth Geneva Conventions. If an individual is not entitled to the protections of the Third Convention as a prisoner of war (or of the First or Second Conventions) he or she necessarily falls within the ambit of Convention IV, provided that its art 4 requirements are satisfied'.

in Guantánamo had the right to challenge the legality of their detention before United States courts.[81]

The second question is more complex. On the one hand, the concept of combatants in the 1949 Geneva Conventions does indeed contain loopholes, so that a person may not necessarily be classifiable, on the basis of these treaties alone, either as a combatant or as a civilian. On the other hand, the ICRC's assertion that there exist only the categories of combatants and civilians is based largely on the provisions of Additional Protocol I, which, having acquired the status of customary law,[82] are also binding on states that are not parties to the Protocol such as the United States.

It remains to be seen how this controversy will eventually be resolved. At any rate, the argument that the provisions concerning prisoners of war and civilians are not entirely adequate when it comes to addressing modern terrorist challenges cannot be rejected out of hand.[83] An undisputed point, however, is that all persons in the power of the adverse party, without exception, are entitled to invoke both human rights—primarily non-derogable core human rights—and the minimum provisions of Article 75 of Additional Protocol I that enjoy customary law status. Detention for an indeterminate period without any prospect of judicial review of its lawfulness or any formal indictment is diametrically opposed to the procedural rights set out in Article 75(4) of Additional Protocol I. It follows that, regardless of which theory is espoused, the long-term detention of persons suspected of terrorism without determination of their prisoner-of-war status, without the option of judicial review of their detention and without bringing charges against them is a violation of fundamental provisions of international human rights and humanitarian law.

(ii) The civilian population

According to Article 4 of GC IV, protected persons are enemy nationals who, as non-combatants, are in the hands of the adverse party or an occupying power. According to the same article, nationals of states that are not parties to the Convention and nationals of neutral or co-belligerent states that have normal diplomatic representation in the country concerned are not considered to be protected civilians.

---

[81] US Supreme Court, *Rasul v Bush*, case (03–334).

[82] See Henckaerts and Doswald-Beck (n 34), vol I, 17 ff, and vol II, Part I, 100 ff.

[83] If such prisoners are classified as combatants, they may not, unless they have committed war crimes, be punished for taking part in the armed conflict, they enjoy considerably more favourable conditions of detention than those charged for or convicted of a crime (GC III, Art 22), and the only statements they need make, under GC III, Art 17, are those required to establish their identity. If they are classified as civilians, on the other hand, while they may be interned if the security of the adverse party makes it 'absolutely necessary' (GC IV, Art 42), they are still entitled to have this decision reconsidered 'as soon as possible' by a court or administrative board and thereafter periodically, at least twice yearly (GC IV, Art 43), and they also enjoy considerably more favourable conditions of detention than criminals (GC IV, Arts 80 ff). Civilians may not be prosecuted by the occupying power, except in cases of war crimes, for offences committed before the occupation (GC IV, Art 70), and they may not, in particular, be deported from their country unless such deportation is necessary for their own security (GC IV, Art 49). This principle also applies to criminal proceedings before military courts of the occupying power, which must sit in the occupied territories (GC IV, Art 66), as well as to pre-trial detention or imprisonment on conviction (GC IV, Art 76). Furthermore, persons may be convicted, as a rule, only on the basis of the law of the occupied country and any laws enacted on exceptional grounds by the occupying power may not be retroactive (GC IV, Arts 64 and 65).

Article 50 of Additional Protocol I dispenses with these restrictions. Irrespective of nationalities, the article classifies everyone as a civilian who is not a member of armed forces, a member of militias belonging to a party to the conflict, a member of the armed forces of an unrecognized government; or a member of the population of a non-occupied territory who on the approach of the enemy spontaneously takes up arms to resist the invading forces (so-called '*levée en masse*'). These persons enjoy the protection of many of the provisions of both GC IV and Additional Protocol I.

GC IV establishes special regimes with more extensive and detailed protective provisions for *inhabitants of occupied territories* (GC IV, Articles 47 ff) and for *civilian internees* (GC IV, Articles 79 ff).

(b) Minimum obligations vis-à-vis all persons under the control of a party to an international armed conflict

In addition to the rules applicable to the category of protected persons, international humanitarian law establishes certain minimum obligations *vis-à-vis all* persons regardless of their nationality and status. In the case of *international* armed conflicts, Article 75 of Additional Protocol I, which has customary law status, contains a list of fundamental guarantees which protect the most important human rights (including due process rights in criminal proceedings) and which is applicable to all persons, regardless of their nationality who are in the power of a party to the conflict and are affected by the conflict, ie the civilian population as well as those taking part in combat.

(c) Obligations vis-à-vis all affected persons in a non-international armed conflict

In a non-international armed conflict, the minimum guarantees of common Article 3 are applicable to all persons *hors de combat*.[84]

In non-international armed conflicts reaching the threshold of conflicts as covered by Additional Protocol II[85] between insurgents and government forces, in which the insurgents have an organized army and exercise control over part of the country, the detailed provisions of Additional Protocol II are applicable, according to Article 2 'without any adverse distinction founded on race, colour, sex, language, religion or belief, political or other opinion, national or social origin, wealth, birth or other status, or on any other similar criteria ... to all persons affected by an armed conflict'.

2. Substantive scope of application

The substantive scope of application of international humanitarian law is determined by its numerous substantive guarantees.

---

[84] For an interpretation of this notion see ECtHR (Grand Chamber), *Korbely v Hungary*, Application No 9174/02 (2008), paras 86 ff.

[85] See above section I.3.

The four Geneva Conventions and their Additional Protocols contain no provisions on the admissibility of reservations. The general rule that reservations are admissible if they are consistent with the objective and purpose of the treaty is therefore applicable. States have entered a number of reservations, with reservations to the Additional Protocols being more numerous than to the four Geneva Conventions.

3. Territorial scope of application

The Geneva Conventions and Additional Protocol I are applicable in territories under the control of a party to the conflict and wherever a party engages in acts that affect persons protected by humanitarian law. This can be either in its own territory or in that of a foreign state. The territorial scope of Additional Protocol II is limited to the parts of a state's own territory in which a non-international armed conflict is taking place.

4. Temporal scope of application

(a) Situation-related scope of application

As already explained in detail (section I above), international humanitarian law is applicable only *during* international or non-international armed conflicts and during the military occupation of foreign territory. The applicability begins, except for obligations that are already binding in peacetime,[86] with the outbreak of the armed conflict, ie 'as soon as the first (protected) person is affected by the conflict, the first portion of territory occupied, the first attack launched, etc'.[87]

The applicability ends, as a rule, with 'the general close of military operations' (GC IV, Article 6(2) and AP I, Article 3(b)), or 'the end of the armed conflict' (AP II, Article 2(2)), ie the cessation of hostilities, unless there is some expectation of a renewed flare-up in the near future. It is irrelevant whether the cessation is marked by a formal peace agreement, a mere truce or the *de facto* termination of military activity. Some provisions remain in force beyond this point. They include, in particular, the provisions regarding prisoners of war, who remained protected by GC III until they are released (GC III, Article 5).

In occupied territories all provisions of GC IV must continue to be respected for a year after the end of military operations. Thereafter a number of specifically

---

[86] They include the enactment of criminal legislation required to bring war criminals to justice (GC I, Art 49; GC II, Art 50; GC III, Art 129; GC IV, Art 146; AP I, Art 80 in conjunction with Art 85), the obligation to instruct armed forces (GC I, Art 47; GC II Art 48; GC III, Art 127; GC IV, Art 144; AP I, Art 83, AP II, Art 19), and material preparations such as the identification of ambulances and military hospitals with the Red Cross or Red Crescent emblem.

[87] Marco Sassòli and Antoine Bouvier, *How Does Law Protect in War?: Cases, Documents and Teaching Materials on Contemporary Practice in International Humanitarian Law* (2nd edn, International Committee of the Red Cross: Geneva, 2006), 116.

defined guarantees remain in force until the occupation comes to an end (GC IV, Article 6(3)). Article 3(b) of Additional Protocol I extends the applicability of humanitarian law in general until the occupation is terminated. In both cases, provisions concerning the protection of interned and deported civilians must be respected until their release and repatriation, even if this occurs only after the end of occupation. In the case of non-international armed conflicts, guarantees for persons who have been detained or indicted remain in force after the end of the conflict for as long as such individuals remain subject to such measures (AP II, Article 2(2)).

Unlike human rights, the guarantees of international humanitarian law, as *lex specialis* governing the extraordinary circumstances of an armed conflict, cannot be *derogated from under any circumstances*.

(b) Entry into force and denunciation

The Geneva Conventions and their Additional Protocols enter into force for the respective contracting party six months after ratification.[88] If the state concerned becomes involved in an armed conflict before this period expires, the treaty concerned takes immediate effect in the case of an international conflict.[89]

Humanitarian law treaties can be denounced. The period of notification of denunciation is one year (six months in the case of AP II). However, where the denouncing party is involved at the time in an armed conflict, the denunciation does not take effect until it ends and protected persons such as prisoners of war and interned or deported civilians have been repatriated. Denunciation does not release parties from customary law obligations, including obligations arising 'from the usages established among civilized peoples, from the laws of humanity and the dictates of the public conscience'.[90] As a substantial proportion of international humanitarian law has now acquired customary status,[91] denunciation would release the state concerned from only a limited number of obligations.

IV. The Elements of a Violation of International Humanitarian Law

What constitutes, in legal terms, a violation of international humanitarian law by a state? This question can be answered, as in the case of the checklist for human rights violations, by running through the following series of questions.

---

[88]   GC III, Art 138; GC IV, Art 153; AP I, Art 95; AP II, Art 23.
[89]   GC III, Art 141; GC IV, Art 157.
[90]   This so-called 'Martens clause' is embodied in GC III, Art 142, GC IV, Art 158, AP I, Art 99 and AP II, Art 25.
[91]   See Chapter 2, section III.3.

Table 5.2. The constitutive elements of a violation of international humanitarian law

Element	Question		Outcome
1. Harm suffered	Has the victim suffered personal harm?	No: ⇨ Yes: ⇩	No violation
2. Scope of application	Is the victim protected by an international humanitarian law guarantee?		
(a) Situation-related	Is an international or non-international armed conflict taking place?	No: ⇨ Yes: ⇩	No violation
(b) Substantive	Is the guarantee in question applicable during the conflict in question? Has the state refrained from entering a reservation to the guarantee?	No: ⇨ Yes: ⇩	No violation
(c) Personal	Does the guarantee protect the category of persons to which the victim belongs?	No: ⇨ Yes: ⇩	No violation
(d) Territorial	Is the person under the control of the relevant party to the conflict?	No: ⇨ Yes: ⇩	No violation
(e) Temporal	Is the conflict still taking place or is it a guarantee that is applicable even after the cessation of hostilities?	No: ⇨ Yes: ⇩	No violation
3. Category of obligation	Has the state violated an obligation (a) to respect? (b) to protect? (c) to fulfil? (d) without discrimination?	No: ⇨ Yes: ⇩	No violation
4. Limitations	Is the guarantee in question absolute or does the violation always constitute prohibited conduct?	Yes: ⇨ No: ⇩	**Violation**
	Can the violation be legally justified?	Yes: ⇨ No: ⇩	No violation **Violation**

V. Simultaneous Application of International Humanitarian Law and Human Rights Law?

What kind of relationship exists between the guarantees of international human rights law and those of international humanitarian law? Can they be applied simultaneously to the same circumstances?

According to an old and now largely discredited *theory of separation*[92] of the two branches of law, human rights were created for peacetime and international humanitarian law for wartime and, thus, their conceptual basis is fundamentally different. This theory has been untenable for some time, at the very least since

---

[92] Eg, Henri Meyrowitz, 'Le droit de la guerre et les droits de l'homme', in *Revue du droit public et de la science politique en France et à l'étranger* (1972), 1095; Jean Pictet, *Le droit humanitaire et la protection des victimes de la guerre* (Institut Henry-Dunant: Leiden, 1973), 13.

the incorporation of the list of human rights relevant guarantees in Article 75 of Additional Protocol I and Article 4 of Additional Protocol II. The theory is furthermore incompatible with the simple fact that human rights must also be respected in wartime[93] and are derogable only to a limited extent.[94]

The ICRC has been the main proponent of the *complementarity theory*, according to which the two branches of law, though separate and non-overlapping, are nonetheless complementary. Meron went a step further with his *convergence theory*, which advocates the cumulative application of human rights guarantees and rules of international humanitarian law, where overlapping areas of regulation so permit, in order to maximize human protection in wartime.[95] According to this approach, the two branches of law constitute two institutionally separate aspects of a single system of human rights protection.[96]

A basis in law for the convergence theory exists, *inter alia*, in common Article 5(2) of the two Human Rights Covenants, according to which '[t]here shall be no restriction upon or derogation from any of the fundamental human rights recognized or existing in any State Party . . . on the pretext that the present Covenant does not recognize such rights or that it recognizes them to a lesser extent'. Conversely, the so-called Martens clause in international humanitarian law[97] requires states, regardless of their obligations under the Geneva Conventions and their Additional Protocols, to respect the obligations 'which the Parties to the conflict . . . remain bound to fulfil by virtue of the principles of the law of nations, as they result from the usages established among civilized peoples, from the laws of humanity and the dictates of the public conscience'. This body of law includes a large proportion of the rights contained in human rights treaties.

Notwithstanding the fact that humanitarian law and human rights law are complementary and overlap to some extent, the relationship between the two branches of law is complex. The International Court of Justice differentiates in this regard between three situations. Some rights fall exclusively within the scope of international humanitarian law;[98] others are guaranteed solely by human rights law;[99] and still others are subject to both branches of law.[100] Where both

---

[93] HRCttee, General Comment No 31 (2004), para 11. ICJ, *Legality of the Threat or Use of Nuclear Weapons* (Advisory Opinion), ICJ Reports 1996, para 25; *Legal Consequences of the Construction of a Wall in the Occupied Palestinian Territory* (Advisory Opinion), ICJ Reports 2004, para 106.

[94] For more detail, see Chapter 4, section IV.2.

[95] Theodor Meron, *Human Rights in Internal Strife: Their International Protection* (Cambridge University Press: Cambridge, 1987), 28.

[96] Meron, ibid.   [97] For example, GC IV, Art 158(5).

[98] For instance, human rights treaties contain no specific provisions regarding the rights of wounded soldiers.

[99] International humanitarian law takes no position, for example, on the right to marriage. Human rights law affords protection, for instance, in cases where GC IV, Art 4(2) leaves nationals of certain countries unprotected (neutral countries; allied countries with normal diplomatic representation in the state concerned).

[100] ICJ, *Legal Consequences of the Construction of a Wall in the Occupied Palestinian Territory* (Advisory Opinion), ICJ Reports 2004, para 106.

branches are applicable, the following scenarios are conceivable:

(1) In applying human rights guarantees, international humanitarian law provisions must be consulted on account of their more specific content[101] in order to determine the exact meaning and scope of the human rights concerned. In concrete terms this means, for example, that deprivation of life under ICCPR, Article 6 is not 'arbitrary' if it is permitted under international humanitarian law[102] or that restrictions on freedom of movement under ICCPR, Article 12 can be justified if their purpose is the evacuation of the civilian population from a particular area by an occupying power where 'the security of the population' or 'imperative military reasons' (GC IV, Article 49(2)) so demand.

(2) Conversely, human rights guarantees may play an important role in giving specific content to open-ended rules of international humanitarian law. The core content of the procedural guarantees in human rights treaties now sheds light on what is meant by the obligation, under common Article 3, to respect 'the judicial guarantees which are recognized as indispensable by civilized peoples' when handing down a death sentence, and in what circumstances a military court, according to GC III, Article 84(2), 'does not offer the essential guarantees of independence and impartiality as generally recognized'.

(3) Lastly, provisions of the two branches of law may in some circumstances be applicable cumulatively. For instance, when states parties to the ICCPR impose a death sentence on prisoners of war pursuant to GC III, Article 100, they must respect all the non-derogable safeguards set out in ICCPR. Article 6(2). At the same time, they may not execute the person sentenced to death before the expiry of the six-month waiting period laid down in GC III, Article 101, although the ICCPR makes no provision for such a delay.

---

[101] The ICJ refers in this connection to *lex specialis* (ibid, paras 105 f); however, it does not use the term to mean specific provisions pre-empting the more general rules of human rights law but rather specific rules that are relevant when it comes to determining the content of the general rule.

[102] See Chapter 9, section II.2.d.

PART II

IMPLEMENTATION OF HUMAN RIGHTS

6

Basic Principles

I. Functions of Implementation

The possibility to implement and to enforce implementation is a characteristic fundamental to any law. If human rights guarantees are to amount to more than lofty declarations of intent, their realization and implementation at the domestic level must not be left to the discretion of states; rather, international monitoring is necessary. Under traditional international law, reciprocal interests provide a strong incentive for states to abide by their obligations. That is, state parties obey treaty provisions so as not to face the consequences when other state parties decide to break them in turn.[1] There is, however, no such incentive for self-enforcement in the case of human rights obligations which lack a clear element of reciprocity. It follows that implementation and enforcement procedures at the international level are particularly necessary in the area of human rights law, a circumstance that may at least partly account for the proliferation of such mechanisms in this branch of law. By contrast, the emphasis in international humanitarian law—in keeping with its historic origins—is on reciprocal obligations. Accordingly, in international humanitarian law, international implementation mechanisms play only a very subordinate role.

Human rights implementation mechanisms may perform the following main functions:

(1) *Stopping ongoing human rights violations* by ensuring that action to do so is indeed taken.

(2) *Remedying violations* by ensuring that states provide reparation where human rights violations cannot be halted, or where by their very nature they occur before mechanisms can intervene (eg extrajudicial killings). The remedial function places violating states under the obligation to make reparation (particularly in the forms of compensation or rehabilitation of the victims).

(3) *Punishing persons responsible for violations* through international criminal law mechanisms and through obligations to prosecute at the domestic level under

---

[1] For example, if state A fails to extradite a person to state B under an extradition treaty, it runs the risk of state B also withholding its cooperation.

Table 6.1. Levels and categories of human rights mechanisms

Domestic level		International level		
	Decentralized (interstate) mechanisms:	**Centralized (international) mechanisms**		
		Human rights mechanisms		*Criminal tribunals*
• Legislation • Administrative procedures • Judicial procedures • Activities of national human rights institutions	• Bilateral technical assistance • Human rights dialogues • Protests • Sanctions	Treaty bodies: • UN Committees • Regional human rights commissions and courts	Charter-based bodies: • Human Rights Council / General Assembly • Security Council • International Court of Justice	• International Criminal Court (ICC) • *Ad hoc* tribunal (ICTY, ICTR, etc)

certain human rights treaties intending to hold individuals acting on behalf of states or of non-state actors accountable.

(4) *Preventing violations* by ensuring states, in future, are effectively aware of their obligations to respect, protect and fulfil human rights, thereby preventing fresh violations.

This chapter presents an overview of the human rights implementation and enforcement regime and its underlying general principles. The subsequent chapters deal first with the international treaty-based human rights bodies established by human rights conventions (treaty-based bodies) to monitor the implementation of the treaties concerned (Chapter 7) and then with the Charter-based human rights protection mechanisms that have been established on the bases of the UN Charter and the founding treaties of regional organizations (Charter-based bodies) (Chapter 8).

II. Domestic Implementation of Human Rights

1. Overview

Responsibility for implementing and enforcing human rights[2] lies primarily with states, as they are the bearers of human rights obligations stemming from both customary and treaty law, and because the principle of territorial sovereignty

---

[2] On the concept of the Responsibility to Protect (R2P) see Chapter 8, section III.1.

enables them to take the necessary measures within their own territory. States cannot shirk this obligation by invoking sovereignty; indeed it is precisely on account of their sovereignty that they bear responsibility for the protection of people within their territory. International monitoring and implementation mechanisms complement domestic judicial procedures, playing a subsidiary role where domestic bodies are unable or unwilling to prevent, end, remedy, or punish human rights violations.

The choice of means of domestic implementation is largely a decision to be taken by individual states. However, international law imposes certain minimum requirements. Thus, states are bound:

- to allow individuals to invoke human rights at the domestic level (*duty to incorporate*) and to seek an effective domestic legal remedy in the event of violations (*duty to provide a legal remedy*);
- to investigate alleged violations (*duty to investigate*) and, in cases of particularly serious violations, to bring criminal charges against perpetrators (*duty to prosecute and punish*);
- to compensate or rehabilitate victims of violations (*duty to provide reparation*); and
- to prevent future violations (*duty to prevent*).

States have a comparatively free hand in choosing how to fulfil these duties and what bodies to entrust with the task. In addition to judicial bodies, they may assign responsibility, for example, to administrative authorities, national human rights commissions, ombudsman's offices, or truth commissions.

Issue in focus: Independent national human rights institutions[3]

In recent years, the UN and regional organizations have stressed the desirability of establishing *independent national human rights institutions*—if possible in all states. According to the 'Paris Principles'[4] adopted by the UN General Assembly in 1993, the structure and mandate of such institutions should enable them to address specific shortcomings in a state's implementation of human rights and to serve as a bridge between different branches of the administration and civil society. Depending on the country concerned, national human rights institutions, which assume a variety of different forms (eg National Human Rights Commission, Ombudspersons, National Human Rights Institutes), perform, *inter alia*, the following functions: systematic and independent monitoring of the human rights situation; investigation of specific violations or problems with implementation; dealing with individual cases and performing ombudsman functions; offering advice to both individuals and government; enhancing awareness among the

---

[3] See the website of the National Human Rights Institutions Forum <www.nhri.net> (accessed 6 February 2009).

[4] 'Principles relating to the status and functioning of national institutions for protection and promotion of human rights', UN Doc A/Res/48/134.

general public, the administration and lawmakers; promoting professional expertise in the area of human rights; and making proposals for the improvement of legislation.

   To be able to perform these functions, national human rights institutions must, according to the 'Paris Principles', have a pluralist membership, be independent in both personal and institutional terms, have a constitutional or at least a legislative basis, and be able to rely on adequate funding. Globally, there are now about 60 national human rights institutions, with each continent represented, that comply with the 'Paris Principles'.

2. Specific duties

(a) Duty to incorporate human rights and to provide effective remedies

The main human rights treaties provide individuals with the right to take action at the domestic level against decisions by state bodies that violate their human rights. Article 2(3)(a) of the ICCPR obliges states parties to 'ensure that any person whose rights or freedoms as herein recognized are violated shall have an effective remedy, notwithstanding that the violation has been committed by persons acting in an official capacity'. At the regional level, ECHR, Article 13 guarantees that anyone whose rights under the Convention are violated 'shall have an effective remedy before a national authority notwithstanding that the violation has been committed by persons acting in an official capacity'. Similar guarantees are contained in ACHR, Article 25 and ArCHR, Article 23. Other treaties take it for granted that such a right exists when they stipulate that victims of alleged human rights violations must exhaust domestic remedies before having recourse to an international body.[5]

   International law does not compel states to allow individuals to invoke human rights treaties directly before domestic bodies. It is sufficient if individuals can seek remedies for alleged violations of domestic constitutional safeguards or legal provisions containing guarantees analogous to the state's international human rights obligations. States are also free to opt either for automatic applicability of human rights treaties in domestic law[6] or for transformation of their content into domestic law through legislation.[7] The only essential requirement is that individuals can invoke at least *the substance* of the human rights binding the state concerned.

---

[5] Eg, CAT, Art 22(5)(b) and CERD, Art 14(7)(a).

[6] Under what is known in international law as 'monism', which exists, for example, in Switzerland, Austria, and the United States of America and is now practised in many Central and Eastern European states.

[7] Under what is known in international law as 'dualism'. The transformation of international law into domestic law occurs either through a statute that reproduces the content of the treaty (thus, the United Kingdom incorporated the content of the ECHR into domestic law through the Human Rights Act 1998) or through a so-called 'act of consent' (*Zustimmungsgesetz*), which merely states that the corresponding treaty has force of law (a procedure followed in Germany).

The lack of effective legal remedies or the denial of access to existing remedies may in itself amount to a human rights violation.[8] However, the entitlement to an effective legal remedy does not create a right of access to a court.[9] It is sufficient if relief may be sought from any judicial or administrative authority, provided the body enjoys sufficient independence *vis-à-vis* the authority that took the original decision and has jurisdiction to quash the impugned decision or to order reparation.[10] Moreover, in order to be effective, a remedy must be dealt with within a reasonable time limit[11] and have suspensive effect in cases of immediate threat of human rights violations with irreversible consequences.[12]

The right to an effective remedy does not mean that all allegations of human rights violations, 'no matter how unmeritorious', must have access to remedy at the domestic level. While persons wishing to lodge complaints are not required to prove that they are victims of an actual violation, such allegations must be 'arguable' under the invoked treaty, ie seem to be at least sufficiently plausible to warrant an examination.[13]

Example: The ECtHR judgment in *Jabari v Turkey*[14]

Ms Jabari applied for asylum in Turkey because she feared she would be stoned in Iran for adultery. However, as she failed to submit the required documents within five days of her arrival, the Turkish authorities rejected her application and ordered that she be returned to Iran. Although she could appeal the deportation order, the court reviewing the order only examined whether the deportation was lawful under Turkish domestic law, had no power to scrutinize the claim that Ms Jabari would be at risk in Iran, and was unable to provide remedies with suspensive effect. Given the real risk of stoning in Iran, the European Court of Human Rights concluded that a decision to deport the applicant would have constituted inhuman treatment, under ECHR, Article 3. It further held that Article 13 had been violated because the remedy provided by Turkish law had not been 'effective'. The Court stated in this regard:

50. In the Court's opinion, given the irreversible nature of the harm that might occur if the risk of torture or ill-treatment alleged materialised and the importance which it attaches to Article 3, the notion of an effective remedy under Article 13 requires independent and rigorous

---

[8] ICCPR, Art 2(3); ACHR, Art 25; ArCHR, Art 23; ECHR, Art 13.

[9] Such a right exists under ICCPR, Art 14; under ECHR, Art 6 in respect of disputes of a civil character (suit at law) and the determination of criminal charges; according to ACHR, Art 8 'in the substantiation of any accusation of a criminal nature made against him or for the determination of his rights and obligations of a civil, labor, fiscal, or any other nature'; and under ArCHR, Art 13 regarding criminal charges and procedures on a person's rights or obligations.

[10] For example, ECtHR (Grand Chamber), *Sürmeli v Germany*, Application No 75529/01 (2006), para 98.

[11] See eg, HRCttee, *Rajapakse v Sri Lanka*, Communication No 1250/2004 (2006), para 9.5.

[12] Ibid, para 50.

[13] HRCttee, *Kazantzis v Cyprus*, Communication No 972/2001 (2003), para 6.6, and *Faure v Australia*, Communication No 1036/01 (2005), para 7.2, as well as ECtHR, *Boyle and Rice v The United Kingdom*, Series A, No 131 (1988), para 52.

[14] ECtHR, *Jabari v Turkey*, *Reports* 2000-VIII.

scrutiny of a claim that there exist substantial grounds for fearing a real risk of treatment contrary to Article 3 and the possibility of suspending the implementation of the measure impugned. Since the Ankara Administrative Court failed in the circumstances to provide any of these safeguards, the Court is led to conclude that the judicial review proceedings relied on by the Government did not satisfy the requirements of Article 13.

(b) Duty to investigate, prosecute and punish

It is clear from the views of the UN Human Rights Committee and the jurisprudence of the European Court of Human Rights and the American Court of Human Rights, that—at least in the event of violations of particularly important rights such as the prohibition of torture and the right to life, or in cases of enforced disappearance of persons—states parties must conduct an *effective investigation* and *prosecute* as well as punish the persons responsible for such violations under domestic law. According to the jurisprudence of the Inter-American Court of Human Rights, amnesty rules which hinder the criminal prosecution of persons responsible for the violation of non-derogable guarantees or crimes against humanity are not compatible with the duty to punish.[15]

Example: The ECtHR judgment in *Ergi v Turkey*[16]

In addition, the Court has attached particular weight to the procedural requirement implicit in Article 2 of the Convention. It recalls that, according to its case-law, the obligation to protect the right to life under Article 2, read in conjunction with the State's general duty under Article 1 to 'secure to everyone within their jurisdiction the rights and freedoms defined in [the] Convention', requires by implication that there should be some form of effective official investigation when individuals have been killed as a result of the use of force by, *inter alia*, agents of the State. Thus, contrary to what is asserted by the Government…, this obligation is not confined to cases where it has been established that the killing was caused by an agent of the State. Nor is it decisive whether members of the deceased's family or others have lodged a formal complaint about the killing with the competent investigatory authority. In the case under consideration, the mere knowledge of the killing on the part of the authorities gave rise ipso facto to an obligation under Article 2 of the Convention to carry out an effective investigation into the circumstances surrounding the death.

Some human rights treaties expressly incorporate obligations to prosecute and punish in their text. For instance, the Convention against Torture and the Convention on the Protection of All Persons from Enforced Disappearances oblige states parties to investigate allegations of torture or enforced disappearance[17] and to ensure that such acts, or attempts to commit such acts, are offences under their criminal law.[18]

---

[15] IACtHR, *Chumbipuma Aguirre and Others v Peru* (Barrios Altos Case), Series C, No 75 (2001) paras 41 ff, and *Almonacid-Arellano et al v Chile*, Series C, No 154 (2006), paras 108 ff.
[16] ECtHR, *Ergi v Turkey, Reports* 1998-IV, para 82.   [17] CAT, Art 12; CPAPED, Art 3.
[18] CAT, Art 4 and CPAPED, Arts 4 and 6. A similar obligation to prosecute is contained in CERD (Art 2 in conjunction with Art 5), and in the Convention on the Prevention and Punishment of the Crime of Genocide (Art III).

These Conventions furthermore enshrine the *principle of universal jurisdiction*. According to this principle, states parties must prosecute a person suspected of having committed acts of torture or enforced disappearance even where the alleged acts occurred abroad and against foreign nationals.[19] This means, for example, that third states have jurisdiction to prosecute former dictators who ordered acts of torture or enforced disappearance if their state of origin is unable or unwilling to do so, for instance on account of amnesty legislation. Alternatively, states have the possibility of extraditing the alleged offender to the state with primary responsibility.[20] This approach, known under the principle of *aut dedere aut judicare*, also exists in international humanitarian law.[21]

These principles are of vital importance for the implementation of human rights because incidences of impunity, ie climates in which those responsible for human rights violations remain unpunished, have increasingly proved to be one of the main reasons for the persistence of systematic and serious human rights violations.

(c) Duty to provide reparation

A number of universal and regional treaties contain explicit provisions requiring states parties to make reparation for human rights violations. This duty is laid down in particularly clear terms in CERD, Article 6 and CPAPED, Article 24(4) and (5). Similarly, CAT, Article 14 provides that the states parties must ensure that 'the victim of an act of torture obtains redress and has an enforceable right to fair and adequate compensation including the means for as full rehabilitation as possible'. Lastly, in cases where children are victims of 'any form of neglect, exploitation, or abuse; torture or any other form of inhuman or degrading treatment; or armed conflict,' Article 39 of the CRC imposes an obligation on states to take 'all appropriate measures to promote physical and psychological recovery and social reintegration' of the child. The general human rights conventions also impose a duty to make reparation in specific circumstances, especially in the event of unlawful arrest or detention.[22]

Furthermore, according to the views of the Human Rights Committee and the jurisprudence of the American as well as the European Courts of Human Rights, states have an obligation to provide compensation or some other form of reparation to persons who have successfully asserted a claim. This jurisprudence is based indirectly on the obligation to provide effective remedies and, in the case of the ECHR and ACHR, on the Courts' subsidiary authority to award fair compensation themselves.[23]

---

[19] In other words, without reference to traditional criminal law criteria of jurisdiction: the territoriality principle and the active and passive personality principle.

[20] CAT, Art 5(2) and CPAPED, Art 9(2) and 11.   [21] Eg, GC IV, Art 146.

[22] ICCPR, Art 9(5); ECHR, Art 5(5); ArCHR, Art 14(7). See also ICCPR, Art 14(6) and Art 10 ACHR and Art 19(2) ArCHR concerning compensation in the event of wrongful conviction for a criminal offence.

[23] ECHR, Art 41: 'If the Court finds that there has been a violation of the Convention or the protocols thereto, and if the internal law of the High Contracting Party concerned allows only

These rules are important because, while international law imposes an obligation on states to make reparation to injured states for their internationally wrongful acts,[24] it is questionable whether under customary law such an obligation also exists towards individuals, including a state's own citizens. It follows that, aside from treaties with corresponding provisions, a general obligation to compensate arguably does not yet exist in the area of human rights. However, the Principles and guidelines on the right to a remedy and reparation for victims of gross violations of international human rights law and serious violations of humanitarian law, adopted by the UN General Assembly in 2005[25] state that 'victims of gross violations of international human rights law and serious violations of international humanitarian law should, as appropriate and proportional to the gravity of the violation and the circumstances of each case, be provided with full and effective reparation' including restitution and compensation.

(d) Duty to prevent

The effective implementation of human rights also imposes an obligation to act in advance, where possible, to prevent violations. This duty is achieved through preventive measures. There are, however, few explicit treaty-based obligations to prevent human rights violations. By CAT, Article 2 each state party is required to take 'effective legislative, administrative, judicial or other measures to prevent acts of torture in any territory under its jurisdiction'.[26] The Convention against Racial Discrimination, the Convention on the Elimination of Discrimination against Women, and the Convention against Enforced Disappearances also provide for preventive action by requiring states to take certain legislative and administrative measures.[27] While there is no evidence of a general obligation to prevent, which if breached would constitute a violation of international law, there are strong grounds for arguing that such an obligation may be inferred from the general obligation to protect under human rights law[28] at least in cases where violations are foreseeable and where the state is in a position to take concrete and effective preventive measures.

---

partial reparation to be made, the Court shall, if necessary, afford just satisfaction to the injured party.' A similar provision is contained in ACHR, Art 63.

[24] Thus, if a state acts against the interests of the national of a foreign state that are protected under human rights law, it is required to make reparation to that state; see Arts 34 ff of the ILC draft Articles on State Responsibility 'Report of the ILC on its fifty-third session' (2001), UN Doc A/56/10, Supplement No 10 (*Official Records of the General Assembly*).

[25] UN General Assembly Resolution 60/147 (2005). However, some states still seem to be somewhat sceptical about whether such rules should be recognized. See, for example, an expert opinion by the International Law Section of the Swiss Ministry of Foreign Affairs of 10 July 2000, published in *Verwaltungspraxis der Bundesbehörden* (VPB), 66.126.

[26] See also CAT, Art 16 according to which each state party is required 'to prevent in any territory under its jurisdiction other acts of cruel, inhuman or degrading treatment or punishment...'.

[27] CERD, Art 2(c) and (d); CEDAW, Art 2; CPAPED, Arts 23 and 24.

[28] See above, Chapter 3, section III.3.

III. International Implementation Mechanisms

Until far into the twentieth century, international law was a highly decentralized legal regime devoid of any law-making or law-implementing bodies at a level above the states. States had the right and the ability to enforce their legal claims against a violating state by themselves, using a variety of means, ranging from negotiations, arbitration and non-violent coercive measures (known as reprisals) to the use of force. Apart from the prohibition of the use of force,[29] these methods known as *decentralized enforcement*, still exist. They have, however, been increasingly supplanted since the end of the Second World War by 'centralized' monitoring and implementation mechanisms by bodies situated at the supranational level.

1. Decentralized implementation

Notwithstanding the existence of numerous centralized implementation mechanisms (see Section 2), human rights continue to form part of general international law and can therefore be enforced by states themselves through traditional bilateral mechanisms. States are entitled to resort to such procedures:

- On the one hand, by invoking the right of *diplomatic protection* where the human rights of their nationals are violated in a foreign state. In invoking diplomatic protection, the state of origin is not enforcing the rights of the victims in question but asserting its own claim to have its nationals treated in accordance with international law, ie affirming its own interests. Nevertheless, where this action is successful, it helps to secure implementation of the human rights of the individual concerned in the specific case;
- On the other hand, as a direct consequence of the fact that a state's human rights obligations are owed to all contracting parties (obligations *erga omnes partes*) or, in the case of customary law obligations, to the community of states as a whole (obligations *erga omnes*). Claimant states are therefore entitled, as 'representatives' of the international community to insist that a violating state abide by human rights obligations even where those affected are exclusively the nationals of the violating state.

Bilateral action against a violating state is permitted even where an international monitoring and implementation mechanism is available. In this sense, human rights treaties are not so-called self-contained regimes, ie legal regimes that can be enforced only by means provided for in the treaty concerned.[30] Decentralized

---

[29] Under Art 2(4) of the UN Charter, states are required to refrain in their international relations from the threat or use of military force against another state.

[30] This classification has practical implications; otherwise states would have their hands tied in the event of violations of a treaty endowed with only rudimentary enforcement mechanisms, such as the UN conventions with treaty bodies that cannot hand down binding decisions.

action may thus directly compete with the treaty-based mechanisms that states can invoke. For instance, a state party to the ICCPR is not obliged to file a state complaint against another state party in the event of a violation of Covenant rights, but can resort to bilateral means. It is also permissible for a state to join with other like-minded countries to take measures such as economic sanctions against a violating state in the interest of furthering the general interest in securing respect for human rights.

What *means* can be deployed by a state or a group of states to induce another state to respect human rights?

(1) States can endeavour by means of diplomacy (representations, communication of lists of political prisoners whose release is demanded, etc) and negotiations to persuade foreign governments to halt particular violations or to improve the overall human rights situation.

(2) States can assist countries with human rights problems to improve the situation by means of advice, training, financial support and practical projects. This approach is particularly helpful where a state is in transition from an authoritarian to a democratic regime or engaged in a process of reform, for example in the aftermath of an armed conflict. Human rights projects have now become a standard component of development cooperation.

Issue in focus: Human rights dialogues

The focus of human rights dialogues between the EU and several Western countries and a number of states in the South is not on criticism of shortcomings in the human rights situation in a particular state, but rather on helping the state concerned to create and strengthen a legal and institutional framework that is in conformity with human rights standards.[31] In theory, only states that demonstrate a willingness to improve their human rights record, or states whose human rights shortcomings are due to a lack of know-how and infrastructure are eligible as partners in this kind of dialogue. In terms of content, bilateral human rights dialogues usually consist of institutionalized contacts with a range of government agencies and, if possible, with representatives of civil society and of practical projects such as training of members of the security forces, expert cooperation in the area of law enforcement and support for human rights defenders. Following the example of the 'Berne Process', a number or EU states along with Switzerland, Australia, Norway and Canada are currently seeking to coordinate their dialogues in terms of content and choice of partner states in order to enhance their effectiveness. Where human rights dialogues are conducted seriously by both parties, they may be viewed as a highly promising and creative tool for non-confrontational bilateral implementation of human rights. Critics say, however, that these dialogues often serve as nothing more than a convenient fig leaf for a state's inconsistent foreign policy *vis-à-vis* an important trading partner that systematically violates human rights.

---

[31] The EU is currently engaged in human rights dialogues with China, Iran, and Uzbekistan.

(3) When dealing with violators of human rights, states are free to take steps which may constitute an unfriendly act in the eyes of the country affected, but which are not in fact prohibited under international law. Traditional examples of such *retorsions* are public condemnations, the severing of diplomatic relations and trade restrictions.

(4) States are also entitled to resort to countermeasures against states parties that seriously violate a human rights treaty or against states that violate customary law with obligations *erga omnes*.[32] Countermeasures are defined as measures prohibited in principle by international law, such as non-application of a treaty or confiscation of foreign property, but permissible when used proportionately against a state that has itself violated international law in order to compel it to perform its obligations. Countermeasures that violate the prohibition of the use of force or other peremptory norms of international law are forbidden in all cases.

Example: Trade sanctions against Myanmar

The measures taken by many states against the military junta in Myanmar are a typical example of decentralized measures that can be brought against states that violate human rights. When an attempt by the UN to get all states to adopt binding measures against Myanmar failed, the EU issued several regulations in 2000 imposing economic sanctions. They were revised and sharpened at the beginning of 2008 in reaction to the violence used against peaceful demonstrations in September 2007:[33]

Article 2
(1) Annex I shall include goods belonging to the following categories:
  (a) round logs, timber and timber products;
  (b) coal and certain metals; and
  (c) precious and semi-precious stones.
(2) It shall be prohibited:
  (a) to import goods listed in Annex I, if such goods (i) originate in Burma/ Myanmar; or (ii) have been exported from Burma/Myanmar;
  (b) to purchase goods located in Burma/Myanmar which are listed in Annex I;
  (c) to transport goods listed in Annex I, if such goods originate in Burma/ Myanmar or are being exported from Burma/ Myanmar to any other country, and their final destination is in the Community; or

---

[32] The conditions governing permissible countermeasures are set out in Arts 49 ff of the ILC draft Articles on State Responsibility (n 24). The ILC left open whether states not directly concerned by a violation of international public law could resort to countermeasures against the offender (see Art 54 of the ILC draft Articles). However, the practice of many states and many legal writers accept this possibility. In our view, a state is entitled to resort to countermeasures against another state, when the latter has grievously and systematically violated human rights, even if the victims of these violations were exclusively citizens of the offending state.

[33] Council Regulation (EC) No 194/2008 of 25 February 2008 renewing and strengthening the restrictive measures in respect of Myanmar (Burma) and repealing Regulation (EC) No 817/2006, *Bulletin of the European Union* L66/1, 10 March 2008.

(d) to participate, knowingly and intentionally, in activities whose object or effect is, directly or indirectly, to circumvent the prohibitions in points (a), (b) or (c).

…

Article 4

(1) It shall be prohibited to sell, supply, transfer or export, directly or indirectly, equipment which might be used for internal repression as listed in Annex II, whether or not originating in the Community, to any natural or legal person, entity or body in, or for use in Burma/Myanmar.

Article 11

(1) All funds and economic resources belonging to, owned, held or controlled by the individual members of the Government of Burma/Myanmar and to the natural or legal persons, entities or bodies associated with them, as listed in Annex VI, shall be frozen.

(2) No funds or economic resources shall be made available, directly or indirectly, to or for the benefit of natural or legal persons, entities or bodies listed in Annex VI.

(3) The participation, knowingly and intentionally, in activities the object or effect of which is, directly or indirectly, to promote the transactions referred to at paragraphs 1 and 2 shall be prohibited.

(4) The prohibition set out in paragraph 2 shall not give rise to liability of any kind on the part of the natural or legal persons or entities concerned, if they did not know, and had no reasonable cause to suspect, that their actions would infringe this prohibition. (…)

2. Centralized monitoring and implementation mechanisms

(a) Types of bodies

Establishing bodies at the international level to monitor the implementation of human rights by states was from the beginning an important part of treaty-making in this area. The regional model, created by the 1950 European Human Rights Convention in the form of the European Commission of Human Rights[34] and the European Court of Human Rights, heavily influenced treaties elaborated by the United Nations. Yet a lack of consensus prevented establishment at the global level of courts with jurisdiction to hand down binding judgments. Instead, the system which evolved at the universal and to some extent also at the regional level consists, in simplified terms, of the following components:

(1) *Monitoring bodies*, which are called for in most human rights treaties (*treaty bodies*) and are mandated to secure compliance with the relevant treaty obligations. These bodies include Committees entrusted with the task of monitoring the principal UN human rights treaties and the regional Commissions and Courts of Human Rights.[35]

---

[34] The Commission was abolished by P 11/ECHR in 1998.   [35] See Chapter 7.

(2) *Intergovernmental (political) bodies based on the UN Charter* and the founding treaties if regional organizations (Charter-based bodies). Chief among these is the UN Human Rights Council.[36] Since the early 1990s, the UN Security Council[37] has also played some role in enforcing human rights through coercive measures under Chapter VII of the Charter.

(3) *The International Court of Justice*[38] which, albeit not accessible for victims of human rights violations, may be asked by states or UN organs to express itself on human rights issues.

(4) *International criminal tribunals*, which can hold individuals accountable for war crimes and crimes against humanity.

(b) Types of procedure

(i) Treaty-based and Charter-based procedures

Depending on the body before which they take place, human rights monitoring and implementation procedures are classified as either treaty-based (conventional) or Charter-based.

- *Treaty-based procedures* (see Chapter 7) follow detailed and strict procedural rules, that are exclusively based on the substantial guarantees of the treaty concerned and, depending on the treaty result in decisions or conclusions with considerable quasi-judicial authority or full fledged judgment;

- By contrast, procedures before *Charter-based bodies* (see Chapter 8) are often determined by circumstances on an *ad hoc* basis; their outcome is frequently influenced by political considerations, they can be discontinued at any stage; and result in resolutions and recommendations which derive their authority mainly from their political significance.

(ii) Different types of treaty-based procedures

The UN human rights treaties provide for different kinds of implementation mechanisms. All treaty monitoring bodies have to examine *state reports* that states parties are required to submit periodically as a form of self-assessment.[39] Most treaty bodies are furthermore empowered to consider communications by a state against another state alleged of having violated human rights (*inter-state complaints*).[40] Moreover, they are authorized under certain circumstances to rule on communications submitted by victims of human rights violations against the violating state (*individual complaints*).[41] Some treaties bodies are also mandated to undertake what amount to fact-finding *inquiries and inspections*.[42]

---

[36] See Chapter 8, section II.   [37] See Chapter 8, section III.
[38] See Chapter 8, section IV.   [39] Chapter 7, section II.   [40] Chapter 7, section IV.1.
[41] Chapter 7, section III.   [42] Chapter 7, sections IV.2 and 3.

These procedures may be divided into:

- *Non-contentious* procedures, such as reporting procedures, or fact-finding procedures and inspections by a body entrusted with such competence by the treaty; and
- *Contentious* procedures, such as individual communications and complaints and interstate complaints.

The extent to which the individual treaty monitoring bodies are mandated to conduct these various procedures is varied and determined by the respective treaty. The different levels of competence may be classified as follows:

(1) *procedures*: In this case, the state party automatically recognizes a particular procedure when it ratifies the treaty in question. Examples of compulsory procedures are the reporting procedures under the UN human rights treaties and the ACPHR and ArCHR and the individual complaint procedure under the ECHR.

(2) *Compulsory procedures with an opting-out clause*: In this case, a particular procedure is automatically applicable unless the state party expressly declares its non-acceptance on ratification. This option corresponds to a standardized reservation and is provided for, *inter alia*, in the case of the inquiry procedure under Article 20, read in conjunction with Article 28, of the Convention against Torture.

(3) *Optional acceptance of a procedure*: by means of a unilateral declaration (eg interstate complaint procedures under the ICCPR) or by ratification of an additional treaty (usually a protocol, eg individual complaint procedures under the ICCPR-OP).

As a rule, treaty-based procedures enjoy considerable legal authority, since they have been explicitly accepted by states. Political mechanisms, on the other hand, have the advantage of being applicable to all states. This is particularly useful in practice, because while most states with a problematic human rights record have ratified some of the core human rights treaties, their recognition of the competence of the monitoring bodies tends to be very limited. As a result, only the Charter-based mechanisms are available to keep their human rights situation under surveillance.

(c) Criminal procedures

International criminal procedures (see section IV) make it possible to reach beyond the level of the state in order to ensure that, in the event of systematic violations of human rights, the persons responsible can be held directly accountable.

(d) Overview: enforcement of international humanitarian law

There was originally no provision under international humanitarian law for monitoring bodies as such. Instead, the states parties themselves were supposed to secure compliance with these obligations by means of criminal prosecution at the domestic level. More recently, international criminal tribunals (see section IV) have become an important means to enforce international humanitarian law, since they generally have jurisdiction to prosecute war crimes and hence to investigate compliance with obligations under international humanitarian law.

Moreover, the ICRC plays a *de facto* role as a monitoring body in this branch of law through its many activities, including visits to prisoners of war. In 1977, AP I, Article 90 laid the basis for the establishment of an international Fact-Finding Commission. Where a state makes a declaration under paragraph 2 of this article, it recognizes 'ipso facto and without special agreement, in relation to any other High Contracting Party accepting the same obligation,' the competence of the Commission during international conflicts to 'inquire into any facts alleged to be a grave breach as defined in the Conventions and this Protocol or other serious violation' of international humanitarian law and 'facilitate, through its good offices, the restoration of an attitude of respect' for it. Although 70 states have since recognized the Commission's competence, it has never been called upon to take action as provided for in the Protocol.

Issue in focus: The Eritrea-Ethiopia Claims Commission[43]

Under the Algiers Agreement of 12 December 2000, Ethiopia and Eritrea agreed on a cessation of hostilities related to border disputes which became an international armed conflict in 1998. They decided to have their common border demarcated authoritatively by a Boundary Commission. At the same time, the Agreement set up the Eritrea-Ethiopia Claims Commission, which had the authority to make binding awards with respect to complaints by parties to the Agreement and individuals alleging violations of the Geneva Conventions by a party to the conflict. In December 2001 both parties filed complaints on their own behalf and on behalf of their nationals regarding violations of the rights of prisoners of war under GC III. On 1 July 2003 the Commission ruled on both complaints.[44]

As Eritrea had not ratified GC III until August 2000, the Commission was compelled to rule on Ethiopia's complaint in the light of customary law. It took the view that a large proportion of the Convention now had the status of such unwritten law and concluded that *Eritrea* had violated customary guarantees of international humanitarian law by refusing to allow ICRC delegates to visit the prisoner-of-war camps, mistreating and killing prisoners of war immediately after they were taken into captivity, failing to ensure humane evacuation conditions for other prisoners of war, threatening them during interrogation and abusing them in the camps. It further held that there had been breaches of the entitlement to adequate conditions

---

[43] See Natalie Klein, 'State Responsibility for International Humanitarian Law Violations and the Work of the Eritrea-Ethiopia Claims Commission So Far' (2004) *German Yearbook of International Law* 214 ff.

[44] Eritrea-Ethiopia Claims Commission, Partial Awards, Ethiopia's Claim 4 and Eritrea's Claim 17, published in (2003) *ILM* 1056 ff and 1083 ff.

of detention and sanitation and to the provision of food, drinking water and medical care. Lastly, the Commission held that to subject prisoners of war to inhumane working conditions constituted a violation of international humanitarian law.

According to the Commission, *Ethiopia* mistreated Eritrean soldiers at capture and afterwards, subjected them to enforced indoctrination, and violated GC III, *inter alia* by failing to provide adequate food and health care in the prisoner-of-war camps as well as by delaying the release of prisoners of war.

IV. International Criminal Jurisdiction

1. Overview

In some circumstances, human rights monitoring and implementation mechanisms run up against practical and conceptual obstacles. Human rights violations by non-state actors during non-international armed conflicts or tensions and disturbances cannot be addressed by treaty mechanisms because non-state actors are not subject to them and cannot recognize their competence. Traditional human rights mechanisms are also at a loss when faced with so-called 'failed states' in which state structures, though they may still exist *de jure*, are unable to exercise their authority. In the case of human rights violations by repressive regimes, the states concerned would have the means to take action against individual perpetrators but are unwilling to do so. In these and other similar cases, international criminal jurisdiction provides the possibility of bringing the perpetrators to justice on the international level.

Encouraged by the successful experience of the Nuremberg (1945) and Tokyo (1946) war crimes Tribunals, from its beginnings, the UN embraced the idea of establishing an international regime of criminal justice to prosecute the most serious violations of international human rights and humanitarian law. As early as 1948, the General Assembly mandated the International Law Commission (ILC) to look into the possibility of setting up an international criminal tribunal. Also, the Convention on the Prevention and Punishment of the Crime of Genocide, drafted in 1948, envisaged the possibility of establishing such a tribunal.[45] The Cold War put an end to these plans for almost half a century. The Security Council, acting under Chapter VII of the UN Charter in response to the genocide and the other massive human rights violations in the former Yugoslavia and in Rwanda, set up *ad hoc* international criminal tribunals in 1993 and 1994 with territorial jurisdiction limited to those states.[46]

The substantive jurisdiction of the International Criminal Tribunal for the Former Yugoslavia (ICTY) with its seat in The Hague relates to crimes that

---

[45] CPPCG, Art VI.
[46] Security Council Resolutions 827 of 25 May 1993 and 955 of 8 November 1994.

were already prohibited by customary law, namely genocide, grave breaches of the Geneva Conventions, violations of the laws and customs of war, and crimes against humanity.[47] The commission, planning and instigation as well as the aiding or abetting of any of these crimes is punishable.[48] In organizational terms, the Tribunal is divided into three Trial Chambers and an Appeals Chamber[49] with 16 permanent judges[50] and an independent Office of the Prosecutor. The second *ad hoc* Tribunal, the International Criminal Tribunal for Rwanda (ICTR), which has its seat in Arusha, Tanzania, has similar substantive jurisdiction but can additionally prosecute breaches of Article 3 common to the Geneva Conventions and breaches of Protocol II. While this Tribunal shares its Appeals Chamber with the ICTY, its Office of the Prosecution and its nine permanent judges serve exclusively at the ICTR.

Despite initial financial and organizational difficulties and, in the case of the ICTY, despite the initial refusal of the states concerned (and of international peace-keeping troops) to arrest and handover the accused, both Tribunals eventually succeeded in charging and convicting many of the main perpetrators. A problematic point, however, is that they were established only after most of the crimes had been committed; moreover, the international community for a long time took no steps in other cases of gross human rights violations to bring the perpetrators to justice.

These flaws were at least partially remedied by the adoption of the Rome Statute[51] of 17 July 1998 establishing a permanent International Criminal Court (ICC) (see section 2 below).

The most recent approach to establishing international criminal jurisdiction is demonstrated by the *ad hoc* criminal courts based on a combination of domestic and international law and with a mixed panel of judges. This category includes the Special Court for Sierra Leone, the Extraordinary Chambers in the Courts of Cambodia,[52] and the Special Panels in East Timor.[53] The purpose of these hybrid

---

[47] Arts 2–5 of the SICTY.   [48] Art 7(1) of the SICTY.

[49] The first-instance Trial Chambers sit in benches of three judges; the Appeals Chamber sits in benches of five.

[50] In addition, there are nine *ad litem* judges.

[51] The Statute was adopted by 120 votes to 7 with 21 abstentions. China, Iraq, Israel, Libya, Qatar, the United States of America, and Yemen voted against.

[52] The Special Court for Sierra Leone is based on a bilateral Agreement between the UN and Sierra Leone dated 16 January 2002 and consists of a first-instance three-judge Trial Chamber and a five-judge Appeals Chamber; two of the former and three of the latter being appointed by the UN Secretary-General and the remainder by the Government of Sierra Leone. See <www.sc-sl. org> (accessed 6 February 2009). The Extraordinary Chambers for Cambodia are based on an agreement between the UN and Cambodia signed on 6 June 2003 after five years of difficult negotiations. The Chambers became operative in 2006 and consist of a five-judge Criminal Chamber and a seven-judge Appeals Chamber. Three to four of the judges are appointed by the Cambodian government, the rest are appointed by the UN. The Chambers have jurisdiction to try the leaders of the Khmer Rouge, who committed gross human rights violations during the 1970s. See <www. eccc.gov.kh/english/> (accessed 18 January 2009).

[53] The former UN Mission of Support in East Timor (UNMISET) and the Government of East Timor administered two Special Panels and a Court of Appeal at the District Court in the capital Dili. Each court was composed of two international judges and one local judge, which adjudicated,

Table 6.2. International criminal tribunals

	Basis	Substantive jurisdiction	Personal jurisdiction	Relationship with domestic courts
International Criminal Court (ICC)	Multilateral treaty (Rome Statute)	War crimes, genocide, crimes against humanity (aggression, once it is defined)	Individuals who have committed a crime and who are nationals of a state party or have committed a crime on the territory of a state party	Subsidiarity, ie having jurisdiction only where domestic criminal courts are unable or unwilling
Ad hoc tribunals (ICTY/ ICTR)	Security Council resolutions	War crimes, crimes against humanity and genocide as prohibited by customary law	Individuals who have committed crimes within the territorial jurisdiction of the tribunals	Priority status: can take over proceedings before domestic courts
Hybrid criminal courts (Sierra Leone, Cambodia)	Bilateral agreement between the UN and the state in which the court has its seat	Violations of GC, Art 3 and AP II, war crimes, crimes against humanity, offences under domestic law	Individuals who have committed crimes within the territorial jurisdiction of the court	Priority status: can take over proceedings before domestic courts

bodies is to assist in making criminal prosecutions possible in circumstances where the domestic criminal justice system is unable, for financial or political reasons, to take legal action against the perpetrators of massive human rights violations. The mixed tribunals, which apply international criminal law with customary status in addition to domestic law, are supposedly less expensive and more efficient than international tribunals.

Issues of procedural law for these tribunals lie beyond the scope of this publication.[54] A summary of the international criminal tribunals and their jurisdictions is shown in Table 6.2.

2. The International Criminal Court (ICC)

The ICC has its seat in The Hague and started work in 2003.

on the basis of international customary law, charges related to massive human rights violations committed in 1999 and 2000. Indonesia refused to surrender suspects to these bodies, setting up a special tribunal itself that acquitted many of the accused and imposed only lenient penalties.

[54] For proceedings before the International Criminal Court, see, *inter alia*, Antonio Cassese, Paola Gaeta and John RWD Jones, *The Rome Statute of the International Criminal Court: A Commentary* (Oxford University Press: Oxford, 2002), and for proceedings before the ICTY see, *inter alia*, John E Ackerman and Eugene O'Sullivan, *Practice and Procedure of the International Criminal Tribunal for the Former Yugoslavia* (Brill: The Hague, 2002).

The Criminal Court with its 18 full-time judges assigned to the pre-trial, trial and appeals chambers may only charge a person and try a case where the following conditions have been cumulatively met:[55]

(1) The alleged act falls within the core international crimes, ie genocide, war crimes and crimes against humanity[56] (Rome Statute, Article 5).
(2) The act occurred after the date of entry into force of the Rome Statute, ie 1 July 2002 (Rome Statute, Article 11).
(3) The act was allegedly committed by a person over 18 years of age (Rome Statute, Article 26).
(4) The preconditions for the exercise of the Court's jurisdiction are fulfilled (Rome Statute, Articles 12 and 13); ie
    (i) a referral of the situation to the Office of the Prosecutor is made by the state party where the conduct in question occurred or of which the accused is a national;
    (ii) the UN Security Council, acting under Chapter VII of the Charter, requests the initiation of proceedings before the ICC;
    (iii) the ICC Office of the Prosecutor initiates proceedings on its own motion (Rome Statute, Articles 13–15).
(5) The Security Council has not adopted a resolution under Chapter VII of the Charter requesting a deferral of either the investigation or the prosecution (Rome Statute, Article 16).
(6) The responsible state is either unwilling or unable to carry out the prosecution (Rome Statute, Article 17).
(7) The case is of sufficient gravity to justify action before the ICC (Rome Statute, Article 17(1)(d)).

Thus, the Court can exercise its jurisdiction in the following cases:[57]

(1) *Ordinary jurisdiction,* ie the ICC is entitled to exercise its jurisdiction, basing itself solely on the Rome Statute, where a crime either occurred on the territory of a state party (territoriality principle) or was committed by a national of a state party (active personality principle). Proceedings based on the Court's ordinary jurisdiction may be initiated by any state party, the Prosecutor, or the Security Council acting under Chapter VII of the Charter, ie where the Security Council considers the situation resulting from the alleged crimes as a breach of or a threat to world peace.

(2) *Extraordinary jurisdiction,* ie a state that is not a party to the Rome Statute can, by means of a declaration, lay the basis for *ad hoc* ICC jurisdiction to prosecute

---

[55] Arts 5–20 of the Rome Statute. The elements of the crime of aggression have thus far not been defined (see Art 5(2)).
[56] On these crimes, see Chapter 2, section II.5.
[57] For a detailed discussion, see Cassese, Gaeta, and Jones (n 54), 559 ff and 619 ff.

crimes specified in the declaration, which must again either have occurred on the territory of the state concerned or have been committed by one of its nationals.

(3) *Jurisdiction derived from the UN Charter,* ie, the Court is empowered to deal with core crimes regardless of the place the crime was committed and the nationality of the alleged perpetrators if the Security Council, acting under Chapter VII of the Charter, refers a situation to the ICC. The Security Council also has competence to defer all measures of investigation and prosecution for one year by adopting a resolution under Chapter VII of the Charter. The deferral may be renewed, for example to facilitate ongoing work on peace treaties.

Table 6.3 presents an overview of these different types of jurisdiction.

To date, three states parties, Uganda, the Democratic Republic of the Congo and the Central African Republic, have referred situations to the ICC.[58] In all these cases, the Office of the Prosecutor decided after a preliminary analysis to open an investigation. Furthermore, the UN Security Council, acting under Chapter VII of the UN Charter, adopted on 31 March 2005 Resolution 1593 (2005) referring the situation in Darfur, Sudan, since 1 July 2002 to the Court for investigation. It took this action although Sudan is not a party to the Rome Statute and no nationals of a state party are involved in the alleged war crimes and crimes against humanity.[59] On 6 June 2005, upon completing a preliminary analysis, the Chief Prosecutor of the Court decided to open the official investigation in Darfur.[60]

Although the first proceedings are now pending, the ICC is faced with a number of problems. While the Rome Statute currently has 108[61] states parties, the United States,[62] China, Russia, and many states located in traditional conflict zones have chosen not to take part. Accusations of jurisdictional selectivity will likely only be

---

[58] While the Democratic Republic of the Congo and the Central African Republic requested the Office of the Prosecutor to conduct comprehensive investigations into core crimes committed since the entry into force of the Rome Statute on their territory, Uganda's request related solely to crimes committed by the Lord's Resistance Army rebel group in the northern part of the country.

[59] Resolution 1593 (2005) was adopted by 11 votes to none with 4 abstentions (China, USA, Brazil and Algeria). However, to address the reservations expressed, in particular by the United States, which preferred to establish a new *ad hoc* tribunal, the Security Council constrained the jurisdiction of the ICC regarding crimes committed by members of future international peacekeeping troops in Darfur. It follows that the Court has no jurisdiction to prosecute crimes committed by foreign state agents from a state that has not ratified the Rome Statute unless such a state explicitly consents to such jurisdiction (ibid, para 6).

[60] For more details see Chapter 2, section II.5.c (Example: The Darfur conflict and war crimes).

[61] Status as of December 2008.

[62] Although the United States refrained from vetoing the referral of the Darfur situation to the ICC, its current opposition to the Court goes far beyond mere non-ratification. Measures to prevent American military and civilian personnel serving abroad from being brought before the Court under any circumstances include both domestic legislation prohibiting all collaboration with the ICC and bilateral agreements prohibiting the surrender of American nationals to the Court. Moreover, the UN Security Council was compelled through pressure from the United States to establish a binding *exceptional arrangement* for nationals of non-states parties taking part in UN-authorized military operations by adopting resolutions under Chapter VII of the UN Charter (Resolution 1422 of 12 June 2002, extended by Resolution 1487 of 12 July 2003). This arrangement, which was difficult to justify with regards to the Rome Statute, excludes personnel taking part in such assignments— barring a contrary decision by the Security Council—from the personal jurisdiction of the ICC. In 2004 the arrangement was not extended. However, the resolution conferring jurisdiction on the

Table 6.3. Jurisdiction of the ICC

	Ordinary jurisdiction		Extraordinary jurisdiction		Jurisdiction derived from the UN Charter
Proceedings triggered by:	Crimes committed on the territory of a state party	Crimes committed by a national of a state party	Crimes committed on the territory of a state that recognizes the jurisdiction of the ICC *ad hoc*	Crimes committed by nationals of a state that recognizes the jurisdiction of the ICC *ad hoc*	Crimes committed on any territory and regardless of the nationality of the accused person
State party	X	X			
Non-state party	—	—	X	X	—
Prosecutor	X	X	—	—	—
Security Council (Chapter VII)	X	X	—	—	X

refuted once the Court is in a position to operate with very few territorial restrictions. The selection of proceedings, the manner in which they are conducted and, in particular, the Court's interpretation of the complementarity clause will no doubt play a decisive role in determining whether these states decide after all to ratify the Statute.

Issue in focus: Accountability for human rights violations and personal immunity from prosecution

---

Future criminal proceedings before international bodies are likely to be increasingly brought against heads of state and other top state representatives. This raises the issue of the possible immunity from prosecution of these individuals. According to a traditional rule of international law, heads of state enjoy absolute immunity. Moreover, their immunity for official acts continues beyond their term of office. A number of developments, however, have undermined this rule. The following points should be noted:

- Members of a government who are in *active* service enjoy immunity in proceedings before the domestic courts of another state.[63] The question of immunity in proceedings before the courts of an official's own state remains a matter of its own law and is unregulated by international law;
- If criminal proceedings against *former* officials relate to official acts, ie acts performed by such persons in an official capacity during their term of office, the accused may, according to the ICJ, invoke immunity in domestic criminal proceedings of other states.[64] According to the British House of Lords, acts of

---

ICC to prosecute crimes committed in Darfur again contains a provision that exempts nationals of non-states parties from being called to account before the Court; see above (n 59).

[63] ICJ, *Case concerning the Arrest Warrant of 11 April 2000, Democratic Republic of the Congo v Belgium*, ICJ Reports 2002, para 54.
[64] Ibid, para 61.

torture cannot, however, be characterized under any circumstances as official acts;[65]

– Former members of government and heads of state cannot invoke immunity from prosecution before courts of other states for acts committed *before* or *after* their term of office or for acts unrelated to their official duties;[66]

– Article 27 of the Rome Statute as well as the statutes of the *ad hoc* tribunals are based on the premise that (present or former) heads of state and members of governments cannot invoke any form of immunity before international criminal tribunals. This rule also applies to the prosecution of genocide before courts of states parties to the Genocide Convention.[67]

V. Summary

The different levels of human rights implementation and the procedures available may be presented in summary form, as shown in Table 6.4.

Table 6.4. Implementation procedures of human rights law and international humanitarian law—an overview

		Petition and complaint procedures		Reporting procedures	
		Treaty bodies	*Extra-conventional bodies*	*Treaty bodies*	*Extra-conventional bodies*
National level		Individual complaint before national courts Individual complaint before internationally established constitutional courts (eg Bosnia)	Procedure before a truth commission	Possibility of periodic reporting through national human rights institutions	
Regional level		Individual complaint: ECHR, ACHR, ACHPR Interstate complaint: ECHR, ACHR, ACHPR	Individual complaint procedure before ACmHR (OAS) Interstate complaint: OSCE Vienna and Moscow mechanisms	ESC and special European treaties Special American treaties ACHPR	Reporting system of the European Commission against Racism
Universal level		Individual communications: ICCPR-OP1, ICESCR-OP, CEDAW-OP, CERD, CAT, ICRMW, CPAPED Interstate complaint: ICCPR, ICESCR-OP, CERD, ICRMW, CAT, CPAPED and within the ILO	Petitions procedure before the Human Rights Council and the Commission on the Status of Women; complaint-oriented thematic mandates of the Human Rights Council	State reporting: ICESCR, ICCPR, CERD, CAT, CEDAW, CRC, ICRMW, CPAPED, CRPD	

[65] Judgments of the House of Lords in the *Pinochet* case, *Regina v Bartle and Others ex parte Pinochet*, of 25 November 1998, 17 December 1998 and 24 March 1999, *ILM*, vol XXXVIII, No 2, March 1999, 30 ff.

[66] ICJ, *Case concerning the Arrest Warrant of 11 April 2000, Democratic Republic of the Congo v Belgium*, ICJ Reports 2002, para 61.

[67] CPPCG, Art IV.

Table 6.4. (*Contd.*)

	Fact-finding procedures		Criminal procedures	Procedures under general international law
	Treaty bodies	*Extra-conventional bodies*		
National level	National visiting system under OPCAT Possibility of monitoring by national human rights institutions National fact-finding mechanisms and truth commissions, etc		Application of domestic criminal law Obligation to prosecute under international convention	Bilateral dialogue, support, criticism or countermeasures
Regional level	Visiting system under European Convention for the Prevention of Torture	OAS: fact-finding by the AmCHR (country reports) OSCE: expert and field missions; fact-finding by the Minorities Commissioner Council of Europe: fact-finding by the European Commission against Racism	Application of international criminal law Internationally established (hybrid) domestic criminal courts (eg Sierra Leone, Cambodia) *Ad hoc* Tribunals (ICTY and ICTR)	Countermeasures by regional organizations such as the EU or the OAS (eg economic sanctions)
Universal level	Preventive: OPCAT Fact-finding by CtteeAT, CtteeERD, etc Fact-finding under Art 90 AP I	UN: fact-finding by country and thematic Special Rapporteurs of the Human Rights Council and by UN field missions ICRC visiting system	International Criminal Court (ICC)	Non-military countermeasures Peacekeeping missions Military sanctions under Chapter VII of the UN Charter Procedures before the ICJ

7

Treaty Bodies

I. Introduction

1. United Nations treaty bodies

Each of the nine core UN human rights conventions provides for setting up of an independent body to monitor the implementation of the respective treaty by the states parties.

These bodies, known as committees, are composed of independent experts, all of whom serve on a voluntary basis. Depending on their workload and available financial means, the committees hold between one and three sessions annually, usually in Geneva.[1] Each session runs for two or three weeks.

The terms of reference of the treaty bodies, ie the means at their disposal to monitor compliance with the provisions of the treaty concerned, differ in scope from one convention to another. All conventions provide for a compulsory *state reporting procedure*, ie states parties must periodically submit a report on the implementation of their treaty obligations to the committee concerned, which subjects it to a critical review in the presence of a delegation from the state party. *Individual communication procedures*, which allow victims of alleged human rights violations to initiate a formal procedure against the violating state before the committee, exist for all treaties except the Convention on the Rights of the Child. Such complaint procedures are not available automatically but only when the state party concerned makes a corresponding declaration or ratifies an optional protocol. Some treaties further provide for a *procedure for interstate communications* (compulsory or optional depending on the treaty), which allows states parties to file a complaint against another state with the committee concerned, irrespective of whether their own interests are at stake or whether they are acting in pursuit of a general interest in the implementation of human rights. The Convention against Torture, the Convention on the Elimination of All Forms of Discrimination against Women, and the Convention for the Protection of All Persons from Enforced Disappearance also have *inquiry procedures*, which allow the committees concerned to conduct an on-site inquiry under certain circumstances. The most recent types of procedure are the *preventive procedure*, created by the 2002 Optional Protocol to the Convention

---

[1] The HRCttee usually holds one of its sessions in New York, whereas the CtteeEDAW met exclusively in New-York until the end of 2007, holding their first meeting in Geneva in January 2008.

against Torture, and the possibility for *urgent actions* in cases of disappearances in accordance with the Convention for the Protection of All Persons from Enforced Disappearance. An overview of the UN treaty bodies is provided in Table 7.1.

Table 7.1. Overview of the UN treaty bodies

Name of the committee	Composition	Procedures[2]
Committee on Economic, Social and Cultural Rights (ICESCR)	18 members elected by ECOSOC	RP: compulsory (Arts 16–17) ISCP: optional (Art 10 OP) ICP: optional (Arts 1–9 OP) IP/PP: optional (Arts 11–12 OP)
Human Rights Committee (ICCPR)	18 members elected by the states parties	RP: compulsory (Art 40) ISCP: optional (Art 41) ICP: optional (FP) IP/PP: —
Committee against Torture (CAT)	10 members elected by the states parties	RP: compulsory (Art 19) ISCP: optional (Art 21) ICP: optional (Art 22) IP: compulsory/opt-out clause (Art 20) PP: optional (OP)
Committee on the Rights of the Child (CRC)	18 members elected by the states parties	RP: compulsory (Art 44) ISCP: — ICP: — IP/PP: —
Committee on the Elimination of Racial Discrimination (CERD)	18 members elected by the states parties	RP: compulsory (Art 9) ISCP: compulsory (Arts 11–13) ICP: optional (Art 14) IP/PP: —
Committee on the Elimination of Discrimination against Women (CEDAW)	23 members elected by the states parties	RP: compulsory (Art 18) ISCP: — ICP: optional (Arts 1–7 OP) IP: optional/opt-out clause (Art 8 OP) PP: —
Committee on the Protection of the Rights of All Migrant Workers and Members of Their Families (ICRMW)	10 members elected by the states parties	RP: compulsory (Art 74) ISCP: optional (Art 76) ICP: optional (Art 77) IP/PP: –
Committee on Enforced Disappearances (CPAPED)	10 members elected by the states parties	RP: compulsory (Art 29) ISCP: — ICP: optional (Art 31) IP: compulsory (Art 33) Urgent action: compulsory (Art 30)
Committee on the Rights of Persons with Disabilities (CRPD)	12 (18 after the 80th ratification or accession) elected by the states parties	RP: compulsory (Art 35) ISCP:— ICP: optional (Arts 1–5OP) IP/PP:—

[2] RP: reporting procedure; ISCP: interstate complaint procedure; ICP: individual communications procedure; IP: inquiry procedure; PP: preventive procedure; OP: Optional Protocol.

Some treaties, such as the Convention on the Prevention and Punishment of the Crime of Genocide, the Convention on the Political Rights of Women, the Convention relating to the Status of Refugees, and the Slavery Convention, make no provision for monitoring bodies. With respect to the Genocide Convention, however, this omission is partly offset by the fact that its Article IX[3] gives states parties the option of having recourse to the International Court of Justice (ICJ).

Even in cases where the committees are empowered to deal with claims from individuals or states parties that a particular right was violated, they do not act as judicial bodies in the true sense of the term. Nevertheless, in practice, these complaint procedures come so close to a judicial examination that the committees are often referred to as 'quasi-judicial bodies'. Moreover, although complaints from individuals are called 'communications' and the committees' decisions are not referred to as judgments but as 'views', the findings may nonetheless be compared to judicial decisions in terms of form. While not legally binding in the strict sense of the word, they possess considerable weight and authority.[4]

2. Regional treaty bodies

(a) Europe

Courts of human rights entitled to hand down binding judgments exist at the regional level. As early as 1950, the European Convention on Human Rights established the European Court of Human Rights, which was not at the time a standing body. However, with the entry into force of Protocol No 11 to the ECHR on 1 November 1998, it became the permanent European Court of Human Rights (hereinafter 'the Court') with its seat in Strasbourg. Both individuals and states have recourse to the Court, which can render binding judgments on violations of the ECHR. Between 1955 and October 2008 the Court handed down over 10,000 substantive judgments and is therefore, in quantitative terms, by far the most successful judicial body in the area of human rights law.[5]

The Court is composed of one judge for each of the states parties to the ECHR and adjudicates in *committees* of three judges, in *chambers* of seven judges and in a *Grand Chamber* of 17 judges.[6] Organizational matters, such as adoption of the rules of procedure and the formation of chambers, are handled by the *Plenary Court*, which has no jurisdiction, however, to rule on applications.

---

[3] Some conventions with their own monitoring mechanisms, such as the Convention against Torture (CAT, Art 30) or the Convention on the Elimination of Racial Discrimination (CERD, Art 22), may also provide for compulsory recognition of the jurisdiction of the ICJ.

[4] For more on the legal character of the decisions taken by the Committees on individual communications and the obligations of states parties in this regard, see section III.1 below.

[5] During the same period over 520,000 complaints were filed with the Commission and, with effect from 1998, with the Court. At the end of November 2008, 96,550 cases were pending with the Court.

[6] ECHR, Art 27.

Table 7.2. Overview of the European treaty bodies

Name of the committee (treaty)	Composition	Areas of competence
European Committee of Social Rights (ESC)	9 members	Compulsory reporting procedure/ collective complaint procedure (AP/ESC)
European Committee for the Prevention of Torture (European Convention for the Prevention of Torture)	1 member per state party	Preventive visits system (compulsory)
Advisory Committee on National Minorities (Framework Convention for the Protection of National Minorities)	16 members	Compulsory reporting procedure
Committee of Experts of the European Charter for Regional or Minority Languages (European Charter for Regional or Minority Languages)	1 member per state party	Compulsory reporting procedure

Responsibility for monitoring compliance with the other European human rights treaties lies, as at the universal level, with individual expert committees, which, except for the Committee of Social Rights, are not empowered to consider individual communications but to undertake, in most cases, a periodic review of the implementation of the relevant treaty through *reporting procedures*. In addition to the Court, the Council of Europe has established a number of human rights treaty bodies, as summarized in Table 7.2.

(b) Other regions

Independent human rights courts have also been established at the (Latin) American (Inter-American Court of Human Rights[7]) and African level (African Court on Human and Peoples' Rights)[8] to enforce the relevant regional human rights conventions. In contrast to the current[9] European model, however, commissions play a primary role in both cases as individuals cannot file cases directly with the Courts but must submit them to the Inter-American Commission on Human Rights and the African Commission on Human and Peoples' Rights respectively.

The Inter-American Commission on Human Rights[10] has seven members. In addition of dealing with individual complaints (named 'petitions') submitted by individuals or non-governmental organizations, it can examine interstate

---

[7] ACHR, Arts 52–69.
[8] Protocol to the African Charter on Human and Peoples' Rights on the Establishment of an African Court on Human and Peoples' Rights of 9 June 1998.
[9] Before the entry into force of P 11/ECHR, the ECHR also had a two-stage system with a first-stage Commission (European Commission of Human Rights).
[10] ACHR, Arts 34–51.

complaints if the state concerned has accepted this competence.[11] The Inter-American Court of Human Rights,[12] with its seat in San José, Costa Rica, is composed of seven part-time judges. It hears cases that have been submitted to it by the Commission or a state party after the Commission has adopted its report, provided the state concerned has accepted its jurisdiction. In addition, the Court, upon request by the member states of the Organization of American States or by organs of the Organization 'may consult the Court regarding the interpretation of this Convention or of other treaties concerning the protection of human rights in the American states' (ACHR, Article 64). As of December 2008, the Court has rendered 192 judgments and issued 19 advisory opinions.

The African Commission on Human and Peoples' Rights[13] has eleven members who serve in their individual capacity. One of its main tasks is to examine state reports on the implementation of the African Charter of Human and Peoples' Rights. It has also the power to examine interstate complaints as well as individual communications. The African Union has created an African Court on Human and Peoples' Rights with its seat in Arusha/Tanzania which, however, has not yet taken up its activities.[14]

The Arab Charter on Human Rights foresees an Arab Human Rights Committee made up of seven members charged with the examination of state reports.[15]

II. State Reporting Procedure

1. Overview

Under the core UN treaties[16] and, at the regional level, under the Protocol of San Salvador,[17] the Inter-American Convention on the Elimination of All Forms of Discrimination against Persons with Disabilities,[18] the ACHPR[19] and its Protocols,[20] the ArCHR,[21] the European Social Charter,[22] the European Framework Convention for the Protection of National Minorities, and the European Charter for Regional or Minority Languages—but not under the ECHR[23] and the ACHR—states parties are required to submit periodic reports

---

[11] The procedure for examining individual and interstate complaints is regulated in ACHR, Arts 46–51.

[12] ACHR, Arts 52–69.   [13] ACHPR, Arts 31 ff.

[14] The judges of this Court were elected in 2006.   [15] ArCHR, Arts 45–48.

[16] ICESCR, Art 16; ICCPR, Art 40; CAT, Art 19; CERD, Art 9; CEDAW, Art 19; CRC, Art 44; ICRMW, Art 73; CPAPED, Art 29; CRPD, Art 35.

[17] P 1/ACHR, Art 19.   [18] IACDAPD, Art VI.   [19] ACHPR, Art 63.

[20] See Protocol to the African Charter on Human and Peoples' Rights on the Rights of Women in Africa (P 2/ACHPR), Article 26, regarding the reporting obligation under this instrument.

[21] ArCHR, Art 48.   [22] ESC, Art 21.

[23] ECHR, Art 52 actually empowers the Secretary General to request the contracting parties to explain how their internal laws ensure the effective implementation of the provisions of the Convention. However, this provision has not acquired any importance in practice.

to a treaty body on progress and difficulties in implementing their obligations under the treaty concerned. The state reporting procedure is generally viewed as the weakest monitoring instrument. Logically, therefore, this mechanism is the only one that is in all cases compulsory, ie a state becomes subject to this obligation as soon as it ratifies the relevant treaty.

States are specifically required to submit reports at regular intervals[24] on difficulties encountered and progress made in domestic implementation of the relevant treaty guarantees. The reports should not focus on specific cases but should present a state's legislation and practical experience and review the status of implementation of treaty obligations as a form of self-assessment. At the UN level, the treaty bodies hold meetings with a delegation from the state party concerned and these meetings are open to the public. The object of the meetings is to identify difficulties in implementation and to seek solutions through a dialogue that should be as constructive as possible.[25] The review of a state report ends with 'Concluding Observations', in which the treaty body takes the opportunity to make specific recommendations to the state concerned.[26] Although the tone of these recommendations is restrained, they often amount to clear directives to lawmakers and the executive branch. The cumulative experience acquired by a committee through the reporting procedure is recorded in so-called 'General Comments',[27] which are brief remarks on specific guarantees that offer valuable guidance on the content and scope of states parties' human rights obligations in respect of a particular right.

2. Example: the state reporting procedure of the Committee on Economic, Social and Cultural Rights

Despite certain differences in approach and methodology, examination of state reports follows essentially the same pattern in all treaty bodies. The following description focuses on the Committee on Economic, Social and Cultural Rights.

[24] Initial reports must generally be submitted within two years of ratification and periodic reports usually every four or five years (in the case of CERD every two years) thereafter. Art 29 of the CPAPED lays down an exception to this rule by not demanding periodic reports of the states parties; it only requires the states parties to submit an initial report within two years after the treaty enters into force. The Committee on Enforced Disappearances may however ask the states parties for additional information on the implementation of the treaty obligations at any time.

[25] Unlike the state report procedures before the UN Committees, the monitoring of state reports by the European Committee on National Minorities does not take place at the seat of this body. Instead, a delegation of the Committee visits the states parties concerned and meets with the government and NGOs on their territory. Based on these visits, the Committee draws up its own report on the progress in the implementation of the treaty obligations by the state concerned.

[26] The Concluding Observations are accessible on the website of the High Commissioner for Human Rights (<http://tb.ohchr.org/default.aspx> (accessed 5 February 2009)) and (since 2000) at <www.universalhumanrightsindex.org> (accessed 5 February 2009), which provides a powerful search tool.

[27] The General Comments are available at <http://tb.ohchr.org/default.aspx> (18 January 2009).

States have traditionally been reluctant to accept the possibility of effective implementation of economic social and cultural human rights. During the Cold War, the Eastern bloc's general scepticism regarding international monitoring and enforcement mechanisms coincided with the West's ideologically motivated reservations *vis-à-vis* this category of human rights. Under the circumstances, it is not surprising that the ICESCR was endowed with a comparatively weak implementation mechanism. First, the only such mechanism was a state reporting procedure and, second, the body entrusted with its monitoring was not independent but a political organ composed of state representatives: the Economic and Social Council (ECOSOC). As ECOSOC was unable to perform this function satisfactorily, however, it adopted a resolution in 1987 establishing an expert body, the Committee on Economic, Social and Cultural Rights, to monitor implementation of the ICESCR.[28] It follows that the Committee is not a treaty body in the strict sense of the term,[29] although its working methods no longer differ from those of the other UN committees.

(a) *The purpose of the reporting procedure*

In its first General Comment, the Committee on Economic, Social and Cultural Rights identified seven objectives to be achieved by the reporting process, namely:

(1) a review by the state party of the legal situation (legislation, procedures, etc) in the area of human rights;
(2) a realistic assessment by the state party of the actual human rights situation;
(3) an opportunity for the state party to draw attention to progress achieved in the realization of human rights;
(4) facilitation of public scrutiny by the state party;
(5) establishment of a basis for evaluation of the state party's progress in the area of human rights;
(6) development of a better understanding of the problems and shortcomings encountered in implementing the Covenant; and
(7) facilitation of the exchange of information among states with a view to developing a better understanding of the common problems they face in realizing human rights.[30]

In practice, achievement of these objectives is often undermined by states parties' lack of reporting discipline. Very few states submit their reports within the prescribed period, and it is not just small and poorer states (which have to commit considerable resources to human rights reporting) whose reports are long overdue or which have failed to submit any report despite being states parties in some cases

[28] ECOSOC Res 1985/17, 28 May 1985.
[29] The legal basis of the CtteeESCR is still reflected in the fact that its members are not elected by the states parties but by ECOSOC and in the fact that the Committee reports to that body and not the General Assembly.
[30] CtteeESCR, General Comment No 1 (1989).

for decades.[31] The reporting mechanism cannot be effective unless states fulfil their reporting obligations not only on time but also in qualitative terms. A common failing is the submission of reports containing a mere catalogue of legislation and statements of intent rather than an informative account of the real situation including statistical details and information on shortcomings as regards to implementation of the Covenant guarantees. This may be remedied to some extent by the detailed NGO reports, known as 'shadow reports', on the situation in the country concerned that are often brought to the attention of the Committee.

(b) Stages of the reporting procedure

The procedure culminating in the review of state reports may be divided into the following five stages:[32]

(1) *Preparation of the state report by the state party*: On ratifying the ICESCR, states undertake, pursuant to Articles 16 and 17 of the Covenant, to submit a full report within two years on measures adopted to implement its provisions and subsequently a periodic report every five years on difficulties encountered and progress made in implementing obligations to be fulfilled immediately and obligations to be met progressively. To ensure that reports on the implementation of the Covenant are properly structured, they should comply as far as possible with the *Reporting Guidelines*[33] drawn up by the Committee, which contain detailed questions regarding the realization of individual guarantees. Ideally, all administrative bodies responsible for implementing Covenant rights should be involved in preparing the report, and inputs from civil society should also be taken into account.

Issue in focus: The Reporting Guidelines of the Committee on Economic, Social and Cultural Rights

---

The following excerpt from the ICESCR Committee's Reporting Guidelines on the right to health (Article 13 ICESCR) indicates the amount of detailed and accurate information this body requires:

4. Please provide, where available, indicators as defined by the WHO [World Health Organization], relating to the following issues: (a) Infant mortality rate (in addition to the

---

[31] As of early 2008, 15 states that had been parties to the ICESCR for at least 15 years had not yet submitted a report. Even European countries frequently fall behind in their reporting obligations; for instance, in 2004, Latvia had been a state party for 12 years without ever having fulfilled its reporting obligation, and in the same year Malta submitted its initial report 14 years after ratification of the Covenant.

[32] See the review of the Committee's working methods contained in the 'Report of the Committee on Economic, Social and Cultural Rights on its 28th and 29th Sessions', UN Doc E/C.12/2002/13, paras 25 ff.

[33] Revised general guidelines regarding the form and contents of reports to be submitted by states parties under Arts 16 and 17 of the International Covenant on Economic, Social and Cultural Rights, UN Doc E/C.12/1991/1.

national value, please provide the rate by sex, urban/rural division, and also, if possible, by socio-economic or ethnic group and geographical area. Please include national definitions of urban/rural and other subdivisions); (b) Population access to safe water (please disaggregate urban/rural); (c) Population access to adequate excreta disposal facilities (please disaggregate urban/rural); (d) Infants immunized against diphtheria, pertussis, tetanus, measles, poliomyelitis and tuberculosis (please disaggregate urban/rural and by sex); (e) Life expectancy (please disaggregate urban/rural, by socio-economic group and by sex); (f) Proportion of the population having access to trained personnel for the treatment of common diseases and injuries, with regular supply of 20 essential drugs, within one hour's walk or travel; (g) Proportion of pregnant women having access to trained personnel during pregnancy and proportion attended by such personnel for delivery. Please provide figures on the maternity mortality rate, both before and after childbirth; (h) Proportion of infants having access to trained personnel for care. (Please provide breakdowns by urban/rural and socio-economic groups for indicators (f) to (h).)

5. Can it be discerned from the breakdowns of the indicators employed in paragraph 4, or by other means, that there are any groups in your country whose health situation is significantly worse than that of the majority of the population? Please define these groups as precisely as possible and give details. Which geographical areas in your country, if any, are worse off with regard to the health of their population?...

Where states breach their reporting obligation by either failing to report at all or by submitting their reports long after the due date, the Committee can decide of its own motion to review the situation in the country concerned. If a state fails to react to such warnings, the Committee informs the state that a review will be undertaken, even in the absence of a report, on the basis of available information. This often prods states to make the effort to submit a report, or at least to send a delegation to attend the scheduled review. Otherwise the Committee reviews the situation in the light of the information it has received.

(2) *Procedure before the Working Group*: State reports are first referred to a five-member Working Group of the Committee, which meets before each of the Committee's sessions. Its main task consists in compiling an advance list of questions to be put to government representatives, in the light of a preliminary review by the member of the Group responsible for each report,[34] (the Country Rapporteur). The list is transmitted to the state party so that it can come to its meeting with the Committee properly prepared. States' written answers to the list of issues should be made available to the Committee before the meeting so that a constructive dialogue can be held. The process of preparing relevant questions is greatly facilitated by the documentation compiled by the secretariat and the shadow reports drawn up by non-governmental organizations.

(3) *Dialogue between the Committee and the government of the state party*: The core of the state reporting procedure consists of a dialogue between the full

---

[34] In each case one member of the Working Group prepares an assessment of the state's report, compiles a list of possible questions and prepares a preliminary draft of the Committee's conclusions.

Committee and a government delegation—composed ideally of highly competent members. The public review begins with a presentation by the delegation of the report and any additional written information submitted by the state party. The report is next examined in terms of the following clusters of issues: existence of discrimination, equality of men and women in the enjoyment of rights; labour rights; subsistence rights; and cultural rights. Each cluster begins with questions from Committee members followed by a response from the government delegation. At this stage in the procedure, representatives of specialized agencies of the United Nations[35] can also intervene in the dialogue.[36]

(4) *The Committee's Concluding Observations*: After the public discussion, the Committee meets in closed session to discuss the Concluding Observations drafted by the County Rapporteur which are then adopted by consensus. The Observations are always presented under the following headings: introduction; positive aspects; factors and difficulties impeding the implementation of the Covenant; principal subjects of concern; and suggestions and recommendations. The Concluding Observations are published on the last day of the session.

Example: Concluding Observations of the Committee on Economic, Social and Cultural Rights on Belgium's report

---

Belgium submitted its third report to the Committee on Economic, Social and Cultural Rights in 2006. In its Concluding Observations in 2008 the Committee found the following:

D. Principal subjects of concern

…

11. The Committee reiterates its concerns expressed in paragraph 5 of its previous concluding observations (E/C.12/1/Add.54) relating to the lack of appropriate and effective mechanisms to ensure compliance, at the federal, regional and community levels, with the State party's obligations under the Covenant.

12. The Committee notes with concern that the vast majority of the Covenant provisions, as well as some of the provisions of article 23 of the Constitution of the State party, which enumerates a number of economic, social and cultural rights but leaves it to national legislation regarding its implementation, do not have direct legal effect under national law, and are therefore rarely invoked separately before, and directly enforced by, national courts and other tribunals or administrative authorities.

13. The Committee notes that despite the existence of several bodies with a mandate to promote and protect human rights, including economic, social and cultural rights, no independent

---

[35] For instance, the International Labour Organization (ILO), the World Health Organization (WHO), and the Food and Agriculture Organization of the United Nations (FAO).
[36] This option is not available as a rule in the other committees. However, they may in some cases listen to the views of such agencies prior to the dialogue.

national human rights institution established in accordance with the Paris Principles (General Assembly resolution 48/134 of 20 December 1993, annex) exists in the State party.

14. The Committee notes that despite the measures adopted by the State party to enhance its legal and institutional mechanisms aimed at combating racial discrimination, de facto discrimination against foreigners and persons belonging to ethnic and national minorities, in particular migrant workers and members of their families, members of the Muslim community and Roma, is still widespread among some sectors of the population, especially in the fields of employment, housing and access to public places such as restaurants and bars.

15. The Committee remains concerned about the high unemployment rates among women, the persistent wage differentials between men and women and the low percentage of women in high-ranking posts in many areas, including in the public administration and university teaching posts.

16. The Committee remains concerned that despite the measures adopted by the State party to increase employment opportunities for young persons, persons over 55 years of age and foreign residents, the unemployment rates of persons belonging to these groups continue to be considerably higher than the European Union average rate.

17. The Committee notes with concern the significant obstructions to the exercise of the right to strike, arising from the practice of employers to start legal proceedings in order to obtain a ban on certain strike-related activities, as well as from the possibility that workers may be dismissed as a result of their participation in a strike.....

20. The Committee remains concerned, in spite of the various initiatives undertaken by the State party to increase the supply of social housing units, about the continuing shortage of social housing units for low-income households and other disadvantaged and marginalized individuals and groups, and about the continuing increase of rents in the private rental sector.

21. The Committee notes with concern that access to health-care facilities, goods and services for persons belonging to vulnerable and disadvantaged groups, such as undocumented migrant workers and members of their families, is limited to access to urgent medical care.

22. The Committee remains concerned about the persistent divergences in terms of performance existing in the educational system of the State party and the lack of adequate mechanisms aimed at ensuring uniformity in the application of educational standards....

(5) *The follow-up procedure*: In its Concluding Observations, the Committee requests that states parties, as a rule, provide information in their next periodic report on steps taken to implement its recommendations, and to submit additional information on particularly pressing issues even before the date the report is due. If the requested additional information is not provided or proves inadequate, the Committee can authorize the Chairperson to take the matter further. Another option is to request the defaulting party to accept a mission consisting of a one- or two-member delegation of the Committee. The purpose of such a visit (which is contemplated only where there seems to be no promising alternative) is, first, to collect the information needed for a dialogue with the state party and, second, to identify the extent to which the state concerned needs technical assistance in implementing Covenant rights or in preparing its reports.[37] Country

[37] See ICESCR, Arts 22–23.

missions of this kind culminate with the formulation of conclusions by the full Committee. So far two on-site missions—deemed highly successful by the Committee—have been undertaken.[38]

(c) *The adoption of General Comments*

Acting without an explicit legal basis, the Committee on Economic, Social and Cultural Rights, like the other UN treaty bodies, presents a broad summary of the experience it has gained from the state reporting procedure in General Comments. These Comments, which are adopted by consensus, play a vitally important role in the case of the ICESCR,[39] since they are the prime source of clarification of states parties' obligations in respect of specific Covenant guarantees.

The Committee's first General Comment, adopted in 1989, deals with the purpose of the reporting procedure. It was followed in 1990 by Comments on technical assistance measures and on the nature of states parties' obligations under the Covenant. The high quality of the latter Comment was not maintained in the years that followed.[40] However, the situation changed in 1997, when the Committee stated its positions on the compatibility of economic sanctions with ICESCR rights and subsequently on the domestic application of such rights.[41] The next Comments in the series, which were based on a standardized outline,[42] dealt with substantive Covenant rights. General Comments have now been published on the rights to primary schooling; education; food; water; and health; as well as the equal right of men and women to the enjoyment of Covenant rights; the right of everyone to benefit from the protection of the moral and material interests resulting from any scientific, literary or artistic production of which he or she is the author; the right to work; and the right to social security.[43]

3. Assessment

The state reporting procedure is sometimes criticized for lacking efficiency. While it is true that coercive aspects are absent from this dialogue-based procedure, the

---

[38] CtteeESCR, 'Report on the 36th and 37th session, Supplement No 2' (UN Doc E/2007/22), para 40.

[39] The General Comments are often based on one-day discussions of general issues ('days of general discussion') that are held at each session of the Committee with the participation of interested parties such as NGOs, experts, Special Rapporteurs and representatives of UN specialized agencies.

[40] During the period from 1991 to 1996, several General Comments—in some cases quite detailed—on topics such as social rights, the rights of persons with disabilities and older persons, and the right to housing were published; however, they covered relatively little new ground.

[41] CtteeESCR, General Comments No 8 (1997) and No 9 (1998).

[42] ECOSOC, *Official Records 2000, Supplement No 2*, UN Doc E/C.12/1999/11, Annex IX. According to this outline, General Comments deal with the following points in the order listed: introduction; normative content of rights; state party obligations; obligations of other actors; possible violations; recommendations to states parties.

[43] A General Comment on Non-Discrimination and Economic, Social and Cultural Rights is currently (December 2008) being drafted.

awareness-raising potential of the process of preparing a country report should not be underestimated, provided, of course, that all relevant administrative bodies are involved and civil society is genuinely given a say. The reporting mechanism also sharpens awareness of the need for positive action to secure the enjoyment of human rights. The orientation towards obtaining an overview of a state's legal system rather than focusing on isolated individual cases clearly has the potential, through the Concluding Observations, to harmonize law worldwide in areas of relevance to human rights. At the same time, the consensus-based procedure enables the committees not only to denounce treaty violations but also to identify ways of tackling them and to commend positive elements. Furthermore, the compulsory nature of the procedure enables the international bodies concerned to develop continuous contacts with states which are unwilling to submit to scrutiny by other monitoring mechanisms.

On the negative side, the international bodies are unable to react speedily and are poorly equipped to bring pressure to bear on a state that shows no willingness to cooperate.[44] Moreover, thorough and informative reporting is particularly burdensome for smaller and poorer states, which may partially account for some states' habitual tardiness in complying with their reporting obligations.[45] On the other hand, if all states parties reported punctually, some committees would find it impossible to review all reports in the meeting time available. Hence some measure of streamlining and standardization of the reporting mechanism is clearly necessary.

Issue in focus: Treaty body reform

In recent years, the proliferation of treaty bodies has led to growing criticism over an overburdening of states with reporting duties, a problem compounded by the fact that the competences of Committees overlap, thus creating duplications. In addition, methodologies adopted by the different treaty bodies lack uniformity and may therefore produce inconsistent outcomes.

This has for a long time triggered calls for reforms of the treaty body system: 'An independent expert appointed by the Secretary-General to carry out a study on enhancing the long-term effectiveness of the United Nations human rights treaty system during the 1980s, suggested, inter alia, the creation of a single monitoring body for all treaties. The Secretary-General's second reform report in 2002 provided new impetus for discussions by calling on the international human rights treaty bodies to "craft a more coordinated approach to their activities and standardize their varied

---

[44] In its General Comment No 30 (2002), paras 2 f, the HRCttee also complains that only a small number of states submit their reports on time. Moreover, state delegations have often failed to show up for the scheduled public meeting on their country's report.

[45] See 'Concept Paper on the High Commissioner's Proposal for a Unified Standing Treaty Body, Report by the Secretariat', UN Doc HRI/MC/2006/2, para 16: 'As of February 2006, only eight of the 194 States that are party to one or more of the seven treaties are up to date with their reports, with the remaining 186 States owing 1,442 reports to the treaty bodies.'

reporting requirements" and suggested that "each State should be allowed to produce a single report summarizing its adherence to the full range of international human rights treaties to which it is a party" (A/57/387, para 54). In his report "In larger freedom" (A/59/2005), the Secretary-General re-emphasized the need to streamline and strengthen the treaty body system, and called for implementation of harmonized guidelines on reporting to all treaty bodies, so that the treaty bodies can operate as a unified system.'[46]

As a consequence, it was decided that the 'reporting guidelines' of the different committees are to be harmonized. Harmonized guidelines on reporting under the international human rights treaties, including guidelines on a common core document and treaty-specific targeted documents were submitted by OHCHR in 2005,[47] and a few countries have started to apply them on a voluntary basis. These guidelines provide, *inter alia*, for an expanded common core document that may cover information on issues such as non-discrimination that are covered by several treaties. Information contained in this expanded core document must not be repeated in the specific reports submitted to each of the committees.

In 2005, the High Commissioner for Human Rights proposed more far-reaching reforms by advancing the idea of replacing the existing treaty bodies by one unified standing treaty body with members working full-time:[48]

The proposal of a unified standing treaty body is based on the premise that, unless the international human rights treaty system functions and is perceived as a unified, single entity responsible for monitoring the implementation of all international human rights obligations, with a single, accessible entry point for rights-holders, the lack of visibility, authority and access which affects the current system will persist. The proposal is also based on the recognition that, as currently constituted, the system is approaching the limits of its performance, and that, while steps can be taken to improve its functioning in the short and medium term, more fundamental, structural change will be required in order to guarantee its effectiveness in the long term. Unlike the current system of seven part-time Committees, a unified standing treaty body comprised of permanent, full-time professionals is more likely to produce consistent and authoritative jurisprudence. A unified standing treaty body would be available to victims on a permanent basis and could respond rapidly to grave violations. As a permanent body, it would have the flexibility to develop innovative working methods and approaches to human rights protection and be able to develop clear modalities for the participation of United Nations partners and civil society, which build on the good practices of the current system. It would also be able to develop a strong capacity to assist States parties in their implementation of human rights obligations...

As States implement human rights obligations in an integrated rather than treaty specific way, and individuals and groups do not enjoy their human rights or experience violations along treaty lines, a unified standing treaty body would provide a framework for a comprehensive, cross-cutting and holistic approach to implementation of the treaties. In contrast to the current system of seven treaty bodies which consider reports which are submitted in accordance with different periodicities, a unified standing treaty body could introduce flexible

---

[46] Ibid, para 5.   [47] 'Report by the Secretariat', UN Doc HRI/MC/2005/3, 1 June 2005.
[48] High Commissioner for Human Rights, 'Plan of Action', UN Doc A/59/2005/Add.3, Annex, para 147. For the details of the proposal see Concept Paper on the High Commissioner's Proposal for a Unified Standing Treaty Body, Report by the Secretariat, UN Doc HRI/MC/2006/2.

and creative measures to encourage reporting, and maximize the effectiveness and impact of monitoring. For example, a single cycle for reporting by each State party on implementation of all treaty obligations could be introduced, which would occur once every three to five years, providing States parties and partners with the opportunity to carry out in-depth, holistic, comprehensive and cross-cutting assessments and analysis of a State's human rights perform-ance against all relevant obligations...[49]

Reactions to the proposal have not been very enthusiastic and its implementation would be difficult as the existing treaties would arguably need to be amended, either by a common protocol or by revisions of each treaty concerned. It remains to be seen whether these discussions will lead to more than incremental reforms of the treaty body system.

III. Individual Complaint Procedures

1. Individual communications to the UN treaty bodies

(a) Overview

Individual complaint procedures before UN human rights treaty bodies are of great practical importance even though the decisions reached are not legally bind-ing. In particular, the Human Rights Committee has succeeded, by virtue of its high-quality jurisprudence, in obtaining, in many cases *de facto* recognition of its decisions, which closely resemble judicial judgments in terms of form and content.

At present a total of 111[50] states recognize the Committee's competence to consider individual communications and more than 1,800 such complaints have been dealt with to date. Some 64 states have authorized the Committee against Torture to rule on cases concerning them, a procedure that has hith-erto given rise to more than 360 complaints. Although recognized by 53 states, with only around 40 complaints received to date, comparatively little use has been made of the corresponding procedure before the Committee on the Elimination of Racial Discrimination. Only about 20 individual complaints have been decided by the Committee on the Elimination of Discrimination against Women. The Committees on Migrant Workers[51] and on the Rights of Persons with Disabilities[52] have not yet ruled on any individual communica-tion and the Committee against Enforced Disappearances has not yet been set

---

[49] 'Concept Paper on the High Commissioner's Proposal for a Unified Standing Treaty Body, Report by the Secretariat', UN Doc HRI/MC/2006/2, para 27.

[50] All figures in this section relate to status as of November 2008.

[51] This individual communications mechanism will enter into force when ten states parties have made a declaration under Art 77 of the ICRMW, which could take quite some time. So far, this number of declarations has not been attained.

[52] The Optional Protocol to ICRPD entered into force on 3 May 2008.

up. For the ICESCR, an Optional Protocol designed to allow individual complaints against violations of this treaty was adopted by the General Assembly on 10 December 2008.

Issue in focus: The Optional Protocol to the International Covenant on Economic Social and Cultural Rights

---

Article 1: Competence of the Committee to receive and consider communications

1. A State Party to the Covenant that becomes a Party to the present Protocol recognizes the competence of the Committee to receive and consider communications as provided for by the provisions of the present Protocol. . . .

Article 2: Communications

Communications may be submitted by or on behalf of individuals or groups of individuals, under the jurisdiction of a State Party, claiming to be victims of a violation of any of the economic, social and cultural rights set forth in the Covenant by that State Party. . . .

Article 3: Admissibility

1. The Committee shall not consider a communication unless it has ascertained that all available domestic remedies have been exhausted. This shall not be the rule where the application of such remedies is unreasonably prolonged.

2. The Committee shall declare a communication inadmissible when:

   (a) It is not submitted within one year after the exhaustion of domestic remedies, except in cases where the author can demonstrate that it had not been possible to submit the communication within that time limit;

   (b) The facts that are the subject of the communication occurred prior to the entry into force of the present Protocol for the State Party concerned unless those facts continued after that date;

   (c) The same matter has already been examined by the Committee or has been or is being examined under another procedure of international investigation or settlement; . . . .

   (e) It is manifestly ill-founded, not sufficiently substantiated or exclusively based on reports disseminated by mass media; . . .

Article 4: Communications not revealing a clear disadvantage

The Committee may, if necessary, decline to consider a communication where it does not reveal that the author has suffered a clear disadvantage, unless the Committee considers that the communication raises a serious issue of general importance.

Article 5: Interim measures

1. At any time after the receipt of a communication and before a determination on the merits has been reached, the Committee may transmit to the State Party concerned for its urgent consideration a request that the State Party take such interim measures as may be necessary in exceptional circumstances to avoid possible irreparable damage to the victim or victims of the alleged violations.

2. Where the Committee exercises its discretion under paragraph 1 of the present article, this does not imply a determination on admissibility or on the merits of the communication.

...

Article 8: Examination of communications

...

4. When examining communications under the present Protocol, the Committee shall consider the reasonableness of the steps taken by the State Party in accordance with part II of the Covenant. In doing so, the Committee shall bear in mind that the State Party may adopt a range of possible policy measures for the implementation of the rights set forth in the Covenant.

(b) *The individual communications procedure of the Human Rights Committee*

Taking the Human Rights Committee as its model, the following section describes the individual communications procedure, which is very similar in the case of all treaty bodies. The procedure developed by the Committee is by far the most important of its kind in the UN treaty system.

An individual communication can be filed only against states that have recognized the Committee's competence in this regard by ratifying the ICCPR-OP1. As soon as a communication is registered with the Committee, the state party concerned is notified and, with a view to keeping the proceedings reasonably short, requested to comment within six months both on the admissibility and on the merits of the case. The author of the communication is then given an opportunity to reply within a period of two months. Where a state party fails to cooperate with the Committee even after receiving reminders, the Committee usually bases its assessment of the facts of the case on the complainant's allegations, provided that they appear credible.

Communications to the Committee have no suspensive effect. Where, as often happens in death penalty cases or cases of imminent risk of torture in the country to which a person is facing deportation or extradition, the individual is in danger of suffering serious and irreparable harm during the period between submission of the communication and the final decision, the Committee[53] is entitled at any point in the proceedings to order interim measures of protection.[54] These measures are binding and a state that disregards them commits a grave breach of the Optional Protocol.[55]

---

[53] The Committee has appointed a Special Rapporteur for New Communications from among its members for this purpose.

[54] Arts 92 ff of the Rules of Procedure of the HRCttee. The other committees also have competence in this regard.

[55] See for example HRCttee, General Comment No 33 (2008), para 19, and *Piandiong et al v The Philippines*, Communication No 869/1999 (2000), para 5, and *Saidova v Tajikistan*, Communication No 964/2001 (2004), para 4.2.

Example: Views of the HRCttee in *Piandiong et al v The Philippines*[56]

1.2 On 7 November 1994, Messrs. Piandiong, Morallos and Bulan were convicted of robbery with homicide and sentenced to death by the Regional Trial Court of Caloocan City. The Supreme Court denied the appeal, and confirmed both conviction and sentence by judgment of 19 February 1997. Further motions for reconsideration were denied on 3 March 1998. After the execution had been scheduled for 6 April 1999, the Office of the President, on 5 April 1999, granted a three month reprieve of execution. No clemency was however granted and on 15 June 1999, counsel presented a communication to the Committee under the Optional Protocol.

1.3 On 23 June 1999, the Committee, acting through its Special Rapporteur for New Communications, transmitted the communication to the State party with a request to provide information and observations in respect of both admissibility and merits of the claims, in accordance with rule 91, paragraph 2, of the Committee's rules of procedure. The State party was also requested, under rule 86 of the Committee's rules of procedure, not to carry out the death sentence against Messrs. Piandiong, Morallos and Bulan, while their case was under consideration by the Committee....

1.5 Counsel for Messrs. Piandiong, Morallos and Bulan filed a petition with the Supreme Court seeking an injunction, which was refused by the Court on 8 July 1999. Counsel also met personally with the Government's Justice Secretary and asked him not to carry out the death sentence in view of the Committee's request. In the afternoon of 8 July 1999, however, Messrs. Piandiong, Morallos and Bulan were executed by lethal injection....

5. *State party's failure to respect the Committee's request for interim measures under Rule 86*

5.1 By adhering to the Optional Protocol, a State party to the Covenant recognizes the competence of the Human Rights Committee to receive and consider communications from individuals claiming to be victims of violations of any of the rights set forth in the Covenant (Preamble and Article 1). Implicit in a State's adherence to the Protocol is an undertaking to cooperate with the Committee in good faith so as to permit and enable it to consider such communications, and after examination to forward its views to the State party and to the individual (Article 5 (1), (4)). It is incompatible with these obligations for a State party to take any action that would prevent or frustrate the Committee in its consideration and examination of the communication, and in the expression of its Views.

5.2 Quite apart, then, from any violation of the Covenant charged to a State party in a communication, a State party commits grave breaches of its obligations under the Optional Protocol if it acts to prevent or frustrate consideration by the Committee of a communication alleging a violation of the Covenant, or to render examination by the Committee moot and the expression of its Views nugatory and futile. In respect of the present communication, the authors allege that the alleged victims were denied rights under Articles 6 and 14 of the Covenant. Having been notified of the communication, the State party breaches its obligations under the Protocol, if it proceeds to execute the alleged victims before the Committee concludes its consideration and examination, and the formulation and communication of its Views. It is particularly inexcusable for the State to do so after the Committee has acted under its rule 86 to request that the State party refrain from doing so....

5.4 Interim measures pursuant to rule 86 of the Committee's rules adopted in conformity with Article 39 of the Covenant, are essential to the Committee's role under the Protocol. Flouting of this Rule, especially by irreversible measures such as the execution of the alleged victim or his/her deportation from the country, undermines the protection of Covenant rights through the Optional Protocol.'

---

[56] HRCttee, *Piandiong et al v The Philippines*, Communication No 869/1999 (2000). Rule 86 is now Rule 92 (UN Doc CCPR/C/3/Rev.8).

Following the comments by the state party and the reply by the author of the communication, a draft decision is prepared, with support from the secretariat, by a member of the Committee acting as Rapporteur. The Committee then examines the communications and discusses the draft during a private meeting;[57] if it is deemed to be admissible, a decision is usually taken concurrently on the merits. At the request of the state concerned, however, the Special Rapporteur on New Communications may decide to divide the procedure into two separate stages, ie grant a so-called 'split'. In such cases, the comments by the state party and the reply by the author in the first stage deals exclusively with the question of admissibility and the procedure is continued on the merits only where the communication is declared to be admissible.[58]

At the admissibility stage, the Committee determines:

- whether its competence is recognized by the state concerned;[59] in practice problems may arise regarding the interpretation of reservations entered by the state party at the time of ratification of the first Optional Protocol;
- whether the authors claim concerns the violation of a right guaranteed by the Covenant;[60]
- whether the author's claim concerns a violation of a right that occurred after the date of entry into force of the Optional Protocol for the respondent state or, as, for instance, in the case of forced disappearance, whether the violation that occurred before the date of entry into force continues beyond it;[61]
- whether the author's claim to be the victim of a violation of one or more ICCPR guarantees is sufficiently substantiated;[62]
- whether available domestic remedies have been exhausted;[63]
- whether the communication is abusive or anonymous;[64] and

---

[57] During the week preceding the Committee's sessions, a working group consisting of the case rapporteurs meets to prepare the discussion of drafts in plenary. Cases that are declared inadmissible unanimously by the Working Group are adopted by the Committee without further discussion unless a member so demands.

[58] In clear-cut cases, the Committee can declare the complaint inadmissible even without first inviting the state party to comment. In such cases a draft decision is prepared by the Special Rapporteur on new Communications.

[59] ICCPR-OP1, Art 1.   [60] ICCPR-OP1, Art 2.

[61] The Committee declares communications admissible not only when the violation is ongoing (for example in the case of detention), but also when, after the entry into force of the Optional Protocol for the state party concerned, a domestic law, a decision by the government, or a judgment confirm a violation that occurred prior to that date. See, eg, HRCttee, *Simunek et al v Czech Republic*, Communication No 516/1992 (1995), paras 4.5 ff. Furthermore, communications may be rendered inadmissible by a reservation regarding the temporal scope of application of the Optional Protocol. See, for example, HRCttee, *Singarasa v Sri Lanka*, Communication No 1033/2001 (2004), para 6.3.

[62] ICCPR-OP1, Art 2; this *prima facie* examination corresponds to the European Court of Human Rights examination of whether an application is inadmissible on the grounds of being 'manifestly unfounded'.

[63] ICCPR-OP1, Arts 2 and 5(2)(b).   [64] ICCPR-OP1, Art 3.

- whether the same matter is not simultaneously being examined under another procedure of international investigation or settlement, ie before another treaty monitoring body or a regional human rights court.[65]

While there is no time limit for filing communications, a case filed after an unduly long delay without a reasonable justification may be deemed abusive.[66]

If these conditions are cumulatively met, the communication is declared admissible and examined on the merits, ie the Committee decides whether a violation of the ICCPR has occurred. If a violation is found, the Committee also rules on the remedy to be provided by the violating state. This decision is taken in a closed session on the basis of a simple majority[67] and communicated to the parties. Any separate opinions by members of the Committee disagreeing with the outcome or the reasoning in support of the decision are attached to the decision. All decisions are published in the Committee's annual report to the UN General Assembly.[68]

As the notion of 'views' indicates, the decisions of the Human Rights Committee are legally non-binding. They nevertheless possess considerable authority because they stem from a body entrusted and empowered by states parties to determine authoritatively whether human rights have been violated in specific cases. Thus, the principle of good faith requires that states at least consider and weigh the reasons why they are not ready to implement a finding of a violation.

Issue in focus: Human Rights Committee,
General Comment No 33 (2008)

---

11. While the function of the Human Rights Committee in considering individual communications is not, as such, that of a judicial body, the views issued by the Committee under

---

[65] ICCPR-OP1, Arts 2 and 5(2)(a). A prior examination by another human rights enforcement body, such as the ECtHR, does not constitute a ground of inadmissibility. However, many European states parties have entered a reservation excluding admissibility under such circumstances. Concurrent consideration of a case in the context of the complaints procedure of the Human Rights Council (Chapter 8, section II.4.d) or as part of a procedure involving Special Procedures of the Human Rights Council (Chapter 8, section II.4.b) does not constitute an impediment. A communication before the CtteeAT is inadmissible if the 'same matter has . . . been, and is . . . being, examined under another procedure of international investigation or settlement' (CAT, Art 22(5)(a)). A pending procedure dealing with the same matter does not constitute a ground of inadmissibility in the case of the CtteeERD.

[66] See for example, HRCttee, *Zundel v Canada*, Communication No 1341/2005 (2007), para 6.5, and *Chytil v Czech Republic*, Communication No 1452/2006 (2007), para 6.

[67] In practice many decisions are taken unanimously. This accounts to some extent for reasoning that is couched in remarkably brief or loose terms, reflecting the lowest common denominator of Committee members' views.

[68] They may also be consulted on the website of the Office of the UN High Commissioner for Human Rights (<http://www.ohchr.org/EN/HRBodies/Pages/HumanRightsBodies.aspx> (accessed 5 February 2009)). A more user-friendly website run by the Netherlands Institute of Human Rights of the University of Utrecht can be found at <http://sim.law.uu.nl/sim/Dochome.nsf> (accessed 5 February 2009).

the Optional Protocol exhibit some important characteristics of a judicial decision. They are arrived at in a judicial spirit, including the impartiality and independence of Committee members, the considered interpretation of the language of the Covenant, and the determinative character of the decisions.

12. The term used in article 5, paragraph 4 of the Optional Protocol to describe the decisions of the Committee is 'views'. These decisions state the Committee's findings on the violations alleged by the author of a communication and, where a violation has been found, state a remedy for that violation.

13. The views of the Committee under the Optional Protocol represent an authoritative determination by the organ established under the Covenant itself charged with the interpretation of that instrument. These views derive their character, and the importance which attaches to them, from the integral role of the Committee under both the Covenant and the Optional Protocol.

...

15. The character of the views of the Committee is further determined by the obligation of States parties to act in good faith, both in their participation in the procedures under the Optional Protocol and in relation to the Covenant itself. A duty to cooperate with the Committee arises from an application of the principle of good faith to the observance of all treaty obligations.

...

20. Most States do not have specific enabling legislation to receive the views of the Committee into their domestic legal order. The domestic law of some States parties does, however, provide for the payment of compensation to the victims of violations of human rights as found by international organs. In any case, States parties must use whatever means lie within their power in order to give effect to the views issued by the Committee.

In contrast to the situation at the regional level, the UN system has no political organ with a mandate to enforce treaty body decisions. Accordingly, the Human Rights Committee assumes the task itself to following up to its decisions. Where it has determined that a violation of the Covenant has occurred, the Committee requests the state concerned to report within three months on the measures it has taken to give effect to the decision.[69] Its response is forwarded to the author of the communication for comment. Where the state fails to respond to the request or where its response is unsatisfactory, the matter is referred to a member of the Committee specifically entrusted with this task, the 'Special Rapporteur for Follow-up'. This member's task is to persuade the government to cooperate. The Committee's annual report gives an account of the measures taken by the Special Rapporteur as an additional means of exerting pressure.[70] The success of this procedure has been varied.[71]

---

[69] The HRCttee bases this practice on the requirement of an effective remedy at the domestic level required by ICCPR, Art 2(3).

[70] HRCttee, General Comment No 33 (2008), para 16.

[71] The Committee's annual reports to the General Assembly contain information about the follow-up to its views.

2. Individual complaints to the European Court of Human Rights

(a) General remarks

Since 1998 a permanent Court of Human Rights has been sitting in Strasbourg.[72] At this time, the former two-stage complaint procedure before both the Commission and the Court[73] was replaced by a new compulsory procedure before the Court alone. The purpose of the procedural reform was primarily to simplify and streamline the procedure but also to enhance the effectiveness of the system. The latter goal was only partially successful. Thus, while the new monitoring regime achieved a massive increase in efficiency, ie in the number of judgments rendered, the Court found itself unable to cope adequately with the dramatic increase in complaints.[74] This led to a considerable increase in the duration of the proceedings and to demands for restrictions on access to the Court.

In 2004, the states parties to the ECHR adopted Protocol No 14, which amends the ECHR with provisions simplifying some aspects of the individual complaint procedure aimed at allowing the Court to cope better with the steadily increasing workload. The new Protocol will enter into force following its ratification by all states parties to the ECHR.[75]

(b) The right of individual petition

The core of the European human rights system, the right of any person to file a complaint (called 'application') with the Court regarding an alleged violation of ECHR rights by a state party, is set out in ECHR, Article 34. This provision confers the right of petition to 'any person, non-governmental organization, or group of individuals claiming to be the victim of a violation by one of the High Contracting Parties of the rights set forth in the Convention or the protocols thereto'. This rules out applications against a particular state party if the impugned act or omission is not attributable to it.

---

[72] With the entry into force of P 11/ECHR on 1 November 1998.

[73] Applications had to be submitted to the former European Human Rights Commission which examined their admissibility, prepared a report with its own views on the facts and the law of the case and tried to achieve a friendly settlement of the case. If such settlement could not be achieved, the Commission and the state party concerned (and since the adoption of P 9/ECHR also the author of the application) could submit the case to the Court.

[74] At the end of 2008, approximately 96,550 complaints were pending before the ECtHR. The standard Council of Europe explanation for this development was that the Court had become the victim of its own success. This perspective should, however, be qualified to take into account the sharp increase in the number of particularly complex cases that followed the admission of Central and East European states to the Council of Europe after the end of the Cold War before they had managed to establish properly functioning judicial systems. In the absence of an effective domestic system of legal redress in certain countries, the Court often found itself having to rule on complaints as the first independent judicial body, and consequently having to investigate the facts of a case.

[75] At the time of this writing (2008), this seems rather unlikely as Russia continues to be unwilling to ratify the Protocol.

(c) Admissibility

Individual applications must be submitted to the Registrar of the Court, who sends the complainant an application form. Once the completed application form is received, the complaint is registered.

In a first step, the admissibility of the application is examined. A committee of three judges can unanimously declare it inadmissible.[76] If this is not done, the Chamber examining the case decides about its admissibility. A complaint may also be declared inadmissible at a later stage in the proceedings—particularly on the grounds of being manifestly ill-founded.[77] All inadmissibility decisions are final.

Pursuant to ECHR, Article 35, an individual application must meet the following admissibility criteria:

(1) Available domestic remedies must have been exhausted in due form and within the prescribed period prior to submission of the application. Domestic remedies need only be sought where they are effective, ie where they can repair the violation and where they have suspensive effect if this is necessary in the circumstances.[78] Domestic remedies are deemed to have been exhausted only if the claim in the complaint regarding the violation of a Convention right was asserted 'in substance', ie at least the essence of the claim, before domestic bodies.

(2) The application must be deposited within six months of the date on which the final domestic decision was taken.

(3) The application may not be anonymous. The applicant's name and address must be provided.

(4) The principle of *res judicata* may not be violated, ie an application may not be the same matter (in terms of the parties, subject matter and rights invoked) as already examined by the Court.

(5) Other procedures of international investigation or settlement—particularly by the UN treaty bodies—may not have dealt with the case.[79]

(6) The application may not be incompatible with the provisions of the Convention, ie the subject matter must fall within the personal, substantive, territorial, and temporal scope of application of the Convention, taking into account any reservations by the state party concerned.

(7) It may not constitute an abuse of the right of application, eg by using grossly offensive language or providing misleading or false information.

(8) The application may not be manifestly ill-founded.

---

[76] Pursuant to P 14/ECHR, which has not yet come into force, a single judge could declare applications to the Court inadmissible if no further examination is needed. The Protocol would also allow a committee of three judges to make an immediate summary determination, where a complaint relates to matters that do not raise complex legal issues and are already settled in the jurisprudence of the Court.

[77] See subsection (d) below.   [78] For instance, in the face of a threat of extradition.

[79] In contrast to the procedure under ICCPR-OP1 where only the simultaneous handling of a complaint is deemed to be a ground of inadmissibility.

(d) In particular: manifest ill-foundedness as a ground of inadmissibility

With the exception of the criteria of manifest ill-foundedness, these admissibility criteria are purely formal and procedural. Closer examination of the substance is required in order to determine whether or not a complaint is manifestly ill-founded.

According to a standard approach, applications are manifestly ill-founded where an examination of the facts 'fails to disclose any appearance of a violation of the rights and freedoms set out in the Convention'. A complaint can be declared manifestly ill-founded at different stages of the procedure, ie from the time of its registration until any oral hearing. If, on the other hand, the Court finds that, after a summary examination of the substantive issues, a violation of ECHR guarantees cannot be ruled out, it declares the application admissible.

In practice, the vast majority of complaints are declared to be manifestly ill-founded because:

(1) the complainant *lacks victim status*, ie is not personally affected or aggrieved and therefore cannot establish his or her claim to have suffered a violation of a right recognized by the ECHR;
(2) the complaint is *insufficiently substantiated*, ie its author does not sufficiently set out the facts of the case and how the attacked action or omission by the state party concerned violate the ECHR;
(3) the claim is *based solely on an error in the application of domestic law* or an error in determining the facts;[80] or
(4) the complaint is *wholly unfounded* according to the Court's so-called 'global formula', whereby it declares that an examination of all aspects of the case has failed to disclose any violation of the ECHR. This occurs, for instance, in the case of muddled complaints or claims regarding insubstantial minor points or where a disproportionate effort of reasoning would be required to handle a complaint.

(e) No significant disadvantage as a ground of inadmissibility

If Protocol No 14 enters into force, the Court will also have the authority under ECHR, Article 35(3) to declare a complaint inadmissible if the victim has not suffered a 'significant' disadvantage through an alleged violation of the Convention. This ground of inadmissibility calls for a summary examination of the facts of the case. However, the Court may not invoke this ground if either (1) respect for human rights as defined in the Convention and the Protocols thereto requires

---

[80] A frequently overlooked fact is that the Court *is not an additional appellate court* but an international body whose jurisdiction is confined to claims of violations of Convention rights and that it cannot under any circumstances review the correct application of domestic law. It follows that while the Strasbourg Court can examine compliance with the due process guarantees contained in ECHR, Arts 5 and 6 in criminal proceedings, it cannot rule on the legitimacy of the verdict.

an examination of the application on the merits, or (2) an independent domestic tribunal has not rendered a decision on the claim of a human rights violation.

This new procedural barrier differs from other admissibility criteria in that it marks the first departure from the principle that every domestic violation of the ECHR can be remedied by an international body. While this possibility may help the Court to address more efficiently its backlog, it seems problematic from a rule of law perspective that someone whose rights under the ECHR have been violated is barred from an effective remedy at the European level.

(f) Interim measures

A complaint under the ECHR does not have suspensive effect. Pursuant to Article 39 of the Rules of Court, however, the chambers can indicate to the state concerned any interim measures that they consider desirable in the interests of the parties or the proper conduct of the proceedings. The Court's established practice is to resort to interim measures only in cases where a summary examination of the facts does not entirely rule out a violation of Convention rights and failure to grant interim measures would cause irreparable harm to the victim. Interim measures tend to be granted in cases of deportation or extradition of complainants to states where they face a risk of torture or inhuman treatment. According to the Court,[81] a state party that disregards interim measures violates the ECHR, specifically Article 34, pursuant to which the contracting parties undertake not to hinder in any way 'the effective exercise' of the right of petition.

(g) Continuation of the procedure

After the admissibility decision, the next steps in the procedure are as follows:

(1) Where the application is not immediately declared inadmissible, it is forwarded to the government concerned for comments; the applicant is also given the opportunity to comment subsequently on the government's submission. Even after this exchange of correspondence, the chamber can still declare the complaint inadmissible; it can make the declaration of admissibility right away, or it can schedule an oral hearing (and rule on admissibility at that point);

(2) If the application is declared admissible, the Chamber examines the facts of the case. Under ECHR, Articles 38 and 39, the Court is required to seek a 'friendly settlement'. If such a settlement is achieved, it draws up a brief report and strikes the case from its list.

(3) Where a friendly settlement cannot be achieved, the Chamber renders a judgment that is, in principle, final (ECHR, Article 43). However, the Chamber can refer to the Grand Chamber any complaint pending before it that raises

---

[81] ECtHR (Grand Chamber), *Mamatkulov and Abdurasulovic v Turkey*, Reports 2005-I, paras 99 ff.

serious questions of interpretation of the ECHR and its protocols or that may result in a deviation from an earlier judgment of the Court, provided that no objection is raised by any of the parties (ECHR, Article 30).

(4) Within three months of the rendering of a judgment by a Chamber, any party may request that it be reviewed by the Grand Chamber; a panel of five judges then decides whether the request should be accepted. If it is accepted, the Grand Chamber renders a final judgment; if it is rejected, the Chamber's judgment becomes final (ECHR, Articles 43 f).

(h) Outcome of the procedure and enforcement of judgments

If the Court concludes that a complaint is substantiated, its only option is to find that there has been a violation of the ECHR. It has no jurisdiction, for instance, to set aside a judgment that is contrary to the Convention, to repeal a domestic law or to order the release of a prisoner. In addition to finding violations, it is further empowered to make binding awards of damages and 'just satisfaction'.[82] The manner in which the judgment is implemented is, broadly speaking, left to the sovereign decision of the state party concerned.

The Court's judgments are binding (ECHR, Article 46). The Committee of Ministers of the Council of Europe[83] monitors states' compliance with awards of damages and their implementation of the substantive content of the judgment (eg amendment of legislation or review of proceedings).[84] To ensure that judgments are executed, the Committee of Ministers invites states to submit reports on measures taken to implement them. While Court judgments were formerly implemented virtually without exception at the national level, albeit in some cases reluctantly and with threats to denounce the ECHR, in recent years there has been a troubling tendency to disregard or not fully to implement some judgments. The Committee of Ministers has so far been all but powerless in the face of this development, having to content itself for the most part with warnings to defaulting states.[85]

Protocol No 14 to the ECHR seeks to remedy this state of affairs by providing the Committee of Ministers with additional means of enforcement. The Committee would thus be entitled, (1) on the basis of a two-thirds majority, to

---

[82] Under ECHR, Art 41 just satisfaction is owed only in cases where domestic law allows only partial reparation to be made and, according to Court jurisprudence, where the finding of a violation of the ECHR does not in itself constitute satisfaction. The ECtHR thus operates on the principle that the victim should be provided with full compensation.

[83] This organ of the Council of Europe is composed of the Foreign Ministers of the Council's member states or, in the Ministers' absence, of their permanent representatives in Strasbourg.

[84] See Rules of the Committee of Ministers for the supervision of the execution of judgments and of the terms of friendly settlements of 10 May 2006.

[85] Although the Committee of Ministers has always had the power to take far-reaching measures such as expulsion of a state from the Council of Europe, the prospects of obtaining majority support in the Committee for this kind of action are limited, except perhaps as a last resort in the event of massive human rights violations.

refer a matter to the Court for clarification if it considers that the supervision
of the execution of a final judgment is hindered by a problem of interpretation.
If, on the other hand, it considers that (2) a state has refused to abide by a judgment, it can decide by a two-thirds majority to refer to the Court the question of
whether the state has properly executed the judgment. If the Court finds that this
is not the case, it refers the matter back to the Committee of Ministers for consideration of further measures. If the Court finds that the state's conduct was not
a violation of the Convention, the matter is also referred back to the Committee,
which declares the case closed.[86] How far these new powers would enable the
Committee of Ministers to reduce the number of Court judgments that fail to be
implemented in the future remains to be seen.

3. Individual complaints to the other regional Courts

At the (Latin) American level, there is a two-step individual complaint procedure.[87] The complaint (called 'petition') is examined for admissibility by the
Inter-American Commission on Human Rights. In case of admissibility, the
Commission seeks to reach a friendly settlement. If that fails, it draws up a report
which both sets out the facts and states the Commission's legal opinion. In this
context, the Commission has the possibility to conduct, with the consent of the
state in whose territory a violation has allegedly been committed, an investigation on that territory. Within three months of the adoption of the report by the
Commission, both the Commission and the defendant state (but not the complainant[88]) can refer the case to the Inter-American Court of Human Rights,
which—if the state has recognized the Court's jurisdiction—renders a judgment.
Its power to order provisional measures '[i]n cases of extreme gravity and urgency,
and when necessary to avoid irreparable damage to persons' has become particularly relevant in cases where the Court ordered states to protect individuals
threatened to be displaced or massacred.[89] The judgments are legally binding. If
the case is not referred to the Court, the Commission's report, which is not binding, is published.

   In Africa, an individual communication is first, and—as long as the African
Court of Human and Peoples' Rights has not become operational—exclusively,
examined by the African Commission on Human and Peoples' Rights.[90] In contrast to its regional counterparts, the procedure before the Commission does not

---

[86] ECHR, Art 46(3–5).   [87] ACHR, Arts 44–51 and 61–69.
   [88] Since 2001, however, the complainant can at least obtain a referral through the Commission.
This fact (partially) accounts for the relatively small number of complaints before the IACtHR,
which has so far handed down only about 90 substantive judgments in individual complaint
procedures.
   [89] Such measures can also be ordered in cases that are still pending with the Commission
(ACHR, Art 63(2)). In IACtHR, *James et al v Trinidad and Tobago*, order of 25 May 1999, para 2(g),
the Court decided that such measures are legally binding.
   [90] ACHPR, Arts 30 ff.

provide complainants a right to have their grievances considered. Thus, as a first step, the Commission decides by a simple majority whether it should consider a complaint.[91] If it decides against consideration of the complaint, the procedure is closed. Otherwise, the next step is an admissibility procedure in which the usual criteria are examined,[92] followed by the examination of the merits.[93] The Commission is entitled to examine complaints not only in light of the African Charter but also with reference to all human rights treaties ratified by the defendant state.[94] The Commission's reports on individual communications 'remain confidential until such a time as the Assembly of Heads of State and Government shall otherwise decide'.[95]

Once the African Court of Human and Peoples' Rights becomes operational there will presumably be a two-step procedure at the African level, as well. The African Commission on Human and Peoples' Rights, the state party against which the complaint has been lodged at the Commission, and the state party whose citizen is a victim of human rights violation (but not the complainant) are entitled to submit cases to the Court.[96] Additionally, '[t]he Court may entitle relevant Non Governmental organizations (NGOs) with observer status before the Commission, and individuals to institute cases directly before it'.[97] The Court, when examining a case on the merits, shall apply 'the provision of the Charter and any other relevant human rights instruments ratified by the States concerned'.[98]

4. Assessment

Individual complaint procedures are commonly viewed as the greatest achievement of the international human rights system and are even equated, especially in the West, with the successful enforcement of human rights. It is no small concession for states to agree to allow individuals to take the initiative in instituting proceedings at the international level that puts the claimant and the government on an equal footing in procedural terms in areas that were traditionally viewed as domestic matters within the sphere of sovereignty. In practical terms, this type of procedure offers individual victims the most direct means of securing effective application of human rights. Furthermore, individual complaint procedures provide a framework conducive to the dynamic development of human rights,

---

[91] ACHPR, Art 55.   [92] ACHPR, Art 56.

[93] If after its considerations the African Commission comes to the conclusion 'that one or more Communications apparently relate to special cases which reveal the existence of a series of serious or massive violations of human and peoples' rights' the complaint is drawn to the attention of the Assembly of Heads of State and Government. This body may request the Commission 'to undertake an in-depth study of these cases and make a factual report, accompanied by its finding and recommendations'. A further decision by the Assembly is required for publication of the results of this study (ACHPR, Art 58).

[94] ACHPR, Arts 60 f. See, eg, ACmHPR, *Democratic Republic of Congo v Burundi, Rwanda and Uganda*, Communication No 227/1999 (2004), para 70.

[95] ACHPR, Art 59.   [96] P 1/ACHPR, Art 5(1).

[97] P 1/ACHPR, Art 5(3).   [98] P 1/ACHPR, Art 7.

since new social and technological developments can be taken into account when deciding specific cases.

Yet this ideal image of an appellate authority to which every victim of a human rights violation has access, which can take binding and enforceable decisions against states, is not quite matched by the facts. Even the European Court of Human Rights does not fully live up to this concept, since the proceedings now run for years and its judgments are sometimes not implemented to the letter by states. At the Inter-American level, the scarcity of Court judgments demonstrates in itself that the image of unimpeded access for victims of human rights violations is largely fictional. In the African regional context, there can be little prospect of an effective complaint procedure in view of the many built-in loopholes that can be invoked to halt the proceedings on political grounds. At the universal level, one is struck by the relatively small number of complaints filed. This may well be due to the fact that UN committees are not empowered to make binding decisions, so that individuals opt for another forum wherever the choice exists, as it does in Europe and the Americas. A more likely reason, however, is that victims of human rights violations (and even more so members of disadvantaged groups) in most states throughout the world lack both the knowledge and the practical means to petition an international body.

IV. Other Procedures

1. Interstate complaint procedures

A state's right to file a communication with a monitoring body against another state is generally an optional provision, except in the case of the ECHR and the Convention against Racial Discrimination. The ICCPR, the Optional Protocol to the ICESCR, and the Conventions against Torture and Racial Discrimination, as well as the regional human rights conventions, with the exception of the Arab Charter on Human Rights, provide for an interstate complaint procedure.[99] This type of complaint reflects the *erga omnes partes* character of treaty-based human rights[100] at the procedural level. The option of triggering proceedings to enforce treaty obligations is, in principle, open not only to states whose interests are directly affected but also to other states parties.

In practice, interstate complaint procedures are hardly used. There has not been a single instance of a state filing a complaint of this kind at the universal level, and only Europe and in one case Africa[101] have experienced such proceedings at the

---

[99] ICCPR, Art 41; CERD, Arts 12–13; CAT, Art 21; ECHR, Art 33; ACHR, Art 45; ACHPR, Art 47.

[100] See Chapter 3, section II.

[101] ACmHPR, *Democratic Republic of Congo v Burundi, Rwanda and Uganda*, Communication No 227/1999 (2004).

regional level. Moreover, the great majority of the 13 complaints filed to date in Strasbourg were not lodged in defence of a European *ordre public* of states with no direct interest of their own in the outcome,[102] but in the context of bilateral conflicts or in cases where the human rights of a state's own nationals had been violated.[103]

What accounts for this reluctance on the part of states? One reason is that the filing of such a complaint, usually viewed by the defendant state as a drastic measure and an unfriendly act, may have a serious adverse impact on political and economic relations between the states involved. The fear of becoming the 'victim' of a counter-complaint by the defendant state may also play a significant role in this regard. Furthermore, this kind of procedure entails substantial procedural expenses since they must substantiate the claims through costly investigations of facts that did not occur as a rule on their own territory. An easier option is to bring pressure to bear through bilateral human rights policy measures (diplomatic representations, public criticism, attachment of conditions to development or economic aid, etc). At the same time, measures taken by the Human Rights Council such as special sessions or investigations by special procedures[104] can produce an outcome similar to that of an interstate complaint by means that are less burdensome for states. A strong resolution by the Human Rights Council may even have more authority from a moral and political point of view than a treaty body decision.

Issue in focus: The interstate complaint procedure

While the different stages of this procedure before the European Court correspond closely to those of the individual procedure (but last for several years owing to the generally complex nature of the facts involved), interstate procedures under the UN treaties differ sharply from individual procedures.

In the interstate complaint procedure under the ICCPR,[105] for example, the first stage of the procedure is entirely bilateral. If a state party considers that another state party has violated the Covenant, it can bring the matter to that state's attention by

---

[102] Three complaints fall into that category. They were filed by Sweden, Norway, Denmark, the Netherlands and partly by France against human rights violations perpetrated by the former military dictatorship in Greece and by Turkey.

[103] The first of these categories comprises two complaints by Greece against the United Kingdom in connection with the independence of Cyprus, four complaints by Cyprus against Turkey (occupation of the northern part of the island by Turkey), a complaint by Austria against Italy (South Tyrol) and a complaint by Ireland against the United Kingdom (Northern Ireland); complaints by Denmark against Turkey and by Georgia against Russia belong to the second category. Only two of these complaints gave rise to a Court judgment (*Ireland v The United Kingdom*, Series A, No 25 (1978), and *Cyprus v Turkey*, Reports 2001-IV). The other procedures concluded either with a friendly settlement or—in the absence of mandatory jurisdiction of the Court—with a decision by the Committee of Ministers. The Case of Georgia against Russia is pending at the time of writing (2008).

[104] See Chapter 8, section II.4.

[105] ICCPR, Art 41 and rr 74–83 of the Rules of Procedure of the Human Rights Committee.

a written communication. The other state has three months in which to respond to the communication. If no agreement is reached within six months, either state has the right to refer the matter to the Human Rights Committee, which examines the complaint to determine admissibility, particularly in terms of exhaustion of domestic remedies. If it is admissible, the Committee seeks to mediate between the states with a view to resolving the matter on the basis of the Covenant. Where this fails, the Committee draws up a report containing the facts and the parties' written and oral submissions. That completes the procedure; the Committee takes no specific decision nor does it publish its substantive suggestions as mediator.[106]

2. Preventive procedures

Complaint procedures are triggered by actual violations and reactive, and they are not primarily designed to prevent future human rights violations, although in some cases they may have a preventive impact. At the European level, the adoption in 1987 of the European Convention for the Prevention of Torture addressed this shortcoming—at least for a core human right, violations of which can cause irreparable harm to the victim. Under the Convention, the European Committee for the Prevention of Torture (ECPT) has jurisdiction to carry out inspections at any time, and if need be unannounced, of places where persons are held in custody and are at risk of ill-treatment. In practice, this means that the Committee is authorized to visit prisons, police stations, locked wards of psychiatric hospitals, facilities for detaining deportable aliens, and all other places where people are deprived of their liberty by order of the public authorities. On the basis of its observations, the Committee makes detailed recommendations to states for measures to reduce the risk of future ill-treatment. The reports are confidential unless the state party concerned agrees to have them published.[107]

In December 2002, after years of negotiations, a substantively similar treaty was finally adopted at the universal level in the form of an Optional Protocol to the 1984 UN Convention against Torture.[108] As at the European level, the aim is to prevent ill-treatment through a system of regular visits to custodial facilities. Unlike its European counterpart, however, the UN mechanism has two layers. States parties are required to set up at the domestic level one or several bodies composed of independent experts who are authorized to undertake visits at any time to all establishments where persons are deprived of their liberty and to interview detainees without witnesses. At the international level, a Subcommittee on Prevention of Torture was established in 2007.[109] It has the

[106] The CAT procedure is identical, while the CERD procedure is even more complex and does not even provide for the publication of a report.

[107] This agreement is granted in most cases.

[108] Optional Protocol to the Convention against Torture and other Cruel, Inhuman or Degrading Treatment or Punishment of 18 December 2002, in force since 22 June 2006.

[109] Composed initially of 10 members and, after the 50th ratification of the Protocol, of 25 members.

same visiting rights as the national body and has the competence to advise states on national mechanisms and supervise their work. Where states fail to cooperate with the Subcommittee, the Committee against Torture is authorized to publish the reports of its subsidiary body, which are normally confidential.

3. Inquiry procedures

The Convention against Torture, the Convention on the Elimination of All Forms of Discrimination against Women, the Convention on the Rights of Persons with Disabilities, the Convention for the Protection of All Persons from Enforced Disappearance, and the Optional Protocol to the ICESCR[110] empower their monitoring bodies to investigate a state party's compliance with relevant treaty rights on their own initiative if reliable and well-founded information indicates that serious and systematic violations of the rights concerned are being perpetrated. Accordingly, the basic thrust of this little-used treaty-based procedure[111] is reactive.

When the treaty bodies receive such information, they can initiate the procedure by their own motion, ie as a first step invite the state party to comment. If the charges are not credibly refuted by the state's response, one or more members of the Committee concerned begin the actual inquiry. In this context, on-site fact-finding is possible but requires the consent of the state concerned. The findings are communicated to the state in a confidential report. A summary account of the results may eventually be published. Inquiry procedures have not really found favour to date. This may be due to competition from the special procedures of the Human Rights Council with their public reports[112] or to weaknesses in the procedure itself, especially the facts that on-site fact-finding requires the consent of the state concerned, that the procedure remains confidential and that it is basically unable to provide a swift remedy for the most serious human rights violations.

4. Collective complaint procedures

Collective complaint procedures correspond to the right of petition of associations or corporate entities at the international level. For the time being, the only such procedure is that established by the European Social Charter monitoring system in an Additional Protocol, adopted in 1995 and entered into force in

---

[110] CAT, Art 20, Art 8 of the Optional Protocol to CEDAW, CPAPED, Art 33 and CRPD, Art 6 which are compulsory in all cases. CAT and the OP to CEDAW contain, however, an opt-out clause. The OP to the ICESCR foresees an optional investigation procedure in its Art 11.

[111] The CtteeAT has hitherto conducted inquiries in seven states. The findings were published in the following cases: Turkey, Egypt, Peru, Sri Lanka, Mexico, Serbia and Montenegro, and Brazil. Except in the case of Sri Lanka, the Committee concluded that there was a pattern of systematic torture.

[112] See Chapter 8, section III.4.b.

1998.[113] Employers and trade unions as well as international NGOs with recognized status can lodge complaints alleging violations of the Social Charter with the European Committee of Social Rights. The Committee's decisions to date have contributed to identifying and monitoring the justiciable content of such rights.

5. Advisory opinion procedures

The advisory opinion procedure offered in the area of human rights by the Inter-American, and to a very limited extent by the European Court of Human Rights,[114] is a non-contentious mechanism. In the case of the Inter-American Court of Human Rights, every member state of the Organization of American States (OAS) as well as its organs, ie in practice the Inter-American Commission on Human Rights, can apply to the Court for an interpretation of the ACHR and other treaties. The states parties may also request a legal opinion regarding the compatibility of their domestic legislation with these international instruments.[115] The San José Court has so far issued 19 such opinions, some of which have had far-reaching implications for the development of human rights protection in (Latin) America. This mechanism has proved effective not only in terms of the qualitative content of its opinions, but also in terms of its procedural economy.

---

[113] Additional Protocol to the European Social Charter Providing for a System of Collective Complaints of November 1995. NGOs are also entitled to file complaints in procedures before the African Commission on Human and Peoples' Rights. As not only victims of human rights violations but also other individuals can initiate proceedings, this procedure actually amounts to an *actio popularis* mechanism.

[114] The Committee of Ministers of the Council of Europe is entitled to request advisory opinions from the Court under ECHR, Art 47 but has hitherto done so only once. On that occasion, the ECtHR decided that it did not have jurisdiction to answer the question raised. The Court may deliver opinions under Art 47 primarily on the substantive rights set out in the ECHR and its Protocols. An advisory opinion procedure is also foreseen for the African Court of Human Rights.

[115] ACHR, Art 64.

8

Charter Based Bodies

I. The UN Charter and Human Rights

Charter based bodies are those created on the basis of the 1945 Charter of the United Nations. Human rights feature prominently in the Charter. Its preamble reaffirms the 'faith in fundamental human rights, in the dignity and worth of the human person, [and] in the equal rights of men and women...' The promotion of 'respect for human rights and for fundamental freedoms for all without distinction as to race, sex, language, or religion' is, according to Article 1, one of the main purposes of the organization. Article 55 stresses the close relationship between peace and just economic and social conditions by recognizing that 'conditions of stability and well-being...are necessary for peaceful and friendly relations among nations' and therefore lists 'universal respect for, and observance of, human rights and fundamental freedoms for all without distinction as to race, sex, language, or religion' as one of the UN's field of activities in the area of international economic and social cooperation. Finally, it obliges member states 'to take joint and separate action in co-operation with the Organization for the achievement of' this purpose (Chapter IX, Articles 55 and 56).

Which organs of the United Nations are entrusted with addressing human rights issues? According to Article 13, the *General Assembly*, *inter alia*, 'shall initiate studies and make recommendations for the purpose of'... 'assisting in the realization of human rights and fundamental freedoms for all without distinction as to race, sex, language, or religion'. Each year, through its Third Committee, the General Assembly holds a discussion on human rights issues, which is based on reports submitted to it by the High Commissioner on Human Rights and some of the Special Procedures mandate holders,[1] and adopts a series of resolutions. It also adopts the text of human rights declarations and conventions on human rights that are usually prepared by one of the bodies specifically entrusted with human rights tasks. In 2006, the General Assembly took a bold step and created the *Human Rights Council* (section II below) as one of its subsidiary organs.

According to the Charter, the *Economic and Social Council* (ECOSOC) is entitled to 'make recommendations for the purpose of promoting respect for,

---

[1] On the Special Procedures, see below section II.4.b.

and observance of, human rights and fundamental freedoms for all' and to 'prepare draft conventions for submission to the General Assembly,' including with
respect to human rights (Article 62) and to set up a commission for the promotion of human rights (Article 68). Based on this provision, ECOSOC set up the
Commission on Human Rights which played the key role in the area of human
rights from 1946 until it was replaced by the Human Rights Council in 2006.
Since then, ECOSOCs role in the area of human rights has become marginal.

The *Security Council* is not mentioned in the Charter as one of the bodies dealing
with human rights. However, in recent decades it has started to play an increasingly
important role in the area of human rights because of their close association to peace
and security (section III below). Although the International Court of Justice cannot be approached by victims of human rights violations, in the course of deciding
disputes between states and rendering advisory opinions to the UN, it occasionally
gets the opportunity to pronounce itself on human rights issues (section IV below).

Finally, several other bodies, such as the Office of the United Nations High
Commissioner for Human Rights and the Commissions on the Status of Women
and on Crime Prevention and Criminal Justice, which both report to ECOSOC,
are entrusted with specific mandates relevant for the protection of human rights
(section V below).

II. The Human Rights Council

1. From the Human Rights Commission to the Human Rights Council

On 15 March 2006, the General Assembly decided to create the Human Rights
Council as the main organ in the UN system to deal with human rights issues.
The Council replaced the Commission on Human Rights that was set up by
ECOSOC in 1946 on the basis of Article 68 of the UN Charter.

Issue in focus: Achievements of the UN Commission on Human Rights

The original mandate of the Commission on Human Rights as adopted by ECOSOC
in 1946 consisted of the following elements: '(a) formulation of an international bill
of rights; (b) formulation of recommendations for an international declaration or
convention on such matters as civil liberties, status of women, freedom of information;
(c) protection of minorities; (d) prevention of discrimination on grounds of race, sex,
language, or religion; and (e) any other matter concerning human rights not covered
by items (a) (b) (c) and (d).'[2]

---

[2] Mandate of the Human Rights Commission adopted by ECOSOC in June 1946 as summarized by Philip Alston, 'The Commission of Human Rights', in Philip Alston, *The United Nations
and Human Rights—A Critical Appraisal* (Clarendon Press: Oxford, 1992), 127.

While responding to serious human rights violations has become one of the Human Rights Commission's main tasks since the early 1990s, its original role was principally one of standard setting. In that role, the Commission, with its 53 member states, attained many notable achievements. It successfully drafted numerous human rights instruments, including the 1948 Universal Declaration, the 1966 Covenants and other key human rights conventions including CAT and CRC. On the basis of ECOSOC Resolution 1235(1967), the Human Rights Commission also built up a system of Special Procedures, ie of independent experts and working-groups entrusted with the mandate to report on human rights violations in specific countries (country mandates) or on the situation of specific rights or groups of victims (thematic mandates). In addition, based on ECOSOC Resolution 1503(1970), the Commission created a confidential procedure to deal with complaints from individuals; such complaints were not decided on an individual basis but served to assess whether they revealed 'a consistent pattern of gross and reliably attested violations of human rights and fundamental freedoms' in the country concerned, a result that led to a confidential dialogue with said country. As well, the Commission set up a Sub-Commission on the Promotion and Protection of Human Rights (until 1999: 'Sub-Commission on Prevention of Discrimination and Protection of Minorities') composed of independent experts who prepared studies on thematic issues. Finally, the Commission was creative in allowing non-governmental organizations to contribute to its work as observers to a degree that went far beyond civil society participation in other parts of the UN system.

Over the years, the Commission on Human Rights came under increasing criticism because of declining credibility. As former Secretary-General Kofi Annan put it: 'States have sought membership of the Commission not to strengthen human rights but to protect themselves against criticism or to criticize others. As a result, a credibility deficit has developed, which casts a shadow on the reputation of the United Nations system as a whole.'[3] When proposing far-reaching reforms of the UN system in spring 2005, the Secretary-General stressed the interdependence of the three main pillars of the UN system: development, security, and human rights. 'Accordingly,' he wrote 'we will not enjoy development without security, we will not enjoy security without development, and we will not enjoy either without respect for human rights'.[4] Therefore, taking up an idea originally advanced by Switzerland[5], he proposed to 'accord human rights a more authoritative position, corresponding to the primacy of human rights in the Charter of the United Nations' by replacing the Commission on Human Rights with a smaller, standing Human Rights Council that would be better placed to

---

[3] 'In larger freedom: towards development, security and human rights for all, Report of the Secretary-General', UN Doc A/59/2005, para 182.

[4] Ibid, para 17.

[5] Wolfgang Amadeus Brülhart, 'From a Swiss Initiative to a United Nations Proposal (from 2003 until 2005)', in Lars Müller (ed), *The First 365 Days of the United Nations Human Rights Council* (Baden, 2007), 15 ff.

'meet the expectations of men and women everywhere'.[6] Thus, the idea was to create the Human Rights Council as the main institutional element of the third pillar of the UN system.

The General Assembly agreed to take up this idea and after difficult negotiations[7] adopted Resolution 60/251 of 15 March 2006, creating the Human Rights Council as one of its subsidiary organs. On 19 June 2006, the new Council met for the first time in Geneva. One year later, on 18 June 2007, it adopted resolution 5/1, entitled 'Institution-Building of the United Nations Human Rights Council',[8] which sets out its working methods as well as the different procedures and tools available to it.

2. Composition, structure and working methods

The Council is composed of forty-seven members elected directly and individually by the majority of the members of the General Assembly. They must represent the different regions of the world according to fixed quota.[9] States are expected to make voluntary pledges and commitments in the area of human rights when presenting their candidatures for election to the Human Rights Council.

The Council is chaired by a President and four Vice-presidents. They have to be elected by the Council from among the five regional groups and constitute the Bureau whose task is limited to organizational and procedural matters. The secretariat of the Council is assumed by the Office of the High Commissioner for Human Rights.

The Council[10] meets throughout the year, holding three to four sessions with a total duration of not less than ten weeks. Special sessions lasting one to two days addressing especially serious human rights violations in a specific country are convened upon request by one third of the Council's members.[11]

---

[6] 'In larger freedom: towards development, security and human rights for all, Report of the Secretary-General', UN Doc A/59/2005, para 185.

[7] Peter Maurer, 'About the Negotiation Process in New York (from 2005 until 2006): Of Ants, Caterpillars and Butterflies', in Müller (n 5), 33 ff.

[8] Reprinted in UN Doc A/HRC/5/21, 4–37.

[9] UN General Assembly Resolution 60/251 (2005), operational para (OP) 7: Group of African States: 13 members of the Council; Group of Asian States: 13; Group of Eastern European States: 6; Group of Latin American and Caribbean States: 8; and Group of Western European and other States: 7.

[10] On the activities of the Council see <http://www2.ohchr.org/english/bodies/hrcouncil/> (accessed 12 January 2009).

[11] Between June 2006 and January 2009, the Human Rights Council held special sessions on the situations in the Occupied Palestinian Territory (5–6 July 2006); and in Lebanon caused by the Israeli military operations (11 August 2006); on the Israeli military incursions in the Occupied Palestinian Territory including the one in Northern Gaza (15 November 2006); on the situation of human rights in Darfur (12–13 December 2006); on the human rights situation in Myanmar (2 October 2007); on the Israeli military incursions in the Occupied Palestinian Territory (23–24 January 2008); on the food crisis and in particular the difficulties in the implementation of the right to nourishment caused by the rise of product costs (22 May 2008); on the situation of human

Working-groups of the Council dealing with specific tasks entrusted to them on an *ad hoc* basis meet in-between sessions.

Member states of the UN that are not members of the Council as well as other states and entities and accredited non-governmental organizations may attend the meetings as observers where they have the right to speak but not to vote.

Example: Special session of the Human Rights Council on Myanmar

---

After the violent interruption of peaceful demonstrations by the security forces of Myanmar in late September 2007, the Slovenian UN delegate asked the president of the Human Rights Council on 27 September 2007 to call a special session with the title 'The human rights situation in Myanmar'. Eighteen members of the Human Rights Council, making up more than a third of all member states, supported this demand. The special session took place on 2 October 2007.[12] Discussions started with the statements of the High Commissioner of Human Rights and of the Special Rapporteur on the Human Rights situation in Myanmar, followed by numerous interventions of member states, observer states and non-governmental organizations, and ended with concluding remarks by the Special Rapporteur. After these deliberations, Portugal submitted a resolution draft, supported by 26 states. After some revisions, the following Resolution of the Human Rights Council was unanimously adopted:[13]

1. *Strongly deplores* the continued violent repression of peaceful demonstrations in Myanmar, including through beatings, killings, arbitrary detentions and enforced disappearances, expresses condolences to the victims and their families, and urges the Government of Myanmar to exercise utmost restraint and to desist from further violence against peaceful protesters;

2. *Urges* the Government of Myanmar to ensure full respect for human rights and fundamental freedoms and to investigate and bring to justice perpetrators of human rights violations, including for the recent violations of the rights of peaceful protesters;

3. *Also urges* the Government of Myanmar to release without delay those arrested and detained as a result of the recent repression of peaceful protests, as well as to release all political detainees in Myanmar, including Daw Aung San Suu Kyi, and to ensure that conditions of detention meet international standards and include the possibility of visiting any detainee;

4. *Further urges* the Government of Myanmar to lift all restraints on peaceful political activity of all persons by, inter alia, guaranteeing freedom of peaceful assembly and association and freedom of opinion and expression, including for free and independent media, and to ensure unhindered access to media information for the people of Myanmar;

5. *Welcomes* the decision of the Government of Myanmar to receive a visit by the Special Envoy to Myanmar of the Secretary-General, Ibrahim Gambari, and calls upon the Government of Myanmar to cooperate fully with him to find a peaceful solution;

---

rights in the East of the Democratic Republic of the Congo (28–29 November 2008); and on the grave violations of human rights in the Occupied Palestinian Territory including the recent aggression in the occupied Gaza Strip (9 January 2009).

[12] See 'Report of the Human Rights Council on its fifth special session', UN Doc A/HRC/S-5/2.
[13] Human Rights Council Resolution S-5/1; UN Doc A/HRC/S-5/2.

6. *Urges* the Government of Myanmar to engage urgently in a reinvigorated national dialogue with all parties with a view to achieving genuine national reconciliation, democratization and the establishment of the rule of law;

7. *Encourages* the Government of Myanmar and the Office of the High Commissioner for Human Rights to engage in a dialogue with a view to ensuring full respect for all human rights and fundamental freedoms;

8. *Urges* the Government of Myanmar to cooperate fully with humanitarian organizations, including by ensuring full, safe and unhindered access of humanitarian assistance to all persons in need throughout the country;

9. *Requests* the Special Rapporteur on the situation of human rights in Myanmar to assess the current human rights situation and to monitor the implementation of this resolution, including by seeking an urgent visit to Myanmar, and to report to the resumed sixth session of the Human Rights Council, and in this respect urges the Government of Myanmar to cooperate with the Special Rapporteur;

10. *Also requests* the Special Rapporteur on the situation of human rights in Myanmar to inform the General Assembly at its sixty-second session on progress in this regard;

11. *Decides* to remain seized of this matter.

After the adoption of this Resolution, three states gave the reasons for their vote and the representative of Myanmar was given the possibility to present his position on the Resolution. Subsequently, Myanmar gave the Special Rapporteur permission to enter the country. The latter reported on the conclusions of his investigations during the sixth ordinary session.[14]

3. Tasks

According to General Assembly Resolution 60/251, the Human Rights Council is entrusted with the following seven, closely interlinked tasks:

(1) *Protection* of victims of human rights violations, in particular to 'address situations of violations of human rights, including gross and systematic violations, and make recommendations thereon' (operational paragraph 3) and to 'respond promptly to human rights emergencies' (operational paragraph 5(f)).

(2) *Promotion* of the protection of human rights not only in general but also in specific countries, in particular through educational, capacity-building, and technical assistance activities which would support the implementation of the obligations and the commitments of the states concerned (operational paragraph 5(a)).

(3) *Reflection* on concepts and policies through providing a forum for dialogue where thematic issues on all human rights can be discussed (operational paragraph 5(b)).

---

[14] See the Report by the Special Rapporteur on the situation of human rights in Myanmar, UN Doc A/HRC/6/14, 7.

(4) *Standard-setting* by making 'recommendations to the General Assembly for the further development of international law in the field of human rights' (operational paragraph 5(c)).

(5) *Prevention* through proposing measures aimed at ensuring that human rights violations do not occur or re-occur (operational paragraph 5(f)). Here too, the provision of technical assistance to countries under consideration plays an important role.

(6) *Integrating a human rights perspective into the work of the UN*, through the promotion of 'the effective coordination and the mainstreaming of human rights within the United Nations system' (operational paragraph 3).

(7) *Follow-up*, foreseen as follow-up discussions 'to recommendations and their implementation' (operational paragraph 12) as well as 'to the goals and commitments related to the promotion and protection of human rights emanating from United Nations conferences and summits' (operational paragraph 5(d)).

4. Tools

In order to enable it to carry out these tasks, the General Assembly provided the Council with four instruments, namely (a) 'a universal periodic review... of the fulfillment by each State of its human rights obligations and commitments' (OP 5 e), (b) a system of special procedures, (c) a system of expert advice (Advisory Committee), and (d) a complaint procedure (OP 6).

(a) Universal Periodic Review[15]

The Universal Periodic Review (UPR) mechanism ensures all member states of the UN are periodically reviewed in terms of whether and to what extent they fulfil their human rights obligations. The review also serves to identify means of enhancing the capacity of the state under review to address its human rights problems and whether it needs to get technical assistance in this regard from the Office of the UN High Commissioner of Human Rights and relevant UN agencies.

The benchmarks for review are relevant standards of the UN Charter as well as the Universal Declaration of Human Rights, human rights instruments to which the state concerned is a party, as well as the voluntary pledges and commitments made by it in the area of human rights. The actual review is based on three documents: information prepared by the state concerned; a compilation prepared by OHCHR of information contained in concluding observations of treaty bodies, reports of special procedures and other relevant UN documents; and a summary

---

[15] This description follows closely the following: United Nations Human Rights Council: Institution Building; Annex to Human Rights Council Resolution 5/1, Part I, A/HRC/21, paras 1–38, and President statement on modalities and practices for the Universal Periodic Review Process, UN Doc A/HRC/8/L.1.

prepared by OHCHR of additional 'credible and reliable' information provided by other stakeholders in the process, ie other governments, NGOs, and National Human Rights Institutions.

The review is conducted by a working group chaired by the President of the Council and composed of the forty-seven members of the Council in the form of a three-hour long interactive dialogue between the state under review and Council members. This process is facilitated by a group of three rapporteurs from different regional groups who are selected by the drawing of lots among the members of the Council. These rapporteurs are tasked with drafting a report about the dialogue that serves as a basis for the discussion and adoption of an outcome document by the plenary of the Council. This outcome document contains an assessment of the human rights situation in the country concerned, as well as recommendations, including those explicitly accepted by the state concerned. The subsequent cycle of reviews will focus, *inter alia*, on the implementation of the preceding outcomes and thus serve as a follow-up mechanism.

Example: Universal periodic review of Switzerland

On 12 June 2008, the Human Rights Council adopted Decision 8/122 entitled 'Outcome of the universal periodic review: Switzerland':

The Human Rights Council,

   Acting in compliance with the mandate entrusted to it by the General Assembly in its resolution 60/251 of 15 March 2006 and Council resolution 5/1 of 18 June 2007, and in accordance with the President's statement PRST/8/1 on modalities and practices for the universal periodic review process of 9 April 2008;

   Having conducted the review of Switzerland on 8 May in conformity with all the relevant provisions contained in Council resolution 5/1;

   Adopts the outcome of the universal periodic review on Switzerland which is constituted of the report of the Working Group on the review of Switzerland (A/HRC/8/41), together with the views of Switzerland concerning the recommendations and/or conclusions, as well as its voluntary commitments and its replies presented before the adoption of the outcome by the plenary to questions or issues that were not sufficiently addressed during the interactive dialogue in the Working Group (A/HRC/8/52 chap. VI and A/HRC/8/41/Add.1).

Excerpts from the Report of the Working Group (UN Doc A/HRC/8/41):

56. The recommendations formulated during the interactive dialogue have been examined by Switzerland and the recommendations listed below enjoy the support of Switzerland:

1. To pursue its efforts in preventing and combating xenophobia (Algeria);

2. To ratify the Optional Protocol to the Convention against Torture (Mexico, United Kingdom) and to create or designate a national mechanism for the prevention of torture (Mexico);

3. To fully, systematically and continuously integrate a gender perspective into the follow-up process to the Universal Periodic Review (Slovenia);

4. To continue to consult stakeholders in the follow-up to the Universal Periodic Review outcome (United Kingdom);

5. To take necessary steps to prevent the incidence of acts of violence with racist and xenophobic undertones by security agents against foreigners, immigrants and asylum-seekers, and to bring to justice the perpetrators of such acts (Nigeria);

6. To continue its efforts to promote the use of non-gender specific language (Canada).

57. The following recommendations will be examined by Switzerland which will provide responses in due time . . . :

1. To establish a national institution on human rights in accordance with the Paris Principles (Algeria, India, Canada, Philippines, United Kingdom, Germany, Jordan, Morocco);

2. To foster internal analysis on the recently adopted law on asylum and its compatibility with international human rights law (Brazil);
. . . [16]

58. One recommendation noted in the present report . . . (the ratification of the International Convention on the Protection of the Rights of All Migrant Workers and Members of Their Families) and another recommendation . . . (the justiciability of the economic, social and cultural rights) above did not enjoy the support of Switzerland.

The UPR is the main innovation introduced with the creation of the Human Rights Council and first experiences have been rather positive. It does not replace the expert-based and more in-depth examination of state reports by the treaty bodies, but is conceived as a system of peer-review based on intergovernmental dialogue and cooperation. It has a great potential to overcome the problem of selectivity given that each and every State will be under scrutiny. The list of commitment made by the state concerned not only allows testing the degree of its willingness to improve the human rights situation but also provides a basis for effective follow-up in the context of later review cycles.

(b) Special Procedures

Special procedures are mechanisms originally established by the Commission on Human Rights and now assumed by the Human Rights Council that address either specific country situations or thematic issues in all parts of the world. Mandate holders are independent experts who either work as individual Special Rapporteurs or as Working Groups. Their mandates are either *thematic*, ie addressing a particular right (eg right to health), a particular group of victims or vulnerable persons (eg internally displaced persons) or a specific problem (eg violence against women), or *country specific*, ie dealing with all relevant human rights problems in a specific country.[17] A summary of the thematic mandates of the Human Rights Council is given in Table 8.1.

---

[16] This list contains 23 points.

[17] Currently (December 2008), the following country mandates exist: Occupied Palestinian territories (since 1967), Myanmar (since 1992), Somalia (since 1993), Cambodia (since 1993), Haiti (since 1995), Burundi (since 2004), Democratic Peoples' Republic of Korea (since 2004), Sudan (since 2005). Former mandates include, eg, South Africa (1967–1995), Chile (1975–1990), Equatorial Guinea (1979–2002), Bolivia (1981–1983), El Salvador (1981–1995), Poland

Table 8.1. Thematic mandates of the Human Rights Council

Mandate	Title / Form	Established in[18]
Adequate housing as a component of the right to an adequate standard of living, and on the right to non-discrimination in this context	Special Rapporteur	2000
People of African descent	Working Group	2002
Arbitrary detention	Working Group	1991
Sale of children, child prostitution and child pornography	Special Rapporteur	1990
Right to education	Special Rapporteur	1998
Enforced or involuntary disappearances	Working Group	1980
Extrajudicial, summary or arbitrary executions	Special Rapporteur	1982
Extreme poverty	Independent Expert	1998
Right to food	Special Rapporteur	2000
Effects of foreign debt and other related international financial obligations of States on the full enjoyment of human rights, particularly economic, social and cultural rights	Independent Expert	2000
Freedom of opinion and expression	Special Rapporteur	1993
Freedom of religion or belief	Special Rapporteur	1986
Right of everyone to the enjoyment of the highest attainable standard of physical and mental health	Special Rapporteur	2002
Situation of human rights defenders	Special Rapporteur	2000
Independence of judges and lawyers	Special Rapporteur	1994
Situation of human rights and fundamental freedoms of indigenous people	Special Rapporteur	2001
Human rights of internally displaced persons	Representative of the Secretary-General	2004
Use of mercenaries as a means of impeding the exercise of the right of peoples to self-determination	Working Group	2005
Human rights of migrants	Special Rapporteur	1999
Minority issues	Independent Expert	2005
Contemporary forms of racism, racial discrimination, xenophobia and related intolerance	Special Rapporteur	1993
Contemporary forms of slavery, including its causes and consequences	Special Rapporteur	2007
Human rights and international solidarity	Independent Expert	2005
Promotion and protection of human rights while countering terrorism	Special Rapporteur	2005
Torture and other cruel, inhuman or degrading treatment or punishment	Special Rapporteur	1985
Adverse effects of the movement and dumping of toxic and dangerous products and wastes on the enjoyment of human rights	Special Rapporteur	1995

(1982–1985), Guatemala (1983–1998), Iran (1984–2002), Afghanistan (1984–2005), Cuba (1990–1998 and 2002–2007), Kuwait under Iraqi occupation (1991–1992), Iraq (1991–2004), Bosnia-Herzegovina and Yugoslavia (1992–2001), Rwanda (1994–2001), Nigeria (1997–1999), East Timor (1999–2002), Democratic Republic of Congo (2004–2008), Chad (2003–2005), Uzbekistan (2004–2007), and Belarus (2004–2007).

[18] Mandates established before 2006 were reviewed and renewed by the Human Rights Council.

Table 8.1. *(Contd.)*

Mandate	Title / Form	Established in
Trafficking in persons, especially in women and children	Special Rapporteur	2004
Human rights and transnational corporations and other business enterprises	Representative of the Secretary-General	2005
Issue of human rights obligations related to access to safe drinking water and sanitation	Independent Expert	2008
Violence against women, its causes and consequences	Special Rapporteur	1994

The mandate holders are selected by a consultative group of the Council and then approved by the full Council. They must have the necessary expertise, experience and independence. In particular, individuals holding decision-making positions in Government or in organizations which may give rise to a conflict of interest are not eligible. Mandate holders are neither UN staff nor representatives of governments but act in their individual capacity as independent experts. They are, however, bound by a code of conduct.[19] The tenure of mandate-holders is limited to a maximum of six years. Mandate holders report annually to the Human Rights Council; they may also be asked to submit annual or bi-annual reports to the General Assembly.

Example: The mandate of the Special Rapporteur on the right to food

The Human Rights Council confirmed the Special Rapporteur's mandate on the right to food on 27 September 2007, giving him the following tasks:[20]

(a) To promote the full realization of the right to food and the adoption of measures at the national, regional and international levels for the realization of the right of everyone to adequate food and the fundamental right of everyone to be free from hunger so as to be able fully to develop and maintain their physical and mental capacities;

(b) To examine ways and means of overcoming existing and emerging obstacles to the realization of the right to food;

(c) To continue mainstreaming a gender perspective and taking into account an age dimension in the fulfilment of the mandate, considering that women and children are disproportionately affected by hunger, food insecurity and poverty;

(d) To submit proposals that could help the realization of Millennium Development Goal No 1 to halve by the year 2015 the proportion of people who suffer from hunger, as well as to realize the right to food, in particular, taking into account the role of international assistance and cooperation in reinforcing national actions to implement sustainable food security policies;

(e) To present recommendations on possible steps with a view to achieving progressively the full realization of the right to food, including steps to promote the conditions for everyone to be free from hunger and as soon as possible enjoy fully the right to food, taking into account lessons learnt in the implementation of national plans to combat hunger;

(f) To work in close cooperation with all States, intergovernmental and non-governmental organizations, the Committee on Economic, Social and Cultural Rights, as well as with

---

[19] Human Rights Council Resolution 5/8 and Annex, reprinted in UN Doc A/HRC/21, 37–45.
[20] UN Doc A/HRC/RES/6/2.

> other relevant actors representing the broadest possible range of interests and experiences, within their respective mandates, to take fully into account the need to promote the effective realization of the right to food for all, including in the ongoing negotiations in different fields.
>
> (g) To continue participating in and contributing to relevant international conferences and events with the aim of promoting the realization of the right to food; (. . .)

Special procedures' mandates are defined by resolutions of the Human Rights Council. These mandates usually call on mandate holders to examine, monitor, advise, and publicly report on human rights situations covered by their mandate. For this purpose, mandate holders carry out country missions, undertake studies, provide advice on technical cooperation at the country level, and engage in general promotional activities. They also engage in follow-up activities.

What does it mean to 'examine' human rights violations? Special Rapporteurs first and foremost, have the task of fact-finding: They collect information, analyse it and, on this basis, describe pertinent events and patterns in order to enable the Human Rights Council to draw its conclusions. Although they have no judicial functions, Special Rapporteurs can only properly fulfil their tasks if they present their findings in light of relevant legal obligations binding the country in question. Besides these basic requirements, the mandates of Special Rapporteurs regularly leave enough room to adopt different approaches and thus to respond to the peculiarities of each case. Alston distinguishes three principal approaches: 'The first emphasizes the fact-finding and documentation function. In this view the function of reporting is to record the facts, to provide a reliable historical record, and to provide the necessary raw material against the background of which political organs can determine the best strategy under the circumstances. In this approach, facts and their substantiation are the key. . . . The second approach assumes that the prosecutorial/publicity function is paramount. . . . The goal in such cases is to mobilize world public opinion and to provide a basis on which the earlier conviction can be justified. The third approach is to emphasize the conciliation function. The rapporteur's role is not to confront the violators but to seek solutions which will improve, even if not necessarily resolve, the situation.'[21]

Many mandates include the possibility of receiving information on specific allegations of human rights violations and sending urgent appeals or letters of allegation to governments asking for clarifications.[22] Thus, Special Procedures can intervene on behalf of specific victims of human rights violations. The Working Group on Arbitrary Detention has even developed a specific complaints mechanism allowing for the examination of individual cases.

[21] Alston (n 2) 167 ff.
[22] In 2007, more than 1,000 communications were sent to Governments in 128 countries. 49% of these were joint communications of two or more mandate holders (<http://www2.ohchr.org/english/bodies/chr/special/docs/SP2007FactsFigures.pdf> (accessed 18 January 2009)).

Issue in focus: The complaints procedure of the Working Group on Arbitrary Detention

The Working Group describes its complaints procedure as follows:[23]

The Working Group acts on information submitted by communications sent to it by the individuals directly concerned, their families, their representatives or non-governmental organizations for the protection of human rights, from Governments and inter-governmental organizations regarding alleged cases of arbitrary detention.

The communication is forwarded to the Government concerned through diplomatic channels with an invitation to communicate to the Working Group within 90 days its comments and observations on the allegations made, both as regards the facts and the applicable legislation and concerning the progress and outcome of any investigations that may have been ordered.

A reply sent by the Government to the Working Group is transmitted to the source for any final comments or observations.

According to the methods of work of the Group, deprivation of liberty is arbitrary if a case falls into one of the following three categories:

A) When it is clearly impossible to invoke any legal basis justifying the deprivation of liberty (as when a person is kept in detention after the completion of his sentence or despite an amnesty law applicable to him) (Category I);

B) When the deprivation of liberty results from the exercise of the rights or freedoms guaranteed by articles 7, 13, 14, 18, 19, 10 and 21 of the Universal Declaration of Human Rights and, insofar as States parties are concerned, by articles 12, 18, 19, 21, 22, 25, 26 and 27 of the International Covenant on Civil and Political Rights (Category II);

C) When the total or partial non-observance of the international norms relating to the right to a fair trial, spelled out in the Universal Declaration of Human Rights and in the relevant international instruments accepted by the States concerned, is of such gravity as to give the deprivation of liberty an arbitrary character (Category III).

In the light of the information collected under this adversary procedure, the Working Group adopts one of the following measures in private session:

(a) If the person has been released, for whatever reason, following the reference of the case to the Working Group the case may be filed; the Group, however, reserves the right to render an opinion, on a case-by-case basis, whether or not the deprivation of liberty was arbitrary, notwithstanding the release of the person concerned;

(b) If the Group considers that the case is not one of the arbitrary deprivation of liberty, it shall render an opinion to this effect;

(c) If the Group considers that further information is required from the Government or the source, it may keep the case pending until that information is received;

(d) If the Group considers that it is unable to obtain sufficient information on the case, it may file the case provisionally or definitively;

(e) If the Group decides that the arbitrary nature of the deprivation of liberty is established, it shall render an opinion to that effect and make recommendations to the Government.

The opinion is sent to the Government, together with the recommendations. Three weeks after this notification, the opinion is also conveyed to the source for information.

The opinions are published in an annex to the report presented by the Working Group to the Commission on Human Rights at each of its annual sessions.

---

[23] <www2.ohchr.org/english/issues/detention/complaints.htm> (accessed 18 January 2009).

(c) *The Human Rights Council Advisory Committee*[24]

The Human Rights Council Advisory Committee replaces the former Sub-Commission on the Promotion and Protection of Human Rights as an expert think-tank. It is composed of 18 independent experts elected by the Council and acting in their individual capacity but under the direction of the Council.

The Advisory Committee provides expertise to the Council by preparing studies and giving research-based advice as requested by the Council. It can propose topics of study to the Council but, unlike its predecessor, it cannot act on its own initiative.

(d) *Complaint Procedure*[25]

Despite its name, the Complaint Procedure set up by the Council is not an instrument to address violations of human rights in individual cases. Rather, it aims at identifying 'consistent patterns of gross and reliably attested violations of all human rights and all fundamental freedoms occurring in any part of the world and under any circumstances'.[26]

Complaints by victims, their families or human rights organizations are examined by a Working Group on Communications composed of five members of the Human Rights Council Advisory Group who decide on the admissibility of a case and transmit it to the state concerned for comments. If cases appear to reveal the existence of consistent patterns of gross and reliably attested violations of human rights, they are transmitted to the Working Group on Situations, which is composed of representatives from the regional groups of the Council. This Working Group prepares a report for the Council and makes recommendations on the course of action to be taken. The whole procedure remains confidential unless the Council decides otherwise. Measures the Council can take are limited to keeping a situation under further review or recommending that OHCHR provide technical cooperation, capacity assistance or advisory services to the state concerned.

The confidentiality of the procedure as well as the limited possibility to take remedial action render the complaint procedure rather weak. It is very similar to the former 1503-procedure of the Commission on Human Rights, although the Council has made some improvements, including such measures as allowing for a more timely examination of complaints; the principle that petitioners will be informed of the outcome of the examination of their complaint; and the possibility for the Working Group on Situations to submit a country situation to the Council for public discussion.

---

[24] Human Rights Council: Institution Building; Annex to Human Rights Council Resolution 5/1, Part I, UN Doc A/HRC/21, paras 65–84.
[25] Ibid, paras 85–109.   [26] Ibid, para 85.

5. Working style: non-selectivity, dialogue, and cooperation

The Commission on Human Rights was often criticized for its 'politicization' of international human rights issues, ie its tendency to single out for harsh criticism some countries rather than others. In order to break the confrontational atmosphere that had marked the Commission's last years of existence, the General Assembly hoped that the Council's actual work would 'be guided by the principles of universality, impartiality, objectivity and non-selectivity, constructive international dialogue and cooperation'.[27]

In this context, states often invoke the principle of non-selectivity to fend off criticism. However, non-selectivity, properly understood, cannot mean to refrain from addressing serious human rights violations in a given state. Rather, the Council acts in a non-selective manner if it shows a willingness to take up every serious human rights issue and to take all measures necessary to improve the situation, regardless of the country's location, size, economic position and political alliances. The UPR is an important step towards non-selectivity. At the same time, the existence of the UPR, with its four-year cycle, should not preclude the Council from resorting to special sessions, as an instrument that allows it to respond immediately to a sudden deterioration of the human rights situation in a particular country.

Regarding the principles of constructive international dialogue and cooperation, the idea is that rather than 'finger-pointing' and 'shaming and blaming' countries with a bad human rights record, the Council should instead help them to improve the situation by offering, among other things, technical assistance provided by the Office of the High Commissioner for Human Rights.

Issue in focus: The group of experts on Darfur

One example for an approach based on dialogue and cooperation is the establishment, by the Council, of a group of experts on Darfur.[28] In March 2007, the Council, acknowledging 'the seriousness of the ongoing violations of human rights and international humanitarian law in Darfur, including armed attacks on the civilian population and humanitarian workers, widespread destruction of villages, and continued and widespread violence, in particular gender-based violence against women and girls, as well as the lack of accountability of perpetrators of such crimes' decided to set up a group of experts, comprising of seven special procedures mandate holders. It entrusted the group with the task of ensuring 'effective follow-up to resolutions and recommendations on Darfur, as adopted by the Council, the Commission on Human Rights and other United Nations human rights institutions, as well as to promote the implementation of relevant recommendations of other United Nations human rights mechanisms, taking into account the needs of the Sudan, ensuring

---

[27] UN General Assembly Resolution 60/251 (2005), OP 4.
[28] Human Rights Council Resolution 4/8 of 30 March 2007.

the consistency of these recommendations and contributing to the monitoring of the human rights situation on the ground'.[29]

The experts group identified a series of relevant recommendations, indicated the steps required of the Government of the Sudan to implement each recommendation over the short and medium term, met on several occasions with a high-level governmental delegation from Sudan to discuss and assess the status of implementation and reported to the Council on progress achieved.[30] This was the first time the main UN human rights body created a process focused on the implementation of recommendations. Experiences were mixed: on the one hand, Sudan started implementing many of the recommendations and cooperated with the group of experts by reporting on steps taken. On the other hand, six months into the implementation process, few improvements could be identified on the ground. In December 2007, the Council decided to dissolve the group before it could complete its work and entrusted the Special Rapporteur on Sudan with the task of continuing the process.[31]

III. The Role of the Security Council

1. Human rights and international security

According to the United Nations Charter, primary responsibility for the maintenance of international peace and security lies with the Security Council,[32] a standing body which is the only UN organ empowered to make decisions that are binding on all member states (UN Charter, Article 25). It can adopt such measures under Chapter VII of the UN Charter in case of a 'threat to the peace, breach of the peace, or act of aggression' (UN Charter, Article 39). When drafting these Articles the authors of the Charter had in mind traditional military operations and instances of armed conflict. Since the end of the Cold War, however, the Security Council has been inclined also to characterize massive human rights violations as an element of a threat to the peace,

---

[29] Ibid, paras 3 and 7.

[30] See Final report on the situation of human rights in Darfur prepared by the group of experts mandated by the Human Rights Council in its resolution 4/8, presided by the Special Rapporteur on the situation of human rights in the Sudan and composed of the Special Rapporteur on extra-judicial, summary or arbitrary executions, the Special Representative of the Secretary-General for children and armed conflict, the Special Rapporteur on violence against women, its causes and consequences, the Special Representative of the Secretary-General on the situation of human rights defenders, the Representative of the Secretary-General on the human rights of internally displaced persons and the Special Rapporteur on the question of torture and other cruel, inhuman or degrading treatment or punishment, UN Doc A/HRC/6/19, 28 November 2007.

[31] See UN Doc A/HRC/6/19, in particular paras 54–9, and Human Rights Council Resolution 6/35. The Special Rapporteur on Sudan presented a follow-up report to the Council in 2008 (UN Doc A/HRC/9/13/Add.1).

[32] The Security Council is made up of fifteen member states. Five of these states are permanent members and can veto the Council's binding decisions. The other ten states are elected by the General Assembly with a 2/3 majority for a period of two years.

thereby recognizing the link between protecting human rights and safeguarding peace. This connection is evident, for example, where repression in one state causes massive flows of refugees and therefore has repercussions abroad or where regimes that practise repression at home begin to direct their aggression beyond their borders. A recent study of Security Council practice shows that the Council is willing to take action where human rights violations: have threatened or led to a breach of world peace; are due to the collapse of state structures; undermine the authority of the United Nations; occur on a particularly large scale or constitute crimes against humanity; prompt a government to request an intervention; or are so appalling that they provoke horror in the international community.[33]

Where a threat to peace of such kind exists, the Security Council is empowered not only to take measures for the peaceful settlement of the dispute (such as making recommendations or initiating negotiations) but also to resort to coercive measures or peacekeeping operations.

Issue in focus: An emerging collective responsibility to protect?

In 2005, UN Secretary-General Kofi Annan commented on the view of the role of states and the international community in the area of human rights law and international humanitarian law in his report on United Nations reform ('In larger freedom: towards development, security and human rights for all, Report of the Secretary General', UN Doc A/59/2005, 21 March 2005):

135. The International Commission on Intervention and State Sovereignty and more recently the High-level Panel on Threats, Challenges and Change, with its 16 members from all around the world, endorsed what they described as an 'emerging norm that there is a collective responsibility to protect' (see A/59/565, paragraph 203). While I am well aware of the sensitivities involved in this issue, I strongly agree with this approach. I believe that we must embrace the responsibility to protect, and, when necessary, we must act on it. This responsibility lies, first and foremost, with each individual State, whose primary raison d'être and duty is to protect its population. But if national authorities are unable or unwilling to protect their citizens, then the responsibility shifts to the international community to use diplomatic, humanitarian and other methods to help protect the human rights and well-being of civilian populations. When such methods appear insufficient, the Security Council may out of necessity decide to take action under the Charter of the United Nations, including enforcement action, if so required.

The unanimously adopted Final Resolution of the World Summit of 2005 (General Assembly Resolution 60/1) recognized the following:

138. Each individual State has the responsibility to protect its populations from genocide, war crimes, ethnic cleansing and crimes against humanity. This responsibility entails the prevention of such crimes, including their incitement, through appropriate and necessary means. We accept that responsibility and will act in accordance with it. The international

---

[33] Betrand G Ramcharan, *The Security Council and the Protection of Human Rights* (Brill: Den Haag, 2002), 211.

community should, as appropriate, encourage and help States to exercise this responsibility and support the United Nations in establishing an early warning capability.

139. The international community, through the United Nations, also has the responsibility to use appropriate diplomatic, humanitarian and other peaceful means, in accordance with Chapters VI and VIII of the Charter, to help to protect populations from genocide, war crimes, ethnic cleansing and crimes against humanity. In this context, we are prepared to take collective action, in a timely and decisive manner, through the Security Council, in accordance with the Charter, including Chapter VII, on a case-by-case basis and in cooperation with relevant regional organizations as appropriate, should peaceful means be inadequate and national authorities are manifestly failing to protect their populations from genocide, war crimes, ethnic cleansing and crimes against humanity. We stress the need for the General Assembly to continue consideration of the responsibility to protect populations from genocide, war crimes, ethnic cleansing and crimes against humanity and its implications, bearing in mind the principles of the Charter and international law. We also intend to commit ourselves, as necessary and appropriate, to helping States build capacity to protect their populations from genocide, war crimes, ethnic cleansing and crimes against humanity and to assisting those which are under stress before crises and conflicts break out.

The mandate of the Special Advisor to the Secretary General on the Responsibility to Protect was created in 2007.

2. From peacekeeping operations to transitional UN administrations

Traditional peacekeeping operations usually focused on the neutral monitoring of ceasefire lines and refrained from interfering in the 'internal affairs' of the states in which troops were stationed. While these traditional mandates succeeded and are still succeeding in maintaining the status quo, they have scarcely ever achieved any long-term easing of tensions in conflict situations. As a result, traditional operations have often continued for decades with corresponding heavy financial implications. It was only after the end of the Cold War that it became possible to expand the scope of peacekeeping mandates to include the authority to cooperate actively in post-conflict reconstruction ('peace-building'). Today, human rights have become a regular part of the mandate of UN peacekeeping operations. These mandates are often fulfilled in collaboration with the field missions of the High Commissioner for Human Rights.

This integrated approach was put into practice for the first time in 1990 after the civil war in El Salvador. The United Nations ONUSAL mission was mandated, *inter alia*, to monitor the human rights situation. To that end, it was authorized, for example, to have unimpeded access to all places of detention. It also had the right to make suggestions for legal and institutional reforms and to receive complaints from victims of human rights violations. To carry out this mission, professionally trained human rights observers were used for the first time. They now form part of virtually all such missions.

Example: Report on ONUSAL's activities in 1994[34]

III. Human rights and the judicial system

8. The human rights situation in El Salvador has improved markedly during ONUSAL's three years of operation ...

9. In the past six months, ONUSAL's Human Rights Division has emphasized the strengthening of national institutions such as the National Council of the Judiciary, the Office of the Attorney-General of the Republic, the National Civil Police and the National Public Security Academy, as well as the development of a new doctrine for the Armed Forces. In July, a mechanism for the joint verification of human rights violations was established with the National Counsel for the Defence of Human Rights, together with a training and specialization programme for officials of the National Counsel. The Division has also continued to conduct seminars and specialized workshops on human rights for members of the judicial system, the Armed Forces and non-governmental organizations (NGOs) active in the field of human rights. These activities have been complemented by the publication of a series of books and pamphlets on human rights.

10. In this phase of the peace process, institution-building is crucial for the consolidation of the progress achieved in the protection of human rights and due process. In view of the future winding-up of ONUSAL, programmes to ensure continuous support for institution-building are being prepared.

ONUSAL played a pioneering role and became a model for other peacekeeping operations, such as the human rights observer mission in Guatemala, which was created in 1994 after the end of the civil war. This mission conducted investigations of human rights violations and assisted in building democratic structures throughout the country ('institution-building'). To that end, more than 250 human rights observers, legal experts and police officers were dispersed to even the remotest parts of the country. Their presence succeeded in focusing public interest on human rights issues, particularly the problem of impunity from prosecution for human rights violations, thereby curbing at least to some extent the phenomenon of politically motivated violence.

Subsequent UN peacekeeping missions were often entrusted with even more ambitious mandates, a development that culminated in some cases with the conferral of full authority to administer a territory. One example is the United Nations Transitional Authority in Cambodia in 1992–1993 (UNTAC), whose mandate comprised of human rights protection, the organization of elections, maintenance of law and order, building a civil administration and the repatriation of refugees. Other examples are the UN's overall administrative responsibility for East Timor (UNTAET) between the country's referendum on independence in

---

[34] 'Report of the Secretary-General on the United Nations Observer Mission in El Salvador' dated 31 October 1994 (UN Doc S/1994/1212) and its addendum of 14 November 1994 (UN Doc S/1994/1212/Add.1).

1999 and its actual attainment of independence in 2002[35] and the UN Mission in Kosovo (UNMIK) since 1999.

Example: UN Security Council Resolution 1272 (1999) of 25 October 1999 on the situation in East Timor

The Security Council ...

Deeply concerned by the grave humanitarian situation resulting from violence in East Timor and the large-scale displacement and relocation of East Timorese civilians, including large numbers of women and children...

Expressing its concern at reports indicating that systematic, widespread and flagrant violations of international humanitarian and human rights law have been committed in East Timor, stressing that persons committing such violations bear individual responsibility, and calling on all parties to cooperate with investigations into these reports ...

Determining that the continuing situation in East Timor constitutes a threat to peace and security,

Acting under Chapter VII of the Charter of the United Nations,

1. Decides to establish, in accordance with the report of the Secretary-General, a United Nations Transitional Administration in East Timor (UNTAET), which will be endowed with overall responsibility for the administration of East Timor and will be empowered to exercise all legislative and executive authority, including the administration of justice...

8. Stresses the need for UNTAET to consult and cooperate closely with the East Timorese people in order to carry out its mandate effectively with a view to the development of local democratic institutions, including an independent East Timorese human rights institution, and the transfer to these institutions of its administrative and public service functions;...

10. Reiterates the urgent need for coordinated humanitarian and reconstruction assistance, and calls upon all parties to cooperate with humanitarian and human rights organizations so as to ensure their safety, the protection of civilians, in particular children, the safe return of refugees and displaced persons and the effective delivery of humanitarian aid;...

15. Underlines the importance of including in UNTAET personnel with appropriate training in international humanitarian, human rights and refugee law, including child and gender-related provisions, negotiation and communication skills, cultural awareness and civilian-military coordination.[36]

---

[35] East Timor, a former Portuguese colony, was occupied by Indonesia illegally, ie in breach of the right of self-determination, following Portugal's withdrawal. After years of guerrilla warfare, Indonesia declared—at a time of domestic political weakness—that it was prepared to hold a referendum on independence under international supervision. An overwhelming majority opted for independence. As soon as the results were announced, militias loyal to Indonesia began to commit massacres among the civilian population with the support of the Indonesian armed forces. These gross and systematic human rights violations eventually led to a military intervention by the international community.

[36] The UN continued to administer East Timor until the country became independent on 20 May 2002. However, UN Security Council Resolution 1410 (2002) decided to maintain a UN support mission in the country for a further 12 months (United Nations Mission of Support in East Timor, UNMISET). Under its mandate, UNMISET was required, *inter alia*, (ibid, para 2): '(a) To provide assistance to core administrative structures critical to the viability and political stability of East Timor; (b) To provide interim law enforcement and public security and to assist in the development of a new law enforcement agency in East Timor, the East Timor Police Service (ETPS); (c) To contribute to the maintenance of the external and internal security of East Timor...'

3. Economic sanctions

Article 41 of the UN Charter explicitly allows economic sanctions as a coercive measure in the event of a threat to peace. While human rights violations have so far never constituted the sole incentive for a Security Council decision to resort to this kind of measure, they have been important considerations in several cases. For instance, when the Security Council chose to impose a global trade embargo on Iraq in 1990,[37] the decisive factor was the invasion of Kuwait, but human rights violations by Saddam Hussein's regime were also taken into account. While the full-scale sanctions imposed two years later on the former Yugoslavia[38] as well as the sectoral embargoes imposed on the parties to the Liberia and Sierra Leone[39] conflicts were motivated primarily by security policy concerns, the widespread war crimes and crimes against humanity committed in these countries against the civilian population where a powerful motive. Human rights violations in Darfur were a key factor in the decision to impose sanctions on Sudan in 2005.[40]

In the 1990s, economic sanctions made headlines less as a potentially effective means of enforcing human rights obligations than as an instrument that threatened to undermine the enjoyment of human rights. The sanctions and disarmament obligations imposed on Iraq after its withdrawal from occupied Kuwait raised the question of whether such measures could be consistent with human rights if they deprived large sectors of the population of their source of income and destroyed part of the state's infrastructure, such as basic health facilities.[41] To make sanctions as compatible as possible with economic, social and cultural rights, efforts have been made to design so-called 'smart sanctions', ie sanctions targeted more directly against those responsible for violations of international law.[42] Accordingly, contemporary sanctions no longer prohibit all

---

[37] UN Security Council Resolution 661 (1990).
[38] UN Security Council Resolution 757 (1992).
[39] UN Security Council Resolutions 788 (1992) and 1521 (2003) on Liberia; and 1132 (1997) on Sierra Leone.
[40] UN Security Council Resolution 1591 (2005).
[41] See CtteeESCR, General Comment No 8 (1997), para 3: 'While the impact of sanctions varies from one case to another, the Committee is aware that they almost always have a dramatic impact on the rights recognized in the Covenant. Thus, for example, they often cause significant disruption in the distribution of food, pharmaceuticals and sanitation supplies, jeopardize the quality of food and the availability of clean drinking water, severely interfere with the functioning of basic health and education systems, and undermine the right to work. In addition, their unintended consequences can include reinforcement of the power of oppressive elites, the emergence, almost invariably, of a black market and the generation of huge windfall profits for the privileged elites which manage it, enhancement of the control of the governing elite over the population at large, and restriction of opportunities to seek asylum or to manifest political opposition. While the phenomena mentioned in the preceding sentence are essentially political in nature, they also have a major additional impact on the enjoyment of economic, social and cultural rights'
[42] In 1998 and 1999 expert meetings on the subject of targeted sanctions, particularly economic sanctions, were held as part of the so-called 'Interlaken Process' initiated by Switzerland. These

economic transactions with a state under sanctions, but instead impose targeted restrictions on trade in armaments and products used for repression as well as limiting the freedom of travel of members of the regime and freezing assets they hold abroad.

4. Authorization of military action

Under Article 42 of the UN Charter, the Security Council may authorize states to intervene militarily in a conflict situation. Since the early 1990s, it has invoked this authority in a number of resolutions, and human rights violations were often one of several factors motivating the decision to resort to such drastic measures. Violations of international human rights guarantees, for instance, were among the key considerations that led to the authorization of a military intervention in the civil war in Somalia in 1992[43] and probably played an even more important role in the decision to authorize an armed intervention in Haiti.[44] In the latter case, there was no real risk of an international conflict, but the flow of refugees triggered by the situation provided reason enough for taking action. More recently, the authorizations to intervene in the civil wars in Sierra Leone and Liberia were strongly motivated by human rights concerns.

Example: Authorization of the intervention in Liberia by
UN Security Council Resolution 1497 of 1 August 2003

The Security Council,
    Deeply concerned over the conflict in Liberia and its effects on the humanitarian situation, including the tragic loss of countless innocent lives, in that country, and its destabilizing effect to the region,
    Stressing the need to create a secure environment that enables respect for human rights, including the well being and rehabilitation of children, protects the well-being of civilians, and supports the mission of humanitarian workers...

Determining that the situation in Liberia constitutes a threat to the international peace and security, the stability in the West Africa subregion, and to the peace process for Liberia, Acting under Chapter VII of the Charter of the United Nations,

1. Authorizes Member States to establish a Multinational Force in Liberia to support the implementation of the...ceasefire agreement, including establishing conditions for initial stages of disarmament, demobilization and reintegration activities, to help establish and maintain security in the period after the departure of the current President and the installation of a successor authority...

---

activities were continued in the Bonn-Berlin Process on arms embargoes, travel sanctions and aviation-related sanctions, and in the Stockholm Process on the implementation and monitoring of sanctions. For further information, see <www.smartsanctions.ch> (accessed 10 February 2009).

[43] UN Security Council Resolution 794 (1992).
[44] UN Security Council Resolution 940 (1994).

Coercive measures of this kind have proven unsuccessful in some cases, often because of the failure to undertake post-war reconstruction in the states concerned or, as in the case of Somalia, the unwillingness of states to allow their troops to carry out the mandate until set goals were achieved, notwithstanding unexpected difficulties on the ground. The outcome of the intervention in East Timor merits a more favourable assessment, since it succeeded in setting the territory on an orderly track towards independence.

Authorization of military action as a means of law enforcement is tarnished with the charge of selectivity. It usually depends on political factors such as whether the international community is prepared to give its approval and whether any states are willing to provide troops for such a mission. The genocide in Rwanda in 1994 is a particularly problematic example of collective inertia on the part of the international community and of its inability to take effective action against the most unspeakable human rights violations.[45] Another problem is that the UN is militarily dependent on NATO for robust military interventions, which tends to undermine its credibility, depending on the region concerned.

Issue in focus: Humanitarian interventions without
Security Council authorization?

The notion of *humanitarian intervention* denotes the use of military force by states to protect the population of a foreign state from human rights violations by its government. Such interventions can be authorized by the Security Council under Chapter VII of the Charter when the human rights situation has become so alarming that it poses a threat to international peace.

But are states allowed to intervene militarily to protect victims in another state in cases where the Security Council is unwilling or—owing to a lack of consensus or a veto by one or more of the Council's permanent members—unable to decide on a response to massive human rights violations that is commensurate with the seriousness of the situation? This question became critical in 1999 in the case of Kosovo, when NATO member states decided, in the face of Security Council inaction, to force Serb troops to withdraw from Kosovo by means of aerial bombardment. Humanitarian intervention arguments were also invoked, alongside the main argument of an immediate threat from weapons of mass destruction, to justify the United States military intervention in Iraq in 2003.

Article 2(4) of the UN Charter prohibits states from using force against a foreign country even for the purpose of protecting human rights. Both interventions mentioned above were arguably inadmissible under international law, and the Security Council approved neither, before or after the event. The question arose, however, as to whether the international community should really be constrained to accept

---

[45] See the report on the independent inquiry commissioned by Secretary-General Annan on UN conduct during the Rwandan genocide: 'Report of the independent inquiry into the actions of the United Nations during the 1994 genocide in Rwanda of 15 December 1999', UN Doc S/1999/1257.

massacres or systematic rape and torture because a state wielding a veto acts as a shield for regimes responsible for such atrocities, or whether a humanitarian intervention without Security Council authorization ought instead to be permissible as a last resort under certain stringent conditions. It has been suggested, for example, that the following conditions, where cumulatively fulfilled, might justify humanitarian interventions: (1) violations of fundamental and vital interests of the international community that amount to a threat to peace; (2) unwillingness or inability of the Security Council to take appropriate measures to counter the threat; (3) exhaustion of all non-military channels, ie use of military force as a last resort (*ultima ratio*); (4) assumption of collective responsibility for the intervention; (5) proportionality of the means deployed; and (6) a form of action that leaves scope for political solutions in keeping with the UN Charter.[46] These ideas have not found political favour, however, because of fears of abuse where intervening states are left free to decide themselves whether these conditions have been met in a particular case.

A possible way forward is indicated in the report 'The Responsibility to Protect,' published in 2002 by the International Commission for Intervention and State Sovereignty, established on the initiative of the Canadian Government. The report concludes that sovereignty confers primary responsibility on states for the protection of their population, but that sovereignty must yield to the obligation of the international community to afford protection where a population is suffering serious harm on account of civil war, insurrections, state repression or state collapse, and the government is unwilling or unable to come to its assistance. According to the report, military interventions may be contemplated but only in the event of large-scale loss of life or ethnic cleansing, and even then only if no other option is available and there is a real prospect of effectively helping the victims. Such interventions would require Security Council authorization. Where that is not granted, intervening states should seek authorization from the General Assembly under the 'Uniting for Peace' resolution[47] and, if possible, act in the framework of regional or sub-regional arrangements under Chapter VIII of the UN Charter.[48]

---

[46] See, for example, Antonio Cassese, 'Ex iniuria ius oritur: Are We Moving towards International Legitimation of Forcible Humanitarian Countermeasures in the World Community?' 1999 *EJIL* 23 ff.

[47] Pursuant to the 'Uniting for Peace' resolution (Resolution 377(V)(A)) adopted by the General Assembly on 3 November 1950 during the Korean crisis, the General Assembly has the right to consider and take action on matters for which the Security Council is responsible in cases where the Security Council is unable to act because its permanent members block each other.

[48] International Commission on Intervention and State Sovereignty, 'The Responsibility to Protect', Ottawa 2001, XI–XIII. A group of experts set up by the UN Secretary-General, the High-level Panel on Threats, Challenges and Change, referred to the International Commission in its report on UN reform but failed to take up this idea. However, it emphasized the duty of the Security Council to take the necessary measures, including coercive military measures, in the event of gross violations of human rights ('A more secure world: our shared responsibility, Report of the High-level Panel on Threats, Challenges and Change', UN Doc A/59/565, 29 November 2004), paras 199–203. In his report on the UN reform, UN Secretary-General Kofi Annan did not address the issue of humanitarian intervention by states without Security Council authorization but stressed the Security Council's responsibility in situations of gross human rights violations ('In larger freedom: towards development, security and human rights for all, Report of the Secretary-General', UN Doc A/59/2005, 21 March 2005, paras 122–126). On the responsibility to protect, see section III.1.

5. Establishment of criminal tribunals and other bodies

The Security Council has made innovative use of the Articles in Chapter VII of the Charter, invoking them as the legal basis for the establishment of bodies with powers of enforcement. The two Criminal Tribunals for the former Yugoslavia and Rwanda[49] are a prime example.

Issue in focus: Is the Security Council competent under international law to establish *ad hoc* tribunals?

In the *Tadić* judgment,[50] the International Criminal Tribunal for the former Yugoslavia (ICTY) had to consider the argument raised by the defence in a criminal case that there was no basis in the UN Charter for the establishment of an international criminal tribunal by means of a Security Council resolution. The Tribunal came to the following conclusion:

32.... In its resolution 827, the Security Council considers that 'in the particular circumstances of the former Yugoslavia', the establishment of the International Tribunal 'would contribute to the restoration and maintenance of peace' and indicates that, in establishing it, the Security Council was acting under Chapter VIII (S.C. Res. 827, U.N. Doc. S/RES/827 (1993)). However, it did not specify a particular article as a basis for this action.

Appellant has attacked the legality of this decision at different stages before the Trial Chamber as well as before this Chamber on at least three grounds:

(a) that the establishment of such a tribunal was never contemplated by the framers of the Charter as one of the measures to be taken under Chapter VII;...

33. The establishment of an international tribunal is not expressly mentioned among the enforcement measures provided for in Chapter VII, and more particularly in Articles 41 and 42...

35. ... It is evident that measures set out in Article 41[51] are merely illustrative examples which obviously do not exclude other measures. All the Article requires is that they do not involve 'the use of force'. It is a negative definition.... Moreover, even a simple literal analysis of the Article shows that the first phrase of the first sentence carries a very general prescription which can accommodate both institutional and Member State action. The second phrase can be read as referring particularly to one species of this very large category of measures referred to in the first phrase, but not necessarily the only one, namely, measures undertaken directly by States. It is also clear that the second sentence, starting with 'These [measures]' not 'Those [measures]', refers to the species mentioned in the second phrase rather than to the 'genus' referred to in the first phrase of this sentence.

---

[49] See Chapter 6, section IV.1.

[50] ICTY (Appeals Chamber), *The Prosecutor v Tadić*, Decision on the Defence Motion for Interlocutory Appeal on Jurisdiction, Case No IT-94-1AR72 (1995).

[51] Art 41 of the Charter reads: 'The Security Council may decide what measures not involving the use of armed force are to be employed to give effect to its decisions, and it may call upon the Members of the United Nations to apply such measures. These may include complete or partial interruption of economic relations and of rail, sea, air, postal, telegraphic, radio, and other means of communication, and the severance of diplomatic relations.'

> 36. Logically, if the Organization can undertake such measures which have to be implemented through the intermediary of its Members, it can a fortiori undertake measures which it can implement directly via its organs, if it happens to have the resources to do so. It is only for want of such resources that the United Nations has to act through its Members. But it is of the essence of 'collective measures' that they are collectively undertaken. Action by Member States on behalf of the Organization is but a poor substitute *faute de mieux*, or a 'second best' for want of the first. This is also the pattern of Article 42 on measures involving the use of armed force.
>
> In sum, the establishment of the international Tribunal falls squarely within the powers of the Security Council under Article 41 ...

As previously mentioned,[52] the Security Council, acting under Chapter VII of the Charter, can mandate the International Criminal Court (ICC) to prosecute international crimes in a specific country, even if the state concerned has not ratified the Rome Statute. The Security Council's decision on 18 September 2004 to set up an independent International Commission of Inquiry in response to allegations that genocide was being committed in the Sudanese region of Darfur was therefore a particularly interesting development.[53] The Commission was mandated to investigate reports of war crimes, crimes against humanity and genocide. In light of its report,[54] the Security Council referred the situation to the ICC in spring 2005.[55]

Another body created by the Security Council is the United Nations Compensation Commission (UNCC), which was established in 1991 in the wake of the Iraqi invasion of Kuwait.[56] The UNCC awarded compensation not only for material damages but also to victims of human rights violations during the Iraqi occupation of Kuwait. The resources for this purpose were drawn from a UN-administered fund that was financed by compulsory contributions from the proceeds of Iraqi oil exports. Claims for compensation could not be lodged by victims of a human rights violation in their own names, but had to be put forward by the victims' state of origin. This mechanism is therefore based on the concept of diplomatic protection[57] and only indirectly on human rights.

IV. The Role of the International Court of Justice

1. Overview

International human rights law and international humanitarian law do not occupy a very prominent place in the case law of the International Court of Justice (ICJ), the main judicial organ of the United Nations. Nevertheless, some

---

[52] See Chapter 6, section IV.2. [53] UN Security Council Resolution 1564 (2004).
[54] 'Report of the International Commission of Inquiry on Darfur to the United Nations Secretary-General', Geneva, 25 January 2005.
[55] UN Security Council Resolution 1593 (2005).
[56] UN Security Council Resolution 687 (1991). [57] See Chapter 1, section II.1.

judgments and advisory opinions have important implications for the doctrine of human rights protection. For instance, the much-cited *obiter dictum* in the *Barcelona Traction* judgment[58] laid the basis for the recognition of the *erga omnes* status of certain fundamental human rights obligations, and other judgments and advisory opinions have made important contributions towards determining which human rights enjoy customary law status.

The main reason why the ICJ has relatively few opportunities to state its views on human rights issues is that individuals can never bring proceedings before the Court; states alone are entitled to initiate contentious proceedings culminating in a judgment that is binding on the parties to the dispute.[59] Neither states nor individuals may request advisory opinions; this procedure is available only to UN organs. ICJ advisory opinions are not legally binding but have considerable legal and political authority.

2. Contentious proceedings

To date, states have generally initiated contentious proceedings on account of violations of human rights and international humanitarian law obligations *vis-à-vis* their *own* citizens (rather than to assert the general interests of the community of states). Some relevant cases in this respect involve the adjudication of alleged violations of international law committed indirectly or directly by the respondent state during armed conflicts on the territory of the complainant state.[60] This was the claim behind both Yugoslavia's case against various NATO member states[61] and the case of the Democratic Republic of the Congo against Uganda. In the latter case, the Court decided that Uganda had to provide reparation for its violations of international humanitarian law on Congolese territory.[62] Finally, the cases of Bosnia and Herzegovina and Croatia against Serbia and Montenegro dealt with violations of the Genocide Convention[63] and the

---

[58] ICJ, *Case concerning the Barcelona Traction, Light and Power Company, Limited (Belgium v Spain)*, ICJ Reports 1970, 32, para 33.

[59] The Court can deal with a complaint by a state against another country only if both parties to the dispute have recognized its jurisdiction by means of a so-called optional clause declaration, a provision to that effect in a treaty or an *ad hoc* agreement following the outbreak of the dispute. See Art 36 of the Statute of the ICJ.

[60] See, eg, ICJ, *Case concerning Military and Paramilitary Activities in and against Nicaragua (Nicaragua v the United States of America)*, ICJ Reports 1986, para 220.

[61] ICJ, *Case concerning the Legality of Use of Force (Serbia and Montenegro v Belgium, Canada, France, Germany, Italy, the Netherlands, Portugal and the United Kingdom)*, ICJ Reports 2004.

[62] ICJ, *Case concerning Armed Activities on the Territory of the Congo (Democratic Republic of the Congo v Uganda)*, ICJ Reports 2005. The Court decided in this case that Uganda had to offer compensation for the human rights violations committed on Congolese territory. A second case concerning *Armed Activities on the Territory of the Congo (New Application: 2002) (Democratic Republic of the Congo v Rwanda)* was declared inadmissible for lack of jurisdiction of the ICJ (ICJ Reports 2006).

[63] ICJ, *Case concerning Application of the Convention on the Prevention and Punishment of the Crime of Genocide (Bosnia and Herzegovina v Serbia and Montenegro)*, ICJ Reports 2007 and *Case concerning Application of the Convention on the Prevention and Punishment of the Crime of Genocide (Croatia v Serbia and Montenegro)* (pending at the time of writing).

case of Georgia against Russia with alleged acts of ethnic cleansing in violation of CERD.[64]

A number of cases concerned claims arising from the concept of *diplomatic protection*, ie the right of a state to intervene in cases where the treatment of its nationals in another state was not in accordance with international law. In the so-called 'Tehran hostage case',[65] the ICJ held that the hostage-taking of American diplomats during the Islamic revolution in 1979 constituted a flagrant violation of the principles of the Charter and of the Universal Declaration of Human Rights. The Court has also accepted jurisdiction with respect to complaints alleging violations of the notification provisions of the Vienna Convention on Consular Relations by the United States upon the imposition of the death penalty on foreign nationals.[66] The lack of notice allegedly made it impossible for the state of origin to provide the accused with consular protection, for instance by providing legal assistance. In the *LaGrand*[67] and *Avena*[68] cases, the ICJ found in favour of the complainants, developing what amounts to a human-rights based claim to consular protection in the event of detention in a third state.

3. Advisory proceedings

As only the UN General Assembly, the Security Council[69] and, within the limits of their mandates, other UN specialized agencies are entitled to request an advisory opinion, issues of major interest to the community of states are generally at stake in such circumstances. Thus, as early as 1951 the ICJ ruled in its Advisory Opinion on the admissibility of reservations to the Genocide Convention[70] on the legal status of the prohibition of genocide. It concluded that this prohibition was of such fundamental importance that no reservations thereto were permissible. In an Advisory Opinion issued in 1996, the Court responded to a request by the General Assembly to rule on the legality of the threat or use of nuclear weapons.[71] Although the judges were unable to agree on whether such a prohibition existed in all circumstances, the Advisory Opinion contains important observations on the right to life and its relationship to international

---

[64] ICJ, *Case concerning Application of the International Convention on the Elimination of All Forms of Racial Discrimination (Georgia v Russian Federation)* (pending at the time of writing).

[65] ICJ, *Case concerning United States Diplomatic and Consular Staff in Tehran (United States of America v Iran)*, ICJ Reports 1980, 3 ff.

[66] Vienna Convention on Consular Relations of 1963, Art 74.

[67] ICJ, *Case concerning the Vienna Convention on Consular Relations, LaGrand Case (Germany v United States of America)*, ICJ Reports 2001, 466 ff.

[68] ICJ, *Case concerning Avena and Other Mexican Nationals (Mexico v United States of America)*, ICJ Reports 2004.

[69] Art 96 of the UN Charter.

[70] ICJ, *Advisory Opinion on Reservations to the Convention on the Prevention and Punishment of the Crime of Genocide*, ICJ Reports 1951, 15.

[71] ICJ, *Legality of the Threat or Use of Nuclear Weapons* (Advisory Opinion), ICJ Reports 1996-I, 226 ff.

humanitarian law. Lastly, the Court placed strong emphasis on human rights and international humanitarian law in its response to the question of the permissibility of the Israeli separation barrier on Palestinian territory referred to it by the General Assembly in 2003.[72] The Court recognized in its Advisory Opinion the extraterritorial applicability of the Human Rights Covenants and dwelt at length on the question of individual rights under international law to food, work, and freedom of movement, as embodied in the ICCPR, the ICESCR, and in international humanitarian law.

V. Other UN Bodies

1. Office of the UN High Commissioner for Human Rights

The Office of the United Nations High Commissioner for Human Rights (OHCHR) occupies a special place among Charter-based institutions. Founded in the wake of the 1993 Vienna World Conference on Human Rights, the Office of the High Commissioner,[73] with its seat in Geneva, is the voice of the United Nations on human rights issues and a source of moral authority whose mission is also to ensure that victims' voices are heard. In addition to its task of providing the Human Rights Council and the treaty bodies with secretarial support, it has functions in its own right. These functions include coordinating the UN's human rights activities, developing early warning systems, commenting on topical human rights issues, and representing the United Nations human rights programme in various UN coordinating mechanisms. The Office of the High Commissioner also organizes human rights field presences as independent missions,[74] as components of UN peacekeeping or peace-building missions,[75] or in the framework of the United Nations Development Programme (UNDP).[76]

The Office of the High Commissioner currently (2008) has field presences in more than forty countries. The legal basis for these missions is usually an agreement between the UN and the individual state or, more rarely, a Security Council resolution. The activities of field presences, whose staffing may vary considerably, typically involve human rights fact-finding, monitoring of the human rights situation and support for the development of rights-based institutions (ie

---

[72] ICJ, *Legal Consequences of the Construction of a Wall in the Occupied Palestinian Territory* (Advisory Opinion), ICJ Reports 2004, especially paras 89 ff.

[73] The current High Commissioner for Human Rights is Navanethem Pillay. Her predecessors were Louise Arbour (2004–2008), Sergio Vieira de Mello (2002–2003), Mary Robinson (1997–2002), José Ayala-Lasso (1994–1997). Betrand Ramcharan was Acting High Commissioner in 2003–2004.

[74] Eg in Burundi, the Democratic Republic of the Congo, Cambodia, the Solomon Islands, Macedonia, Colombia, and Guatemala.

[75] Eg in Angola, Sierra Leone, Liberia, Central African Republic, Guinea-Bissau, Abkhazia/Georgia, and Tajikistan.

[76] Eg in Madagascar, Chad, South Africa, Somalia and the Occupied Palestinian Territory.

capacity-building). There are at present particularly large monitoring missions in the Sudan (since 2004) and in Nepal (since 2005).

2. UN Commissions

The Commission on the Status of Women is a functional subsidiary body of ECOSOC. It is composed of representatives from forty-five states, elected by ECOSOC for four-year terms, and its mandate is to promote women's rights. This body has assumed responsibility for the codification of human rights treaties relating specifically to women, such as the Convention on the Political Rights of Women and the Convention on the Elimination of All Forms of Discrimination against Women. The Commission's mandate now also includes the implementation of the Platform for Action, adopted by the Beijing Fourth World Conference on Women. In order to support the implementation of the Platform, the Commission has even established a confidential petition system. Despite its many activities, a recurring complaint is that the Commission remains in the shadow of the Human Rights Council because of its institutional constraints as well as its meagre financial resources and meeting time, not to mention the limited attention its activities receive from states.[77]

The Commission on the Status of Women is not the only UN commission active in the area of human rights. Over the last 30 years, the Commission on Crime Prevention and Criminal Justice, which is primarily responsible for implementing the UN's crime prevention programme, has adopted an impressive body of recommendations on the rules of conduct governing the treatment of prisoners and the manner in which criminal proceedings are carried out.[78]

VI. Extra-conventional Human Rights Organs of Regional Organizations

1. Europe

Human rights organs that have their legal basis not in a human rights convention but the charter of an international organization also exist at the regional level, albeit to a lesser extent than at the UN level.

---

[77] For more detail, see Christina Hausammann, *Menschenrechte, Impulse für die Gleichstellung von Frau und Mann in der Schweiz* (Helbing & Lichtenhahn: Basle, 2002), 32 ff.

[78] See, for example, the 'Basic Principles for the Treatment of Prisoners' (1990), the 'Body of Principles for the Protection of All Persons under Any Form of Detention or Imprisonment' (1988), the 'Basic Principles on the Use of Force and Firearms by Law Enforcement Officials' (1990), the 'Basic Principles on the Independence of the Judiciary' (1985), and the 'Code of Conduct for Law Enforcement Officials' (1979).

The Organization for Security and Co-operation in Europe (OSCE), which had adopted a pan-European approach from the outset and had always regarded human rights as a component of any comprehensive security architecture,[79] created, in 1992, the Office of the OSCE High Commissioner on National Minorities which was established in response to mounting ethnic tensions in Central and Eastern Europe after the fall of the Berlin wall. Today, although the High Commissioner's main task still consists of conflict prevention, particularly through the development of an early warning system, his or her on-site missions and confidential fact-finding activities are also of major importance from a human rights perspective, since their aim is to ensure the broadest possible enforcement of human rights protection for minorities.[80]

Another pillar of OSCE human rights protection comes in the form of long-term field missions. These missions, which vary in terms of size and mandate, are conducted in crisis regions in the Balkans, Eastern Europe, the Caucasus, and Central Asia,[81] often in close cooperation with the UN and the Council of Europe. Their mandate frequently includes human rights monitoring and rule-of-law institution-building in the reconstruction phase following armed conflicts.

In the Council of Europe, the Parliamentary Assembly and the Committee of Ministers[82] undertake standard setting by adopting new human rights conventions and recommendations.[83] In 1999, the Council of Europe established the office of an independent European Commissioner for Human Rights. The Commissioner is elected by the Parliamentary Assembly of the Council of Europe and has a wide-ranging mandate in the area of human rights education and enforcement. The incumbent has also been assigned ombudsman-related functions.[84] To date, the

---

[79] The OSCE was founded in 1975 by the so-called 'Helsinki Final Act' at the Conference on Security and Co-operation in Europe (CSCE), ie as a loosely knit conference of all European states plus the United States and Canada. The Act contains three 'baskets' of recommendations relating to political and military issues, economics and—in the so-called 'humanitarian basket'—human rights such as freedom of movement. At follow-up conferences in Paris, Copenhagen and Moscow from 1989 to 1991 progress was made on the humanitarian basket including explicit recognition of certain rights. The Charter of Paris of 21 November 1990 declared that the Cold War was over, and the CSCE built its first institutional structures. This process was completed in 1994 when the CSCE became the OSCE and permanent structures were put in place.

[80] Office of the OSCE High Commissioner on National Minorities: <http://www.osce.org/hcnm/> (accessed 18 January 2009).

[81] The OSCE currently has missions and other field activities in 18 countries: Bosnia and Herzegovina, Croatia, Serbia, Montenegro, Macedonia, Kosovo, Albania, Moldova, Belarus, Ukraine, Georgia, Armenia, Azerbaijan, Kazakhstan, Turkmenistan, Kyrgyzstan, Uzbekistan, and Tajikistan. The mission in Georgia is currently preparing to close down in 2009.

[82] On the role of the Committee of Ministers in the area of monitoring the implementation of judgments of the European Court of Human Rights see Chapter 7, section III.2.h.

[83] See the examples in Chapter 2, sections II.3.c and IV.

[84] Resolution 99(50) of the Committee of Ministers of the Council of Europe describes the mandate as follows: 'The Commissioner shall: (a) promote education in and awareness of human rights in the member States; (b) contribute to the promotion of the effective observance...of human rights in the member States; (c) provide advice and information on the protection of human rights and prevention of human rights violations...; (d) facilitate the activities of national ombudsmen or similar institutions in the field of human rights; (e) identify possible shortcomings in the

Commissioner's work has included visiting countries[85] as well as organizing seminars, expressing opinions and making recommendations on current issues.[86]

The European Commission against Racism and Intolerance, established by the Council of Europe in 1993, is specifically entrusted with the task of combating racism, xenophobia, and anti-Semitism. Its members are independent experts appointed by national governments, one for each member state of the Council of Europe. Following country visits, the Commission draws up detailed country reports that analyse the situation in the state concerned from a legal and factual perspective and conclude with suggestions for improvement. As a rule, these reports are published. In addition, the Commission issues general policy recommendations concerning possible ways of addressing current problems.[87]

2. The Americas

In the Americas, the mandate of the Inter-American Commission on Human Rights in the framework of the Organization of American States (OAS) includes, in addition to its Convention-based functions,[88] certain extra-conventional responsibilities *vis-à-vis* all member states of the Organization, ie also those not party to the American Convention on Human Rights, such as the United States and Canada. These obligations include dealing with individual complaints regarding alleged violations of the American Declaration on the Rights and Duties of Man against those states,[89] although referral to the Inter-American Court of Human Rights is ruled out in such cases, since the Court's jurisdiction is derived exclusively from the American Convention on Human Rights.

law and practice of member States concerning the compliance with human rights…, promote the effective implementation of these standards by member States and assist them, with their agreement, in their efforts to remedy such shortcomings…'

[85] The Commissioner has already visited almost all Council of Europe member states, including, for example, Chechnya and Ingushetia, Poland, Portugal and Turkey in 2003, Cyprus, Sweden, Luxembourg, Croatia and others in 2004, Liechtenstein and Switzerland in 2005, Russia, Rumania and France in 2006, Austria, Germany and the Ukraine in 2007 and San Marino and Georgia in 2008.

[86] In 2002 and 2003, for example, on the human rights of detainees in Chechnya and on derogations from human rights in Northern Ireland, in 2006 on the human rights of Sinti and Roma.

[87] As of December 2008, the Commission had issued 11 general policy recommendations, including on problems such as discrimination against Muslims or racism on the Internet. Moreover, at least two country reports have so far been prepared for each Council of Europe member state. Protocol 12 to the ECHR on a general prohibition of discrimination was also drafted in response to a Commission suggestion.

[88] See Chapter 7, section III.3.

[89] Art 20(b) of the Statute of the Inter-American Commission on Human Rights, October 1979.

PART III

SUBSTANTIVE GUARANTEES

The third part of this book discusses a selection of substantive human rights guarantees. Its organization is based on an understanding of human rights as legal concepts that address basic human needs and vulnerabilities and highlights the indivisibility of civil and political rights on the one hand and economic, social and cultural rights on the other.

The first rights to be examined are those protecting the person as an individual: Obviously the need to survive as an individual is the most fundamental prerequisite to the enjoyment of human rights; it is protected by the different dimensions of the right to life but also by the rights to food, shelter, and health as necessary conditions of subsistence (Chapter 9). Torture and other forms of ill-treatment destroy the personality and are therefore prohibited in an absolute manner (Chapter 10). Given that we all strive to be recognized the way we are, the prohibition of discrimination protects, *inter alia*, our identity as individuals with a specific gender, origin, ethnicity, and religion (Chapter 11).

As social beings most individuals wish to marry, have a family, make friends and lead private lives. People must therefore be protected against state interference in all these areas (Chapter 12). As rational beings, humans strive to develop and use their intellects, to interact with others, to shape and participate in society, and to fulfil spiritual needs. This is done either alone or in community with others, through intellectual or artistic activities, and through religious beliefs. Individuals are protected by a large number of rights in this area, including, freedom of thought, conscience and opinion, the right to education, cultural rights, and freedom of religion (Chapter 13). In a wider social sphere, humans are economic beings in need of protection against being exploited and loosing their property (Chapter 14).

Individuals who fall into the hands of the state as detainees or as persons accused of having committed a crime are particularly vulnerable and are therefore protected, *inter alia*, against arbitrary detention and by fair trial guarantees (Chapter 15). As citizens, people are also political beings eager to influence the public sphere, and these interests are protected by political rights (Chapter 16).

Finally, also at risk and in need of special protection are migrants, people who are forcibly displaced inside their country, and refugees compelled to flee across international borders (Chapter 17).

9

Protection of Human Existence:
Right to Life and Subsistence Rights

I. Overview

Human life is protected under international law by an array of rights.

The *right to life* plays a central role in this regard, and is generally characterized, alongside the prohibition of torture and the right to food, as one of the most fundamental human rights.[1] Despite its name (right *to* life) it does not guarantee human existence as such. Rather, it protects against deprivation of life by state action or as a consequence of its omissions. Although the right is non-derogable in times of a public emergency, the right to life is not absolute. Treaty law provides for three exceptions to the rule that prohibits the taking of human life:

(1) Killing by state agents cannot be characterized as a violation of the right to life if the lethal outcome is unavoidable in circumstances of self-defence, defence of others, or any other legitimate and proportional police action that, although not intended, may result in death.

(2) Execution of a death sentence imposed in a fair trial in a state where capital punishment has not been abolished does not constitute a violation of human rights if certain specific procedural and substantive conditions are met.

(3) Killings in the context of armed conflicts are permissible if they are compatible with the requirements set out in international humanitarian law. Beyond the state obligation to respect, the duty to protect is of cardinal importance to the effective realization of the right to life as evidenced by the wording of relevant provisions stipulating that this right 'shall be protected by law'.[2]

Where killings are aimed at the systematic destruction of a particular national, racial, ethnic or religious group, they meet the definition of the international crime of *genocide*. Deemed to be the most serious of all crimes, genocide entails

---

[1] See, eg, HRCttee, *Baboeram et al v Suriname*, Communications Nos 146/1983 and 148–154/1983 (1985), para 13.2; ECtHR (Grand Chamber), *McCann and Others v the United Kingdom*, Series A, No 324 (1995), para 147; and ACmHPR, *Forum of Conscience v Sierra Leone*, Communication No 223/1998 (2000), para 19.

[2] ICCPR, Art 6; ACHR, Art 4; ArCHR, Art 5; ECHR, Art 2.

individual criminal responsibility at the national and international level as well as the responsibility of the state on whose behalf the individuals act.

The *right to food*, the core of the right to an adequate standard of living, is the only right characterized as 'fundamental' in the text of the UN human rights covenants. However, although many people die from hunger or lack of medical care under circumstances that could have been avoided if the state had taken appropriate measures, the threat to life from a lack of food, and indeed also from lack of health care, is far less widely perceived to be a human rights issue. Human existence, though, is not just about survival, it is also about a minimum level of dignity that is not guaranteed for the many hundreds of millions of people who are undernourished, homeless or deprived of adequate medical care even if these deprivations are not immediately life-threatening. The protection of human life must therefore also embrace *subsistence rights* and the *right to health*.

II. The Right to Life

Relevant provisions: UDHR, Article 3; ICCPR, Article 6; CPPCG; CRC, Article 6(2); CRPD, Article 10; ACHR, Article 4; ACHPR, Article 4; ArCHR, Articles 5–7; ECHR, Article 2; P 6/ECHR; P 13/ECHR; GC I–IV, Article 3; GC III, Articles 13 and 100 ff; GC IV, Articles 27, 32, 68, and 75; AP I, Article 75(2); AP II, Articles 4(2) and 6(4); Rome Statute, Articles 6, 7(1)(a) and 8; SICTY, Articles 2(a), 4 and 5(a); SICTR, Articles 2, 3(a) and 4(a).

1. The notion of life

Article 6(1) of the ICCPR and equivalent guarantees in the regional conventions stipulate that every human being has the inherent right to life. While the notion of human life as such does not need further clarification, the question arises as to when such life begins and when it ends. These issues are often defined for purposes of domestic law, eg referring to birth as the time when the legal capacity as human being begins[3] or considering a person deceased upon the 'irreversible cessation of circulatory and respiratory functions or ... of all functions of the entire brain, including the brain stem'.[4]

With the exception of Article 4(1) of the ACHR, under which the scope of the right to life extends to the moment of conception, the treaty texts are silent on the highly controversial issue of when life begins. In a recent decision, the Grand Chamber of the ECtHR determined that, given the absence of European legislation on the issue, states parties are basically free to settle the question themselves.

---

[3] See, eg, German Civil Code of 18 August 1896, § 1: 'The legal capacity of a human being begins on the completion of birth.'

[4] California Health and Safety Code, Section 7180 (available at <http://www.leginfo.ca.gov/cgi-bin/calawquery?codesection=hsc&codebody=&hits=20> (accessed 22 October 2008)).

In the case at hand, as British law did not recognize individual rights of a fecundated egg cell, the Court decided that the destruction of human embryos did not fall under the protection of ECHR, Article 2.[5] Although the Human Rights Committee addressed abortion issues on several occasions, its focus was always on the rights of the mother.[6] In any case, life, as protected by human rights law, starts no later than birth. Thus, for example, euthanasia programmes for severely handicapped newborn babies[7] would constitute a gross violation of the right to life.

At the other end of the spectrum, the controversy surrounds not the identification of the time of death but whether mentally competent individuals derive from the right to life a right to euthanasia, ie the deliberate termination of their life with the assistance of a third person. The controversy extends to the question of whether the state's duty to protect requires that the termination of life be punishable also in the case of persons who are incurably ill.[8]

The right to life may be violated even if nobody is killed. This is the case, for example, where the victim of indiscriminate fire by the police 'fortuitously' survives,[9] or where a person manages to escape an attempt by a police officer to kill him.[10]

2. Duty to respect life

(a) Overview

According to ICCPR, Article 6 '[n]o one shall be arbitrarily deprived of his life.' The duty to respect life obliges states and their organs to refrain from any intentional killing unless it is permissible under the circumstances described below. Thus, acts such as murder of political opponents, killing of persons in custody (including in the context of disappearances), or massacres of civilians automatically constitute violations of the right to life.

---

[5] ECtHR (Grand Chamber), *Evans v The United Kingdom*, Application No 6339/05 (2007), paras 53 ff. The ECtHR had to decide whether the destruction of embryos, ie fecundated egg cells, which had been raised outside of the mother's womb and had not yet been implanted in the womb, violated ECHR, Art 2. According to British law, the agreement of keeping the fecundated egg-cells during the in vitro fertilization process can be revoked individually by either parent at any time. In that event, the fecundated egg cells are destroyed.

[6] See the cases mentioned below, at section II.3.c.

[7] See HRCttee, Concluding Observations Netherlands (2001), para 6, in which the Committee asked the Netherlands to investigate reports of the killing of newborn severely handicapped infants.

[8] See section II.3.c below.

[9] See ECtHR (Grand Chamber), *Makaratzis v Greece, Reports* 2004-XI, paras 49 ff. According to this judgment ECHR, Art 2 may be invoked in the event of non-lethal use of force only where the resort to force was not intended to inflict humiliation, pain or debasement on the victim, and hence did not fall within the substantive scope of ECHR, Art 3 concerning the prohibition of torture and cruel, inhuman or degrading treatment. For a similar conclusion in the context of armed conflict see ECtHR, *Makhauri v Russia*, Application No 58701/00 (2007), para 117. See also IACtHR, *Case of the Rochela Massacre v Colombia*, Series C, No 163 (2007), para 127.

[10] ACmHPR, *Kazeem Aminu v Nigeria*, Communication No 205/1997 (2000), para 18.

Although subject to restrictive conditions, state actions may be permissible even if they result in death where they are the consequence of lawful use of violence by police and other law-enforcement personnel (see (b) below); take the form of an execution of a death penalty imposed by a court (see (c) below); or take place in accordance with international humanitarian law in the context of an armed conflict (see (d) below).

(b) The prohibition of arbitrary killing by law enforcement officials

While ICCPR, Article 6(1) and most regional conventions[11] prohibit the 'arbitrary' deprivation of human life, ECHR, Article 2 is differently structured. It stipulates in paragraph 2 that deprivation of life is not a human rights violation 'when it results from the use of force which is no more than absolutely necessary: (a) in defence of any person from unlawful violence; (b) in order to effect a lawful arrest or to prevent escape of a person lawfully detained; (c) in action lawfully taken for the purpose of quelling a riot or insurrection'.

It follows that human rights law does not entirely prohibit a state, as the holder of the monopoly on the use of force, from employing lethal force by its police and security personnel. Thus, pursuant to ECHR, Article 2, law enforcement officials may use force, notwithstanding a potentially fatal outcome, in self-defence, in the defence of others, to arrest a person and to quell an insurrection where the force used is no more than that which is absolutely necessary. Article 2(2) should not be read as enumerating the circumstances in which the state is allowed intentionally to kill, but rather as listing the conditions in which the right to life is not violated notwithstanding deprivation of life because the use of force in pursuit of one of the delineated aims is absolutely necessary and proportionate.[12] Under these circumstances, force may be used in the above-mentioned cases even where there is no certainty that a fatal outcome can be avoided.[13] Force with the deliberate aim of killing may be used *in extremis* and as a last resort in circumstances

---

[11] ACHR, Art 4; ACHPR, Art 4; and ArCHR, Art 5.

[12] See, eg, ECtHR (Grand Chamber), *Ramsahai and Others v The Netherlands*, Application No 52391/99 (2007), para 287: '[T]he term 'absolutely necessary' in Article 2 § 2 indicates that a stricter and more compelling test of necessity must be employed than that normally applicable when determining whether State action is "necessary in a democratic society" under the second paragraph of Articles 8 to 11 of the Convention.' The potentially lethal use of force to arrest a person who poses no threat to the life and person of others and is not suspected of having committed a violent offence is always a disproportionate response: ECtHR (Grand Chamber), *Nachova and Others v Bulgaria*, Reports 2005-VII, para 95. The use of violence, which would not normally cause death but exceptionally does so because of the health predisposition of the victim, is not in itself disproportional: ECtHR, *Scavuzzo-Hager v Switzerland*, Application No 41773/98 (2006).

[13] ECtHR (Grand Chamber), *McCann and Others v The United Kingdom*, Series A, No 324 (1995), para 148: 'The Court considers that the exceptions delineated in paragraph 2 indicate that this provision extends to, but is not concerned exclusively with, intentional killing...[T]he text of Article 2, read as a whole, demonstrates that paragraph 2 does not primarily define instances where it is permitted intentionally to kill an individual, but describes the situations where it is permitted to "use force" which may result, as an unintended outcome, in the deprivation of life. The use of force, however, must be no more than "absolutely necessary" for the achievement of one of the

of genuine self-defence and necessity, and only in such circumstances.[14] If that condition is not met, the intentional killing of a human being other than in an armed conflict is always a violation of the right to life, even, for instance, in the case of the extrajudicial killing of a terrorist.

It follows also from the less detailed jurisprudence of the Human Rights Committee and the other regional conventions that the use of lethal force is a violation of the right to life unless it is proportionate to the requirements of law enforcement[15] in the circumstances of the specific case.[16] Given the special importance to be attached to the safeguarding of human life, these conditions should be no less strictly construed than in the case of the ECHR.

Furthermore, all conventions introduce an additional protective element by stipulating that the right to life is to be protected by law: states parties are required to set out in concrete terms the circumstances in which security forces may use force, in particular the preconditions for shooting to kill.[17] However, even where certain forms of killing are permitted by law, they may nevertheless constitute a breach of a state's obligation to protect life through law in cases where the legislation in question permits or tolerates lethal actions that are incompatible with the right to life.[18]

These are very high thresholds for the use of lethal force, and thus it should not come as a surprise that authorities planning the use of force are obliged to take precautionary measures with the aim of avoiding potentially lethal outcomes in order to be clear of responsibility under the right to life. The approach taken by the European Court of Human Rights in 1995 in the *McCann* case[19] is very rigid. Today, it constitutes the standard that is applicable to determine the permissibility of extrajudicial killings:[20] according to this standard, the use of force as such must be absolutely necessary for the achievement of a legitimate aim, the planning and control of the operation must ensure that every step is taken to safeguard life, and force is resorted to only when a risk to the life of others cannot be dealt with in any other way. These requirements are also applicable, in

---

purposes set out in sub-paragraphs (a), (b) or (c) . . .' See also ECtHR (Grand Chamber), *Ramsahai and Others v The Netherlands*, Application No 52391/99 (2007), para 286.

[14] See, eg, ECtHR, *Bubbins v The United Kingdom, Reports* 2005-II.

[15] HRCttee, *Suárez de Guerrero v Colombia*, Communication No 45/1979 (1982), para 13.2, mentions self-defence and the defence of others as well as carrying out the arrest of a person or preventing the escape of detained persons as legitimate grounds.

[16] Ibid, paras 13.2 and 13.3. See also the similar case law of the IACtHR, eg, *Villagrán-Morales et al v Guatemala* (the 'street children' case), Series C, No 63 (1999), paras 141 ff, and of the IACmHR, *Corumbiara v Brazil*, Report No 32/04, Case 11.556 (2004), paras 171 ff.

[17] HRCttee, General Comment No 6 (1982), para 3: 'The deprivation of life by the authorities of the State is a matter of the utmost gravity. Therefore, the law must strictly control and limit the circumstances in which a person may be deprived of his life by such authorities.' See also ECtHR (Grand Chamber), *Makaratzis v Greece, Reports* 2004-IX paras 57 ff.

[18] HRCttee, *Suárez de Guerrero v Colombia*, Communication No 45/1979 (1982), para 13.3.

[19] ECtHR (Grand Chamber), *McCann and Others v The United Kingdom*, Series A, No 324 (1995).

[20] See also ECtHR (Grand Chamber), *Makaratzis v Greece, Reports* 2004-XI, paras 56 ff.

principle, under the other conventions. Thus, in the *Guerrero* case, the Human Rights Committee held Colombia to task over the fact that the victims had not been warned and had been offered no opportunity to surrender.[21]

Example: The ECtHR judgment in *McCann v the United Kingdom*[22]

This judgment of the European Court of Human Rights deals with the lawfulness of a state's use of force with a lethal outcome in the context of an attempt by British security forces to arrest members of the Irish Republican Army (IRA) in Gibraltar. According to intelligence reports, the IRA members were preparing a bomb attack in Gibraltar. The security forces had been informed prior to the operation that the persons to be arrested were carrying a bomb. As they approached the suspects, one IRA member made a sudden movement. The security agents took it to be an attempt to detonate the bomb and deliberately shot the suspects dead. The assumption proved to be false. Taking into account the state of knowledge of the agents who fired the fatal shots, the Court held that the intentional killing of the alleged terrorists was consistent with the ECHR, since the agents honestly believed that they were in a situation of necessity. However, this finding was not sufficient to relieve the state of its responsibility under human rights law. Rather, the Court held that:

148.…the text of Article 2 (art. 2), read as a whole, demonstrates that paragraph 2 (art. 2–2) does not primarily define instances where it is permitted intentionally to kill an individual, but describes the situations where it is permitted to 'use force' which may result, as an unintended outcome, in the deprivation of life. The use of force, however, must be no more than 'absolutely necessary' for the achievement of one of the purposes set out in sub-paragraphs (a), (b) or (c)…

150. In keeping with the importance of this provision in a democratic society, the Court must, in making its assessment, subject deprivations of life to the most careful scrutiny, particularly where deliberate lethal force is used, taking into consideration not only the actions of the agents of the State who actually administer the force but also all the surrounding circumstances including such matters as the planning and control of the actions under examination…

The Court concluded that the operation had not been planned and controlled in a manner designed to guarantee that lethal force would be resorted to only if absolutely necessary.

213. In sum, having regard to the decision not to prevent the suspect from travelling into Gibraltar, to the failure of the authorities to make sufficient allowances for the possibility that their intelligence assessments might, in some respects at least, be erroneous and to the automatic recourse to lethal force when the soldiers opened fire, the Court is not persuaded that the killing of the three terrorists constituted the use of force which was no more than absolutely necessary in defence of persons from unlawful violence within the meaning of Article 2 § 2 (a) of the Convention.

The killing of the alleged terrorists therefore constituted a violation of the right to life.

---

[21] HRCttee, *Suárez de Guerrero v Colombia*, Communication No 45/1979 (1982), para 13.2.

[22] ECtHR (Grand Chamber), *McCann and Others v The United Kingdom*, Series A, No 324 (1995). See also, eg, *Andronicou and Constantinou v Cyprus*, Reports 1997-VI, *Ergi v Turkey*, Reports 1998-IV, paras 79 ff, and *Güleç v Turkey*, Reports 1998-IV, paras 63 ff on the lawfulness of the use of force by the state to quell violent demonstrations.

Clearly, the right to life is also violated where an agent of the state inflicts wounds on an individual that would not be lethal if treated properly but bars the victim's access to available health care and, as a consequence of which, the person concerned dies.[23] The same must be true where life-saving access to health care or food is blocked by deliberate state action, even if the state has not caused the life-threatening condition.

(c) The death penalty and efforts to abolish it

Customary international law does not prohibit the death penalty as such. However, there is now a largely uncontested view that customary law prohibits the execution of persons below 18 years of age at the time of commission of the crime, pregnant women, and persons suffering from a mental disorder.[24]

According to treaty law, capital punishment is a permissible criminal sanction provided that certain strict conditions are met. These restrictions are set forth in detail in the ICCPR, the regional human rights conventions and international humanitarian law instruments.[25] Optional protocols to the ICCPR and regional conventions go one step further by prohibiting the imposition of the death penalty in peacetime and even during armed conflict.[26]

(i) Preconditions

As regards Article 6 of the ICCPR, as well as arguably the regional conventions, states that have not abolished capital punishment in their domestic law or are not parties to a treaty on the abolition of the death penalty may impose and carry it out under the following conditions, which are to be narrowly construed.

(1) The death penalty may be imposed, as an absolutely exceptional measure, only for what constitutes, in objective and subjective terms, *the most serious crimes*[27] *committed with intent.*[28] The 'most serious' condition is not met,

---

[23] HRCttee, *Mulezi v The Democratic Republic of the Congo*, Communication No 962/2001 (2004), para 5.4.

[24] See, eg, CHR resolution 2003/67, para 4(a) and (g). The United States of America has entered the following reservation to Art 6 (5) ICCPR: '[T]he United States reserves the right, subject to its Constitutional constraints, to impose capital punishment on any person (other than a pregnant woman) duly convicted under existing or future laws permitting the imposition of capital punishment, including such punishment for crimes committed by persons below eighteen years of age.' Germany and Sweden have objected to the admissibility of this reservation. See also, in support of the prohibition of such a reservation, IACmHR, *Patterson v The United States of America*, Report No 25/05, Case 12.439 (2005). On 1 March 2005 in the *Roper v Simmons* case (03-633), the United States Supreme Court, referring to international standards and practice, held that the death penalty for juvenile offenders is unconstitutional. Nineteen US states were affected by this decision.

[25] ICCPR, Art 6(5); ACHR, Art 4(5); GC IV, Art 68(4); AP I, Arts 76(3) and 77(5); AP II, Art 6(4).

[26] See (ii) immediately below.

[27] For instance, the HRCttee found the definition of the offence of 'opposition to order and national security' to be excessively vague. See, eg, Concluding Observations Vietnam (2002), para 7, and also Concluding Observations Kuwait (2000), paras 13 f.

[28] HRCttee, General Comment No 6 (1982), para 6.

for instance, by economic crimes, corruption, robbery,[29] trading in hazardous waste,[30] adultery or homosexual acts, or abductions that do not cause death.[31] It may safely be argued that only wilful homicide and wilful infliction of extremely serious bodily and mental harm can be characterized as sufficiently serious.[32] Criminal provisions that make the death penalty mandatory for certain offences, ie without allowing the offender's degree of culpability and other personal circumstances to be taken into consideration, constitute in all cases a violation of the Covenant.[33]

(2) Criminal legislation that provides for the death penalty must be *framed in such a way as to be consistent with other human rights guarantees* set forth in the ICCPR.[34] In particular, such legislation may not prescribe methods of execution that breach the absolute prohibition of inhuman treatment, ie cause suffering or humiliation beyond the pain and anguish inherent in an execution. For instance, public executions, owing to their degrading character,[35] or gas chamber executions, on account of the time it takes to die,[36] fail to meet this condition. However, upon a close interpretation of the ICCPR, it cannot be argued in legal terms that the imposition and implementation of the death penalty constitute *per se* inhuman treatment and are therefore prohibited under international law. The European Court of Human Rights nevertheless hinted at the possibility of such a broad conclusion, but eventually confined itself to noting that capital punishment in peacetime has become all but unacceptable[37] and invariably constitutes inhuman treatment where it is imposed after an unfair trial.[38]

---

[29] HRCttee, Concluding Observations Republic of Korea (1992), para 8.

[30] HRCttee, Concluding Observations Cameroon (1994), para 9.

[31] HRCttee, Concluding Observations Guatemala (2001), para 17; IACtHR, *Raxcacó-Reyes v Guatemala*, Series C, No 133 (2005), para 72.

[32] Cf Sarah Joseph, Jenny Schultz, and Melissa Castan, *The International Covenant on Civil and Political Rights* (2nd edn, Oxford University Press: Oxford, 2004), 167.

[33] See, eg, HRCttee, *Pagdayawon Rolando v The Philippines*, Communication No 1320/204 (2007), para 5.2; *Carpo et al v The Philippines*, Communication No 1077/2002 (2003), para 8.3; *Hussain and Singh v Guyana*, Communication No 862/1999 (2005), para 6.2. See also IACtHR, *Hilaire et al v Trinidad and Tobago*, Series C, No 94 (2002), paras 103 ff, *Boyce et al v Barbados*, Series C, No 169 (2007), paras 47 ff, and the settled jurisprudence of the IACmHR, see eg *Lallion v Grenada*, Report No 55/02, Case 11.765 (2002), para 63.

[34] This obvious requirement is not explicitly mentioned in the regional conventions but must also apply at that level.

[35] Report of the Special Rapporteur on extrajudicial, summary or arbitrary executions of 22 December 2003, UN Doc E/CN.4/2004/7, para 53.

[36] HRCttee, *Ng v Canada*, Communication No 469/1991 (1993), para 16.4.

[37] ECtHR (Grand Chamber), *Öcalan v Turkey*, *Reports* 2005-IV, paras 162 ff, citing the Chamber's judgment in the same case, Application No 46221/99 (2003), paras 189 ff. The judgment in *Shamayev and 12 Others v Georgia and Russia*, *Reports* 2005-III, para 333, seems, however, to contradict this conclusion.

[38] ECtHR (Grand Chamber), *Öcalan v Turkey*, *Reports* 2005-IV, paras 167 ff. See also ACmHPR, *Civil Liberties Organisation and Others v Nigeria*, Communication No 218/1998 (1998), paras 24 ff.

(3) Furthermore, a death sentence may be imposed only in accordance with criminal laws that were *in force at the time of commission of the crime.* This requirement relates to the prohibition of retrospective laws.[39] If, subsequent to the commission of the crime, a lighter penalty is introduced or the death penalty is abolished, the more lenient provision is always applicable (the *lex mitior* principle).

(4) A death sentence is deemed not to constitute a violation of the right to life only if it is imposed in a *fair trial* before a *competent court.* National laws that provide for the death penalty, and the criminal proceedings themselves, must therefore comply with the procedural safeguards set out in ICCPR, Article 14 and its regional equivalents.[40] Military courts in particular are scarcely ever capable of meeting these requirements in proceedings against civilians.[41]

(5) As mentioned, the execution of persons below 18 years of age at the time of commission of the crime and of pregnant women is prohibited.[42] Article 4(5) of the ACHR also prohibits the execution of persons who are over 70 years of age.

(6) Lastly, it is explicitly stipulated in ICCPR, Article 6(4) and ACHR, Article 4(6) that anyone sentenced to death should be given the opportunity to seek pardon or commutation of the sentence.[43]

(ii) Abolition of the death penalty

A clear trend towards abolition of the death penalty has emerged in recent decades. In international law, this development is reflected at two levels.

Firstly, ACHR, Article 4(3) prohibits states that have abolished the death penalty from re-establishing it. In its second paragraph, the same article forbids states parties to the convention from extending the applicability of capital punishment to crimes that did not warrant the death penalty before ratification.[44] According to ICCPR, Article 6(2), capital punishment may persist only in countries that

---

[39] It is explicitly mentioned in ICCPR, Art 6(2).

[40] This is the settled jurisprudence of the HRCttee: See eg, *Chikunova v Uzbekistan*, 1043/2002 (2007), para 7.5. See also ECtHR (Grand Chamber), *Öcalan v Turkey, Reports* 2005-IV, para 166. In its Views on *Smartt v Guyana*, Communication No 867/1999 (2004), para 6.3, the HRCttee found that the right to life had been violated because defence counsel for the person sentenced to death was absent throughout the criminal proceedings. This jurisprudence is shared by the ACmHPR (see eg *Forum of Conscience v Sierra Leone*, Communication No 223/1998 (2000), para 19, and *International Pen and Others v Nigeria*, Communications Nos 137/1994, 139/1994, 154/1996, and 161/1997 (1998), para 103) and the IACmHR (*Moreno Ramos v The United States of America*, Report No 1/05, Case 12.430 (2005), para 71).

[41] See ECtHR (Grand Chamber), *Öcalan v Turkey, Reports* 2005-IV, paras 112 ff. See also ACmHPR, *Civil Liberties Organisation and Others v Nigeria*, Communication No 218/1998 (1998), paras 24 ff. HRCttee, General Comment No 32, para 22 does not entirely outlaw trials of civilians by military courts, without, however, referring to the issue of capital punishment.

[42] ICCPR, Art 6(5); ACHR, Art 4(5).

[43] See, eg, HRCttee, *Chisanga v Zambia*, Communication No 1132/2002 (2005), para 7.

[44] See IACtHR, *Raxcacó-Reyes v Guatemala*, Series C, No 133, paras 58 ff.

'*have not* abolished the death penalty',[45] and Article 6(6) indicates that the Covenant's aim is to secure its abolition.[46] Construing these provisions both grammatically and teleologically reveals a clear-cut preference in the Covenant for outright abolition of the death penalty. It also suggests that states that have abolished capital punishment may not reintroduce it. Accordingly, the Human Rights Committee emphasizes that states which have abolished the death penalty are under an obligation not to expose people to the risk of its application by extraditing them to a country where they would be executed;[47] views all measures taken to restrict application of the death penalty or to abolish it completely as progress in the enjoyment of the right to life;[48] and encourages states that have not yet done so to abolish capital punishment if they have not imposed or carried out capital sentences for some time.[49]

Secondly, protocols to the ICCPR, ACHR, and ECHR prohibit the death penalty under all circumstances, as summarized in Table 9.1.

(iii) Removal where there is a risk of capital punishment

Is it permissible to extradite or otherwise remove an individual to a country where he or she would face the death penalty?

It is generally accepted that this risk is not an absolute impediment to extradition on human rights grounds for states that have not abolished the death penalty under their domestic law. In the case law of the monitoring bodies, however, it is clear that if treatment prior to execution (eg the conditions on death-row[50]) or the method of execution (eg asphyxiation in a gas chamber[51]) were themselves inhuman, then handing a person over to a state that would execute him or her amounts to prohibited inhuman treatment.[52] In our opinion, the same must apply where, even in

---

[45] Emphasis added.

[46] According to ICCPR, Art 6(6), 'Nothing in this article shall be invoked to delay or to prevent the abolition of capital punishment by any State Party to the present Covenant'. See also ACHR, Art 4(2) prohibiting the extension of such punishment to crimes to which it did not apply at the time of ratification.

[47] HRCttee, *Judge v Canada*, Communication No 829/1998 (2003), para 10.4. See immediately below at (iii).

[48] See, eg, HRCttee, General Comment No 6 (1982), para 6. See also IACtHR, *Right to Information on Consular Assistance in the Framework of the Guarantees of the Due Process of Law* (Advisory Opinion), OC-16 (1999), paras 134 ff.

[49] See, eg, HRCttee, Concluding Observations Suriname (2004), para 10. The question as to whether ECHR, Art 2 prohibits the reintroduction of the death penalty has little practical relevance in the European system today inasmuch as (almost) all states members of the Council of Europe have ratified the additional protocols concerning its abolition. Although these protocols may, in theory, be denounced, any reintroduction of capital punishment, at least in peacetime, would in any case violate the ECHR itself and (presumably) European customary law; ECtHR (Grand Chamber), *Öcalan v Turkey*, Reports 2005-IV, paras 162 ff, citing the Chamber's judgment in the same case (2003), paras 189 ff.

[50] ECtHR, *Soering v The United Kingdom*, Series A, No 161 (1989), paras 90–91 and 100–111.

[51] HRCttee, *Ng v Canada*, Communication No 469/1991 (1993), paras 16.1–16.4.

[52] On the prohibition of inhuman treatment as a barrier to removal to another country see Chapter 17, section III.4.

Table 9.1. Treaties prohibiting the death penalty

Instrument	Content
P 6/ECHR (1983)	Prohibition of the death penalty in peacetime; national law may provide for the death penalty in respect of acts committed in times of war or of imminent threat of war.
ICCPR-OP2 (1989)	Prohibition of the death penalty; a reservation may be made that provides for the application of the death penalty in time of war pursuant to a conviction for a most serious crime of a military nature committed during wartime.
P 2/ACHR (1990)	Same as ICCPR-OP2.
P 13/ECHR (2002)	Absolute prohibition of the death penalty in peacetime and wartime.

the absence of inhuman treatment, it is foreseeable that the death penalty would be carried out in violation of the standards set out above.[53] In such a case, the duty to protect life would forbid a state to remove an individual under its jurisdiction in order to avoid enabling another state to violate the right to life.

What about states that have abolished the death penalty for themselves? Are they entitled to extradite or otherwise remove a person to a country where he or she would risk being sentenced to death and executed albeit in a way compatible with the requirements set out by ICCPR, Article 6 and the corresponding regional conventions? Originally, the Human Rights Committee held that states were not in breach of the Covenant in such cases, even if they themselves had abolished the death penalty.[54] In 2003, however, the Committee changed its view, holding that all states that had abolished the death penalty, regardless of whether they had ratified ICCPR-OP2, had an obligation to protect the right to life of all persons within their jurisdiction. They were therefore prohibited from extraditing a person who would be exposed to the risk of capital punishment. In contrast, the European Court of Human Rights continues to consider as an absolute impediment to extradition and other forms of removal only the cases where the death penalty would be imposed and executed in violation of human rights standards.[55]

Example: Views of the HRCttee in *Judge v Canada*[56]

10.4...Paragraph 1 of article 6 [ICCPR], which states that 'Every human being has the inherent right to life...', is a general rule: its purpose is to protect life. States parties that have abolished the death penalty have an obligation under this paragraph to so protect in all

---

[53] Preceding sub-section (i).
[54] HRCttee, *Kindler v Canada*, Communication No 470/1991 (1993), and *Cox v Canada*, Communication No 539/1993 (1994).
[55] ECtHR, *Bader and Kanbor v Sweden*, *Reports* 2005-XI, paras 41 ff.
[56] HRCttee, *Judge v Canada*, Communication No 829/1998 (2003).

circumstances... In effect, paragraphs 2 to 6 have the dual function of creating an exception to the right to life in respect of the death penalty and laying down limits on the scope of that exception. Only the death penalty pronounced when certain elements are present can benefit from the exception. Among these limitations are that found in the opening words of paragraph 2, namely, that only States parties that 'have not abolished the death penalty' can avail themselves of the exceptions created in paragraphs 2 to 6. For countries that *have* abolished the death penalty, there is an obligation not to expose a person to the real risk of its application. Thus, they may not remove, either by deportation or extradition, individuals from their jurisdiction if it may be reasonably anticipated that they will be sentenced to death, without ensuring that the death sentence would not be carried out.

10.5 The Committee acknowledges that by interpreting paragraphs 1 and 2 of article 6 in this way, abolitionist and retentionist States parties are treated differently. But it considers that this is an inevitable consequence of the wording of the provision itself ...

10.6 For these reasons, the Committee considers that Canada, as a State party which has abolished the death penalty, irrespective of whether it has not yet ratified the Second Optional Protocol... violated the author's right to life under article 6, paragraph 1, by deporting him to the United States, where he is under sentence of death, without ensuring that the death penalty would not be carried out. The Committee recognises that Canada did not itself impose the death penalty on the author. But by deporting him to a country where he was under sentence of death, Canada established the crucial link in the causal chain that would make possible the execution of the author.

(d) *The right to life in situations of armed conflict*

According to the ICCPR and the regional conventions, the right to life is non-derogable in times of public emergency, so that its protective scope extends also, in principle, to situations of armed conflict. This raises the question as to whether acts of killings during armed conflicts are always incompatible with the right to life.

A negative answer is explicitly given by ECHR, Article 15, para 2 which prohibits derogation from Article 2 'except in respect of deaths resulting from lawful acts of war'. This provision declares killings during times of armed conflict as compatible with Article 2 if (1) the state concerned has made a declaration of derogation within the limits of Article 15, and (2) the specific act of killing is compatible with the requirements of international humanitarian law, ie the body of law that determines when the taking of life is permissible during armed conflict. If, despite the existence of an armed conflict, no derogation has been declared, Article 2 continues to apply fully and the standards on the use of lethal force described above[57] carry on determining whether acts of killing constitute a violation of the right to life.[58]

Unlike under the ECHR, there is no reference to the exception of 'lawful acts of war' in the emergency provisions prohibiting derogation from the right to life of the ICCPR and the other regional conventions. It is nonetheless accepted that

[57] In this Chapter, section II.2.b.
[58] See the jurisprudence of the ECtHR on the armed conflict in Chechnya, discussed further below in this sub-section.

loss of life attributable to lawful acts of war is not deemed to constitute arbitrary deprivation of life and hence is not a violation of the right to life. This has been explicitly confirmed by the International Court of Justice when it stressed that '[i]n principle, the right not arbitrarily to be deprived of one's life applies also in hostilities. The test of what is an arbitrary deprivation of life, ... then falls to be determined by ... the law applicable in armed conflict which is designed to regulate the conduct of hostilities. Thus whether a particular loss of life, through the use of a certain weapon in warfare, is to be considered an arbitrary deprivation of life contrary to Article 6 of the Covenant, can only be decided by reference to the law applicable in armed conflict and not deduced from the terms of the Covenant itself.'[59] Thus, where the two bodies of law simultaneously apply, the provisions of international humanitarian law determine whether hostilities entailing loss of life in times of armed conflict constitute a violation of the right to life.

International humanitarian law does not impose a general prohibition on intentional killing since it accepts war as an inevitable occurrence and furthermore adopts no position with regard to the lawfulness of armed conflict. However, the fundamental principle of distinction requires that the 'parties to the conflict must at all times distinguish between civilians and combatants' and that attacks may only be directed against combatants and never against civilians unless and for such time as they take a direct part in hostilities.[60] The principle therefore permits the killing of combatants by combatants provided they use permissible methods and permissible weapons for the purpose. On the other hand, the following categories of deprivation of life, in particular, are prohibited:

(1) *The killing of persons 'hors de combat':* 'Persons taking no active part in the hostilities, including members of armed forces who have laid down their arms and those placed "hors de combat" by sickness, wounds, detention, or any other cause', may never be killed[61] and their lives must be protected as well as possible under the circumstances.[62]

---

[59] ICJ, *Legality of the Threat or Use of Nuclear Weapons* (Advisory Opinion), ICJ Reports 1996, para 25. In the same paragraph the Court also observed 'that the protection of the International Covenant of Civil and Political Rights does not cease in times of war, except by operation of Article 4 of the Covenant whereby certain provisions may be derogated from in a time of national emergency. Respect for the right to life is not, however, such a provision.' See also ICJ, *Legal Consequences of the Construction of a Wall in the Occupied Palestinian Territory* (Advisory Opinion), ICJ Reports 2004, para 106.

[60] Jean-Marie Henckaerts and Louise Doswald-Beck, *Customary International Humanitarian Law*, Vol I: Rules (Cambridge University Press: Cambridge, 2005), Rules 1 and 6; AP I, Art 48; AP II, Art 13.

[61] This is the wording of common Art 3 of the Geneva Conventions pertaining to non-international armed conflicts; pursuant to customary law, it is also applicable to international armed conflicts; see the ICJ in *Case concerning Military and Paramilitary Activities in and against Nicaragua (Nicaragua v United States of America)*, ICJ Reports 1986, 114, paras 218 ff.

[62] ECtHR, *Varnava and Others v Turkey*, Applications Nos 16064-73/90 (2008), para 130: 'International treaties, which have attained the status of customary law, impose obligations on combatant States as regards care of wounded, prisoners of war and civilians; Article 2 of the

(2) *Deadly attacks on civilians*: Civilians are persons who do not belong to armed forces and take no part in the hostilities.[63] The rule according to which the civilian population as such, as well as individual civilians, must not be made the object of military attacks is of special importance for their protection. It is now enshrined in Article 51(2) of Additional Protocol I but is also applicable, as a fundamental principle of customary international humanitarian law, to states that have not ratified the Additional Protocol.[64] Parties to an armed conflict must therefore distinguish between military and civilian objects and may direct their operations only against military objectives.[65] Military objectives are 'those objects which by their nature, location, purpose or use make an effective contribution to military action and whose partial or total destruction, capture or neutralization, in the circumstances ruling at the time, offers a definite military advantage'.[66] The destruction of objects of an exclusive military character such as military personnel and their weapons and equipment, defence facilities, defence ministries or facilities belonging to the arms industry regularly meet these requirements. In contrast, in the case of so-called dual use objects such as ports, streets, bridges, canals, and other infrastructural facilities, fuel-supply, and communication facilities, and militarily relevant terrain such as bridgeheads or hills, the requirement of definite military advantage must be present in the specific case.[67] In case of doubt 'whether an object which is normally dedicated to civilian purposes, such as a place of worship, a house or other dwelling or a school, is being used to make an effective contribution to military action, it shall be presumed not to be so used'[68] unless it comes to light that it has been diverted for military purposes. Therefore, with respect to the right to life, intentionally killing members of armed forces is permissible, whereas civilians must never be made targets. If they are killed because they are in the immediate vicinity of a military target or present at the location of a dual-use object, the attack is prohibited if the collateral damages 'would be excessive in relation to the concrete and direct military advantage anticipated', ie prohibited for lack of proportionality.[69]

(3) *Indiscriminate attacks:* Such prohibited attacks comprise '(a) those which are not directed at a specific military objective; (b) those which employ a method or means of combat which cannot be directed at a specific military objective; or (c) those which employ a method or means of combat the effects of which

Convention certainly extends so far as to require Contracting States to take such steps as may be reasonably available to them to protect the lives of those not, or no longer, engaged in hostilities.'

    [63] AP I, Art 50. See also Chapter 5, section III.1.a.ii.
    [64] *Customary International Humanitarian Law* (n 60), Rules 1 and 7–10.
    [65] AP I, Art 48.
    [66] AP I, Art 52(2); *Customary International Humanitarian Law* (n 60), Rule 8.
    [67] See Dieter Fleck (ed), *The Handbook of Humanitarian Law in Armed Conflicts* (2nd edn, Oxford University Press: Oxford, 2008), para 443.
    [68] AP I, Art 52(3).
    [69] AP I, Art 51(5)(b); *Customary International Humanitarian Law* (n 60), Rule 14.

cannot be limited as required by this Protocol; and consequently, in each such case, are of a nature to strike military objectives and civilians or civilian objects without distinction'.[70] It follows that the term 'indiscriminate' is applicable, *inter alia*, to an attack by bombardment 'which treats as a single military objective a number of clearly separated and distinct military objectives located in a city, town, village or other area containing a similar concentration of civilians or civilian objects'.[71] Another category of indiscriminate attacks comprises those directed against a military objective but causing disproportional collateral damages. International humanitarian law prohibits an attack if it 'may be expected', in addition to inflicting military losses on the enemy, 'to cause incidental loss of civilian life...which would be excessive in relation to the concrete and direct military advantage anticipated'.[72] In its Advisory Opinion on the legality of the threat or use of nuclear weapons, the ICJ left open the question as to whether such weapons are in all circumstances incompatible with the requirement of distinction or whether they could be used without violating the prohibition of indiscriminate attacks.[73]

The *precautionary measures principle* obliges states, in advance of any attack, to take steps to ensure that the prohibition of attacks on civilian objects and the prohibition of indiscriminate attacks are fully respected in practice.[74] They must therefore verify that the selected objective is of a military character and choose means and methods that minimize incidental loss of life. Further, military objectives may not be located in a civilian environment, and the civilian population must be removed, to the maximum extent feasible, from the vicinity of military objectives.[75]

Issue in focus: The precautionary principle in human rights law—the armed conflict in Chechnya

---

The European Court of Human Rights had to rule for the first time in 2005, in the context of the conflict in Chechnya, on the conformity of warfare with human rights norms.[76] As Russia had not declared a state of emergency in Chechnya, the authorization for lawful military operations contained in the derogation clause of ECHR, Article 15 was inapplicable. The Court consequently had to assess operations resulting in the deprivation of life solely on the basis of the exception clauses contained

---

[70] AP I, Art 51(4); *Customary International Humanitarian Law* (n 60), Rules 11 and 12. According to AP I, Art 57(2)(b) 'An attack shall be cancelled or suspended if it becomes apparent...that the attack may be expected to cause incidental loss of civilian life, injury to civilians, damage to civilian objects, or a combination thereof, which would be excessive in relation to the concrete and direct military advantage anticipated.'

[71] AP I, Art 51(5).   [72] AP I, Art 51(5).

[73] ICJ, *Legality of the Threat or Use of Nuclear Weapons* (Advisory Opinion), ICJ Reports 1996.

[74] See AP I, Art 57(3) and (4); *Customary International Humanitarian Law* (n 60), Rules 15–25.

[75] AP I, Art 58; *Customary International Humanitarian Law* (n 60), Rules 23 and 24.

[76] The HRCttee has no jurisprudence on this set of issues owing to the absence of complaints.

in ECHR, Article 2(2) according to which lethal force is permissible, *inter alia*, 'in defence of any person from unlawful violence' and 'in action lawfully taken for the purpose of quelling a riot or insurrection'. Furthermore, the Court was faced in all these cases with considerable evidentiary difficulties.

In the *Isayeva and Others* case,[77] the facts before the ECtHR were as follows. The applicants and their relatives fled from the fighting in Grozny in 1999 with a large number of other civilians. At the border of the neighbouring Republic of Ingushetia, the column of cars was forced to turn around because, contrary to previous announcements, the cross-border corridor remained closed. Shortly afterwards, two military aircraft fired missiles at the convoy, killing relatives of the applicants. While the applicants and numerous witnesses stated that the column of refugees consisted exclusively of civilians, Russia alleged that the planes had been shot at from a truck travelling in the convoy. The Court accepted in principle that the state was justified, in the situation that existed at the time in Chechnya, in taking exceptional measures to regain control. The use of lethal weapons would thus have been justifiable if the planes had indeed come under fire. However, Russia had failed to produce any evidence of such an attack. The Court therefore retained certain doubts as to whether Russia's invocation of Article 2, para 2, to the effect that the missile attack was intended to protect persons from unlawful violence, was reasonable. Nevertheless, in view of the prevailing climate of violence in Chechnya, the Court proceeded to examine the facts in the light of that claim. However, as the authorities were doubtless aware that a refugee convoy was on the move from Grozny, extreme caution should have been exercised in planning the use of military force in that area. Moreover, the planes fired 12 missiles straight at the convoy, spraying thousands of pieces of shrapnel within a radius of several hundred metres. Hence, even on the assumption that a legitimate aim was being pursued, the military operation had not been planned and executed with the requisite care for the lives of civilians; there had therefore been a violation of Article 2.

The Court reached a similar conclusion in the *Zara Isayeva v Russia* case.[78] After Russian troops enticed armed rebels out of Grozny by means of a ruse, a group of at least several hundred fighters took cover in a neighbouring village as was foreseen by the authorities. However, the authorities failed to warn the villagers in advance of the arrival of the armed rebels and the military began bombarding the village without warning as soon as the fighters moved in. During the attack, relatives of the applicant and many others seeking to escape the bombardment lost their lives. The Court concluded that the deployment of heavy and indiscriminate combat weapons in a populated area, outside of a wartime situation as described in ECHR, Article 15 and without prior evacuation of the civilian population, was impossible to reconcile with the degree of caution expected from a law-enforcement body in a democratic society. This was so even if the attack was mounted in pursuit of a legitimate aim. Furthermore, once the population had finally been informed by loudspeaker of the opening of a humanitarian corridor, the commanders of the operation had failed to order a cessation of the shelling of fleeing civilians and to inform pilots about the route of the safe passage.

---

[77] ECtHR, *Isayeva, Yusopova and Bazayeva v Russia*, Applications Nos 57947-9/00 (2005).
[78] ECtHR, *Isayeva v Russia*, Application No 57950/00 (2005).

The ECtHR also held that there had been a violation of the right to life in the *Kashiyev and Akayeva* case.[79] Relatives of the applicant were killed in a government-controlled district of Grozny in largely unexplained circumstances. As Russia submitted no explanations regarding the circumstances of the killings, the Court assumed that they had occurred during an identity check that could only have been conducted by Russian soldiers.

In the case of *Khatsiyeva and Others*,[80] the Court had to clarify whether the intentional killing of six people was in accordance with the ECHR. The parties to the proceeding agreed that a Russian military helicopter equipped with a machine gun had killed the victims. However, the complainants claimed that the victims had been farmers busy cutting grass and unarmed when they were attacked. The Government, on the other hand, asserted that the farmers were carrying machine guns and tried to flee despite warning shots. The Court was not able to clarify this point but assumed that the helicopter pilots were convinced that they were attacking armed rebels. Furthermore, the facts showed that the pilots had asked their superiors at the military command center for permission before attacking and received explicit orders to attack them. The orders were given without any further clarifications sought as to the victims and the sight conditions in the area. It also remained unclear whether the targets had taken aim at the helicopter or whether there existed a risk that they might do so. Therefore, the Court found it very unlikely that the military command center could have determined the identity of the victims before it gave the order to attack. For these reasons, the Court considered that the commanders responsible did not clarify the factual situation with appropriate thoroughness. Therefore, the use of force was not considered absolutely necessary to fulfil one of the legitimate aims set down in ECHR, Article 2, para 2 and Russia was deemed to have violated the right to life by its actions.

(4) *Prohibited methods of warfare*: Finally, international humanitarian law further forbids the killing of combatants through prohibited methods of warfare, with weapons that cause superfluous injury or unnecessary suffering,[81] or by means that are otherwise expressly prohibited.[82]

Issue in focus: Prohibition of the use of anti-personnel mines

---

The rules governing the use of anti-personnel mines provide a particularly interesting example of the interplay between international humanitarian law and the right

---

[79] ECtHR, *Kashiyev and Akayeva v Russia*, Applications Nos 57942 and 57945/00 (2005). The ECtHR dealt with similar cases, amongst others, *Tangieva v Russia*, Application No 57935/00 (2007), and *Musayev and Others v Russia*, Application No 57941/00 (2007), in which it considered the right to life to have been violated.

[80] ECtHR, *Khatsiyeva and Others v Russia*, Application No 5108/02 (2008).

[81] This prohibition is contained, for instance, in the Convention of 10 October 1980 on Prohibitions or Restrictions on the Use of Certain Conventional Weapons which May be Deemed to be Excessively Injurious or to Have Indiscriminate Effects and in its protocols.

[82] For example, AP I, Art 40 and Rule 46 *Customary International Humanitarian Law* (n 60) outlaw orders that no quarter be given, AP I, Art 42 and *Customary International Humanitarian Law* (n 60), Rule 48 prohibit the attack on persons parachuting from an aircraft in distress.

to life under human rights law. Anti-personnel mines can rarely be employed against combatants alone and mine clearance in the aftermath of a conflict is an extremely burdensome task. Mines often continue for decades to constitute a hazard for the civilian population, greatly hampering reconstruction and encumbering daily life in former conflict areas. This being the case, several conventions have restricted the use of such weapons beyond the general rules of armed conflict.

The Convention on Prohibitions or Restrictions on the Use of Certain Conventional Weapons which May be Deemed to be Excessively Injurious or to Have Indiscriminate Effects (CCW) of 10 October 1980 and its Protocol on Prohibitions or Restrictions on the Use of Mines, Booby-Traps and Other Devices (Protocol II) of 10 October 1980 restrict the lawful use of all mines, including, for instance, anti-vehicle mines, in international conflicts.[83] The restrictions were made more stringent, albeit only for anti-personnel mines, by Protocol II as amended on 3 May 1996. Lastly, a new Protocol V[84] to this Convention requires the marking of all explosive remnants of war without exception as soon as feasible after the cessation of hostilities and their subsequent clearance.

The Convention on the Prohibition of the Use, Stockpiling, Production and Transfer of Anti-Personnel Mines and on Their Destruction (the Ottawa Convention) of 18 September 1997 prohibits under all circumstances not only the use of anti-personnel mines but also their sale, stockpiling and production. The Convention further requires states parties, under Article 5(1), 'to destroy or ensure the destruction of all anti-personnel mines in mined areas under its jurisdiction or control, as soon as possible but not later than ten years after the entry into force of this Convention for that State Party'.

Notwithstanding the fact that non-exploded ordnance originating from cluster bombs often has the same fatal, though unintended, outcome as anti-personal mines, the Ottawa Convention does not prohibit the use of cluster bombs. Therefore, on 30 May 2008, 107 participating states at the Dublin Conference on cluster munitions adopted the text of the new Convention on Cluster Munitions.[85] Its key obligations are not only for states to refrain from the use of cluster munitions, but also to abstain from developing, producing, otherwise acquiring, stockpiling, retaining or transferring to anyone, directly or indirectly, such munitions (Article 1).

None of the treaties mentioned has its own enforcement mechanism allowing victims to bring a complaint against a state alleged to have violated its obligations. This weakness is mitigated by the fact that where deaths ensue from the prohibited use of such weapons, not only the convention concerned but also the right to life under the ICCPR and the regional conventions would be violated as the fatalities would not be deemed to result from lawful military operations in keeping with international humanitarian law. Mine victims are accordingly free in such cases to file a communication with the Human Rights Committee or the regional courts.

---

[83] Pursuant to an amendment of 21 December 2001, the entire treaty regime is also applicable during non-international armed conflicts to states that have ratified this Protocol.

[84] Protocol on Explosive Remnants of War (Protocol V to the 1980 Convention, 28 November 2003).

[85] The text is available at <www.clusterconvention.org> (accessed 1 November 2008). The Convention was opened for signature on 3 December 2008.

(5) *Death penalty:* International humanitarian law contains provisions that place restrictions on the imposition of the death penalty.[86] Article 3 common to the Geneva Conventions imposes a general prohibition on 'the passing of sentences and the carrying out of executions without previous judgment pronounced by a regularly constituted court, affording all the judicial guarantees which are recognised as indispensable by civilised peoples'.[87] Article 75(4) of Additional Protocol I and Article 6 of Additional Protocol II enumerate in detail the rights that must be respected during such trials. Furthermore, international humanitarian law prohibits the execution of pregnant women and mothers of small children, as well as persons who had not attained the age of 18 years at the time the offence was committed.[88]

3. Duty to protect

(a) General

The ICCPR, the ACHR, the ArCHR, and the ECHR consistently require states parties to protect the right to life by law, thus underscoring the cardinal importance of obligations aimed at safeguarding the right to life. This duty to protect against attempts on the life of a person by third parties or against dangerous situations[89] is breached where, for instance, domestic criminal legislation fails to sanction certain homicide offences or provides excessive justificatory grounds for security forces.

Issue in focus: 'Honour killings' and the state's duty to prosecute

---

In some countries a man's honour is traditionally perceived to depend on the honourable conduct of female family members, ie their conformity with established norms. Where a woman fails to conduct herself as required by society's image of women, not only does she become an object of universal contempt but her male relatives also consider their honour to have been tainted. Women and girls are quite frequently killed in order to restore honour as thus defined. The Special Rapporteur on violence against women described the problem as follows:

Honour killings in Pakistan...have recently received international attention...They are also reported in Turkey..., Jordan, Syria, Egypt, Lebanon, Iran, Yemen, Morocco and other Mediterranean and Gulf countries. It also takes place in countries such as Germany, France and the United Kingdom within the migrant communities. Honour killings are carried out by husbands, fathers, brothers or uncles, sometimes on behalf of tribal councils. The killing is mainly carried out by under-aged males of the family to reduce the punishment. They are then treated as heroes. The action is further endorsed by their fellow inmates in prison, if they are sent there, who wash these young boys' feet and tell them that they are now 'complete' men.

---

[86] GC III, Arts 100, 101, and 107 in respect of prisoners of war and GC IV, Arts 68, 71 and 75 in respect of civilians.
[87] Art 3(1)(d) common to the four Geneva Conventions.
[88] GC IV, Art 68(4); AP I, Arts 76(3) and 77(5); AP II, Art 6(4).
[89] On the duty to protect in general see Chapter 3, section III.3.

The act is regarded as a rite of passage into manhood. Ironically, it is not unheard of for female relatives to either carry out the murder or be accomplice to it.[90]

Perpetrators of 'honour killings' benefit in a number of states from domestic criminal law provisions that recognise such motives for homicide as a ground of mitigation, or even exempt honour killings from prosecution. At the time of the Special Rapporteur's study, such provisions existed, *inter alia*, in the criminal codes of Peru, Bangladesh, Argentina, Ecuador, Egypt, Guatemala, Iran, Israel, Jordan, Syria, Lebanon, Turkey, Palestine and Venezuela.[91] Immunity from prosecution and grounds of mitigation of the sentence provided for by these provisions, as well as the lack of criminal sanction of such cases, constitute a violation of the duty to protect life and thus amount to a human rights violation.

Legislative action is not sufficient by itself to honour this type of obligation. When a person's life is materially put at risk by the action of an individual,[92] by natural dangers[93] or by the dangers inherent to a building, technical facility, or enterprise,[94] states parties are further required to take all feasible measures to provide protection[95] if they know of the danger and have the possibility to react. The scale and particulars of the required measures have been discussed above.[96]

Issue in focus: The right to security of person as a codified obligation to protect in the context of the right to life?

The right to liberty and security of person enshrined in ICCPR, Article 9, ACHR, Article 7, ArCHR, Article 14, and ECHR, Article 5 protects individuals primarily against wrongful imprisonment.[97] The Human Rights Committee accords the security aspect special importance in its own right, thereby adding a new dimension to the protective scope of this guarantee. It holds that the right to security of person is violated if a state knowingly declines to afford protection to a person notwithstanding the existence of a serious threat to his or her life from third parties.[98] It follows that this provision is also deemed to have been violated if, in the event, the threatened person is not killed.

---

[90] Report of the Special Rapporteur on violence against women, its causes and consequences of 28 January 2002, UN Doc E/CN.4/2002/83, paras 21 ff.

[91] Ibid, para 35.

[92] ECtHR (Grand Chamber), *Osman v The United Kingdom, Reports* 1998-VIII.

[93] ECtHR, *Budayeva and Others v Russia*, Applications Nos 15339/02, 21166/02, 20058/02, 11673/02 and 15343/02 (2008).

[94] ECtHR (Grand Chamber), *Öneryildiz v Turkey, Reports* 2004-XII.

[95] These obligations to protect have been interpreted at particularly great length by the ACmHPR. Thus, according to the Commission, states also have a responsibility in the context of a civil war to protect civilians within their jurisdiction from killings, irrespective of the perpetrators, and to ensure that civilians are treated in accordance with the rules of international humanitarian law; ACmHPR, *Amnesty International and Others v Sudan*, Communications Nos 48/1990, 50/1991, 52/1991, 89/1993 (1999), para 50.

[96] Chapter 3, section III.3. See also the discussion of the *McCann* judgment of the ECtHR, section II.2.b above.

[97] See Chapter 15, section II.

[98] See, eg, HRCttee, *Mojica v Dominican Republic*, Communication No 449/1991 (1994), paras 5.5 f, and *Jayawardena v Sri Lanka*, Communication No 916/2000 (2002), para 7.2. The ECtHR

(b) Obligation to protect persons in state custody

The obligation to protect the right to life is particularly stringent in circumstances where individuals are in state custody, and thus in a particularly vulnerable situation.[99] As a result, the case law of the European Court of Human Rights and the Human Rights Committee not only recognizes a comprehensive duty to protect the lives of those in custody,[100] but also provides for a reversal of the burden of proof: if a person dies while in custody, it is incumbent on the state to prove its authorities bear no responsibility for the death.[101]

Example: The ECtHR judgment in *Anguelova v Bulgaria*[102]

In the light of the importance of the protection afforded by Article 2, the Court must subject complaints about deprivations of life to the most careful scrutiny, taking into consideration all relevant circumstances. Persons in custody are in a vulnerable position and the authorities are under an obligation to account for their treatment. Consequently, where an individual is taken into police custody in good health but later dies, it is incumbent on the State to provide a plausible explanation of the events leading to his death... In assessing evidence, the Court adopts the standard of proof 'beyond reasonable doubt'... However, such proof may follow from the co-existence of sufficiently strong, clear and concordant inferences or of similar unrebutted presumptions of fact. Where the events in issue lie wholly, or in large part, within the exclusive knowledge of the authorities, as in the case of persons within their control in custody, strong presumptions of fact will arise in respect of injuries and death occurring during that detention. Indeed, the burden of proof may be regarded as resting on the authorities to provide a satisfactory and convincing explanation...

Based on these principles, the Court found that Bulgaria had violated the right to life in failing to explain the circumstances of the death of a young Roma man who had been detained for several hours at a police station following his arrest for attempted theft. The cause of death was determined to be a cerebral hematoma caused by a blow by, or against, a blunt object.

In situations of custody, the state is required not only to afford protection against risks from third parties but also to take reasonable measures to prevent suicide in

---

aligned itself with this jurisprudence after some delay: see, eg, *Çiçek v Turkey*, Application No 25704/94 (2001), para 164.

[99] See in particular ECtHR, *Paul and Audrey Edwards v The United Kingdom*, Reports 2002-II.

[100] HRCttee, *Dermit Barbato and Dermit Barbato v Uruguay*, Communication No 84/1981 (1982), para 9.2: 'While the Committee cannot arrive at a definite conclusion as to whether Hugo Dermit committed suicide, was driven to suicide or was killed by others while in custody; yet, the inescapable conclusion is that in all the circumstances the Uruguayan authorities either by act or by omission were responsible for not taking adequate measures to protect his life, as required by article 6(1) of the Covenant.'

[101] ECtHR, *Anguelova v Bulgaria*, Reports 2002-IV, paras 110 f. Similarly, HRCttee, *Telitsina v Russia*, Communication No 888/1999 (2004), para 7.3. See also HRCttee, *Burrell v Jamaica*, Communication No 546/1993 (1996), para 9.5, and IACtHR, *Durand and Ugarte v Peru*, Series C, No 68 (2000), para 65. The ECtHR also applies this reversal of the burden of proof if a person is killed or injured in an area that is under complete control of state agents during an armed conflict. See, eg, ECHR *Akkum and Others v Turkey*, Reports 2005-II, para 211, and *Goygova v Russia*, Application No 74240/01 (2007), para 94.

[102] ECtHR, *Anguelova v Bulgaria*, Reports 2002-IV, paras 110–111.

cases of manifestly mentally ill and suicidal prisoners.[103] A state is under no such obligation, however, where a prisoner of sound mind wilfully exposes himself or herself to risk through a hunger strike. If the prisoner on hunger strike has become confused to the point of being unable to make an unimpaired decision or has lapsed into a coma, 'a conflict between an individual's right to physical integrity and [the state's] positive obligation' under the right to life arises.[104] Such an issue has yet to be ruled upon by a human rights organ in an individual case. The Declaration on Hunger Strikers adopted by the World Medical Association leaves the decision in such cases to the doctor treating the person concerned.[105] A decision to force-feed made once it has been established that such action is necessary to save the person from harm does not amount to a human rights violation; in contrast, force-feeding without establishing such medical necessity in a convincing way and undertaken in a manner that inflicts unnecessary suffering may amount to a violation of the prohibition of inhuman treatment.[106]

Where a person released from state custody kills another human being, the responsibility of the state for a breach of its duty to protect is engaged only if it failed to ascertain with the requisite care whether the person's release represented a danger to the public at large.[107]

(c) Special obligations at the beginning and the end of life?

The question as to whether states have specific obligations to protect at the beginning and the end of life focuses attention on the substantive scope of application of the right to life. In particular, these stages raise ethical-juridical issues relating to the conformity of abortion and (active) euthanasia to human rights norms. As mentioned above,[108] international human rights law, with the exception of ACHR, Article 4(1), which extends the protection of life to the moment of conception, does not clearly define the beginning and end of life and leaves such

---

[103] ECtHR, *Keenan v the United Kingdom, Reports* 2001-III, para 89. In this case, the ECtHR held that there had been no violation of the right to life. In the *Trubnikov v Russia* judgment, Application No 49790/99 (2005), on the question of suicide prevention, the Court found that the Russian authorities had not violated their obligations to protect, but that they had violated their investigatory obligations. In ECtHR, *Rénolde v France,* Application No 5608/05 (2008), the Court came to the conclusion that France had violated the right to life because the authorities had not considered admission to a psychiatric institution or at least appropriate medical treatment although it was evident that the victim was 'very disturbed' and suffered from obvious mental health problems (paras 80–110). The fact that he was placed in solitary confinement despite his mental health problems and without proper treatment for them furthermore amounted to inhuman treatment (paras 119–130). See also ECtHR, *Kilavuz v Turkey,* Application No 8327/03 (2008), paras 87–96.

[104] ECtHR, *Nevmerzhitsky v Ukraine, Reports* 2005-II, para 93.

[105] World Medical Association Declaration on Hunger Strikers adopted by the 43rd World Medical Assembly, Malta, November 1991, and editorially revised at the 44th World Medical Assembly Marbella, Spain, September 1992, Guidelines for the Management of Hunger Strikers, para 4.

[106] ECtHR, *Nevmerzhitsky v Ukraine, Reports* 2005-II, para 94.

[107] ECtHR, *Mastromatteo v Italy, Reports* 2002-VIII, paras 69 ff.

[108] See section II.1 above.

decisions to domestic legislation. Nevertheless, the question of the existence of a state duty to protect, which is in any case never absolute, is a key issue that arises on a regular basis in these borderline areas.

Possible obligations to protect the unborn child must be weighed against the right to life and the right to self-determination of a pregnant woman. The Human Rights Committee thus criticizes the absolute prohibition of abortion, drawing attention to the serious risks to the lives and physical and mental integrity of women who consequently seek them illegally.[109] In the case of a minor forced to give birth to an anencephalic baby with absolutely no chances of survival, the Human Rights Committee concluded that the refusal to allow a therapeutic abortion and the resulting physical and mental health risks suffered by the minor amounted to inhuman treatment as well as a violation of the right to privacy.[110]

Although the case law of the Strasbourg bodies[111] has so far left unsettled the question of the extent to which a duty to protect unborn life flows from the right to life, it seems to proceed on the assumption that an absolute prohibition of abortion would be in conflict with human rights norms. States are therefore allowed a certain measure of discretion to permit abortion not only where there is a risk to the mother's life and person but also on other grounds. The right to privacy, for its part, does not afford absolute protection for the mother's freedom to interrupt her pregnancy. On the contrary, this entitlement may be restricted, providing states with the discretionary power to permit abortions only when certain conditions are met.

At the other end of the life spectrum, the European Court of Human Rights denied the existence of a right to choose the time of one's own death and held that an absolute prohibition of assisted suicide was consistent with ECHR, Article 2.[112] A statutory regime that permits euthanasia provided certain conditions are met, however, does not appear, *per se*, to be contrary to the right to life.[113]

Consistent with the approach of not recognizing a 'right to death', states have a duty to protect persons in their custody from suicide, as shown above (section (b)).

---

[109] HRCttee, General Comment No 28 (2000), para 10; Concluding Observations Colombia (2004), para 13; Concluding Observations Poland (2004), para 8; and Concluding Observations Chile (2007), para 8.

[110] HRCttee, *Huamán v Peru*, Communication No 1153/2003 (2005), paras 6.3 and 6.4.

[111] The ECtHR expressly left this question unresolved in *Open Door and Dublin Well Women v Ireland*, Series A, No 246-A (1992), para 66. The former ECmHR, in *X v The United Kingdom* Application No 8416/79, DR 19 (1980), para 23, affirmed the permissibility of abortion in the early stages of pregnancy, observing that any right to life of the foetus was in any case limited by the mother's claim to protection of her life and health. In *RH v Norway*, decision on admissibility, Application No 17004/90 (1992), the Commission accepted that the foetus could be protected by the right to life but emphasized at the same time that states were allowed a considerable margin of discretion when it came to regulating the question of abortion.

[112] ECtHR, *Pretty v The United Kingdom*, Reports 2002-III.

[113] See HRCttee, Concluding Observations Netherlands (2001), para 5, in which the Committee expressed concern about euthanasia and assisted suicide legislation in the Netherlands but, apart from questioning the permissibility of such acts in the case of children between the ages of 12 and 16, refrained from finding that the Netherlands had violated ICCPR, Art 6.

Example: The ECtHR judgment in *Pretty v The United Kingdom*[114] (assisted suicide)

The European Court of Human Rights addressed in this judgment the issues raised by assisted suicide. The Court had to determine whether and to what extent criminalizing assisted suicide was incompatible with the right to life of a terminally ill woman suffering from an incurable and degenerative muscular disease that would eventually result in death through asphyxiation. The applicant was no longer capable of terminating her own life and sought to obtain an assurance from the British authorities that her husband would not be prosecuted if he fulfilled her desire to end her life. This request was turned down. The European Court of Human Rights expressed doubt as to whether a right to determine the time of one's death could be inferred from the right to life or otherwise derived from the wording of the Convention. While the Court acknowledged that the criminal-law prohibition could place the applicant in a very difficult situation, it held that no obligation to end suffering could be derived from the prohibition of inhuman treatment—which was to be construed in harmony with the right to life—that would require a state to render certain actions intended to terminate life free from prosecution. Furthermore, the Court determined that although the right to respect for private life was restricted by the prohibition of assisted suicide, even a blanket ban on it, where based in law, was deemed to be a proportionate interference owing to the high risk of abuse, ie justified in order to afford protection to persons who, owing to deficient mental capacity, were unable to assess the consequences of such a decision. Hence the British prohibition did not breach the right to respect for private life.

4. Duty to fulfil

Effective protection of life entails the state obligation to fulfil, ie to take positive measures beyond the obligation to protect. The obligation to fulfil comprises the following basic duties:

(1) *Obligation to investigate*: States are required, first, to investigate all unexplained deaths, particularly those having occurred in custody, with the requisite independence and diligence, ie of their own motion and in a manner that ensures that those responsible are identified.[115] Where a state refuses to undertake such investigations or conducts them without due diligence, it violates the right to life and is liable to pay compensation to the relatives of the deceased person.[116]

---

[114] ECtHR, *Pretty v The United Kingdom*, Reports 2002-III.

[115] See HRCttee, *Baboeram et al v Suriname*, Communications Nos 146/1983 and 148–154/1983 (1985), para 16 (killing of an arrested person by the military police); *Rubio and Parents v Colombia*, Communication No 161/83 (1987), para 10.3 (enforced disappearances); ECtHR (Grand Chamber), *Ramsahai and Others v The Netherlands*, Application No 52391/99 (2007), paras 321 ff, and ECtHR, *Finucane v The United Kingdom*, Reports 2003-VIII, paras 67 ff.

[116] See, eg, IACtHR, *Velázquez-Rodríguez v Honduras*, Series C, No 4 (1988), para 166; ECtHR, *Yasa v Turkey*, Reports 1998-VI, para 100, and HRCttee, *Chaparro et al v Colombia*, Communication No 612/1995 (1997), para 8.8.

Although proof of direct state responsibility for deprivation of life is unattainable in many cases due to evidentiary difficulties, such as in the case of killings by paramilitary groups, a state can still frequently be held responsible for violation of its obligation to investigate. In a case where it was impossible to prove that state authorities and not insurgents had laid anti-personnel mines that killed farmers in Chechnya, for instance, Russia was held responsible under the right to life because the authorities had failed to carry out an effective criminal investigation into the deaths.[117]

(2) *Obligation to prosecute and punish*: The obligation to prosecute and punish either state agents or private perpetrators under criminal law for unlawful killings is closely related to the obligation to investigate. As the Human Rights Committee rightly stressed, the problem of impunity for infringements 'may well be an important contributing element in the recurrence of the violations'.[118] Amnesty provisions are at odds with the aim of combating impunity, but are sometimes seen as a necessary part of peace-building and reconciliation processes in the aftermath of armed conflict or periods of extreme violence. However, where an amnesty provision rules out the possibility of investigating unsolved killings, it is clearly incompatible with the right to life.[119] Moreover, where the use of lethal force involves breaches of international humanitarian law amounting to war crimes, states are required either to punish those responsible or to extradite them to the state that has prime jurisdiction in the matter or to transfer them to an international criminal tribunal.[120]

(3) *Obligations to fulfil in situations of state custody*: Specific obligations to take positive measures in respect of fulfilment of the right to life exist in circumstances of state custody, namely in circumstances of detention and during sojourns in (state run) psychiatric hospitals. Detainees must be provided with sufficient food[121] and with adequate medical care if they are sick. Additionally, their state of health must be monitored.[122] Thus, states are required, even if they lack financial resources, to at least provide detainees

---

[117] ECtHR, *Albekov and Others v Russia*, Application No 68216/01 (2008).

[118] HRCttee, General Comment No 31 (2004), para 18.

[119] HRCttee, *Rodríguez v Uruguay*, Communication No 322/1988 (1994), para 12.4. The IACtHR held that, at the very least, amnesty provisions that preclude the possibility of punishing persons responsible for violations of non-derogable rights are incompatible with the human rights obligation to punish; *Chumbipuma Aguirre et al v Peru* (*Barrios Altos* case), Series C, No 75 (2001), paras 41 ff.

[120] Hans-Peter Gasser, *Humanitäres Völkerrecht—Eine Einführung* (Nomos: Zurich etc, 2007), 99 f; GC I, Arts 49 and 50; GC II, Arts 50 and 51; GC III, Arts 129 and 130; GC IV, Arts 146 and 147; AP I, Art 85; Rome Statute, Art 8.

[121] ACmHPR, *Malawi African Association and Others v Mauritania*, Communication No 54/1991, 61/1991, 98/1993, 164–196/1997 and 210/1998 (2000), para 120.

[122] HRCttee, *Lantsova v Russia*, Communication No 763/1997 (2002), para 9.2; ECtHR, *Taïs v France*, Application No 39922/03 (2006), paras 93 ff, and ACmHPR, *International Pen and Others v Nigeria*, Communications Nos 137/1994, 139/1994, 154/1996, and 161/1997 (1998), para 104.

suffering from life-threatening illnesses with medical care.[123] The right to life is violated, for example, if a person in a state of severe alcoholic intoxication at the time of arrest is left without medical attention, despite serious symptoms, and subsequently dies[124] or if the patient of a psychiatric clinic shares the same fate due to lack of medical care.[125]

(4) *Obligation to fulfil in situations of state-caused dependence outside custody*: The obligation of states to provide goods and medical services necessary for survival has been recognized by the Inter-American Court of Human Rights if people are unable to satisfy there subsistence needs as a consequence of the behaviour of state authorities. This happened, for example, when Paraguay refused to protect the land rights of indigenous communities who, as a consequence, were no longer able to pursue their traditional lifestyle leading to the death of some of their members.[126]

(5) *Obligation to take measures to enhance the protection of life*: At the programmatic level of the right to life, states have a duty to take concrete steps to enhance the protection of life in areas in which it is particularly endangered. The Human Rights Committee, which can express its views on such matters primarily through its state reporting procedure, has called on states to adopt measures to reduce infant mortality and to increase average life expectancy,[127] to bring about nuclear disarmament or to prevent war.[128]

5. The collective dimension of the right to life: prohibition of genocide

(a) Introduction

The Nazi Holocaust focused the attention of the international community on the phenomenon of genocide, ie the planned annihilation of entire national, ethnic, racial, or religious groups. The abhorrent nature of this crime, not only in quantitative terms but also because it selects victims solely on the basis of their affiliation to a group, makes genocide the most serious of all crimes. Although the crime was codified in the 1948 Convention on the Prevention and Punishment of the Crime of Genocide, the Convention has failed to prevent further cases of it from occurring. It was only after the end of the Cold War that it became possible,

---

[123] HRCttee, *Lantsova v Russia*, Communication No 763/1997 (2002), para 9.2.
[124] ECtHR, *Anguelova v Bulgaria*, *Reports* 2002-IV, paras 123 ff. See also the report of the Special Rapporteur on extrajudicial, summary or arbitrary executions of 22 December 2003, UN Doc E/CN.4/2004/7, paras 35 f.
[125] IACtHR, *Ximenes-Lopes v Brazil*, Series C, No 149 (2006), paras 121 ff.
[126] IACtHR Case of the *Yakye Axa Indigenous Community v Paraguay*, Series C, No 125 (2005), paras 162 ff, and Case of the *Sawhoyamaxa Indigenous Community v Paraguay*, Series C, No 146 (2006), paras 159 ff.
[127] HRCttee, General Comment No 6 (1982), para 5.
[128] HRCttee, General Comment No 14 (1984).

as is shown through the establishment of the International Criminal Tribunals for the former Yugoslavia and Rwanda, to set up international courts to prosecute and punish perpetrators. Today, the International Criminal Court also has jurisdiction over the crime of genocide.

Issue in focus: What circumstances can lead to genocide?[129]

Genocide typically develops over eight stages: (1) classification ('us and them'); (2) symbolization (manifestation of hate symbols); (3) dehumanization ('they' are actually not human beings); (4) organization (by the state, armed militias or mobs); (5) polarization (driving the groups apart through propaganda and laws); (6) preparation (identifying and separating out the victims, etc); (7) extermination; and (8) denial ('it didn't happen').

The prohibition of genocide has not only been enshrined in treaty law; genocide, as a criminal offence, is also a peremptory norm of international law (*jus cogens*)[130] and must be prosecuted by all states regardless of the official status of the alleged perpetrators.[131]

(b) Definition under international criminal law

According to Article II of the Genocide Convention:

… genocide means any of the following acts committed with intent to destroy, in whole or in part, a national, ethnical, racial or religious group, as such:

(a) Killing members of the group;
(b) Causing serious bodily or mental harm to members of the group;
(c) Deliberately inflicting on the group conditions of life calculated to bring about its physical destruction in whole or in part;
(d) Imposing measures intended to prevent births within the group;
(e) Forcibly transferring children of the group to another group.

The definition of genocide thus consists of the following elements:[132]

(1) The perpetrator commits one of the following acts: kills or causes serious bodily or mental harm to one or more persons; forces one or more persons into life-threatening circumstances; imposes measures intended to prevent births; or takes away the children of one or more persons belonging to the group concerned. Thus, contrary to a widely held view, killing is not a prerequisite for

---

[129] Gregory H Stanton, 'The Eight Stages of Genocide', paper presented at the Yale University Center for International and Area Studies, 1998, <www.genocidewatch.org/8stages.htm> (accessed 18 December 2008).

[130] ICJ, *Case concerning Application of the Convention on the Prevention and Punishment of the Crime of Genocide (Bosnia and Herzegovina v Serbia and Montenegro)*, ICJ Reports 2007, para 161.

[131] CPPCG, Art IV.

[132] 'Elements of Crimes, Report of the Preparatory Commission for the International Criminal Court', UN Doc PCNICC/2000/1/Add.2

the commission of the crime of genocide. It is furthermore irrelevant whether the acts were committed in time of peace or in time of war.[133] Moreover, not only the direct commission of such acts but also incitement, attempt and complicity are punishable pursuant to the Genocide Convention and other sources of law.[134]

(2) The victims belong to a particular national, ethnic, racial or religious group. The perpetrator thus selects his or her victims solely on the basis of their membership of a group. Political or social groups are not covered by the definition of genocide.

(3) The perpetrator acts with the specific intent to destroy a group as such, or at least a substantial part of it.[135] In other words, the intent to destroy a group in part 'means seeking to destroy a distinct part of the group as opposed to an accumulation of isolated individuals within it'.[136] This subjective element, which must contain an actual plan, is often difficult to prove.

(4) The acts occur in the context of a pattern of similar conduct directed against the same group, or could themselves effect the destruction of the group.

Example: The judgment of the International Criminal Tribunal for the Former Yugoslavia concerning the genocide in Srebrenica[137]

In the *Krstić* case, the defence argued, in its submission to the Appeals Chamber of the ICTY, that it had never been the intent of the accused to annihilate a substantial part of the Bosnian Muslim population; his conduct during the Srebrenica massacre had therefore been erroneously held to constitute genocide by the Trial Chamber. The Appeals Chamber rejected this view with the following reasoning:

12. The intent requirement of genocide under Article 4 of the Statute is…satisfied where evidence shows that the alleged perpetrator intended to destroy at least a substantial part of the protected group. The determination of when the targeted part is substantial enough to meet this requirement may involve a number of considerations. The numeric size of the targeted part of the group is the necessary and important starting point, though not in all cases the ending point of the inquiry. The number of individuals targeted should be evaluated not only in absolute terms, but also in relation to the overall size of the entire group. In addition to the numeric size of the targeted portion, its prominence within the group can be a useful consideration. If a specific part of the group is emblematic of the overall group, or is essential to its survival, that may support a finding that the part qualifies as substantial within the meaning of Article 4.

13. The historical examples of genocide also suggest that the area of the perpetrators' activity and control, as well as the possible extent of their reach, should be considered. Nazi Germany may have intended only to eliminate Jews within Europe alone; that ambition probably did

---

[133] CPPCG, Art I.   [134] CPPCG, Art III; Rome Statute, Art 25(3).

[135] ICTY (Appeals Chamber), *The Prosecutor v Krstić*, 'Srebrenica', Case No IT-98-33-A (2004), para 12.

[136] ICTY (Trial Chamber), *The Prosecutor v Krstić*, Case No IT-98-33-T (2001), para 590.

[137] ICTY (Appeals Chamber), *The Prosecutor v Krstić*, 'Srebrenica', Case No IT-98-33-A (2004).

not extend, even at the height of its power, to an undertaking of that enterprise on a global scale... The intent to destroy formed by a perpetrator of genocide will always be limited by the opportunity presented to him...

14. These considerations, of course, are neither exhaustive nor dispositive. They are only useful guidelines. The applicability of these factors, as well as their relative weight, will vary depending on the circumstances of a particular case.

15. In this case, having identified the protected group as the national group of Bosnian Muslims, the Trial Chamber concluded that the part... Radislav Krstić targeted was the Bosnian Muslims of Srebrenica...Although this population constituted only a small percentage of the overall Muslim population of Bosnia and Herzegovina at the time, the importance of the Muslim community of Srebrenica is not captured solely by its size. As the Trial Chamber explained, Srebrenica [was] of immense strategic importance to the Bosnian Serb leadership...

16. In addition, Srebrenica was important due to its prominence in the eyes of both the Bosnian Muslims and the international community. The town of Srebrenica was the most visible of the 'safe areas' established by the UN Security Council in Bosnia...

17. Finally, the ambit of the genocidal enterprise in this case was limited to the area of Srebrenica...From the perspective of the Bosnian Serb forces alleged to have had genocidal intent in this case, the Muslims of Srebrenica were the only part of the Bosnian Muslim group within their area of control...

21. The Trial Chamber determined that Radislav Krstić had the intent to kill the Srebrenica Bosnian Muslim men of military age. This finding is one of intent to commit the requisite genocidal act—in this case, the killing of the members of the protected group, prohibited by Article 4(2)(a) of the Statute...

23. The Trial Chamber's determination of the substantial part of the protected group was correct. The Defence's appeal on this issue is dismissed.

(c) State obligations

Genocide is not only an individual crime under international criminal law, but also entails obligations for states parties. On ratifying the Convention, contracting states are required:

(1) *Not to commit genocide.* Albeit not expressly stipulated by the wording of the Genocide Convention, not only individuals but states parties as well are obliged to abstain from genocide. Thus, the Convention not only establishes criminal responsibility but creates a duality of responsibilities.[138] According to the ICJ the obligation of a state party not to commit genocide flows from Article I of the Convention as '[i]t would be paradoxical if States were...under an obligation to prevent [the] commission of genocide by persons over whom they have a certain influence, but were not forbidden to commit such acts through their own organs, or persons over whom they have such firm control that their conduct is attributable to the State concerned under international law'.[139]

---

[138] See also Art 25 (4) of the Rome Statute according to which '[n]o provision in this Statute relating to individual criminal responsibility shall affect the responsibility of States under international law'.

[139] ICJ, *Case concerning Application of the Convention on the Prevention and Punishment of the Crime of Genocide (Bosnia and Herzegovina v Serbia and Montenegro)*, ICJ Reports 2007, para 166.

(2) *To prevent genocide.* The obligation to prevent, pursuant to Article I, must first be fulfilled within the state's own territory. Additionally, the duty to prevent and the corresponding obligation to act, arises when state authorities 'learn of, or should normally have learned of, the existence of a serious risk that genocide will be committed' by another state or non-state actors operating in a foreign country. 'From that moment onwards, if the State has available to it means likely to have a deterrent effect on those suspected of preparing genocide, or reasonably suspected of harbouring specific intent..., it is under a duty to make such use of these means as the circumstances permit. However, if neither genocide nor any of the other acts listed in Article III of the Convention are ultimately carried out, then a State that omitted to act when it could have done so cannot be held responsible *a posteriori*, since the event did not happen which, under the rule set out above, must occur for there to be a violation of the obligation to prevent.'[140]

(3) *Not to aid and assist genocide.* States must neither conspire to commit genocide (Article III(b)) nor must they directly and publicly incite the commission of genocide (Article III(c)). They are also obliged to abstain from acts which could be characterized as complicity in genocide (Article III(e)), ie not to render aid or assistance to the perpetrator with a view of enabling or facilitating the commission of the crime. However, according to the ICJ, 'there is no doubt that the conduct of an organ...furnishing aid or assistance to a perpetrator of the crime of genocide cannot be treated as complicity in genocide unless at the least that organ or person acted knowingly, that is to say, in particular, was aware of the specific intent *(dolus specialis)* of the principal perpetrator'.[141]

(4) *To punish genocide.* Article VI imposes the obligation to prosecute and punish perpetrators of genocide on the state in whose territory the act was committed. Alternatively, persons charged with genocide may be tried by an international penal tribunal whose jurisdiction has been recognized by the states parties involved. Today, such jurisdiction lies primarily with the ICTY, the ICTR, and the ICC.

(5) To *extradite* persons charged with genocide either to the state that has jurisdiction to prosecute or to an international tribunal and, in particular, not to classify genocide as non-extraditable political crime (Article VII).

(d) International enforcement

The Genocide Convention provides for three mechanisms to ensure enforcement of its obligations at the international level.

The primary means of enforcement is criminal prosecution by a national or international tribunal.[142] All international criminal tribunals today have

---

[140] Ibid, para 431.   [141] Ibid, para 421.   [142] CPPCG, Arts IV–VI.

jurisdiction to punish genocide as an international criminal offence.[143] At the political level, any contracting party may, pursuant to Article VIII of the Genocide Convention, call upon the competent organs of the United Nations, in other words the Security Council, to take action for the prevention and punishment of genocide.[144] Lastly, as a third mechanism the Convention authorizes states parties, under Article IX, to refer disputes relating to the interpretation, application and fulfilment of the Convention to the ICJ.[145]

In 2004 the UN Secretary-General appointed an Advisor for the Prevention of Genocide whose mandate includes the development of an early warning mechanism to identify potentially genocidal situations.

III. Subsistence Rights and the Right to Health

1. General observations

The scope of human-rights-based protection of life is not confined to minimizing the risk of being killed. Access to the basic necessities of life, such as food, shelter and, in the case of life-threatening health problems, minimum medical treatment is equally relevant if not even more important for survival in situations where such access is being blocked or where basic goods are simply not available. It follows that the right to life not only as a civil and political right but also as part of economic, social and cultural rights plays a major role in safeguarding human existence. It does so through providing entitlements to an adequate standard of living and the right to health set forth in ICESCR, Articles 11 and 12. These guarantees, however, are not limited to ensuring mere survival. In addition, they guarantee the minimal conditions necessary for a life in dignity.

As already discussed,[146] economic, social, and cultural rights contain the triple obligation to respect, protect and fulfil. This is also true for the rights discussed here.

A peculiarity of subsistence rights is the fact that they guarantee 'adequate' food and housing as well as (despite a lack of an explicit reference in the text of the Covenant) health care. The Committee on Economic, Social and Cultural Rights developed criteria for assessing what 'adequate' means for each of these rights. Despite different formulations, the following are core

---

[143] See Chapter 6, section IV.

[144] The establishment of the International Criminal Tribunals for the Former Yugoslavia and Rwanda under Chapter VII of the UN Charter is based ultimately on this provision.

[145] On the basis of this article, applications instituting proceedings against Yugoslavia were filed with the ICJ by Bosnia in 1996 and Croatia in 1999.

[146] Chapter 3, section III.6.

elements that are in any case necessary to make relevant goods and services adequate:[147]

- *Availability*: Obviously, the rights to adequate food, housing and health care cannot be enjoyed if food, shelter and accommodations, health services and medication are not available in sufficient quantity as well as quality.
- *Accessibility*: The fact that food, housing and health care are available does not automatically mean that they are accessible to everyone. Accessibility has different dimensions including the fact that they are physically within reach (location) and that persons are not legally or *de facto* denied access. Furthermore, relevant goods and services must be economically affordable for the poor in order to be truly accessible.
- *Acceptability*: Relevant goods and services must be culturally acceptable, *ie* respectful of the beliefs and traditions of people, communities and minorities as well as gender-sensitive.

2. The right to food

Relevant provisions: UDHR, Article 25; ICESCR, Article 11; CRC, Articles 24(2) and 27; CRPD, Article 28; ArCHR, Article 38; P 1/ACHR, Article 12; GC II, Article 26; GC IV, Article 55; AP I, Article 54; AP II, Articles 5(1)(b) and 14; Rome Statute, Article 8(2)(b)(xxv).

(a) The content of the right to food

According to the wording of ICESCR, Article 11(1), states parties recognize the right of everyone to adequate food. Paragraph 2 further establishes the fundamental right to protection against hunger. The Committee on Economic, Social and Cultural Rights and the Commission on Human Rights have made it clear that this guarantee also embraces the right to an adequate supply of drinking water.[148]

The text of the provision remains vague and provides little guidance as to when the right to food has been fully realized. However, the Committee on Economic, Social and Cultural Rights has identified two elements that make up the content of the right to food:[149]

(1) The *availability of food* in a quantity and quality sufficient to satisfy the dietary needs of individuals, free from adverse substances, and acceptable within a given culture;

---

[147] In its General Comment No 4, the Committee identified the following factors as elements of adequacy in the context of the right to adequate housing: 'availability', 'affordability', 'accessibility' and 'cultural adequacy'. In its general comment No 12, the Committee identified relevant elements of the right to adequate food as 'availability', 'acceptability', and 'accessibility'.

[148] CtteeESCR, General Comment No 15 (2002), para 3; CHR, resolution 2001/25, para 9.

[149] CtteeESCR, General Comment No 12 (1999), para 8, and General Comment No 15 (2002), para 12.

(2) The *accessibility* of such food in ways that are sustainable and that do not interfere with the enjoyment of other human rights.

Where sufficient food is available and access to food has been made sustainable, the right to food has been fully realized. However, this does not imply that states parties are required to provide an unlimited supply of food or risk violating the right in question. Rather, the core content of the right to food flows from the interrelationship between the two elements set out above and the different layers of obligations corresponding to this right.

Issue in focus: The right to water

Despite the fact that water is a limited natural resource and a public good fundamental for life and health, a right to water was only recently developed in international human rights law.

On the universal level, a right to water as part of the right to an adequate standard if living is mentioned in CEDAW, Article 14(2)(h), CRC, Article 24(2)(c), and CRPD, Article 28(2)(a). Additionally, an obligation to provide protected persons with the necessary water is firmly rooted in international humanitarian law.[150] Similar guarantees exist in Article 14(2)(c) of the African Charter on the Rights and Welfare of the Child and in Article 15(a) of the Protocol to the African Charter on Human and Peoples' Rights on the Rights of Women in Africa, as well as in some soft law instruments.[151] In contrast, neither the ICESCR nor the European Social Charter or the Additional Protocol to the American Convention on Human Rights in the Area of Economic, Social and Cultural Rights expressly contain this guarantee. However, according to the Committee on Economic, Social and Cultural Right a right guaranteeing access to water of satisfactory quantity and quality to meet vital human and basic hygienic needs may be derived from the right to an adequate standard of living of ICESCR, Article 11 and the right to health of ICESCR, Article 12.[152]

In 2001 the former Commission on Human Rights expanded the mandate of its special Rapporteur on the right to food to the right to drinking water. In March 2008, the Human Rights Council decided to create a separate mandate and appoint an Independent Expert on the issue of human rights obligations related to access to safe drinking water and sanitation.[153]

The corresponding obligations of States include a duty of states to refrain from interfering with the individual's use of water on its territory or that of neighbouring states[154] by, eg, polluting water resources or the construction of infrastructure

---

[150] GC III, Arts 20, 26, 29 and 46; GC IV, Arts 85, 89 and 127; AP I, Arts 54 and 55; AP II, Arts 5 and 14.

[151] Eg, Council of Europe, Committee of Ministers, Rec(2001)14 to member states on the European Charter on Water Resources.

[152] CtteeESCR, General Comment No 15 (2002), para 3.

[153] Human Rights Council Resolution 7/22.

[154] CtteeESCR, General Comment No 15 (2002), para 31. See also on this topic the Convention on the Law of Non-Navigational Uses of International Watercourses of 1997 (not yet in force, but which is recognized as an authoritative codification on the customary international law governing the issue), the ILC Resolution on Confined Transboundary Groundwater of 1994, and the Draft

projects such as dams endangering the access to water of an acceptable quality. On the other hand a prohibition to privatize water infrastructure may not be deduced from human rights law. However, in situations where water service are controlled by private companies states 'must prevent them from compromising equal, affordable, and physical access to sufficient, safe and acceptable water. To prevent such abuses an effective regulatory system must be established'.[155] Furthermore, the duty to protect requires states to prevent other individuals[156] and other states, eg a riparian state, to make access to water impossible by polluting or inequitably extracting water from water resources. Finally, the obligation to fulfil requires a state to take measures with a view to ensuring access of all individuals under its jurisdiction to water.

(b) Obligations to respect

The obligation to respect flowing from the right to food obliges states (1) *to respect private access to available food*, and prohibits (2) *the destruction of accessible food and the food supply infrastructure*. The first category prohibits denial of access for individuals or members of particular groups to food that is readily available; whether this occurs through legislation or proactive measures by the authorities is immaterial. The following are some examples of such proscribed conduct:

- Laying landmines in areas used for the production of necessary foodstuffs.
- Imposing a ban on the provision of food to persons who are without access to a food supply (eg by blocking humanitarian access to the hungry during an armed conflict or in the aftermath of a natural disaster).
- Destroying food sources with a view to driving out the local population.[157]
- Requisitioning foodstuffs without compensation, confiscating farmland used for the production of necessary foodstuffs, or failing to respect the land rights of indigenous peoples resulting in non-access to traditional sources of food (eg hunting, fishing, gathering).
- Using hunger as a weapon, ie intentionally starving the civilian population (an act which constitutes a war crime).[158]

The prohibition of the destruction of foodstuffs and its infrastructural facilities is of special relevance during armed conflicts and therefore occupies a prominent place in international humanitarian law.[159] Moreover, such conduct violates ICESCR, Article 11.[160]

---

articles on the Law of Transboundary Aquifers of 2008 adopted by the UN General Assembly in Resolution A/RES/63/124 on 11 December 2008.

[155] CtteeESCR, General Comment No 15 (2002), para 24.   [156] Ibid, para 23.

[157] ACmHPR, *Social and Economic Rights Action Centre and the Centre for Economic and Social Rights v Nigeria*, Communication No 155/96 (2001), paras 64 ff.

[158] Rome Statute, Art 8(2)(b)(xxv); AP I, Art 54(1); and AP II, Art 14.

[159] AP I, Art 54(2) and AP II ,Art 14.

[160] See, eg, the report of the Special Rapporteur of the United Nations Commission on Human Rights on human rights violations in Iraqi-occupied Kuwait of 16 January 1992, UN Doc E/CN.4/1992/26, paras 224 ff.

(c) Obligations to protect

Obligations to protect play an important role in the context of the right to food. The Committee on Economic, Social and Cultural Rights thus emphasizes in its General Comment No 12 (1999) that this human right is violated where the state fails to protect people through legislation or proactive measures against attacks by third parties aimed at blocking access to food.[161] It follows that states have a duty, for instance, to take action during food shortages to prevent the hoarding of food-stuffs for subsequent sale at significantly inflated prices with the result that poorer sectors of the population can no longer afford to feed themselves properly; to see to it that patients or children in private care, for instance in retirement homes, nursing homes and private orphanages, are properly fed; to take action against disruption of the food chain by private parties; and to oppose social traditions which dictate that, during food shortages, women should receive less food than men.

(d) Obligations to fulfil

Obligations to fulfil the core content of the right to food are of immediate effect and include the right to freedom from hunger.[162] States parties thus have an obligation during times of famine or humanitarian disaster either to supply the starving population with foodstuffs, or to seek support from the international community[163] if they are unable to do so. It is furthermore clear from international humanitarian law, from case law pertaining to the right to life, from the prohibition of inhuman treatment and from the right to adequate conditions of detention that more far-reaching obligations to fulfil exist where persons are no longer in a position to satisfy their basic needs themselves owing to state action. This is so, for example, in situations of state custody,[164] during armed conflicts,[165] or when states render it impossible for indigenous communities to live in accordance with their traditional lifestyles of gathering, hunting, or planting food for themselves.[166]

---

[161] CtteeESCR, General Comment No 12 (1999), para 19.

[162] CtteeESCR, General Comment No 12 (1999), para 17.

[163] Pursuant to the general obligation clause of Art 2(1) ICESCR, states bear responsibility for the realization of ICESCR rights not just through their own action but also, where necessary, 'through international assistance and co-operation'.

[164] See for an example from the viewpoint of civil and political rights: HRCttee, *Hill and Hill v Spain*, Communication No 526/1993 (1997), para 13: 'With respect to the author's allegations regarding their treatment during detention, particularly during the first 10 days when they were in police custody . . . , the Committee notes that the information and documents submitted by the State party do not refute the author's claim that they were not given any food during the first five days of police detention. The Committee concludes that such treatment amounts to a violation of article 10 of the Covenant.' GC III Art 26 recognizes an immediate right to food for prisoners of war, specifying that 'it shall be sufficient in quantity, quality and variety to keep prisoners of war in good health and to prevent loss of weight or the development of nutritional deficiencies'.

[165] GC IV Art 55 imposes a subsidiary obligation on the occupying power to supply the civilian population with foodstuffs 'if the resources of the occupied territory are inadequate'.

[166] IACtHR, Case of the *Yakye Axa Indigenous Community v Paraguay*, Series C, No 125 (2005), paras 162 ff, and Case of the *Sawhoyamaxa Indigenous Community v Paraguay*, Series C, No 146 (2006), paras 159 ff.

Lastly, the ICESCR imposes programmatic obligations to fulfil in respect of a number of measures aimed at enhancing food production enumerated in Article 11(2),[167] which are to be realized progressively. These obligations are designed to guarantee the availability of adequate food for all persons within the jurisdiction of a state by regulating markets, supplementing private-sector initiatives, and laying the basis for long-term food security.

Issue in focus: The right to food and economic sanctions

The realization of the right to an adequate standard of living is particularly difficult for states subject to economic sanctions under Chapter VII of the UN Charter. In such cases the international community determines to a large extent, through its design of the sanctions regime, the extent to which the state concerned is still capable of meeting its obligation to fulfil. Against the background of the comprehensive sanctions imposed on Iraq in the 1990s, the Committee on Economic, Social and Cultural Rights adopted a position on this controversial issue in General Comment No 8 (1997). It found that sanctions 'almost always have a dramatic impact on the rights recognized in the Covenant. Thus, for example, they often cause significant disruption in the distribution of food, pharmaceuticals and sanitation supplies, jeopardize the quality of food and the availability of clean drinking water, severely interfere with the functioning of basic health and education systems, and undermine the right to work.' (para 3). The Committee stressed the need 'to distinguish between the basic objective of applying political and economic pressure upon the governing elite of the country to persuade them to conform to international law, and the collateral infliction of suffering upon the most vulnerable groups within the targeted country' (para 4) and underlined that 'the terms of sanctions and the manner in which they are implemented' should be in accordance with human rights requirements (para 9). This obligation arises, according to the Committee, from the fact that economic and social rights remain in effect during sanctions in respect of two sets of obligations:

10.... The first set relates to the affected State. The imposition of sanctions does not in any way nullify or diminish the relevant obligations of that State party. As in other comparable situations, those obligations assume greater practical importance in times of particular hardship... While sanctions will inevitably diminish the capacity of the affected State to fund or support some of the necessary measures, the State remains under an obligation to ensure the absence of discrimination in relation to the enjoyment of these rights, and to take all possible measures, including negotiations with other States and the international community, to reduce to a minimum the negative impact upon the rights of vulnerable groups within the society.

11. The second set of obligations relates to the party or parties responsible for the imposition, maintenance or implementation of the sanctions... In this respect, the Committee considers that there are three conclusions:...

---

[167] ICESCR, Art 11(2) mentions measures to 'improve methods of production, conservation and distribution of food by making full use of technical and scientific knowledge, by disseminating knowledge of the principles of nutrition and by developing or reforming agrarian systems in such a way as to achieve the most efficient development and utilization of natural resources'.

12. First, [economic, social and cultural] rights must be taken fully into account when designing an appropriate sanctions regime...

13. Second, effective monitoring, which is always required under the terms of the Covenant, should be undertaken throughout the period that sanctions are in force...

14. Third, the external entity has an obligation 'to take steps, individually and through international assistance and cooperation, especially economic and technical' in order to respond to any disproportionate suffering experienced by vulnerable groups within the targeted country.

This approach has since been adopted to a large extent by the international community. The Security Council has not imposed a comprehensive economic sanctions regime since the Iraq sanctions but only so-called 'smart sanctions', ie sanctions directed specifically against representatives of the government of a state that has violated international law.[168]

3. The right to adequate housing

Relevant provisions: UDHR, Article 25; ICESCR, Article 11; ICCPR, Article 17; CRC, Article 27(3); CRPD, Article 28; CEDAW, Article 14(2)(h); CERD, Article 5(e)(iii); ICRMW, Article 43(1)(d); ACHR, Article 11; ArCHR, Article 38; ESCrev, Article 31; ECHR, Article 8; GC IV, Article 53; AP I, Article 69.

(a) The content of the right to adequate housing

The right to an adequate standard of living pursuant to ICESCR, Article 11(1) includes a right to adequate housing. The text of the Covenant, however, sheds no further light on the normative content of this right. According to the Committee on Economic, Social and Cultural Rights, full realization of the right to housing demands that the following parameters be met:[169]

(1) The *availability* of habitable housing, ie housing that provides the inhabitants with adequate space and protects them from cold, damp and other health-threatening environmental hazards; guarantees their physical safety; gives them access to energy, drinking water and sanitation facilities; affords a certain measure of security in terms of legal protection against eviction, harassment or other threats; and is culturally acceptable.

(2) *Accessibility* of such housing for everyone, including disadvantaged groups, without discrimination, and in a manner that does not jeopardize other basic needs.

The specific meaning of these parameters and the concrete duties flowing from them depend on the category of state obligations within the right to adequate housing.

---

[168] On 'smart' sanctions see Chapter 8, section III.3 and the Interlaken Process (<www.smartsanctions.ch> (accessed 6 February 2009)), in particular the publication *Targeted Financial Sanctions—A manual for design and implementation, Contributions from the Interlaken Process*, 2001.
[169] CtteeESCR, General Comment No 4 (1991), para 8. See also on the normative content of this right the report of the Special Rapporteur on adequate housing of 25 January 2001, UN Doc E/CN.4/2001/51, paras 23 ff.

(b) Obligations to respect

In reviewing reports, the Committee on Economic, Social and Cultural Rights attaches special importance to action against the widespread state practice of unlawful or forced evictions.[170] As such evictions are diametrically opposed to the criterion of accessibility and also violate other human rights,[171] the Committee considers them serious violations of the right to adequate housing.

Issue in focus: The concept of forced evictions

The Committee on Economic, Social and Cultural Rights[172] understands the concept of forced evictions as follows:

3.... The term 'forced evictions'... is defined as the permanent or temporary removal against their will of individuals, families and/or communities from the homes and/or land which they occupy, without the provision of, and access to, appropriate forms of legal or other protection. The prohibition on forced evictions does not, however, apply to evictions carried out by force in accordance with the law and in conformity with the provisions of the International Covenants on Human Rights....

5. Although the practice of forced evictions might appear to occur primarily in heavily populated urban areas, it also takes place in connection with forced population transfers, internal displacement, forced relocations in the context of armed conflict, mass exoduses and refugee movements. In all of these contexts, the right to adequate housing and not to be subjected to forced eviction may be violated through a wide range of acts or omissions attributable to States parties...

6. Many instances of forced eviction are associated with violence, such as evictions resulting from international armed conflicts, internal strife and communal or ethnic violence.

7. Other instances of forced eviction occur in the name of development. Evictions may be carried out in connection with conflict over land rights, development and infrastructure projects, such as the construction of dams or other large-scale energy projects, with land acquisition measures associated with urban renewal...

The Basic Principles and Guidelines on Development based Evictions and Displacement, of the Special Rapporteur on adequate housing[173] provide detailed guidance for cases where forced evictions are justified by the necessity of realizing development projects.

---

[170] See CtteeESCR, General Comment No 7 (1997) and the report of the Special Rapporteur on adequate housing of 8 March 2004, UN Doc E/CN.4/2004/48.

[171] The ACmHPR derives this aspect of the right to housing from the following entitlements: the right to property (ACHPR, Art 14), the right to health (ACHPR, Art 16) and family rights (ACHPR, Art 18(1)); ACmHPR, *Social and Economic Rights Action Centre and the Centre for Economic and Social Rights v Nigeria*, Communication No 155/96 (2001), paras 60 ff. The ECtHR has condemned the forced eviction and subsequent destruction of dwellings in the presence of the former inhabitants as inhuman treatment and hence a violation of ECHR, Art 3; see Chapter 10, section II.1.c. Forced evictions are also a violation of the rights for respect of the home and private life, see Chapter 12, section II.1.c.

[172] CtteeESCR, General Comment No 7 (1997), paras 3 and 5 ff.

[173] Basic Principles and Guidelines on Development based Evictions and Displacement, in Report of the Special Rapporteur on adequate housing as a component of the right to an adequate standard of living, UN Doc A/HRC/4/18, Annex I.

The right to privacy recognized in ICCPR, Article 17, ACHR, Article 11, ArCHR, Article 21, and ECHR, Article 8, though not providing a right to housing as such, includes the right to respect for a person's home as one of its components.[174] It thus affords protection, albeit not absolute, not only against state interference in a person's home, for instance through unlawful house searches or electronic surveillance measures,[175] but also against forced eviction. The European Court of Human Rights made this determination in several cases against Turkey, which was censured for the displacement of Kurds from their villages through the deliberate destruction of their homes.[176] In another judgment, the Court held that prohibiting so-called 'travellers' from living in a caravan on their own land was interference with the right in question.[177] The rights mentioned above also afford protection against, for instance, hazardous or annoying intrusions such as odours or noise pollution.[178]

International humanitarian law also contains provisions aimed at protecting private homes by categorically prohibiting the destruction and plundering of private property and attacks on private houses.[179] It equally prohibits evictions carried out in the form of forced evacuations and deportations that are not necessary for the safety of the civilian population or justified by considerations of military necessity.[180]

(c) Obligations to protect

Obligations to protect rest primarily with the legislature, which is required to adopt laws ensuring that occupants of private homes are protected against arbitrary eviction by private parties, that dwellings meet certain quality standards and that occupants are protected against intrusions by third parties. Achievement of these aims calls for the development of appropriate legal protection and provision of legal remedies that can serve as the basis for action against arbitrary eviction, disturbances by third parties, discriminatory evictions and health endangering housing conditions attributable to third parties.[181]

(d) Obligations to fulfil

The right to adequate housing obliges states to undertake a large number of measures, both legislative and other. The measures include the regulation and

---

[174] On this right see Chapter 12, section II.1.c.
[175] See, eg, ECtHR, *Camenzind v Switzerland*, *Reports* 1997-VIII, paras 32 ff, and IACtHR, *Escué-Zapata v Colombia*, Series C, No 165 (2007), para 95.
[176] See, eg, ECtHR (Grand Chamber), *Akdivar and Others v Turkey*, *Reports* 1996-IV, paras 88 ff. See also the similar jurisprudence of the IACtHR; eg Case of the *Ituango Massacres v Colombia*, Series C, No 148 (2006), paras 192 ff.
[177] ECtHR (Grand Chamber), *Chapman v The United Kingdom*, *Reports* 2001-I, paras 75 ff, and *Connors v The United Kingdom*, Application No 66746/01 (2004), paras 68 and 81 ff.
[178] For more details on this question, see Chapter 12, section II.1.c.
[179] GC IV, Art 33 and AP II, Art 4(2)(g), and GC IV, Art 53; AP I, Art 52.
[180] See Chapter 17, section IV.2.
[181] CtteeESCR, General Comment No 4 (1991), para 17, and, on the basis of the right to privacy as guaranteed by ECHR, Art 8, ECtHR, *Moldovan and Others v Romania*, *Reports* 2005-VII, paras 102 ff.

promotion of private housing, making subsidized housing available for disadvantaged groups and the provision of sites for nomadic 'travellers',[182] all of which must be designed incrementally to ensure the full realization of the right.

In addition, this right entails minimum obligations which must, in principle, be realized immediately. They include making available emergency housing for victims of, for instance, natural disasters or armed conflict, for the homeless and for other persons in distress. The housing must afford protection against environmental factors and other hazards, thereby securing survival. Further immediate obligations to fulfil arise in circumstances in which state action renders the unassisted fulfilment of this right impossible. Thus, in the event of, for instance, state expropriation of private property or forced relocations of people to make way for development projects, either replacement or full compensation is required.

Issue in focus: Street children and human rights violations

The following excerpts from the Concluding Observations of the Committee on Economic, Social and Cultural Rights on Nigeria's country report[183] demonstrate the consequences of a violation of the right to adequate housing for a particularly vulnerable group.

23. The Committee expresses its deep concern about the rising number of homeless women and young girls, who are forced to sleep in the streets where they are vulnerable to rape and other forms of violence.

. . .

27. The Committee is appalled at the great number of homeless people and notes with concern the acute housing problem in Nigeria where decent housing is scarce and relatively expensive. The urban poor, especially women and children, are forced to live in make-shift cheap dumps or shelters in appalling and degrading conditions representing both physical and mental illnesses hazards.

---

4. The right to health

Relevant provisions: UDHR, Article 25; ICESCR, Article 12 and Article 7(b); CERD, Article 5(e)(iv); CEDAW, Article 12; CRC, Article 24; CRPD, Article 25; Preamble to the Constitution of the World Health Organization (WHO); P 1/ACHR, Article 10; IACDAPD; ACHPR, Article 16; ArCHR, Article 39; GC I–IV, Article 3(2); GC III, Articles 29–32; GC IV, Articles 16–23, 38, 55–57; AP I, Articles 10–15; AP II, Articles 7–11; ESCrev, Articles 11 and 13; ECHRB and its Additional Protocols on the Prohibition of Cloning Human Beings and on Transplantation of Organs and Tissues of Human Origin.

---

[182] See European Committee of Social Rights, *European Roma Rights Center v Greece*, Complaint No 15/2003 (2004), and *European Roma Rights Center v Italy*, Complaint No 27/2004 (2005).
[183] CtteeESCR, Concluding Observations Nigeria (1998), para 23.

(a) General considerations

The right to health under ICESCR, Article 12 contains a variety of exceptional features. Rather than a right to be healthy, which no state can guarantee to every individual, the provision enshrines a right to conditions that allow the leading of a healthy life and a right to adequate health care in case of illness. States parties are thus required to supplement individual health care by endeavouring to create conditions and services conducive to the highest possible standard of health for all persons under their jurisdiction. The fact that health does not depend solely on an individual's constitutional predisposition but that state action can have a major impact on people's state of health is demonstrated, for example, by the vastly different life expectancies in countries of the North and South.[184]

Issue in focus: The right to protection of health under the European Social Charter

Part I of the revised ESC stipulates under point 11 that '[e]veryone has the right to benefit from any measures enabling him to enjoy the highest possible standard of health attainable'. The provision requires the contracting states, '[w]ith a view to ensuring the effective exercise of the right to protection of health, ... either directly or in cooperation with public or private organisations, to take appropriate measures designed *inter alia*: 1. to remove as far as possible the causes of ill-health; 2. to provide advisory and educational facilities for the promotion of health and the encouragement of individual responsibility in matters of health; 3. to prevent as far as possible epidemic, endemic and other diseases, as well as accidents.' This right is supplemented by the right to safe and healthy working conditions (Article 3), the right to (medical) assistance (Article 13), and rights for persons with disabilities (Article 15).

The links between the right to health and other human rights are particularly complex, a fact that provides strong evidence of the indivisibility and interdependence of human rights. This is so in three respects. First, violations of other rights—such as the rights to food and housing, the prohibition of torture and the right to adequate conditions of detention—have an impact on the right to health.[185] Not surprisingly, the substantive scope of the right to health therefore overlaps that of many other rights.[186] On the other hand, medical treatment or examinations conducted without consent or denial of access to treatment may adversely affect other rights including the right to privacy[187] and the prohibition

---

[184] See, eg, the World Bank Annual Report 2006, which states that the average life expectancy in Africa is 46 years, whereas in Europe it is 69 years (p 30).

[185] See, eg, IACtHR, Case of the *Sawhoyamaxa Indigenous Community v Paraguay*, Series C, No 146 (2006), paras 177–178.

[186] The CtteeESCR laid particular emphasis on this connection in the case of the right to drinking water which, according to its General Comment No 15 (2002), is embodied in both Art 11 and Art 12 of the ICESCR.

[187] See Chapter 12, section II.1.a.

of subjecting someone without his free consent to medical experimentation as prohibited by ICCPR, Article 7.[188] Lastly, poor health, physical or mental disability, or contraction of an infectious disease often provide a pretext for violations of the right to non-discrimination.

(b) The content of the right to health

In view of the complexity of the factors that exert an influence on health, it is not surprising that the precise normative content of this right remains unclear in several respects. The wording of the various relevant provisions is in most cases of little assistance. Nevertheless, Articles 7 and 12 of the ICESCR, by referring to the measures required to ensure environmental and industrial hygiene and healthy working conditions,[189] make it clear that this right not only covers health care as such but also entails obligations in respect of the necessary conditions for the protection of health. The Committee on Economic, Social and Cultural Rights has shed additional light on the normative content of the right to health.[190] According to the Committee, this right is satisfied where the following is ensured:

(1) The *availability* of qualitatively and quantitatively adequate public health facilities, ie of general and psychiatric hospitals, health centres and care facilities for persons with disabilities that are adequately staffed and equipped and guarantee acceptable preventive, therapeutic and palliative treatment, as well as the availability of drugs and other necessary items; and

(2) Non-discriminatory *accessibility* for all, with consideration for disadvantaged groups, to health services and health-related information throughout the territory of a state party.[191]

States' concrete obligations with a view to the attainment of the highest possible standard of health vary in terms of the different categories of obligation.

(c) Obligations to respect

Obligations to respect play an important role in the context of the right to health. In systematic terms they may be categorized as follows:

(1) States parties to the ICESCR (but also to the ICCPR and the regional conventions[192]) are prohibited from ordering *coercive diagnostic or therapeutic*

---

[188] Report of the Special Rapporteur on torture of 23 December 2003, UN Doc E/CN.4/2004/56, para 56.

[189] ICESCR, Art 12(2)(c) and Art 7(b).

[190] CtteeESCR, General Comment No 14 (2000), paras 7 ff. See also the reports of the Special Rapporteur on the right to health of 13 February 2003, UN Doc E/CN.4/2003/58, paras 22 ff, and of 1 March 2004, 'Mission to the World Trade Organization', UN Doc E/CN.4/2004/49/Add.1, paras 33 ff.

[191] See also ACmHPR, *Purohit and Moore v The Gambia*, Communication No 241/2001 (2003), para 80.

[192] Thus, eg, coercive medical treatment always constitutes interference with the right to privacy and family life under ICCPR, Art 17 and ECHR, Art 8.

measures. However, this prohibition is not absolute. Mandatory medical treatment may be conducted without the consent of the person concerned under the ICESCR, Article 4 limitations clause, ie in cases determined by law and insofar as such treatment is perceived to be proportionate to the achievement of a legitimate aim. Such general welfare goals may include, for instance, protection of the health of third parties in the event of a highly infectious disease, clarification of the circumstances of a crime, or protection of the life and person of nursing staff or of individuals without capacity to consent. Article 7 of the ICCPR absolutely prohibits subjecting a person without his or her free consent to medical or scientific experimentation.[193]

(2) The *obstruction or denial of access to existing health facilities* by agents of the state also constitutes a violation of the obligation to respect. According to the Committee on Economic, Social and Cultural Rights, examples of such unlawful conduct include the denial of access to contraceptives directly or indirectly through censorship of information regarding contraception, the prohibition of traditional healing methods and practices, or the limiting of access to health facilities for certain groups such as women or foreign nationals without legal status.[194] The Human Rights Committee found that the denial of permission to travel abroad to receive medical attention, resulting in the death of a person, constituted a violation of the right to life under ICCPR, Article 6.[195]

(3) Article 12 of the ICESCR further prohibits states from *polluting the environment in a manner that is harmful to human health*, for instance through state-owned industrial facilities or the testing of weapons that release harmful substances.[196]

(4) The prohibition of *the destruction of health care facilities* and of *attacks on medical personnel* is of major practical importance during armed conflicts and occupies a prominent place in international humanitarian law.[197] The same is true of the absolute prohibition of the *requisitioning* of medical equipment or civilian hospitals[198] and of *obstruction of the passage of relief consignments*[199] and *medical transports.*[200] Lastly, the numerous Hague Law rules prohibiting

---

[193] AP I, Art 11 contains a similar prohibition in respect of international armed conflicts.

[194] CtteeESCR, General Comment No 14 (2000), para 34, and Birgit Toebes, 'The Right to Health', in Asbjørn Eide, Catarina Krause, and Allan Rosas (eds), *Economic, Social and Cultural Rights: A Textbook* (2nd edn, Brill: Dordrecht etc, 2001), 179 ff.

[195] HRCttee, *Mulezi v Democratic Republic of the Congo*, Communication No 962/2001 (2004), para 5.4.

[196] CtteeESCR, General Comment No 14 (2000), para 34, and ACmHPR, *Social and Economic Rights Action Centre and the Centre for Economic and Social Rights v Nigeria*, Communication No 155/96 (2001), paras 50 ff. This prohibition also flows from guarantees of privacy; see below, Chapter 12, section II.1.a.

[197] GC IV, Art 18; AP I, Art 12; AP II, Art 9.

[198] GC IV, Arts 55(2) and 57; AP I, Art 14.   [199] GC IV, Art 23; AP I, Art 70.

[200] GC IV, Art 17 and Arts 21–31; AP II, Art 11.

the use of weapons that disproportionately endanger the life and health of civilians may be understood as specific concretizations of the concept of the right to health.[201]

Issue in focus: The European Convention for the Protection of Human Rights and Dignity of the Human Being with regard to the Application of Biology and Medicine[202]

This Convention seeks to protect human rights in the area of medical treatment. It establishes the principle that the interests of human beings have primacy over those of scientific research and guarantees non-discriminatory access to health care of appropriate quality.[203] The Convention prohibits, except in emergencies, all forms of coercive medical treatment. Moreover, it sets out detailed rules governing the requirement of consent, the protection of persons without the capacity to consent, and the obligation to provide individuals with information regarding their own state of health. Other areas covered by the agreement include a prohibition of discrimination on the grounds of genetic heritage, a limitation on the permissibility of genetic testing including prenatal choosing of a child's sex and protection of persons taking part in medical research programmes.[204] Article 17 of the Convention may give rise to problems in this regard, since it permits research on persons without the capacity to consent under certain circumstances and thus clashes with the prohibition of scientific experimentation without consent under ICCPR, Article 7. The last substantive chapter of the Convention lays down human-rights-based principles governing transplant medicine, prohibiting any use of the human body or body parts for financial gain; it does not, however, prohibit the patenting of human genes. The rights recognised in this Convention do not afford absolute protection but may be subject to limitations, provided they are based on law and necessary to protect public health, to prevent crime or to protect the fundamental rights of third parties.

This Convention is deemed to be a core treaty, whose scope may be extended through additional protocols. To date, a protocol prohibiting cloning has been adopted as well as protocols with supplementary rules governing transplant medicine and biomedical research.[205]

---

[201] See section II.2.d above ('Issue in focus: Prohibition of the use of anti-personnel mines').

[202] European Convention for the Protection of Human Rights and Dignity of the Human Being with regard to the Application of Biology and Medicine (Convention on Human Rights and Biomedicine) of 4 April 1997.

[203] Convention on Human Rights and Biomedicine, Arts 2 and 3.

[204] The permissibility of embryo research depends on the relevant provisions of domestic law; the creation of embryos for research purposes, on the other hand, is prohibited (Convention on Human Rights and Biomedicine, Art 18).

[205] Additional Protocol on the Prohibition of Cloning Human Beings of 12 January 1998, Additional Protocol concerning Transplantation of Organs and Tissues of Human Origin of 24 January 2002, and Additional Protocol concerning Biomedical Research of 25 January 2005. Additional protocols to protect human embryos and foetuses and on human genetics are currently (2008) being drafted.

(d) Obligations to protect

To meet these obligations, states are required primarily to take legal action against infringements of the right to health by private actors. Authorities are further required to take appropriate protective measures against private conduct such as hazardous emissions from a private business that seriously endangers people's health.

Human-rights-motivated health legislation must include, for instance, the following provisions:[206]

(1) non-discriminatory access to private health-care facilities;

(2) eradication of private discrimination against sick people and people with disabilities;

(3) prevention of traditional practices and customs from, for instance, impeding access to pre- or post-natal care or violating women's right to health. The Committee, when examining state reports, deems, *inter alia*, the following practices as incompatible with the right to health: food taboos, forced marriages for young girls, force-feeding of women prior to marriage, private discrimination against children and adults with disabilities and, in particular, female genital mutilation;[207]

(4) healthy working conditions in private-sector workplaces through the establishment of minimum regulations governing, for example, exposure to hazardous emissions or necessary protective measures;[208] and

(5) elimination as far as possible of environmental impacts generated by private households and businesses that are harmful to health.[209]

Issue in focus: The prohibition of female genital mutilation

How should the practice of genital mutilation of women and girls be categorized in human rights terms? This is a controversial issue. Female genital mutilation plainly involves inhuman treatment, which furthermore affects victims on the basis of gender without objective justification and is therefore discriminatory.[210] Conversely, from the standpoint of human rights policy, the idea of placing the mothers, grandmothers and other relatives of the victims in the same category as torturers acting

---

[206] CtteeESCR, General Comment No 14 (2000), para 35.

[207] CtteeESCR, Concluding Observations Senegal (2001), para 24; Egypt (2000), para 16; Mali (1994), para 14; General Comment No 14 (2000), para 22; and CtteeEDAW, General Recommendation No 14 (1990).

[208] ICESCR, Art 7(b). This obligation is also set out in numerous ILO conventions; see eg the Chemicals Convention, 1990 (No 170), the Safety and Health in Mines Convention, 1995 (No 176), and the Safety and Health in Agriculture Convention, 2001 (No 184).

[209] For instance, the ECtHR held that the granting of a state permit for a goldmine whose operations endangered the health of the local population was a violation of the right to private life under ECHR, Art 8; *Taşkin and Others v Turkey, Reports* 2004-X, paras 111 ff.

[210] The HRCttee characterizes such practices as violations of ICCPR, Arts 2, 7 and 26. See, eg, HRCttee, Concluding Observations Uganda (2004), para 10.

on behalf of the state is questionable, and is unlikely to persuade societies attached to their traditions to relinquish such practices. The treaty bodies therefore tend to address the issue of female genital mutilation as a right to health issue and to emphasize the obligations to protect of the states concerned. The Committee on the Elimination of Discrimination against women qualified 'the practice of female circumcision' as harmful to the health of women and recommended mainly public health measures.[211] The Committee on the Rights of the Child, for instance, adopted the following approach in its Concluding Observations on Mali in 2001:

> 28. The Committee notes the efforts of the State party to introduce measures to eradicate the practice of female genital mutilation (FGM) and other harmful traditional practices affecting the health of girls, including early and forced marriages... The Committee remains concerned... that harmful traditional practices such as excision and early and forced marriages continue to be widely practised within the State party. The Committee also notes with concern that approximately 75 per cent of women in the State party are in favour of maintaining the practice of excision. The Committee recommends that the State party strengthen its efforts to combat and eradicate the persistent practice of FGM and other traditional practices harmful to the health of girls. The Committee urges the State party to continue its efforts to conduct sensitization programmes for practitioners and the general public in order to change traditional attitudes and discourage harmful practices. In this regard, the Committee also encourages the establishment of alternative career training programmes for practitioners. The Committee encourages the State party to continue its collaboration with, *inter alia*, neighbouring States to identify good practices undertaken in the campaign to combat and eradicate the practice of FGM... affecting the health of girls.

(e) Obligations to fulfil

This social right entails an obligation for states to incorporate at least its core content in their domestic law.[212] In other words, a minimum standard of health care must be ensured. Where this minimum content is not realized, the Committee on Economic, Social and Cultural Rights considers there to be a violation of ICESCR, Article 12, unless a state can show that the required minimum standard has proved unattainable despite heavy investment of its resources and recourse to available international assistance. The core content of the right to health includes, for example, ensuring that basic health facilities exist and that essential medicines are both available and accessible to disadvantaged groups as well as ensuring that adequate food, water and housing necessary to prevent detriment to health are available. The Committee equally assigns high priority to the availability of pre- and post-natal care for all women, comprehensive vaccination programmes against the most dangerous infectious diseases, measures to prevent and contain epidemic and endemic diseases, health education measures and qualitatively adequate public training for members of the medical profession. The Inter-American Court of Human Rights deduced from the right to life and the

---

[211] CtteeEDAW, General Recommendation No 14 (1990) which deals exclusively with this issue.

[212] In circumstances of state custody, on the other hand, the state has an obligation to ensure the full realization of the right to health, see Chapter 3, section III.6.

right to humane treatment a duty of states to take measures to ensure the monitoring of their health infrastructure in order for said rights to be safeguarded in these institutions.[213] Measures above and beyond this minimum core are to be introduced progressively, ie depending on the availability of resources.[214]

Issue in focus: The right to health and international assistance

Are states obliged to promote the right to health in other states, for instance through trade policy, by relaxing patent regulations for drugs, or by exerting influence on other states or international organizations? The Committee on Economic, Social and Cultural Rights has adopted the following approach to this question.[215]

To comply with their international obligations in relation to article 12, States parties have to respect the enjoyment of the right to health in other countries, and to prevent third parties from violating the right in other countries, if they are able to influence these third parties by way of legal or political means, in accordance with the Charter of the United Nations and applicable international law. Depending on the availability of resources, States should facilitate access to essential health facilities, goods and services in other countries, wherever possible and provide the necessary aid when required. States parties should ensure that the right to health is given due attention in international agreements and, to that end, should consider the development of further legal instruments. In relation to the conclusion of other international agreements, States parties should take steps to ensure that these instruments do not adversely impact upon the right to health. Similarly, States parties have an obligation to ensure that their actions as members of international organizations take due account of the right to health. Accordingly, States parties which are members of international financial institutions, notably the International Monetary Fund, the World Bank, and regional development banks, should pay greater attention to the protection of the right to health in influencing the lending policies, credit agreements and international measures of these institutions.

---

[213] IACtHR, *Albán Cornejo et al v Ecuador*, Series C, No 171 (2007), para 121.
[214] See generally CtteeESCR, General Comment No 14 (2000), paras 43–45.
[215] CtteeESCR, General Comment No 14 (2000), para 39. See also the report of the Special Rapporteur on the right to health of 1 March 2004, Mission to the World Trade Organization, UN Doc E/CN.4/2004/49/Add.1, para 11.

10

Protection of Human Integrity: Prohibition of Ill-treatment and of Enforced Disappearance

I. Overview

International human rights treaties contain a range of guarantees designed to safeguard the individual's physical and mental integrity. The prohibition of torture and inhuman or degrading treatment or punishment proscribes serious interference with a person's physical or mental integrity that can negate the very basis of human dignity by traumatizing its victim. A special stigma is attached to torture as one of the most shocking form of arbitrary state conduct. Therefore, the ban on torture occupies for good reason a special position in international human rights protection and has the status of an absolute and non-derogable norm in all treaties. The status of the ban on torture as part of customary law and as a peremptory norm of international law (*jus cogens*) is undisputed. Yet even this categorical prohibition is insufficient to prevent torture from continuing to manifest itself as a rather common practice in many states today.

A particularly offensive form of cruelty is the widespread practice of enforced disappearance,[1] ie deprivation of a person's liberty by or with the knowledge of state agents while denying that the person is in their custody. This crime, which is often perpetrated systematically, not only breaches the prohibition of inhuman treatment but also, by definition, grossly violates or threatens other fundamental human rights. Moreover, it violates not only the rights of missing persons but also the rights of their families.

The right to health and the right to privacy, discussed in other Chapters,[2] also protect certain aspects of the integrity of the human person.

---

[1] Section III below.
[2] For the right to health, see Chapter 9, section III.4; and for the right to private life, see Chapter 12.

II. The Prohibition of Torture and Inhuman or Degrading Treatment or Punishment

Relevant provisions: UDHR, Article 5; ICCPR, Article 7; CAT; OPCAT; CRC, Article 37; CRPD, Article 15; ACHR, Article 5; ACHPR, Article 5; ArCHR, Article 8; ECHR, Article 3; GC, Article 3; GC III, Articles 13–14, 17, 87, 89 and 99; GC IV, Articles 27, 31–32, 37, 100 and 118 f; AP I, Articles 11 and 75; AP II, Article 4; Rome Statute, Articles 7(1)(f) and (2)(e) and Article 8(2)(a)(ii) and (c) (i); SICTY, Articles 2(b) and 5(f); SICTR, Articles 3(f) and 4(a).

1. Torture and inhuman or degrading treatment or punishment

(a) The definition of torture

Article 7 of the ICCPR, all regional human rights treaties, and diverse provisions of international humanitarian law prohibit torture but contain no definition of the concept. A legal definition is found, however, in Article 1(1) of the Convention against Torture, which states that torture is:

any act by which severe pain or suffering, whether physical or mental, is intentionally inflicted on a person for such purposes as obtaining from him or a third person information or a confession, punishing him for an act he or a third person has committed or is suspected of having committed, or intimidating or coercing him or a third person, or for any reason based on discrimination of any kind, when such pain or suffering is inflicted by or at the instigation of or with the consent or acquiescence of a public official or other person acting in an official capacity. It does not include pain or suffering arising only from, inherent in or incidental to lawful sanctions.

Thus, torture is severe physical or mental suffering that is intentionally inflicted by or with the consent or acquiescence of state agents where it is undertaken in pursuit of a specific purpose and where the suffering is not the inevitable consequence of a lawfully imposed penalty.

The definition in the Convention against Torture does not fully correspond to what emerges from the Covenant, the regional treaties, and international humanitarian and customary law because it excludes cases of torture by private actors in the absence of any involvement of the state. The reason for this restrictive approach is that the Convention against Torture derives far-reaching state obligations from the definition relating, *inter alia*, to prosecution, extradition and reparations.[3] States were not prepared to assume such obligations for cases of torture by non-state actors. Accordingly, the definition in the other treaties is broader inasmuch as it is not limited to state and state-condoned acts but also covers cases of private abuse.[4]

---

[3] See section II.5 below.   [4] HRCttee, General Comment No 20 (1992), para 2.

Torture is also prohibited by international criminal law. According to the Rome Statute, torture is 'the intentional infliction of severe pain or suffering, whether physical or mental, upon a person in the custody or under the control of the accused; except that torture shall not include pain or suffering arising only from, inherent in or incidental to, lawful sanctions'.[5] It is punishable as a crime against humanity when committed as part of a widespread or systematic attack directed against any civilian population.[6] Torture is a war crime[7] when, in the context of an international or non-international armed conflict, severe physical or mental suffering is inflicted on a protected person within the meaning of the four Geneva Conventions or on a person *hors de combat* within the meaning of common Article 3. The Rome Statute equally requires that the abuse has the purpose of obtaining information or a confession, or of punishing, intimidating or coercing the victim. Abuse that occurs for reasons based on discrimination can also be considered torture within the Statute.[8] According to both definitions, torture is practised in pursuit of a specific purpose and can be perpetrated not only by state agents but also by non-state actors.

(b) Torture and inhuman or degrading treatment or punishment

The ICCPR, the Convention against Torture,[9] and the regional treaties differentiate between torture and inhuman or degrading treatment or punishment.[10] What is the difference between these categories of ill-treatment and how do they relate to each other? The comments of international courts and other bodies on the subject are often somewhat vague. Nevertheless, two separate theoretical models may be devised in the light of their jurisprudence:

(1) *Degree of severity theory:* According to this traditional approach, the three elements are differentiated primarily in terms of the *intensity* of the suffering inflicted. Torture, the severest form of abuse, involves particularly harsh and manifestly inhuman conduct, while at the other end of the spectrum degrading treatment is a comparatively mild form of inhumanity, whereas inhumane treatment lies somewhere between these two. The 'degree of severity theory',[11] ie basing the distinction primarily on the severity of the ill-treatment, is particularly evident in the ECtHR's *Ireland v the United Kingdom* judgment (1979), in which torture is defined as an aggravated form of cruel, inhuman, and degrading treatment or punishment.[12] Accordingly, the Court of

---

[5] Rome Statute, Art 7(2)(e).   [6] Rome Statute, Art 7(1)(f).
[7] Rome Statute, Art 8(2)(a)(ii) and (c)(i).
[8] Elements of Crimes, UN Doc ICC-ASP/1/3, Art 8(2)(a)(ii) and (c)(i).
[9] Art 16 of CAT mentions these forms of abuse without defining their content, but the prohibition is also limited to state or state-condoned acts.
[10] ICCPR, Art 7 and CAT, Art 16 also prohibit cruel treatment and punishment.
[11] This theory is espoused by many legal scholars; see, for example, Manfred Nowak, *UN Covenant on Civil and Political Rights, CCPR Commentary* (2nd edn, Engel: Kehl, 2005), 160 ff.
[12] ECtHR, *Ireland v The United Kingdom*, Series A, No 25 (1978), para 167.

Human Rights held that an interrogation technique whereby suspects were forced to remain for long periods spread-eagled against a wall while being blasted with loud music and deprived of sleep and food was not torture but inhuman treatment because it caused serious but not extremely severe suffering.[13] This differentiation criterion was maintained when the Court explicitly held for the first time in 1996 that torture had in fact occurred, stating[14] that the special stigma of torture could be attached only to deliberate ill-treatment causing very serious and cruel suffering. In the Court's view, these conditions were met in the case of so-called 'Palestinian hanging', which involves stripping victims naked, tying their arms together behind their backs and leaving them suspended by their arms for long periods.

(2) *Purpose theory:* The 'severity theory' is not only problematic because it seems exceedingly difficult to distinguish between the different levels of severity but also because it fails to reflect that, because of the absolute guarantee of the prohibitions in question, no legal consequences at all are attached to the different qualifications as torture or inhuman or degrading treatment.[15] The more satisfactory model, in our view, differentiates the three forms of abuse not in terms of intensity but rather in terms of *purpose*.[16] Viewed from this perspective, torture is a form of severe physical or mental abuse that is inflicted (1) deliberately and (2) for a purpose mentioned in CAT, Article 1 (eg, in order to force a person to provide information[17]), provided a certain level of severity is reached. Thus, the special stigma attached to *torture* lies not only in the severity of the ill-treatment but also in the intent to break a person's will or—as in the case of intimidating a third person—make him or her an instrument of an illegitimate action. *Degrading treatment or punishment* occurs, on the other hand, where the assault on a person's physical or mental integrity has the effect of degrading or humiliating the victim, *ie* where the

---

[13] This classification has since been qualified by the ECtHR: 'The Court has previously examined cases in which it concluded that there had been treatment which could only be described as torture...However, having regard to the fact that the Convention is a "living instrument which must be interpreted in the light of present-day conditions"..., the Court considers that certain acts which were classified in the past as "inhuman and degrading treatment" as opposed to "torture" could be classified differently in future. It takes the view that the increasingly high standard being required in the area of the protection of human rights and fundamental liberties correspondingly and inevitably requires greater firmness in assessing breaches of the fundamental values of democratic societies'; *Selmouni v France* (Grand Chamber), *Reports* 1999-V, para 101, and *Elci and Others v Turkey*, Application Nos 23145/93 and 25091/94 (2003), para 634.

[14] ECtHR, *Aksoy v Turkey*, *Reports* 1996-VI, paras 63–64.

[15] In contrast, many provisions of CAT apply only to cases of torture.

[16] Cf Rod Morgan and Malcolm D Evans, *Preventing Torture: A study of the European Convention for the Prevention of Torture and Inhuman or Degrading Treatment or Punishment* (Diane Pub Co: Oxford, 1998), 73 ff, and Nigel S Rodley, *The Treatment of Prisoners in International Law* (2nd edn, Oxford University Press: Oxford, 1999), 29 and 75.

[17] This purpose as defining characteristic of torture is also reflected in GC III, Art 17(4) according to which '[n]o physical or mental torture, nor any other form of coercion, may be inflicted on prisoners of war *to secure from them information of any kind whatever*' (emphasis added).

suffering consists exactly in this debasement,[18] regardless of whether a corresponding intention exists.[19] *Inhuman treatment or punishment* remains as a catch-all concept for cases in which intensive mental and/or physical suffering either (1) is unjustifiably caused by specific circumstances (such as conditions of detention); or (2) arises from a punishment that is unlawful in terms of its nature or manner of imposition.[20]

Example: The ECtHR judgment in *Aktaş v Turkey*[21]

Invoking the legal definition in Article 1 of the CAT, the European Court moved in its recent case law closer to the second model by focusing on the purpose of inflicting pain as much as on the degree of suffering. It reasoned, for instance, in 2003 that:

In determining whether a particular form of ill-treatment should be qualified as torture, consideration must be given to the distinction, embodied in Article 3, between this notion and that of inhuman or degrading treatment... [I]t appears that it was the intention that the Convention should, by means of this distinction, attach a special stigma to deliberate inhuman treatment causing very serious and cruel suffering... In addition to the severity of the treatment, there is a purposive element, as recognised in the [Convention against Torture], which defines torture in terms of the intentional infliction of severe pain or suffering with the aim, inter alia, of obtaining information, inflicting punishment or intimidating.

The Committee against Torture follows the purpose theory in its jurisprudence.[22] The recent case law of the Inter-American Court of Human Rights explicitly qualifies acts of ill-treatment in light of the purpose theory[23] and believes that not only physical but also mental mistreatments can be qualified as torture.[24]

The Human Rights Committee gives no importance to the distinction of the different methods used. While the Human Rights Committee held in an older General Comment that the difference between categories of ill-treatment

---

[18] ECtHR, *Pretty v The United Kingdom*, Reports 2002-III, para 52: 'Where treatment humiliates or debases an individual, showing a lack of respect for, or diminishing, his or her human dignity, or arouses feelings of fear, anguish or inferiority capable of breaking an individual's moral and physical resistance, it may be characterised as degrading and also fall within the prohibition of Article 3...'. See also ECtHR (Grand Chamber), *Ramirez Sanchez v France*, Application No 59450/00 (2006), para 118: 'In considering whether a punishment or treatment is "degrading" within the meaning of Article 3, the Court will have regard to whether its object is to humiliate and debase the person concerned and whether, as far as the consequences are concerned, it adversely affected his or her personality in a manner incompatible with Article 3.'

[19] ECtHR, *Price v The United Kingdom*, Reports 2001-VII, para 30.

[20] It may serve also to characterize cases where suffering is inflicted deliberately and for a specific purpose but is obviously not severe enough to be classified as torture.

[21] ECtHR, *Aktaş v Turkey*, Reports 2003-V, paras 313–314.

[22] CtteeAT, *Dimitrijevic v Serbia and Montenegro*, Communication No 172/2000 (2005), para 7.5. See also Manfred Nowak and Elizabeth McArthur, *The United Nations Convention against Torture: A Commentary* (Oxford University Press: Oxford, 2008), 51.

[23] For a clear statement see IACtHR, *Bueno-Alves v Argentina*, Series C, No 164 (2007), paras 79 ff.

[24] IACtHR, *Cantoral Benavides v Peru*, C/69 (2000), paras 95 ff, and *Maritza Urrutia v Guatemala*, Series C, No 103 (2003), paras 91 ff.

depends on the nature, purpose and severity of the treatment applied,[25] and found instances of torture in some early cases,[26] it refrains today from assigning cases of ill-treatment to a specific category; instead it makes a general finding of a violation of ICCPR, Article 7.

(c) Case law

The regional courts have characterized the following as torture: severe ill-treatment during custody and interrogation, undertaken for the purpose of obtaining a statement or confession, of intimidating the victim or a third party, or of inflicting punishment.[27] The notion of torture also covers rape by state agents in custodial circumstances[28] or, eg, force-feeding, not prompted by valid medical reasons but rather with the aim of forcing a person to stop his or her protest, and performed in a manner which unnecessarily exposes him or her to great physical pain and humiliation.[29] The European Court of Human Rights has explicitly lowered the required threshold of severity of abuse in recent years.[30] In *Selmouni v France*, for example, the Court characterized repeated beatings and severe humiliation[31] of a foreigner in pre-deportation custody as torture on the ground 'that certain acts which were classified in the past as "inhuman and degrading treatment" as

[25] HRCttee, General Comment No 20 (1992), para 4. See also Sarah Joseph, Jenny Schultz and Melissa Castan, *The International Covenant on Civil and Political Rights* (2nd edn, Oxford University Press: Oxford, 2004), 148–9.

[26] For example, HRCttee, *Rubio and Parents v Colombia*, Communication No 161/1983 (1987), paras 10.2, 10.4 and 11; for an overview, see Nowak (n 11) 162.

[27] For example, ECtHR, *Aktaş v Turkey*, *Reports* 2003-V, paras 313 ff; *Selmouni v France*, *Reports* 1999-V, paras 96 ff; *Çakici v Turkey* (Grand Chamber), *Reports* 1999-IV, para 92; *Salman v Turkey* (Grand Chamber), *Reports* 2000-VII, para 114 and IACtHR, *Bueno-Alves v Argentina*, Series C, No 164 (2007). See, however, also ECtHR (Grand Chamber), *Ilhan v Turkey*, *Reports* 2000-VII, para 87, where the ECtHR makes its finding primarily on the basis of the severity of the abuse but also on the basis of failure to provide the victim with medical attention. See also IACtHR, *Humberto Sánchez v Honduras*, Series C, No 99 (2003), para 99.

[28] ECtHR (Grand Chamber), *Aydin v Turkey*, *Reports* 1997-VI, para 83: 'Rape of a detainee by an official of the State must be considered to be an especially grave and abhorrent form of ill-treatment given the ease with which the offender can exploit the vulnerability and weakened resistance of his victim. Furthermore, rape leaves deep psychological scars on the victim which do not respond to the passage of time as quickly as other forms of physical and mental violence.' See also ECtHR, *Maslova and Nalbandov v Russia*, Application No 839/02 (2008), paras 107–8. Similar findings were made by, for example, the Appeals Chamber of the ICTY in its judgment in *The Prosecutor v Kunarac et al*, Case No IT-96-23&23/1-A (2002), para 150, and the Special Rapporteur on Torture, report of 23 December 2003, UN Doc E/CN.4/2004/56, para 55.

[29] ECtHR, *Ciorap v Moldova*, Application No 12066/02 (2007), para 89.

[30] Cf ECtHR, *Elci and Others v Turkey*, Application Nos 23145/93 and 25091/94 (2003), paras 632 ff, where maltreatment of lawyers who had represented Kurds before the State Security Court, involving insults, assaults, being stripped naked, and hosed down with cold water, blindfold interrogations and inadequate conditions of detention, were characterized as torture. However, the Court held that the less serious ill-treatment suffered by other complainants was inhuman and degrading treatment, basing itself primarily on the less severe nature of the abuse (ibid, para 647).

[31] ECtHR, *Selmouni v France*, *Reports* 1999-V, paras 24 and 103 ff: '...various forms of ill-treatment. These included being repeatedly punched, kicked, and hit with objects;...having a police officer show him his penis, saying "Look, suck this", before urinating over him...'

opposed to "torture" could be classified differently in future. It [took] the view that the increasingly high standard being required in the area of the protection of human rights and fundamental liberties correspondingly and inevitably requires greater firmness in assessing breaches of the fundamental values of democratic societies.'[32] The Inter-American Court of Human Rights has developed similar jurisprudence. In particular, it held that exclusively psychological ill-treatment may also be classified as torture, especially when its aim is to break the resistance of the accused.[33] According to the Court, threats of violence during interrogation may also be classified as torture.[34] The Special Rapporteur on Torture has expressly characterized the enforced disappearance of persons as torture.[35]

Cases classified as *inhuman treatment* have included specific conditions of detention on death row[36] but not the duration alone of said detention;[37] sentencing a person to death after an unfair trial;[38] beatings, other ill-treatment, threats of violence,[39] and any use of physical force in detention that does not appear to be necessitated by the conduct of the person concerned;[40] failure to provide medical treatment for a fatally ill person;[41] lack of medical or psychiatric treatment for a prisoner entailing severe suffering;[42] forced feeding of vomit inducing products to secure evidence in a criminal procedure;[43] continuation of administrative detention despite medically indicated grounds for release;[44] extended incommunicado detention;[45] detention of a five-year-old unaccompanied child

---

[32] Ibid, para 101.

[33] See, eg, IACtHR, *Cantoral Benavides v Peru*, Series C, No 69 (2000), paras 95 ff, and *Maritza Urrutia v Guatemala*, Series C, No 103 (2003), paras 91 ff.

[34] IACtHR, *Maritza Urrutia v Guatemala*, Series C, No 103 (2003), para 94. The IACmHR described as torture the arrest of a 14-year-old child, who was subsequently forced to accompany the police during an operation in a *favela* at risk to his life; *Neri da Fonseca v Brazil*, Report No 33/04, Case 11.634 (2004), paras 63 ff.

[35] Interim report of 3 July 2001, UN Doc A/56/156, paras 9 ff.

[36] For example, ECtHR, *Soering v The United Kingdom*, Series A, No 161 (1989), para 111, and *Poltoratskiy v Ukraine*, *Reports* 2003-V, paras 129 ff; HRCttee, *Williams v Jamaica*, Communication No 609/1995 (1997), para 6.5, and *Wilson v The Philippines*, Communication No 868/1999 (2003) para 7.4.

[37] HRCttee, *Edwards v Jamaica*, Communication No 529/1993 (1997), para 8.2.

[38] HRCttee, *Larrañaga v The Philippines*, Communication No 1421/2005 (2006), para 7.11.

[39] For example, HRCttee, *Kennedy v Trinidad and Tobago*, Communication No 845/1998 (2002); ECtHR, *Gäfgen v Germany*, Application No 22978/05 (2008), para 66: '[T]o threaten an individual with torture may constitute at least inhuman treatment.'

[40] See, *inter alia*, ECtHR, *Ribitsch v Austria*, Series A, No 336 (1995), para 38.

[41] See, for example, the report of the Special Rapporteur on Torture of 23 December 2003, UN Doc E/CN.4/2004/56, paras 50 ff, and also, indirectly, ECtHR, *D v The United Kingdom*, *Reports* 1997-III, paras 50 ff.

[42] HRCttee, *Rouse v The Philippines*, Communication No 1089/2002 (2005), para 7.8; ECtHR, *Keenan v The United Kingdom*, *Reports* 2001-III and *Kotsaftis v Greece*, Application No 39780/06 (2008); ACmHPR, *Huri-Laws v Nigeria*, Communication No 225/1998 (2000), para 41.

[43] ECtHR (Grand Chamber), *Jalloh v Germany*, Application No 54810/00 (2006), para 82.

[44] HRCttee, *C v Australia*, Communication No 900/1999 (2002), para 8.4.

[45] HRCttee, *El-Megreisi v Libyan Arab Jamahiriya*, Communication No 440/1990 (1994), para 5.4; ACmHPR, *Amnesty International and Others v Sudan*, Communication Nos 48/1990, 50/1991, 52/1991, 89/1993 (1999), para 54, and *Liesbeth Zegveld and Messie Ephrem v Eritrea*,

in a closed transit centre without qualified personnel and surveillance appropriate to the child's age;[46] detention for several days without food and water;[47] failure to inform detainees' relatives of their whereabouts[48] or their execution as well as location of the burial site;[49] and destruction of the houses of complainants before their eyes by state agents[50] or by private actors with the implicit consent of state agents.[51]

According to the case law of the treaty bodies and the regional courts, the following constitute *inhuman punishment*: any form of corporal punishment, even where it is imposed as a legally prescribed criminal penalty, irrespective of the act perpetrated;[52] prolonged solitary confinement;[53] the execution of a person by gas asphyxiation[54] or by stoning[55] and execution without prior notice as to the date of execution,[56] but not execution by lethal injection.[57] According to the European Court of Human Rights, the sentencing of an adult to lifelong detention is not *per se* incompatible with ECHR, Article 3, except if this sentence cannot be reviewed

Communication No 250/2002 (2003), para 55; IACmHR, *Levoyer Jiménez v Ecuador*, Report No 66/01, Case 11.992 (2001), paras 82 ff.

[46] ECtHR, *Mayeka and Mitunga v Belgium*, Application No 13178/03 (2007), paras 50 ff.

[47] HRCttee, *Miha v Equatorial Guinea*, Communication No 414/1990 (1994), para 6.4. Cf also IACtHR, *Neptune v Haiti*, Series C, No 180 (2008), para 137, and ACmHPR, *Achutan and Amnesty International v Malawi*, Communication Nos 64/1992, 68/1992 and 78/1992 (1995), para 7.

[48] For example, ECtHR (Grand Chamber), *Çaciki v Turkey*, *Reports* 1999-IV, para 98; HRCttee, *Jegatheeswara Sarma v Sri Lanka*, Communication No 950/2000 (2003), para 9.5; IACtHR, *Humberto Sánchez v Honduras*, Series C, No 99 (2003), para 101, and ACmHPR, *Law Office of Ghazi Suleiman v Sudan*, Communication Nos 222/98 and 229/99 (2003), para 44.

[49] For example, HRCttee, *Alibovea v Tajikistan*, Communication No 985/2001 (2005), para 6.7, and *Sultanova v Uzbekistan*, Communication No 915/2000 (2006), para 7.10.

[50] For example, ECtHR, *Yöyler v Turkey*, Application No 26973/95 (2003), para 74, and *Dulas v Turkey*, Application No 25801/94 (2001), para 55.

[51] CtteeAT, *Dzemajl et al v Serbia and Montenegro*, Communication No 161/2000 (2002).

[52] For example, HRCttee, *Boodlal Sooklal v Trinidad and Tobago*, Communication No 928/2000 (2001), para 4.6; *Higginson v Jamaica*, Communication No 792/1998 (2002), para 4.6, and IACtHR, *Caesar v Trinidad and Tobago*, Series C, No 123 (2005), para 70. By contrast, CAT, Art 1(1) does not explicitly prohibit corporal punishment where it is prescribed by law. The CtteeAT takes the view, however, that criminal sanctions of this kind are in breach of the Convention; see, for example, the Concluding Observations on Yemen (2004), para 6, and Saudi Arabia (2002), para 4.

[53] HRCttee, General Comment No 20 (1992), para 6. See also ECtHR (Grand Chamber), *Öcalan v Turkey*, *Reports* 2005-IV, para 191, according to which complete sensory deprivation and social isolation can never be justified even by the requirements of state security and therefore always constitute inhuman punishment. This conclusion is however not automatically valid for cases of (long) isolated detention, ie where the detainee is deprived of all contact with his inmates, for example for security reasons; ECtHR (Grand Chamber), *Ramirez Sanchez v France*, Application No 59450/00 (2006), paras 125 ff.

[54] HRCttee, *Ng v Canada*, Communication No 469/1991 (1994), para 16.4.

[55] ECtHR, *Jabari v Turkey*, *Reports* 2000-VIII.

[56] ACmHPR, *Interights et al v Botswana*, Communication No 240/2001 (2004), para 41.

[57] HRCttee, *Kindler v Canada*, Communication No 470/1991 (1993), paras 15.3–15.4 in conjunction with 9.7; *Cox v Canada*, Communication No 539/1993 (1994), para 17.3. In the European context at least, imposition of the death penalty after an unfair trial also constitutes a breach of this prohibition; ECtHR (Grand Chamber), *Öcalan v Turkey*, *Reports* 2005-IV, paras 167 ff.

de iure or *de facto* after a certain lapse of time, ie where no prospect whatsoever of an earlier (conditional) release exists.[58] On the other hand, according to the Human Rights Committee, the sentencing of a person to 75 years' imprisonment with hard labour does not violate this prohibition.[59]

The following are examples of conduct explicitly classified as *degrading treatment*: strip searches in the presence of prison staff of the opposite sex;[60] routine weekly strip searches without clear justification;[61] the forced shaving-off of a prisoner's hair without objective justification;[62] displaying a prisoner to the media in a cage;[63] harassment by prison warders involving repeated soaking of a prisoner's bedding;[64] the chaining of an elderly prisoner to his hospital bed for a night without objective justification;[65] eight consecutive condemnations to several months of detention each of a conscientious objector in a country that does not offer any civil service as an alternative;[66] and, according to recent case law of the European Court of Human Rights, also grievous and systematic discrimination on racist grounds.[67] The treatment of a woman with paralysed limbs and suffering from kidney problems who was prevented from bringing the battery charger for her electric wheelchair into prison, had to sleep in the wheelchair, and was accompanied to the toilet by a male officer was also found to be degrading.[68] The European Court of Human Rights has classified detention under particularly severe conditions[69] and lack of medical care in a prison[70] as degrading rather than inhuman treatment—in our view inappropriately and evidently on the basis of the 'degree of severity' theory.

Examples of *degrading punishment* include public executions[71] or certain forms of physical punishment.[72]

---

[58] ECtHR (Grand Chamber), *Kafkaris v Cyprus*, Application No 21906/04 (2008), paras 97 ff.

[59] HRCttee, *Teesdale v Trinidad and Tobago*, Communication No 677/1996 (2002), para 9.8.

[60] ECtHR, *Valasinas v Lithuania*, *Reports* 2001-VIII, para 117.

[61] ECtHR, *Van der Ven v The Netherlands*, *Reports* 2003-II, paras 53 ff.

[62] ECtHR, *Yankov v Bulgaria*, *Reports* 2003-XII, paras 109 ff.

[63] HRCttee, *Polay Campos v Peru*, Communication No 577/1994 (1997), para 8.5.

[64] HRCttee, *Young v Jamaica*, Communication No 615/1995 (1997); para 5.2.

[65] ECtHR, *Henaf v France*, *Reports* 2003-XI, paras 47 ff.

[66] ECtHR, *Ülke v Turkey*, Application No 39437/98 (2006), para 52.

[67] ECtHR, *Moldovan and Others v Romania* (No 2), *Reports* 2005-VII, para 111.

[68] ECtHR, *Price v The United Kingdom*, *Reports* 2001-VII, paras 25–30. The Court concluded: 'There is no evidence in this case of any positive intention to humiliate or debase the applicant. However, the Court considers that to detain a severely disabled person in conditions where she is dangerously cold, risks developing sores because her bed is too hard or unreachable, and is unable to go to the toilet or keep clean without the greatest of difficulty, constitutes degrading treatment contrary to Article 3 of the Convention. It therefore finds a violation of this provision in the present case' (ibid, para 30). For a similar constellation see *Scoppola v Italy*, Application No 50550/06 (2008). This case is currently under examination by the Grand Chamber of the ECtHR.

[69] See, eg, ECtHR, *Kalashnikov v Russia*, *Reports* 2002-VI, paras 95 ff, and *Dougoz v Greece*, *Reports* 2001-II, para 48. It should be noted that the jurisprudence of the HRCttee on the compatibility of conditions of detention with human rights law is not based on Art 7 but on Art 10 of the ICCPR.

[70] ECtHR, *Keenan v The United Kingdom*, *Reports* 2001-III, paras 109 ff.

[71] Nowak (n 11) 171.

[72] See, eg, ECtHR, *Tyrer v The United Kingdom*, Series A, No 26 (1978), paras 28 ff (three strokes of the birch on the naked buttocks of a 15-year-old boy). See also ACmHPR, *Doebbler v*

(d) Threshold of applicability

Not every case of infliction of pain or suffering violates the prohibition of torture and inhuman or degrading treatment or punishment. The ill-treatment must reach a certain threshold of severity, ie a minimum degree of intensity, to be covered by the prohibition. As reflected in the jurisprudence of the treaty bodies and regional human rights courts, this threshold cannot be determined in the abstract but is heavily dependent on the circumstances involved. For decades the ECtHR has based its reasoning in such cases on a standard formula, stressing that 'ill-treatment must attain a minimum level of severity before it will be considered to fall within the provision's scope. The assessment of this minimum is relative and depends on all of the circumstances of the case including the duration of its treatment, the physical or mental effects and, in some cases, the age, sex, and health of the individual.'[73] The specific circumstances of individual cases, such as the duration of the ill-treatment or the sex, age or behaviour of the victim, are therefore often decisive when it comes to determining whether 'less' severe ill-treatment falls outside the scope of international human rights protection against torture and inhuman or degrading treatment.[74] The bounds of this relativistic approach are reached where physical force is used in custodial circumstances without objective justification, ie treatment that may be viewed as unnecessary and therefore diminishes the victim's dignity, rendering the treatment inhuman.[75]

The need to determine where the threshold lies between conduct not covered by the prohibition of torture and inhuman or degrading treatment that falls within the substantive scope of the prohibition does not mean that exceptions could be justified with arguments that a certain treatment is proportional. Rather, the absolute nature of the prohibition means that any infringement above the threshold automatically constitutes a violation.[76] It follows that one should be careful in not setting the threshold of applicability of this fundamental human right at a too low a level that trivializes and ultimately undermines the concept of torture.[77] In our view it is more appropriate to assess the compatibility of comparatively minor

---

Sudan, Communication No 236/2000 (2003), paras 29 ff (between 25 and 40 lashes carried out in public on the bare backs of women using a wire and plastic whip that leaves permanent marks).

[73] For example, *Aktaş v Turkey*, *Reports* 2003-V, para 312.

[74] Ill-treatment falling short of the threshold of applicability may, however, come within the substantive scope of ICCPR, Art 10 or that of ICCPR, Art 17 or ECHR, Art 8.

[75] Since 1995 the ECtHR has been using the following standard formula to explain the need for a relative approach: 'The Court emphasizes that, in respect of a person deprived of his liberty, any recourse to physical force which has not been made strictly necessary by his own conduct diminishes human dignity and is in principle an infringement of the right set forth in Article 3.'

[76] Relative factors thus merely assist in determining whether treatment is covered by the substantive scope of application of the prohibition in a specific case. Nevertheless, the analysis of these relative factors comes close to an examination of proportionality in certain cases dealt with by the ECtHR; see for a clear example, ECtHR (Grand Chamber), *Jalloh v Germany*, Application No 54810/00 (2006), paras 76 ff.

[77] The example of forced head shaving referred to in ECtHR, *Yankov v Bulgaria* (n 62) is questionable in this regard.

infringements with human rights law in the light of the right to privacy which is subject to certain limitations. In this sense, the European Court of Human Rights increasingly recognizes that a right to personal autonomy, in particular regarding choices about one's own body flows from the protection of private life[78] which therefore provides protection also beneath the lower threshold of applicability of ECHR, Article 3.[79] Hence, forms of interference such as forced head shaving, body searches, or restrictive dress codes in custodial circumstances may be covered by the right to privacy, a guarantee that can be limited under certain circumstances.

Issue in focus: Interrogating alleged terrorists

States facing strong threats of terrorism frequently stress the need for harsher interrogation methods in the war on terror. These methods, they argue, are acceptable so long as they do not reach the actual level of torture. In its first judgment in a state complaint procedure, the European Court of Human Rights had to deal with Great Britain's claim that the so-called 'five technique'[80] interrogations of people suspected of being involved in terrorist action in North Ireland did not violate ECHR, Article 3. The Court concluded in 1978 that the combination of these interrogation methods was not compatible with Article 3.[81]

In Israel the government allowed the Israeli security service to use 'moderate physical pressure' during interrogations. In a seminal judgment, the Supreme Court of Israel concluded[82] that even though there was danger of terrorist action, Israel's use of violence during interrogations remained inadmissible. It justified its decision with the following general principles:

First, a reasonable investigation is necessarily one free of torture, free of cruel, inhuman treatment of the subject and free of any degrading handling whatsoever.... Human dignity also includes the dignity of the suspected being interrogated...

This conclusion is in perfect accord with (various) International Law treaties...which prohibit the use of torture, cruel, inhuman treatment and degrading treatment...These prohibitions are absolute. There are no exceptions to them and there is no room for balancing. Indeed, violence directed at a suspect's body or spirit does not constitute a reasonable investigation practice...

Second, a reasonable investigation is likely to cause discomfort. It may result in insufficient sleep. The conditions under which it is conducted risk being unpleasant. Indeed, it is possible to

---

[78] ICCPR, Art 17 and corresponding provisions of the regional human rights conventions. See Chapter 12, section II.1.a.

[79] Thus, pointedly, ECtHR, *Wainwright v The United Kingdom*, Application No 12350/04 (2006), para 46: 'The treatment undoubtedly caused the applicants distress but does not, in the Court's view, reach the minimum level of severity prohibited by Article 3. Rather the Court finds that this is a case which falls within the scope of Article 8 of the Convention and which requires due justification under the second paragraph of Article 8.'

[80] ECtHR, *Ireland v The United Kingdom*, Series A, No 25 (1978), para 96.

[81] Ibid, para 167.

[82] Israeli Supreme Court sitting as the High Court of Justice, Judgment concerning the Legality of the General Security Service's Interrogation Methods, *The Public Committee against Torture in Israel et al v The State of Israel*, 6 September 1999, HCJ 5100/94.

conduct an effective investigation without resorting to violence. Within the confines of the law, it is permitted to resort to various machinations and specific sophisticated activities which serve investigations today...In the end result, the legality of an investigation is deduced from the propriety of its purpose and from its methods. Thus, for instance, sleep deprivation for a prolonged period, or sleep deprivation at night when this is not necessary to the investigation time wise may be deemed a use of an investigation method which surpasses the least restrictive means.[83]

Based on these principles, the Supreme Court categorized certain methods of interrogation as absolutely prohibited. Such illegal methods were beatings, sleep withdrawal, exposure to loud music, being forced to adopt a painful position during interrogation and intensive shaking of people in such positions.

The Human Rights Committee had also concerned itself with the question of admissible methods of interrogation. In its 2006 Concluding Observations on the state report of the USA it took the following position:

13. The Committee is concerned with the fact that the State party has authorized for some time the use of enhanced interrogation techniques, such as prolonged stress positions and isolation, sensory deprivation, hooding, exposure to cold or heat, sleep and dietary adjustments, 20-hour interrogations, removal of clothing and deprivation of all comfort and religious items, forced grooming, and exploitation of detainees' individual phobias. Although the Committee welcomes the assurance that, according to the Detainee Treatment Act of 2005, such interrogation techniques are prohibited by the present Army Field Manual on Intelligence Interrogation, the Committee remains concerned that (a) the State party refuses to acknowledge that such techniques, several of which were allegedly applied, either individually or in combination, over a protracted period of time, violate the prohibition contained by article 7 of the Covenant; (b) no sentence has been pronounced against an officer, employee, member of the Armed Forces, or other agent of the United States Government for using harsh interrogation techniques that had been approved; (c) these interrogation techniques may still be authorized or used by other agencies, including intelligence agencies and 'private contractors'; and (d) the State party has provided no information to the fact that oversight systems of such agencies have been established to ensure compliance with article 7.[84]

The case law of the Human Rights Committee contains scarcely any statements on how to define the lower threshold. This may be due to the fact that the ICCPR, unlike the ECHR, contains in Article 10 a right to humane conditions of detention, which can be applied to many cases that fall beneath the threshold of applicability of the prohibition of inhuman treatment. The question of whether state conduct falls within the scope of ICCPR, Article 7 is therefore less crucial, at least in custodial circumstances. Accordingly, in such situations, the Committee often contents itself with finding that conditions of detention which are contrary to human rights law constitute a violation of ICCPR, Article 10. The Committee examines whether Article 7 has also been violated in such cases only if, in addition to the unacceptable conditions of detention, it can be determined that specific acts of violence were perpetrated

---

[83] Ibid, para 23.
[84] HRCttee, Concluding Observations USA (2006), para 13. See also, James Ross, Black letter abuse: the US legal response to torture since 9/11 (2007) *IRRC* 561 ff.

by prison staff.[85] The threshold of applicability also seems to be of little relevance in the ACHR regime, since Article 5 contains not only—in paragraph 2—a prohibition of torture and inhuman and degrading treatment and the right to humane conditions of detention but also—in paragraph 1—a general and non-derogable right to humane treatment, ie specifically to respect for physical, mental and moral integrity. A right to human dignity is also foreseen in Article 5.

Issue in focus: The right to humane conditions of detention

The right to humane conditions of detention as enshrined in ICCPR, Article 10(1) (and, at the regional level, in ACHR, Article 5(2)), protects not only remand or convicted prisoners but all persons deprived of their liberty.[86] It has been characterized by the Human Rights Committee as non-derogable[87] (although it is not in the list contained in the Article on states of emergency). As a right that complements the prohibition of inhuman treatment, this guarantee gives rise primarily to obligations to fulfil, which involve ensuring that detention does not entail any infringement of the integrity of detainees that goes beyond the restrictions and suffering necessarily associated with deprivation of liberty.[88] For instance, states must ensure minimum facilities in prison cells (minimum space, lighting, fresh air, sanitary installations, etc), an adequate supply of food and clothing, and adequate medical care. Although considerable financial resources are needed to meet these humane incarceration requirements, the Committee does not, for instance, consider that these obligations should be fulfilled progressively but views them as immediately applicable irrespective of the level of development of the state concerned.[89]

The standards of humanity in detention have been given detailed meaning by the UN and regional organizations in a series of (soft law) recommendations and minimum standards[90] that help to determine whether conditions of detention amount to a violation of human rights.

---

[85] See, for example, HRCttee, *Boodoo v Trinidad and Tobago*, Communication No 721/1996 (2002), paras 6.1 ff, and *Sirageva v Uzbekistan*, Communication No 907/2000 (2005), para 6.2.

[86] HRCttee, General Comment No 21 (1992), para 2.

[87] HRCttee, General Comment No 29 (2001), para 13(a).

[88] See HRCttee, General Comment No 21 (1992), para 3.

[89] HRCttee, *Mukong v Cameroon*, Communication No 458/1991 (1994), para 9.3.

[90] Standard Minimum Rules for the Treatment of Prisoners, Adopted by the First United Nations Congress on the Prevention of Crime and the Treatment of Offenders, held at Geneva in 1955, and approved by the Economic and Social Council by its resolutions 663 C (XXIV) of 31 July 1957 and 2076 (LXII) of 13 May 1977; Basic Principles for the Treatment of Prisoners Adopted and proclaimed by General Assembly resolution 45/111 of 14 December 1990; Body of Principles for the Protection of All Persons under Any Form of Detention or Imprisonment Adopted by General Assembly resolution 43/173 of 9 December 1988; United Nations Rules for the Protection of Juveniles Deprived of their Liberty Adopted by General Assembly resolution 45/113 of 14 December 1990. At the regional level, the 2006 European Prison Rules (Recommendation Rec(2006)2 of the Committee of Ministers to member states on the European Prison Rules) are particularly important.

2. The absolute nature of the prohibition

There is no explicit provision in the wordings of the ICCPR or the regional treaties recognizing the absolute nature of the prohibition of torture, ie stating that it is not subject to limitation.[91] However, its absolute character is explicitly affirmed in CAT, Article 2, according to which '[n]o exceptional circumstances whatsoever...may be invoked as a justification of torture'. International humanitarian law also prohibits torture in Article 3 common to the Geneva Conventions in all armed conflicts 'at any time and in any place whatsoever'. Furthermore, the case law of the Human Rights Committee and the regional human rights courts makes it crystal clear that no exceptions to the prohibition of torture and inhuman or degrading treatment will be tolerated.[92] This remains the case irrespective of the existence of a general—for instance terrorist—threat,[93] of the victim's past[94] or present[95] criminal conduct or in the case of degrading or inhuman punishment, irrespective of the consequences that failure to execute the punishment might entail.[96] The fact that the prohibition remains absolute even in cases of extradition or deportation is also undisputed.[97] In 2008, the European Court of Human Rights rejected in a seminal judgment the view that torture may be permissible to save the lives of third parties in the case of terrorists[98] and the claim that the extradition or deportation of a terrorist threatening state security should be assessed in the light of less strict standards.[99]

3. The duty to respect

As evidenced by the negative wording of this guarantee and its classification as a prohibition, ICCPR, Article 7 puts the emphasis on the duty to respect. They violate this guarantee whenever the conduct of their agents crosses the threshold

---

[91] However, they unanimously characterize the prohibition of torture as a non-derogable guarantee.

[92] HRCttee, General Comment No 20 (1992), para 3. See also, for example, IACtHR, *Loayza-Tamayo v Peru*, C/33 (1997), para 57, and ECtHR, *Aksoy v Turkey*, *Reports* 1996-VI, para 62.

[93] See, for example, ECtHR (Grand Chamber), *Ramirez Sanchez v France*, Application No 59450/00 (2006), para 115: 'Even in the most difficult of circumstances, such as the fight against terrorism, the Convention prohibits in absolute terms torture or inhuman or degrading treatment or punishment.' Similarly, IACtHR, *Cantoral Benavides v Peru*, Series C, No 69 (2000), para 96.

[94] See, eg , ECHR, *D v The United Kingdom*, *Reports* 1997-III, para 47.

[95] ECtHR, *Kalashnikov v Russia*, *Reports* 2002-VI, para 95.

[96] ECtHR, *Tyrer v The United Kingdom*, Series A, No 26 (1978), paras 28 ff.

[97] The Grand Chamber of the ECtHR makes this particularly clear in *Chahal v The United Kingdom*, *Reports* 1996-V, para 80 See also CtteeAT, *Dadar v Canada*, Communication No 258/2004 (2005), para 8.8. On this topic, see Chapter 17, section III.4.

[98] On this point see, for example, the controversial contributions by Alan Dershowitz, Elaine Scarry and Richard A Posner, in Sanford Levinson (ed), *Torture—A Collection* (Oxford University Press: Oxford, 2004), 257 ff.

[99] ECtHR (Grand Chamber), *Saadi v Italy*, Application No 37201/06 (2008), especially paras 137 ff. See Chapter 17, section III.4 for more information on this judgment.

of applicability. Accordingly, the treaty monitoring bodies have repeatedly held that the state is also in breach of its obligation to respect when its agents, acting in an official capacity or feigning to do so, encroach on the area protected by this guarantee acting against express instructions and hence *ultra vires*.[100] A state is also in direct breach of its obligation to respect where the staffs of autonomous or privatized state units such as private schools, privatized prisons, or private psychiatric clinics violate the prohibition or where contractual security personnel ill-treat persons in their custody. As early as 1993 the European Court of Human Rights established the principle that a state cannot release itself from its obligations under ECHR, Article 3 by delegating its tasks to private actors.[101]

As it is notoriously difficult to obtain evidence in cases of alleged ill-treatment in custodial circumstances, the jurisprudence of the treaty monitoring bodies provides for a *reversal of the burden of proof* in such cases. If a person who was healthy before being taken into custody leaves detention facilities with physical signs of ill-treatment, the state is required to prove that these signs are not attributable to a breach of this prohibition.[102]

States are not only prohibited from practising torture or inflicting inhuman treatment or punishment themselves but must also refrain from extraditing, expelling or otherwise handing people over to another state where there are well-founded reasons to believe that they would risk such treatment. The prohibition of extradition, expulsion, or *refoulement* where there is a risk of torture or inhuman, or degrading treatment usually becomes relevant in the case of foreigners[103] but a state's own nationals are equally protected by this prohibition.

4. The duty to protect

In contrast to the right to life, the wording of ICCPR, Article 7, ECHR, Article 3, and ACHR, Article 5 does not expressly oblige states parties to afford legal protection against torture or inhumane or degrading treatment to persons subject to their jurisdiction.[104] Nevertheless, the treaty bodies recognize that states parties are under an obligation to enact legislative provisions that criminalize private conduct encroaching on the areas protected by these guarantees.[105] States are further

---

[100] Explicitly stated by the IACtHR, *Velásquez-Rodríguez v Honduras*, Series C, No 4 (1988), paras 169 ff.

[101] ECtHR, *Costello-Roberts v The United Kingdom*, Series A, No 247-C (1993), para 27.

[102] See, for example, HRCttee, *Terán Jijón v Ecuador*, Communication No 277/1988 (1992), para 5.2; ECtHR, *Aktaş v Turkey*, Reports 2003-V, para 291; and IACtHR, *Humberto Sánchez v Honduras*, Series C, No 99 (2003), para 100.

[103] See Chapter 17, section III.4. On the prohibition of extradition, expulsion and *refoulement* where there is a risk of the death penalty, see Chapter 9, section II.2.c.iii.

[104] CAT, Art 16 on the other hand, explicitly imposes such an obligation. Moreover, international humanitarian law, in GC IV, Art 27 requires states to protect women 'against any attack on their honour, in particular against rape, enforced prostitution, or any form of indecent assault'.

[105] HRCttee, General Comments Nos 20 (1992), para 13, and 30 (2002), para 8; ECtHR, *Mahmut Kaya v Turkey*, Reports 2000-III, para 15; IACtHR, *Velásquez-Rodríguez v Honduras*,

required to provide a person with effective protection against ill-treatment by third parties if they are aware of the risk and in a position to avert it.[106] The treaty monitoring bodies and regional human rights courts apply particularly stringent standards in respect of this guarantee where a person is under full state control (eg in cases of assault by fellow inmates[107]) or where the victims of infringements by private actors are members of a particularly vulnerable group (eg children[108]).

On the other hand, the prohibition of inhuman treatment entails no obligation for states parties to provide immunity from prosecution in a case of assisted suicide to spare a fatally ill person from inhuman suffering.[109]

5. The duty to fulfil

To ensure effective protection from serious attacks on personal integrity as prohibited by guarantees outlawing torture and inhuman or degrading treatment, the state is also required to fulfil specific positive obligations. These are set out in detail in the UN Convention against Torture of 1984, but are also inferable to some extent from the general prohibitions of torture under the ICCPR and the regional human rights conventions.

(1) *Obligations to fulfil in circumstances of state custody or care*: The European Court of Human Rights has inferred from ECHR, Article 3 that states have a duty to ensure that conditions of detention, or living conditions in situations where people find themselves in state custody or care against their will, are humane

---

Series C, No 4 (1988), paras 184–5. By contrast, the CAT requires states to criminalize acts constituting torture or cruel, inhuman or degrading treatment only if they are perpetrated or sanctioned by state agents (CAT, Art 4 in conjunction with Arts 1 and 16).

[106] See ECtHR, *Moldovan and Others v Romania*, Reports 2005-VII, para 98, as well as ECtHR, *Case of 97 members of the Gldani Congregation of Jehovah's Witnesses and 4 Others v Georgia*, Application No 71156/01 (2007), para 96. On the circumstances entailing obligations to protect, see Chapter 3, section III.3.

[107] See, for example, ECtHR, *Pantea v Romania*, Reports 2003-VI, paras 189 ff, and *Keenan v The United Kingdom*, Reports 2001-III, para 110, and *Rodić and 3 Others v Bosnia and Herzegovina*, Application No 22893/05 (2008), paras 64 ff, and HRCttee, *Wilson v The Philippines*, Communication No 868/1999 (2003), para 7.3.

[108] ECtHR, *A v The United Kingdom*, Reports 1998-VI, para 22 (regular beatings of a nine-year-old child); similarly, *Z and Others v The United Kingdom*, Reports 2001-V, paras 73–4 (abuse and neglect of children by their parents), and *E and Others v The United Kingdom*, Application No 33218/96 (2002), paras 89 ff (sexual abuse of children by their mother's partner).

[109] ECtHR, *Pretty v The United Kingdom*, Reports 2002-III, para 55: 'The Court cannot but be sympathetic to the applicant's apprehension that without the possibility of ending her life she faces the prospect of a distressing death. It is true that she is unable to commit suicide herself due to physical incapacity and that the state of law is such that her husband faces the risk of prosecution if he renders her assistance. Nonetheless, the positive obligation on the part of the State which is relied on in the present case would not involve the removal or mitigation of harm by, for instance, preventing any ill-treatment by public bodies or private individuals or providing improved conditions or care. It would require that the State sanction actions intended to terminate life, an obligation that cannot be derived from Article 3 of the Convention.' For more details on this judgment see Chapter 9, section II.3.c, and Chapter 12, section II.1.a.

and not degrading.[110] Lack of financial resources cannot serve to justify detention conditions, which violate Article 3.[111] Should a state detain sick persons[112] or persons with a physical[113] or mental[114] disability, it must ensure that the prison infrastructure is adequate to their special needs. In the case of conditions of detention, the Human Rights Committee bases such obligations primarily on the right to adequate conditions of detention under ICCPR, Article 10.

The state also violates its duty to fulfil where it gives up its supervision of a person without taking any specific measures, leaving the aforementioned to their fate, although their age or state of health would require assistance. In this spirit, the European Court of Human Rights considered that the deportation of a five-year-old child, who had been residing in a registration centre, without making sure that the child would be taken care of in the state of destination, violated ECHR, Article 3 with regard to the child as well as the mother, who only learnt of the deportation conditions immediately before it was carried out.[115]

(2) *Obligations to fulfil in circumstances other than state custody or care*: The question as to whether and to what extent a state's refusal to provide services can be classified as inhuman or degrading treatment even outside state custody or care is largely unresolved. In other words, can an obligation to provide what is necessary to avoid inhuman or degrading living conditions be inferred from the existing prohibition? In our view, a state's refusal to help people in need may, in extraordinary circumstances, constitute not only a violation of the relevant subsistence rights but may also amount to inhuman treatment where the degree of sufferings exceeds the threshold of the prohibition of inhuman treatment and the state could, without difficulty, provide the necessary services (basic food and shelter, essential health care, etc). This would be particularly true in situations where the suffering is at least partially a consequence of an omission of the authorities to provide protection against dangers emanating from third persons or situations. In the case of survivors of a racist attack who, without financial means to improve their condition, had to live in a house destroyed by the attackers for many years, the European Court of Human Rights accepted that the failure of the state to alleviate these inhumane living conditions violated ECHR, Article 3.[116]

---

[110] See, for example, ECtHR, *Keenan v the United Kingdom*, *Reports* 2001-III, paras 111 ff, and *Kalashnikov v Russia*, *Reports* 2001-VI, paras 95 ff.

[111] ECtHR, *Dybeku v Albania,* Application No 41153/06 (2008) para 50.

[112] For example, ECtHR, *Mechenkov v Russia*, Application No 35421/05 (2008).

[113] ECtHR, *Vincent v France*, Application No 6253/03 (2006). The Court found Art 3 had been violated in the given case, where the complainant who needed a wheelchair to move around was held in a prison whose doors were too small for the wheelchair to get through. Therefore, the complainant could not leave his cell alone, but had to be lifted out of his wheelchair for this purpose. Because of this, he was excluded from all communal activities in the prison. In another prison, the same problem meant that he had been unable to use the shower for more than a month.

[114] ECtHR, *Dybeku v Albania*, Application No 41153/06 (2008), paras 35 ff.

[115] ECtHR, *Mayeka and Mitunga v Belgium*, Application No 13178/03 (2007), paras 66 ff.

[116] ECtHR, *Moldovan and Others v Romania*, *Reports* 2005-VII, paras 110 ff.

(3) *Obligations to prevent*: Pursuant to CAT, Article 10, every state party is bound by obligations to prevent torture. The state must therefore take all necessary steps, such as training police, civil and military prison staff, and doctors, to prevent state or state-condoned torture and other abuse that constitutes inhuman or degrading treatment[117] in the territory under its jurisdiction.[118] Furthermore, Article 11 of the Convention requires states to keep the country's rules governing admissible methods of interrogation and the treatment of prisoners under systematic review. States that have ratified the Optional Protocol to the Torture Convention have the specific duty to establish and maintain a national preventive mechanism by setting up an independent visiting body that can inspect places where persons are deprived of their liberty with a view to identify factors and circumstances conducive to ill-treatment.

(4) *Obligations to investigate, prosecute and extradite*: Article 13 of the CAT requires states parties to conduct an impartial investigation of any allegation by a person that he or she has been subjected to torture or to inhuman or degrading treatment.[119] Articles 4 to 9 of the CAT oblige states to make torture a punishable crime under domestic law and prosecute and punish its agents who are responsible for acts of torture as defined by CAT, Article 1. States are obliged to establish the jurisdiction of their courts for any such act of torture committed on its territory, or by its nationals or against victims with their nationality. They are also obliged to try other offenders present on their territory based on the principle of universality, or extradite them (*aut dedere, aut iudicare*).[120] Although there is no explicit mention of obligations in the wording of ICCPR, Article 7 or in the equivalent provisions of the regional human rights treaties, both the treaty monitoring bodies and the regional human rights courts recognize an obligation to investigate, prosecute and punish.[121] Moreover the regional courts, and arguably also the Human Rights Committee,[122] recognize an individual right of torture victims to have acts of torture criminally prosecuted.[123]

---

[117] CAT, Art 16 in conjunction with Art 10.

[118] The 2002 Optional Protocol to CAT and the 1987 European Convention on the Prevention of Torture have created an international mechanism to assist states in preventing torture; see Chapter 7, section IV.2.

[119] CAT, Art 16 in conjunction with Art 13.

[120] CAT, Art 6. See CtteeAT, *Guengueng et al v Senegal*, Communication No 181/2001 (2006), paras 9.5 ff. This decision concerned the ex-president of Chad, Habré, who had been living in Senegal for years.

[121] See, eg, HRCtee, *Singarasa v Sri Lanka*, Communication No 1033/2001 (2004), para 7.4, and ECtHR, *Assenov and Others v Bulgaria*, Reports 1998-VIII, para 102.

[122] HRCttee, General Comment No 31 (2004), para 18, according to which failure to prosecute a person who has committed acts of torture can in itself constitute a breach of the Covenant.

[123] ECtHR, *Aksoy v Turkey*, Reports 1996-VI, para 98, and IACtHR, *Velásquez-Rodríguez v Honduras*, Series C, No 4 (1988), paras 175–176.

(5) *Obligation to compensate:* Under CAT, Article 14 all victims of torture within the meaning of CAT, Article 1 have a legally enforceable right to fair and adequate compensation, including the means for as full a rehabilitation as possible. The UN treaty bodies and the regional human rights courts deduce the existence of such obligations from the general prohibitions of torture.[124]

Issue in focus: Torture and state immunity against civil proceedings?

Does the prohibition of torture impose an obligation on the states parties to the ECHR to place their courts at the disposal of torture victims to enforce their claims for compensation *vis-à-vis* a torturing state? Does this entitlement override the principle of immunity of third states *vis-à-vis* civil claims internal to the state? The European Court of Human rights addressed this question in the *Al-Adsani v The United Kingdom* case.[125] A Kuwaiti citizen sought to enforce his claim to compensation from Kuwait in respect of injury to his physical and mental health caused by torture in Kuwait in May 1991 before English courts, which declared that they lacked jurisdiction due to third state immunity. While the Court unanimously concluded that the United Kingdom had not violated ECHR, Article 3 a majority of the judges held that this refusal did not amount to a violation of the right to have civil claims heard by an independent court (ECHR, Article 6). They noted 'the growing recognition of the overriding importance of the prohibition of torture' but did not 'find it established that there is yet acceptance in international law of the proposition that States are not entitled to immunity in respect of civil claims for damages for alleged torture committed outside the forum State'.[126] Therefore, the United Kingdom was not obliged to grant Al-Adsani access to its courts.

A substantial minority of dissenting judges noted that '[b]y accepting that the rule on prohibition of torture is a rule of *jus cogens*, the majority recognize that it is hierarchically higher than any other rule of international law, be it general or particular, customary or conventional, with the exception, of course, of other *jus cogens* norms. For the basic characteristic of a *jus cogens* rule is that, as a source of law in the now vertical international legal system, it overrides any other rule which does not have the same status. In the event of a conflict between a *jus cogens* rule and any other rule of international law, the former prevails.' They concluded that as the right to be protected against took precedence over the non-peremptory rules on state immunity granting such immunity to Kuwait violated ECHR, Article 6.[127]

---

[124] For example, HRCttee, General Comment No 20 (1992), para 14, and *Wilson v The Philippines*, Communication No 868/1999 (2003), para 9; IACtHR, *Velásquez-Rodríguez v Honduras*, Compensatory Damages, C/7 (1989); ECtHR, *Tas v Turkey*, Application No 24396/94 (2000), paras 100 ff.

[125] ECtHR (Grand Chamber), *Al-Adsani v The United Kingdom*, Reports 2001-XI.

[126] Ibid, para 66.

[127] Ibid, Dissenting Opinion by Judges Rozakis and Caflisch joined by Judges Wildhaber, Costa, Cabral Barreto, and Vajic.

III. The Prohibition of Enforced Disappearance of Persons

Relevant provisions: CPAPED, Inter-American Convention on the Forced Disappearance of Persons; Rome Statute, Article 7(2)(i).

1. What is enforced disappearance?

The widespread practice[128] of enforced disappearance of persons represents one of the most serious human rights violations. According to the international criminal law definition in Article 7(2)(i) of the Rome Statute:

(i) 'Enforced disappearance of persons' means the arrest, detention or abduction of persons by, or with the authorization, support or acquiescence of, a State or a political organization, followed by a refusal to acknowledge that deprivation of freedom or to give information on the fate or whereabouts of those persons, with the intention of removing them from the protection of the law for a prolonged period of time.

An almost identical human rights definition of enforced disappearance is contained in Art II of the Inter-American Convention on Forced Disappearance of Persons. The 2006 International Convention for the Protection of All Persons against Enforced Disappearance defines this human rights violation in Article 2 similarly, as:

the arrest, detention, abduction or any other form of deprivation of liberty by agents of the State or by persons or groups of persons acting with the authorization, support or acquiescence of the State, followed by a refusal to acknowledge the deprivation of liberty or by concealment of the fate or whereabouts of the disappeared person, which place such a person outside the protection of the law.

The main difference between the two definitions is the fact that, whereas under the Rome Statute non-state actors constituting a political organization can be criminally responsible, the International Convention for the Protection of All Persons against Enforced Disappearance is binding upon states and their organs only.

It follows that, from a human rights perspective, enforced disappearance has four components: (1) deprivation of a person's liberty; (2) by state agents such as the police, the armed forces or intelligence services, or by private actors with the acquiescence of state agents; (3) a subsequent refusal to inform the victim's relatives or anybody else of the deprivation of liberty. This act of secrecy and deceit is inherent to the nature of enforced disappearance, making the victim particularly

---

[128] See, for example, the report of the Working Group on Enforced and Involuntary Disappearances of 10 January 2008, UN Doc A/HRC/7/2, paras 27–420 and Annex III. The number of cases under active consideration at the end of 2007 stood at 41,257 and concerned 78 states.

vulnerable; as a consequence thereof, the victim (4) cannot seek the protection of due process guarantees, as his or her disappearance has effectively removed him or her from the protection of the law, and in particular from any effective remedy.

This human rights violation which is by definition clandestine constitutes a dual assault on human integrity. On the one hand, it completely removes the missing persons, who generally live in constant fear of death and torture, from human rights protection. On the other, it places their relatives, who are entirely in the dark about the fate of the disappeared person, under extremely severe mental stress. It may also create serious economic problems for families where the disappeared person was the breadwinner. Furthermore, relatives often suffer other disadvantages (eg under the law of succession, family law, and social insurance law) because it remains unclear whether or not the disappeared person is deceased.

2. Enforced disappearance under general human rights law

None of the general human rights conventions contain a specific prohibition of enforced disappearance of persons. However, as is evidenced by international jurisprudence, it violates a number of existing human rights of both the disappeared persons and their relatives.

Issue in focus: Disappearances as composite human rights violation in the case law of the Human Rights Committee

In its views in *Jegatheeswara Sarma v Sri Lanka*,[129] the Human Rights Committee spelt out in general terms which rights of which persons are violated or threatened by the practice of enforced disappearance:

9.3 Any act of such disappearance constitutes a violation of many of the rights enshrined in the Covenant, including the right to liberty and security of person (article 9), the right not to be subjected to torture or to cruel, inhuman or degrading treatment or punishment (article 7), and the right of all persons deprived of their liberty to be treated with humanity and with respect for the inherent dignity of the human person (article 10). It also violates or constitutes a grave threat to the right to life (article 6).

9.4 The facts of the present case clearly illustrate the applicability of article 9 of the Covenant concerning liberty and security of the person. The State party has itself acknowledged that the arrest of the author's son was illegal and a prohibited activity. Not only was there no legal basis for his arrest, there evidently was none for the continuing detention. Such a gross violation of article 9 can never be justified . . .

9.5 As to the alleged violation of article 7, the Committee recognizes the degree of suffering involved in being held indefinitely without any contact with the outside world, and observes that, in the present case, the author appears to have accidentally seen his son some 15 months

---

[129] HRCttee, *Jegatheeswara Sarma v Sri Lanka*, Communication No 950/2000 (2003). For earlier references, see also *Quinteros Almeida and Mother v Uruguay*, Communication No 107/1981 (1983), and General Comment No 6 (1982), para 4.

after the initial detention. He must, accordingly, be considered a victim of a violation of article 7. Moreover, noting the anguish and stress caused to the author's family by the disappearance of his son and by the continuing uncertainty concerning his fate and whereabouts, the Committee considers that the author and his wife are also victims of violation of article 7 of the Covenant. The Committee is therefore of the opinion that the facts before it reveal a violation of article 7 of the Covenant both with regard to the author's son and with regard to the author's family.

9.6 As to the possible violation of article 6 of the Covenant, the Committee notes that the author has not asked the Committee to conclude that his son is dead. Moreover, while invoking article 6, the author also asks for the release of his son, indicating that he has not abandoned hope for his son's reappearance. The Committee considers that, in such circumstances, it is not for it to appear to presume the death of the author's son. Insofar as the State party's obligations... would be the same with or without such a finding, the Committee considers it appropriate in the present case not to make any finding in respect of article 6.

In the case of *Grioua v Algeria*,[130] the Human Rights Committee pointed out that 'intentionally removing a person from the protection of the law for a prolonged period of time may constitute a refusal to recognize that person before the law if the victim was in the hands of the State authorities when last seen and, at the same time, if the efforts of his or her relatives to obtain access to potentially effective remedies, including judicial remedies (Covenant, Article 2, paragraph 3) have been systematically impeded. In such situations, disappeared persons are in practice deprived of their capacity to exercise entitlements under law, including all their other rights under the Covenant, and of access to any possible remedy as a direct consequence of the actions of the State, which must be interpreted as a refusal to recognize such victims as persons before the law' (ICCPR, Article 16).

Thus, according to the Committee's jurisprudence, the following guarantees are breached by the practice of enforced disappearance: the right to liberty and security of person; the prohibition of torture and inhuman treatment *vis-à-vis* missing persons and their relatives; the right to humane conditions of detention; the right to life where the killing of the disappeared person by state agents can be proved or where on confirmation of the person's death no adequate investigation was conducted; and the right to be recognized as a person before the law, provided access to remedies was systematically impeded.

A nearly[131] identical approach is adopted by the Inter-American Court of Human Rights.[132] The jurisprudence of the European Court of Human Rights

---

[130] HRCttee, *Grioua v Algeria*, Communication No 1327/2004 (2007), para 7.8.

[131] In contrast to the HRCttee, the IACtHR consistently denies the violation of the right to recognition as a person before the law in cases of enforced disappearance, see *La Cantuta v Peru*, Series C, No 162, (2006), paras 118 ff.

[132] See, for example, IACtHR, *Velásquez-Rodríguez v Honduras*, Series C, No 4 (1988), *Humberto Sánchez v Honduras*, Series C, No 99 (2003), and *Villagrán-Morales et al v Guatemala*, Series C, No 63 (1999), concerning the disappearance of street children, and *Blanco Romero et al v Venezuela*, Series C, No 138 (2005), and, for a detailed analysis, IACmHR, *Pasache Vidal et al v Peru*, Report No 101/01, Case 10.247 (2001). With regard to African jurisprudence, see, for example, ACmHPR, *Mouvement Burkinabé des Droits de l'Homme et des Peuples v Burkina*

seems more restrictive and less inclined to do full justice to the multiple character of the human rights violations involved insofar as it only treats enforced disappearance as a violation of ECHR, Article 3 *vis-à-vis* the disappeared person[133]
if it can be proved 'beyond reasonable doubt', ie on the basis of concrete evidence,
that the victim was actually ill-treated during his or her detention.[134] Otherwise,
its approach is similar to that of the other monitoring bodies. For instance, the
Court characterizes enforced disappearance as a gross violation of a person's right
to liberty and security under ECHR, Article 5 and requires states to investigate the
fate of missing persons.[135] The Court holds, like the Human Rights Committee,
that the prohibition of torture and inhuman treatment under ECHR, Article 3
is also violated *vis-à-vis* the relatives of the disappeared person.[136] If the corpse of
the disappeared person is found, it generally assumes that a violation of the right
to life has occurred.[137] If no body is found, concrete evidence must be adduced in
the individual case or in a specific general situation[138] to demonstrate that a person has died and that the state may be held responsible.[139] However, the rigidity

Faso, Communication No 204/1997 (2001), paras 41 ff, and *Zegveld and Ephrem v Eritrea,*
Communication No 250/2002 (2003), paras 46 ff.

[133] See, eg, ECtHR, *Orhan v Turkey,* Application No 25656/94 (2002), paras 353–354.

[134] Eg, ECtHR, *Aktaş v Turkey, Reports* 2003-V, paras 314 ff, where the autopsy provided clear
evidence of acts of torture. See also *Aziyevy v Russia,* Application No 77626/01 (2008), paras 99 ff,
and *Alikhadzhiyeva v Russia,* Application No 68007/01 (2007), paras 76 ff.

[135] See, eg, ECtHR (Grand Chamber), *Çakici v Turkey, Reports* 1999-IV, para 104.

[136] See, eg, ECtHR, *Kurt v Turkey, Reports* 1998-III, para 134. It qualified this principle, however, in the following judgments: *Çakici v Turkey* (Grand Chamber), *Reports* 1999-IV, para 98,
Timurtas v Turkey, Reports 2000-VI, paras 95 ff, and *Orhan v Turkey,* Application No 25656/94
(2002), paras 358 ff.

[137] Eg, ECtHR, *Aktaş v Turkey, Reports* 2003-V, para 292.

[138] This is the case for Chechnya. See amongst many *Aziyevy v Russia,* Application No 77626/01
(2008), para 76: 'The Court notes with great concern that a number of cases have come before it
which suggest that the phenomenon of 'disappearances' is well known in Chechnya...A number
of international reports point to the same conclusion. The Court agrees with the applicants that,
in the context of the conflict in Chechnya, when a person is detained by unidentified servicemen
without any subsequent acknowledgment of the detention, this can be regarded as life-threatening.
The absence of Lom-Ali and Umar-Ali Aziyev or of any news of them for over seven years supports
this assumption. For the above reasons the Court considers that it has been established beyond
reasonable doubt that Lom-Ali and Umar-Ali Aziyev must be presumed dead following their
unacknowledged detention by State servicemen.'

[139] As clearly stated in ECtHR, *Tas v Turkey,* Application No 24396/94 (2000), para 63:
'Whether the failure on the part of the authorities to provide a plausible explanation as to a detainee's fate, in the absence of a body, might also raise issues under Article 2 of the Convention depends
on all circumstances of the case, and in particular on the existence of sufficient circumstantial
evidence, based on concrete elements, from which it may be concluded to the requisite standard of
proof that the detainee must be presumed to have died in custody.' In its more recent jurisprudence,
the Court therefore concluded on a number of occasions that even where no body was found the
disappeared person was dead and consequently the right to life had been violated. It took into
account, in particular, the time that had elapsed since the person's disappearance as an important though not decisive element. In cases against Turkey brought by relatives of persons disappeared in the context of operations against Kurdish groups, the Court also took into consideration
the general situation in the Kurdish areas of south-eastern Turkey. Where a person was wanted
for political activities on behalf of the Kurdistan Workers Party (PKK), the ECtHR took this as

of this standard is partly mitigated by the fact that the Court generally infers from the right to life an obligation on states to investigate unexplained deaths in the event of enforced disappearance of persons.[140]

3. Obligations under the Convention for the Protection of All Persons Against Enforced Disappearances

After many years of preparatory work by the former Commission on Human Rights, the Human Rights Council, at its very first session in June 2006, was able to finalize the work on an International Convention for the Protection of All Persons against Enforced Disappearances. The Convention, of which the main content has been described above,[141] was subsequently adopted by the UN General Assembly in December 2006. Its purpose is not primarily to bridge gaps in substantive law but rather to toughen and expand states' obligations to act against a practice that is manifestly contrary to human rights. Accordingly, the Convention contains a range of specific and detailed obligations: to take measures to make such acts punishable under domestic criminal law and to investigate, prosecute, punish, or extradite the offender (Articles 3 to 14, 25); to assist and rehabilitate victims (Articles 15, 24); not to 'expel, return ("refouler"), surrender or extradite a person to another state where there are substantial grounds for believing that he or she would be in danger of being subjected to enforced disappearance' (Article 16); and to take specific legal and administrative measures (eg keeping registers of detainees, respecting the right to information) to ensure no one can be held in secret detention (Articles 17–23). Some of these obligations are not new. The duties to investigate or to rehabilitate, for example, can already be inferred from the general obligation to provide victims with an effective remedy in the ICCPR and the regional conventions.

strong evidence that a disappeared person was dead. See for example ECtHR, *Özdemir v Turkey*, Application No 54169/00 (2007), paras 45 ff.

[140] ECtHR in *Tas v Turkey*, Application No 24396/94 (2000), paras 71–2 and 76; *Aktaş v Turkey*, Reports 2003-V, para 307; *Orhan v Turkey*, Application No 25656/94 (2002), para 348; *Timurtas v Turkey*, Reports 2000-VI, para 90; *Mahmut Kaya v Turkey*, Reports 2000-III, para 108.

[141] See Chapter 2, section II.2.b.i.

11

Protection of Human Identity:
Prohibition of Discrimination, and
Protection of Minorities

Relevant provisions: UDHR, Article 2; ICESCR, Article 2(2) and Article 3; ICCPR, Article 2(1), Article 3, Articles 26 and 27; CERD; CEDAW; CRC, Article 2; CRPD, Articles 3–6; ACHR, Article 24; ACHPR, Articles 2 and 3; ECHR, Article 14; P 12/ECHR; European Framework Convention for the Protection of National Minorities; European Charter for Regional or Minority Languages; international humanitarian law, for example: Article 3 common to GCs I–IV, GC I, Articles 12 and 31, GC II, Article 12, GC III, Article 16, GC IV, Articles 13 and 27, AP I, Articles 9, 75 and 85(4)(c); AP II, Article 2(2); ILO Discrimination (Employment and Occupation) Convention, 1958 (No 111); ILO Indigenous and Tribal Peoples Convention, 1989 (No 169).

I. Overview

1. What is discrimination?

The temptation to treat people unfairly because of their 'otherness' is an inherent characteristic of human nature. In all cultures people have been socially ostracized, banished, or persecuted on account of their religion, race, ethnic origin, sex or for other similar reasons. The fact that the rights guaranteed by states must be enjoyed by all human beings in equal measure is therefore a principle that constantly needs to be championed and defended. This is expressly recognized by the UN Charter, which states in Article 1(3) that one of the main functions of the United Nations consists in 'promoting and encouraging respect for human rights and for fundamental freedoms for all without distinction as to race, sex, language, or religion'. The non-discrimination principle is in effect one of the cornerstones of international human rights protection. It protects persons who, solely on account of their membership of a particular group or of specific innate characteristics, are subjected to exclusion, prejudice or hatred and treated as second-class human beings.

At its core, discrimination is treating differently, without an objective and reasonable justification, persons in similar situations.[1] More specifically, the concept of discrimination under international law denotes specific cases of unequal treatment that have the purpose or effect of making adverse distinctions on the grounds of race, sex, birth, ethnic origin, religion, political opinion, or other similar reasons, ie distinctions that are based on characteristics which constitute a (virtually) indispensable component of a person's identity. In all cases, unfavourable treatment on the basis of such characteristics constitutes a negative statement regarding attributes of individuals that are either unalterable or can only be changed at the cost of their dignity.

This close link with the identity of an individual and his or her dignity is relevant for all grounds of discrimination. What we are depends to a large extent on our gender, religion, ethnic origin, or language; these characteristics define each individual. We are neither able, nor can it be reasonably expected from us, to renounce what makes us unique as a person. It is therefore an assault on human dignity if we are unfavourably treated not on account of our behaviour, but on account of characteristics we possess as human beings.

Violations of this kind are highly relevant to human rights. As emphasized by the social philosopher Charles Taylor, '. . . our identity is partly shaped by recognition or its absence, often by the *mis*recognition of others, and so a person or group of people can suffer real damage, real distortion, if the people or society around them mirror back to them a confining or demeaning or contemptible picture of themselves. Non-recognition or misrecognition can inflict harm, can be a form of oppression, imprisoning someone in a false, distorted, and reduced mode of being.'[2]

International law conceptualizes discrimination as unjustified debasement of individuals on the grounds of identity-related characteristics and embodies several approaches and categories of prohibitions to discriminate.

2. Typology of prohibitions of discrimination

(a) Starting point: equality before the law and equal protection of the law

The principle of equality before the law and equal protection of the law constitutes the starting point for conceptualizing non-discrimination. The idea that human beings should not be treated unfavourably because of their race, ethnic origin, sex, religion, social origin, etc, but dealt with *on an equal footing with others* irrespective of these characteristics is fundamental to the principle of non-discrimination.

Equality of legal treatment is an essential feature of any political and legal system based on the rule of law. Accordingly, the Aristotelian maxims of 'treating

---

[1] ECtHR, *Willis v The United Kingdom*, *Reports* 2002-IV, para 48.
[2] Charles Taylor and Amy Gutmann (eds), *Multiculturalism and 'The Politics of Recognition'* (Princeton University Press: Princeton, 1992), 13 f.

equals equally' (equalizing justice) and 'to each his or her due' (distributive just-ice) are fundamental to the concept of justice. The solution is not absolute equality of treatment, but rather treatment that fairly reflects the factual circumstances. Broadly speaking, it is prohibited to make legal distinctions in similar circum-stances that are not based on any objective grounds and for which no reasonable ground is discernible (equal treatment precept). Furthermore, it is inadmissible to place on the same footing factual circumstances that are essentially different that require differentiated treatment (differentiation precept).

A general precept of equal treatment is set out in the first sentence of ICCPR, Article 26 and in similar terms in ACHR, Article 24, ACHPR, Article 3 and ArCHR, Article 11: 'All persons are equal before the law and are entitled . . . to the equal protection of the law.' Equality *before* the law means the right to the same interpretation and application of the law as all others (equal application of the law), and equal protection *of* the law is the right to be treated equally by the laws, ie the right to provisions whose substance is formulated in equal terms (equality in legislation).

Issue in focus: Equality before the law and
the prohibition of arbitrariness

The entitlement to equal application of the law in accordance with the first sentence of ICCPR, Article 26 is violated when, without objectively justifiable grounds, similar cases are treated unequally or circumstances requiring differential treatment are dealt with in the same way. The principle of equality in the application of the law also entails a general entitlement to non-arbitrary application of domestic legislation. As stressed by the Human Rights Committee, 'an individual may be deprived of his right to equality before the law if a provision of law is applied to him or her in arbitrary fashion, such that an application of law to an individual's detriment is not based on reasonable and objective grounds'.[3]

The entitlement to non-arbitrary application of the law is a free-standing entitlement and not just an accessory right.[4] As is the case for the prohibition of discrimination in ICCPR, Article 26, the non-arbitrary application of the law is applicable not only to the areas covered by the Covenant's other substantive guarantees, but also to issues that are not regulated by the ICCPR. The Human Rights Committee therefore considered, for example, whether Estonia's refusal to grant citizenship to a former Soviet army officer ought to be deemed arbitrary even though the ICCPR, as for all other human rights treaties, contains no provision regarding the right to obtain citizenship. The Committee considered:

In the present case, the State party has invoked national security, a ground provided for by law, for its refusal to grant citizenship to the author in the light of particular personal circumstances . . . While the Committee recognizes that the Covenant explicitly permits, in

---

[3] HRCttee, *Borzov v Estonia*, Communication No 1136/2002 (2004), para 7.2, and *Tsarjov v Estonia* Communication No 1223/2003 (2007), para 7.3.
[4] On this distinction, see below section II.1.

certain circumstances, considerations of national security to be invoked as a justification for certain actions on the part of a State party, the Committee emphasizes that invocation of national security on the part of a State party does not, ipso facto, remove an issue wholly from the Committee's scrutiny...While the Committee cannot leave it to the unfettered discretion of a State party whether reasons related to national security existed in an individual case, it recognizes that its own role in reviewing the existence and relevance of such considerations will depend on the circumstances of the case and the relevant provision of the Covenant. Whereas articles 19, 21 and 22 of the Covenant establish a criterion of necessity in respect of restrictions based on national security, the criteria applicable under article 26 are more general in nature, requiring reasonable and objective justification and a legitimate aim for distinctions that relate to an individual's characteristics enumerated in article 26, including 'other status'. The Committee accepts that considerations related to national security may serve a legitimate aim in the exercise of a State party's sovereignty in the granting of its citizenship, at least where a newly independent state invokes national security concerns related to its earlier status.[5]

(b) *The nexus between equal treatment and non-discrimination*

The principle of equality before the law leaves open the question of what criteria should be applied to determine whether two sets of circumstances are equal. Views as to what constitutes equality or inequality often differ according to place, time and social attitudes and often involve value judgments of an *ad hoc* nature. On the other hand, prohibitions of discrimination reflect a consensus on the criteria that may not be invoked to justify unequal treatment.

Prohibitions of discrimination are rather frequent in international law. As mentioned at the outset, the UN Charter embodies the principle of promoting and encouraging respect for human rights without distinction as to 'race, sex, language, or religion'.[6] Similarly, most universal and regional human rights treaties require states parties to give effect to the rights contained in the respective treaty 'without distinction of any kind, such as race, colour, sex, language, religion, political or other opinion, national or social origin, property, birth or other status'.[7] A violation of these so-called *accessory* prohibitions of discrimination occurs where people are denied full enjoyment of a human right guaranteed by a particular convention on account of one of these grounds. Such an example would be the restriction of the freedom of expression or religion solely due to the person in question belonging to a particular race or religious group. It follows that accessory prohibitions can be invoked only in conjunction with the application of specific human rights guarantees. These grounds are to be distinguished from *autonomous* prohibitions of discrimination, which offer protection against adverse distinctions on one of the enumerated grounds by any state act, ie also in areas where specific human rights afford no protection.[8] The

---

[5] HRCttee, *Borzov v Estonia*, Communication No 1136/2002 (2004), paras 7.2 f.
[6] UN Charter, Art 1(2); see also UN Charter, Art 13(1)(b) and Art 55(c).
[7] ICCPR, Art 2(1); similarly ICCPR, Art 2(2), Convention on the Rights of the Child, Art 2(2), ECHR, Art 14, ACHR, Art 1, ACHPR, Art 2, and ArCHR, Art 3(1).
[8] For more detail, see below section II.1.

second sentence of Article 26 of the ICCPR is the only provision of a universal treaty that affords this form of autonomous all-embracing protection against discrimination. On a regional level, the AP 12/ECHR offers autonomous protection against discrimination.

A distinction must also be made between the general and *group specific* prohibitions of discrimination applicable to particular categories of persons. They include, in particular, guarantees embodied in the International Convention on the Elimination of All Forms of Racial Discrimination of 1966,[9] the Convention on the Elimination of All Forms of Discrimination against Women of 1979,[10] and the Convention on the Rights of Persons with Disabilities of 2006. Other instruments, especially the International Labour Organization conventions, are designed to protect workers against discrimination.[11]

3. Protection of minorities as collective protection against discrimination

Prohibitions of discrimination in international human rights instruments are formulated as individual rights—even though people are often subjected to unfavourable or even demeaning treatment due to their belonging to a particular *group*—whether it be religious, racial or ethnic. However, historical experience shows that a strictly individualistic perspective is often inadequate when it comes to affording effective protection against marginalization and oppression to ethnic, religious, linguistic, and other similar minorities. Protection of minorities under international law is therefore conceptually closely linked to protection against discrimination.

Alongside the right of peoples to self-determination, which is embodied in Article 1 of the two UN Human Rights Covenants but has no status as an individual human right,[12] international law has adopted three different approaches to the protection of minorities. On the individual level, members of ethnic, religious, or linguistic minorities have a right to enjoy their own culture, to profess and practise their own religion, and to use their own language with other members of their group (ICCPR, Article 27). On the collective level, there are regional instruments for the protection of national minorities and minority languages adopted by the Council of Europe in 1995 and 1992 respectively. Finally, at the global level, international law has begun to protect indigenous peoples, with the International Labour Organization's Indigenous and Tribal Peoples Convention (No 169) and the 2007 United Nations Declaration on the Rights of Indigenous Peoples playing a particularly important role in conceptual terms.

---

[9] See below section IV.   [10] See below section III.
[11] For example, the following ILO Conventions: Equal Remuneration Convention, 1951 (No 100); Discrimination (Employment and Occupation) Convention, 1958 (No 111); Workers with Family Responsibilities Convention, 1981 (No 156); and Maternity Protection Convention, 2000 (No 183).
[12] HRCttee, *Kitok v Sweden*, 197/1985 (1988), para 6.3.

II. General Prohibitions of Discrimination

1. Accessory and autonomous prohibitions of discrimination

As already stated, *accessory prohibitions of discrimination* can be invoked only in conjunction with the substantive guarantees set out in the relevant treaties. For instance, ICCPR, Article 2(1) prohibits the discriminatory application of civil and political rights on grounds of 'race, colour, sex, language, religion, political or other opinion, national or social origin, property, birth or other status'. Similar provisions are contained in ICESCR, Article 2(2); CRC, Article 2; ACHR, Article 1; ACHPR. Article 2; ArCHR, Article 3; and ECHR, Article 14. According to the jurisprudence of the European Court of Human Rights, the accessory prohibition of discrimination in ECHR, Article 14 can be invoked where a person suffers discrimination in an area directly protected by a substantive guarantee of the ECHR. In addition, where domestic law expands the scope of application of a right embodied in the ECHR beyond that guaranteed by the Convention, individuals are entitled to invoke Article 14 even if the discrimination does not infringe the right in question but touches upon the wider ambit of the national law guarantees.[13] As French law generally allows single persons to adopt a child, the Court concluded that to refuse a lesbian candidate the right to enter the adoption procedure was a violation of Article 14, although the Court expressly left the question open as to whether a right to adopt was protected by ECHR, Article 8.[14] In a subsequent judgment, the Court held that the right to property did not give a right to acquire property, but that where a state provided a social security system with certain entitlements, ECHR, Article 14 could be invoked in conjunction with the right to property to claim that the system was discriminatory.[15]

Prohibitions of accessory discrimination are violated not only where a violation of a human rights guarantee is exclusively affecting persons who possess one of the enumerated characteristics (eg a prohibition of acts of worship affecting only members of one particular belief), but also where an interference would be permissible *per se* but is only applied to such persons (eg prohibition of a demonstration owing to the objective risk of violent clashes directed solely against members of an ethnic minority and not everyone likely to resort to violence).

---

[13] ECtHR (Grand Chamber), *EB v France*, Application No 43546/02 (2008), para 48: 'The prohibition of discrimination enshrined in Article 14 thus extends beyond the enjoyment of the rights and freedoms which the Convention and the Protocols thereto require each State to guarantee. It applies also to those additional rights, falling within the general scope of any Convention Article, for which the State has voluntarily decided to provide.'

[14] ECtHR (Grand Chamber), *EB v France*, Application No 43546/02 (2008), paras 49 ff.

[15] ECtHR (Chamber) *Stec and Others v The United Kingdom*, Application Nos 65731/01 and 65900/01 (2006), para 51.

Example: The ECtHR case relating to certain aspects of
the laws of the use of languages in education in Belgium[16]

The language of education in public schools in Belgium was determined by their
location in districts belonging to one of the two linguistic groups. French-language
schools, however, were permitted in six Flemish-speaking districts on the periphery
of Brussels. These schools had been granted special status on account of the
relatively large number of French-speaking inhabitants. Enrolment in the schools
was restricted, however, to children whose (French-speaking) parents lived in the six
districts concerned, while Flemish-language schools in the same districts admitted
children irrespective of their parents' place of residence or of their mother tongue.

The Court held that it is justifiable to give preference to minority languages in
education and that P 1/ECHR, Article 2 (right to education) '...does not require
of States that they should, in the sphere of education or teaching, respect parents'
linguistic preferences...'. However, where a contracting party provides the possibility
of enrolment in schools offering mother-tongue instruction although it is not required
to do so by the provisions of the ECHR, it must secure access to all persons on the
same conditions. That had not been done in the case before the Court. The place
of residence requirement was applicable only to the children of French-speaking
parents in the Flemish-speaking part of Belgium, and not to the children of Flemish-
speaking parents in the French linguistic region. On that ground, the Court held
that there had been a violation of P1/ECHR, Article 2 read in conjunction with
ECHR, Article 14.

In addition to the possibility of invoking ICCPR, Article 26 in conjunction with
other Covenant guarantees, the article contains an *autonomous prohibition of discrimination*, which, as the Committee on Human Rights has maintained since
the *Zwaan-de Vries* case,[17] requires states to refrain from practising discrimination in the enactment or application of the law, even in areas where protection
is not afforded by the Covenant. This means that substantial areas of state action
are open to human rights supervision by way of the prohibition of discrimination, which are not protected by the ICCPR but instead are considered economic, social and cultural rights, as well as areas falling entirely outside the scope
of human rights protection.

Example: Gender discrimination in unemployment law—the views of
the HRCttee in *Zwaan-de Vries v the Netherlands*[18]

Ms. Zwaan-de Vries became unemployed and consequently received unemployment
benefits for ten months. An application for further benefits was refused because

---

[16] ECtHR, *Case relating to certain aspects of the laws of the use of languages in education in Belgium*,
Series A, No 6 (1968) (the *Belgian Linguistics Case*).
[17] HRCttee, *Zwaan-de Vries v The Netherlands*, Communication No 182/1984 (1987).
[18] Ibid.

Ms. Zwaan-de Vries failed to meet the condition according to which married women had to prove that they were their family's breadwinner, a condition that married men were not required to fulfil. Ms. Zwaan-de Vries contended that this amounted to a violation of ICCPR, Article 26. The Dutch Government argued, *inter alia*, that the ICCPR was not applicable inasmuch as a right to social security was embodied only in the ICESCR (Article 9).

The Human Rights Committee rejected this argument on the ground that Article 26 does not merely reproduce the accessory prohibition of discrimination contained in Article 2 of the Covenant; rather, it concerns obligations states parties have to respect whenever they enact and apply their laws. The ICCPR does not require the enactment of legislation providing for social security, but if a state enacts such legislation it must ensure that it is non-discriminatory. In the case before the Committee, there were no reasonable grounds for treating married women less favourably than married men. It followed that the legal requirement for women but not for men to prove their status as breadwinners constituted a violation, based on sex, of the prohibition of discrimination contained in Article 26.

2. The prohibition of direct discrimination

Discrimination, whether autonomous or accessory, can be either direct or indirect.[19] *Direct discrimination* always occurs where an adverse distinction in legislation or in the application of a basically non-discriminatory law is directly related to one of the prohibited grounds of distinction without adequate objective justification.

This notion shows that not all distinctions subjectively perceived by the person concerned as victimization constitute discrimination in the legal sense. Rather, the following four conditions must be *cumulatively* met for direct discrimination in the legal sense to occur:

(1) *Unequal treatment*: The concept of discrimination implies primarily the existence of unequal treatment in the sense of the presence of distinctions, limitations, exclusions or preferences. To determine whether disparate treatment exists, one has to examine whether comparable situations, ie situations being similar in aspects that are relevant for the decision, have been treated differently.

(2) *Unfavourable treatment*: The concept of discrimination further implies that the individuals or groups concerned are experiencing a disadvantage compared with other individuals or groups in similar situations. The manner in which the unfavourable treatment occurs is irrelevant, ie whether it involves a distinction, exclusion, limitation, punishment, preferential treatment of the other group, or some other element. The unfavourable treatment must be the purpose or the effect of the distinction. It follows that the existence of a

---

[19] On indirect discrimination, see below section II.3.

discriminatory intent is not a necessary element of discrimination, which can occur where the outcome is discriminatory although nobody actually wanted to discriminate.

(3) *Based on a suspect classification*: Discrimination consists essentially of adverse distinctions on the basis of a characteristic that is not intrinsically negative but forms part of a person's identity. The characteristics enumerated in the provisions regarding discrimination are called *prohibited grounds* or *suspect classifications* because they should not serve as a basis for making distinctions. The list of suspect classifications cannot be determined exhaustively on an abstract level but must be established on the basis of the specific convention in question. While the various provisions prohibiting discrimination contain different lists of such grounds, there is a solid core that includes race or colour; ethnic or national origin or membership of a national minority; sex; religion; language; social origin or birth; and political conviction. The reference to prohibited distinctions based on 'other status' in most provisions makes it clear that the list is not exhaustive and can be extended by jurisprudence to include characteristics—such as age or disability—that are structurally similar to the enumerated grounds because they are an essential component of a person's identity and cannot be relinquished. Prohibitions of discrimination usually evolve in reaction to historical experience of the marginalization of particular groups, and it is conceivable that awareness of new forms of marginalization will develop over the course of time.

(4) *Without justification*: Adverse distinctions based on any of these grounds create a *presumption* that such treatment constitutes a form of debasement. This is why they are 'suspect' when used for purposes of classification but not automatically prohibited. Yet discrimination can be held to have occurred only where unequal treatment cannot be justified on legitimate grounds. The lack of a sufficient justification for the distinction confirms that debasement is the purpose or effect. Conversely, debasement or discrimination cannot occur where an adverse distinction may be justified on serious and objective grounds. It follows that there is no such thing as 'justified discrimination'; rather, a distinction is either justified or it constitutes discrimination because a valid justification is absent. But when are distinctions justifiable even though they are based on a suspect characteristic? According to a standard formula used by the Human Rights Committee, 'not every distinction constitutes discrimination, in violation of article 26, but that distinctions must be justified on reasonable and objective grounds, in pursuit of an aim that is legitimate under the Covenant'.[20] Essentially, this implies that the question

---

[20] For example, HRCttee, *Love et al v Australia*, Communication No 983/2001 (2003), para 8.2. The ECtHR adopts a three-step approach to the examination of cases of accessory discrimination. As a first step, it examines whether comparable situations have been treated differently. It next examines whether the distinction made has any objective and reasonable justification.

to be examined is whether the distinction *can be justified because it (i) pursues legitimate aims and (ii) is proportionate, ie suitable, necessary and reasonable to achieve that aim.* Where the answer is in the affirmative, the distinction, despite appearances to the contrary, is not really being made on account of a prohibited characteristic but instead on another legitimate ground.

Issue in focus: The jurisprudence of the HRCttee on the prohibition of direct discrimination

---

In the *Karakurt v Austria* case, the Committee held that differential treatment of foreigners from the EU and other states was not prohibited provided that preferential treatment was accorded under international agreements on free movement of persons and was therefore justifiable. However, such justification could not be inferred automatically but had to be examined in light of the issue involved. Thus, due to the lack of a genuine link between the issue of freedom of movement and the question of who could best represent workers' interests, there were insufficient grounds to justify restricting the right to stand for election to a company's work-council to the country's own nationals and to nationals of EU states.[21]

In the *Love v Australia* case, the Committee concluded that differences in the mandatory retirement age could amount to discrimination on the basis of age. Although age was not one of the characteristics mentioned in Article 26, it was covered by the term 'other status' within the meaning of the article. In the case of pilots, however, important grounds (especially considerations of flight safety) could be invoked to justify an earlier retirement age.[22]

Addressing the question of differential treatment of couples, the Committee emphasized in *Young v Australia* and *X v Colombia* that cohabiting couples need not be treated on an equal footing with married couples, since the decision not to enter into marriage reflects the free choice of the partners concerned. However, where a state grants cohabiting partners certain rights (in the cases in point, pension benefits for the surviving partner), it must also grant them to same-sex couples in order to avoid discrimination on the basis of sexual orientation.[23]

In *Haraldsson and Sveinsson v Iceland* the Committee ruled a fishing-quotas system to be discriminatory as it allowed owners of quotas received for free in the

---

As a final step, it examines whether there is a relationship of proportionality between the means employed and the aim sought. It follows that the decisive element in determining the permissibility of a distinction is whether the aim pursued by the distinction can be justified and whether the means employed to achieve the aim are suitable, necessary and reasonable, ie proportionate. See, for example, ECtHR, *Case relating to certain aspects of the laws of the use of languages in education in Belgium*, Series A, No 6 (1968), para 10. Similarly, ECtHR (Grand Chamber), *Stec and Others v The United Kingdom*, Application Nos 65731/01 and 65900/01 (2006), para 51.

[21] HRCttee, *Karakurt v Austria*, Communication No 965/2000 (2002), para 8.4: '...no general rule can be drawn therefrom to the effect that such an agreement in itself constitutes a sufficient ground with regard to the requirements of article 26 of the Covenant. Rather, it is necessary to judge every case on its own facts.'

[22] HRCttee, *Love et al v Australia*, Communication No 983/2001 (2003), para 8.2 ff.

[23] HRCttee, *Young v Australia*, Communication No 941/2000 (2003), para 10.4, and *X v Colombia*, Communication No 1361/2005 (2007), para 7.2.

mid-1980s to sell them at market-value to fishermen who had entered the business at a later stage. It noted 'that every quota system introduced to regulate access to limited resources privileges, to some extent, the holders of such quotas and disadvantages others without necessarily being discriminatory' but underscored 'the specificities of the present case: On the one hand, the first Article of the Fisheries Management Act No 38/1990 states that the fishing banks around Iceland are common property of the Icelandic nation. On the other hand, the distinction based on the activity during the reference period which initially, as a temporary measure, may have been a reasonable and objective criterion, became not only permanent with the adoption of the Act but transformed original rights to use and exploit a public property into individual property: Allocated quotas no longer used by their original holders can be sold or leased at market prices instead of reverting to the State for allocation to new quota holders in accordance with fair and equitable criteria. The State party has not shown that this particular design and modalities of implementation of the quota system meets the requirement of reasonableness.'[24]

The principle of non-discrimination requires states not only to refrain from making adverse distinctions based on a prohibited characteristic, but also to take action against traditional patterns of discrimination in the private sphere and against the *de facto* disadvantages suffered by certain population groups.[25] This dimension of the obligation is set out in clear terms in common Article 3 of the Covenants, which requires states parties '*to ensure* the equal right of men and women to the enjoyment of all . . . rights set forth in the present Covenant'. To date, however, the jurisprudence of the Human Rights Committee and of the regional Courts regarding the substance of these positive aspects of the obligation remains vague. Nevertheless, it is accepted that temporary affirmative measures aimed at achieving *de facto* equality for socially marginalized or otherwise disadvantaged groups *vis-à-vis* the rest of the population do not constitute discrimination but, provided they are applied proportionately, represent legitimate distinctions.[26] Thus, the European Court of Human Rights has stressed that Article 14 of the ECHR 'does not prohibit a member State from treating groups differently in order to correct "factual inequalities" between them; indeed in certain circumstances a failure to attempt to correct inequality through different treatment may in itself give rise to a breach of the Article'.[27]

---

[24] HRCttee, *Haraldsson and Sveinsson v Iceland*, Communication No 1306/2004 (2007), para 12.4.

[25] See CtteeESCR, General Comment No 16 (2005), para 18, and HRCttee, General Comments Nos 28 (2000), paras 3 ff, and 18 (1989), para 5.

[26] CtteeHSC, General Comment No 16 (2005), para 15, and ECtHR (Chamber) *Stec and Others v The United Kingdom*, Application Nos 65731/01 and 65900/01 (2006), paras 60 ff.

[27] ECtHR (Grand Chamber), *DH v Czech Republic*, Application No 57325/00 (2007), para 175.

3. Indirect discrimination

Laws or their application may result in distinctions that, though unrelated to any prohibited grounds, in practice have detrimental effects that exclusively or at least disproportionately affect people with such characteristics. Although a law that restricts certain entitlements to persons who are liable to military service is not based on the prohibited ground of gender, in states where only men are required to perform military service it categorically excludes women from the enjoyment of the respective entitlements. In such cases, the ostensibly neutral criterion of liability to military service is applied in a manner that automatically disadvantages *all* women. Overcoming this form of discrimination requires finding other reasonable grounds unrelated to gender in order to justify the differentiation. Persons with characteristics corresponding to those enumerated in the anti-discrimination provisions can also suffer disadvantages when no distinction is made although it is necessary under the circumstances. For example, the rule in Switzerland whereby graves in public cemeteries are assigned in the order of burial entails no disadvantage except for practising Muslims who wish to be buried facing in the direction of Mecca which, depending on the layout of the cemetery, cannot always be guaranteed.[28] In such cases the question arises whether *indirect discrimination* exists.[29]

As the Human Rights Committee has recognized, indirect discrimination occurs where: (1) a measure is formulated in 'neutral' terms, ie without making prohibited distinctions; (2) the measure has detrimental effects in its practical application that exclusively or disproportionately affect a group with characteristics that are classified as critical in anti-discrimination provisions; and (3) these adverse distinctions cannot be adequately justified on serious and objective grounds.[30]

Underlying the prohibition of indirect discrimination is the idea that ostensibly neutral practices can perpetuate or reinforce *de facto* disadvantages that are in effect based on long-term and deliberate marginalization. Such conduct that completely disregards the special needs of a particular group amounts to a violation of the dignity of the persons concerned, just as in the case of direct discrimination.

Issue in focus: The Convention on the Rights of Persons with Disabilities (CRPD)—more than a non-discrimination convention

---

Unlike the first international convention dealing exclusively with the human rights of persons with disabilities, the Inter-American Convention on the

---

[28] Judgment of the Swiss Federal Court (BGE) 125 I 300.

[29] See for example, HRCttee, *Prince v South Africa*, Communication No 1474/2006 (2007), para 7.5, and ECtHR (Grand Chamber), *DH v Czech Republic*, Application No 57325/00 (2007), paras 175 and 185 ff.

[30] HRCttee, *Althammer et al v Austria*, Communication No 998/2001 (2003), para 10.2. At the European level, this issue is dealt with primarily by the European Court of Justice (ECJ): eg ECJ, Case C-170/84 *Bilka-Kaufhaus GmbH v Weber von Hartz* (1986); ECJ, Case C-184/89 *Nimtz v Freie und Hansestadt Hamburg* (1991); ECJ, Case C-360/90 *Arbeitswohlfahrt der Stadt Berlin Ev v Boetel,* (1992).

Elimination of All Forms of Discrimination against Persons with Disabilities 1999, the Convention on the Rights of Persons with Disabilities of 2006 is not an anti-discrimination convention in the narrow sense but it takes a more holistic approach[31] by aiming to 'promote, protect and ensure the full and equal enjoyment of all human rights and fundamental freedoms by all persons with disabilities, and to promote respect for their inherent dignity' (Article 1). This goal is to be achieved based on the following general principles: '(a) [r]espect for inherent dignity, individual autonomy including the freedom to make one's own choices, and independence of persons; (b) [n]on-discrimination; (c) [f]ull and effective participation and inclusion in society; (d) [r]espect for difference and acceptance of persons with disabilities as part of human diversity and humanity; (e) [e]quality of opportunity; (f) [a]ccessibility'; (g) [e]quality between men and women; and (h) [r]espect for the evolving capacities of children with disabilities and respect for the right of children with disabilities to preserve their identities (Article 2). As this treaty aims to realize fully 'all human rights and fundamental freedoms for all persons with disabilities' (Article 4(1)), the Convention contains a comprehensive list of human rights guarantees, tailored to the specific needs of persons with disabilities. These rights may be classified into the following categories:

Certain rather general guarantees, such as the right to life and the prohibition of torture (Articles 10 and 15), emphasize the meaning of these fundamental guarantees for the rights holders of this treaty. Other provisions such as the right to education or the right to work (Articles 24 and 27) are, without expanding the obligations of states, stipulating in detail the measures states have to take in order to fulfil the guarantees concerned *vis-à-vis* persons with disabilities. Further rights such as the right to accessibility (Article 9) or the right to personal mobility (Article 20) go beyond equivalent guarantees in other human rights conventions. The right to live independently and to be included in the community (Article 19) is a completely new guarantee.

Finally, many substantive guarantees oblige states to take measure with a view to enabling the rights holders to enjoy these rights on an equal basis with others' and hence to ensure the principle of equal opportunities of individuals with disabilities.

III. The Prohibition of Discrimination Against Women

1. Discrimination against women as a structural issue

The history of human rights was for a long time a distinctly male history. In the eighteenth-century American and French declarations of human rights, the 'rights of man' or *'droits de l'homme'* were perceived in gender-specific terms.[32] Today's conventions rest on the premise that internationally

---

[31] The Convention does not define the notion of disability.
[32] Olympe de Gouges tried to counterbalance this in 1791 with her *'Déclaration des droits de la femme et de la citoyenne'* ('Declaration of the Rights of Women and Female Citizen'), which stated

recognized human rights must be applicable, on an equal footing, to women and men.

Nevertheless, the persistently unfavourable treatment of women through-out the world seems to be a systematic and structural phenomenon.[33] Arguably, there is no country that has achieved full equality of men and women in all areas of life. In many places the unfavourable treatment of women is perceived to be 'normal' and is not recognized as discrimination because the status of women is categorized as an unalterable fact on cultural and religious grounds. Moreover, women's rights are not treated as human rights on the grounds that such rights are directed against the state, while discrimination against women also occurs within the family or in the work-place, ie in the private sphere. There is often a tendency to treat the mechanisms of daily physical, psychological and structural oppression that impede the equal development of women as mere individual and private problems rather than human rights issues.[34]

Contemporary international law has developed three approaches aimed at eliminating discrimination against women. These are:

(1) The prohibition of discrimination on the basis of 'sex' protects women *and* men against adverse distinctions and thus constitutes a *symmetrical* prohib-ition as it gives both sexes entitlements to equal treatment and to equality of opportunity.

(2) The prohibition of discrimination against women affords protection only to persons of the female sex and therefore operates *asymmetrically*. This prohib-ition limits entitlements to equal treatment and equality of opportunity to women and furthermore gives women, at least in principle, the right to *de facto* equality in the sense of equality of result.

(3) The aforementioned types of prohibition, which oblige states to refrain from taking measures that discriminate against women, are frequently insufficient to protect women against gender-specific violations of their rights. To achieve

in Art 1: '*La Femme naît libre et demeure égale à l'homme en droits*' (Woman is born free and remains equal to man in her rights).

[33] Although globally women account for two thirds of work performed and produce 50% of the world's food, they benefit from only 10% of available income and possess less than 10% of private property; UN Publication: 'The World's Women 2000: Trends and Statistics' (available at <http://unstats.un.org/unsd/demographic/products/indwm/index.htm> (accessed 18 January 2009)). They are heavily under-represented in all the world's parliaments (ibid). Irrespective of a country's level of economic development, women are victims of domestic violence on an incomparably greater scale than men. The EU estimates the number of victims of trafficking in women and girls each year at close to 700,000 (see <http://europa.eu.int/comm/justice_home/news/8mars_en.htm#a1> (accessed 18 January 2008)). In many countries, state legislation continues to grant women fewer rights than men in the areas of family law, successions, labour law, in procedural law as well as other branches.

[34] Charlotte Bunch, *Women's Rights as Human Rights: Towards a Re-Vision of Human Rights* (1990) *HRQ* 486 ff.

that aim, *special norms protecting women* are required to oblige states to adopt affirmative measures.

The three approaches reflect different understandings of the status and role of women in society: They provide different answers to the question as to whether women should be treated in the same way as men, and hence equally, or whether fundamental gender differences demand differentiated treatment.[35] The first approach rests on the assumption that abolishing gender differences in domestic law is sufficient to create conditions in which women are able to enjoy equal rights. The second assumes that fundamental differences between men and women are a deeply entrenched reality, so that special provisions for women are necessary to achieve their equality with men. The last approach takes male power and its potential for abuse as the point of departure and stresses that specific norms to protect women against the exercise of male dominance are a necessity.

2. Symmetrical prohibitions of discrimination

Symmetrical prohibitions of discrimination are contained in the anti-discrimination provisions of the human rights conventions (especially ICCPR, Article 26 and ECHR, Article 14), which classify *gender* as a prohibited characteristic of discrimination and allow women *and* men[36] to take action against adverse distinctions.[37] Article 5 of the P7/ECHR, which guarantees spouses 'equality of rights and responsibilities of a private law character between them, and in their relations with their children, as to marriage, during marriage and in the event of its dissolution', is also symmetrically formulated.

Underlying the concept of symmetrical prohibition of discrimination is the assumption that, despite gender-specific differences, women and men are fundamentally the same. Enforcement of this prohibition thus serves the aim of abolishing differences between the sexes. It follows from this perspective that action must be taken first and foremost against laws and decisions that entrench gender stereotypes.

---

[35] This question was at the centre of the feminist debate of the last quarter of the twentieth century (Christina Hausammann, *Menschenrechte–Impulse für die Gleichstellung von Mann und Frau in der Schweiz* (Helbing & Lichtenhahn: Basle, 2002), 9, referring, *inter alia*, to Carol Gilligan, *In a Different Voice* (Harvard University Press, 1982); Mary Daly, *Gyn/Ecology* (Women's Press: London, 1987); Ute Gerhard *et al* (eds), *Differenz und Gleichheit, Menschenrechte haben (k)ein Geschlecht* (Ulrike Helmer Verlag: Frankfurt am Main, 1990); Susanne Okin, *Justice, Gender and the Family* (Basic Books: New York, 1990); Sandra Harding, *Whose Science? Whose Knowledge?* (Open University Press: Milton Keynes, 1991); and Scott Joan, 'Deconstructing equality-versus-difference', in Marianne Hirsch and Evelyn Keller Fox (eds), *Conflicts in Feminism* (Routledge: New York and London, 1990).

[36] In *Pauger v Austria*, Communication No 415/1990 (1992), the HRCttee held that a pension which was lower for widowers than for widows violated ICCPR, Art 26.

[37] For more detail, see above section II.

Issue in focus: The prohibition of symmetrical discrimination in international jurisprudence

(1) Accessory prohibition of discrimination (ECHR, Article 14)[38]

In the case of *Schuler-Zgraggen v Switzerland*,[39] the applicant had been employed as a secretary. Owing to a disability, she was assessed as being between 60 and 70 per cent incapacitated and obtained a corresponding invalidity pension. When she gave birth to a child, the pension was cancelled. She appealed the decision and offered to submit specific evidence to the Federal Insurance Court. The offer was rejected on the grounds that such evidence was irrelevant as she would in any case, in the light of everyday experience, have given up her job or at least worked less after the birth of the child. As noted by the European Court of Human Rights, this assumption of typical female behaviour constituted 'the sole basis for the reasoning [of the Federal Insurance Court], thus being decisive, and introduce[d] a difference of treatment based on the ground of sex only'. As Switzerland had been unable to put forward any convincing reasons why such a difference in treatment of the sexes should be regarded as compatible with the Convention, the Court concluded that there had been a breach of Article 14 in conjunction with Article 6 of the ECHR.

In the case of *Stec and Others v The United Kingdom*,[40] the Grand Chamber of the European Court had to examine the human rights conformity of a British piece of legislation, which allowed women to receive retirement benefits at the age of 60, whereas men could only do so at the age of 65. The court based itself on the assumption that this difference aimed to counterbalance women's existing economical disadvantages on the work market. The legislation in question was considered to be pertinent and objective until social and economic changes would make such special treatment of women unnecessary. The Court found that the prohibition of discrimination had not been violated because the development towards complete gender equality in the labour market remained incomplete and member states of the Council of Europe still had not harmonized their legislation on this issue. Furthermore, British authorities had already planned to take action for an equalization of the age of retirement but possessed a considerable margin of appreciation as to determine the appropriate moment for adopting such legislation. Based on the same ratio, the Court considered a rule which only provides a pension for widows but not for widowers to be (still) compatible with Article 14 of the ECHR.[41]

---

[38] Another example: ECtHR, *Abdulaziz and Others v The United Kingdom*, Series A, No 94 (1985): A provision of United Kingdom immigration law that gives only foreign wives but not foreign husbands permission to enter the country for the purpose of family reunification violates Art 14 taken together with Art 8 of the ECHR.

[39] ECtHR, *Schuler-Zgraggen v Switzerland*, Series A, No 263 (1993).

[40] ECtHR (Grand Chamber) *Stec and Others v The United Kingdom*, Application Nos 65731/01 and 65900/01 (2006), paras 60 ff.

[41] ECtHR, *Runkee and White v The United Kingdom*, Application No 42949/98 and 53134/99 (2007).

(2) **Autonomous prohibition of discrimination (ICCPR, Article 26)**[42]

In the *Mauritian Women Case* the Human Rights Committee held that a law automatically granting foreign wives of Mauritian men unlimited residence status but requiring foreign husbands of Mauritian women to apply for a residence permit was discriminatory.[43]

Similarly, a law under which only a husband is entitled to represent matrimonial property violates ICCPR, Article 26.[44]

While the Committee, in Concluding Observations on state reports, often expresses appreciation of the progress made in the area of equality for men and women in the public service, it regularly notes with concern that the number of women in senior positions is still very low.[45]

Symmetrical prohibitions of discrimination are laudable in terms of their goal of removing, as far as possible, all gender-related criteria from the legal system, thereby eliminating distinctions based on sex. There is a risk, however, that the symmetry of the prohibition may obscure the fact that many women have specific gender related needs or suffer from particular social or economic vulnerabilities, thereby largely disregarding *de facto* disparities that are often of a structural nature and are not reflected in the legal system.[46]

3. Asymmetrical prohibitions of discrimination: Convention on the Elimination of All Forms of Discrimination Against Women

The fact that it is often insufficient simply to grant formal equality of status to men and women is the basis for asymmetrical protection against discrimination as embodied in the Convention on the Elimination of All Forms of Discrimination against Women (CEDAW) of 18 December 1979. Article 1 defines the term discrimination against women as 'any distinction, exclusion or restriction made on the basis of sex which has the effect or purpose of impairing or nullifying the recognition, enjoyment or exercise by women, irrespective of their marital status, on a basis of equality of men and women, of human rights and fundamental freedoms in the political, economic, social, cultural, civil or any other field'. This concept of discrimination is rooted in the idea that *women* should not be confronted with impediments to their development and hence to the full enjoyment of human rights on account of their gender. Article 2 lists the core obligations of states: they must not only condemn and refrain from all forms of discrimination

---

[42] See also HRCttee, *Zwaan-de Vries v The Netherlands* (see n 17).
[43] HRCttee, *Aumeeruddy-Cziffra et al v Mauritius*, Communication No 35/1978 (1981).
[44] HRCttee, *Ato de Avellanal v Peru*, Communication No 202/1986 (1988).
[45] Eg, HRCttee, Concluding Observations Germany (2004), para 13, Concluding Observations Tajikistan (2005), para 7, Concluding Observations Madagascar (2007), para 9, and Concluding Observations Former Yugoslav Republic of Macedonia (2008), para 9.
[46] In such circumstances, symmetrical prohibitions may end up privileging the men who invoke them.

against women, but also adopt concrete legislative and administrative measures to eliminate discrimination against women and to ensure their equality.

Issue in focus: Article 2 of the Convention on the Elimination of All Forms of Discrimination against Women

States Parties condemn discrimination against women in all its forms, agree to pursue by all appropriate means and without delay a policy of eliminating discrimination against women and, to this end, undertake:

(a) To embody the principle of the equality of men and women in their national constitutions or other appropriate legislation if not yet incorporated therein and to ensure, through law and other appropriate means, the practical realization of this principle;

(b) To adopt appropriate legislative and other measures, including sanctions where appropriate, prohibiting all discrimination against women;

(c) To establish legal protection of the rights of women on an equal basis with men and to ensure through competent national tribunals and other public institutions the effective protection of women against any act of discrimination;

(d) To refrain from engaging in any act or practice of discrimination against women and to ensure that public authorities and institutions shall act in conformity with this obligation;

(e) To take all appropriate measures to eliminate discrimination against women by any person, organization or enterprise;

(f) To take all appropriate measures, including legislation, to modify or abolish existing laws, regulations, customs and practices which constitute discrimination against women;

(g) To repeal all national penal provisions which constitute discrimination against women.

Furthermore, the Convention imposes a large number of specific obligations on states with a view to realizing equality in all spheres of life.[47] Some examples are the obligation to ensure equal rights and opportunities to hold public office, equal rights in family law (especially in respect of the dissolution of marriage), equal remuneration for work of equal value, and realization of the right of access to all educational facilities. The obligation contained in certain provisions[48] to take action against stereotypical roles for men and women and against various forms of sexual exploitation is of special importance for ensuring the *de facto* equality of women and men. The CEDAW also deals with categories of women confronted with specific problems, requiring states parties to take measures against the exploitation of women through trafficking and prostitution (Article 6) and to counter discrimination against women in rural areas (Article 14).

---

[47] Including political and public life (Arts 7 and 8), nationality (Art 9), education (Art 10), employment and social security (Art 11), health care (Art 12), and marriage and the family (Art 16).
[48] CEDAW, Arts 5 and 10.

Beyond the prohibition of discrimination, the obligations imposed by the Convention require states to take proactive measures, which are described in detail in the text, to facilitate the realization of *de facto* substantive equality. Accordingly, equality must be realized in both women's relations with the state and in the private sphere.[49] Affirmative measures that are designed to accelerate *de facto* equality between women and men, and which must be discontinued 'when the objectives of equality of opportunity and treatment have been achieved', do not constitute discrimination even where they place men at a disadvantage until the goal has been reached.

As the Committee on the Elimination of Discrimination against Women has stressed, these provisions embody three core obligations on states, namely: (1) the obligation to ensure that there is no direct or indirect discrimination against women in their laws and that women are protected against discrimination in public and private sphere; (2) the obligation to improve the *de facto* position of women through concrete and effective policies and programmes; and (3) the obligation to address prevailing gender relations and persistence of gender-based stereotypes.[50] These duties aim not only to eliminate discrimination in the legal order, but also to address the imbalances women face in the public and the private sphere. From the perspective of the CEDAW, what is necessary is the modification of social and cultural patterns of conduct of men and women leading to the elimination of prejudices and traditional practices that are based on the idea of inferiority/superiority of the two sexes or on stereotyped roles. In this context, the Committee identifies the persistence of traditions and prejudices assigning the 'natural' role of women as being within the family as one of the main obstacles to the full enjoyment of their rights.[51] In order to overcome such prejudices and patterns, the Committee views temporary special measures for women ('affirmative action') such as special education, literacy campaigns or quotas as a particularly important 'part of a necessary strategy by States parties directed towards the achievement of de facto or substantive equality of women with men in the enjoyment of their human rights'.[52]

Issue in focus: The impact of CEDAW[53]

In 1995, the Committee on the Elimination of Discrimination against Women evaluated the impact of the CEDAW on the legal situation of women in the states parties. It came to the following conclusions:

38. The direct impact of the Convention and the work of the Committee has been dramatic in many countries. A number of countries that had focused little, if any, attention on the

---

[49] In general, see CEDAW, Art 2(e). For specific examples, see CEDAW, Arts 11(2), 13 and 15(2).
[50] CtteeEDAW, General Recommendation No 25 (2004), paras 6 and 7.
[51] CtteeEDAW, Progress Achieved in the Implementation of the Convention on the Elimination of Discrimination against Women, UN Doc A/CONF177/7 (1995), para 45j.
[52] CtteeEDAW, General Recommendation No 25 (2004), para 18.
[53] CtteeEDAW, Progress Achieved in the Implementation of the Convention on the Elimination of Discrimination against Women, UN Doc A/CONF177/7 (1995).

human rights of women in the past, do so today in large part because of the Convention. The development of the Committee has given rise to an increasing awareness of the importance of the human rights of women and the importance of measures to secure those rights.

39. Ratification of and accession to the Convention have frequently been preceded by the amendment of specific discriminatory laws and the introduction of broad-ranging policies to achieve equality of women and men. The spread of ratification and accession has in some instances preceded, and in others influenced, legal and policy change. The constitutions of many States Parties now incorporate clauses providing equality before the law or equal protection before the law. Moreover, a number of constitutions have incorporated the Convention into domestic law. Legislation to address sex discrimination has been introduced in many States Parties, both generally and within specific contexts. The Convention has positively influenced litigation, on occasion even in States that are not parties to it, with judicial officers concluding that the provisions of the Convention must be respected as established norms for interpreting the constitution and evaluating discrimination claims.

40. Since the adoption of the Convention, most States Parties have established national machineries to promote the advancement of women . . . Still others have pursued the provisions of the Convention through national plans and policy directives. Others have introduced equal-opportunity ombudspersons and some have introduced temporary special measures of affirmative action, . . . Ratification and accession have frequently been followed by the elimination of legal restrictions that impeded, (particularly, rural) women from obtaining access to land, capital and technology. While progress towards exercising these rights has been less rapid, it is certainly the case that most States Parties have gone a long way towards removing formal discrimination . . .

44. The impact of the Convention and the work of the Committee has not been confined to States, but has permeated civil society. Non-governmental organizations dedicated to the promotion of the Convention have been established. The Convention has also served to focus the work of existing women's non-governmental organizations, allowing them to forge a better collaboration between themselves and Governments. Furthermore, the Convention has contributed to the development of the concept by non-governmental organizations of the empowerment of women. Both non-governmental organizations and individual women have turned to the Convention as the framework for equality, using it to campaign for women's rights at all levels.

4. Special protection for women

(a) Overview

The first international efforts to provide special protection for women were attempts to suppress trafficking in women and forced prostitution. They go back to the late nineteenth century and led to the adoption of the Agreements on Protection against the Trafficking in Girls of 1904 and 1910 and on the Suppression of Trafficking of Mature Women of 1921 and 1933. Notable contemporary instruments include the Convention for the Suppression of the Traffic in Persons and of the Exploitation of the Prostitution of Others of 2 December 1949 and the Protocol to Prevent, Suppress and Punish Trafficking in Persons, Especially Women and Children, supplementing the United Nations Convention against Transnational Organized Crime of 15 November 2000 (Palermo Protocol).

Action to protect women in employment also has a long history. As early as 1919 the International Labour Organization adopted a Convention concerning the Employment of Women before and after Childbirth, and since the days of the League of Nations a series of conventions have sought to restrict night work for women as a particularly harmful form of employment.

Specific forms of protection for women can also be inferred from the general human rights obligation to protect,[54] for instance, against forced marriage or female genital mutilation.[55]

Particularly comprehensive obligations to protect are found in international humanitarian law (see (b) below) and in the context of violence against women (see (c) below).

(b) Protection of women in armed conflict

International humanitarian law contains a number of provisions aimed at protecting women. The prohibition of adverse distinctions based on sex contained in all instruments[56] does not exclude more favourable treatment of women where this is required by reason of their gender specific needs rather it ensures that women benefit from at least the same guarantees as men. This is particularly important in the case of wounded or sick women combatants or where such combatants fall into the hands of the enemy as prisoners of war.[57]

Special emphasis is placed on the protection of female members of the civilian population. In international armed conflicts, they are protected against attacks on their physical, sexual, and mental integrity, and especially 'against any attack on their honour, in particular against rape, enforced prostitution, or any form of indecent assault'.[58] In non-international armed conflicts,[59] Article 4 of Additional Protocol II expressly prohibits 'outrages upon personal dignity, in particular humiliating and degrading treatment, rape, enforced prostitution and any form of indecent assault', a form of protection enjoyed by women and men alike. In occupied territories women can be interned as civilians but must be held in separate quarters from men. The principle of segregation is also applicable to women who are interned or detained in non-international armed conflicts.[60] Lastly, international humanitarian law contains a number of provisions

---

[54] See ECtHR, *X and Y v The Netherlands*, A/91 (1985).

[55] See Chapter 12, section IV (prohibition of forced marriages) and Chapter 9, section III.4.d (female genital mutilation). See also CtteeEDAW, General Recommendation No 14 (1990) female circumcision.

[56] GC I and GC II, Art 12; GC III, Art 16; GC IV, Art 27; AP I, Art 75; and AP II, Art 4.

[57] See GC III, Art 14.

[58] GC IV, Art 27(2). Similarly, AP I, Arts 75(2)(b) and 76(1) which, unlike GC IV, Art 27, protect not only women who are nationals of the adverse party to the conflict but also women from neutral states and states with which the state party in question is jointly conducting the war.

[59] See also common Art 3 guaranteeing that 'persons not taking part in the hostilities...shall in all circumstances be treated humanely, without any adverse distinction founded', *inter alia*, on sex.

[60] GC IV, Art 85; AP I, Art 75(5); AP II, Art 5(2)(a).

protecting pregnant women, nursing mothers and mothers with children under the age of seven, eg in the context of internment and prosecution, or in connection with the supply of food and medical necessities.[61] It should also be noted that pregnant women may not be executed.[62]

(c) Protection of women against violence[63]

Outside the realm of international humanitarian law, violence against women, including domestic violence, was long perceived as a social phenomenon or a criminal law matter rather than as a human rights issue. This accounts for the fact that the CEDAW is silent on the question of violence against women.[64] It was felt that women's lifestyles were deeply rooted in cultural and social traditions and patterns and that it would be more appropriate to change them through educational and social measures. Although this view was criticized by the international women's movement, the movement's human rights approach of 'women's rights are human rights' campaign remained unsuccessful for a long time.

The breakthrough came at the 1993 World Conference on Human Rights in Vienna. In its final Declaration, states recognized that the rights of women and girls were an integral part of human rights. They declared that gender-based violence and all forms of sexual harassment and exploitation, including those resulting from cultural prejudice and international trafficking, were incompatible with the dignity and worth of the human person and must be eliminated.[65] This consensus was reaffirmed and further developed in the Platform for Action adopted by the UN Fourth World Conference on Women held in Beijing in 1995.[66]

After the Vienna Conference, the UN General Assembly adopted the Declaration on the Elimination of Violence against Women on 12 December 1993.[67] Article 1 of the Declaration defines violence against women as any act of gender-based violence that results in, or is likely to result in, physical, sexual, or psychological harm or suffering to women, including threats of such acts, coercion, or arbitrary deprivation of liberty, whether occurring in public or in private life. As examples, the Declaration refers in Article 2 to physical, sexual, and psychological violence occurring in the family, including: battery; sexual abuse of

---

[61] For example, GC IV, Arts 23, 50, 89, 91, 127 and 132 and AP I, Art 76(2).

[62] AP I, Art 76(3) and AP II, Art 6(4) which also prohibits the execution of mothers of young children.

[63] See on this topic the detailed information in 'In-depth study on all forms of violence against women', Report of the Secretary-General, UN Doc A/61/122/Add. 1 (2006).

[64] CtteeEDAW, however, has stressed that such violence is covered by the definition of discrimination as embodied in Article 1 of the Convention; see CtteeEDAW, General Recommendation No 19 (1992), Violence against Women, para 6.

[65] Vienna Declaration and Programme of Action adopted by the World Conference on Human Rights on 25 July 1993, para 18.

[66] Part D of the Platform for Action, contained in UN Doc A/CONF.177/20 (1995), Annex II.

[67] UN General Assembly Resolution A/RES/48/104 on the Elimination of Violence against Women of 20 December 1993. In 1994 the Commission on Human Rights established the mandate of Special Rapporteur on Violence against Women to implement the Declaration.

female children in the household; dowry-related violence; marital rape; female genital mutilation and other traditional practices harmful to women; non-spousal violence and violence related to exploitation; physical, sexual and psychological violence occurring within the general community, including rape, sexual abuse, sexual harassment and intimidation at work, in educational institutions and elsewhere; trafficking in women and forced prostitution; and physical, sexual and psychological violence perpetrated or condoned by the state, wherever it occurs. States are required to condemn violence against women and are prohibited from invoking any cultural traditions or religious precepts to justify it. Not only must states refrain from engaging in such violence, they must also prevent, investigate and punish acts of violence against women, whether perpetrated by state agents or private persons. Finally, states must create mechanisms that enable women to take legal action against perpetrators and to obtain compensation and redress (Article 4).

The obligations to prevent, protect, investigate, and punish are particularly important in the context of domestic violence, which is a taboo area in many countries. Even though the Declaration is not binding *per se*, it sets out specific obligations that arguably already existed under the 'hard' obligations to protect under human rights treaties. Thus, the Committee concluded in one of its first views on an individual communication under the Optional Protocol to the CEDAW that a state violates Articles 5(a) and 16 of the Convention if a woman battered by her husband for years cannot find any protection from the state. In this case the law did not provide any possibility of barring the husband from the woman's apartment, of obtaining a protection order, or of providing her and her children with the option of finding refuge in a shelter.[68]

Issue in focus: Risk factors for violence against women[69]

In 2006, UN Secretary General Kofi Annan identified the following risk factors for violence against women:

98. A range of studies identify risk factors at the levels of the individual, family, community, society and State. These have been summarized in one public health model and include:

(a) At the level of the individual: youth; a history of abuse as a child; witnessing marital violence in the home; the frequent use of alcohol and drugs; low educational or economic status; and membership in marginalized and excluded communities. These factors are associated with both the perpetrators and victims/survivors of violence.

(b) At the level of the couple and family: male control of wealth and decision-making authority within the family; a history of marital conflict; and significant interpersonal disparities in economic, educational or employment status.

---

[68] CtteeEDAW, *AT v Hungary*, Communication No 2/2003 (2005), para 9.4.
[69] 'In-depth study on all forms of violence against women', Report of the Secretary-General, UN Doc A/61/122/Add. 1 (2006), paras 98–9 (footnotes omitted).

(c) At the level of the community: women's isolation and lack of social support; community attitudes that tolerate and legitimize male violence; and high levels of social and economic disempowerment, including poverty.

(d) At the level of society: gender roles that entrench male dominance and female subordination; and tolerance of violence as a means of conflict resolution.

(e) At the level of the State: inadequate laws and policies for the prevention and punishment of violence; and limited awareness and sensitivity on the part of law enforcement officials, courts and social service providers.

99. These analyses point to power disparities based on discrimination and inequalities as the underlying determinants of violence against women. As a leading researcher on domestic violence noted, although such violence 'is greatest in relationships and communities where the use of violence in many situations is normative, notably when witnessed in childhood, *it is substantially a product of gender inequality and the lesser status of women compared with men in society*.' A number of the risk factors cited above are tied to human rights violations. For example, girls and young women face violations of a range of rights guaranteed by the Convention on the Rights of the Child. Some of these violations constitute forms of violence and others increase the risk of violence.

International criminal law can also be invoked to combat and punish gender-based violence. In addition to the relevant war crimes that have already been mentioned, '[r]ape, sexual slavery, enforced prostitution, forced pregnancy, enforced sterilization, or any other form of sexual violence of comparable gravity' constitute crimes against humanity when committed by agents of state or members of private groups as part of a planned or systematic attack against a civilian population.[70]

IV. The Prohibition of Racial Discrimination

1. Race and the prohibition of racial discrimination

In light of historic experiences such as the German Holocaust, colonialism, or the South-African apartheid system, race is regarded as a particularly odious reason for treating persons differently. This is especially true when racist action takes violent forms. As was stressed by the European Court on Human Rights, racially motivated violence is 'a particular affront to human dignity and, in view of its perilous consequences, requires from the authorities special vigilance and a vigorous reaction. It is for this reason that the authorities must use all available means to combat racism and racist violence, thereby reinforcing democracy's vision of a society in which diversity is not perceived as a threat but as a source of enrichment.'[71]

The notions of diversity and tolerance are important in the context of fighting racism. Nevertheless, and although the same persons might benefit from both

---

[70] Rome Statute, Art 7(1)(g).
[71] ECtHR (Grand Chamber), *Nachova and Others v Bulgaria*, *Reports* 2005-VII, para 145.

legal regimes, it is necessary clearly to distinguish between the prohibition of racial discrimination and the protection of minorities (section V below): While minority protection is about the right to be different, the prohibition of discrimination aims at eliminating differences and making legal systems as well as societies 'colour-blind'.

In international human rights law, race is one of the suspect criteria in all provisions prohibiting discrimination, including ICCPR, Articles 2(3) and 26, ICESCR, Article 2(2), and the anti-discrimination provisions of the regional conventions. In terms of examining whether an accessory or autonomous prohibition has been violated, the general principles discussed above (section II above) apply. In particular, a distinction based on race is not discriminatory 'if the criteria for such differentiation, judged against the objectives and purposes of the Convention, are legitimate'.[72]

To go beyond prohibiting racism and to achieve a situation where race no longer plays any role, the International Convention on the Elimination of All Forms of Racial Discrimination was adopted on 21 December 1965. It strives to eliminate 'any distinction, exclusion, restriction or preference based on race, colour, descent, or national or ethnic origin which has the purpose or effect of nullifying or impairing the recognition, enjoyment or exercise, on an equal footing, of human rights and fundamental freedoms in the political, economic, social, cultural or any other field of public life' (Article 1). Thus, people should not be impeded from enjoying guaranteed rights solely on account of their colour, origin or descent.

The notion of race poses a number of challenges. Biological concepts of race distinguish populations on the basis of inherited physical characteristics such as the color of skin or facial features. However, such distinctions do not say anything about the personality or behavior of the individuals concerned. Scientific research has shown that the percentage of genetic variations between individuals within a given population is far bigger than genetic differences shared between all the members of one 'racial' group and those of another such group.[73] 'Race' is thus a social construct 'based on observable physical characteristics (eg skin color) that have acquired socially significant meaning...In addition to physical features, ascribed and other characteristics such as given name, dress, and diet may also contribute to racial categorizations ...'[74] Such determinations, although simply constructs, have a powerful effect on the lives of those affected. As a study by the US National Research Council stresses:

[t]he social meaning given to racial classifications activates beliefs and assumptions about individuals in a particular racial category. Consequently, if someone is perceived or identifies himself or herself as belonging to the African American or another racial

---

[72] CtteeERD, General Recommendation XIV (1993), para 2.

[73] Panel on Methods for Assessing Discrimination, Rebecca M Blank, Marilyn Dabady, and Constance F Citro (eds), National Research Council, *Measuring Racial Discrimination* (The National Academies Press: Washington, 2004), 26.

[74] Ibid, 27 (references omitted).

group—regardless of the person's precise physical or other characteristics—that classification creates a social reality that can have real and enduring consequences. For instance, racial classification can affect access to resources (e.g., education, health care, and jobs), the distribution of income and wealth, political power, residential living patterns, and interpersonal relationships. Moreover, the consequences of racial classification over time can create boundaries among racially defined groups that affect people today.[75]

Thus, 'race' is the outcome of collective ascription. It is typically used to refer to a group of people who are perceived as being different and possibly inferior by other groups on account of particular physical and/or cultural attributes. Accordingly, race is particularly associated with social relations involving oppression, subjugation, hatred of 'the other', and defence of what is perceived to be 'one's own'.[76]

The sentiments set out in the preambular paragraphs demonstrate that the drafters of the Convention on the Elimination of All Forms of Racial Discrimination (CERD) were influenced by the experiences of colonialism and the then apartheid regime in South Africa. In the case of systems with legal norms providing explicitly for the exclusion of particular groups, it is easy to identify those entitled to protection against racial discrimination. Where there are no such declarations or where physical differences between members of different groups are hardly visible, it becomes difficult to establish who should be protected as a member of a 'racial' group. The Committee on the Elimination of All Forms of Racial Discrimination (CtteeERD) puts the emphasis on the self-identification of the individuals concerned,[77] an approach that is problematic in light of the history of racial discrimination and the social mechanisms leading to it. The CtteeERD has considered the situation of diverse groups such as so-called travellers in the United Kingdom and Switzerland, Roma in Bulgaria, Germany and the Czech Republic, Tibetans in China, Dalits in India, Mapuches in Chile, Chiapans in Mexico, Blacks in Costa Rica, Aborigines in Australia, Serbs, Croatians and Albanian Muslims in the former Yugoslavia, immigrants in France and Italy, Hungarians in Romania, Turks in Bulgaria, and Hutus and Tutsis in Rwanda and Burundi, but declined to classify Muslim immigrants in Denmark as being discriminated against on the basis of 'race' rather than 'religion'.[78]

The difficulties of determining whether discrimination is based on 'race' are particularly acute in the case of immigrants. The Convention permits states to make distinctions between citizens and non-citizens (Article 1(2)) provided that differential treatment based on citizenship or immigration status serves a

---

[75] Ibid, 27.
[76] Sandra Fredman (ed), *Discrimination and Human Rights—The Case of Racism* (Oxford University Press: Oxford, 2001), 11.
[77] CtteeERD, General Recommendation VIII (1990).
[78] CtteeERD, *PSN v Denmark*, Communication No 36/2006 (2007), para 6.4, and *AWRAP v Denmark*, Communication No 37/2006 (2007), para 6.4.

legitimate aim and is proportional to the achievement of such an objective.[79] In particular, states are prohibited from making distinctions between different groups of migrants, asylum-seekers, or refugees solely on the basis of nationality, citizenship, or naturalization (Article 1(3)). According to the Committee, such a prohibition entails an obligation to ensure that immigration policies or provisions regarding access to citizenship do not have the effect of discriminating against particular groups of persons on the basis of race, colour, descent, or national or ethnic origin.[80]

2. Elimination of racial discrimination

The Convention on the Elimination of All Forms of Racial Discrimination obliges states parties to pursue a policy of elimination of racial discrimination and promotion of understanding among races and ethnic groups. Furthermore, to achieve these goals, states parties are under an obligation as set out in Article 2 to take specific political, legal and social measures. Thus, the emphasis is on taking positive steps with a view to developing a society where race is no longer used to justify differential treatment.

Issue in focus: Article 2 of the Convention on the Elimination of All Forms of Racial Discrimination

States Parties condemn racial discrimination and undertake to pursue by all appropriate means and without delay a policy of eliminating racial discrimination in all its forms and promoting understanding among all races, and, to this end:

(a) Each State Party undertakes to engage in no act or practice of racial discrimination against persons, groups of persons or institutions and to ensure that all public authorities and public institutions, national and local, shall act in conformity with this obligation;

(b) Each State Party undertakes not to sponsor, defend or support racial discrimination by any persons or organizations;

(c) Each State Party shall take effective measures to review governmental, national and local policies, and to amend, rescind or nullify any laws and regulations which have the effect of creating or perpetuating racial discrimination wherever it exists;

(d) Each State Party shall prohibit and bring to an end, by all appropriate means, including legislation as required by circumstances, racial discrimination by any persons, group or organization;

(e) Each State Party undertakes to encourage, where appropriate, integrationist multiracial organizations and movements and other means of eliminating barriers between races, and to discourage anything which tends to strengthen racial division.

---

[79] CtteeERD, General Recommendation XXX (2004), para 4.   [80] Ibid, paras 9 and 13.

States parties must furthermore criminalize the dissemination of racist ideas and racial violence, prohibit racist organizations (Article 4), and guarantee equal treatment in areas such as employment, housing and education and '[t]he right of access to any place or service intended for use by the general public, such as transport, hotels, restaurants, cafés, theatres and parks' (Article 5). The Convention thus not only addresses discrimination by state authorities, but also discrimination by private actors. It is clear that the goal of elimination of racial discrimination 'in the political, economic, social, cultural or any other field of public life' (Article 1) must have a broad understanding. Affected persons must be assured of effective protection and of available legal remedies against acts of racial discrimination (Article 6). This, too, touches on the question of the applicability of the non-discrimination principle among private actors; such horizontal effect can only become effective to the extent that states enact corresponding legislation and take the requisite measures. The Netherlands, for instance, was negligent in this regard when it failed to take adequate action against the residents of a street who had prevented a Moroccan person from renting an apartment there.[81]

Lastly, states undertake to adopt 'effective measures, particularly in the fields of teaching, education, culture and information, with a view to combating prejudices which lead to racial discrimination and to promoting understanding, tolerance and friendship among nations and racial or ethnical groups' (Article 7).

Outside treaty obligations, states adopted a very comprehensive declaration and action plan at the World Conference against Racism, Racial Discrimination, Xenophobia and Related Intolerance, held in Durban, South Africa, from 31 August to 8 September 2001.[82] The General Assembly (Resolution 61/149) decided to convene a review conference in 2009 on the implementation of the Durban Declaration and Programme of Action.

Issue in focus: The jurisprudence of the ECtHR on the prohibition of racial discrimination

---

Recently, the European Court of Human Rights had to deal with an increasing number of cases of alleged racial discrimination, in particular with complaints of Roma's against Central and Eastern European countries. As the following standard paragraph of the Court stresses, this form of discrimination constitutes a particularly severe violation of ECHR, Article 14:

Discrimination on account of, inter alia, a person's ethnic origin is a form of racial discrimination. Racial discrimination is a particularly invidious kind of discrimination and, in view of its perilous consequences, requires from the authorities special vigilance and a vigorous reaction. It is for this reason that the authorities must use all available means to

---

[81] CtteeERD, *LK v The Netherlands*, Communication No 4/1991 (1993). See also *Sadic v Denmark*, Communication No 25/2002 (2003), and *Habassi v Denmark*, Communication No 10/1997 (1999).
[82] UN Doc A/ CONF.189/12 (2001).

combat racism, thereby reinforcing democracy's vision of a society in which diversity is not perceived as a threat but as a source of enrichment...[83]

According to the Strasbourg jurisprudence, this categorization has different consequences:

Unlike in the case of other suspect classifications, differential treatment of persons on grounds of their racial or ethnic origin cannot be objectively justified in a democratic society based on the principles of plurality and respect of different cultures.[84]

In the case of *Moldovan v Romania*, the court determined that discrimination by the authorities on racial grounds could exceptionally fall under the category of inhumane treatment and therefore constitute a violation of Article 3 ECHR.[85]

As regards the duty to investigate in cases of deprivation of life torture and inhuman or degrading treatment, the Court applies particularly stringent criteria where acts of violence seem to have been motivated by racist attitudes. In the *Nachova v Bulgaria* case, the Grand Chamber stressed the following:

States have a general obligation under Article 2 of the Convention to conduct an effective investigation in cases of deprivation of life. That obligation must be discharged without discrimination, as required by Article 14 of the Convention... [W]here there is suspicion that racial attitudes induced a violent act it is particularly important that the official investigation is pursued with vigour and impartiality, having regard to the need to reassert continuously society's condemnation of racism and ethnic hatred and to maintain the confidence of minorities in the ability of the authorities to protect them from the threat of racist violence. Compliance with the State's positive obligations under Article 2 of the Convention requires that the domestic legal system must demonstrate its capacity to enforce criminal law against those who unlawfully took the life of another, irrespective of the victim's racial or ethnic origin... [W]hen investigating violent incidents and, in particular, deaths at the hands of State agents, State authorities have the additional duty to take all reasonable steps to unmask any racist motive and to establish whether or not ethnic hatred or prejudice may have played a role in the events. Failing to do so and treating racially induced violence and brutality on an equal footing with cases that have no racist overtones would be to turn a blind eye to the specific nature of acts that are particularly destructive of fundamental rights. A failure to make a distinction in the way in which situations that are essentially different are handled may constitute unjustified treatment irreconcilable with Article 14 of the Convention... In order to maintain public confidence in their law enforcement machinery, Contracting States must ensure that in the investigation of incidents involving the use of force a distinction is made both in their legal systems and in practice between cases of excessive use of force and of racist killing. Admittedly, proving racial motivation will often be extremely difficult in practice. The respondent State's obligation to investigate possible racist overtones to a violent act is an obligation to use best endeavours and not absolute... The authorities must do what is reasonable in the circumstances to collect and secure the evidence, explore all practical means of discovering the truth and deliver fully reasoned, impartial and objective decisions, without omitting suspicious facts that may be indicative of a racially induced violence...

---

[83] ECtHR (Grand Chamber), *DH v Czech Republic*, Application No 57325/00 (2007), para 176.

[84] Ibid. '[N]o difference in treatment which is based exclusively or to a decisive extent on a person's ethnic origin is capable of being objectively justified in a contemporary democratic society built on the principles of pluralism and respect for different cultures...'

[85] ECtHR, *Moldovan and Others v Romania*, Application Nos 41138/98 and 64320/01 (2005), para 111.

The Grand Chamber would add that the authorities' duty to investigate the existence of a possible link between racist attitudes and an act of violence is an aspect of their procedural obligations arising under Article 2 of the Convention, but may also be seen as implicit in their responsibilities under Article 14 of the Convention taken in conjunction with Article 2 to secure the enjoyment of the right to life without discrimination. Owing to the interplay of the two provisions, issues such as those in the present case may fall to be examined under one of the two provisions only, with no separate issue arising under the other, or may require examination under both Articles. This is a question to be decided in each case on its facts and depending on the nature of the allegations made.[86]

As confirmed for example in the case of *Šečić v Croatia*, the Court also applies these principles in cases of assault by non-state actors where there is the suspicion that the offender's motives were of a racist nature.[87]

V. Protection of Minorities and of Indigenous Peoples

1. Concepts

The numerous ethnically or religiously motivated conflicts in recent years demonstrate to what extent the protection of minority groups and peoples is one of the most urgent issues facing contemporary international law. Many of these conflicts revolve around questions of collective identity, and the oppression of such groups is usually based on their race, religion, ethnic origin, and other similar grounds, ie *collective discrimination*.

Alongside general human rights law and international humanitarian law, which protect members of minorities as individuals, international law has three specific sets of legal rules for the purpose of protecting the rights of threatened minorities:

(1) Historically, the *right of peoples to self-determination* has been closely linked with the idea of decolonization. Its original purpose was to enable peoples living under foreign domination to decide under certain circumstances to establish their own state and hence to secede from the state in which they were living. Although this right was incorporated in common Article 1 of the two Human Rights Covenants of 1966 and is an important prerequisite for the enjoyment of human rights, it does not, *per se*, constitute a human right capable of being invoked by individuals in the event of a violation.[88] It will therefore not be considered further in this context.[89]

---

[86] ECtHR (Grand Chamber), *Nachova and Others v Bulgaria, Reports* 2005-VII, paras 160 f.

[87] ECtHR, *Šečić v Croatia*, Application No 40116/02 (2007), paras 67 ff.

[88] HRCttee, *Ominayak and the Lubicon Lake Band v Canada*, Communication No 167/1984 (1990), para 32.1.

[89] For further background reading, see, for example, Antonio Cassese, *Self-Determination of Peoples* (Cambridge University Press: Cambridge, 1995), especially 141 ff.

Issue in focus: Human Rights Committee, General Comment No 12

---

1. In accordance with the purposes and principles of the Charter of the United Nations, article 1 of the International Covenant on Civil and Political Rights recognizes that all peoples have the right of self-determination. The right of self-determination is of particular importance because its realization is an essential condition for the effective guarantee and observance of individual human rights and for the promotion and strengthening of those rights. It is for that reason that States set forth the right of self-determination in a provision of positive law in both Covenants and placed this provision as article 1 apart from and before all of the other rights in the two Covenants.

2. Article 1 enshrines an inalienable right of all peoples as described in its paragraphs 1 and 2. By virtue of that right they freely 'determine their political status and freely pursue their economic, social and cultural development'. The article imposes on all States parties corresponding obligations...

5. Paragraph 2 affirms a particular aspect of the economic content of the right of self-determination, namely the right of peoples, for their own ends, freely to 'dispose of their natural wealth and resources without prejudice to any obligations arising out of international economic cooperation, based upon the principle of mutual benefit, and international law. In no case may a people be deprived of its own means of subsistence'. This right entails corresponding duties for all States and the international community...

---

(2) The notion of *protection of minorities* hinges on the idea that the identity of ethnic, religious, linguistic and other minorities and their members necessitates protection against the majority ethnic group *within* an existing state. This notion stems from minority protection treaties adopted by the League of Nations.[90] Guarantees of minority rights can be formulated in either individual or collective terms.

(3) It is only in recent decades that the international community has taken steps to adopt special legal provisions for the *protection of indigenous peoples.* By means of collective or individual rights, the aim of such legal provisions is to secure the cultural and economic survival of members of threatened minorities whose economic, cultural and political organization is intimately bound up with the territory that they have inhabited since time immemorial.

2. Protection of minorities

(a) Protection of individual rights

Members of ethnic, religious, or linguistic minorities can invoke the human rights to which they are entitled whenever they suffer adverse distinctions on account of their membership to a specific group or community. In this regard, general prohibitions of discrimination and rights such as religious freedom are particularly important. Yet in spite of their collective dimension, these rights are

---

[90] See Chapter 1, section II.2.

formulated in individual terms and their suitability for the protection of minorities as such is therefore limited.

Article 27 of the ICCPR goes a step further by stating that '[i]n those states in which ethnic, religious or linguistic minorities exist, persons belonging to such minorities shall not be denied the rights, *in community with the other members of their group*, to enjoy their own culture, to profess and practise their own religion, or to use their own language'. Article 30 of the Convention on the Rights of the Child confirms the applicability of this right to children.

However, the Covenant and the Convention fail to specify what is meant by minorities in these provisions. The Human Rights Committee defines members of a minority as persons, 'who belong to a group and who share in common a culture, a religion and/or a language'[91] and who are outnumbered in the state as a whole by the majority.[92] This concept is clearly inspired by a notion proposed by Capotorti and widely used in the UN system. He defines a minority as a 'group, numerically inferior to the rest of the population of a State, in a non-dominant position, whose members—being nationals of the State—possess ethnic, religious or linguistic characteristics differing from those of the rest of the population, and show, if only implicitly, a sense of solidarity directed towards preserving their culture, traditions, religion or language'.[93] The Human Rights Committee goes beyond this definition insofar as it extends the protection of Article 27 to include members of minorities who are either citizens of other states or stateless.[94] The Committee has so far denied minority status in two cases, with the first concerning members of the English-speaking population of French-speaking Quebec who were not deemed to have minority status because they constitute the majority in Canada as a whole.[95] The second case addressed members of the Namibian Rehoboth Baster Community, descendants of indigenous Khoi and white Afrikaners. The Committee found that the Community members were not entitled to invoke Article 27 because they were unable to prove that their way of life, based on raising cattle on grazing lands they had used for 125 years, could give rise to a distinctive culture.[96] Most other cases concerned indigenous peoples (see section 3 below) whose classification as minorities in the sense of Article 27 caused no difficulties.

Although it is formulated as an individual right of members of minorities, ICCPR, Article 27 serves to protect collective ways of life. According to Nowak, it gives members of minorities 'a privileged, unrestricted right to common

---

[91] HRCttee, General Comment No 23 (1994), para 5.1.

[92] HRCttee, *Ballantyne et al v Canada*, Communication Nos 359/1989 and 385/1989 (1993).

[93] F Capotorti, *Study on the Rights of Persons Belonging to Ethnic, Religious and Linguistic Minorities, United Nations* (United Nations Economic and Social Council: New York, 1991), para 468.

[94] HRCttee, General Comment No 23 (1994), para 5.2.

[95] HRCttee, *Ballantyne et al v Canada*, Communication Nos 359/1989 and 385/1989 (1993), para 11.2.

[96] HRCttee, *Diergaardt et al v Namibia*, Communication Nos 760/1997 (2000), para 10.6.

enjoyment of their culture, language and religion'.[97] Hence Article 27 prohibits all forms of coercive integration and assimilation.[98] As the article is directed towards ensuring 'the survival and continued development of the cultural, religious and social identity of the minorities concerned', the rights set out in Article 27 'must be protected as such and should not be confused with other personal rights conferred on one and all under the Covenant. States parties, therefore, have an obligation to ensure that the exercise of these rights is fully protected and they should indicate in their reports the measures they have adopted to this end.'[99] This applies in particular to the right to use one's own language, a right that exceeds the scope of the freedom of expression inasmuch as it is not just the individual use of minority languages but their existence as such that is protected.[100] The entitlement to protection of 'their own culture' is also a cultural right that goes beyond the sum of culture-related rights set out in the Covenant. The purpose of protecting cultural identity is not solely to ensure that states refrain from interfering with minorities' cultural autonomy. Rather, it goes further by necessitating specific measures to protect such identity against interference by third parties and in some circumstances requires positive promotional measures.[101]

(b) Protection of collective rights

The weakness of approaches to minority protection based on individual rights lies in the inherent difficulty of assessing and addressing structural disadvantages encountered by minorities and the impossibility of fulfilling certain minority demands of a collective nature, eg for their own schools, instruction in their own language, minimum or proportional representation in administrative and political bodies (eg reserved seats), recognition of their language as an official language, or use of their own signs (eg place and street names) and symbols (eg flags and insignia) in public places. Such issues were dealt with in the League of Nations minority treaties, which were formulated in terms of collective rights.[102] This tradition was discontinued in the UN and there is still no treaty under which rights are conferred on minorities as such. Although Article 1 of the 1992 UN General Assembly Declaration on the Rights of Persons Belonging to National or Ethnic, Religious and Linguistic Minorities[103] calls on states to protect the

---

[97] Manfred Nowak, *UN Covenant on Civil and Political Rights, CCPR Commentary* (2nd edn, Engel: Kehl, 2005), para 45.
[98] The Convention on the Rights of the Child contains a prohibition of assimilation in the area of education. Although Art 29(1)(c) expressly permits the inculcation of respect for 'the national values of the country in which the child is living', it stresses that states parties also agree 'that the education of the child shall be directed to: ... (c) The development of respect for the child's ... cultural identity, language and values'.
[99] HRCttee, General Comment No 23 (1994), para 9.
[100] See HRCttee, General Comment No 23 (1994), para 5.3.
[101] HRCttee, General Comment No 23 (1994), paras 6.1 and 6.2.
[102] See Chapter 1, section II.2.
[103] Declaration on the Rights of Persons Belonging to National or Ethnic, Religious and Linguistic Minorities, adopted by UN General Assembly Resolution 47/135 of 18 December 1992.

existence and the national or ethnic, cultural, religious and linguistic identity of minorities within their territories and to encourage conditions for the promotion of that identity, the Declaration focuses, as clearly indicated by its title, on the individual rights of *members* of such minorities.

By contrast, collective protection of minorities exists, at least to some extent, in Europe. The most important instrument is the Framework Convention for the Protection of National Minorities, which was adopted by the Council of Europe on 1 February 1995 and entered into force in 1998. Although according to Article 1 the Convention concerns 'national minorities', as the drafters were unable to agree on a precise definition of what constitutes 'national minorities' it remains unclear whether protection is enjoyed only by minorities whose members possess the nationality of their state of residence or also by minorities constituting the majority in another state (such as the Hungarian minorities in Romania and Slovakia). The Advisory Committee charged with monitoring the application of the Convention adopts a broad definition and also questions states about 'new' minorities or those that are not composed of a state's own nationals. However, the extension of the definition to immigrant minorities is rejected by a number of states.[104]

As is clear from its description as a Framework Convention, the treaty merely establishes principles. These principles are, however, legally binding and it is up to individual states to decide how they should be implemented at the domestic level. In terms of substance, the Convention embodies, in addition to the non-discrimination principle and civil liberties such as freedom of expression, religion and assembly, specific guarantees for which there is no equivalent in human rights treaties. For instance, Article 3 stipulates that: 'Every person belonging to a national minority shall have the right freely to choose to be treated or not to be treated as such.' In areas inhabited by national minorities, the states parties endeavour to ensure that their language is used in relations with the administrative authorities and can be studied at school (Articles 10 and 14).

The Council of Europe's European Charter for Regional or Minority Languages of 5 December 1992 seeks to protect multilingualism without, however, establishing justiciable rights for individuals or groups. States are required to respect the use of minority languages in public and private life. Additionally, states must promote the use of minority languages by means of educational, judicial and administrative programmes and through the media.[105]

---

[104] Rainer Hofmann, 'The Work of the Advisory Committee under the Framework Convention for the Protection of National Minorities, with Particular Emphasis on Germany', in Martin Scheinin and Reeta Toivanen (eds), *Rethinking Non-Discrimination and Minority Rights* (Institute for Human Rights: Åbo Akademi, 2004), 64 and 91.

[105] Minority protection is also implemented institutionally at the European level by the OSCE High Commissioner on National Minorities, whose mandate does not, however, include treaty monitoring (see Chapter 8, section VI.1).

3. The protection of indigenous peoples

(a) Protection of individual rights

Indigenous peoples are a territory's 'original inhabitants', ie descendants of the population of a state's territory who lived there before the now dominant population assumed control as a result of migration or conquest. The definition also encompasses peoples living in tribes, who are socially, culturally, and economically different from the majority population and whose way of life is regulated wholly or partially by their own customs and traditions.[106]

Even where they do not regard themselves as a minority but rather as an autonomous community unwilling to have anything to do with the state concerned, indigenous peoples can invoke Article 27 of the ICCPR. The views of the Human Rights Committee on communications by members of these peoples deal for the most part with the use of natural resources and questions of membership to a particular indigenous community.

Generally, indigenous peoples have a deep-rooted and often spiritual relationship with the land on which they live and with the natural resources that they use. For such peoples land and resources are not merely property and means of production, but the very basis of their existence, traditions and beliefs. Accordingly, the land and resources must be available for use by all members of the community freely and collectively.[107] The Human Rights Committee recognizes that economic activities may be deemed to form part of a minority's own culture when they constitute an essential element of its cultural tradition, as in the case of Maori fisheries in New Zealand or Sami reindeer breeding in Finland and Sweden.[108] State measures or state-tolerated private activities that have an adverse impact on traditional economic activities are permissible, however, if the minority concerned is consulted in advance, the adverse impact is kept to a minimum and members of the minority can continue to pursue their way of life. Consequently, Article 27 was not violated by the granting of a permit for a small quarry in northern Finland in which work was suspended during the period used for reindeer pasturing, nor was there a violation where a logging permit was granted for a relatively small area in which reindeer lived on tree lichen in winter.[109] By contrast, a

---

[106] See the definition of indigenous peoples in Art 1 of the ILO Indigenous and Tribal Peoples Convention (No 169) and in the draft United Nations Declaration on the Rights of Indigenous Peoples, UN Doc E/CN.4/Sub.2/1994/56.

[107] José R Martínez Cobo, 'Study of the Problem of Discrimination against Indigenous Populations', UN Doc E/CN.4/Sub.2/1986/7, Vol. V, paras 196 f.

[108] HRCttee, *Kitok v Sweden*, Communication No 197/1985 (1988), para 9.2; *Mahuika et al v New Zealand*, Communication No 547/1993 (2000), para 9.3. In *Mahuika*, para 9.4, and in *Länsman et al v Finland*, Communication No 511/1992 (1994), para 9.3, the Committee recognized that a minority does not lose its right to protection of its own culture where it modernizes its traditional economic activity.

[109] HRCttee, *Länsman et al v Finland*, Communication No 511/1992 (1994), paras 9.1–9.8; *Länsman et al v Finland*, Communication No 671/1995 (1996), paras 10.4–10.6; *Äärelä and Näkkäläjärvi v Finland*, Communication No 779/1997 (2001), para 7.6.

permit for large-scale oil and gas exploration was deemed to be incompatible with the way of life of the Lubicon Lake Cree Indians in Canada.[110]

On the question of membership to such communities, the Committee decided that persons who are descendants of indigenous peoples can be prevented from sharing those peoples' way of life only where this seems reasonable and necessary to preserve the identity of the people concerned. These conditions were fulfilled in the case of Mr Kitok, who wished to take up the way of life of a reindeer-breeding Sami, because the pasture areas available for reindeer husbandry were too small to permit further breeding. They were however not realized in the case of Ms Lovelace, who had lost the right to live in her tribe's reservation following her marriage to a white man and who wished to resume the Indian way of life after her divorce. There were no serious reasons in this case to prohibit her return.[111] Both cases show that individual entitlements under Article 27 can clash with the collective rights it implicitly contains, and that in some circumstances majority interests within a community may take precedence over those of an individual or of a minority within the minority.[112]

The Inter-American Court of Human Rights deduces from the right to protection of property the obligation of states to respect the particularities of the lifestyle of indigenous communities and most importantly their right to use their land according to their traditions.[113]

(b) Protection of collective rights

As evidenced by the generally poor success rate of individual claims of violations of ICCPR, Article 27 the individual rights approach of the Covenant has its limitations in addressing the problems of those wishing to preserve their traditional communal, tribe- or clan-based way of life and to defend their natural resources against state interference. For some time now indigenous peoples have therefore been demanding protection of their collective rights.

Such protection is afforded, at least to some extent, by the ILO Indigenous and Tribal Peoples Convention of 27 June 1989 (No 169). It sets out guarantees for indigenous and tribal peoples such as the right to their own territory and their own way of life, culture and language. Thus, they may set their own priorities for development (Article 7) and apply their own laws, including rules governing the punishment of offences, provided that they are compatible with

---

[110] HRCttee, *Ominayak and the Lubicon Lake Band v Canada*, Communication No 167/1984 (1990), para 33.

[111] HRCttee, *Lovelace v Canada*, Communication No 24/1977 (1981), para 17, and *Kitok v Sweden*, Communication No 197/1985 (1988), para 9.8.

[112] A similar fate was suffered by the Maoris who, unlike the majority of their people, were opposed to a settlement with the Government on the sharing of fishery rights between indigenous inhabitants and the immigrant population (HRCttee, *Mahuika et al v New Zealand*, Communication No 547/1993 (2000), paras 9.5–9.8). An important point for the rejection of the communication was that the Government had conducted extensive consultations with the tribes concerned and a majority of the tribes had consented to the settlement.

[113] Eg, IACtHR, *Mayagna (Sumo) Awas Tingni Community v Nicaragua*, Series C, No 79 (2001). See Chapter 14, section III.3.c.

international human rights law (Articles 8 and 9), and their land rights must be respected (Article 14).

For a long time, the majority of states were reluctant to recognize the rights of indigenous peoples. This was evidenced by the low ratification rate of ILO Convention No 169,[114] and by the fact that the negotiations on a Declaration by the UN General Assembly were deadlocked for more than a decade. A breakthrough came on 13 September 2007 when, with a large majority, the General Assembly adopted the United Nations Declaration on the Rights of Indigenous Peoples.[115] The declaration contains both collective and individual rights. Indigenous peoples possess the right to self-determination which is defined as the right to 'freely determine their political status and freely pursue their economic, social and cultural development' (Article 3); therefore, they are entitled to have 'autonomy or self-government in matters relating to their internal and local affairs, as well as ways and means for financing their autonomous functions' (Article 4) and 'to maintain and strengthen their distinct political, legal, economic, social and cultural institutions, while retaining their right to participate fully, if they so choose, in the political, economic, social and cultural life of the State' (Article 5; similarly Article 20). Also, they can exercise their cultural and religious traditions and use their language (Articles 11–13). As a consequence, indigenous peoples and their members 'have the right not to be subjected to forced assimilation or destruction of their culture' (Article 8(1)). The particularly deep attachment of indigenous peoples to their land is protected by Article 10, stating that they 'shall not be forcibly removed from their lands or territories. No relocation shall take place without the free, prior and informed consent of the indigenous peoples concerned and after agreement on just and fair compensation and, where possible, with the option of return.' Indigenous peoples also 'have the right to redress, by means that can include restitution or, when this is not possible, just, fair and equitable compensation, for the lands, territories and resources which they have traditionally owned or otherwise occupied or used, and which have been confiscated, taken, occupied, used or damaged without their free, prior and informed consent' (Article 20(1)).

Protection of cultural traditions of indigenous peoples coupled with the right to keep their own institutions may create dangers for the human rights of individuals subjected to such pre-modern traditions against their will. This is particularly relevant where indigenous institutions exercise judicial functions. For these reasons, Article 34 insists that judicial systems and customs can only be maintained 'in accordance with international human rights standards'. More generally, Article 46(2) underlines that '[i]n the exercise of the rights enunciated in the present Declaration, human rights and fundamental freedoms of all shall be respected'.

---

[114] A total of 20 states in December 2008.
[115] UN General Assembly Resolution A/Res/61/295 (2007). The resolution was adopted with 143 votes in favour to 4 against, with 11 abstentions.

12

Protection of Private Life

I. Overview

Private life is where we as individuals decide about matters we do not want to share with others; where we determine a way of life or style of living that reflects our (egocentric) attitudes, values, tastes and preferences; where we take pleasure in intimate relationships with a lover, shape our family life, or enjoy being together with our friends. Private life is at home where we want to keep out the state or people who are strangers to us. Private life is where we leave the public sphere behind us to be with and among ourselves.[1] As 'right to be left alone' it protects the space 'in which the individual is free to be itself'.[2]

The right to private life ranks high among the traditional civil liberties. As 'freedom to autonomy' at home it represents one of the two key aspects of the western tradition of freedom, 'freedom to participate' in the public realm being the other facet of an understanding that guarantees freedom both in the private as well as in the public sphere.[3]

The right is reflected in the ICCPR as well as in all regional conventions but terminology is not uniform. Article 17 of the ICCPR and some of the regional conventions[4] talk about protection from interference with 'privacy' whereas Article 8 of the ECHR guarantees the right to respect for 'private life'. Among these two notions, 'private life' seems to be more comprehensive as a concept and is used in this chapter as an overarching notion covering both the right to respect for privacy (section II), the right to family (section III) and the right to marry and found a family (section IV).

International human rights law protects this right in different ways. On one level it guarantees the *right of everyone to personal autonomy*, ie the right to make autonomous decisions regarding personal matters, for example, one's personal relations, one's lifestyle, or whether to undergo medical treatment. On a second level, international human rights law enshrines the right to privacy *in spatial*

---

[1] See Manfred Nowak, *UN Covenant on Civil and Political Rights, CCPR Commentary* (2nd edn, Engel: Kehl, 2005), 377–9 for the history and the different shades of the notion of privacy.

[2] Lord Mustill in *R v Broadcasting Standards Commission, ex p BBC (Liberty Intervening)* [2000] 3 All ER 989.

[3] See Nowak (n 1) 377 with references. [4] ACHR, Art 11; ArCHR, Art 21.

terms by prohibiting, in principle, state access to a person's residence either physically or, for example, through electronic or other means of surveillance. On a third and final level, the right to private life protects the *right to live together within the family*. This aspect of the right prohibits—albeit not absolutely— authorities, for instance, from forcibly separating children from their parents or spouses from each other. The right to private life is supplemented by the *right to marry and to found a family* which, in principle, precludes the state from prohibiting a man and woman of marriageable age from marrying and founding a family.

II. The Right to Protection of Privacy

Relevant provisions: UDHR, Article 12; ICCPR, Article 17; CRC, Article 16; CRPD, Article 22; ACHR, Article 11; ArCHR, Article 21; ECHR, Article 8.

1. Scope of protection of the right to privacy

The right to privacy provides protection in a large number of circumstances that are somewhat difficult to define in general terms.[5] The purpose of the right is to secure for the individual autonomy in private matters. The relevant treaty provisions as well as the case law of the Human Rights Committee, and in particular, the European Court of Human Rights, recognize different dimensions of the right that can be grouped into (a) respect of privacy, (b) respect of communication, and (c) respect of home.

Example: The ECtHR judgment in *Pretty v The United Kingdom*[6] (private life)

In this judgment the European Court of Human Rights described the scope of the protection afforded to private life as follows:

[T]he concept of "private life" is a broad term not susceptible to exhaustive definition. It covers the physical and psychological integrity of a person...It can sometimes embrace aspects of an individual's physical and social identity...Elements such as, for example, gender identification, name and sexual orientation and sexual life fall within the personal sphere protected by Article 8...Article 8 also protects a right to personal development, and the right to establish and develop relationships with other human beings and the outside world...Although no previous case has established as such any right to self-determination as being contained in Article 8 of the Convention, the Court considers that the notion of personal autonomy is an important principle underlying the interpretation of its guarantees.

---

[5] For instance, HRCttee General Comment No 16 (1988) on ICCPR, Art 17 contains no general definition of the substantive scope of application of this right.

[6] ECtHR, *Pretty v The United Kingdom*, *Reports* 2002-III, para 61.

(a) Respect of privacy

The right to respect of privacy is intended to secure space for individual self-determination and development without outside interference.[7] Such autonomy is clearly affected if an individual's private behaviour is monitored by authorities. Therefore, *freedom from state surveillance* in one's own private sphere is essential to protect the individual's private life. Typical violations of this right include all forms of surveillance of a person's home, especially by means of telephone tapping.[8] The extent to which the increasing surveillance of public space, eg by video cameras, is covered by these guarantees is still far from clear.[9]

The jurisprudence of the European Court of Human Rights holds that the right to privacy includes, second, a right to protection of privacy in the media. Thus, Article 8 of the ECHR requires states, on request, to prohibit a newspaper from publishing photographs taken without the consent of the person concerned and showing him or her engaged in strictly private activities.[10] Furthermore, the storage, use and exploitation of all kinds of private data, ie in particular biometric and genetic data,[11] as well as police records on a person's political activities[12] are also covered by the guarantee, which means that core aspects of data protection have a human rights dimension. The right to be informed about the existence of personal data collection and the right to the rectification or possible deletion of false data is also protected.

According to the jurisprudence of the European Court of Human Rights (which is not yet paralleled in that of the Human Rights Committee), the notion of privacy encompasses, third, a person's *right to make choices about one's own body* and thus to protection of *physical and mental integrity*[13] in cases that fall short of the threshold of applicability of the prohibition of inhuman and degrading treatment.[14] Accordingly, interference with physical integrity such as compulsory

---

[7] Nowak (n 1) 377 ff.

[8] HRCttee, Concluding Observations Poland (1999), para 22; ECtHR, *Kopp v Switzerland*, *Reports* 1998-II, para 50.

[9] See Nowak (n 1), 388. In ECtHR, *Martin v The United Kingdom*, Application No 63608/00 (2003), the Court admitted that the video camera surveillance of the entrance to a private home fell within the field of protection offered by ECHR, Art 8. An amicable solution was found and the case closed. See also Resolution 1604 (2008) of the Parliamentary Assembly of the Council of Europe on video surveillance of public areas, para 5, where the Council explicitly says that 'video surveillance may impinge on human rights such as privacy and data protection'.

[10] ECtHR, *Von Hannover v Germany*, *Reports* 2004-VI.

[11] See, for example, HRCttee, General Comment No 16 (1988), para 10; ECtHR, *Leander v Sweden*, Series A, No 116 (1987), para 48, and *S and Marper v The United Kingdom* (Grand Chamber), Application No 30562/04 and 30566/04 (2008), paras 66 ff.

[12] ECtHR, *Segerstedt-Wiberg and Others v Sweden*, Application No 62332/00 (2006), para 72.

[13] See, for example, ECtHR, *X and Y v The Netherlands*, Series A, No 91 (1985), and *Pretty v The United Kingdom*, *Reports* 2002-III, para 61. Similarly, with regard to the ICCPR, see Nowak (n 1) 385 f.

[14] The ECtHR explicitly recognized this function of ECHR, Art 8 for example in its judgments in *Raninen v Finland*, *Reports* 1997-VIII, para 63, and *Wainwright v The United Kingdom*, Application No 12350/04 (2006), para 46.

blood tests, compulsory medical treatment of schoolchildren, as well as insults or minor forms of humiliation falling outside the scope of protection of the prohibition of inhuman or degrading treatment constitute an encroachment on an area protected by ECHR, Article 8. This also applies to any medical treatment undertaken without the consent of the person concerned.[15] While Article 8 does not guarantee no 'right to any specific level of medical care' the Court recognizes that states parties have to take active measures to ensure that individuals are conscious of their claims as to the protection of their physical integrity in the private sphere, for example when dealing with a private doctor and that they really can assert them.[16] Another important aspect is the right to have access to information relevant in the context of health problems and their treatment. The Court recognized that ECHR, Article 8 entitled an army veteran who had been exposed to tests on nerve gas in the 1960s and subsequently suffered because of breathing difficulties the right to receive information on these tests. The Court accepted that the uncertainty caused by the lack of information as to whether or not he had been put at risk through his participation in the tests 'could reasonably be accepted to have caused him substantial anxiety and stress' and considered 'that a positive obligation arose to provide an "effective and accessible procedure" enabling the applicant to have access to "all relevant and appropriate information"... which would allow him to assess any risk to which he had been exposed during his participation in the tests'.[17] Overall, the present stage of case law does not yet allow determining the content of the right to privacy in the area of health and its limitations with sufficient precision.

Example: The ECtHR judgment in *Pretty v The United Kingdom*[18] (right to make choices about one's own body)

In this case the European Court of Human Rights had to determine whether a right to choose the time of one's own death could be derived from the right to private life. The United Kingdom argued 'that the right to private life cannot encapsulate a right to die with assistance, such being a negation of the protection that the Convention was intended to provide'.[19] The Court did not agree with this argument and defined the scope of the right of individual self-determination as follows:

62.... The Court would observe that the ability to conduct one's life in a manner of one's own choosing may also include the opportunity to pursue activities perceived to be of a physically or morally harmful or dangerous nature for the individual concerned. The extent to which a State can use compulsory powers or the criminal law to protect people from the consequences of their chosen lifestyle has long been a topic of moral and jurisprudential discussion, the fact that the interference is often viewed as trespassing on the private and personal sphere adding to the vigour of the debate. However, even where the conduct poses a danger to health or,

---

[15] See ECtHR, *Pretty v The United Kingdom*, *Reports* 2002-III, para 63.
[16] ECtHR, *Tysiac v Poland*, Application No 5410/03 (2007), paras 107 ff.
[17] ECtHR (Grand Chamber), *Roche v The United Kingdom*, *Reports* 2005-X, especially para 155.
[18] ECtHR, *Pretty v The United Kingdom*, *Reports* 2002-III.   [19] Ibid, para 62.

arguably, where it is of a life-threatening nature, the case-law of the Convention institutions has regarded the State's imposition of compulsory or criminal measures as impinging on the private life of the applicant within the meaning of Article 8 § 1 and requiring justification in terms of the second paragraph.

For that reason the Court accepted that ECHR, Article 8 protects the right of a mentally competent person to refuse medical treatment even where the refusal might lead to a fatal outcome, because the imposition of medical treatment without the consent of such a person would interfere with his or her physical integrity. A person is thus free to choose to die by refusing medical treatment. The Court further reasoned:

65. The very essence of the Convention is respect for human dignity and human freedom. Without in any way negating the principle of sanctity of life protected under the Convention, the Court considers that it is under Article 8 that notions of the quality of life take on significance. In an era of growing medical sophistication combined with longer life expectancies, many people are concerned that they should not be forced to linger on in old age or in states of advanced physical or mental decrepitude which conflict with strongly held ideas of self and personal identity…

The Court stated that it was not prepared to exclude the possibility that there had been interference with the right to private life of a person who, unable to end her life herself because of a disease that would lead to an undignified and distressing death, was prevented by law from seeking assistance in committing suicide. However, it held that the prohibition of euthanasia pursued legitimate public interests, particularly that of protecting the weak and vulnerable who might no longer be in a position to make a free choice; moreover, the interference was proportionate in view of the high interest of safeguarding life.[20]

A fourth component of the right to privacy is the *right to protection of one's own identity*. This aspect has so far been reflected in the jurisprudence primarily as the entitlement to protection of one's name as a core expression of identity.[21] However, states are generally given a wide margin of discretion in regulating the use of names. The Human Rights Committee nevertheless characterized a state's refusal to allow persons who had converted to Hinduism to change their names as a violation of this aspect of the right to privacy; it also held 'if a state were to compel all foreigners to change their surnames, this would constitute interference in contravention of article 17'.[22] The European Court of Human Rights concluded that a law concerning married couples' family name that discriminated between men and women was a violation of the Convention[23] and held that the right of parents to choose a first name for their children is also protected by the Convention.[24] Protection of identity furthermore includes knowledge of

---

[20] Ibid, paras 68 ff.
[21] The ACHR however, enshrines an explicit right to a name in Art 18.
[22] HRCttee, *Coeriel and Aurik v The Netherlands*, Communication No 453/1991 (1994), paras 10.2–10.5.
[23] ECtHR, *Burghartz v Switzerland*, Series A, No 280-B (1994), para 25.
[24] ECtHR, *Guillot v France, Reports* 1996-V, paras 21 f, and *Johansson v Finland*, Application No 10163/02 (2007), paras 28 ff.

one's parentage. The state must therefore take legal measures to ensure that, for instance, adoptive[25] or extramarital[26] children are able to exercise this right in practice. The right to privacy also protects a person's sexual identity as a core component of human identity. Thus, states are required, for example, to recognize the new gender of transsexual persons after a sex change for all official purposes and, in particular, to change relevant entries in birth registers and identity papers.[27] Finally, dress and hairstyle are protected as part of a person's identity, so that state regulations governing dress and hairstyle are permissible only if they are based on law and necessary to achieve a legitimate goal.[28]

A fifth aspect of the right to privacy under ICCPR, Article 17 and ECHR, Article 8 is the right to *respect for existing intimate relationships between individuals*.[29] The jurisprudence of the treaty monitoring bodies focuses in this context on the protection of consensual sexual relations between adults including consensual same-sex relationships.[30] This right is violated, for example, if consensual homosexual relations between adults are a crime;[31] if a country's armed forces investigate the sexual orientation of their servicemen or servicewomen;[32] or if a rule of national penal law makes a difference between the age of sexual maturity for heterosexual and homosexual relations.[33] The right to respect for relationships between individuals has been extended by the European Court of Human Rights

---

[25] ECtHR, *Mikulić v Croatia, Reports* 2002-I, para 54: 'The Court has held that respect for private life requires that everyone should be able to establish details of their identity as individual human beings and that an individual's entitlement to such information is of importance because of its formative implications for him or her.' This right is made explicit in CRC, Art 7 which stipulates that all children must be registered immediately after birth so that they may know who their parents are.

[26] ECtHR, *Jäggi v Switzerland*, Application No 58757/00 (2006). In this case, the probable father of the 68-year-old complainant had successfully resisted all efforts to clarify his paternity. After the death of the probable father, the complainant demanded that his body be exhumed so as to enable a DNA test. This demand was refused. As he had been trying to ascertain his father's identity for the greater part of his life and was suffering mental disturbances because of these uncertainties, the Court decided that his interests outweighed those of the surviving family and decided that Art 8 had been violated (ibid, paras 40 ff).

[27] ECtHR (Grand Chamber), *I v The United Kingdom*, Application No 25680/94 (2002), paras 51 ff.

[28] See Nowak (n 1) 385 f.

[29] This right also has a negative dimension, ie it also protects the rejection of certain ties. For instance, any compulsory determination of paternity constitutes an interference with this right, Mark E Villiger, *Handbuch der Europäischen Menschenrechtskonvention* (2nd edn, Schulthess: Zürich, 1999), 357 f.

[30] HRCttee, *Toonen v Australia*, Communication No 488/1992 (1994), para 8.2; and ECtHR, *Modinos v Cyprus*, Series A, No 259 (1993) para 24.

[31] HRCttee, *Toonen v Australia*, Communication No 488/1992 (1994), paras 8.3 ff; ECtHR, *Modinos v Cyprus*, Series A, No 259 (1993), para 25. On the other hand, the ECtHR held that a criminal conviction for serious bodily harm due to consensual sado-masochistic activities was admissible, but stated that such practices also came within the scope of protection of ECHR, Art 8; *Laskey, Jaggard and Brown v The United Kingdom, Reports* 1997-I, paras 36 ff.

[32] ECtHR, *Smith and Grady v The United Kingdom, Reports* 1999-VI.

[33] ECtHR, *Wolfmeyer v Austria*, Application No 5263/03 (2005). The Court decided that Art 8 read in conjunction with ECHR, Art 14 had been violated, despite the fact that national courts declared the norm contrary to the constitution and refused to enforce it.

to cover certain business relations with third parties involving confidential matters, specifically the relationship between a lawyer and his or her client.[34]

A particular aspect of this right is the relationship between couples or single parents and their children. The right to respect of one's decision to have a child is therefore subsumed under the right to privacy by recent jurisprudence of the European Court of Human Rights.[35] This claim encompasses the right to have access to methods of artificial reproduction.[36] On the other hand, the Court left open the question whether the right to privacy includes a freestanding right to adoption.[37] However, if a state party allows every individual to seek an adoption authorization non-respect for this right is covered by the Article 8 guarantee.[38] Therefore, the refusal to authorize an adoption because of the sexual orientation of the applicant may amount to discrimination breaching ECHR, Article 14 in conjunction with the right to privacy, unless it is justified by legitimate reasons.[39] Despite lacking jurisprudence, it seems obvious that coercive state measures of birth control fall within the sphere protected by this guarantee and must therefore respect the barriers it imposes.

Based on the Strasbourg jurisprudence, the respect of a person's wish to the contrary, ie not to have children, also comes within the scope of protection of this limitable right.[40] The treaty monitoring bodies have not yet conclusively determined whether abortions fall within the sphere of applicability of the right to privacy. Whilst the former European Commission of Human Rights explicitly left the question open,[41] the Court acknowledged, 'that legislation regulating the interruption of pregnancy touches upon the sphere of private life, since whenever a woman is pregnant her private life becomes closely connected with the developing foetus'.[42] Based on this, it judged that in the case of a very short-sighted woman who was not granted permission to abort, although medical experts had confirmed that the pregnancy endangered her eyesight and the national law allowed for the right to abort in the case of medical indication, the right to privacy was

---

[34] ECtHR, *Niemietz v Germany*, Series A, No 251-B (1992), para 29; *Wieser and Bicos Beteiligungen GmbH v Austria*, Application No 74336/01 (2007), paras 42 ff.

[35] ECtHR (Grand Chamber), *Evans v The United Kingdom*, Application No 6339/05 (2007), para 71.

[36] ECtHR (Grand Chamber), *Dickson v The United Kingdom*, Application No 44362/04 (2007), para 66. Based on this judgment, a person condemned to lifelong detention may call upon the protection of ECHR, Art 8 to this end (ibid, paras 66 ff).

[37] ECtHR (Grand Chamber), *EB v France*, Application No 43546/02 (2008), para 46.

[38] Ibid, para 49.

[39] The complaint was accepted for this reason. On the accessory discrimination prohibition, see Chapter 11, section II.1.

[40] ECtHR (Grand Chamber), *Evans v The United Kingdom*, Application No 6339/05 (2007), para 71.

[41] In 1978 the former ECmHR came to the enigmatic conclusion that ECHR, Art 8 could not be interpreted as meaning 'that pregnancy and its termination are, as a principle, solely a matter of the private life of the mother' (*Brüggemann and Scheuten v Germany*, Application No 6959/75, DR 10 (1977), 100, para 61). On the issue of abortion see also Chapter 9, section II.3.c.

[42] ECtHR, *Tysiac v Poland*, Application No 5410/03 (2007), para 106.

violated because the national legislation failed to provide for any effective mechanism to determine whether the conditions for a legal abortion were given.[43] The Human Rights Committee regularly criticizes states that prohibit termination of pregnancy under all circumstances or with only exceedingly restrictive exceptions, referring to the threat posed by illegal abortions to the lives of the women concerned, who in their desperation may resort to unsafe methods of terminating pregnancy.[44] In an individual case, the Committee concluded that to deny the possibility of an abortion to a 17-year-old minor carrying an anencephalic foetus destined to die shortly after birth not only constituted inhuman treatment because of the intense suffering imposed on the young mother but also amounted to violation of her right to privacy, taking into consideration that her decision to terminate the pregnancy would have been in accordance with domestic law.[45] This, however, does not amount to an autonomous right to abortion. Rather, the right to privacy may shape and limit state prohibitions on abortion .

The *right to protection of a person's honour and reputation* as a sixth component of the right to privacy concerns an individual's social standing. This right is not only guaranteed by the ICCPR, which contains wording to that effect, but also by ECHR, Article 8[46] and ACHR, Article 11.[47] Accordingly, the state may not undermine a person's honour and reputation itself[48] and it must provide remedies against attacks by private parties.[49]

A particularly grievous attack on several aspects of the right to privacy, which aims to guarantee all individuals the freedom necessary to develop their personality,[50] is the withdrawal of legal capacity, as a person becomes dependent on his or her legal representative for nearly all questions pertaining to his life.[51]

To what extent the treaty monitoring bodies would be prepared to include other dimensions of personal lifestyle within the scope of protection of this right, remains to be seen. However, it is clear that, despite its wide field of protection, no general right to freedom of any kind of action can be derived from the right to privacy.

---

[43] Ibid, paras 114 ff.

[44] It generally refers, however, to the right to life (ICCPR, Art 6) rather than to the protection of privacy. See, for example, HRCttee, Concluding Observations Poland (2004), para 8; Concluding Observations Colombia (2004), para 13; Concluding Observations Morocco (2004), para 29.

[45] HRCttee, *Huamán v Peru*, Communication No 1153/2003 (2005), paras 6.3–6.4.

[46] Villiger (n 29), 356 f.

[47] IACtHR, *Case of the Miguel Castro-Castro Prison v Peru*, Series C, No 160 (2006), paras 358 ff.

[48] HRCttee, *Birindwa and Tshisekedi v Zaire*, Communication Nos 241/1987 and 242/1987 (1989), para 12.7.

[49] HRCttee, General Comment No 16 (1988), para 11.

[50] ECtHR, *Shtukaturov v Russia*, Application No 44009/05 (2008), para 83.

[51] Ibid, paras 85 ff. This is particularly the case, where, as in this case, this measure is pronounced for an undetermined time span and the patronized person can only take legal action against this measure with the help of his or her legal representative, the latter having demanded the measure in the first place. Under the ICCPR, such a case could also be assessed based on the right to recognition as a person before the law in ICCPR, Art 16.

(b) Respect of communication

Article 17 of the ICCPR and the regional conventions[52] explicitly recognize a basic right to respect for and hence non-interference with correspondence and modern means of communication. The relevant jurisprudence relates almost exclusively to the issue of whether it is permissible to restrict correspondence by and with persons in custody.[53] Monitoring of correspondence between a detainee and his lawyer constitutes an interference with this right and is only permissible if it is not arbitrary (ICCPR, Article 17(1); ACHR, Article 11(2); ArCHR, Article 21), ie carried out in accordance with the law and necessary to achieve a legitimate aim (ECHR, Article 8(2)). The Court has stated that:

the prison authorities may open a letter from a lawyer to a prisoner when they have reasonable cause to believe that it contains an illicit enclosure which the normal means of detection have failed to disclose. The letter should, however, only be opened and should not be read. Suitable guarantees preventing the reading of the letter should be provided, *eg* opening the letter in the presence of the prisoner. The reading of a prisoner's mail to and from a lawyer, on the other hand, should only be permitted in exceptional circumstances when the authorities have reasonable cause to believe that the privilege is being abused in that the contents of the letter endanger prison security or the safety of others or are otherwise of a criminal nature. What may be regarded as 'reasonable cause' will depend on all the circumstances but it presupposes the existence of facts or information which would satisfy an objective observer that the privileged channel of communication was being abused.[54]

Interference with the right to respect for correspondence may in particular be justified in cases of suspected terrorists where it is necessary to ensure maximal security during the trial.[55]

(c) Respect of the home[56]

Article 17 of the ICCPR and regional conventions[57] explicitly recognize a right to respect of the home, which includes protection against state and private interference involving, for instance, state-conducted searches, forced evictions by state authorities, or the destruction of housing by them.[58] According to the jurisprudence of the European Court of Human Rights, the wording of

---

[52] ACHR, Art 11(2); ArCHR, Art 21; ECHR, Art 8.
[53] HRCttee, *Pinkney v Canada*, Communication No 27/1978 (1981); ECtHR, *Campbell v The United Kingdom*, A/233 (1992), paras 33 ff; *Rinzivillo v Italy*, Application No 31543/96 (2000), paras 25 ff; and *Erdem v Germany*, Application No 38321/97 (2001), paras 53 ff.
[54] ECtHR, *Campbell v The United Kingdom*, Series A, No 233 (1992), para 47.
[55] ECtHR, *Erdem v Germany*, Application No 38321/97 (2001), paras 66 ff.
[56] See also Chapter 9, section III.3 on the right to adequate housing.
[57] ACHR, Art 11(2); ArCHR, Art 21; ECHR, Art 8.
[58] HRCttee, *Rojas García v Colombia*, Communication No 687/1996 (2001), and *Sultanova v Usbekistan*, Communication No 915/2000 (2006), para 7.9, as well as ECtHR, *Moldovan and Others v Romania*, Reports 2005-VII, paras 102 ff.

ECHR, Article 8 may also be construed as providing protection for business premises.[59]

One particularly interesting aspect of this right is the protection it provides, together with the right to privacy, against *harmful emissions* and similar environmental hazards. Hence environmental pollution can raise human rights issues.[60] In this regard, the European Court of Human Rights stated that a person's home:

> will usually be the place, the physically defined area, where private and family life develops. The individual has a right to respect for his home, meaning not just the right to the actual physical area, but also to the quiet enjoyment of that area. Breaches of the right to respect for the home are not confined to concrete or physical breaches, such as unauthorised entry into a person's home, but also include those that are not concrete or physical, such as noise, emissions, smells or other forms of interference. A serious breach may result in the breach of a person's right to respect for his home if it prevents him from enjoying the amenities of his home.[61]

Issue in focus: Protection of privacy and environmental protection

The European Court of Human Rights began in the mid-1990s to derive from the right to protection of home and private life an entitlement to protection against harmful emissions and hence, to some extent, the right to a healthy environment. In the *Lopez-Ostra* case, the Court decided that Spain had violated ECHR, Article 8 by failing to intervene when a company began to treat waste from tanneries in a manner that generated foul-smelling fumes adversely affecting the health of Ms Lopez-Ostra and her family. The Court ruled that by remaining passive, the state had failed to strike a fair balance between the public interest of the town in having the waste-treatment plant and the victim's effective enjoyment of her right to respect of her home and her private and family life.[62]

In *Guerra v Italy* the local authorities had done nothing to reduce the risks associated with fertilizer production in the vicinity of the town of Manfredonia although the central government had rated the risks as 'high'. The Court stated that severe environmental pollution could affect individuals' well-being and prevent them from enjoying their homes, thereby entailing a violation of the right to respect of their private and family life. Moreover, the authorities had also violated ECHR, Article 8 by failing to provide the complainants with information that would have enabled them to assess the risks from the plant that they and their families might run by continuing to live in Manfredonia.[63]

---

[59] ECtHR, *Niemitz v Germany*, Series A, No 251-B (1992), paras 27 ff, and *Sallinen and Others v Finland*, Application No 50882/99 (2005), paras 89 ff.

[60] ECtHR (Grand Chamber), *Tahsin Acar v Turkey*, Reports 2004-III (emissions from a goldmine).

[61] ECtHR, *Giacomelli v Italy*, Application No 59909/00 (2007), para 76. Similar *Hatton and Others v the United Kingdom* (Grand Chamber), *Reports* 2003-VIII, para 96.

[62] ECtHR, *Lopez-Ostra v Spain*, Series A, No 303C (1994), para 58.

[63] ECtHR (Grand Chamber), *Guerra and Others v Italy*, Reports 1998-I, para 60.

In the *Hatton* case, a Chamber of the European Court of Human Rights first concluded that the United Kingdom had failed to fulfil its duty to take reasonable and appropriate measures to secure the victims' rights under ECHR, Article 8 when the relevant authorities allowed a large number of night flights at Heathrow airport without sufficiently assessing the impact on the sleep of people living in the approach corridors.[64] The Grand Chamber confirmed the applicability of Article 8 to the case of noise emissions but made a different assessment of the facts, holding that government measures for protection against noise were sufficient.[65]

In the *Taşkin and Others v Turkey* case, the Court addressed the question of emissions from a privately owned goldmine. It confirmed its jurisprudence by deciding that the authorities had violated ECHR, Article 8 when, ignoring expert reports warning against the harmful impact on the environment and the local population, they permitted the extraction of gold by sodium cyanide leaching. In addition, the authorities failed to shut down the mine when the Supreme Administrative Court decided, in light of the expert reports, that the operation of the mine was unlawful.[66]

In the *Fadeyeva v Russia* case,[67] the question of the permissibility of emissions from a former state steel plant was discussed. The applicant lived in a municipal apartment for which the rent was far below the normal market rate. Her apartment, like many others, was located in a security zone surrounding the steel plant in which toxic emissions greatly exceeded the acceptable norms. The emissions were such that no one should have been living in the area at all. A Russian court therefore held that the applicant should be assigned an apartment outside the zone as a matter of priority. She was subsequently placed on a waiting list as number 6820. The responsible authorities took no action over the following five years to resettle her and the other inhabitants of the security zone. The ECtHR concluded that although there was no obligation under ECHR, Article 8 to provide the applicant with free housing and it was not the Court's role to dictate the precise measures that Russia should adopt in order to comply with its positive duties under that article, the state's failure to assist the applicant in finding an apartment at a comparable rent outside the security zone constituted a violation of Article 8.

Similarly, in the case *Giacomelli v Italy*,[68] the compatibility of emissions, here from an installation for storing and treating hazardous waste, with the right to protection of the home stood to discussion. Ms Giacomelli, whose house was only 30 meters away from the installation, claimed that the state authorizations to enlarge massively its capacity were not acceptable. The Court concluded that ECHR, Article 8 was violated because the authorizations had been issued without prior examination of

---

[64] ECtHR, *Hatton and Others v The United Kingdom*, Application No 36022/97 (2001), para 95.

[65] ECtHR (Grand Chamber), *Hatton and Others v The United Kingdom*, *Reports* 2003-VIII, paras 120 ff.

[66] ECtHR, *Taşkin and Others v Turkey*, *Reports* 2004-X, para 108 ff. See also *Moreno Gómez v Spain*, *Reports* 2004-X, paras 53–63 (violation of ECHR, Art 8 because the authorities refused to take steps against night-time disturbances by discotheques, although noise emissions had far exceeded the maximum permitted levels for some time).

[67] ECtHR, *Fadeyeva v Russia*, *Reports* 2005-IV.

[68] ECtHR, *Giacomelli v Italy*, Application No 59909/00 (2007).

the project's compatibility with the protection of the environment, as foreseen in the national regulations, and the competent authorities had refused to shut down the installation until it fulfilled the legal requirements, despite the fact that national tribunals had confirmed the unlawfulness of the authorizations.

2. The duty to respect

The right to privacy requires states parties to refrain primarily from interfering with the private sphere, with physical and mental integrity, and with the free conduct of relations with intimate partners and other persons. However, the obligation to respect is not absolute. While ECHR, Article 8 allows proportionate interference with this right in pursuit of public interests or to protect the rights of others where such interference is in accordance with the law, ICCPR, Article 17, ACHR, Article 11(2), and ArCHR, Article 21(2) prohibit 'arbitrary' interference with the guarantees involved. The Human Rights Committee's interpretation of this notion resembles a limitation clause inasmuch as it regards interference with protected interests as lawful only where it takes 'place on the basis of law, which itself must comply with the provisions, aims and objectives of the Covenant'.[69]

The jurisprudence of the European Court of Human Rights recognizes protection of public morals as legitimate grounds for interference where the purpose is the protection of minors but not where it involves prohibiting private relations of any kind (including homosexual relationships) between adults.[70] Interference with physical and mental integrity and surveillance measures can be justified on grounds of protecting public order or national security. Economic grounds are frequently invoked by states to justify interference where annoying or harmful emissions, such as those caused by a major airport,[71] violate the right to privacy. Given the open-ended nature of these grounds, it is not surprising that the existence of a permissible ground for interference is usually easily recognized in the jurisprudence and that the case is generally decided on the basis of the principle of proportionality.

Protection of the rights and freedoms of others—permissible grounds for interference contained implicitly in ICCPR, Article 17 and set out explicitly in the text of ECHR, Article 8—is of particular importance. It enables states to fulfil their obligations to protect against violations by third parties and to take

---

[69] HRCttee, General Comment No 16 (1988), para 3, and *Toonen v Australia*, Communication No 488/1992 (1994), para 8.3.

[70] See, eg, ECtHR, *Dudgeon v The United Kingdom*, Series A, No 45 (1981), paras 47 and 60 f, and *ADT v The United Kingdom*, *Reports* 2000-IX, paras 31 ff. In *Laskey, Jaggard and Brown v The United Kingdom*, *Reports* 1997-I, the Court found that the criminal sentence for sadomasochistic actions, which took place with the agreement of all involved, could be justified with the argument of the protection of health.

[71] ECtHR, *Hatton and Others v The United Kingdom*, Application No 36022/97 (2001), and the Grand Chamber's judgment on appeal, *Reports* 2003-VIII.

action to prevent domestic violence, ill-treatment of children and other violations in the private sphere of a kind that would not be possible without forcibly entering people's homes, monitoring telephone conversations, and performing other forms of interference with private life.

3. The duty to protect

In view of the obvious fact that threats in the private sphere emanate more frequently from private actors than from the state, it is not surprising that the right to privacy under both ICCPR, Article 17(2), ACHR, Article 11(3), and ArCHR, Article 21(2) expressly require states to protect privacy by law. States thus have an explicit obligation to protect this right also in relations between private parties.[72] Although the text of ECHR, Article 8 contains no explicit provision, a corresponding obligation is recognized in the Strasbourg case law. Accordingly, the Court confirmed as early as 1985 that states were bound to provide legal remedies to punish interference with privacy by third parties[73] and it regularly recognizes an obligation of the States Parties to ensure the contact of a child with the parent who has right of custody or visiting rights, for example in the case of a kidnapping by one of the parents.[74]

4. The duty to fulfil

Lastly, Article 17 of the ICCPR and the corresponding provisions in the regional conventions impose positive obligations on states. States are, eg, required to adapt places of detention in a way that secures some measure of privacy for persons in custody. The Human Rights Committee requires states to ensure that, in the event of divorce, children have as much contact with both parents as possible, bearing in mind the best interests of the child, and that court orders regarding visiting rights can be enforced in practice.[75]

The dividing line between the obligation to respect and the obligation to fulfil is not always easy to discern. Is it more appropriate, for instance, to treat the obligation to register a change of name and the obligation to inform adoptive children of the names of their biological parents as an issue of non-respect for privacy or one linked to the provision of state services? As the European Court of Human Rights has stressed, although 'the boundaries between the State's positive and negative obligations under [ECHR, Article 8] do not lend themselves to precise definition, [t]he applicable principles are, none the less, similar. In both contexts regard must be had to the fair balance that has to

---

[72] HRCttee, General Comment No 16 (1988), paras 1 and 6.
[73] ECtHR, *X and Y v The Netherlands*, Series A, No 91 (1985), para 23.
[74] ECtHR, *Monory v Romania and Hungary*, Application No 71099/01 (2005), paras 73 ff.
[75] See HRCttee, *LP v Czech Republic*, Communication No 946/2000 (2002).

be struck between the competing interests of the individual and of the community as a whole; and in both contexts the State enjoys a certain margin of appreciation'.[76]

Example: The ECtHR judgment in *Odièvre v France*[77]

The judgment of the European Court of Human Rights in the *Odièvre* case clearly demonstrates the complex interweaving of obligations to respect, protect and fulfil that is particularly common in the area of protection of privacy as well as the multilayered considerations of proportionality that need to be taken into account in order to reach an appropriate decision. The case concerned a complaint by an adoptive child, who challenged the compatibility with human rights of a French legal provision allowing mothers under certain circumstances to give birth to their child anonymously, thereby preventing the child from establishing the identity of his or her mother. The Court considered:

The expression 'everyone' in Article 8 of the Convention applies to both the child and the mother. On the one hand, people have a right to know their origins...The child's vital interest in its personal development is also widely recognised in the general scheme of the Convention...On the other hand, a woman's interest in remaining anonymous in order to protect her health by giving birth in appropriate medical conditions cannot be denied. In the present case, the applicant's mother never went to see the baby at the clinic and appears to have greeted their separation with total indifference...The Court's task is not to judge that conduct, but merely to take note of it. The two competing interests with which the Court is confronted in the present case are not easily reconciled;...

In addition to that conflict of interest, the problem of anonymous births cannot be dealt with in isolation from the issue of the protection of third parties, essentially the adoptive parents, the father and the other members of the natural family. The Court notes in that connection ... that non-consensual disclosure could entail substantial risks, not only for the mother herself, but also for the adoptive family..., and her natural father and siblings, each of whom also has a right to respect for his or her private and family life.

There is also a general interest at stake, as the French legislature has consistently sought to protect the mother's and child's health during pregnancy and birth and to avoid abortions, in particular illegal abortions...The right to respect for life, a higher-ranking value guaranteed by the Convention, is thus one of the aims pursued by the French system.

---

[76] ECtHR, *Keegan v Ireland*, Series A, No 290 (1994), para 49; similarly, also ECtHR (Grand Chamber) *Dickson v The United Kingdom*, Application No 44362/04 (2007), paras 69 ff.

[77] ECtHR (Grand Chamber), *Odièvre v France*, *Reports* 2003-III, paras 44 ff. For a comparable complex case, see the judgment of the Grand Chamber of the ECtHR in *Evans v The United Kingdom*, Application No 6339/05 (2007), paras 71 ff. In this instance, the ECtHR had to find whether a British law, which declared that both the egg and sperm donor could decide individually to have the cells destroyed during the IVF procedure, until the fecundated egg cell was implanted, was compatible with Art 8. In other words, the question was whether Art 8, as foreseen in British law, allows the sperm donor to destroy the fecundated egg cells, thereby protecting his claim not to become a father against his will; or whether it is the mother's claim to receive the egg cells and become a mother, also protected by Art 8, which should prevail. Given the uncompromising contrary positions of both claims, the Grand Chamber concluded that the British law had weighed out a fair balance between the private and public interests at hand and that therefore the states margin of appreciation could not be withdrawn, also in the light of Art 8.

The Court observes that in the present case the applicant was given access to non-identifying information about her mother...that enabled her to trace some of her roots, while ensuring the protection of third-party interests.

The French legislation...seeks to strike a balance and to ensure sufficient proportion between the competing interests...Overall, the Court considers that France has not overstepped the margin of appreciation which it must be afforded in view of the complex and sensitive nature of the issue of access to information about one's origins...Consequently, there has been no violation of Article 8 of the Convention.

III. The Right to Respect of Family Life

Relevant provisions: UDHR, Article 12; ICESCR, Article 10(1); ICCPR, Articles 17 and 23(1); CEDAW, Article 16(1); CRC, Article 16; CRPD, Article 23; ACHR, Article 17(1); ACHPR, Article 18(1) and (2), ArCHR, Article 33; ECHR, Article 8.

The right to respect of family life is less complex than the right to privacy. Nevertheless, its application requires clarification regarding the definition of the family, which is by no means easy in light of the great diversity of patterns of family life in different cultures.

In view of the universal applicability of the Covenant, the Human Rights Committee has not defined the notion of the family contained in Articles 17 and 23 of the ICCPR in abstract terms; rather, it recognizes as 'family' in the sense of the Covenant all interpersonal relations that are held to constitute a family in the society concerned.[78] Accordingly, the substantive scope of application of the right to family life is determined primarily by domestic law. Specifically, the Committee refused to recognize a lesbian couple in New Zealand as a family.[79] On the other hand, in a decision against France it declared itself willing, in keeping with the Polynesian culture of the French overseas territory of Tahiti, to consider the relationship to dead ancestors under the definition of the term family.[80]

In view of the more uniform cultural traditions prevailing in Europe, the European Court of Human Rights has been able to formulate a more precise definition of the family. First, it recognizes marital and extra-marital relationships between men and women as family ties.[81] In the case of homosexual couples, on the other hand, only the right to respect of private life can be invoked.[82] This is also valid with regard to the relationship of a parent to a stillborn child.[83] The

---

[78] HRCttee, General Comments Nos 16 (1988), para 5, and 19 (1990), para 2.

[79] HRCttee, *Joslin et al v New Zealand*, Communication No 902/1999 (2002).

[80] HRCttee, *Hopu and Bessert v France*, Communication No 549/1993 (1997), para 10.3.

[81] ECtHR, *Mikulić v Croatia*, Reports 2002-I, para 51: '[T]he notion of "family life" in Article 8 is not confined solely to marriage-based relationships but may also encompass other *de facto* "family ties" where sufficient constancy is present.'

[82] For example, ECmHR, *Röösli v Germany*, Application No 28318/95, DR 85A (1996), para 151; ECtHR, *Dudgeon v The United Kingdom*, Series A, No 45 (1981), para 41.

[83] ECtHR, *Znamenskaya v Russia*, Application No 77785/01 (2005), para 27, and *Hadri-Vionnet v Switzerland*, Application No 55525/00 (2008), paras 51 f.

term family further includes the relationship between parents and their children and between grandparents and their grandchildren. Finally, the establishment of a relationship with a natural or adoptive child and its continued existence come within the scope of protection of ECHR, Article 8.[84] On the other hand, respect of family life does also protect against the creation, against the will of those concerned, of family bonds on the basis of legal presumptions and contrary to biological facts.[85]

In all cases, the Committee and its European counterpart recognize only genuine relationships, ie 'the real existence in practice of close personal ties' between relatives as family life.[86] The more distant the kinship relations are, or the less they are recognized under domestic law, the higher the standard of proof required. In such cases, the persons must live together, have close economic ties or maintain a regular relationship in order to be recognized as family.[87] According to the Human Rights Committee there is a strong presumption that the relationship between biological parents and their children qualifies as 'family' and their relationship will be protected by ICCPR, Article 17 unless exceptional circumstances exist.[88]

The jurisprudence of the treaty monitoring bodies on the respect of family life addresses, in particular, questions of the removal of parents' guardianship rights over children,[89] the custody of children after a divorce or separation[90] and a father's right of access to a child born out of wedlock.[91]

Issue in focus: The separation of children from parents in the light of CRC, Article 9 and ICCPR, Article 24

Where children are separated by state order from one or both parents, the jurisprudence of the Strasbourg Court generally focuses on the parent(s) as the main victim(s) of a violation of human rights. A different and often more appropriate perspective

---

[84] ECtHR, *Keegan v Ireland*, Series A, No 290 (1993), para 44.

[85] ECtHR, *Mizzi v Malta*, Application No 26111/02 (2006). It was not possible for the complainant to question his paternity of a child born by his wife whilst they were married.

[86] ECtHR (Grand Chamber), *K and T v Finland*, Application No 25702/94 (2001), para 149, and *Marckx v Belgium*, Series A, No 31 (1979), para 31. HRCttee, *Balaguer Santacana v Spain*, Communication No 417/1990 (1994), para 10.2.

[87] For example, ECtHR, *Keegan v Ireland*, Series A, No 290 (1993), para 44, as well as *Gül v Switzerland*, *Reports* 1996-I, para 32.

[88] HRCttee, *Tcholatch v Canada*, Communication No 1052/2002 (2007), para 8.2.

[89] For example, HRCttee, *Buckle v New Zealand*, Communication No 858/1999 (2000), paras 2.1 ff and 9.1 f, and *Tcholatch v Canada*, Communication No 1052/2002 (2007), paras 8.3 ff as well as ECtHR (Grand Chamber), *K and T v Finland*, Application No 25702/94 (2001), paras 148 ff, and ECtHR, *W v The United Kingdom*, Series A, No 121 (1987), paras 58 ff.

[90] HRCttee, *Hendriks v The Netherlands*, Communication No 201/1985 (1988), paras 10.2 ff; HRCttee, *LP v Czech Republic*, Communication No 946/2000 (2002), para 7.3; and, eg, ECtHR, *Hoppe v Germany*, Application No 28422/95 (2002), paras 44 ff.

[91] See, eg, ECtHR (Grand Chamber), *Sahin v Germany*, Application No 30943/96 (2003), and *Sommerfeld v Germany*, *Reports* 2003-VIII.

is adopted by the specific right of CRC, Article 9 and the general right of ICCPR, Article 24,[92] which highlight the *best interests of the child* as the core criterion for decision-making in this regard. According to the Convention on the Rights of the Child, states must ensure that a child is not separated from his or her parents against the parents' will, 'except when competent authorities subject to judicial review determine, in accordance with applicable law and procedures, that such separation is necessary for the best interests of the child'.

The Human Rights Committee and the European Court of Human Rights have developed a rich case law on the issue of family unity in the area of immigration law, in particular the admissibility of breaking up families as a consequence of the deportation of one of the parents[93] or the denial of permission to join one's family members from a third state.[94]

Issue in focus: Family unity and immigration law

The Human Rights Committee has repeatedly addressed the question of whether it is permissible to deport the foreign parents of children who have acquired citizenship of the state of residence. In *Winata v Australia*, the Committee did not exclude the possibility that such deportation would constitute interference with the right to privacy and family life under ICCPR, Articles 17 and 23 which, to be consistent with the Covenant, would require to be based on law and necessary to achieve a legitimate aim. At the same time, the Committee emphasized that states had the right to enforce their immigration law in such cases. However, in doing so they were required to respect the child's rights under ICCPR, Article 24. In the case in point, the Committee held that, in view of the fact that the parents had lived in the country, without permission but also blamelessly, for 14 years and that their 13-year-old son had been born there, Australia had violated the right to privacy and family life, in conjunction with the child's right to special protection because the state had failed to invoke any factors that would have justified the removal beyond a reference to the general interest in ensuring immigration law enforcement.[95]

The *Madafferi* decision concerned the separation of an Italian from his Australian wife and three children, who had also acquired Australian citizenship. Before entering the country, the husband had served a prison sentence in Italy and was therefore unable to legalize his residence in Australia after the expiry of his tourist visa. The Committee held that there had been a violation of Articles 17 and 23 in conjunction

---

[92] See, eg, HRCttee, *Bakhtiyari and Family v Australia*, Communication No 1069/2002 (2003), para 9.7, and *Madafferi and Family v Australia*, Communication No 1011/2001 (2004), para 9.8.

[93] HRCttee, *Winata and Li v Australia*, Communication No 930/2000 (2001), paras 7.2 f; *Bakhtiyari and Family v Australia*, Communication No 1069/2002 (2003), para 9.6; *Madafferi and Family v Australia*, Communication No 1011/2001 (2004), paras 9.7 ff; ECtHR, *Berrehab v The Netherlands*, Series A, No 138 (1988), paras 19 ff.

[94] HRCttee, *AS v Canada*, Communication No 68/1980 (1981), paras 5.1 and 8.2(b); ECtHR, *Gül v Switzerland*, *Reports* 1996-I.

[95] HRCttee, *Winata and Li v Australia*, Communication No 930/2000 (2001), para 7.3.

with Article 24 of the ICCPR because the husband, contrary to the advice of doctors consulted by the authorities, had been kept a long period in deportation custody although he had developed serious mental problems there. Under the circumstances, the part of the family that spoke English only could not be reasonably expected to follow the seriously ill husband to Italy and start a new life there without his support.[96]

The Committee had to deal with a reverse situation in 2007. Libya stopped a wife and her three children from leaving the country by confiscating their passports, thereby making it impossible for them to join the husband, who was living in Switzerland as a recognized refugee and whose application for reuniting the family had been accepted by Swiss authorities. As the husband, as a political refugee, could not be expected to return to join his family in his country of origin, the Committee considered Libya's refusal to constitute a violation of, amongst others, the respect of family life.[97]

According to an earlier jurisprudence, the European Court of Human Rights refused to accept that there was any interference with family life if the entire family could be reasonably expected to leave elsewhere by following the deported person to his or her home country (the so-called 'elsewhere approach'). Only in cases where this option was unavailable or seemed unreasonable did the Court find it necessary to examine whether the interference with family life was justified, ie whether it was in accordance with the law, pursuing a legitimate aim and proportionate. Nowadays (and for good reason) the Court tends to examine the question of whether the continuation of family life abroad is possible and can be reasonably expected from those concerned as an aspect of the proportionality of the interference. Accordingly, in the *Boultif v Switzerland* case it found that there had been clear interference with family life when the authorities refused to renew the residence permit of an Algerian married to a Swiss citizen who had been sentenced for robbery, as a result of which he had to leave the country. The Court held that, given the non-recurrence and only moderately serious nature of the offence, it was unreasonable to expect his Swiss wife to emigrate to Algeria where life would have been very difficult for her; the expulsion order was therefore held to be disproportionate.[98] According to the Court, the following points have to be considered in such cases:

48....In assessing the relevant criteria in such a case, the Court will consider the nature and seriousness of the offence committed by the applicant; the duration of the applicant's stay in the country from which he is going to be expelled; the time which has elapsed since the commission of the offence and the applicant's conduct during that period; the nationalities of the various persons concerned; the applicant's family situation, such as the length of the marriage; other factors revealing whether the couple lead a real and genuine family life; whether the spouse knew about the offence at the time when he or she entered into a family relationship; and whether there are children in the marriage and, if so, their age. Not least, the Court will also consider the seriousness of the difficulties which the spouse would be likely to encounter in the applicant's country of origin, although the mere fact that a person might face certain difficulties in accompanying her or his spouse cannot in itself preclude expulsion.

---

[96] HRCttee, *Madafferi and Family v Australia*, Communication No 1011/2001 (2004), para 9.8.
[97] HRCttee, *El Dernawi v Libyan Arab Jamahiriya*, Communication No 1143/2002 (2007), para 6.3.
[98] ECtHR, *Boultif v Switzerland,* Application No 54273/00 (2001), paras 39 ff.

In the *Üner* case, the Grand Chamber of the ECtHR reaffirmed these criteria and added two additional ones:

58:...—the best interests and well-being of the children, in particular the seriousness of the difficulties which any children of the applicant are likely to encounter in the country—the solidity of social, cultural and family ties with the host country and with the country of destination.[99]

In cases of expulsion of second-generation immigrants, the Court puts, apart from the seriousness of the offence, considerable weight on the quality of family life, degree of integration into the state of residence and strengths of ties (or lack of such ties) with the native country. In *Baghli v France*, a prohibition to re-enter France for ten years was held to be compatible with ECHR, Article 8 because the complainant had been sentenced to three years' imprisonment for dealing heroin, had only loose ties with his parents and his brothers and sisters, had no children of his own, had performed his military service in Algeria, spoke Arabic, and had refrained from acquiring French nationality despite being entitled to do so before his conviction.[100]

A right to obtain a residence permit with a view to reunite with family members already resident in a foreign state, ie a family-related right to immigration, can be derived from the right to family life only in exceptional circumstances.[101] In the *Gül v Switzerland* case,[102] the complainant was a Turkish national who had come to Switzerland. Four years later he was joined by his wife who had major health problems. Their two children remained in Turkey. In 1990 the couple and a child born in Switzerland were granted a humanitarian residence permit, primarily on account of the wife's state of health. The complainant subsequently applied for a residence permit for a son who had remained in Turkey but the application was refused. The European Court of Human Rights reasoned that 'where immigration is concerned, Article 8 (...) cannot be considered to impose on a State a general obligation to respect the choice by married couples of the country of their matrimonial residence and to authorise family reunion in its territory. In order to establish the scope of the State's obligations, the facts of the case must be considered...In this case, therefore, the Court's task is to determine to what extent it is true that [the son's] move to Switzerland would be the only way for Mr Gül to develop family life with his son.'[103] The Court rejected the application on the ground that although the family had been permitted to remain in Switzerland on humanitarian grounds, it would have been able to return to Turkey and live together with the son there.

As regards limitations on the duty of the state to respect family life, ICCPR, Article 17 prohibits 'arbitrary' interferences. The same is true for the regional conventions with the exception of ECHR, Article 8(2) which outlaws any interference unless it is 'in accordance with the law and is necessary in a democratic society in the interests of national security, public safety or the economic

---

[99] ECtHR (Grand Chamber), *Üner v The Netherlands*, Application No 46410/99 (2006), para 58.
[100] ECtHR, *Baghli v France*, Application No 34374/97 (1999), paras 36 f and 48 f.
[101] See eg ECtHR, *Tuquabo-Tekle and Others v The Netherlands*, Application No 60665/00 (2005).
[102] ECtHR, *Gül v Switzerland*, *Reports* 1996-I.   [103] Ibid, paras 38–39.

well-being of the country, for the prevention of disorder or crime, for the protection of health or morals, or for the protection of the rights and freedoms of
others.' In this context, states often invoke public order, the country's economic
interest, and prevention of punishable acts as grounds justifying interference
with family life in the form of expulsion of a family member. States have also
a duty to protect families from interferences by third parties as well as to fulfil,
eg by providing a permit under immigration law to allow a family to reunite on
their territory.[104]

IV. The Right to Marry and to Found a Family

Relevant provisions: UDHR, Article 16; ICESCR, Article 10; ICCPR, Article
23(2–4); CERD, Article 5(d)(iv); CEDAW, Article 16; CRPD, Article 23(1);
ACHR, Article 17(2–5); ArCHR, Article 33; ECHR, Article 12.

1. The right to marry

Both the ICCPR and the regional treaties guarantee the right to marry on the basis
of free consent. However this right relates solely to heterosexual partnerships,[105]
but, according to the European Court of Human Rights also protects transsex-
uals if they wish to marry a person of their original biological gender.[106] This
conclusion follows logically from the state obligation to recognize the new gender
of transsexual persons. The Court's earlier case law held that no right to divorce
could be derived from the right to marry,[107] but in light of developments in
Europe in the last few decades this case law might be overruled should the Court
have an opportunity to revisit it.

Article 23 of the ICCPR recognizes the right of persons of marriageable age
to marry and makes no provision for limitations. Nevertheless, the existence of
implicit restrictions on this guarantee is uncontested. They include, for instance,
the prohibition of incestuous marriages and polygamy, as well as the requirement that those intending to marry should have some capacity of discernment,
but they do not cover unreasonable restrictions such as a prohibition of marriage
between members of different ethnic groups. Article 12 of the ECHR recognizes
the existence of limitations by stipulating that the right to marry may be exercised
solely in accordance with national laws. The European Court of Human Rights

---

[104] See also the considerations above in this Chapter, section II.2–II.4 which apply *mutatis
mutandis* to the right to respect of family life.
[105] HRCttee, *Joslin et al v New Zealand*, Communication No 902/1999 (2002), para 8.2.
[106] ECtHR (Grand Chamber), *Goodwin v The United Kingdom*, Reports 2002-VI, and *I v
The United Kingdom*, Application No 25680/94 (2002); conversely, see, *inter alia*, *Sheffield and
Horsham v The United Kingdom*, Reports 1998-V.
[107] ECtHR, *Johnston and Others v Ireland*, Series A, No 112 (1986), paras 52 ff, and regarding
the ICCPR see Nowak (n 1), 398.

construes this provision as a traditional limitation clause, ie legal restrictions on this guarantee must be based on law, serve a legitimate aim and be proportionate. It considered that these requirements had not been met in the case of a legally ordered temporary prohibition of marriage imposed as a punishment following a divorce;[108] it came to the same conclusion in the case of a marriage impediment between step parents and step children which could only be lifted by parliament in individual cases.[109]

Issue in focus: The prohibition of forced marriage

ICCPR, Article 23(3), ICESCR, Article 10, ACHR, Article 17(3), and ArCHR, Article 33(1) stipulate that marriages cannot be entered into 'without the free and full consent' of both partners. Hence this guarantee prohibits not only all forced marriages ordered by the state or by parents but also, according to the Human Rights Committee, all forms of polygamy as 'equality of treatment with regard to the right to marry implies that polygamy is incompatible with this principle [and] an inadmissible discrimination against women'.[110] States are thus placed under an obligation to verify the existence of consent to marriage. The Committee furthermore requires states parties, in fulfilment of this obligation, to set a minimum age for marriage on the basis of equal criteria for men and women with a view to guaranteeing the existence of free consent and preventing child marriages.[111] This principle is also spelt out in the Convention on the Elimination of Discrimination against Women, which stipulates in Article 16(1)(b) that women must be guaranteed, on a basis of gender equality, the same right freely to choose a spouse and to enter into marriage only with their free and full consent. According to paragraph 2 of this article, the marriage of children shall have no legal effect. Lastly, both ICCPR, Article 23(4) and CEDAW, Article 16(1)(c) state the principle that domestic matrimonial and divorce law should ensure that men and women have the same rights during marriage and at its dissolution. However, a right to divorce cannot be deduced from any of these provisions. The fact that a considerable number of states have entered reservations regarding these human rights norms indicates that some of these principles are still contested in many societies.

---

2. The right to found a family

The right to found a family protects, first and foremost, the right to procreate or to adopt children. Discriminatory or compulsory family planning schemes are not compatible with this right.[112] To date this right has played virtually no role in the jurisprudence of the treaty monitoring bodies; however, it may potentially be invoked in connection with the issue of whether a right of access to

---

[108] ECtHR, *F v Switzerland*, Series A, No 128 (1987), paras 32 ff.
[109] ECtHR, *B and L v The United Kingdom*, Application No 36536/02 (2005).
[110] HRCttee, General Comment No 28 (2000), para 24.
[111] HRCttee, General Comment No 28 (2000), para 23.
[112] HRCttee, General Comment No 19 (1990), para 5.

new techniques of reproductive medicine exists.[113] The wording of the Covenant recognizes an unlimited right to found a family, but here again the existence of implicit limitations may be assumed. States must be allowed, for instance, to impose certain restrictions on adoption, precisely in order to protect the child's best interests.

[113] The ECtHR subsumes the right to decide freely about having children under the right to privacy, see section II.1.a.

13

Protection of the Intellectual and Spiritual Sphere

Humans are rational beings who need to develop and use their intellects. Scientific and artistic works are the product of this capacity. At the same time, people have spiritual needs that many seek to fulfil, alone or in community with others, through religious activities. Human rights law protects the intellectual and spiritual sphere of human life by means of a large number of rights, including the freedom of thought, conscience and opinion (section I), the right to education (section II), cultural rights (section III) and freedom of religion (section IV).

I. Freedom of Thought, Conscience, and Opinion

Relevant provisions: UDHR, Articles 18 and 19; ICCPR, Articles 18 and 19; CERD, Article 5(c)(vii); CRPD, Article 21; ICRMW, Article 12; ACHR, Articles 12 and 13; ACHPR, Article 8 and 9; ArCHR, Articles 30 and 32; ECHR, Articles 9 and 10.

Article 19(1) of the ICCPR guarantees everyone 'the right to hold opinions without interference', and Article 18(1) protects freedom of thought and conscience. All regional conventions have equivalent guarantees. Freedom of thought, conscience and opinion allows persons to think freely, unfettered by state influence, to remain true to their conscience and to form an opinion. It protects strictly internal processes and must therefore be clearly distinguished from the expression of opinions[1] and the manifestation of religious convictions.[2] As demonstrated by the historical record of totalitarian regimes, states are quite capable of seeking to encroach even on this most intimate sphere of human life.

Freedom of thought, conscience and opinion prohibits states in absolute terms[3] from punishing individuals solely on account of their thoughts or from coercing people to think in a particular way by means of psychotropic substances,

---

[1] See Chapter 16, section II.
[2] Manfred Nowak, *UN Covenant on Civil and Political Rights, CCPR Commentary* (2nd edn, Engel: Kehl, 2005), 440 referring to the drafting history of ICCPR, Art 19(1).
[3] HRCttee, *Malakhovsky and Pikul v Belarus*, Communication No 1207/2003 (2005), para 7.2.

'brainwashing' and similar methods. Coercive and ideologically motivated re-education in places of detention is also prohibited.[4] This prohibition does not cover permissible methods of state opinion-shaping, propaganda, advertising or public education provided there is no coercive element.[5]

Freedom of thought, conscience, and opinion promote ideological pluralism, one of the indispensable foundations of a democratic society.[6] By guarding the individual's intellectual autonomy, this right protects a critical private sphere. As strictly passive behaviour forming part of a person's inner life, the exercise of this freedom cannot encroach on legitimate public interests or rights in a manner that could justify limitations. Accordingly, it is applicable without restriction and is non-derogable.[7]

II. The Right to Education

Relevant provisions: UDHR, Article 26; ICESCR, Articles 13 and 14; CEDAW, Article 10; CERD, Article 5(e)(v); CRC, Articles 28 and 29; CRPD, Article 24; ICRMW, Article 30; P 1/ACHR, Article 13; ACHPR, Article 17; ArCHR, Article 41; P 1/ECHR, Article 2; GC III, Article 38; GC IV, Articles 50 and 94; AP I, Article 52.

A minimum of education is a prerequisite for the development of opinions, capacity for reflection and intellectual abilities in general. Lack of formal education in the modern world makes the full development of the human personality nearly impossible. Furthermore, education is a prerequisite for the enjoyment of many other rights such as freedom of opinion and political rights. Lack of proper schooling is one of the main causes of poverty and exploitation and inhibits the realization of major economic and social rights.[8] Formal education is an essential requirement for employment and for securing a proper livelihood for oneself and one's family. Lastly, education guarantees the passing of cultural traditions, experience, and values from one generation to the next. The right to education is thus classified as a social, economic, and cultural right.[9] However, it simultaneously comprises aspects of classic civil liberties by protecting, for example, the freedom of parents' educational choices against state interference.[10] Accordingly, the right to education reflects to a great extent the interdependence of different categories of human rights and their indivisibility.[11]

---

[4] HRCttee, *Kang v Republic of Korea*, Communication No 878/1999 (2003), para 7.2.
[5] Nowak (n 2), 442.
[6] ECtHR, *Kokkinakis v Greece*, Series A, No 260-A (1993), para 31.
[7] ICCPR, Art 18(1) in conjunction with Art 4(2). See HRCttee, General Comment No 10 (1983), para 1.
[8] See CtteeESCR, General Comment No 13 (1999), para 1.
[9] CtteeESCR, General Comment No 11 (1999), para 2.
[10] The right to education in P 1/ECHR, Art 2 is formulated wholly in terms of a civil liberty.
[11] CtteeESCR, General Comment No 11 (1999), para 2.

1. The core right to primary education

The core component of the right to education is the right to primary schooling. As a first indispensable step towards the full realization of the right to education, states parties recognize through ICESCR, Article 13(2)(a) and equivalent guarantees in regional conventions that 'primary education shall be compulsory and available free to all'.[12] Pursuant to ICESCR, Article 14, states that have not yet been able to secure that right are bound, within two years, to adopt a detailed action plan for its progressive implementation within a reasonable period. This wording refers to a goal to be achieved on a step-by-step basis. However, by requiring states to adopt and implement an action plan for the establishment of compulsory and free primary education, Article 14 deprives them of the considerable latitude generally afforded under ICESCR, Article 2(1) for the achievement of Covenant goals. In view of the fundamental importance of primary education for personality development and a person's future, and bearing in mind the fact that this goal can be achieved even in relatively poor countries provided the existence of sufficient political will, the Committee for Economic, Social and Cultural Rights has gone a step further, holding that a state party in which a significant number of individuals are deprived of the most basic forms of education is, *prima facie*, failing to discharge its obligations under the Covenant. Such a charge can only be refuted if the state can demonstrate that it is unable to achieve the Covenant goal despite using all its available resources.[13] The right to free primary education therefore constitutes the core content of the right to education under the ICESCR. An interesting point is that, unlike other social rights for which state intervention is subsidiary, ie required only if private parties are unable to satisfy their basic needs themselves, responsibility for ensuring that children receive primary education lies primarily with the state.

According to the Committee for Economic, Social and Cultural Rights, certain conditions must be met in order to ensure that the right to primary education is effectively fulfilled. A basic prerequisite is that schools are *available* and equipped with the necessary facilities and teaching materials. Furthermore, the schooling provided must be *accessible*, a requirement that comprises legal dimensions (non-exclusion of specific groups), physical dimensions (sufficiently close to where children live) and economic dimensions (no school fees). Lastly, instruction and school activities must be *acceptable* in terms of form and substance to children and their parents, eg from a cultural point of view.[14]

2. The right to receive an education

Availability, accessibility, and acceptability are criteria that states are required to realize, according to ICESCR, Article 13(2), not only at the primary level but at all

---

[12] CRC, Art 28(1)(a) contains a similar provision.
[13] CtteeESCR, General Comment No 3 (1990), para 10.
[14] CtteeESCR, General Comment No 13 (1999), para 6.

levels of the education system. States must create or nurture a system of higher education and make technical and vocational educational facilities as well as universities generally available and accessible to all, and to that end not only establish a system of scholarships or study grants for those without the necessary financial means but also take steps towards the progressive introduction of free education at these levels. However, unlike the right to primary education, these obligations are not justiciable and individually enforceable but are goals to be achieved progressively.

3. The right to equal access to existing educational establishments

The right to equal access to existing educational establishments is justiciable. It is implicitly contained in the right to education under ICESCR, Article 13(1) and clearly set out in the first sentence of P 1/ECHR, Article 2, which states that '[n]o person shall be denied the right to education'. In principle, access must be guaranteed, at least at the primary level, to all children, including refugee children and children with disabilities.[15]

Apart from primary schooling, the right to equal access to education protects only persons who satisfy the necessary requirements for the relevant course of studies (eg in terms of previous schooling or successful completion of an entrance examination).

If the available number of study places is limited, the right to education cannot be invoked to secure an increase in supply.[16] Rather, it entails a right to non-discriminatory access to existing educational opportunities. It is violated where a person is denied access on grounds or in ways that are discriminatory. A violation thus occurred in the case of a Belgian regulation which allowed Flemish-speaking parents who lived in French-speaking districts on the periphery of Brussels to send their children to schools in neighbouring Flemish-speaking districts but withheld the same right from French-speaking parents and their children. The Court held that the denial of access could not be justified on administrative grounds or because of lack of capacity but was based solely on linguistic grounds.[17]

Unequal treatment that is based on objective and serious grounds is not discriminatory. The fact that private schools are not given the same financial support as public schools and that pupils attending private schools do not receive free learning materials and meals or free school transport does not constitute discrimination when parents are free to choose whether to enrol their children in either a public or private school.[18]

---

[15] Art 22 of the Refugee Convention requires states to accord refugees the same treatment as is accorded nationals with respect to elementary education and treatment not less favourable than that accorded to foreigners generally in the same circumstances in the case of education at higher levels. Article 24 of the CRPD obliges states parties to 'ensure an inclusive education system at all levels and life long learning' with a view to developing the full potential of children with disabilities.

[16] ECtHR (Grand Chamber), *Leyla Şahin v Turkey, Reports* 2005-XI, para 137.

[17] ECtHR, *Belgian Linguistics Case*, Series A, No 6 (1968), para 7.

[18] HRCttee, *Blom v Sweden,* Communication No 191/1985 (1988), paras 10.2–10.3.

Article 24(2) of the CRPD spells out what non-discriminatory access to education means in the case of children with disabilities. According to this provision,
states parties shall ensure that such persons are neither excluded from the general
education system on the basis of disability nor from free and compulsory primary
education, or from secondary education; that they 'can access an inclusive, quality and free primary education and secondary education on an equal basis with
others in the communities in which they live'; that 'reasonable accommodation'
to their specific needs is provided; and that they receive effective individualized
support 'to facilitate their effective education', and to maximize their 'academic
and social development, consistent with the goal of full inclusion'.

The European Court of Human Rights has derived from the right to equal
access a right *not to be excluded* from existing establishments without legitimate
grounds and the right to official recognition of school leaving certificates acquired
in accordance with the relevant regulations.[19] This right was found to have been
violated, for instance, in the case of a boy suspended from a British school for
nearly a whole academic year because he and his parents refused to accept the
school's habitual use of corporal punishment.[20]

4. The right to education as a civil liberty

The right to education comprises several civil liberties. The freedom of educational choice attributed to parents of underage children is explicitly embodied
in international treaties. Parents have the right to ensure that their children are
educated[21] in conformity with their own religious and moral convictions.[22] The
same right is also explicitly set out in terms of religious freedom under ICCPR,
Article 18(4) and ECHR, Article 9, which, *inter alia*, prohibit religious indoctrination in public schools.[23] Where pupils must attend a compulsory course in the
history of religion and ethics as an alternative to religious instruction, the lesson
must be given in a neutral and objective way, bearing in mind the convictions
of parents who are non-believers.[24] In addition, in such cases parents must be
given the opportunity to have their children exempted from instruction, and the
exemption scheme must be practicable, ie organized in such a way that parents
can effectively exercise their right of exemption without having to acquaint themselves with the religious content of courses.[25]

---

[19] ECtHR, *Belgian Linguistics Case*, Series A, No 6 (1968).
[20] ECtHR, *Campbell and Cosans v The United Kingdom*, Series A, No 48 (1982), para 41.
[21] They must, however, ensure that their children receive adequate primary schooling.
[22] ICESCR, Art 13(3), final clause; P 1/ECHR, Art 2.
[23] ECtHR, *Kjeldsen, Busk Madsen and Pedersen v Denmark*, Series A, No 23 (1976), para 53.
[24] HRCttee, *Hartikainen et al v Finland*, Communication No 40/1978 (1981), para 10.4, and
General Comment No 22 (1993), para 6.
[25] This requirement was not fulfilled in the case of a Norwegian law which permitted exemption
only for individual lessons and required parents to state why the content of the lessons at issue was
contrary to their convictions. Norway amended the law after the HRCttee held in *Leirvåg et al v*

Parents' educational rights also include the right 'to choose for their children schools, other than those established by the public authorities' (ICESCR, Article 13(3)), ie the right to send them to a private school. They are further guaranteed the liberty to establish such schools (ICESCR, Article 13(4)). In both cases, however, authorities can, according to these provisions, insist that the education imparted conforms to minimum standards laid down by the state.

Issue in focus: Disciplinary punishment in schools

The Convention on the Rights of the Child requires states to ensure that 'school discipline is administered in a manner consistent with the child's human dignity' (Article 28(2)). Inadmissible forms of punishment include corporal punishment, public humiliation and food deprivation.[26] The European Court of Human Rights held that three painful blows with a birch rod on the bare posterior of a juvenile offender amounted to degrading punishment within the meaning of ECHR, Article 3.[27]

III. Right to Take Part in Cultural Life and Protection of Artistic and Scientific Creation

Relevant provisions: UDHR, Article 27; ICESCR, Article 15; ICCPR, Article 19; CRC, Articles 13 and 31; CRPD, Article 30; CEDAW, Article 13(d); ICRMW, Articles 42(1)(g) and 45(1)(d); ACHR, Article 13 and P 1/ACHR, Article 14; ACHPR, Articles 9 and 17; ArCHR, Article 42; ECHR, Article 10; AP I, Article 53; AP II, Article 16.

Culture understood as 'the sum of the material and spiritual activities and products of a given social group which distinguishes it from other similar groups' and thus as a 'system of values and symbols, that a specific cultural group reproduces over time and which provides individuals with the required signposts and meanings for behaviour and social relationship in everyday

---

Norway, Communication No 1155/2003 (2004), paras 14.6 and 14.7, that ICCPR, Art 18 had been violated. In the case of *Folgerø and Others v Norway*, Application No 15472/02 (2007), the Grand Chamber of the ECtHR had to examine whether the (new) Norwegian law was compatible with human rights. It concluded in a judgment adopted by a small majority of judges that not providing for the possibility to get complete dispensation from the class in question constituted a violation of the right to education (paras 84 ff). See also, ECtHR, *Zengin v Turkey*, Application No 1448/04 (2007).

[26] CtteeRC, General Comment No 1 (2001), para 8, and CtteeESCR, General Comment No 13 (1999), para 41.

[27] ECtHR, *Tyrer v The United Kingdom*, Series A, No 26 (1978), para 26. The blows were ordered by a juvenile court as punishment for misconduct at school (assaulting another pupil). By contrast, the ECtHR held in *Costello-Roberts v The United Kingdom*, Series A, No 247-C (1993), para 32, that the disciplining of a seven-year-old boy by means of three light blows with a gym shoe fell short of the threshold of severity that would have constituted a violation of ECHR, Art 3.

life'[28] is protected by several human rights guarantees including freedom of religion (section IV below), the right to education (section II above), the right of members of minorities to enjoy their own culture within their group (Chapter 11, section V.2) and the rights of indigenous communities (Chapter 11, section V.3). Other rights, such as the right to privacy and protection of the family or the right to marry (Chapter 12) also protect specific cultural practices.

The notions of 'literary or artistic production' and 'creative activity' found in ICESCR, Article 15 (paragraphs 1(c) and 3 respectively) along with equivalent provisions in regional conventions deal with a narrow concept of the term culture. It basically embodies artistic activities and productions such as music, painting, and sculpture, literature and theatre, architecture, and scientific findings. It consists of highly disparate elements, some of which are closely related to freedom of expression and other civil liberties designed to protect artistic creation and scientific findings, while others guarantee access to cultural life and the scientific achievements.

1. The right to take part in cultural life and artistic freedom

Under ICESCR, Article 15(1)(a), states parties recognize the right of everyone 'to take part in cultural life'. The article thus establishes an immediately binding duty to respect people's freedom to participate actively or passively in cultural life while prohibiting any state interference that cannot be justified in accordance with Article 4 of the Covenant. The civil liberty emanating from this right protects both the attendance of cultural events and the enjoyment of culture through media such as literature and cinema. This component is justiciable and may be termed *passive artistic freedom*. Paragraph 3, by requiring states parties 'to respect the freedom indispensable for . . . creative activity', codifies what could be called *active artistic freedom* as the justiciable[29] right of artistic creation. In cases where individuals are hindered by private parties and non-state actors from participating in cultural life, Article 15(1)(a) and (3) trigger a state's duty to protect. In terms of state obligations to fulfil, Article 15 requires states parties to promote culture and to take steps to conserve cultural assets.[30] These obligations are to be achieved progressively and as far as available resources permit.

Freedom of artistic expression is guaranteed by Article 19 but may be subject to limitations, provided that such limitations are prescribed by law and are necessary to protect legitimate public interests or the rights of others. The latter

---

[28] Rodolfo Stavenhagen, Cultural Rights and Universal Human Rights, in: Asbjørn Eide, Catarina Krause and Allan Rosas (eds), *Economic, Social and Cultural Rights* (Brill: Dordrecht/Boston/London, 1995), 66.

[29] CtteeESCR, General Comment 3 (1990), para 5.

[30] Asbjørn Eide (ed), *The Universal Declaration of Human Rights, A Commentary* (Aschehoug: Oslo, 1992), 294 f.

includes, in particular, the entitlement of third parties to protection of their honour and reputation.

Example: Artistic freedom and public morals—the ECtHR judgment in *Müller and Others v Switzerland*[31]

In the case of an artist prosecuted for pornographic publication after having painted and exhibited sexually offensive pictures at an art festival in Freiburg (Switzerland) that was open to the general public, the European Court of Human Rights stated that 'freedom of expression, as secured in paragraph 1 of Article 10 [ECHR]..., constitutes one of the essential foundations of a democratic society, indeed one of the basic conditions for its progress and for the self-fulfilment of the individual. Subject to paragraph 2..., it is applicable not only to "information" or "ideas" that are favourably received or regarded as inoffensive or as a matter of indifference, but also to those that offend, shock or disturb... Such are the demands of that pluralism, tolerance and broadmindedness without which there is no "democratic society"... Those who create, perform, distribute or exhibit works of art contribute to the exchange of ideas and opinions which is essential for a democratic society. Hence the obligation on the State not to encroach unduly on their freedom of expression.'(paragraph 33). However, the limitations of Article 10(2) are also applicable to artists, who undertake, 'in accordance with the express terms of that paragraph, "duties and responsibilities"; their scope will depend on [the artist's] situation and the means he uses' (paragraph 34).

The Court emphasized that 'the paintings in question depict in a crude manner sexual relations, particularly between men and animals... They were painted on the spot—in accordance with the aims of the exhibition, which was meant to be spontaneous—and the general public had free access to them, as the organizers had not imposed any admission charge or any age-limit. Indeed, the paintings were displayed in an exhibition which was unrestrictedly open to—and sought to attract—the public at large. The Court recognizes, as did the Swiss courts, that conceptions of sexual morality have changed in recent years. Nevertheless, having inspected the original paintings, the Court does not find unreasonable the view taken by the Swiss courts that those paintings, with their emphasis on sexuality in some of its crudest forms, were "liable grossly to offend the sense of sexual propriety of persons of ordinary sensitivity".' (paragraph 36).

The Court therefore concluded that there had been no violation of the ECHR.

---

2. Scientific rights

Scientific freedom and freedom of research are codified in two separate parts of ICESCR, Article 15. Under paragraph 1(b) the states parties 'recognise the right of everyone to enjoy the benefits of scientific progress and its applications', while paragraph 3 embodies a justiciable[32] right in stating that 'states parties... *undertake to*

---

[31] ECtHR, *Müller and Others v Switzerland*, Series A, No 133 (1988).
[32] CtteeESCR, General Comment No 3 (1990), para 5.

respect the freedom indispensable for scientific research . . .'. Freedom of scientific research also flows from freedom of opinion and expression.

Article 15 thus protects passive and active freedom of research, ie freedom to be informed of research findings and freedom to undertake research oneself. States parties are further required, in terms of their obligations to fulfil, to promote actively scientific progress and to ensure that the benefits of such progress are enjoyed by the population as a whole.

3. Protection of intellectual property

As a final component, Article 15(1)(c) of the ICESCR recognizes a person's right to benefit from protection of moral and material interests resulting from any scientific, literary or artistic production of which he or she is the author. This entitlement to *freedom* of intellectual property is justiciable, provided a state has enacted legislation affording protection for rights to intangible assets.

The Committee on Economic, Social and Cultural Rights has stressed that the duty to respect this right includes the obligation, *inter alia*, to abstain 'from infringing the right of authors to be recognized as the creators of their scientific, literary or artistic productions and to object to any distortion, mutilation or other modification of, or other derogatory action in relation to, their productions that would be prejudicial to their honour or reputation'.[33] According to the Committee, the obligation to protect includes 'the duty of States parties to ensure the effective protection of the moral and material interests of authors against infringement by third parties. In particular, States parties must prevent third parties from infringing the right of authors to claim authorship of their scientific, literary, or artistic productions, and from distorting, mutilating or otherwise modifying, or taking any derogatory action in relation to such productions in a manner that would be prejudicial to the author's honour or reputation. Similarly, States parties are obliged to prevent third parties from infringing the material interests of authors resulting from their productions. To that effect, States parties must prevent the unauthorized use of scientific, literary and artistic productions that are easily accessible or reproducible through modern communication and reproduction technologies, eg by establishing systems of collective administration of authors' rights or by adopting legislation requiring users to inform authors of any use made of their productions and to remunerate them adequately.'[34] Finally, the duty to fulfil obliges states 'to provide administrative, judicial or other appropriate remedies enabling authors, especially those belonging to disadvantaged and marginalized groups, to seek and obtain redress in case their moral and material interests have been infringed, or the failure to provide adequate opportunities for the active and informed participation of authors and groups of authors in any decision-making process that has an impact on their

---

[33] CtteeESCR, General Comment No 17 (2005), para 30.   [34] Ibid, para 31.

right to benefit from the protection of the moral and material interests resulting from their scientific, literary, or artistic productions.'[35]

Issue in focus: Violation of ICESCR, Article 15 in wartime

Massive violations of rights under ICESCR, Article 15 often occur where countries are occupied in the course of international armed conflicts. In Iraqi-occupied Kuwait (1990–1991), for example, the occupying troops systematically plundered and destroyed museums, libraries, universities and research institutes. Research data compiled over a period of 20 years on matters such as fisheries and fish farming and the impact of petroleum pollution on marine life and drinking water disappeared from the Kuwait Institute for Scientific Research. Research and dissertation material at Kuwait University was destroyed or removed. It was feared that Iraqi researchers might publish some of the findings under their own name.[36] Massive looting of museums and other cultural institutions also occurred after the US invasion of Iraq in spring 2003.[37]

International humanitarian law contains a number of provisions aimed at protecting cultural property. The main source of these provisions is the Hague Convention of 14 May 1954 for the Protection of Cultural Property in the Event of Armed Conflict. According to AP I, Article 53 and AP II, Article 16, it is prohibited 'to commit any acts of hostility directed against the historic monuments works of art or places of worship which constitute the cultural or spiritual heritage of peoples' and 'to use such objects in support of the military effort'.

IV. Freedom of Religion

Relevant provisions: UDHR, Article 18; ICCPR, Article 18; CRC, Article 14; CERD, Article 5(c)(vii); ICRMW, Article 12; ACHR, Article 12; ACHPR, Article 8; ArCHR, Article 30; ECHR, Article 9; GC III, Articles 34–37; GC IV, Articles, 27, 58 and 93; AP I, Article 52.

Freedom of religion and belief, as embodied in Article 18 of the ICCPR and all the regional human rights conventions, protects a person's spiritual freedom, ie his or her relationship with the transcendental. In addition to freedom of thought, which is also protected by Article 18 (above at section I), and to freedom of opinion and expression,[38] this right protects 'theistic, nontheistic and atheistic beliefs', ie religions and beliefs in the broader sense,[39] focusing on positive or

---

[35] Ibid, para 46.

[36] 'Report of the Special Rapporteur of the UN Commission on Human Rights on human rights violations in Iraqi-occupied Kuwait of 16 January 1992', UN Doc E/CN.4/1992/26, paras 210 ff.

[37] UNESCO first assessment mission to Baghdad, 17–20 May 2003.

[38] See Chapter 16.

[39] HRCttee, General Comment No 22 (1993), para 2. ECtHR, *Kokkinakis v Greece*, Series A, No 260-A (1993), para 31.

(eg in the case of agnosticism and atheism) negative statements regarding transcendental questions. Even beliefs that are considered shocking or repulsive by most are protected although certain of their manifestations may be limited in accordance with Article 18(3).[40]

1. The right not to have a religion

Freedom of religion has both a negative and a positive component. In *negative* terms, freedom of religion means that nobody may be compelled to profess a particular belief, to join a religious community or to engage in specific religious activities (ICCPR, Article 18(2)). This prohibition is absolute and is violated, for example, where a state prohibits members of a particular religion from converting to another religion,[41] where a person is compelled to adopt another religion,[42] where members of parliament forfeit their seats if they refuse to swear an oath on the Bible when taking up office,[43] and where a person is compelled to reveal his religious beliefs in court.[44]

2. The right to have and manifest a religion

In *positive* terms, freedom of religion gives people the right to adopt a belief of their choice and to manifest their faith, with all its customs and traditions, 'individually or in community with others and in public or private, . . . in worship, observance, practice and teaching' (ICCPR, Article 18(1)). This includes, for instance, the right to establish and attend places of worship, to impart and receive religious instruction, to manifest one's beliefs openly, to write and use religious

---

[40] See for example, HRCttee, *Prince v South Africa*, Communication No 1474/2006 (2007), paras 7.2–7.3. In this case, the Committee admitted that smoking and chewing cannabis products is an integral part of the Rastafari religion and is therefore protected by religious freedom. It did not however consider that religious freedom had been violated, because the prohibition of possession and consumption of cannabis is foreseen in the law, is in the public interest, and is proportional also for followers of this religion. Accordingly, the Committee considered the local lawyer's association had not breached the ICESCR by refusing to grant the complainant admission in the lawyer's register based on his record, ie his repeated conviction for possession of cannabis and his announcement that he would continue to consume cannabis. However, in *MAB et al v Canada*, Communication No 570/1993 (1994), the Committee held that 'the "Assembly of the Church of the Universe", whose beliefs and practices, according to the authors, necessarily involve the care, cultivation, possession, distribution, maintenance, integrity and worship of the "Sacrament" of the Church' which 'is generally known under the designation cannabis sativa or marijuana' (para 2.1) does not qualify as religion as 'a belief consisting primarily or exclusively in the worship and distribution of a narcotic drug cannot conceivably be brought within the scope of article 18 of the Covenant' (para 4.2).
[41] Accordingly, the HRCttee has criticized Islamic states that have enacted such provisions; eg Concluding Observations Yemen (2002), para 20.
[42] ACmHPR, *Amnesty International and Others v Sudan*, Communication Nos 48/1990, 50/1991, 52/1991, 89/1993 (1999), paras 74 and 76.
[43] ECtHR (Grand Chamber), *Buscarini and Others v San Marino*, Reports 1999-I, para 34.
[44] ECtHR, *Alexandridis v Greece*, Application No 19516/06 (2008), paras 31 ff.

literature and to perform religious rites and ceremonies, as well as other religious acts.[45] A violation occurs, for example, where an imprisoned Muslim is prevented without cause from wearing a beard and is deprived of sacred literature[46] or where a member of a Christian Evangelical group is dismissed from her job in the public service after having disclosed her religious commitment.[47] A military judge in a secular state who is removed from office for espousing fundamentalist views and giving judicial support to members of his own group is not a victim of interference with his freedom of religion as he is not being punished for his religious views but rather for improper performance of his official duties.[48]

The freedom to manifest one's religion and beliefs and to live one's life in a manner consistent with religious precepts is not absolute. Article 18(3) of the ICCPR and the regional conventions permit limitations provided that they are prescribed by law and 'are necessary to protect public safety, order, health or morals or the fundamental rights and freedoms of others'. Thus, disciplinary action taken against a public servant for absenting himself without permission during a religious holiday does not breach religious freedom.[49]

Issue in focus: Conscientious objection to military service

Can freedom of religion and belief and freedom of conscience be invoked by conscientious objectors to military service? In its early jurisprudence, the Human Rights Committee answered in the negative on the grounds that the Covenant does not provide for such a right.[50] However, in its General Comment on freedom of religion adopted in 1993, the Committee changed its view: 'The Covenant does not explicitly refer to a right to conscientious objection, but the Committee believes that such a right can be derived from article 18, inasmuch as the obligation to use lethal force may seriously conflict with the freedom of conscience and the right to manifest one's religion or belief. When this right is recognised by [a state's] law or practice, there shall be no differentiation among conscientious objectors on the basis of the nature of their particular beliefs...'[51] Since then, states which make no provision for alternative civilian service for conscientious objectors or which impose a period of civilian service that is disproportionately long compared with military service are regularly criticized when the state's report is reviewed.[52]

---

[45] See for example, HRCttee, *Prince v South Africa*, Communication No 1474/2006 (2007), para 7.2 (use of cannabis by a member of the Rastafari religion).

[46] HRCttee, *Boodoo v Trinidad and Tobago*, Communication No 721/1996 (2002), para 6.6.

[47] ECtHR, *Ivanova v Bulgaria*, Application No 52435/99 (2007).

[48] ECtHR, *Kalaç v Turkey, Reports* 1997-IV, paras 27 ff.

[49] ECtHR, *Kosteski v The Former Yugoslav Republic of Macedonia*, Application No 55170/00 (2006), para 38.

[50] For example, HRCttee, *LTK v Finland*, Communication No 185/1984 (1985), para 5.2.

[51] HRCttee, General Comment No 22 (1993), para 11.

[52] For example, HRCttee, Concluding Observations France (1997), para 19; Concluding Observations Colombia (2004), para 17; and Concluding Observations Serbia and Montenegro (2004), para 21; Concluding Observations Greece (2005), para 15; Concluding Observations Republic of Korea (2006), para 17, and Concluding Observations Chile (2007), para 17.

In its views on an individual complaint in 1999, the Committee also assumed that the Covenant protects conscientious objectors but concluded that the author of the communication had been unable to show that he had an insurmountable objection of conscience to military service.[53] In 2007, the Committee considered in the case of two South Korean conscientious objectors that their freedom of religion and conscience had been violated because Korea could not show that the absence of a civil alternative to the obligatory military service, and forthwith the punishment of the objector of conscience for religious reasons, was necessary for safeguarding national security. It noted:

in relation to relevant State practice, that an increasing number of those States parties to the Covenant which have retained compulsory military service have introduced alternatives to compulsory military service, and considers that the State party has failed to show what special disadvantage would be involved for it if the rights of the authors' under article 18 would be fully respected. As to the issue of social cohesion and equitability, the Committee considers that respect on the part of the State for conscientious beliefs and manifestations thereof is itself an important factor in ensuring cohesive and stable pluralism in society. It likewise observes that it is in principle possible, and in practice common, to conceive alternatives to compulsory military service that do not erode the basis of the principle of universal conscription but render equivalent social good and make equivalent demands on the individual, eliminating unfair disparities between those engaged in compulsory military service and those in alternative service. The Committee, therefore, considers that the State party has not demonstrated that in the present case the restriction in question is necessary, within the meaning of article 18, paragraph 3, of the Covenant.[54]

On the other hand, the Committee held that Article 18 of the Covenant cannot be invoked where a person is punished for refusing to pay taxes because he or she is unable, on conscientious grounds, to support the armed forces.[55] Furthermore, the Committee has held—albeit on the basis of the principle of equality before the law in ICCPR, Article 26—that the duration of alternative civilian service violates the Covenant at least in cases where it amounts to double the length or more of military service.[56]

The European Court of Human Rights has also, in principle, recognized a right to conscientious objection in its recent case law.[57] However, recognized conscientious objectors cannot derive from the ECHR a right of refusal to perform alternative civilian service.[58] On the other hand, a state is prohibited from

---

[53] HRCttee, *Westerman v The Netherlands*, Communication No 682/1996 (1999), para 9.5.

[54] HRCttee, *Yoon and Choi v Republic of Korea*, Communication Nos 1321/2004 and 1322/2004 (2007), para 8.4.

[55] HRCttee, *JP v Canada*, Communication No 446/1991 (1991), para 4.2, and *KV and CV v Germany*, Communication No 568/1993 (1994), para 4.3.

[56] HRCttee, *Foin v France*, Communication No 666/1995 (1999), *Maille v France*, Communication No 689/1996 (2000), and *Venier and Nicolas v France*, Communication Nos 690–691/1996 (2000).

[57] ECtHR (Grand Chamber), *Thlimmenos v Greece*, *Reports* 2000-IV, para 50: 'The ... case-law to the effect that the Convention did not guarantee the right to conscientious objection to military service had to be reviewed in the light of present-day conditions. Virtually all Contracting States now recognised the right to alternative civilian service.'

[58] ECmHR, *X v Germany*, 77705/76, DR 9, 203 f, para 1, with reference to ECHR, Art 4(3)(b) according to which forced labour does not include 'in case of conscientious objectors in countries where they are recognised, service exacted instead of compulsory military service'.

> excluding a conscientious objector who has served his sentence from access to the profession of chartered accountant on account of his status as a convicted person.[59]

Particular difficulties arise where religious tensions between communities exist. Here, limitations may be justified if they are necessary to protect public safety and order or if they stem from the state's duty to protect against religious violence or discrimination. However, such limitations on the freedom to manifest one's religion should be imposed as a measure of last resort. As highlighted by the European Court of Human Rights, the state must remain neutral in its relations with different religious communities and recognize the value of religious pluralism. Where tensions arise between such communities, it is not the role of the authorities to remove the cause of tension by means of prohibitions but to promote dialogue between the groups concerned.[60] Neutrality in religious matters is, for instance, violated where registration is only possible with the consent of the main religious community in the country.[61]

Issue in focus: Protection of religious lifestyles in a multicultural environment

---

In the multicultural context of immigrant societies, as well as in secular states, frictions between state laws and religious precepts are frequently unavoidable. Freedom of religion helps to ease such tensions as it allows the different communities to co-exist and the state to be neutral in religious matters. However, how does the case law of international monitoring bodies seek to address situations where there is a conflict between state and religious commands?

The European Court of Human Rights, in its judgment on the permissibility of the dissolution of the Turkish Welfare Party,[62] has summarized its case law on religious tolerance and its limits as follows:

90.... [The Court] reiterates that, as protected by Article 9, freedom of thought, conscience and religion is one of the foundations of a "democratic society" within the meaning of the Convention. It is, in its religious dimension, one of the most vital elements that go to make up the identity of believers and their conception of life, but it is also a precious asset for atheists, agnostics, sceptics and the unconcerned. The pluralism indissociable from a democratic society, which has been dearly won over the centuries, depends on it...

---

[59] In the judgment in *Thlimmenos v Greece*, *Reports* 2000-IV, paras 41 ff, the Grand Chamber of the ECtHR held that this exclusion constituted accessory discrimination in respect of freedom of religion (ECHR, Art 14 read in conjunction with Art 9). On analogous Inter-American case law, see IACmHR, *Sahli Vera et al v Chile*, Report No 43/05, Case 12.219 (2005).

[60] ECtHR, *Metropolitan Church of Bessarabia and Others v Moldova*, *Reports* 2001-XII, paras 115–116.

[61] Ibid, para 123.

[62] ECtHR (Grand Chamber), *Refah Partisi (the Welfare Party) and Others v Turkey*, *Reports* 2003-II, paras 90 ff.

91. Moreover, in democratic societies, in which several religions coexist within one and the same population, it may be necessary to place restrictions on this freedom in order to reconcile the interests of the various groups and ensure that everyone's beliefs are respected (see *Kokkinakis*,...). The Court has frequently emphasised the State's role as the neutral and impartial organiser of the exercise of various religions, faiths and beliefs, and stated that this role is conducive to public order, religious harmony and tolerance in a democratic society. It also considers that the State's duty of neutrality and impartiality is incompatible with any power on the State's part to assess the legitimacy of religious beliefs (see, *mutatis mutandis, Cha'are Shalom Ve Tsedek v France* [GC], no. 27417/95, § 84, ECHR 2000-VII) and that it requires the State to ensure mutual tolerance between opposing groups (see, *mutatis mutandis, Metropolitan Church of Bessarabia and Others v Moldova*, no. 45701/99, § 123, ECHR 2001-XII).

92. The Court's established case-law confirms this function of the State. It has held that in a democratic society the State may limit the freedom to manifest a religion, for example by wearing an Islamic headscarf, if the exercise of that freedom clashes with the aim of protecting the rights and freedoms of others, public order and public safety (see *Dahlab v Switzerland* (dec.), no. 42393/98, ECHR 2001-V).

While freedom of religion is in the first place a matter of individual conscience, it also implies freedom to manifest one's religion alone and in private or in community with others, in public and within the circle of those whose faith one shares. Article 9 lists a number of forms which manifestation of a religion or belief may take, namely worship, teaching, practice and observance. Nevertheless, it does not protect every act motivated or influenced by a religion or belief (see *Kalaç v Turkey*, judgment of 1 July 1997, *Reports* 1997-IV, p. 1209, § 27).

The obligation for a teacher to observe normal working hours which, he asserts, clash with his attendance at prayers, may be compatible with the freedom of religion (see *X v the United Kingdom*, no. 8160/78, Commission decision of 12 March 1981, Decisions and Reports (DR) 22, p. 27), as may the obligation requiring a motorcyclist to wear a crash helmet, which in his view is incompatible with his religious duties (see *X v the United Kingdom*, no. 7992/77, Commission decision of 12 July 1978, DR 14, p. 234).

The Human Rights Committee similarly decided that a regulation according to which a member of the Sikh religious community could not be released from the obligation to wear safety headgear when engaged in certain kinds of work was compatible with the freedom of religion as the state regulation was aimed solely at protecting the complainant's health.[63]

As regards the prohibition of wearing an Islamic headscarf at school or university, the European Court of Human Rights decided that in the case of female teachers in Switzerland such prohibition could be justified with the necessity of safeguarding the secular character of state schools.[64] In the case of women university students in Turkey, however, the justification was seen in the need to protect other students from pressure by fundamentalist groups.[65] In both cases, the decisions rested to a large extent on the Court's theory of the states' margin of appreciation.[66] In contrast, the Human Rights Committee arguably applying a stricter standard of scrutiny, held

---

[63] HRCttee, *Singh Bhinder v Canada*, Communication No 208/1986 (1989).
[64] ECtHR, *Dahlab v Switzerland*, *Reports* 2001-V.
[65] ECtHR (Grand Chamber), *Leyla Şahin v Turkey*, *Reports* 2005-XI.
[66] On this approach see Chapter 16, section II.2.

> that the exclusion of an author from a state-run university in Uzbekistan on the ground that she had refused to remove her headscarf during lectures violated the freedom of religion because the state party had failed to invoke any specific grounds that would justify such a prohibition.[67]

Religious freedom also has a collective component, which includes the right to found a religious community and to congregate;[68] the right of such communities to organize themselves and to appoint their spiritual leaders; and the right to engage in religious activities, to offer religious instruction,[69] to propagate beliefs, to solicit new members,[70] and to obtain and use (voluntary) contributions from individuals, organizations and companies. These rights are violated where the activities of a Christian church are prosecuted as illegal even though the church has, according to applicable laws, no means of securing recognition as a religious association,[71] where the state registration necessary to the activities of a religious community is refused without serious and objective grounds,[72] or where the legal personality of a religious community was only granted approximately 20 years after the request,[73] where the state interferes without legal cause in the internal affairs of a Muslim minority organization,[74] where Jehovah's Witnesses are prohibited from opening a prayer room without the permission of the local Orthodox bishop and the Ministry of Religious Affairs,[75] or where a state refuses to take reasonable action to protect members of a religious minority from violent attacks performed by members of the religious majority.[76]

---

[67] HRCttee, *Hudoyberganova v Uzbekistan*, Communication No 931/2000 (2004), especially para 6.2.

[68] This right is also valid for prisoners: ECtHR, *Dmitrijevs v Latvia*, Application No 61638/00 (2006), para 79.

[69] See for example, HRCttee, *Malakhovsky and Pikul v Belarus*, Communication No 1207/2003 (2005), para 7.2.

[70] HRCttee, *Sister Immaculate Joseph and 80 Teaching Sisters of the Holy Cross of the Third Order of Saint Francis in Menzingen of Sri Lanka v Sri Lanka*, Communication No 1249/2004 (2005), para 7.2.

[71] ECtHR, *The Metropolitan Church of Bessarabia and Others v Moldova*, Reports 2001-XII, paras 105 and 129 f.

[72] HRCttee, *Malakhovsky and Pikul v Belarus*, Communication No 1207/2003 (2005), paras 7.4–7.5, and ECtHR, *The Moscow Branch of the Salvation Army v Russia*, Application No 72881/01 (2006), 58 ff, and *Church of Scientology of the City of Moscow v Russia*, Application No 18147/02 (2007), paras 81 ff. The ECtHR examines such cases under freedom of assembly anchored in ECHR, Art 11. However, it takes religious freedom into account for the interpretation of this notion.

[73] ECtHR, *Religionsgemeinschaft der Zeugen Jehovas and Others v Austria*, Application No 40825/98 (2008).

[74] ECtHR (Grand Chamber), *Hasan and Chaush v Bulgaria*, Reports 2000-XI, paras 61 ff and 86.

[75] ECtHR, *Manoussakis and Others v Greece*, Reports 1996-IV, para 47.

[76] ECtHR, *Case of 97 members of the Gldani Congregation of Jehovah's Witnesses and 4 Others v Georgia*, Application No 71156/01 (2007), paras 129 ff.

3. The right to change religion

Unlike the ECHR (Article 9(1)) and the ACHR (Article 12(1)), the ICCPR does not explicitly provide for a right to change one's religion. However, such a right is, as the Human Rights Committee has stressed,[77] implicit in the freedom to 'adopt a religion or belief' of one's choice as embodied in ICCPR, Article 18. This right cannot be limited and is obviously violated where a state prohibits members of a particular religion from converting to another religion on pain of prosecution[78] or forces them to remain a member of a religious community they wish to leave.

4. The right of parents to provide religious education to their children

Parents have the right to decide on their children's religious education (ICCPR, Article 18(4)), subject to respect for the children's best interests. While the state may offer religious instruction, it has the duty, where such instruction is based on a specific religion, to give parents the opportunity to opt for alternatives or to exempt their children from instruction.[79]

The right of parents to make decisions regarding the religious education of their children is directed against the state. Within the family, the right may clash with the freedom of religion of the child. Article 14(1) of the CRC obliges the state rather than the parents to respect this right. However, by stating in paragraph 2 that states must 'respect the rights and duties of the parents and, when applicable, legal guardians, *to provide direction* to the child in the exercise of his or her right in a manner consistent *with the evolving capacities* of the child'[80] the CRC highlights the fact that the parents' educational rights must find their limits where the child has reached an age and level of maturity that allows him or her to decide on its own convictions.

5. The prohibition of discrimination on the basis of belief

The right to have, manifest and change one's religion entails the right not to be discriminated against on the basis of belief. This dimension is discussed in the context of the prohibition of discrimination.[81]

---

[77] HRCttee, General Comment No 18 (1989), para 5.
[78] Accordingly, the HRCttee has criticized Islamic states that have enacted such provisions, eg Concluding Observations Yemen (2002), para 20.
[79] This dimension was covered in section II.4 above, under the right to education.
[80] Emphasis added.   [81] See Chapter 11.

14

Protection of the Human Person in the Economic Sphere

In today's world, economic activities have become a fundamental aspect of the human existence. They are a necessary means to earn an adequate standard of living; at the same time many persons find satisfaction and fulfilment in exercising professional activities. Private property may also contribute to securing an adequate standard of living and contribute to individual development. At the same time, the economic sphere can be a source of exploitation of individuals which, in extreme cases may amount to forced labour and modern forms of slavery. This Chapter deals first with protection from these worst forms of economic exploitation (section I), then shortly addresses the right to work and human rights protection of workers (section II), and finishes with a discussion of property related rights (section III).

I. Protection from the Worst Forms of Economic Exploitation

Relevant provisions: UDHR, Article 4; ICESCR, Articles 6–8; ICCPR, Article 8; CRC, Articles 32 and 34–36; CRPD, Article 27; ICRMW, Article 11; Slavery Convention; Supplementary Convention of 7 September 1956 on the Abolition of Slavery, the Slave Trade, and Institutions and Practices Similar to Slavery; ACHR, Article 6; ACHPR, Article 15; ArCHR, Article 10; ECHR, Article 4; ESC, Article 1(2); Rome Statute, Article 7(l)(c) and (g) and Article 8(2)(b)(xxii) and (e)(vi).

1. The prohibition of slavery and its contemporary forms

The fight against slavery, the worst form of economic exploitation of human beings, began at the Congress of Vienna in 1815.[1] It therefore ranks among the earliest international endeavours to protect human rights. Nowadays the prohibition of slavery forms an integral part of international customary law and is considered *jus cogens*.[2] In treaty law, slavery is prohibited by the 1926 Slavery

---

[1] For more detail see Chapter 1, section II.2.   [2] See Chapter 2, section III.2.

Convention, the 1956 Supplementary Slavery Convention, ICCPR, Article 8, ICRMW, Article 11, CRPD, Article 27(2), and by all the regional human rights conventions. In addition to slavery, the above also prohibit serfdom or servitude.

Slavery, in its original sense, refers to the ownership of individuals[3] who do not benefit from legal capacity and can be exploited or sold by their masters with impunity[4] (so-called 'cattle slavery'). The Rome Statute classifies slavery as a crime against humanity and defines the notion as 'the exercise of any or all of the powers attaching to the right of ownership over a person includ[ing] the exercise of such power in the course of trafficking in persons, in particular women and children'.[5]

Serfdom differs from slavery in legal terms in that serfs have not lost their legal capacity as such but must place their labour at the disposal of their master until such time as the latter declares his or her willingness to change the relationship. It may be narrowly defined as the status of a person 'who is by law, custom or agreement bound to live and labour on land belonging to another person and to render some determinate service to such other person, whether for reward or not, and is not free to change his [or her] status'.[6]

Although slavery and serfdom in the strict legal sense are now outlawed throughout the world, they still exist in the social reality of some countries.[7] Practices amounting to the exploitation of human beings as though they held no legal capacity or were equivalent in status to serfs remain frequent. They include the trafficking and sexual exploitation of women and children, enforced prostitution, human trafficking for economic exploitation, the worst forms of child labour, forced recruitment of child soldiers and traditional or contemporary forms of debt bondage.[8] Elements of slavery and serfdom are often combined and treated together by the relevant special procedures of the United Nations Human Rights Council as 'contemporary forms of slavery'.[9]

Slavery, serfdom and their contemporary equivalents are subject to absolute prohibitions, which are non-derogable in states of emergency.[10] In terms of the *obligation to respect*, states are required under international law to abstain from

---

[3] According to Art 1 of the Slavery Convention, slavery is 'the status or condition of a person over whom any or all of the powers attaching to the right of ownership are exercised'.

[4] See ACmHPR, *Malawi African Association and Others v Mauritania*, Communication Nos 54/1991, 61/1991, 98/1993, 164–196/1997 and 210/1998 (2000), paras 132–5.

[5] Rome Statute, Art 7(2)(c).   [6] Supplementary Slavery Convention, Art 1(b).

[7] See ACmHPR, *Bah Ould Rabah v Mauritania*, Communication No 197/97 (2004).

[8] They also include, according to Art 1(c) of the Supplementary Slavery Convention, traditional practices in certain societies, whereby '(i) a woman, without the right to refuse, is promised or given in marriage on payment of a consideration in money or in kind to her parents, guardian, family or any other person or group; or (ii) the husband of a woman, his family, or his clan, has the right to transfer her to another person for value received or otherwise; or (iii) a woman on the death of her husband is liable to be inherited by another person'.

[9] Special Rapporteur on modern forms of slavery, Special Rapporteur on the sale of children, child prostitution and child pornography, and Special Rapporteur on trafficking in persons, especially women and children.

[10] ICCPR, Art 4(2); ECHR, Art 15(2); ACHR, Art 6(3).

practising slavery and serfdom themselves and from enacting laws that permit private slavery and serfdom. According to earlier jurisprudence, however, servitude cannot be held to exist where a state refuses to discharge young men from the army or the navy whose parents consented to their enlistment for a nine-year tour of duty when they were 15 or 16 years old.[11]

As the prohibitions of slavery, serfdom or servitude, and contemporary forms of slavery are usually violated by private actors, in practice, *the duty to protect* is the most important aspect of state obligations. States have a duty to make the above punishable offences,[12] to prosecute such offences and to take further appropriate steps to eradicate such practices and to protect the vulnerable, including through international cooperation involving, *inter alia*, mutual judicial assistance.[13] States violate the obligation to protect if they tolerate slavery despite having knowledge of violations all while being in a position to intervene. States must therefore take action against, for instance, debt bondage, a situation in which a debtor undertakes to work without pay for a creditor until he or she has liquidated a debt, and which, in practice, results in a form of slavery inasmuch as the debtor must constantly incur new debts in order to subsist.[14] In such cases, which include the practice known as 'bonded labour', adults and often children are compelled to pay off debts by means of their labour that were incurred in some cases by their ancestors *vis-à-vis* large landowners or industrialists. High interest rates make it virtually impossible to pay off the debts, making those concerned lifelong victims of this form of economic exploitation.[15] In the European context, the European Court of Human Rights classified the specific situation of a minor foreign citizen without regulated foreigner status as serfdom. The young woman's passport was confiscated by her employer and she was made to work seven days a week up to fifteen hours a day without salary and practically never leaving the apartment. As French legislation provided no possibility of acting effectively against her employer, France was found to have violated the obligations to protect inherent in ECHR, Article 4(1).[16]

Obligations to fulfil arise with respect to the rehabilitation and reintegration of victims.

---

[11] ECmHR, *W, X, Y and Z v The United Kingdom*, Application Nos 3435–3438/67 (1968), Collection of Decisions 28, paras 20–1.

[12] Slavery Convention, Art 6; Supplementary Slavery Convention, Art 6.

[13] See for example, with regard to trafficking in women and children, HRCttee, General Comment No 28 (2000), para 12.

[14] Art 1 of the Supplementary Convention defines debt bondage as 'the status or condition arising from a pledge by a debtor of his personal services or of those of a person under his control as security for a debt, if the value of those services as reasonably assessed is not applied towards the liquidation of the debt or the length and nature of those services are not respectively limited and defined'.

[15] See, for example, HRCttee, Concluding Observations India (1997), para 29; CtteeESCR, Concluding Observations Mali (1994), para 345, Congo (2000), para 210, and Nepal (2001), paras 525 and 538; CtteeRC, Concluding Observations India (2004), para 72 f; CtteeERD, Concluding Observations Nepal (2004), para 18, and Italy (2008), para 17.

[16] ECtHR, *Siliadin v France*, Reports 2005-VII, paras 121 ff and 143 ff.

Individuals who are responsible for slavery can be brought to justice not only under domestic criminal provisions but also, in some circumstances, under *international criminal law*. Where enslavement, sexual slavery and enforced prostitution are perpetrated as part of a widespread or systematic attack directed against the civilian population in execution of a plan by a state or group, they constitute crimes against humanity.[17] Sexual slavery and enforced prostitution during an international or non-international armed conflict can furthermore be deemed to be war crimes.[18]

Issue in focus: Trafficking in women and enforced prostitution

Trafficking in women for sexual exploitation is currently one of the least recognized yet most serious human rights problems, particularly in Europe. It is estimated that up to 800,000 women fall victim to international trafficking each year.[19]

The trafficking phenomenon has traditionally been treated as a criminal matter rather than a human rights issue. The Convention for the Suppression of the Traffic in Persons and of the Exploitation of the Prostitution of Others of 2 December 1949 deals primarily with the punishment of offenders (Articles 1 and 2), measures relating to foreign nationals (Article 17) and the repatriation of victims (Article 19). Although states are required to take steps aimed at prevention and rehabilitation, no individual entitlements for victims are recognized. A similar approach is adopted in the Protocol to Prevent, Suppress and Punish Trafficking in Persons Especially Women and Children of 15 November 2000, supplementing the United Nations Convention against Transnational Organized Crime adopted on the same day. The Convention and Protocol seek to improve international police and judicial cooperation, set minimum standards for domestic legislation, establish mechanisms to counter money laundering, and enhance the protection of victims and witnesses. Provision is made in particular for the prosecution of offenders (Protocol, Article 5), the protection of victims (Article 6) and for stricter border controls (Article 11). States should consider whether to give victims the option of remaining on a temporary or permanent basis in the receiving state where repatriation is deemed to be inappropriate (Article 8). A similar approach is adopted in the European Convention on Action against Trafficking in Human Beings of 16 May 2005. However, it additionally contains specific obligations to extend support to the victims of such crimes (Articles 12 and 13) and requires states to issue a residence permit to victims if either their personal situation or the institution of criminal proceedings against the perpetrators so indicates (Article 14).

Article 6 of the CEDAW is a human-rights-oriented provision inasmuch as it obliges states to 'take all appropriate measures, including legislation, to suppress all

---

[17] Rome Statute, Art 7(l)(c) and (g). The concept of enslavement is to be understood as defined in the Slavery Convention and the Supplementary Convention; in the case of sexual slavery, sexual exploitation is an additional element (Elements of Crimes, Doc ICC-ASP/1/3, Art 7(1)(c), footnote 11, and Art 7(1)(g) and (2).

[18] Rome Statute, Art 8(2)(b)(xxii) and (e)(vi).

[19] US Department of State, *Trafficking in Persons Report*, June 2008, 7.

forms of traffic in women and exploitation of prostitution of women'. Although this article, which is quite vague in terms of content, stops short of creating an individual right, state compliance can be reviewed in the context of the reporting procedure before the Committee on the Elimination of Discrimination against Women.

Trafficking in women and enforced prostitution are not directly addressed in the ICCPR. However, the Human Rights Committee has emphasized that such practices violate ICCPR, Article 8, read in conjunction with the non-discrimination provisions of ICCPR, Articles 3 and 26,[20] and that states have specific obligations to fulfil their duties, to protect the victims,[21] and to punish the perpetrators.[22]

2. Prohibition of forced labour

Forced labour differs from slavery in that it is ordered by public authorities in order to serve the public interest. The prohibition of forced labour in the ICCPR and the regional human rights conventions is couched in absolute terms but is nevertheless derogable in states of emergency.[23] Forced labour is defined as 'all work or service which is exacted from any person under the menace of any penalty and for which the said person has not offered himself voluntarily' and which does not fall within the scope of a recognized exception. This definition, set out in International Labour Organization (ILO) Convention No 29,[24] does not contain the element of ownership which distinguishes forced labour from slavery. This approach is recognized by the European and the Inter-American Court of Human Rights as the authoritative basis for interpreting the human rights concept of forced labour.[25] Thus, the criteria of involuntariness and threat of a penalty provide the best key to easy identification of forced labour. Problems of delimitation may, however, arise. The European Court of Human Rights concluded, for instance, in a case in which the burden was not excessive and the complainant was aware of it when he voluntarily decided to practise law, that the obligation to act on behalf of indigent defendants from time to time on a *pro bono* basis did not constitute forced labour, notwithstanding the compulsory element.[26]

The treaties recognize, in exception clauses, that the following circumstances do not fall within the definition of forced labour despite meeting its

---

[20] See HRCttee, General Comment No 28 (2000), para 12, and for example Concluding Observations Brazil (2005), para 15.

[21] Eg HRCttee, Concluding Observations Slovakia (2003), para 10, and Barbados (2007), para 8.

[22] Eg HRCttee, Concluding Observations Lithuania (2004), para 14, Brazil (2005), para 15.

[23] ICCPR, Art 8(3)(a) in conjunction with Art 4(4); ECHR, Art 4(2) in conjunction with Art 15(2); ACHR, Art 6 in conjunction with Art 27.

[24] ILO Forced Labour Convention of 28 June 1930 (No 29), Art 2.

[25] ECtHR, *Van der Mussele v Belgium*, A/70 (1983), paras 32–43; IACtHR, *Case of the Ituango Massacres v Colombia*, Series C, No 148 (2006), paras 157–160. The HRCttee, while stressing the autonomous nature of this notion in ICCPR, Art 8, acknowledges that, 'the definitions of the relevant ILO instruments may be of assistance in elucidating the meaning of the terms' (*Faure v Australia*, Communication No 1036/2001 (2005), para 7.5).

[26] ECtHR, *Van der Mussele v Belgium*, Series A, No 70 (1983), para 40.

conditions: (1) forced labour as a criminal sanction or labour normally required in the context of either lawful detention compatible with human rights norms or conditional release from such detention; (2) military service or alternative civilian service for conscientious objectors;[27] (3) services exacted in the context of emergencies or calamities threatening the life or well-being of the community; and (4) work and services that form part of normal civic obligations.[28] This gives rise to a number of questions, such as what constitutes work 'normally required' in detention and in the performance of civic obligations. Labour performed during lawful detention can, in any case, be labelled as 'normally required' if it is aimed primarily at the reintegration of the prisoners.[29] It is permissible therefore, for instance, to require a prisoner to perform such work as is necessary to obtain a sum of money on release that will enable him or her to reintegrate into society.[30] A civic obligation is also 'normal' if it is not of 'a punitive purpose or effect' and is 'provided for by law in order to serve a legitimate purpose under the Covenant'.[31] 'Normal' obligations in this sense are, for example, the obligation to serve on a jury panel,[32] the obligation to join the local fire brigade as an alternative to the payment of a compensatory charge,[33] or the obligation to participate in a work program for unemployed youth in order to receive unemployment benefits.[34]

3. Protection of children from exploitation

Children are exploited throughout the world because they are a source of cheap labour and can be taken advantage of, owing to their defencelessness, to serve other purposes. It is estimated that there are globally at least 110 million child workers under 12 years of age and that some 1.8 million children and adolescents are employed in the sex industry.[35] Child labour is often dangerous and harmful to health, and usually prevents the children concerned from attending school or obtaining an adequate education.

Although child labour as such is not prohibited by human rights law, it is restricted in a number of ways. Pursuant to Article 32 of the Convention on the Rights of the Child, children and adolescents below the age of 18 years[36] have

---

[27] However, the European Committee of Social Rights held that a legal provision to the effect that alternative civilian service should run for 18 months longer than military service was a violation of the right, under Art 1(2) ESC, to earn one's living in an occupation freely entered upon: *Quaker Council for European Affairs v Greece*, Complaint No 8/2000 (2001), para 25.

[28] ICCPR, Art 8(3)(b) and (c); ECHR, Art 4(3); ACHR, Art 6(3).

[29] See HRCttee, *Radosevic v Germany*, Communication No 1292/2004 (2005), para 7.3.

[30] ECtHR, *Van Droogenbroeck v Belgium*, Series A, No 50 (1982), paras 59–60.

[31] HRCttee, *Faure v Australia*, Communication No 1036/2001 (2005), para 7.5.

[32] ECtHR, *Adami v Malta*, Application No 17209/02 (2006) para 47.

[33] ECtHR, *Schmidt v Germany*, Series A, No 291-B (1994), para 23.

[34] HRCttee, *Faure v Australia*, Communication No 1036/2001 (2005), in particular para 7.5.

[35] International Programme on the Elimination of Child Labour, *IPEC Action Against Child Labour: Highlights 2002*, Geneva 2003, 13–14.

[36] CRC, Art 1 defines the child as every human being below the age of 18 years.

the right 'to be protected from economic exploitation and from performing any work that is likely to be hazardous or to interfere with the child's education, or to be harmful to the child's health or physical, mental, spiritual, moral or social development'. To that end, states must fix a minimum age for admission to employment, regulate the hours and conditions of employment, and ensure the effective enforcement of such provisions, all while 'having regard to the relevant provisions of other international instruments'. This is primarily a reference to ILO conventions. For instance, Convention No 138 of 26 June 1973 concerning Minimum Age for Admission to Employment (Minimum Age Convention) specifies 15 years as the minimum age in general and 14 years as the minimum age for developing countries and countries in transition 'whose economy and educational facilities are insufficiently developed'.

The following particularly reprehensible forms of child labour are absolutely prohibited under ILO Convention No 182:[37]

(a) all forms of slavery or practices similar to slavery, such as the sale and trafficking of children, debt bondage and serfdom, and forced or compulsory labour, including forced or compulsory recruitment of children for use in armed conflict;
(b) the use, procuring, or offering of a child for prostitution, for the production of pornography, or for pornographic performances;
(c) the use, procuring, or offering of a child for illicit activities, in particular for the production and trafficking of drugs as defined in the relevant international treaties;
(d) work which, by its nature or the circumstances in which it is carried out, is likely to harm the health, safety, or morals of children.

These forms of exploitation of children are also, for the most part, prohibited under the Convention on the Rights of the Child. Thus, the general prohibition of harmful child labour contained in CRC, Article 32 is made more specific in Article 33, which prohibits 'the use of children in the illicit production and trafficking of [narcotic drugs and psychotropic] substances', and Article 34, which requires states parties to protect children 'from all forms of sexual exploitation and sexual abuse', including prostitution and pornography. The Optional Protocol to the Convention on the Rights of the Child of 25 May 2000 on the sale of children, child prostitution, and child pornography also prohibits such practices and obliges states to take concrete steps, such as making such offences punishable under criminal law or enhancing international cooperation, for instance in the area of mutual judicial assistance.

---

[37] Art 3 of ILO Convention No 182 of 17 June 1999 concerning the Prohibition and Immediate Action for the Elimination of the Worst Forms of Child Labour (Worst Forms of Child Labour Convention).

At the regional level, detailed provisions on the protection of children against exploitation can be found in Article 34(3) of the ArCHR and Articles 15 and 16 of the African Charter on the Rights and Welfare of the Child. In Europe, the European Committee of Social Rights held that states must incorporate an explicit prohibition of all forms of violence against children in their penal legislation.[38]

Issue in focus: Prohibition of the use of child soldiers

The question of child soldiers raises a particular set of issues. Many non-state armed groups as well as some state-run armies have in recent years used hundreds of thousands of boys and girls, usually recruited under duress, for the most dangerous types of warfare or to terrorize the civilian population. Child soldiers frequently run the highest risk of being killed, are often victims of sexual violence and exploitation, and may frequently be traumatized for the remainder of their lives.

Pursuant to Article 38 of the CRC and Article 77(2) of Additional Protocol I to the Geneva Conventions, children as young as 15 may be recruited by armed forces of contracting parties and used in armed conflicts. ILO Convention No 182 raises the age restriction to 18 years and makes no provision for exceptions. On the other hand, while the Optional Protocol to the Convention on the Rights of the Child of 25 May 2000 on the Involvement of Children in Armed Conflicts requires states parties to take 'all feasible measures to ensure that members of their armed forces who have not attained the age of 18 years do not take a direct part in hostilities' (Article 1) and to refrain from the compulsory recruitment of persons under 18 (Article 2), it allows them to recruit those who have reached the age of 15 for voluntary military service (Article 3).

At the regional level, Article 22(2) of the 1999 African Charter on the Rights and Welfare of the Child which defines as child 'every human being below the age of 18 years' obliges states to 'take all necessary measures to ensure that no child shall take a direct part in hostilities and refrain in particular, from recruiting any child'.[39] Article 10(2) of the ArCHR prohibits 'the exploitation of children in armed conflict'.

Child victims of these forms of exploitation are entitled to rehabilitation.[40]

II. Overview: the Right to Work and the Protection of Workers

Responsibility for the protection of workers has been vested in the International Labour Organization since its establishment after the First World War.[41] The

---

[38] European Committee of Social Rights, *World Organisation Against Torture v Portugal*, 34/2006 (2006).

[39] Art 2 of the Charter.

[40] CRC, Art 39; Optional Protocol to the Convention on the Rights of the Child of 25 May 2000 on the Sale of Children, Child Prostitution and Child Pornography, Art 8.

[41] See Chapter 1, section II.4.

ILO has adopted more than 180 conventions on all aspects of working life. In addition to the above-mentioned Forced Labour Convention (No 29), Minimum Age Convention (No 138) and Worst Forms of Child Labour Convention (No 182), a further five conventions on trade union rights, forced labour, and non-discrimination[42] are characterized as core conventions that should be ratified by every state. Together with the remaining ILO conventions, they specify in great detail the content of human rights safeguards in the area of employment.

Among human rights treaties, the 1961 European Social Charter is of fundamental importance for the protection of workers at the regional level, inasmuch as twelve of its nineteen substantive guarantees[43] set out in detail the right to employment and other employment-related rights. Three provisions of the International Covenant on Economic, Social and Cultural Rights address the subject (Articles 6–8). Other human rights treaty provisions include the above-mentioned work-related rights in the Convention on the Rights of the Child, safeguards against discrimination in employment for women and victims of racial discrimination,[44] and provisions for the protection of employment-related rights of migrant workers.[45] In Africa, ACHPR, Article 15 sets out the right to equitable working conditions and to equal pay for equal work; in the Americas, Articles 6–8 of the Protocol of San Salvador provide for the right to work and for other workplace rights. Article 34 of the ArCHR also secures the right to work with its different components.

Taken together, these rights constitute the self-contained field of 'international labour law', which is highly complex and far transcends the scope of this book. A few brief remarks on the core set of rights contained in the International Covenant on Economic, Social and Cultural Rights will therefore have to suffice in this context.[46]

The *right to work*[47] set out in ICESCR, Article 6 is not an entitlement to obtain employment from the state. The article consists primarily of a civil liberty, namely the freedom to choose one's work freely and to be able to earn a living by means of the work chosen. It thus guarantees not only freedom to choose among different available employment options without state interference but also freedom to choose a specific profession. This right is not absolute and may be limited under Article 4 of the Covenant provided that such limitation is determined by law and introduced solely for the purpose of 'promoting the general

---

[42] ILO Freedom of Association and Protection of the Right to Organise Convention, 9 July 1948 (No 87); Right to Organise and Collective Bargaining Convention, 1 July 1949 (No 98); Convention concerning Equal Remuneration for Men and Women Workers for Work of Equal Value (Equal Remuneration Convention), 29 June 1951 (No 100); Abolition of Forced Labour Convention, 25 June 1957 (No 105); and Discrimination (Employment and Occupation) Convention, 25 June 1958 (No 111).

[43] ESC, Arts 1–10 and 18–19.   [44] CEDAW, Arts 11 and 14; CERD, Art 5(e).

[45] ICRMW, Arts 25–27, 40 and 52–54.

[46] On the rights of migrant workers and their families see Chapter 17, section III.

[47] See CtteeESCR, General Comment No 18 (2005).

welfare in a democratic society'. Persons who have not completed the necessary training may therefore be denied access to certain professions, and young people or vulnerable persons may be excluded from certain activities that are dangerous or harmful to health. In addition, ICESCR, Article 6, paragraph 2 contains a (non-justiciable) social right inasmuch as the state is required to assist in ensuring full realization of the right to work through measures such as 'technical and vocational guidance and training programmes' and through 'policies and techniques to achieve steady economic, social and cultural development and full and productive employment'.

Article 7 of the ICESCR sets out the *right to just and favourable conditions of work*, under which the Covenant groups together a series of miscellaneous rights. Women's right to working conditions that are no less favourable than those of men; fair wages and equal pay for equal work without distinctions of any kind; and equal career advancement opportunities based on criteria such as competence and seniority are non-discrimination provisions whose enforcement must be guaranteed by the state, not only for civil servants but also for those in the private sector. Ensuring remuneration that provides all workers a wage sufficient for a decent living, especially within the meaning of Article 11 of the Covenant, imposes an obligation on the state to prescribe and enforce minimum wages in cases where employers and employees and their organizations are unable to reach agreement. The right to safe and healthy working conditions, to protection from unreasonably long working hours, and to periodic holidays with pay are also to be realized and secured through legislation, and it is precisely here that the relevant ILO conventions can serve as a source of detailed guidance for the interpretation of these Covenant rights.

Lastly, Article 8 of the ICESCR on *trade union rights* safeguards the rights of workers and their organizations *vis-à-vis* employers, rights that also fall largely into the category of civil liberties. Workers have the right to form trade unions and to join the trade union of their choice. The right to choose incorporates by implication the right not to join a union. Trade unions may form national and international federations and function freely. Although these rights are not absolute, they may not, according to paragraph 1(c), be subject to limitations other than 'those prescribed by law and which are necessary in a democratic society in the interests of national security or public order or for the protection of the rights and freedoms of others'. Provision is also made for the right to strike, on condition, however, that 'it is exercised in conformity with the laws of the particular country'; moreover, it may be restricted by law for members of the armed forces, the police and the administration of the state.[48] Domestic legislation may, in particular, rule out so-called 'political' strikes, ie strike action called not with the aim of successfully asserting collective interests *vis-à-vis* employers but in pursuit

---

[48] ICESCR, Art 8(1)(d) and (2). See also ECtHR (Grand Chamber), *Demir and Baykara v Turkey*, Application No 34503/97 (2008).

of other objectives.[49] The freedom to form and join trade unions is also explicitly recognized in the right to freedom of association set out in ICCPR, Article 22, ECHR, Article 11, ArCHR, Article 35 and is implicitly recognized in ACHR, Article 16.

Issue in focus: The right to social security

Article 9, the shortest provision of ICESR, requires the states parties to 'recognize the right of everyone to social security, including social insurance'. In 2007 the CtteESCR adopted General Comment 19 which defines the content of this often ignored right as follows:

1.... The right to social security is of central importance in guaranteeing human dignity for all persons when they are faced with circumstances that deprive them of their capacity to fully realize their Covenant rights.

2. The right to social security encompasses the right to access and maintain benefits, whether in cash or in kind, without discrimination in order to secure protection, inter alia, from (a) lack of work-related income caused by sickness, disability, maternity, employment injury, unemployment, old age, or death of a family member; (b) unaffordable access to health care; (c) insufficient family support, particularly for children and adult dependents.

4. The wording of article 9 of the Covenant indicates that the measures that are to be used to provide social security benefits cannot be defined narrowly and, in any event, must guarantee all peoples a minimum enjoyment of this human right. These measures can include:

(a) Contributory or insurance-based schemes such as social insurance, which is expressly mentioned in article 9. These generally involve compulsory contributions from beneficiaries, employers and, sometimes, the State, in conjunction with the payment of benefits and administrative expenses from a common fund;

(b) Non-contributory schemes such as universal schemes (which provide the relevant benefit in principle to everyone who experiences a particular risk or contingency) or targeted social assistance schemes (where benefits are received by those in a situation of need). In almost all States parties, non-contributory schemes will be required since it is unlikely that every person can be adequately covered through an insurance-based system.

41. The Committee acknowledges that the realization of the right to social security carries significant financial implications for States parties, but notes that the fundamental importance of social security for human dignity and the legal recognition of this right by States parties mean that the right should be given appropriate priority in law and policy. States parties should develop a national strategy for the full implementation of the right to social security, and should allocate adequate fiscal and other resources at the national level. If necessary, they should avail themselves of international cooperation and technical assistance in line with article 2, paragraph 1, of the Covenant.

---

[49] The fact that the right to strike is confined to conflicts with employers may be inferred in the case of the ESC from the wording of Art 6(4), which provides for such a right in the context of conflicts of interest related to collective bargaining. According to the European Committee of Social Rights, a total prohibition of striking for certain professions, as for example employees in the health, energy, transport or communication industries, violates the right to strike guaranteed by the ESC; *Confederation of Independent Trade Unions in Bulgaria, Confederation of Labour Podkrepa and European Trade Union Confederation v Bulgaria*, Complaint No 32/2005 (2006).

42. There is a strong presumption that retrogressive measures taken in relation to the right to social security are prohibited under the Covenant. If any deliberately retrogressive measures are taken, the State party has the burden of proving that they have been introduced after the most careful consideration of all alternatives and that they are duly justified by reference to the totality of the rights provided for in the Covenant, in the context of the full use of the maximum available resources of the State party. The Committee will look carefully at whether: (a) there was reasonable justification for the action; (b) alternatives were comprehensively examined; (c) there was genuine participation of affected groups in examining the proposed measures and alternatives; (d) the measures were directly or indirectly discriminatory; (e) the measures will have a sustained impact on the realization of the right to social security, an unreasonable impact on acquired social security rights or whether an individual or group is deprived of access to the minimum essential level of social security; and (f) whether there was an independent review of the measures at the national level.

III. Protection of Property

Relevant provisions: UDHR, Article 17; CEDAW, Articles 15(2) and 16(1)(h); CERD, Article 5(c)(v); CRPD, Article 12(5); ICRMW, Article 15; ACHR, Article 21; ACHPR, Article 14; ArCHR, Article 31; P 1/ECHR, Article 1; GC III, Article 18; GC IV, Articles 33, 53 and 97; AP I, Articles 51–54; AP II, Article 4(2); Rome Statute, Article 8(2)(a)(iv).

1. The right to protection of property as a human right

The characterization of the right to property as a human right has been controversial. While the Universal Declaration of Human Rights recognizes this right in Article 17, the two UN Covenants make no mention of it, particularly because of a lack of consensus between the West and the countries of the South and Communist East regarding whether compensation should be 'full' or just 'fair' or 'appropriate' in cases of expropriation and nationalization. Some aspects of the right to property, however, are protected under specialized universal instruments and also, in particularly unambiguous terms, under international humanitarian law and international criminal law. Even at the regional level, the incorporation of this right was not an entirely smooth process. Thus, the drafters of the ECHR were reluctant to include it in the core text of the Convention, so that the basis for the right to property is contained in the first Additional Protocol of 1954. By contrast, at the African and Inter-American level this right is part of the main conventions.

2. Protection of property at the universal level

(a) *Protection of property under the Covenants*

It should not be inferred from the fact that the right to property has not been included in the two UN Covenants that these instruments afford no legal protection in the area of property. In fact, several rights are highly relevant for the protection of property.

The obligation to respect the right to food and housing under ICESCR, Article 11 precludes states from, for instance, destroying land and crops or otherwise removing them from the possession of their owners or from evicting inhabitants from dwellings they rightfully own.[50] Under some circumstances the obligations to protect flowing from these rights require lawmakers, administrative authorities, and courts to take action against infringements of property rights by third parties.

The right of access to a court and the right to a fair hearing in civil disputes under ICCPR, Article 14(1) impose an obligation on states to make judicial bodies available to review the permissibility of expropriations and other forms of property confiscation and to determine whether the compensation provided is in conformity with applicable law.

The autonomous non-discrimination provision of ICCPR, Article 26 forbids, in the area of confiscation of private property and compensation for confiscation, any differentiation based on prohibited grounds of discrimination.[51] The prohibition of discrimination with respect to property can also play a role in the relationship between private actors. For instance, under CEDAW, Article 16(1) states are required to ensure the same rights for both spouses 'in respect of the ownership, acquisition, management, administration, enjoyment and disposition of property'.

Example: Views of the HRCttee in *Simunek et al v Czech Republic*[52]

In *Simunek et al v Czech Republic*, the Human Rights Committee was not being asked to pass judgment on the confiscation of the complainant's property by Czechoslovakia under Communist rule; such confiscations, taken against suspected political opponents of the then Communist regime or those expelled or forced to flee the country, had taken place before the entry into force of the Covenant or its Optional Protocol. Rather, the issue before the Committee was the conformity with human rights norms of a Czech law providing for either the restitution of unlawfully confiscated real estate or for compensation after the fall of the Communist regime. The legislation in question limited restitution to persons who, at the time of the entry into force of the law in 1991, possessed Czech citizenship and resided in the country. The Committee found that these conditions, as applied to the authors of the communication who had found refuge abroad, were discriminatory and thus violated ICCPR, Article 26. It reasoned that the Czech Government had not advanced any material grounds that would justify depriving certain victims of the original violation of property rights of their entitlement to restitution. In view of the fact that the state was responsible for the authors' departure by forcing them to seek refuge abroad

---

[50] See Chapter 9, section III.3.b.
[51] HRCttee, *Simunek et al v Czech Republic*, Communication No 516/1992 (1995), para 11.3.
[52] HRCttee, *Simunek et al v Czech Republic*, Communication No 516/1992 (1995).

as victims of political persecution, it was unreasonable to 'require them permanently to return to the country as a prerequisite for the restitution of their property or for the payment of appropriate compensation'.[53]

Furthermore, the right to privacy and family life (ICCPR, Article 17) may potentially be invoked to secure protection of certain aspects of the right to property. For instance, the corresponding provision of the ECHR (Article 8) entails not only a prohibition of the destruction of residential property and of eviction from one's land but also an entitlement to protection from harmful emissions and hence to unimpeded enjoyment of the property.[54] Arguably, similar prohibitions are implicit in the protection of privacy in the ICCPR.

Lastly, the entitlement of minorities to protection under ICCPR, Article 27 is also of relevance to property. It covers, *inter alia*, the right to collective use of natural resources by indigenous peoples and hence prohibits activities by states and third parties that adversely affect traditional fishing, hunting, or herding.[55]

(b) Protection of property under international humanitarian law

International humanitarian law provides direct and diverse protection for the property rights of anyone falling into the 'protected persons' category in times of armed conflict.

The absolute prohibition of pillage under the second paragraph of GC IV, Article 33 and AP II, Article 4(2)(g) protects the private property of the civilian population during international and non-international conflicts. The war crime of pillaging consolidates this protection by establishing the principle of individual responsibility not only of members of the armed forces but also of non-state armed groups.[56] Reprisals against the property of protected persons[57] and collective punishment[58] are also prohibited in all circumstances without exception.

Article 53 of GC IV deals with the protection of private property in occupied territory. It prohibits '[a]ny destruction by the Occupying Power of real or personal property belonging individually or collectively to private persons, or to the State, or to other public authorities, or to social or cooperative organizations...except where such destruction is rendered absolutely necessary by military operations'.

The personal property of prisoners of war and civilian internees is safeguarded by GC III, Article 18, and GC IV, Article 97.

Lastly, the prohibition of attacks on civilian objects, of indiscriminate attacks, and of the use of certain weapons such as mines against civilian objects may be invoked in general terms to protect property in times of war.[59]

---

[53] Ibid, para 11.6. The Committee has applied the same reasoning in dozens of similar cases.
[54] See Chapter 12, section II.1.c.   [55] See Chapter 11, section V.3.
[56] Rome Statute, Art 8(2)(a)(iv), (b)(xvi), and (e)(v).   [57] GC IV, Art 33(3).
[58] GC IV, Art 33(1); AP I, Art 75(2)(d); AP II, Art 4(2)(b).
[59] See Chapter 9, section II.2.d.

3. Protection of property under the regional conventions

While the regional human rights conventions (P 1/ECHR, Article 1; ACHR, Article 21; ACHPR, Article 14; ArCHR, Article 31) do not protect the freedom to acquire property, they do protect its continued possession and peaceful enjoyment. Due to the rich case law available, the following section deals with this right primarily from the standpoint of the ECHR.

(a) Scope of the protection afforded to property and possessions

Article 1 of P 1/ECHR on 'protection of property' states: 'Every natural or legal person is entitled to the peaceful enjoyment of his possessions.' The concept of possessions covers ownership of both real estate and movables and of intangible assets.[60] However, as it has been construed by the European Court as having an autonomous meaning, the applicability of this entitlement is not confined to property rights under domestic legal regimes.[61] The Court thus affirmed that this right was protected in a case in which the purchaser of a painting had never become its owner under domestic law.[62] The guarantee also covers property claims that create a quasi-ownership status, for example, a 99-year lease, ownership of a concession, or even a firm's regular clientele base,[63] titles acquired under public law, and monetary claims provided that they have 'a sufficient basis in national law, for example where there is settled case law of the domestic courts confirming' them.[64] It does not, on the other hand, cover future income,[65] unless it is already owed.[66] Entitlements to pension benefits would be an example for the latter.

The right to property can be invoked only in the event of restrictions on ownership and quasi-ownership status imposed by a state after the entry into force of P 1/ECHR. It follows that all complaints to the European Court of Human Rights against cases of nationalization of property during communist rule in Central and Eastern European countries are doomed to fail. By contrast, the Court considers that state measures that were initiated before the entry into force of P 1/ECHR but continue after that date to impede the peaceful enjoyment of existing property constitute ongoing interference whose lawfulness it is competent to examine.[67]

---

[60] ECtHR (Grand Chamber), *Anheuser-Busch Inc. v Portugal*, Application No 73049/01 (2007), para 72.

[61] Ibid, para 63.

[62] ECtHR, *Beyeler v Italy*, Reports 2000-I, paras 100–106.

[63] ECtHR, *Van Marle and Others v The Netherlands*, Series A, No 101 (1986), paras 41–42.

[64] ECtHR (Grand Chamber), *Draon v France*, Application No 1513/03 (2005), para 65. The Court asserts that in such case 'the concept of "legitimate expectation" can come into play' (ibid).

[65] ECtHR (Grand Chamber), *Stec and Others v The United Kingdom*, Application No 65731/01 and 65900/01 (2006), para 53.

[66] ECtHR (Grand Chamber), *Anheuser-Busch Inc v Portugal*, Application No 73049/01 (2007), para 64.

[67] ECtHR (Grand Chamber), *Loizidou v Turkey*, Reports 1996-VI, para 41.

According to a standard formula used by the European Court of Human Rights, P 1/ECHR, Article 1 consists of three clearly distinguishable rules:[68]

The first rule, set out in the first sentence of the first paragraph, is of a general nature and enunciates the principle of the peaceful enjoyment of property; the second rule, contained in the second sentence of the first paragraph, covers deprivation of possessions and subjects it to certain conditions; the third rule, stated in the second paragraph, recognises that the Contracting States are entitled, amongst other things, to control the use of property in accordance with the general interest... The rules are not, however, 'distinct' in the sense of being unconnected. The second and third rules are concerned with particular instances of interference with the right to peaceful enjoyment of property and should therefore be construed in the light of the general principle enunciated in the first rule.

(b) Duty to respect property

According to the second sentence of Article 1 of P 1/ECHR, '[n]o one shall be deprived of his possessions except in the public interest and subject to the conditions provided for by law and by the general principles of international law'. The case law of the European Court of Human Rights distinguishes three situations where the state is under an obligation (albeit not absolute) to respect the enjoyment of property:

(1) *Expropriations*: The rule laid down in the second sentence of Article 1(1), according to which a private individual may be deprived of his or her possessions only under certain conditions, covers both cases of formal expropriation, ie compulsory transfer of title to the state, and cases of *de facto* expropriation, in which the person concerned remains the formal owner but can no longer use the property in practice or is severely impeded in his or her enjoyment thereof.[69] Pursuant to this clause, both types of restrictions on the right to property may be imposed only where domestic law so permits in the specific case and on condition that the expropriation serves the public interest. In addition, the principle of proportionality must also be respected, ie a fair balance must be struck between the demands of the general interest and the specific harm that will be done to the person concerned, ensuring 'a reasonable relationship... between the means employed and the aim sought to be realised by any measure depriving a person of his possessions'.[70]

This principle plays a decisive role when it comes to determining whether the state is liable to provide compensation for the loss of property incurred. Although Article 1(1) of P 1/ECHR makes no provision for a right to full compensation, the Court acknowledges that the seizing of property without compensation that is reasonably related to its value will normally constitute

---

[68] ECtHR (Grand Chamber), *Jahn and Others v Germany*, Reports 2005-VI, para 79.
[69] ECtHR, *Jahn and Others v Germany*, 46720/99, 72203/01 and 72552/01 (2004), paras 65–70, confirmed by the Grand Chamber in its judgment, *Reports* 2005-VI, paras 79–80.
[70] ECtHR (Grand Chamber), *Jahn and Others v Germany*, Reports 2005-VI, para 93.

a disproportionate interference with the right to property. The Court also recognizes, however, that public interest, for example in the case of economic reforms or measures aiming to create greater social justice, can result in below market value compensations being considered proportional.[71] Seizing property without compensation 'will normally constitute a disproportionate interference and a total lack of compensation can be considered justifiable under Article 1 of Protocol No 1 only in exceptional circumstances', but even in such cases 'the lack of compensation does not of itself make the State's taking of the applicants' property unlawful'; rather, one has to determine 'whether, in the context of a lawful deprivation of property, the applicants had to bear a disproportionate and excessive burden' in the particular case at hand.[72] Furthermore, expropriations and other forms of taking of property may be imposed only on condition that 'the general principles of international law' are respected. This wording refers to the so-called minimum standard of treatment of aliens as embodied in customary international law, which prohibits the expropriation of property belonging to foreign nationals without 'fair' or 'appropriate' compensation.[73]

(2) *Restrictions on the right of disposal*: The second paragraph of the article stipulates in circuitous terms that the right to property shall not 'in any way impair the right of a State to enforce such laws as it deems necessary to control the use of property in accordance with the general interest or to secure the payment of taxes or other contributions or penalties'. This clause permits states parties to levy property taxes or impose restrictions on the ownership and use of property through tenancy and leasehold provisions that limit the owner's right to terminate tenancy or set ceilings on rent.[74] In addition, restrictions on a testator's right of disposal, restrictions under construction law and the law of enforcement,[75] and the seizure of assets in connection with criminal proceedings[76] are permissible. All these restrictions are scrutinized by the Court in terms of their legal basis, the motives for the interference, as well as their proportionality, ie the balance to be struck between the demands of the general interest and the requirement of protection of the interests of the owners.[77]

---

[71] ECtHR (Grand Chamber), *Scordino v Italy*, Application No 36813/97 (2006), paras 96–98.

[72] See ECtHR (Grand Chamber), *Jahn and Others v Germany, Reports* 2005-VI, paras 94 and 95.

[73] See, for example, Ian Brownlie, *Principles of Public International Law* (6th edn, Oxford University Press: Oxford, 2003), 508 ff.

[74] See, for instance, ECtHR, *Mellacher v Austria*, Series A, No 169 (1989) and ECtHR (Grand Chamber), *Hutten-Czapska v Poland*, Application No 35014/97 (2006).

[75] For example, ECtHR, *Vendittelli v Italy*, Series A, No 293-A (1994), and (Grand Chamber), *Scordino v Italy*, Application No 36813/97 (2006), paras 96 ff.

[76] For example ECtHR, *AGOSI v The United Kingdom*, Series A, No 108 (1986), paras 52–61, *Forminster Enterprises Limited v Czech Republic*, Application No 38238/04 (2008), paras 63–69.

[77] For example, ECtHR (Grand Chamber) *Hutten-Czapska v Poland*, Application No 35014/97 (2006), paras 163–7. The Court requires, in particular, that a 'fair balance' be struck between public and private interests.

(3) *Other restrictions on property ownership*, such as restrictions on use due to a temporary building ban[78] or the destruction of private property by armed forces during military operations,[79] which cannot be characterized either as an expropriation under the second sentence of paragraph 1 or a restriction on use under paragraph 2 are examined by the Strasbourg Court to determine whether they are compatible with the first sentence of paragraph 1, namely that '[e]very natural or legal person is entitled to the peaceful enjoyment of his possessions'. If the Court finds that the public interest does not outweigh the private interest, the restriction will be found to be in violation of the right of property.

Example: The ECtHR judgment in *Loizidou v Turkey*[80]

The applicant, who had fled to the south following the occupation of the northern part of the island of Cyprus in 1972, was the owner of real estate in northern Cyprus. Following the proclamation of the Republic of Northern Cyprus, which is not recognized internationally, the *de facto* partition of the island made it impossible for the applicant to access her property. The ECtHR emphasized that this restriction limited not only the applicant's freedom of movement but also her right of use, which, notwithstanding the occupation and the owner's flight, remained valid. This interference could not be viewed either as a deprivation of property under the second sentence of the first paragraph or as a control of use under the second paragraph of Article 1 of P 1/ECHR, but violated the right to peaceful enjoyment of possessions under the first sentence of the first paragraph inasmuch as *de facto* denial of access to property was equivalent to an unjustified legal impediment.

In a second judgment,[81] the Court awarded the applicant compensation for the harm she had suffered on account of denial of access.

(c) Obligations to protect and fulfil

Like other human rights, the right to property entails obligations to protect private property from interference by third parties. However, owing to the lack of jurisprudence in this regard, it is difficult to determine the scale of such obligations with any precision. There are nonetheless ample grounds for affirming the existence of a state obligation, within the limits of the authorities' knowledge and available resources, to protect private property. Examples of the above include a state obligation to protect against damage caused by (authorized) demonstrations

---

[78] ECtHR, *Sporrong and Lönnroth v Sweden*, A/52 (1982).

[79] See, for example, ECtHR, *Altun v Turkey*, Application No 24561/94 (2004), para 62. The Court has never determined whether, in line with its jurisprudence in respect of the right to life (see Chapter 9, section II), every restriction on the ownership of property that is incompatible with international humanitarian law automatically violates the right to property under the ECHR. In our opinion, this question should be answered in the affirmative.

[80] ECtHR (Grand Chamber), *Loizidou v Turkey*, Reports 1996-VI, paras 61 ff.

[81] ECtHR, *Loizidou v Turkey (Grand Chamber)*, 'Just satisfaction', Reports 1998-IV.

or to provide both judicial and enforcement bodies for the protection of property from private interference. On the other hand, while the state is empowered to place restrictions on private property in the public interest, the authorities are not obliged, for instance, to create conditions conducive to optimum returns from real estate ownership.[82]

Issue in focus: Protection of property under the ACHR and the collective rights of use of indigenous peoples[83]

The Inter-American Court of Human Rights has a rich jurisprudence on the protection of the collective property of indigenous peoples. In the *Awas Tingni Community v Nicaragua* case,[84] members of an indigenous group alleged that Nicaragua was undermining the group's traditional land use by granting concessions to third parties. The IACtHR first had to shed light on the relationship between the right to property under ACHR, Article 21 and traditional collective rights of use:

149. Given the characteristics of the instant case, some specifications are required on the concept of property in indigenous communities. Among indigenous peoples there is a communitarian tradition regarding a communal form of collective property of the land, in the sense that ownership of the land is not centered on an individual but rather on the group and its community. Indigenous groups, by the fact of their very existence, have the right to live freely in their own territory; the close ties of indigenous people with the land must be recognized and understood as the fundamental basis of their cultures, their spiritual life, their integrity, and their economic survival. For indigenous communities, relations to the land are not merely a matter of possession and production but a material and spiritual element which they must fully enjoy, even to preserve their cultural legacy and transmit it to future generations...

In light of these special characteristics, the Court concluded that the use of the land by such groups established an entitlement to collective ownership without the existence of a formal title. It followed that the right to property was applicable to the case, a fact that was also acknowledged in the Nicaraguan Constitution:

153.... Nevertheless, the Court notes that the limits of the territory on which that property right exists have not been effectively delimited and demarcated by the State. This situation has created a climate of constant uncertainty among the members of the Awas Tingni Community, insofar as they do not know for certain how far their communal property extends geographically and, therefore, they do not know until where they can freely use and enjoy their respective property. Based on this understanding, the Court considers that the members of the Awas Tingni Community have the right that the State

(a) carry out the delimitation, demarcation, and titling of the territory belonging to the Community; and

(b) abstain from carrying out, until that delimitation, demarcation, and titling have been done, actions that might lead the agents of the State itself, or third parties acting with its acquiescence or its tolerance, to affect the existence, value, use or enjoyment of the property

---

[82] Jochen A Frowein and Wolfgang Peukert, *Europäische Menschenrechtskonvention, EMRK-Kommentar* (2nd edn, Engel: Kehl, 1996), 788.

[83] On the protection of indigenous groups under international law, see Chapter 11, section V.3.

[84] IACtHR, *Mayagna (Sumo) Awas Tingni Community v Nicaragua*, Section C, No 79 (2001).

located in the geographical area where the members of the Community live and carry out their activities.

Based on the above..., the Court believes that, in light of article 21 of the Convention, the State has violated the right of the members of the Mayagna Awas Tingni Community to the use and enjoyment of their property, and that it has granted concessions to third parties to utilize the property and resources located in an area which could correspond, fully or in part, to the lands which must be delimited, demarcated, and titled.[85]

In 2006, the Court summed up its jurisprudence on property rights of indigenous peoples in the case *Sawhoyamaxa Indigenous Community v Paraguay* in the following manner:

The following conclusions are drawn from the foregoing: 1) traditional possession of their lands by indigenous people has equivalent effects to those of a state-granted full property title; 2) traditional possession entitles indigenous people to demand official recognition and registration of property title; 3) the members of indigenous peoples who have unwillingly left their traditional lands, or lost possession thereof, maintain property rights thereto, even though they lack legal title, unless the lands have been lawfully transferred to third parties in good faith; and 4) the members of indigenous peoples who have unwillingly lost possession of their lands, when those lands have been lawfully transferred to innocent third parties, are entitled to restitution thereof or to obtain other lands of equal extension and quality. Consequently, possession is not a requisite conditioning the existence of indigenous land restitution rights. The instant case is categorized under this last conclusion.[86]

More recently, the Court recognized that in addition to indigenous peoples, communities living in tribes, even if they have not inhabited a particular area since time immemorial, may make claims pertaining to their collective property 'because both share distinct social, cultural, and economic characteristics, including a special relationship with their ancestral territories, that require special measures under international human rights law in order to guarantee their physical and cultural survival'.[87]

---

[85] On the question of land rights of indigenous peoples, see also IACmHR, *Maya Indigenous Communities of the Toledo District v Belize*, Report No 40/04, Case 12.053 (2004), and *Dann v The United States of America*, Report No 75/02, Case 11.140 (2002).

[86] IACtHR, *Case of the Sawhoyamaxa Indigenous Community v Paraguay*, Series C, No 146 (2006), para 128.

[87] IACtHR, *Case of the Saramaka People v Suriname*, Series C, No 172 (2007), para 86.

15

Protection of Persons Deprived of their Liberty and Fair Trial Guarantees

Relevant provisions: UDHR, Articles 9, 10, 11; ICCPR, Articles 9, 10, 14; CRC, Article 40; ACHR, Articles 7–9; ACHPR, Articles 6 and 7; ArCHR, Articles 12–16; ECHR, Articles 5–7 and P 7/ECHR, Articles 2–4.

I. Overview

People who fall into the hands of the state as a result of being arrested, charged with offences, or convicted are particularly vulnerable to human rights violations. As a result, guarantees of protection of persons deprived of their liberty and accused persons were among the earliest precursors of human rights, as evidenced by the English Magna Carta Libertatum of 1215, the Habeas Corpus Act of 1679, and the Bill of Rights of 1689.[1]

Modern human rights treaties address this subject from three angles: first, they guarantee procedural protection against arrest, imprisonment and other forms of deprivation of liberty (section II); second, they contain detailed procedural guarantees with respect to criminal trials (section III); and, third, they establish minimum guarantees for the treatment of persons deprived of their liberty (section IV).

Issue in focus: Procedural guarantees in civil and administrative law proceedings

---

Human rights treaties afford protection to the individual not only in criminal trials but also in court proceedings related to civil and certain administrative law matters. ICCPR, Article 14, ECHR, Article 6 and ACHR, Article 8 guarantee access to an independent and impartial tribunal established by law and a fair and public hearing both in the determination of criminal charges and in cases of determination of

---

[1] The Magna Carta Libertatum or 'Great Charter of Liberties' prohibited imprisonment without a lawful judgment. Pursuant to the Habeas Corpus Act, no subject could be taken into custody without due process of law.

rights and obligations in a 'suit at law' (ICCPR, Article 14(1)) or disputes regarding 'civil rights and obligations' (ECHR, Article 6(1)). These guarantees are important in order 'to ensure that no individual is deprived, in procedural terms, of his/her right to claim justice'.[2]

The terms 'suit at law' (ICCPR) and 'civil rights and obligations' (ECHR) cover not only proceedings relating to strictly private-law matters but also certain administrative proceedings. On this matter, the Human Rights Committee in its General Comment No 32 on ICCPR, Article 14 states the following:

16. The concept of determination of rights and obligations 'in a suit at law' (*de caractère civil/ de carácter civil*) is...complex. It is formulated differently in the various languages of the Covenant that, according to article 53 of the Covenant, are equally authentic, and the *travaux préparatoires* do not resolve the discrepancies in the various language texts. The Committee notes that the concept of a 'suit at law' or its equivalents in other language texts is based on the nature of the right in question rather than on the status of one of the parties or the particular forum provided by domestic legal systems for the determination of particular rights.[3] The concept encompasses (a) judicial procedures aimed at determining rights and obligations pertaining to the areas of contract, property and torts in the area of private law, as well as (b) equivalent notions in the area of administrative law such as the termination of employment of civil servants for other than disciplinary reasons,[4] the determination of social security benefits[5] or the pension rights of soldiers,[6] or procedures regarding the use of public land[7] or the taking of private property. In addition, it may (c) cover other procedures which, however, must be assessed on a case by case basis in the light of the nature of the right in question.

17. On the other hand, the right to access a court or tribunal as provided for by article 14, paragraph 1, second sentence, does not apply where domestic law does not grant any entitlement to the person concerned. For this reason, the Committee held this provision to be inapplicable in cases where domestic law did not confer any right to be promoted to a higher position in the civil service,[8] to be appointed as a judge[9] or to have a death sentence commuted by an executive body.[10] Furthermore, there is no determination of rights and obligations in a suit at law where the persons concerned are confronted with measures taken against them in their capacity as persons subordinated to a high degree of administrative control, such as disciplinary measures not amounting to penal sanctions being taken against a civil servant,[11] a member of the armed forces, or a prisoner. This guarantee furthermore does not apply to extradition, expulsion and deportation procedures.[12] Although there is no right of access to a court or

---

[2] HRCttee, General Comment No 32 (2007), para 9.
[3] HRCttee, *YL v Canada*, Communication No 112/1981 (1986), paras 9.1 and 9.2.
[4] HRCttee, *Casanovas v France*, Communication No 441/1990 (1994), para 5.2.
[5] HRCttee, *Garcia Pons v Spain*, Communication No 454/1991 (1995), para 9.3.
[6] HRCttee, *YL v Canada*, Communication No 112/1981 (1986), para 9.3.
[7] HRCttee, *Äärelä and Näkkäläjätvi v Finland*, Communication No 779/1997 (2001), paras 7.2–7.4.
[8] HRCttee, *Kolanowski v Poland*, Communication No 837/1998 (2003), para 6.4.
[9] HRCttee, *Kazantzis v Cyprus*, Communication No 972/2001 (2003), para 6.5, *Jacobs v Belgium*, Communication No 943/2000 (2004), para 8.7, and *Rivera Fernández v Spain*, Communication No 1396/2005 (2005), para 6.3.
[10] HRCttee, *Kennedy v Trinidad and Tobago*, Communication No 845/1998 (1999), para 7.4.
[11] HRCttee, *Perterer v Austria*, Communication No 1015/2001 (2004), para 9.2 (disciplinary dismissal).
[12] HRCttee, *Zundel v Canada*, Communication No 1341/2005 (2007), para 6.8, *Esposito v Spain*, Communication No 1359/2005 (2007), para 7.6.

tribunal as provided for by article 14, paragraph 1, second sentence, in these and similar cases, other procedural guarantees may still apply.

Case law under the European Convention on Human Rights takes a similar approach. For both ICCPR, Article 14(1) and ECHR, Article 6(1) three conditions must be fulfilled in order to derive from these provisions an entitlement to judicial proceedings on the basis of the above-mentioned principles:

First, the dispute must be of a substantive nature, ie the result must have a concrete impact on the existence or scope of the rights or obligations in question;[13] it follows that complaints in the form of an *actio popularis* do not benefit from an entitlement to judicial proceedings.[14]

Second, the person concerned must actually possess rights or obligations under domestic law; for example, there is no right to a judicial determination in the event of the refusal to promote a police officer[15] or to appoint a person to the office of judge[16] where no legal entitlement of this kind exists.

Third, the rights and obligations in question must be 'of a civil nature', which means they must relate to pecuniary or proprietary entitlements or contracts between parties of basically equal status and not to a relationship in which the individual is subject to the state's authority. The term 'of a civil nature' in this sense covers, for instance, administrative entitlements in the area of social security law,[17] pension entitlements of civil servants[18] or soldiers,[19] authorizations to carry on a business or to practise a profession,[20] and property matters,[21] including land sales and expropriation. No protection is afforded, on the other hand, for disputes regarding taxes[22] or customs duties, the right to stand for election,[23] or asylum and deportation proceedings,[24] although other special procedural guarantees are applicable to expulsions.[25]

The jurisprudence of the Human Rights Committee differs from that of the European Court of Human Rights with respect to public service. While magistrates, public officials and civil servants involved in the exercise of powers conferred by

---

[13] ECtHR, *Benthem v The Netherlands*, Series A, No 97 (1985), para 32.

[14] ECtHR, *Balmer-Schafroth and Others v Switzerland*, *Reports* 1997-IV, para 40.

[15] HRCttee, *Kolanowski v Poland*, Communication No 837/1998 (2003), para 6.4.

[16] HRCttee, *Kazantzis v Cyprus*, Communication No 972/2001 (2003), para 6.5.

[17] HRCttee, *Garcia Pons v Spain*, Communication No 454/1991 (1995); ECtHR, *Schuler-Zgraggen v Switzerland*, Series A, No 263 (1993), para 46.

[18] ECtHR, *Francesco Lombardi v Italy*, Application No 43039/98 (2000).

[19] HRCttee, *YL v Canada*, Communication No 112/1981 (1986), para 9.2.

[20] ECtHR, *Kraska v Switzerland*, Series A, No 254-B (1993), paras 23 ff. HRCttee, *Jansen-Gielen v The Netherlands*, Communication No 846/1999 (2001) (proceedings to determine whether a person has the requisite mental capacity for a particular occupation).

[21] ECtHR, *Mahieu v France*, Application No 43288/98 (2001).

[22] ECtHR (Grand Chamber), *Ferrazzini v Italy*, *Reports* 2001-VII, paras 24 ff, and *Jussila v Finland* 73053/01 (2006), paras 29 ff.

[23] ECtHR, *Pierre-Bloch v France*, *Reports* 1997-VI, para 50.

[24] ECtHR (Grand Chamber), *Maaouia v France*, *Reports* 2000-X, paras 37 ff. In *VMRB v Canada*, Communication No 236/1987 (1988) the Human Rights Committee left open the question of whether deportation proceedings fall under ICCPR, Art 14.

[25] See Chapter 17, section III.3.

public law can only invoke ECHR, Article 6 in cases involving economic claims,[26] ICCPR, Article 14 read in conjunction with the right of equal access to public service under Article 25(c) of the Covenant, affords protection against, for instance, the termination of public employment,[27] save in cases involving disciplinary dismissal from public service.[28]

Based on the first sentence of Article 14(1) providing for equality of all persons before the courts and tribunals the Human Rights Committee decided that the procedural guarantees of ICCPR, Article 14 are fully applicable in cases not covered by the notion of 'suit at law' where a state provides a court procedure for such cases, although it has no obligation to do so under ICCPR, Article 14. Thus, a public official dismissed for disciplinary reasons could claim a violation of his rights under ICCPR, Article 14(1) because the bodies adjudicating disciplinary matters were in fact independent tribunals.[29]

II. Protection Against Arbitrary Deprivation of Liberty

Pursuant to ICCP, Article 9 and similar rights in ACHR, Article 7, ACHPR, Article 6, ArCHR, Article 14 and ECHR, Article 5, persons may be arrested, detained or otherwise deprived of their liberty (1) only on grounds established by law. They must (2) be informed promptly of the reasons for their arrest and (3) brought promptly before a judicial authority to determine the lawfulness of the deprivation of liberty. Anyone arrested or detained on suspicion of having committed a criminal offence must (4) be charged and brought to trial or must be released. Lastly, (5) anyone who has been the victim of unlawful deprivation of liberty has a right to compensation. These five principles[30] constitute the core entitlements of protection under human rights law in the event of deprivation of liberty.

The notion of deprivation of liberty must be broadly interpreted. It includes not only arrest, pre-trial detention and imprisonment on conviction but also includes the following: coercive internment in locked wards of psychiatric hospitals; detention of foreigners as illegal immigrants or pending extradition or deportation;[31] the obligation for asylum seekers to await the decision on their request in the airport transit area without the possibility to leave it;[32] arrest as

---

[26] ECtHR (Grand Chamber), *Pellegrin v France*, *Reports* 1999-VIII, paras 66 ff.

[27] HRCttee, *Casanovas v France*, Communication No 441/1990 (1994), para 5.2 (dismissed civil servant); HRCttee, *Pastukhov v Belarus*, Communication No 814/1998 (2003), para 7.3 (dismissed judge).

[28] HRCttee, *Perterer v Austria*, Communication No 1015/2001 (2004), para 9.2.

[29] Ibid.

[30] ArCHR, Art 14(4) adds the right of everyone deprived of liberty by arrest or detention to request a medical examination.

[31] ECHR, Art 5(1); HRCttee, General Comment No 8 (1982), para 1.

[32] ECtHR, *Amuur v France*, *Reports* 1996-III.

a disciplinary penalty in military service;[33] and internal exile to a small island where there is no opportunity for normal social contact.[34]

1. Right to protection against arbitrary deprivation of liberty

(a) Lawfulness

According to ICCPR, Article 9(1) and corresponding rights in the regional conventions, '[n]o one shall be deprived of his liberty except on such grounds and in accordance with such procedure as are established by law'.[35]

Thus, in order to be compatible with human rights law, each act of deprivation of liberty must be *lawful*, ie based on and compatible with the substantive and procedural requirements of domestic legislation.[36] The principle of lawfulness is, for example, breached where a person is arrested without a warrant, although production of a warrant is prescribed by law,[37] or where the confinement of an offender in a locked ward of a psychiatric hospital has no legal basis.[38] This prerequisite is also violated where persons are only released from prison several months after having fully served their sentence or where detainees are not released despite a court order to that effect.[39]

(b) Permissible grounds

Deprivation of liberty must not only be compatible with domestic law but also rest on a permissible ground as provided for by the human rights conventions. The ECHR is particularly clear as to what constitutes a permissible ground for the deprivation of liberty under international law. Its Article 5(1) contains the following detailed list of such grounds:

(1) execution of a sentence after conviction by a competent court;
(2) the arrest or 'detention of a person for non-compliance with the lawful order of a court or in order to secure the fulfilment of any obligation prescribed by law';
(3) the arrest of suspected offenders and pre-trial detention where there is a risk of flight or where it is necessary to prevent the commission of further offences;
(4) detention of a minor 'for the purpose of educational supervision or . . . for the purpose of bringing [him or her] before the competent legal authority';

---

[33] HRCttee, *Vuolanne v Finland*, Communication No 265/1987 (1989), para 9.4; ECtHR, *Engel and Others v The Netherlands*, Series A, No 22 (1976), paras 57–59.
[34] ECtHR, *Guzzardi v Italy*, Series A, No 39 (1980), paras 92 ff.
[35] Similarly, ACHR, Art 7(2); ACHPR, Art 6; ArCHR, Art 14(2); ECHR, Art 5(1).
[36] ECtHR, *Weber v Switzerland*, Application No 3688/04 (2007), paras 31 ff.
[37] IACtHR, *Suárez-Rosero v Ecuador*, Series C, No 35 (1997), paras 48 ff.
[38] ECtHR, *Erkalo v The Netherlands*, Reports 1998-VI.
[39] HRCttee, *Weismann Lanza and Lanza Perdomo v Uruguay*, Communication No 8/1977 (1980); *Ramírez v Uruguay*, Communication No 4/1977 (1980); ACmHPR, *Constitutional Rights Project and Civil Liberties Organisation v Nigeria*, Communication No 148/1996 (1999); ECtHR (Grand Chamber), *Assanidze v Georgia*, Reports 2004-II, paras 169 ff.

(5) detention 'for the prevention of the spreading of infectious diseases, of persons of unsound mind, alcoholics or drug addicts or vagrants'; and

(6) detention of foreigners to prevent their unauthorized entry into the country or with a view to ensuring their deportation or extradition.

Detention on other grounds, for instance preventive detention of persons suspected of terrorism,[40] constitutes a violation of ECHR, Article 5.

The International Covenant on Civil and Political Rights and corresponding rights found in regional conventions are less restrictive. They permit all grounds of detention that are not 'arbitrary'.[41] This notion comprises elements of unreasonableness, injustice, unpredictability and unfairness. It implies that deprivation of liberty in a specific case must be justifiable in light of all the circumstances.[42] Thus, in addition to the grounds allowing legitimate deprivation of liberty listed in ECHR, Article 5, further grounds may be permissible under these instruments. In contrast to the ECHR, the ICCPR does not prohibit preventive detention. Nevertheless, detention in such cases must be prescribed by law, must be confined to cases in which deprivation of liberty is necessary to protect public security or the rights of others and must satisfy the Article 9 procedural guarantees.[43]

Arbitrariness within the meaning of the ICCPR is present, for instance, where persons are arrested and detained solely on account of the expression of critical political opinions.[44] An initially lawful detention becomes arbitrary when it is upheld for longer than necessary. The Human Rights Committee has repeatedly held that the automatic and compulsory detention of asylum-seekers in Australia without any possibility for release until they were granted asylum or deported exceeds the bounds of legitimate needs and is therefore a violation of the Covenant.[45] It is permissible, on the other hand, to keep an asylum-seeker who has attempted to abscond in detention until such time as deportation takes place or it becomes clear that he or she cannot be deported.[46]

The concept of 'arbitrary' deprivation of liberty also exists under the ECHR.[47] Deprivation of liberty on a ground that is permissible *per se* becomes arbitrary

---

[40] ECtHR, *Lawless v Ireland*, Series A, No 3 (1961), paras 14 ff. In such cases, however, as held by the ECtHR in the same judgment, a derogation from ECHR, Art 5 may be justified in a public emergency within the meaning of ECHR, Art 15.

[41] Similarly, ACHR, Art 7(3), ACHPR, Art 6, and ArCHR, Art 14(1).

[42] HRCttee, *Mukong v Cameroon*, Communication No 458/1991 (1994), para 9.8. Similarly, ACHPR, *Amnesty International and Others v Sudan*, Communications Nos 48/1990, 50/1991, 52/1991, 89/1993 (1999), para 59.

[43] HRCttee, General Comment No 8 (1982), para 4.

[44] HRCttee, *Mukong v Cameroon*, Communication No 458/1991 (1994), para 9.8, *Mpandanjila et al v Zaire*, Communication No 138/1983 (1986).

[45] HRCttee, *A v Australia*, Communication No 560/1993 (1997), paras 9.2–9.4; *C v Australia*, Communication No 900/1999 (2002), para 8.2; and *Baban et al v Australia*, Communication No 1014/2001 (2003).

[46] HRCttee, *Jalloh v The Netherlands*, Communication No 794/1998 (2002), para 8.2.

[47] ECtHR (Grand Chamber) *Çakici v Turkey*, Reports 1999-IV, para 104.

in the absence of an adequate relationship between the ground invoked and the place and conditions of detention. It follows that the imprisonment of a severely mentally disturbed man who was not criminally responsible violated Article 5 even though he was held in the psychiatric wing of the prison.[48]

Enforced disappearances by the state constitute a particularly manifest form of arbitrary deprivation of liberty.[49]

2. Right to be informed promptly of the reasons for deprivation of liberty

A person who does not know why he or she is being detained by the authorities is placed in an extremely stressful situation and is furthermore unable to make effective use of the right to have the lawfulness of the detention reviewed.[50] Persons deprived of their liberty therefore have a right under ICCPR, Article 9(2) and ECHR, Article 5(2) to be informed 'promptly' of the reasons for a deprivation of liberty.[51] This right is applicable not only to criminal-law arrests but to all forms of deprivation of liberty.[52] Furthermore, the information must be given in a language that the person concerned understands.[53]

'Promptly' (or '*dans le plus court délai*' in the French version of the ICCPR and the ECHR) does not necessarily mean immediately but rather without an inexcusable delay. The Human Rights Committee held that this right was violated in cases where arrested persons were not informed for seven[54] or more[55] days of the charges against them; it was not violated, however, in the case of a foreigner who was arrested late at night following the discovery of drugs but was not informed of the charges against him until an interpreter was available the following morning.[56] The European Court of Human Rights found a delay of a few hours in providing information after arrest to be acceptable.[57] A particularly serious violation of the right to be informed occurs in cases where

---

[48] ECtHR, *Aerts v Belgium*, *Reports* 1998-V, paras 45 ff.

[49] See, for example, HRCttee, *Jegatheeswara Sarma v Sri Lanka*, Communication No 950/2000 (2003); ECtHR, *Kurt v Turkey*, *Reports* 1998-III, para 124; IACmHR, *Morales Zegarra et al v Peru*, Report No 57/99, Cases 10.827/11.984 (1999), para 62. On enforced disappearances, see Chapter 10, section III.

[50] ECtHR, *Van der Leer v The Netherlands*, Series A, No 170-A (1990), para 28.

[51] ArCHR, Art 14(3) requires information 'at the time of arrest'. ACHR, Art 7(4) does not specify when the information must be given. ACHPR, Art 6 does not mention the issue at all.

[52] ECtHR, *Van der Leer v The Netherlands*, Series A, No 170-A (1990), para 27. This presumably also applies to the right to be informed 'promptly' under ICCPR, Art 9(2).

[53] Expressly stipulated in ArCHR, Art 14(3) and ECHR, Art 5(2).

[54] HRCttee, *Grant v Jamaica*, Communication No 597/1994 (1996), para 8.1.

[55] Eg, HRCttee, *Kelly v Jamaica*, Communication No 253/1987 (1991), para 5.8 (26 days after arrest) and *Marques de Morais v Angola*, Communication No 1128/2002 (2005), para 6.2 (40 days after arrest).

[56] HRCttee, *Griffin v Spain*, Communication No 493/92 (1995), para 9.2.

[57] ECtHR, *Fox, Campbell and Hartley v The United Kingdom*, Series A, No 182 (1990), paras 41 ff.

people are arrested and detained without being informed of the charges against them.[58]

3. Right to review of the lawfulness of the deprivation of liberty

Three situations must be distinguished in the context of the right to judicial review of deprivation of liberty:

(1) Upon arrest or detention, persons who are suspected of having committed a *criminal offence* must be brought 'promptly before a judge or other officer authorized to exercise judicial power' (ICCPR, Article 9(3), and ACHR, Article 7(5), ArCHR, Article 14(5), and ECHR, Article 5(3)). Such judicial control over the detention must not only be prompt, but also automatic[59] in order to ensure that arbitrary deprivations of liberty last no longer than necessary. Moreover, respect for this right is one of the most effective means of preventing torture and enforced disappearance.[60] Domestic law must determine the authority responsible for undertaking the judicial review of deprivations of liberty. It is essential, however, that the designated judge or judicial officer (even where he or she does not formally hold the office of judge) exercises this task in an independent judicial manner. The designated person must be able to freely review the circumstances militating for and against deprivation of liberty by reference to legal criteria and order the release of the person concerned in the absence of grounds for detention.[61] The requirement of independence is not met, for example, in the case where the designated authority is a public prosecutor involved in investigating the case concerned or someone who obtains instructions from the public prosecutor's office.[62] It is not met either by a commanding officer in the armed forces responsible for maintaining discipline in his unit who plays an important role in the subsequent criminal proceedings.[63] The Human Rights Committee requires an examination of the specific circumstances and holds that delays of more than 'a few days'[64] or five days[65] are too long. In its Concluding Observations

---

[58] ACmHPR, Constitutional Rights Project, *Civil Liberties Organization and Media Rights Agenda v Nigeria*, Communications Nos 140/94, 141/94 and 145/94 (1999), para 51.

[59] ECtHR, *De Jong, Baljet and Van den Brink v The Netherlands*, Series A, No 77 (1984), para 51; *Aquilina v Malta* (Grand Chamber), *Reports* 1999-III, para 49, and *McKai v The United Kingdom* (Grand Chamber), Application No 543/03 (2006), para 34.

[60] ECtHR (Grand Chamber), *Aquilina v Malta*, *Reports* 1999-III, para 49.

[61] ECtHR (Grand Chamber), *Aquilina v Malta*, *Reports* 1999-III, para 47, and *McKai v The United Kingdom*, Application No 543/03 (2006), paras 35 ff.

[62] HRCttee, *Kulomin v Hungary*, Communication No 521/1992 (1996), para 11.3; ECtHR, *Schiesser v Switzerland*, Series A, No 34 (1979), paras 31 ff.

[63] ECtHR (Grand Chamber), *Hood v The United Kingdom*, *Reports* 1999-I, paras 57 ff.

[64] HRCttee, *Stephens v Jamaica*, Communication No 373/1989 (1995), para 9.6 (a delay of 8 days violates Art 9 ICCPR).

[65] HRCttee, *Nazarov v Uzbekistan*, Communication No 911/2000 (2004), para 6.2.

on reports submitted to it by states parties the Human Rights Committee consistently insists on a delay of not more than 48 hours.[66] For the ECHR, 'promptly' in the context of this right means less than four days,[67] bearing in mind the specific circumstances of the case concerned; as a rule, this means that a review must be undertaken within 48 hours of a person's arrest.[68]

(2) In cases of *deprivation of liberty on grounds not based in criminal law*, the person concerned has the right at any time to demand review of the lawfulness of the detention by a court, which must decide 'without delay' or 'speedily' on the application for release (ICCPR, Article 9(4), ACHR, Article 7(6) ArCHR, Article 14(6), and ECHR, Article 5(4)). The reviewing body must be a genuine court, ie a body that enjoys functional and organizational autonomy and independence.[69] Thus, in contrast to the preliminary examination in the case of the detention of criminal suspects, it is not sufficient in such cases for the decision to be taken by an officer authorized to exercise judicial power. What is meant by 'without delay' depends again on the specific circumstances of each case; however, the delay cannot as a rule exceed a few days. The Human Rights Committee decided that a seven-day legal bar on access to a court for detained asylum-seekers was too long.[70] The European Court of Human Rights held that a 31-day delay in a case of detention pending extradition[71] and, *a fortiori*, a 20-month delay in a case of confinement in a psychiatric hospital[72] were clear violations of the ECHR.

(3) Where the deprivation of liberty continues for some time, the grounds that originally warranted detention may subsequently cease to exist. Accordingly, the right under ICCPR, Article 9(4), ACHR, Article 7(6), ArCHR, Article 14(6), and ECHR, Article 5(4), of access at any time to a court further implies a right in the event of long-term detention to *periodic review of the relevant grounds*. In the case of pre-trial detention, the periodic review must be undertaken 'at short intervals',[73] and for other kinds of detention, at reasonable intervals.[74] This means that there is no right of renewed access to a court where a further examination seems unreasonable, eg because the circumstances remain unchanged and only a short period has elapsed since the previous review.[75]

---

[66] Eg, HRCttee, Concluding Observations Namibia (2004), para 13; Gabon (2000), para 13; Kuwait (2000), para 21.

[67] ECtHR, *Brogan and Others v The United Kingdom*, Series A, No 145-B (1988), para 59 (a delay of 4 days and 6 hours is too long even in the case of a suspected terrorist in Northern Ireland).

[68] In *Grauzinis v Lithuania*, Application No 37975/97 (2000), para 25, the ECtHR held that a delay of 48 hours was adequate.

[69] ECtHR (Grand Chamber), *DN v Switzerland*, Reports 2001-III, para 42.

[70] HRCttee, *Torres v Finland*, Communication No 291/1988 (1990), para 7.2.

[71] ECtHR, *Sanchez-Reisse v Switzerland*, Series A, No 107 (1986).

[72] ECtHR (Grand Chamber), *Musial v Poland*, Reports 1999-II, para 43.

[73] ECtHR, *Assenov and Others v Bulgaria*, Reports 1998-VIII, para 162.

[74] ECtHR, *Megyeri v Germany*, Series A, No 237-A (1992), para 22.

[75] ECtHR, *Rutten v The Netherlands*, Application No 32605/96 (2001), para 50.

Issue in focus: Periodic review of the preventive detention of dangerous criminals

The right to periodic review of detention under ICCPR, Article 9(4) and ECHR, Article 5(4) is particularly important in cases where dangerous and potentially recidivist offenders are kept in custody after serving their sentence (or from the outset in the case of persons of unsound mind without criminal capacity) in order to protect the public.

In the *Rameka v New Zealand* case, the Human Rights Committee held that the preventive detention of offenders after the expiry of the non-parole period arising from their sentence had to be justified by compelling reasons that were periodically reviewable by an independent authority.[76] It concluded that ICCPR, Article 9(4) had been violated because in a case where the penalty amounted to seven and a half years' imprisonment, a first review of the indefinite detention order was possible only after ten years, ie 30 months after the end of the actual duration of the penalty. It follows that preventive detention without any possibility of periodic review of the reasons for the detention would, *a fortiori*, constitute a violation of the Covenant.

The European Court of Human Rights confirms in its case law that anyone who remains compulsorily confined on account of aggressiveness or dangerousness or for other mental reasons for a lengthy or indefinite period is entitled to demand a periodic review of the reasons for the continued deprivation of liberty.[77]

---

4. Entitlement to trial within a reasonable time or to release

According to ICCPR, Article 9(3), ECHR, Article 5(3), and ACHR, Article 7, where a person is arrested on suspicion of having committed an offence, legal proceedings must be brought against him or her within a 'reasonable time',[78] or the person concerned must be released. This limits the duration of permissible pretrial detention. What may be considered a reasonable period cannot be assessed in terms of an absolute maximum[79] but depends on the complexity of the case,[80] the conduct of the detainee and other specific circumstances in each case. After a

---

[76] HRCttee, *Rameka et al v New Zealand*, Communication No 1090/2002 (2003), para 7.3.

[77] For example, ECtHR, *Rutten v The Netherlands*, Application No 32605/96 (2001), para 50; *X v The United Kingdom*, Series A, No 46 (1981), para 52; *Musiał v Poland* (Grand Chamber), *Reports* 1999-II, para 43.

[78] This requirement is not applicable to detention on other grounds such as detention pending extradition: ECtHR, *Quinn v France*, Series A, No 311 (1995), para 53. However, the person concerned must be released on completion of the extradition proceedings or if such proceedings are not being pursued 'with due diligence' (ibid, para 48, and *Chahal v The United Kingdom* (Grand Chamber), *Reports* 1996-V, para 112).

[79] ECtHR, *W v Switzerland*, Series A, No 252-A (1993), para 30.

[80] ECtHR, *Chraidi v Germany*, Application No 65655/01 (2006), paras 34 ff: According to this judgment, a period of pre-trial detention of five and a half years did not violate ECHR, Art 5(3) because the criminal procedure, which dealt with questions of international terrorism, was extremely complex. The Court did stress however, that a detention of such length would have violated the Convention in the absence of such exceptional circumstances. According to the HRCttee, on the other hand, this right is violated by a detention period of 34 months in the absence of special circumstances; *Siewpersaud et al v Trinidad and Tobago*, Communication No 938/2000 (2004), para 6.1.

certain period has elapsed, the domestic authorities must, however, invoke relevant and sufficient grounds to justify the continued pre-trial detention, ie grounds such as the risk of absconding or of reoffending must still exist in the case concerned.[81]

5. Right to compensation in the event of unlawful deprivation of liberty

The right to compensation for all victims of unlawful arrest or detention, contained in ICCPR, Article 9(5), ACHR, Article 10, ArCHR, Article 14(7), and ECHR, Article 5(5) is a specific element of the general entitlement to compensation for human rights violations. Unlawful in this context means deprivation of liberty in violation of domestic law or in violation of the specific guarantees afforded by ICCPR, Article 9(5), ArCHR, Article 14(7), and ECHR, Article 5.[82] The Human Rights Committee has observed 'that the fact that the author was subsequently acquitted does not in and of itself render the pre-trial detention unlawful'.[83] In contrast, someone who was detained even after a judicial decision to release him is automatically entitled to compensation.[84]

III. Human Rights of Defendants in Criminal Trials

The human rights principles governing criminal proceedings are established in very great detail by ICCPR, Articles 14 and 15, ACHR, Articles 8 and 9, ArCHR, Articles 15–17 and 19, ACHPR, Article 7, ECHR, Articles 6 and 7, CRC, Article 40, and other provisions. The relevant jurisprudence is very complex and a detailed review of its content lies beyond the scope of this book. Accordingly, this section will merely provide a brief account of the principal rights, following the structure of Article 14 of the ICCPR.[85]

1. Right to equality before courts and to a fair and public hearing

(a) The right to equality before the court and the right to a fair trial

Article 14(1) of the ICCPR contains the right to equality before courts and tribunals[86] which guarantees, in a general manner, 'equal access and equality of arms,

---

[81] ECtHR, *IA v France*, Reports 1998-VII, para 102. See also ACmHPR, *Achutan and Amnesty International v Malawi*, Communications Nos 64/1992, 68/1992 and 78/1992 (1995).

[82] HRCttee, *A v Australia*, Communication No 560/1993 (1997), para 9.5; ECtHR, *Brogan and Others v the United Kingdom*, Series A, No 145-B (1988), para 66.

[83] HRCttee, *WBE v The Netherlands*, Communication No 432/1990 (1992), para 6.5.

[84] HRCttee, *Chambala v Zambia*, Communication No 856/1999 (2003), para 7.3.

[85] For a more detailed guidance see HRCttee, General Comment No 32 (2007): Art 14: Right to equality before courts and tribunals and to a fair trial.

[86] The regional human rights conventions contain no explicit guarantees of this right but arguably guarantee it implicitly, at least in the context of criminal trials.

and ensures that the parties to the proceedings in question are treated without any discrimination'.[87] The right of *equal access* concerns access to first instance procedures and does not address the issue of the right to appeal or other remedies.[88] The principle of equality of arms is a particularly important aspect of any fair trial. As the Human Rights Committee has stressed, it ensures 'that the same procedural rights are to be provided to all the parties unless distinctions are based on law and can be justified on objective and reasonable grounds not entailing actual disadvantage or other unfairness to the defendant'.[89] The principle of equality of arms is, for example, violated where only the prosecutor, but not the defendant, is allowed to appeal a certain decision;[90] the defendant is not served a properly motivated indictment;[91] the defendant is not given the opportunity to comment on a brief likely to have a bearing on the court's decision;[92] or where a court fails to take important evidence into account.[93]

(b) The right to be tried by a competent, independent, and impartial tribunal established by law

This right, enshrined in ICCPR, Article 14(1), ACHR, Article 8(1), and ECHR, Article 6(1), ensures that criminal convictions can be rendered only by a competent, independent, and impartial tribunal. As the Human Rights Committee has stressed, '[t]his right cannot be limited, and any criminal conviction by a body not constituting a tribunal is incompatible with this provision'.[94] Where criminal penalties such as police fines are imposed by an administrative authority, domestic law must ensure that the sanctioned person can submit the case to a judge for subsequent determination of guilt and sentencing. The requirement that the tribunal be established by law rules out *ad hoc* courts set up to adjudicate individual cases.

To be considered independent, tribunals must not take instructions from the legislature or the executive in their adjudicatory activities, must be free from outside influence, and must have judges appointed for a specific term of office.[95] The

---

[87] HRCttee, General Comment No 32 (2007), para 8.

[88] HRCttee, General Comment No 32 (2007), para 12; and *IP v Finland*, Communication No 450/1991 (1993), para 6.2.

[89] HRCttee, General Comment No 32 (2007), para 13, referring to *Dudko v Australia*, Communication No 1347/2005, (2007) para 7.4.

[90] HRCttee, *Weiss v Austria*, Communication No 1086/2002 (2003), para 9.6.

[91] HRCttee, *Wolf v Panama*, Communication No 289/1988 (1992), para 6.6.

[92] HRCttee, *Äärelä and Näkkäläjärvi v Finland*, Communication No 779/1997 (2001), para 7.4; ECtHR, *Mantovanelli v France*, Reports 1997-II, paras 33 ff.

[93] HRCttee, *Wright v Jamaica*, Communication No 349/1989 (1992), para 8.3 (imposition of the death penalty despite medical evidence to the effect that the victim's death occurred when the accused was in custody).

[94] HRCttee, General Comment No 32 (2007), para 18.

[95] ECtHR, *Campell and Fell v The United Kingdom*, Series A, No 80 (1984), para 78. This right is also enshrined in general terms in Art 26 ACHPR, which stipulates that states parties have the duty to guarantee the independence of the courts. See ACmHPR, *Centre for Free Speech v Nigeria*, Communication No 206/1997 (1999), para 16.

requirement of independence thus refers to the institutional aspects and, in particular, 'to the procedure and qualifications for the appointment of judges, and guarantees relating to their security of tenure until a mandatory retirement age or the expiry of their term of office, where such exist, the conditions governing promotion, transfer, suspension and cessation of their functions, and the actual independence of the judiciary from political interference by the executive branch and legislature'.[96]

The requirement of impartiality relates to the attitude of the judges in a specific case. It has two aspects: First, it means that judges must not harbour preconceptions regarding the case, must remain uninfluenced by public opinion or other external pressures and must refrain from treating one of the parties favourably or unfavourably—for reasons such as kinship, friendship, or enmity. Second, the tribunal must also appear to a reasonable observer to be impartial, and judges must not be allowed to participate in a trial where the circumstances indicate that they might be influenced by any of these factors even if subjectively they remain impartial.[97]

Issue in focus: Military Courts

Military courts exist in many countries. Taking into account their character and often close relationship with the political power in the country, the question arises as to whether they are really independent and impartial.

The African Commission on Human and Peoples Rights invariably characterizes proceedings before special military courts whose members are appointed by the executive as a violation of ACHPR, Article 7(1)(d).[98] The Inter-American Commission on Human Rights has repeatedly expressed the view in its settled jurisprudence that military courts are only competent to receive claims against military persons for crimes they committed during their time of service.[99] The Commission can find support of this view in the jurisprudence of the Inter-American Court of Human Rights, which additionally stipulates, that procedures brought before military courts are only admissible when the crime in question actually violates military interests.[100]

The European Court of Human Rights is even stricter where civilians are tried. It qualified the Turkish National Security Courts which 'were set up pursuant to the Constitution to deal with offences affecting Turkey's territorial integrity and national unity, its democratic regime and its State security' as lacking independence and impartiality as, although civilian in character, these courts always have a member of

---

[96] HRCttee, General Comment No 32 (2007), para 19.

[97] HRCttee, General Comment No 32 (2007), para 18; and *Karttunen v Finland*, Communication No 387/1989 (1992), para 7.2; similarly, ECtHR, (Grand Chamber) *Kyprianou v Cyprus*, Application No 73797/01 (2005), paras 118 ff.

[98] See, for example, ACmHPR, *Malawi African Association and Others v Mauritania*, Communications Nos 54/1991, 61/1991, 98/1993, 164–196/1997 and 210/1998 (2000), para 98.

[99] Eg, IACmHR, 'Report on the Situation of Human Rights in Peru', OEA/Ser. L/V/II.106, 2 June 2000.

[100] See for example, IACtHR, *Durand and Ugarte v Peru*, Series C, No 68, para 117.

the Military Legal Service as one of its three judges. Such judges, although sitting in an individual capacity allowing them to act independently, 'remain subject to military discipline and assessment reports are compiled on them by the army for that purpose' and '[d]ecisions pertaining to their appointment are to a great extent taken by the administrative authorities and the army'.[101]

The Human Rights Committee seems to be less restrictive. It has no general concerns where military courts rule on criminal charges brought against members of the armed forces. As regards cases where military courts try civilians, it has noted that '[w]hile the Covenant does not prohibit the trial of civilians in military or special courts, it requires that such trials are in full conformity with the requirements of article 14 and that its guarantees cannot be limited or modified because of the military...character of the court concerned. The Committee also notes that the trial of civilians in military...courts may raise serious problems as far as the equitable, impartial and independent administration of justice is concerned. Therefore, it is important to take all necessary measures to ensure that such trials take place under conditions which genuinely afford the full guarantees stipulated in article 14. Trials of civilians by military...courts should be exceptional, ie limited to cases where the State party can show that resorting to such trials is necessary and justified by objective and serious reasons, and where with regard to the specific class of individuals and offences at issue the regular civilian courts are unable to undertake the trials.'[102]

(c) The right to a fair and public hearing and to public pronouncement of the judgment

The ICCPR and some regional conventions[103] protect this right explicitly. Fairness of the hearing goes beyond the requirement of independence and impartiality of the judges and 'entails the absence of any direct or indirect influence, pressure or intimidation or intrusion from whatever side and for whatever motive. A hearing is not fair if, for instance, the defendant in criminal proceedings is faced with the expression of a hostile attitude from the public or support for one party in the courtroom that is tolerated by the court, thereby impinging on the right to defence.'[104] For instance, a racially biased jury selection would adversely affect the fairness of the procedure, and tribunals are obliged to take steps against members of the public in a courtroom calling for the defendant to be sentenced to death.[105]

As regards the requirement of a public hearing, it should be noted that where justice is administered in secret, the accused is placed at the mercy of arbitrary decision-making by judges who escape public scrutiny, or the public

---

[101] ECtHR (Grand Chamber), *Incal v Turkey, Reports* 1998-IV, paras 68 and 69.
[102] HRCttee, General Comment No 32 (2007), para 18, and *Madani v Algeria*, Communication No 1172/2003 (2007), para 8.7.
[103] CCPR, Art 14(1), ECHR, Art 6(1), and to some extent also ACHR, Art 8(5).
[104] HRCttee, General Comment No 32 (2007), para 25.
[105] HRCttee, *Gridin v Russia*, Communication No 770/1997 (2000), para 8.2 in conjunction with para 3.5.

may suspect certain defendants of using inadmissible means to influence the court in their favour behind closed doors.[106] The public character of hearings and of the pronouncement of judgments (though not of the prior deliberations) is therefore one of the core guarantees of the right to a fair trial and implies that the proceedings at first instance should be conducted orally and with a public hearing. Public hearings are not necessary, on the other hand, at higher levels of the proceedings if the appellate power of the body concerned is confined to points of law.[107] The right to a public hearing, unlike most other rights pertaining to criminal proceedings, is not absolute. The media and the public may be excluded 'from all or part of a trial for reasons of morals, public order (*ordre public*) or national security in a democratic society, or when the interest of the private lives of the parties so requires, or to the extent strictly necessary in the opinion of the court in special circumstances where publicity would prejudice the interests of justice'.[108] The last point justifies exclusion of the public, for example, when this appears necessary for the protection of witnesses.[109]

2. The presumption of innocence

According to Article 14(2) of the ICCPR and corresponding provisions of the regional human rights conventions,[110] everyone charged with a criminal offence shall have the right to be presumed innocent until proven guilty according to law. This right implies in particular that tribunals and other authorities must refrain from any act that could influence the outcome of the proceedings to the detriment of the accused. This fundamental principle of the protection of the human rights of defendants is breached, for instance, where senior governmental representatives express at a press conference, during or before a trial, that an accused person is guilty.[111] Furthermore, the presumption of innocence means that the burden of proof rests on the prosecution and that the court must make every effort to uncover the truth until the charge has been proven beyond reasonable doubt. Where doubt exists, the adjudicating body must decide in favour of the accused (*in dubio pro reo*).[112]

[106] ECtHR, *Pretto and Others v Italy*, Series A, No 71 (1983), para 11.

[107] ECtHR, *Axen v Germany*, Series A, No 72 (1983); *Helmers v Sweden*, Series A, No 212-A (1991), paras 33 and 38.

[108] ICCPR, Art 14(1). Similarly, ECHR, Art 6(1) and ACHR, Art 8(5). The principle of public proceedings is not contained in the ACHPR; however, the ACmHPR deduces its applicability to the African context from the provisions of the ICCPR and the other regional conventions; see ACmHPR, *Civil Liberties Organisation and Others v Nigeria*, Communication No 218/1998 (1998), paras 35 ff.

[109] Explicitly stipulated in Rome Statute, Art 68(2).

[110] ACHR, Art 8(2); ACHPR, Art 7(1)(b); ArCHR, Art 16; ECHR, Art 6(2).

[111] HRCttee, *Gridin v Russia*, Communication No 770/1997, paras 3.5 and 8.3; ECtHR, *Allenet de Ribemont v France*, Series A, No 308 (1995), paras 37 ff.

[112] HRCttee, General Comment No 32 (2007), para 30.

3. Rights of the defendant during the trial

(a) Right to be informed of the charge

The purpose of this right is to ensure that the accused can prepare a defence and exercise his or her rights in the proceedings. According to the clearly worded provisions of ICCPR, Article 14(3)(a) ACHR, Article 7(4), ArCHR, Article 16(1) and ECHR, Article 6(3)(a), the accused must be informed *promptly*, ie without inexcusable delay, *in detail*, and *in a language that he or she understands*. The information must specify the *nature*, ie the category of the offence, and the *cause* of the charge, ie its essential elements. The right exists from the time the person concerned is formally charged under domestic law or is publicly named as an accused person.[113] The right is not applicable while the suspect is only *under police* investigation; in such cases, if the person is remanded in custody, the obligation to inform is applicable, rather, under ICCPR, Article 9(2).[114]

(b) Right to adequate time and facilities for the preparation of a defence

This right as embodied in ICCPR, Article 14(3)(b), ACHR, Article 8(2)(c), ArCHR, Article 13(2), and ECHR, Article 6(3)(b) provides defendants not only adequate time to prepare a defence in criminal proceedings but also the requisite 'facilities'. This term covers material requirements such as access to relevant documents, the opportunity to choose and contact a lawyer, and the right of counsel to communicate freely and confidentially with the defendant.[115] The amount of time needed for the preparation of the defence depends on the complexity of the case[116] and can range from a few days to several months. A notable point is that international humanitarian law guarantees a minimum of two weeks in criminal proceedings against prisoners of war.[117] There is a sound basis for arguing that the period allowed for the main hearing in a case—possibly with the exception of petty cases—should not fall short of this minimum even outside the context of armed conflicts. In all events, this right is violated where the accused is held incommunicado, ie deprived of all contact with the outside world,[118] or has no meeting with counsel until the first day of the trial.[119]

(c) The right to be tried without undue delay

Criminal charges are burdensome for the individuals concerned, especially if they are being held in pre-trial detention or if they are innocent; at the same time,

---

[113] HRCttee, General Comment No 32 (2007), para 31.
[114] HRCttee, *Kelly v Jamaica*, Communication No 253/1987 (1991), para 5.8.
[115] HRCttee, General Comment No 32 (2007), paras 33 and 34, and, for example, ECtHR (Grand Chamber), *Öcalan v Turkey*, Reports 2005-IV, paras 132 ff, and ACmHPR, *Avocats sans Frontières v Burundi*, Communication No 231/1999 (2000), para 27.
[116] HRCttee, *Little v Jamaica*, Communication No 283/1988 (1991), para 8.3.
[117] GC III, Art 105(3).
[118] HRCttee, *Drescher Caldas v Uruguay*, Communication No 43/1979 (1983), para 13.3.
[119] ECtHR, *Twalib v Greece*, Reports 1998-IV, para 40.

long delays and backlogs are detrimental to the interest of justice. Trials should therefore not last longer than necessary. The right to be tried without undue delay as provided for by ICCPR, Article 14(3)(c), ACHR, Article 8(1), ACHPR, Article 7(1)(c), and ECHR, Article 6(1) relates not only to the time a trial should commence, but also to the time it should end and the time until the judgment on appeal, meaning that all stages of the proceedings must be expeditious.[120] The clock begins to run as soon as the person concerned is notified of the allegation that he or she has committed a criminal offence, hence not from the date of official issuing of charges but from the time of arrest or preliminary questioning.[121] What constitutes 'undue' delay depends on the particular circumstances of the case, especially its complexity and the conduct of the accused.[122] In absence of special circumstances, a delay of, for example, 4 years and 3 months in the appeal court review of a death sentence is too long, but a delay of 18 months between arrest and the beginning of trial in a murder case is not.[123] A delay of 33 months in drafting a judgment was too long because even though the workload of the court was indeed excessive, the state had taken no steps to lighten it.[124]

(d) The right to a defence

The right of defence comprises several components:

- An effective defence requires first and foremost that the accused be able to attend the proceedings.[125] Proceedings in absentia are permissible only where the accused declines to attend despite being informed of the proceedings sufficiently in advance and in sufficient detail, or where his or her attendance cannot be assured despite due diligence.[126]

- Second, accused persons may choose whether to defend themselves personally or through counsel of their own choosing,[127] and must be informed of this right if they have no legal assistance. These two forms of defence are not mutually exclusive and defendants 'assisted by a lawyer have the right to instruct their lawyer on the conduct of their case, within the limits of professional

---

[120] HRCttee, General Comment No 32 (2007), para 35.

[121] ECtHR (Grand Chamber), *Reinhardt and Slimane-Kaïd v France, Reports* 1998-II, para 93.

[122] HRCttee, General Comment No 32 (2007), para 35, and, eg, HRCttee, *Siewpersaud et al v Trinidad and Tobago*, Communication No 938/2000 (2004), para 6.2; ECtHR, *Mansur v Turkey*, Series A, No 319-B (1995), para 61.

[123] HRCttee, *Johnson v Jamaica*, Communication No 588/1994 (1996), para 8.8, and *Morrison v Jamaica*, Communication No 635/1995 (1998), para 21.3.

[124] ECtHR, *B v Austria*, Series A, No 175 (1990), paras 52 ff.

[125] ICCPR, Art 14(3)(e) and ArCHR, Art 16(3). This right is also implicitly contained in the ECHR.

[126] HRCttee, General Comment No 32 (2007), para 36 and *Monguya Mbenge v Zaire*, Communication No 16/1977 (1983), para 14.1; *Maleki v Italy*, Communication No 699/1996 (1999), para 9.3. See also ECtHR (Grand Chamber), *Sejdovic v Italy*, Application No 56581/00 (2006), paras 81 ff, and *Hermi v Italy*, Application No 18114/02 (2006), paras 58 ff.

[127] ICCPR, Art 14(3)(d); ACHR, Art 8(2)(d); ArCHR, Art 16(3); ACHPR, Art 7(1)(c); and ECHR, Art 6(3)(c).

responsibility, and to testify on their own behalf'.[128] An accused person has the right to insist on presenting his or her own defence. In such cases, counsel may be appointed by the court against the defendant's will only where the interests of justice and of a fair trial so require, therefore, 'domestic law should avoid any absolute bar against the right to defend oneself in criminal proceedings without the assistance of counsel'.[129]

- Third, if an accused has insufficient means to pay for legal assistance, a defence counsel must be assigned free of charge 'where the interests of justice so require'.[130] Whether this requirement exists depends on the gravity of the offence, the severity of the penalty it attracts, and the complexity of the case.[131] The personal circumstances of the accused may also be relevant; it was a human rights violation, for instance, to deny a young uneducated drug addict free legal assistance in proceedings which, though relating to a relatively minor offence, led upon conviction to a longer sentence because of the triggering of a suspended prison sentence imposed in earlier proceedings.[132] Free legal assistance must always be provided in proceedings that may entail the death penalty.[133] The defence must be effective in order to meet human rights requirements; while this right is not necessarily violated where the services of defence counsel are of poor professional quality, a violation occurs where counsel commits gross and obvious errors. In this regard, the Human Rights Committee has underlined that '[u]nlike in the case of privately retained lawyers,[134] blatant misbehaviour or incompetence, for example the withdrawal of an appeal without consultation in a death penalty case,[135] or absence during the hearing of a witness in such cases[136] may entail the responsibility of the State concerned for a violation of article 14, paragraph 3(d), provided that it was manifest to the judge that the lawyer's behaviour was incompatible with the interests of justice.[137] There is

---

[128] HRCttee, General Comment No 32 (2007), para 37.

[129] HRCttee, General Comment No 32 (2007), para 37 referring to *Correia de Matos v Portugal*, Communication No 1123/2002 (2006), paras 7.4 and 7.5. In contrast, the ECtHR decided that a provision providing for the appointment of counsel against the defendant's will in each criminal case is compatible with the ECHR; see ECtHR, *Correia de Matos v Portugal*, No 48188/99 (2001). See also ECtHR, *Croissant v Germany*, Series A, No 237-B (1992), para 30.

[130] ICCPR, Art 14(3)(d); ArCHR, Art 16(4); ECHR, Art 6(3)(c). ACHR, Art 8(2)(e) leaves it to domestic law to determine whether such counsel is provided free of charge.

[131] For example, ECtHR, *Boner v The United Kingdom*, Series A, No 300-B (1994), para 41.

[132] ECtHR, *Quaranta v Switzerland*, Series A, No 205 (1991), paras 34 ff.

[133] According to the consistent jurisprudence of the HRCttee; see, for example, HRCttee, *LaVende v Trinidad and Tobago*, Communication No 554/1993 (1998). See also HRCttee, General Comment No 32 (2007), para 38.

[134] HRCttee, *HC v Jamaica*, Communication No 383/1989 (1992), para 6.3.

[135] HRCttee, *Kelly v Jamaica*, Communication No 253/1987 (1991), para 9.5.

[136] HRCttee, *Hendricks v Guyana*, Communication No 838/1998 (2002), para 6.4. For the case of an absence of an author's legal representative during the hearing of a witness in a preliminary hearing see *Brown v Jamaica*, Communication No 775/1997 (1999), para 6.6.

[137] HRCttee, *Taylor v Jamaica*, Communication No 705/1996 (1998), para 6.2; *Chan v Guyana*, Communication No 913/2000 (2005), para 6.2; *Hussain v Mauritius*, Communication No 980/2001 (2003), para 6.3.

also a violation of this provision if the court or other relevant authorities hinder appointed lawyers from fulfilling their task effectively.'[138]

- Finally, the right to a defence also includes the right of the accused 'to examine, or have examined, the witnesses against him and to obtain the attendance and examination of witnesses on his behalf under the same conditions as witnesses against him'.[139] This right is an important aspect of the principle of equality of arms[140] and has two components: cross-examination of witnesses for the prosecution and the right to examine one's own witnesses for the defence. In contrast to many other guarantees in criminal proceedings, this right is not absolute: where the defence refrains from cross-examining a witness for the prosecution[141] or where the court rightly refuses to examine a witness whose testimony can in no way buttress the case of the defence,[142] the right is not violated.[143] In exceptional cases, witnesses may be protected against reprisals by remaining anonymous. This means that they do not appear before the accused and the public and that their identity is not published. In such cases, however, it must still be possible to conduct an effective examination.[144]

(e) *The right to the assistance of an interpreter*

A defendant who is unable to follow proceedings because he or she cannot understand or speak the language used in court is not in a position to present an effective defence. In such cases, the accused is entitled 'to have the free assistance of an interpreter'.[145] This right is applicable not only to the trial itself but to every stage of the proceedings.[146] It also includes the right to have all statements and documents of relevance to the trial translated,[147] and it is applicable not only to foreigners but also to nationals of the state concerned.[148] It does not, however, give defendants an entitlement to the free assistance of an interpreter if they are sufficiently proficient in the language used in court to follow the proceedings and are able to express themselves effectively.[149] 'Free' assistance means that the costs of interpretation or translation may not be included in the costs of the proceedings

---

[138] HRCttee, General Comment No 32 (2007), para 38. See also HRCttee, *Arutunyan v Uzbekistan*, Communication No 917/2000 (2004), para 6.3.

[139] ICCPR, Art 14(3)(e); ACHR, Art 8(2)(f); ArCHR, Art 16(4); ECHR, Art 6(3)(d).

[140] HRCttee, General Comment No 32 (2007), para 39.

[141] HRCttee, *Compass v Jamaica*, Communication No 375/1989 (1993), para 10.3.

[142] HRCttee, *Wright v Jamaica*, Communication No 349/1989 (1992), paras 8.4 f.

[143] HRCttee, General Comment No 32 (2007), para 39.

[144] ECtHR, *Lüdi v Switzerland*, Series A, No 238 (1992), paras 49 and 50, and *Doorson v The Netherlands*, Reports 1996-II, paras 72 f.

[145] ICCPR, Art 14(3)(f); ACHR, Art 8(1)(a); ArCHR, Art 16(4); and ECHR, Art 6(3)(e).

[146] HRCttee, General Comment No 32 (2007), para 40; ECtHR, *Kamasinski v Austria*, Series A, No 168 (1989), para 74.

[147] ECtHR, *Luedicke, Belkacem and Koç v Germany*, Series A, No 29 (1978), para 48.

[148] HRCttee, General Comment No 32 (2007), para 40.

[149] HRCttee, General Comment No 32 (2007), para 40; *Barzhig v France*, Communication No 327/1988 (1991), para 5.6.

or claimed back from an accused if he or she subsequently acquires income or property.[150]

(f) The right not to be compelled to testify against oneself

This right enshrined in ICCPR, Article 14(3)(g), ACHR, Article 8(2)(g), and ArCHR, Article 16(6) is related—but not identical—to the presumption of innocence. The wording makes it clear that this right is applicable only to defendants and not to witnesses.[151] The guarantee prohibits different forms of pressure, ranging from psychological pressure to the threat of punishment, actual ill-treatment, or even torture.[152] This right is effective only where silence may not be taken into account in the determination of guilt or innocence.[153] The Human Rights Committee has made clear that '[d]omestic law must ensure that statements or confessions obtained in violation of article 7 of the Covenant are excluded from the evidence, except if such material is used as evidence that torture or other treatment prohibited by this provision occurred, and that in such cases the burden is on the State to prove that statements made by the accused have been given of their own free will'.[154]

(g) The right to have a conviction and sentence reviewed by a higher tribunal

Everyone convicted of a crime is entitled, according to ICCPR, Article 14(5), ACHR, Article 8(2)(h), and ArCHR, Article 16(7)[155] to have the judgment reviewed by a higher court in accordance with domestic law.[156] The right to review under the Covenant is not confined to serious offences but is applicable to all kinds of offences and penalties.[157] As the Human Rights Committee has made clear, this guarantee 'is violated not only if the decision by the court of first instance is final, but also where a conviction imposed by an appeal court[158] or a court of final instance,[159] following acquittal by a lower court, according

---

[150] ECtHR, *Luedicke, Belkacem and Koç v Germany*, Series A, No 29 (1978), para 46.

[151] See, for instance, Manfred Nowak, *UN Covenant on Civil and Political Rights, CCPR Commentary* (2nd edn, Engel: Kehl, 2005), 345.

[152] HRCttee, *Kelly v Jamaica*, Communication No 253/1987 (1991), para 5.5. See also ECtHR (Grand Chamber), *Jalloh v Germany*, Application No 54810/00 (2006), para 99, and for the jurisprudence on the right not to incriminate oneself, *O'Halloran and Francis v The United Kingdom*, Applications Nos 15809/02 and 25624/02 (2007), paras 45 ff.

[153] Stipulated explicitly in Rome Statute, Art 67(1)(g).

[154] HRCttee, General Comment No 32 (2007), para 41 (referring to CAT, Art 15), and *Singarasa v Sri Lanka,* Communication No 1033/2001 (2004), para 7.4; *Kelly v Jamaica*, Communication No 253/1987, para 7.4.

[155] More restrictive, P 7/ECHR, Art 7.

[156] The reference to domestic law does not limit this right but relates to the modalities of the review. HRCttee, General Comment No 32 (2007), para 45.

[157] HRCttee, General Comment No 32 (2007), para 45.

[158] HRCttee, *Gomaríz Valera v Spain*, Communication No 1095/2002 (2005), para 7.1.

[159] HRCttee, *Terrón v Spain*, Communication No 1073/2002 (2004), para 7.4.

to domestic law cannot be reviewed by a higher court. Where the highest court of a country acts as first and only instance, the absence of any right to review by a higher tribunal is not offset by the fact of being tried by the supreme tribunal of the state party concerned; rather, such a system is incompatible with the Covenant, unless the state party concerned has made a reservation to this effect.'[160] The corresponding provision in P 7/ECHR is more restrictive, since the guarantee is not applicable where a person is tried in first instance by the country's highest tribunal or where the law rules out any possibility of review in the case of offences of a minor character.[161]

(h) The right to compensation for a miscarriage of justice

Persons convicted by a final decision are entitled to compensation for the punishment already suffered where a new or newly discovered fact shows conclusively that there has been a miscarriage of justice and the conviction is reversed or a pardon is granted (ICCPR, Article 14(6), ACHR, Article 10, ArCHR, Article 19(2), and P 7/ECHR, Article 3). This right is not applicable where it is proven that the convicted person is responsible for the non-disclosure in due time of the facts concerned. Nor is it applicable where the conviction is set aside by a pardon, amnesty or on appeal, ie before the judgment becomes final.[162]

(i) Ne bis in idem

No one may be prosecuted again for an offence for which he or she has already been convicted or acquitted in accordance with the law of that country (ICCPR, Article 14(7), ACHR, Article 8(4), ArCHR, Article 19(1), ACHPR, Article 7(2), and P 7/ECHR, Article 4). This does not preclude the reopening of a case in accordance with the law if there is evidence of new or newly discovered facts or if there was a fundamental defect in the previous proceedings that affected the outcome of the case.[163] There is no prohibition against charging and convicting persons in their own country although they have already been convicted in another country.[164]

Issue in focus: The applicability of procedural guarantees during armed conflicts

---

Under international human rights law, only the right not to be tried or punished twice for the same offence and the prohibition of retrospective legislation are specifically

---

[160] HRCttee, General Comment No 32 (2007), para 47, and *Terrón v Spain*, Communication No 1073/2002 (2004), para 7.4.

[161] P 7/ECHR, Art 2(2). According to this provision, the guarantee is furthermore inapplicable where the conviction by a higher tribunal follows an appeal by the prosecution against acquittal. This exception is presumably also applicable to ICCPR, Art 14(5).

[162] HRCttee, General Comment No 32 (2007), para 53.

[163] HRCttee, General Comment No 32 (2007), para 56 and P 7/ECHR, Art 4(2).

[164] HRCttee, General Comment No 32 (2007), para 57 referring to *ARJ v Australia*, Communication No 692/1996 (1997), para 6.4 and *AP v Italy*, Communication No 204/1986 (1987), para 7.3.

mentioned as non-derogable. Other due process guarantees in criminal proceedings can, in principle, be derogated from during armed conflicts (provided that such derogations do not go beyond what is strictly required by the exigencies of the particular situation and provided they meet other necessary preconditions[165]). The guarantees of fair trial, however, may never be derogated from in a manner that would circumvent the protection of non-derogable rights.[166] Accordingly, it is inadmissible to derogate from the procedural guarantees in a trial leading to the imposition of the death penalty.[167] Similarly, as the prohibition of torture and cruel, inhuman and degrading treatment 'is also non-derogable in its entirety, no statements or confessions or, in principle, other evidence obtained in violation of this provision may be invoked as evidence' in criminal trials, except if a statement or confession obtained in violation of this prohibition is used as evidence that torture or other treatment prohibited by this provision occurred.[168] The Human Rights Committee holds the view—rightly in our opinion—that the presumption of innocence and the right to a defence are also non-derogable by virtue of the nature of these guarantees.[169]

In the event of derogation, the numerous procedural guarantees afforded by international humanitarian law remain in any case applicable if the person concerned comes within the scope of their protection. Pursuant to Article 3 common to the Geneva Conventions, the conviction and execution of persons in non-international armed conflicts who, as civilians or as wounded, sick or detained fighters, are not (or are no longer) taking an active part in the hostilities (persons *hors de combat*) is prohibited unless such action is based on a 'previous judgment pronounced by a regularly constituted court, affording all the judicial guarantees which are recognized as indispensable by civilized peoples'. More generally, no civilian or person *hors de combat* may, according to customary international humanitarian law applicable in both international and non-international armed conflict, 'be convicted or sentenced, except pursuant to a fair trial affording all essential judicial guarantees'.[170] These guarantees are now largely identical to the core guarantees of Article 14 of the ICCPR .

Articles 75(3) and (4) of Additional Protocol I afford guarantees to persons in the power of a party to an international armed conflict upon arrest and in criminal proceedings which are largely consistent with the provisions of ICCPR, Articles 9 and 14. However, the list does not include, for instance, the right to free assistance of defence counsel or an interpreter and the right to a public hearing (it does include the right to public pronouncement of the judgment). Articles 5(2) and (3) of Additional Protocol II contain the same guarantees for criminal proceedings during non-international armed conflicts as Additional Protocol I, with the exception of the right to examine witnesses for the prosecution and the right to public pronouncement of the judgment.

---

[165] For more detail, see above, Chapter 4, section IV.2.

[166] See also IACtHR, *Judicial Guarantees in States of Emergency* (Advisory Opinion), Series A, No 9 (1987), and *Habeas Corpus in Emergency Situations* (Advisory Opinion), Series A, No 8 (1987).

[167] HRCttee, General Comments No 29 (2001), para 15, and No 32 (2007), para 6.

[168] HRCttee, General Comment No 32 (2007), para 6. See also Art 15 CAT.

[169] HRCttee, General Comments No 29 (2001), para 11, and No 32 (2007), para 6.

[170] Jean Louis Henckaerts and Louise Doswald-Beck, *Customary International Humanitarian Law*, vol I : Rules (Cambridge University Press: Cambridge, 2005), rule 100. Rule 101 prohibits the retroactive application of criminal law.

4. No penalty without law and the prohibition of retrospective criminal legislation

The fact that liability for punishment is confined to acts that were prohibited by law and punishable at the time of their commission is a core human rights principle with non-derogable status. Human rights treaties consequently recognize and enshrine the principle of 'no penalty without law' and prohibit the prosecution of a person for an act or omission that 'did not constitute a criminal offence, under national or international law, at the time it was committed'.[171] This guarantee is violated not only where there is no law at all, but also where the law is so vague that the perpetrators could not have known what was prohibited even by exercising due care.[172]

Issue in focus: The relationship between human rights and substantive domestic criminal law

The complex relationship between international human rights and states' substantive criminal law is based on the following principles:

(1) On the whole, human rights treaties allow states considerable discretion in determining what constitutes a criminal act. However, states may not criminalize acts or omissions that are permissible under human rights law. Where a limitation on a freedom or a right in a specific case would constitute a human rights violation, the exercise of that right must not be made punishable under criminal law.

(2) The following have a direct bearing on substantive criminal law: the guarantee of the right to life, which permits the imposition of the death penalty only for the most serious crimes,[173] and CEDAW, Article 2(g) which stipulates that all national penal provisions which constitute discrimination against women must be repealed.

(3) States must enact criminal provisions to protect certain human rights guarantees, for instance by making genocide, racial discrimination, or torture punishable crimes, where they are specifically required to do so by human rights treaties[174] or under international criminal law.[175]

(4) The duty to criminalize certain behaviour in domestic law can furthermore ensue from human rights obligations to protect private persons from interference by third parties.[176]

The principle of no penalty without a law also includes the *prohibition of retroactive legislation*. This means that no law may be applied to an offence that was

---

[171] ICCPR, Art 15(1); ACHR, Art 9; ArCHR, Art 15; ACHPR, Art 7(2); and ECHR, Art 7(1).
[172] ECtHR, *Kokkinakis v Greece*, Series A, No 260-A (1993), para 52, *Jorgic v Germany*, Application No 74613/01 (2007), paras 100 ff, and *Korbely v Hungary* (Grand Chamber), Application No 9174/02 (2008), paras 70 ff.
[173] ICCPR, Art 6(2).   [174] CPPCG, Art V; CERD, Art 4; CAT, Art 4; CRC, Art 32(2).
[175] See Chapter 2, section II.5.   [176] See Chapter 3, section III.3.

committed before the law came into force (*nullum crimen sine lege*) and that stiffer penalties introduced after the commission of a punishable act are not applicable to that act (*nulla poena sine lege*). There is no retroactive effect if a particular offence was a war crime, a crime against humanity or any other crime under international law at the time of its commission with the respective elements of the crime only later being incorporated in domestic criminal law,[177] because international public law alone already gives sufficient grounds for prosecution. There is no retrospective effect either if a criminal provision is repealed and replaced by another provision that is substantively the same as the earlier one, provided that no heavier penalty is imposed than under the older law.[178] Retroactive effect is permissible by way of exception where a new law is more lenient than an older one (*lex mitior*).[179]

Issue in focus: The Berlin Wall marksmen cases

The question of retroactive application of criminal law arose after the fall of the Berlin Wall in 1989 in connection with the criminal convictions of those responsible for the killing of persons attempting to flee the former German Democratic Republic (GDR) for the Federal Republic of Germany. Although the German courts applied GDR criminal law, the accused argued that their conduct had not been liable to criminal prosecution in the GDR. The European Court of Human Rights held that, even at the material time, the killings had been clear infringements of human rights; hence the complainants, as senior Party officials and members of the GDR National Defence Council, should have been held responsible even then for human rights violations which were explicitly subject to prosecution under GDR law.[180] It followed that there had been no retroactive effect.[181]

The Human Rights Committee similarly held in the *Baumgarten* case concerning the former Head of Border Troops and Deputy Defence Minister that the GDR's Criminal Code had itself provided for the punishment of human rights violations. In view of the fact that the killings at the Wall had been manifestly disproportionate and that the GDR had already been criticized on that account by the Committee during the discussion of its state report, such killings had been prohibited by criminal law even at the material time, so that there was no retroactive effect despite the earlier jurisprudence of the GDR courts.[182]

---

[177] ICCPR, Art 15(2); ECHR, Art 7(2).

[178] HRCttee, *Westerman v The Netherlands*, Communication No 682/1996 (1999), para 9.2. This also applies where a more severe approach is adopted in judicial interpretation, but the perpetrator could not have relied on the case law remaining the same and could reasonably have foreseen the development in the jurisprudence: ECtHR, *SW v The United Kingdom*, Series A, No 335-B (1995), para 36.

[179] ECtHR, *G v France*, Series A, No 325-B (1995), para 26.

[180] The first chapter of the Special Part of the GDR's 1968 Criminal Code expressly stipulated that anyone who committed crimes against human rights would be punished.

[181] ECtHR (Grand Chamber), *Streletz, Kessler and Krenz v Germany*, Reports 2001-II, paras 102 ff. The same reasoning was used against a border guard in the *K-HW v Germany* (Grand Chamber), Reports 2001-II, paras 102–106.

[182] HRCttee, *Baumgarten v Germany*, Communication No 960/2000 (2003), para 9.5.

IV. Overview: the Right of Detainees to Humane Treatment

Persons deprived of their liberty or serving a prison sentence may not be tortured or subject to ill-treatment (ICCPR, Article 7, and numerous other conventions) and they have a right to humane treatment (ICCPR, Article 10(1), ACHR, Article 5(2), ArCHR, Article 20(1)[183]). These guarantees have already been considered in detail.[184]

Furthermore, Article 10(2)(a) of the ICCPR guarantees accused persons the right to be segregated from convicted prisoners. They need not be accommodated in separate buildings but at least in separate quarters.[185] In keeping with the presumption of innocence, the paragraph adds that accused persons in detention must be accorded treatment 'appropriate to their status as unconvicted persons'.

According to Article 10(3) of the ICCPR, the treatment of convicted prisoners must be aimed at their 'reformation and social rehabilitation'. This provision is violated, for example, where a perpetrator is detained for 13 years in solitary confinement for refusing to change his political opinion.[186]

Issue in focus: Children and adolescents in detention and criminal proceedings

---

When children and adolescents are arrested and detained on suspicion of having committed an offence, they must be separated from adults and brought as speedily as possible to adjudication (Article 10(2)(b) ICCPR) in order to limit the time spent in custody.

According to ICCPR, Article 14(4), criminal proceedings against juveniles 'shall be such as will take account of their age and the desirability of promoting their rehabilitation'. What this means in concrete terms is not specified in the Covenant[187] but is clarified to some extent in the Convention on the Rights of the Child. According to CRC, Article 40(1), children or adolescents alleged as, accused of, or recognized as having infringed penal law must 'be treated in a manner consistent with the promotion of the child's sense of dignity and worth, which reinforces the child's respect for the human rights and fundamental freedoms of others and which takes into account the child's age and the desirability of promoting the child's reintegration and the child's assuming a constructive role in society'. With this end in view, states parties must establish a minimum age of criminal responsibility (paragraph 3). In criminal proceedings, accused children and adolescents are automatically entitled to have legal or other appropriate assistance in the preparation and presentation of

---

[183] There is no corresponding provision in the ECHR; inhuman conditions of detention are assessed in the light of ECHR, Art 3.

[184] See above, Chapter 10, section II.

[185] HRCttee, *Pinkney v Canada*, Communication No 27/1978 (1981), para 30.

[186] HRCttee, *Kang v Republic of Korea*, Communication No 878/1999 (2003), para 7.3.

[187] See HRCttee, General Comment No 32 (2007), paras 42 ff.

their defence, and the judicial proceedings should take place in the presence of their parents or legal guardian unless this is considered not to be in the best interest of the child (paragraph 2(b)).

Where children and adolescents are sentenced to deprivation of liberty, states must make available measures such as 'counselling; probation; foster care; education and vocational training programmes and other alternatives to institutional care' to ensure that juvenile offenders 'are dealt with in a manner appropriate to their well-being' (CRC, Article 40(4)). If they are sentenced to imprisonment, they have a right to be segregated from adults (ICCPR, Article 10(3)).

16

Protection of Participation in Political Life

I. Overview

A person's identity, ambitions and opportunities as a social being are largely determined by his or her social environment. Political rights, understood in a broad sense, are designed to enable people to communicate as freely as possible with others and to enjoy, as far as possible, equality of opportunity under the law to participate in shaping their social context. Political rights in a narrow sense (section V) guarantee citizens both the right to vote under equal conditions and at regular intervals in free elections and the right to stand for election. These rights cannot be realized unless the freedom to inform oneself as well as others and the freedom to communicate with others are respected during the run-up to elections. These freedoms include the right of free access to all sources of desired information without state interference and the right to form and express one's own political opinion, both of which are protected by freedom of expression (section II). Of equal importance for the formation of opinions and their public manifestation is the right, protected by freedom of assembly (section III), to meet freely with other persons, be it for a private meeting or for a demonstration on public grounds. Lastly, all free political activity depends on like-minded people being able to join together in political parties or other organizations. This right is protected by freedom of association (section IV).

While this chapter focuses on the core political function of these rights, one should not forget that the freedoms of expression, assembly and association are equally crucial in areas of personal autonomy and development unrelated to the realm of politics. Hence, unlike the rights to vote and stand in elections, which can be invoked only by citizens, they protect all persons within the jurisdiction of a state regardless of their nationality.[1]

---

[1] However, the ECHR—but not the ICCPR or the ACHR—contains a special rule in Art 16, according to which the freedoms of expression, assembly and association cannot be construed as preventing the contracting parties from imposing restrictions on the political activities of foreigners. This exception now rightly plays only a very marginal role, at least in the recent jurisprudence of the European Court of Human Rights; see, for example, ECtHR, *Piermont v France*, Series A, No 314 (1995). ArCHR, Article 32 goes even further by restricting freedom of association and peaceful assembly to citizens.

II. Freedom of Opinion and Expression

Relevant provisions: UDHR, Article 19; ICESCR, Article 15(3); ICCPR, Articles 19 and 20; CRC, Article 13; CRPD, Article 21;CERD, Article 5(d)(viii); ICRMW, Article 13(2); ACHR, Article 13; ACHPR, Article 9, ArCHR, Article 32; ECHR, Article 10.

1. The scope of protection

The freedom of opinion and expression constitutes an essential prerequisite not only for personal growth but also for a pluralist democratic society.[2] This freedom protects not only the right to have an opinion but also the right to receive and disseminate all kinds of information and all forms 'of subjective ideas and opinions capable of transmission to others'.[3] In addition to guaranteeing the freedom to choose one's language of expression,[4] it protects the freedom to transmit ideas and impressions non-orally through symbols, books, paintings, or other forms of artistic expression,[5] the freedom to disseminate scientific findings and, lastly, the freedom to choose the medium used to impart or receive such opinions.[6] Its substantive scope of application is, in principle,[7] unlimited in terms of the content of the information and ideas disseminated, although certain expressions can be outlawed under applicable limitation clauses. As stressed by the European and Inter-American Courts of Human Rights, freedom of expression also protects expression that offends, disturbs, or shocks[8] as well as spontaneous and emotional statements. A call for an election boycott, for example, falls within the scope of

---

[2] See, for example, ECtHR (Grand Chamber), *Zana v Turkey, Reports* 1997-VII, para 51, and ACmHPR, *Constitutional Rights Project, Civil Liberties Organization and Media Rights Agenda v Nigeria*, Communications Nos 140/1994, 141/1994, 145/1995 (1999), para 36.

[3] HRCttee, *Ballantyne et al v Canada*, Communications Nos 359 and 385/1989 (1993), para 11.3; IACtHR, *Kimel v Argentina*, Series C, No 177 (2008), para 53.

[4] Accordingly, the IACtHR held that forbidding family members belonging to a minority from speaking their mother tongue when in custody breaches freedom of expression; IACtHR, *López-Álvarez v Honduras*, Series C, No 141 (2006) para 166.

[5] HRCttee, *Shin v Republic of Korea*, Communication No 926/2000 (2004), para 7.2; ECtHR, *Müller and Others v Switzerland*, Series A, No 133 (1988), and *Vajnai v Hungary*, Application No 33629/06 (2008).

[6] ECtHR, *Autronic AG v Switzerland*, Series A, No 178 (1990), para 47; IACtHR, *Olmedo Bustos et al v Chile ('The Last Temptation of Christ' case)*, Series C, No 73 (2001), para 65.

[7] It is somewhat unclear, however, whether the jurisprudence of the HRCttee or the ECtHR excludes racist statements from the scope of this right or whether such statements can or even must be restricted by law on the basis of relevant limitation clauses in order to be outlawed. In our view, the latter approach is more appropriate. See, for example, ECtHR, *Jersild v Denmark*, Series A, No 298 (1994), para 35; HRCttee, *Faurisson v France*, Communication No 550/1993 (1996); and Chapter 3, 'Issue in focus: Permissible limitations of civil rights'.

[8] See, for example, ECtHR (Grand Chamber), *Refah Partisi (the Welfare Party) and Others v Turkey, Reports* 2003-II, para 89, and IACtHR, *Ivcher-Bronstein v Peru*, Series C, No 74 (2001), para 152.

protection of this freedom.[9] The type of idea expressed by a statement or its commercial character is also immaterial,[10] as is the location or context of statements made.[11] Furthermore, the protective scope of the guarantee covers not only the freedom to impart information but also the freedom to seek and receive information.[12] Finally, the European Court of Human Rights recognizes that this guarantee offers protection against the secret registration of personal data about a person's political activities by the state.[13]

A distinction must be made between freedom of *expression*, which can be restricted, and freedom of *opinion*, ie the freedom to have an opinion, which is explicitly embodied only in ICCPR, Article 19(1)[14] and is absolute.[15] Measures such as brainwashing or coercive ideological re-education systems in prisons[16] can thus never be justified under the ICCPR. As freedom of opinion protects exclusively passive behaviour or a process occurring within a person's mind, there can be no legitimate grounds for coercive state indoctrination. Although the regional conventions lack the explicit language found in ICCPR, Article 19, they too provide absolute protection for this freedom.

2. Duty to respect

Freedom of expression obliges states first and foremost to allow information to be freely imparted and received, and to refrain from subsequently inflicting penalties or other forms of adverse treatment on persons who impart or receive information. This right is violated not only by censorship or publication bans but also when indirect measures of coercion are used. Examples of the latter include revoking the citizenship of the majority shareholder and director of a private television broadcasting company which televised various reports on human rights violations[17] or sanctioning a lawyer with imprisonment for being in contempt of

---

[9] According to the HRCttee, *Svetik v Belarus*, Communication No 927/2000 (2004), para 7.3, punishing a person for encouraging voters not to participate in an election is a violation of freedom of expression if voting is not compulsory in the state concerned.

[10] HRCttee, *Ballantyne et al v Canada*, Communications Nos 359 and 385/1989 (1993), para 11.3; ECtHR, *Casado Coca v Spain*, Series A, No 285-A (1994), para 35.

[11] Thus, the ECtHR has repeatedly held that 'the freedom of speech guarantee extends to lawyers pleading on behalf of their clients in court': see ECtHR (Grand Chamber), *Kyprianou v Cyprus*, Application No 73797/01 (2005), para 151.

[12] HRCttee, *Gauthier v Canada*, Communication No 633/1995 (1999); ECtHR, *Gaskin v The United Kingdom*, Series A, No 160 (1989); IACtHR, *Olmedo Bustos et al v Chile* ('The Last Temptation of Christ' case), Series C, No 73 (2001), para 66.

[13] ECtHR, *Segerstedt-Wiberg and Others v Sweden*, Application No 62332/00 (2006), para 107.

[14] The freedom to have an opinion is also protected by the freedom of conscience, see Chapter 13, section I.

[15] This right is furthermore, according to ICCPR, Art 4, non-derogable in a state of emergency. See HRCttee, General Comment No 10 (1983), para 1.

[16] HRCttee, *Kang v Republic of Korea*, Communication No 878/1999 (2003), para 7.2.

[17] IACtHR, *Ivcher-Bronstein v Peru*, Series C, No 74 (2001), paras 145 ff. Because the victim was not a citizen, the domestic courts also had ordered the suspension of his majority rights in the media firm.

court because of comments protesting the manner in which judges were trying to stop his cross-examination of a witness in a murder case.[18] It is also considered indirect coercion to sanction individuals for participating in an illegal assembly merely for distributing the Universal Declaration of Human Rights,[19] or to launch criminal proceedings against a journalist for alleged defamation of a minister and to keep the proceedings pending for several years,[20] thereby also violating the right to a trial without undue delay. In some of these cases, the severity of the interference was such that it had a 'chilling effect' on the exercise of expression beyond the actual case.[21]

As in the case of other freedoms, the obligation to respect freedom of expression is not absolute. Restrictions are, according to ICCPR, Article 19(3), permissible if they 'are provided by law and necessary (a) For respect of the rights or reputations of others; (b) For the protection of national security or of public order (ordre public), or of public health or morals.' The regional conventions contain similar limitation clauses with ECHR, Article 11(2) adding that restrictions may be made in the name of 'preventing the disclosure of information received in confidence, or . . . maintaining the authority and impartiality of the judiciary'.

The following examples illustrate the application of limitation clauses:

- The European Court of Human Rights has developed extensive case law on the legitimacy of interference in order to protect the *rights of others*. In such cases, the Court generally attaches considerable weight to the public interest of receiving information if the interference is aimed at protecting the reputation of a politician.[22] By contrast, it attaches greater weight to the right to privacy than to freedom of expression where a publication does not really serve the public interest. Accordingly, freedom of expression was not violated by a ban on publication of photos showing a social celebrity engaged in strictly private activities.[23] The aim of protecting the rights of others has also been invoked to protect the religious feelings of third parties[24] and to justify limitations on

---

[18] ECtHR (Grand Chamber), *Kyprianou v Cyprus*, Application No 73797/01 (2005), paras 149–83.

[19] HRCttee, *Velichkin v Belarus*, Communication No 1022/2001 (2005).

[20] HRCttee, *Majuwana Kankanamge v Sri Lanka*, Communication No 909/2000 (2004), para 9.4. The Committee held that there had been a violation of ICCPR, Art 19, read in conjunction with Art 2(3).

[21] Eg, ECtHR (Grand Chamber), *Kyprianou v Cyprus*, Application No 73797/01 (2005), para 181 (disproportionate sentence for a lawyer who got into a heated argument with the court while defending a client in a murder case); ECtHR, *Tønsberg Blad As and Haukom v Norway*, Application No 510/04 (2007), para 102 (defamation proceedings against a newspaper).

[22] See for example, ECtHR (Grand Chamber), *Lindon, Otchakovsky-Laurens and July v France*, Applications Nos 21279/02 and 36448/02 (2007), paras 42 and 46, and *Wirtschafts-Trend Zeitschriften Verlagsgesellschaft GmbH v Austria*, Application No 58547/00 (2005), para 37. Similarly, HRCttee, *Bodrožić v Serbia*, Communication No 1180/2003 (2005), para 7.2, and IACtHR, *Kimel v Argentina*, Series C, No 177 (2008), paras 87 ff.

[23] ECtHR, *Von Hannover v Germany*, Reports 2004-VI, paras 65 ff.

[24] ECtHR, *İA v Turkey*, Application No 42571/98 (2005). In this case, the Court held that passages in a book suggesting that Prophet Muhammad 'broke his fast through sexual intercourse,

press freedom in the interest of fair competition. Where limitations on exercising the freedom of expression are based on the rights of others, the Court adopts a comparatively strict level of scrutiny in assessing the legitimacy of interference.[25]

• States regularly invoke *national security* as a permissible ground for restricting freedom of expression in order to protect military secrets in the context of an ongoing or potential armed conflict. The European Court of Human Rights has given states a wide margin of appreciation in assessing the need for restrictions on press freedom during periods of unrest. For instance, it considered justified the punishment of a former mayor who voiced his support for an insurrectionary movement during an interview.[26] By contrast, the Human Rights Committee decided that the prosecution of a political activist who had distributed printed material in South Korea expressing support for North Korean political positions had been disproportionate and hence a violation of freedom of expression.[27] It is a violation of freedom of expression when the publication of official secrets is sanctioned albeit the information had already been made public.[28] The same is true where a public official is dismissed from service because he forwarded to a newspaper an internal memo which had not been classified as confidential and spoke of irregularities in the department of the public prosecutor.[29] On the other hand, the European Court of Human Rights considers that there is no violation of freedom of expression where a journalist is sanctioned for making public secret state documents, even if these documents were leaked to him by an official.[30] Similarly, the Human Rights Committee found no violation in the case of a journalist who was punished for releasing the results of surveys on the presidential elections during the 23-day period prior to the elections, during which the publication of survey results was prohibited by the national election law.[31]

• The European Court of Human Rights and the Human Rights Committee generally give states a particularly wide margin of discretion in assessing whether a restriction on freedom of expression is necessary to *protect public*

after dinner and before prayer' and 'did not forbid sexual intercourse with a dead person or a live animal' were 'not only comments that offend or shock, or a "provocative" opinion, but also an abusive attack on the Prophet of Islam' (para 39). It concluded that a fine amounting to the equivalent of 16 US$ imposed 'in respect of the statements in issue was intended to provide protection against offensive attacks on matters regarded as sacred by Muslims. In that respect it finds that the measure may reasonably be held to have met a "pressing social need"' (para 30).

[25] As an instructive example, see ECtHR, *Hertel v Switzerland, Reports* 1998-VI, paras 42 and 47–51.

[26] ECtHR (Grand Chamber), *Zana v Turkey, Reports* 1997-VII, paras 52–62.

[27] HRCttee, *Kim v Republic of Korea*, Communication No 574/1994 (1999), para 12.4.

[28] See, for example, ECtHR, *Vereniging Weekblad Bluf! v The Netherlands*, Series A, No 306-A (1995), paras 43–46.

[29] ECtHR (Grand Chamber), *Guja v Moldova*, Application No 14277/04 (2008).

[30] ECtHR (Grand Chamber), *Stoll v Switzerland*, Application No 69698/01 (2007).

[31] HRCttee, *Jong-Cheol v Republic of Korea*, Communication No 968/2001 (2005).

morals, eg in order to protect the youth or to enforce a ban on pornography.[32] This approach is based on the fact that the ways in which morals are conceived in the different states with their particular cultural traditions are extremely varied, making it inappropriate for an international body to rule on such national concepts.

Issue in focus: The 'margin of appreciation' theory in the jurisprudence of the ECtHR

In its settled jurisprudence, the European Court of Human Rights limits the scope of its examination of the proportionality of interference with a human right often by according states a 'margin of appreciation', thus allowing them to exercise a large degree of discretion in assessing the facts and interpreting the law in a given area. However, according to the Court's standard formula, national authorities' power of appreciation is not unrestricted but 'goes hand in hand with European supervision'.[33] A certain amount of judicial circumspection is nevertheless justified by reference to the subsidiary character of the Convention guarantees and national authorities' closer contact and familiarity with the specific circumstances to be assessed.[34]

The extent to which such margin of appreciation is granted is not uniform. Relevant factors in determining whether this approach is applicable include: the type of public interest pursued; the degree of uniformity of the case law in the state concerned; the area of protection affected by the interference; and the type of state obligation involved.[35] Judicial circumspection seems appropriate in cases where the Court is called to assess local circumstances. Today, however, it would seem that the Court often invokes this legal approach in particularly controversial cases, sometimes even in cases with a strong bearing on core aspects of the right of individuals (such as the right to be informed of one's natural family[36] or the legitimacy of state prohibitions on compliance with religious dress codes[37]), so that it can declare them inadmissible or dismiss them without any real substantive examination.

Article 20 of the ICCPR *obliges* states parties to restrict freedom of expression in cases of war propaganda and advocacy of racial hatred.[38] This mandatory restriction is made more specific in CERD, Article 4, pursuant to which the states

---

[32] See, for example, ECtHR, *Müller and Others v Switzerland*, Series A, No 133 (1988), para 35; HRCttee, *Hertzberg et al v Finland*, Communication No 61/1979 (1982), para 10.3.

[33] ECtHR, *Handyside v The United Kingdom*, Series A, No 24 (1976), paras 48–49.

[34] Ibid.

[35] For instance, the ECtHR allows a comparatively wide margin of appreciation for interference on the ground of public morals, while the margin is narrower for interference on the ground of national security where there is a clash with democracy-related private interests. For a detailed analysis, see Jörg Künzli, *Zwischen Rigidität und Flexibilität—Der Verpflichtungsgrad internationaler Menschenrechte* (Berlin: Duncker & Humblot, 2001), 343 ff.

[36] See, for example, ECtHR, *Odièvre v France*, Reports 2003-III, paras 35, 40 and 49.

[37] See, for example, ECtHR, *Dahlab v Switzerland*, Reports 2001-V; *Leyla Şahin v Turkey* (Grand Chamber), Reports 2005-XI.

[38] See HRCttee, General Comment No 11 (1983). Many states have entered reservations to Art 20.

parties to the Convention undertake, *inter alia*, to 'declare an offence punishable by law all dissemination of ideas based on racial superiority or hatred [and] all incitement to racial discrimination' and to prohibit all organizations that promote such ideas. Whether and to what extent ICCPR, Article 20 accords victims of such propaganda an individual right—in the sense of an explicit obligation to protect—has not yet been clarified by the Human Rights Committee.

Many Western states made reservations to these provisions out of fear that they would undermine the freedom of expression. The Human Rights Committee, in the *Faurisson* case did not resort to Article 20 of the ICCPR but came to the conclusion that a conviction for denial of the Holocaust was a permissible restriction on ICCPR, Article 19. It noted 'that the rights for the protection of which restrictions on the freedom of expression are permitted by article 19, paragraph 3, may relate to the interests of other persons or to those of the community as a whole. Since the statements made by the author, read in their full context, were of a nature as to raise or strengthen anti-semitic feelings, the restriction served the respect of the Jewish community to live free from fear of an atmosphere of anti-semitism.'[39] Furthermore, the Committee accepted that such restrictions are necessary as the denial of the existence of the Holocaust could be characterized 'as the principal vehicle for anti-semitism'.[40] Similarly, in the case of *Malcolm Ross v Canada*, the Committee concluded that the removal of a teacher who had publicly called upon Christians 'to hold those of the Jewish faith and ancestry in contempt as undermining freedom, democracy and Christian beliefs and values'[41] was 'necessary to protect the right and freedom of Jewish children to have a school system free from bias, prejudice and intolerance'.[42] In light of these decisions, Article 20 of the ICCPR should be understood as referring to specific measures necessary to protect the rights of others including the right to be protected against acts of violence or discrimination rather than imposing additional undue restrictions on the freedom of expression.

The approach taken by the European Court of Human Rights is slightly different. In the case of sanctions for blasphemy and religious defamation, the Court emphasized that the exercise of the freedom of expression 'carries with it duties and responsibilities. Among them, in the context of religious beliefs, may legitimately be included a duty to avoid expressions that are gratuitously offensive to others and profane (...). This being so, as a matter of principle it may be considered necessary to punish improper attacks on objects of religious veneration.'[43] The Court then goes on to 'weighing up the conflicting interests of the exercise

---

[39] HRCttee, *Faurisson v France*, Communication No 550/1993 (1996), para 9.6.
[40] Ibid, para. 9.7.
[41] HRCttee, *Ross v Canada*, Communication No 736/1997 (2000), para 11.5.
[42] Ibid, para 15.6.
[43] See ECHR, *İ.A. v Turkey*, Application No 42571/98 (2005), para 24. See also *Otto-Preminger-Institut v Austria*, Series A, No 295-A (1994), para § 49, and *Murphy v Ireland*, *Reports* 2003-IX, para 67.

of two fundamental freedoms, namely the right of the applicant to impart to the public his views on religious doctrine on the one hand and the right of others to respect for their freedom of thought, conscience and religion on the other hand'.[44] This approach raises the question whether a blasphemous or defamatory act really could affect someone's freedom to have a religion or belief and to manifest it as guaranteed by Article 19 of the ECHR. Furthermore, it carries the risk of actually protecting religions rather than individuals, a step that would seriously jeopardize the free exercise of expression.

Issue in focus: Threats to media freedom in the OSCE area

The OSCE Representative on Freedom of the Media identified, *inter alia*, the following obstacles to press freedom in Europe:[45]

— Restrictions on freedom of reporting during election campaigns;
— Media concentration in the hands of tycoons, who in some cases also hold political office;
— Structural censorship involving indirect interference (eg through tax inspections, compulsory fire department measures, harassment, etc);
— Direct censorship through the enforced disappearance or killing of journalists or by pressuring the editors of a publication to dismiss journalists who are disliked;
— Indirect censorship by bringing trumped-up charges against journalists; and
— Increasingly dangerous working conditions of journalists in conflict zones.

---

3. Duties to protect and to fulfil

States must also take positive steps to protect freedom of expression against interference by private actors. There is, however, very little international case law to date in this area. The Human Rights Committee held in an early case that a state-controlled private broadcasting company's internal censorship *vis-à-vis* its journalists constituted interference with this guarantee.[46] The European Court of Human Rights similarly held that where a commercial television company cited domestic legislation and refused to broadcast an animal protection association's commercial, it was restricting the latter's freedom of expression. The Court further held that the state should not have tolerated such a restriction.[47]

In the absence of relevant jurisprudence, it is at present difficult to assess the extent to which states actually have an obligation to fulfil this right, for instance through media promotion.

---

[44] Ibid, para 27.
[45] Report by the Representative to the Permanent Council of the OSCE of 11 December 2003.
[46] HRCttee, *Hertzberg et al v Finland*, Communication No 61/1979 (1982), paras 9.1 and 10.2.
[47] ECtHR, *VgT Verein gegen Tierfabriken v Switzerland*, Reports 2001-VI, paras 44–79.

Issue in focus: Repression of human rights defenders

In recent decades there has been a global escalation in repressive state measures against persons who champion human rights causes. The measures range from harassment, threats, detention, and prosecution to enforced disappearances and extrajudicial killings of activists.[48] According to the Special Representative of the UN Secretary-General (since 2008: Special Rapporteur) on the situation of human rights defenders,[49] such measures are directed primarily against journalists, lawyers and doctors who are members of NGOs or who collaborate with international organizations and against relatives of victims of human rights abuses. This *de facto* curtailment of freedom of expression tends to occur in states which have civil society organizations but seek to conceal human rights violations and hence to rein in the activities of independent observers. The curtailment of freedom of expression in such cases pursues the illegitimate aim of covering up violations of other rights, thereby not only massively breaching obligations to ensure the domestic implementation of human rights, but also seriously impeding the work of the international monitoring bodies.

In addition to violating freedom of expression and other relevant human rights, such measures go against the detailed guarantees set out in the UN General Assembly Declaration of 9 December 1998 on the Right and Responsibility of Individuals, Groups and Organs of Society to Promote and Protect Universally Recognized Human Rights and Fundamental Freedoms.

III. Freedom of Assembly

Relevant provisions: UDHR, Article 20; ICCPR, Article 21; CRC, Article 15; CERD, Article 5(d)(ix); ICRMW, Articles 26 and 40; ACHR, Article 15; ACHPR, Article 11; ArCHR, Article 24; ECHR, Article 11.

1. Scope of protection

The freedom to gather together with other persons is fundamental for the exercise of any form of democracy. Article 21 of the ICCPR and equivalent guarantees in regional conventions consequently protect all gatherings that are organized deliberately and with a specific end in view. The scope of protection afforded by this right includes both the organization of and participation in such assemblies. Assemblies[50] can be held in different ways, for instance as stationary gatherings

---

[48] See, for example, ACmHPR, *Huri-Laws v Nigeria*, Communication No 225/1998 (2000).

[49] See, for example, the reports of the Special Representative of the Secretary-General of 15 January 2004, UN Doc E/CN.4/2004/94, paras 29 ff and of 31 January 2008, UN Doc A/HRC/7/28, paras 19 ff.

[50] Some assemblies are also protected by other guarantees, for instance religious assemblies by freedom of religion and strictly private assemblies by the right to privacy.

on public or private premises that are either accessible to the general public or restricted to a private group of participants, but also as marches or demonstrations.[51] The subject matter addressed by an assembly is also immaterial: the right can be invoked by political parties or by other organizations irrespective of their purpose.

The caveat is that this freedom protects only peaceful assembly.[52] Accordingly, its substantive scope of protection excludes assemblies in which demonstrators resort to violence. Acts of civil disobedience, however, such as sit-ins or the use by participants of passive means of protest, are not considered to be acts allowing classifying assemblies as violent.[53] Furthermore, the violent nature of an assembly may not be inferred solely from the opinions expressed during the event.[54]

2. Duty to respect

Any state interference before or during a peaceful gathering, whether in the form of a conditional authorization, an outright ban, or the dispersal of an assembly, as well as any subsequent punishment of the participants, constitutes a restriction of the right to freedom of assembly. The question arises whether the requirement of a permit should in itself be characterized as interference with this civil liberty. The Human Rights Committee has held that it does,[55] while older Strasbourg case law concluded that the requirement to obtain permission does not constitute a restriction and thus cannot be challenged.[56]

Freedom of assembly is not absolute. Restrictions may be placed on its exercise if they are 'imposed in conformity with the law and...are necessary in a democratic society in the interests of national security or public safety, public order (*ordre public*), the protection of public health or morals or the protection of the rights and freedoms of others' (ICCPR, Article 21). States typically invoke the grounds of protection of national security or public safety and maintenance of public order in support of restrictions. The rights of others, such as their right to enjoy property, also constitute a legitimate ground for interference. In assessing compliance with the limitation provisions, the European Court of Human Rights often gives states parties a relatively wide margin of appreciation.

---

[51] See ECtHR, *Ezelin v France*, Series A, No 202 (1991), para 53.

[52] Moreover, ACHR, Art 15 explicitly restricts protection to assemblies 'without arms'.

[53] See Manfred Nowak, *UN Covenant on Civil and Political Rights, CCPR Commentary* (2nd edn, Engel: Kehl, 2005), 487; Jochen A. Frowein and Wolfgang Peukert, *Europäische Menschenrechtskonvention, EMRK-Kommentar* (2nd edn, Engel: Kehl, 1996), 411. However, according to these authors, sit-ins that seal off a building are not peaceful.

[54] See Nowak (n 53), 486.

[55] HRCttee, *Kivenmaa v Finland*, Communication No 412/1990 (1994), para 9.2.

[56] ECmHR, *Rassemblement jurassien v Switzerland*, Application No 8191/78, DR 17 (1979), 119, para 3.

3. Duties to protect and to fulfil

The European Court of Human Rights recognized as early as 1988 that freedom of assembly carries inherent obligations to protect. Accordingly, a contracting party is obliged to protect a demonstration against disruption by private opponents. The Court stressed that although a demonstration may annoy or give offence to persons opposed to the opinion it seeks to promote, freedom of assembly requires that participants in a demonstration should be able to express their ideas without fear, even on highly controversial issues. In a democracy the right to conduct a counter-demonstration cannot extend to inhibiting the right of those participating in the original demonstration. Hence, in order to prevent the effective exercise of the right from being undermined, the state has a duty to take reasonable measures to protect peaceful demonstrations.[57]

The duty to make peaceful assemblies possible by making public spaces available for demonstrations can arguably be derived from the duty to fulfil under the freedom of assembly.[58]

IV. Freedom of Association

Relevant provisions: UDHR, Article 20; ICCPR, Article 22; CEDAW, Article 7; CERD, Article 5; CRC, Article 15; CRPD, Article 29; ICRMW; ACHR, Article 16; ACHPR, Article 10; ArCHR, Article 24; ECHR, Article 11.

1. Scope of protection

Human rights protect not only the physical gathering of people in assemblies but also allow them to join together in legally constituted associations. Freedom of association accordingly protects the right of *individuals* to form and join civil society associations and organizations of any kind.

The precise nature and purpose of the association is immaterial: protection is enjoyed by members of political parties[59] as well as associations established for athletic, economic, social or cultural purposes.[60] Freedom of association also

---

[57] ECtHR, *Plattform 'Ärzte für das Leben' v Austria*, Series A, No 139 (1988), paras 32 and 34.

[58] See also ECtHR, *Appleby and Others v The United Kingdom*, Reports 2003-VI, paras 47 and 52, on freedom of assembly in a private shopping mall. In the literature, David Harris, Michael O'Boyle and Chris Warbrick, *Law of the European Convention on Human Rights* (2nd edn, Oxford University Press: Oxford, 1995), p 419 raise the question of whether the state has the authority, in the context of its positive obligations, to require private actors to make their property available.

[59] Explicitly stated in, for example, ECtHR (Grand Chamber), *United Communist Party of Turkey and Others v Turkey*, Reports 1998-I, paras 24 f and ACmHPR, *Lawyers for Human Rights v Swaziland*, Communication No 251/2002 (2005), para 61.

[60] Explicitly stipulated by ACHR, Art 16.

includes the right to form and to join trade unions.[61] On the other hand, public entities established by law do not count as associations within the meaning of this guarantee.[62]

In its positive dimension, freedom of association protects the freedom of individuals to form and join an association, enjoy continuing membership and carry out its statutory activities in practice[63] without being subjected to state restrictions and repression on that account.[64] In negative terms, it protects against being compelled to become or remain a member of a given association.[65]

Does the right also protect associations as such? The Human Rights Committee seemed to answer the question in the affirmative when it recognized 'the right of such an association freely to carry out its statutory activities'.[66] However, as OP/ICCPR, Article 1 permits individuals only to invoke Covenant rights in the individual communications procedure, the right protects members of the association rather than the association itself. In contrast, as the ECHR protects not only natural but also legal persons,[67] the right can be invoked by the association itself as well as by its members. Therefore, the freedom of association also protects the freedom of these associations to choose and exclude their members.[68]

2. State obligations

The states parties to the ICCPR and the regional conventions are obliged first and foremost to avoid impeding the establishment, existence, and activities of private-law associations and to refrain from inhibiting the freedom to join such bodies. Restrictions on freedom of association include overly complicated registration

---

[61] This right is also protected by ICESCR, Art 8.

[62] See, for example, HRCttee, *Wallmann et al v Austria*, Communication No 1002/2001 (2004), para 9.4, and ECtHR, *Chassagnou and Others v France*, Reports 1999-III, para 100. According to both decisions, the character of an association under domestic law as private or public is immaterial when it comes to determining whether an association or its members can invoke this right. Rather, the term association must be construed autonomously.

[63] See ECtHR (Grand Chamber), *United Communist Party of Turkey and Others v Turkey*, Reports 1998-I, para 33, explicitly holding that this guarantee protects not only the founding of a party but also its continued existence. For a similar viewpoint, HRCttee, *Belyatsky et al v Belarus*, Communication No 1296/2004 (2007), para 7.2. See also IACtHR, *Baena Ricardo et al v Panama*, Series C, No 72 (2001), paras 153–73 on the right to join and play an active part in a trade union.

[64] See, for example, ECtHR, *Maestri v Italy (Grand Chamber)*, Reports 2004-I and *Grande Oriente d'Italia di Palazzo Giustiniani v Italy (No 2)*, Application No 26740/02 (2007). In these cases, the Court considered a rule barring members of Masonic lodges from standing for election to a regional parliament to be in violation, of ECHR, Art 11 read in conjunction with ECHR, Art 14.

[65] See ECtHR, *Sigurjónsson v Iceland*, Series A, No 264 (1993), paras 33–37; and *Sørensen v Denmark and Rasmusen v Denmark* (Grand Chamber), Applications Nos 52562/99 and 52620/99 (2006), para 54.

[66] For example, HRCttee, *Belyatsky et al v Belarus*, Communication No 1296/2004 (2007), para 7.2.

[67] See Chapter 4, section I.2.

[68] ECtHR, *Associated Society of Locomotive Engineers & Firemen (ASLEF) v The United Kingdom*, Application No 11002/05 (2007), para 39.

procedures and other formal impediments,[69] substantive restrictions on associ-ations' activities, restrictions on other rights of members by virtue of their mem-bership, the passing of a penal sentence on members of the association,[70] and, most seriously of all, the prohibition or the forced dissolution of an association.[71]

As in the case of other civil liberties, interference with the right does not neces-sarily constitute a violation. Rather, the relevant provisions permit interference in accordance with the usual limitation clauses. Thus, ICCPR, Article 22(2) allows restrictions provided they 'are prescribed by law and . . . necessary in a democratic society in the interests of national security or public safety, public order (ordre public), the protection of public health or morals or the protection of the rights and freedoms of others.' In addition, this provision does 'not prevent the impos-ition of lawful restrictions on members of the armed forces and of the police in their exercise of this right.' In practice, the grounds of national security or pub-lic safety and that of public order are most often invoked to justify restrictions. While such motives are valid as such, states must show that imposed restrictions are really necessary in the circumstances of the specific case. Thus, for instance, the Human Rights Committee held that convicting someone to detention on account of being a member of a student's association that allegedly supported North Korea was not a necessary measure for safeguarding national security. For this reason, the conviction violated Article 22.[72]

Issue in focus: Compatibility of the banning of political parties with human rights law

Much of the recent case law of the European Court of Human Rights on freedom of association has focused on the legitimacy of banning political parties.[73] Although the Court allows states a certain margin of appreciation in assessing the need for a ban, it nonetheless adopts a relatively strict approach in examining the implications of such action for a democratic system of governance. It uses the following standard line of reasoning:

[T]he exceptions set out in Article 11 are, where political parties are concerned, to be con-strued strictly; only convincing and compelling reasons can justify restrictions on such parties'

---

[69] See HRCttee, *Zvozskov et al v Belarus*, Communication No 1039/2001 (2006).

[70] HRCttee, *Lee v Republic of Korea*, Communication No 1119/2002 (2005).

[71] See for example, HRCttee, *Koneenko et al v Belarus*, Communication No 1274/2004 (2006).

[72] In the case of *Lee v Republic of Korea*, Communication No 1119/2002 (2005), the HRCttee decided that to convict the author of the communication to detention on account of being a mem-ber of a students' association that allegedly supported North Korea was not a necessary measure for safeguarding national security. For this reason, the conviction violated ICCPR, Art 22.

[73] ECtHR, *United Communist Party of Turkey and Others v Turkey* (Grand Chamber), *Reports* 1998-I; *The Socialist Party of Turkey and Others v Turkey* (Grand Chamber), *Reports* 1998-III; *Freedom and Democracy Party (Özdep) v Turkey* (Grand Chamber), *Reports* 1999-VIII; *Refah Partisi (the Welfare Party) and Others v Turkey*, Applications Nos 41340/98, 41342/98, 41343/98 and 41344/98 (2001) and Reports 2003-II (Grand Chamber). On this subject, see also ACmHPR, *Dawda Jawara v The Gambia*, Communication No 147/1995 and 149/1996 (2000).

freedom of association. In determining whether a necessity within the meaning of Article 11 § 2 exists, the Contracting States have only a limited margin of appreciation, which goes hand in hand with rigorous European supervision embracing both the law and the decisions applying it, including those given by independent courts.[74]

The Court held that a prohibition based solely on the name of a party, without concrete evidence that the party represents any real threat to the state and its democratic structure and without taking into account that the party's activities are aimed at finding a democratic resolution of minority issues, constitutes a violation of freedom of association; there is an even more straightforward violation where a party is declared illegal immediately after its foundation.[75] Even a party that aspires to change a state's constitutional structure cannot be prohibited as long as it seeks to achieve that goal by democratic means and as long as the change it promotes is compatible in substance with fundamental democratic principles, ie if it is not advocating the abolition of the freedoms guaranteed by the ECHR.[76] According to the Court, these requirements were not fulfilled in the case of a party whose leadership promoted a discriminatory legal structure in the form of different legal systems for members of different religions (specifically the introduction of Sharia law) while failing to distance itself sufficiently from the idea of using violence, if necessary, to gain power in the state.[77]

A ban on a party seeking to establish a totalitarian regime may also be justified under the abuse clauses of ICCPR, Article 5, ECHR, Article 17, or ACHR, Article 29(a), which state that no provision implies any right to engage in an activity or to perform an act aimed at the destruction of the guarantees enshrined in these treaties. These clauses play only a minor role in the jurisprudence of the Human Rights Committee and the regional Courts, however, since the limitation clauses pertaining to freedom of expression, assembly and association generally allow states to take legal action against such activities where necessary.

State duties to protect are, in principle, inherent in the right to freedom of association but there is as yet little relevant case law by international adjudicatory bodies. The European Court of Human Rights recognized an obligation of the state to protect employees in the private sector against forced membership in a particular trade union.[78] Based on the same freedom, the Inter-American Court of Human Rights found that the state has an obligation to investigate criminal actions taken against trade union activists.[79]

In regard to the duty to fulfil, effective implementation of freedom of association requires the state, *inter alia*, to ensure through the enactment of

---

[74] ECtHR (Grand Chamber), *United Communist Party of Turkey and Others v Turkey*, Reports 1998-I, para 46.

[75] Ibid, paras 53 ff.

[76] ECtHR (Grand Chamber), *Refah Partisi (the Welfare Party) v Turkey*, Reports 2003-II, para 98.

[77] Ibid, paras 117 ff.

[78] ECtHR (Grand Chamber), *Sørensen v Denmark and Rasmussen v Denmark*, Applications Nos 52562/99 and 52620/99 (2006), paras 57–8.

[79] IACtHR, *Cantoral-Huamaní and García-Santa Cruz v Peru*, Series C, No 167 (2007), para 146.

appropriate domestic legislation that individuals are not coerced by third parties, such as their employers, to join or not to join an association.[80] States must also ensure that domestic law affords the greatest possible freedom of action for founding such associations. Moreover, they must provide associations with the option of taking legal action against other associations that unlawfully disturb their activities.

V. The Right to Take Part in Elections and Public Affairs

Relevant provisions: UDHR, Article 21; ICCPR, Article 25; CERD, Article 5(c); CEDAW, Article 7(f); CRPD, Article 29; ACHR, Article 23; ACHPR, Article 13; P 2/ACHPR, Articles 1–3; ArCHR, Article 24(2)–(4); P 1/ECHR, Article 3.

1. Introduction

Human rights that protect freedom of expression, assembly and association are particularly important for a country's political life. In addition, the ICCPR and the regional conventions embody political rights in a narrow sense that guarantee direct participation in elections and referendums and in public affairs in general. Unlike the other treaty guarantees, they are formulated as citizens' rights, ie they can be exercised only by nationals of the state party concerned.

These rights are not based on a universally valid concept of democracy nor do they prescribe a particular electoral system, since a state's political system is usually the product of diverse historical, cultural and religious factors. Accordingly, ICCPR, Article 25(a) embodies the minimal consensus its drafters could achieve, namely that all states parties should be obliged to allow their citizens to 'take part' directly or indirectly 'in the conduct of public affairs' without defining any standards that a political system must fulfil.

At the regional level, the European Court of Human Rights goes further, holding that a pluralistic, democratic form of government is a component of the European public order guaranteed by the ECHR.[81] In support of this view, it cites the preamble to the ECHR, according to which human rights 'are best maintained...by an effective political democracy' and European states have 'a common heritage of political traditions, ideals, freedom and the rule of law'. The Court further emphasizes that the ECHR was designed to maintain and promote the ideals and values of a democratic society.[82]

---

[80] Nowak (n 53), 498; Harris, O'Boyle, and Warbrick (n 58), 423 and 425–30.
[81] ECtHR (Grand Chamber), *United Communist Party of Turkey and Others v Turkey, Reports* 1998-I, para 45.
[82] Ibid.

2. Right to take part in periodic elections

The right to take part in periodic elections, recognized both in the ICCPR and in regional conventions, embodies primarily a right of all citizens to participate in free and universal elections based on equal suffrage—at least to the legislative body—and hence an obligation to fulfil which must be discharged through positive measures. The precise substance of these electoral rights has yet to be clarified by case law of international bodies. It is generally accepted, however, that elections can scarcely be considered free in a one-party system,[83] and that elections are only in conformity with human rights standards when freedom of expression, assembly and association are respected in the run-up to the polls and when the results of free and fair elections are recognized by the government regardless of the outcome.[84] Elections must further be held within reasonable intervals, although none of the treaties specifies a maximum duration of the interval between polls.[85] Both majority and proportional representation voting systems meet international human rights requirements.[86]

Obligations to respect, for their part, exist, for example, with regard to the principle of voting secrecy. Moreover, this right also entails obligations to protect, since states have an obligation to prosecute, according to the jurisprudence of the Human Rights Committee, in the event of intimidation of voters by private groups.[87]

Article 25 of the ICCPR and equivalent rights in regional conventions enshrine both the right to vote freely and to stand for election. The right to secret ballots expressly contained in Article 25(b) is of particular importance for ensuring free elections.[88] States have a dual obligation in this regard: to respect voting secrecy and to take organizational measures aimed at ensuring that secrecy is possible.

According to the terms of the treaties, the obligations on states inherent in electoral rights are not subject to limitation. However, the Human Rights Committee as well as the European and Inter-American Courts of Human Rights recognize the existence of implicit limitations. According to the

---

[83] HRCttee, General Comment No 25 (1996), para 17.

[84] In 1993 the Nigerian Government annulled the results of presidential elections which had been described as fair by international observers. The ACmHPR held that this action violated the right to take part in the state's public affairs under ACHPR, Art 13(1) and the right to self-determination of the Nigerian people; ACmHPR, *Constitutional Rights Project and Civil Liberties Organisation v Nigeria*, Communication No 102/1993 (1998), paras 49–50.

[85] See, for example, HRCttee, General Comment No 25 (1996), para 9, according to which '[s]uch elections must be held at intervals which are not unduly long and which ensure that the authority of government continues to be based on the free expression of the will of electors'.

[86] Guy S Goodwin-Gill, *Free and Fair Elections, International Law and Practice* (2nd edn, Inter-Parliamentary Union: Geneva, 2006), 28.

[87] HRCttee, *Svetik v Belarus*, Communication No 927/2000 (2004), para 7.3.

[88] Switzerland entered a reservation to this provision because of the many cantonal and local election laws that continue to provide for the election of public authorities by citizens attending a public meeting through a show of hands.

Human Rights Committee, '[a]ny conditions which apply to the exercise of the rights protected by article 25 should be based on objective and reasonable criteria'.[89] The European Court of Human Rights stresses that the test for the compatibility of restrictions on the right to vote and stand for elections is less stringent than in the case of the freedoms of expression, assembly and association and is limited to 'two criteria: whether there has been arbitrariness or a lack of proportionality, and whether the restriction has interfered with the free expression of the opinion of the people. In this connection, the wide margin of appreciation enjoyed by the Contracting States has always been underlined. In addition, the Court has stressed the need to assess any electoral legislation in the light of the political evolution of the country concerned, with the result that features unacceptable in the context of one system may be justified in the context of another.'[90] In cases of disenfranchisement, however, the Court applies a more stringent test by affirming that 'it has to satisfy itself that the conditions do not curtail the rights in question to such an extent as to impair their very essence and deprive them of their effectiveness; that they are imposed in pursuit of a legitimate aim; and that the means employed are not disproportionate'.[91]

In fact, in the area of the *right to vote*, few legitimate grounds for limitation are conceivable apart from regulations establishing a minimum age, requirements as to the time of residence in the electoral area and requiring mental capacity. The Human Rights Committee has stated that, as a general principle, restrictions on the right to vote on the ground of physical disability or lack of education fail to meet the requirement of reasonableness.[92] Moreover, where registration of voters is required or residence requirements exist, they should not be imposed in such an unreasonable manner as to prevent persons wishing to vote from exercising their electoral rights.[93] The drawing of electoral districts in such a way that the weight carried by individual votes is extremely varied is also incompatible with human rights.[94] The European Court of Human Rights decided that the delegation of sovereign powers to a supranational organization did not affect the obligation of individual states to secure the right to vote to everyone within their jurisdiction without exception.[95] On the other hand, the Human Rights Committee held that the requirement of a certain duration of residence in the territory was

---

[89] HRCttee, General Comment No 25 (1996), para 4, See also ECtHR, *Podkolzina v Latvia*, Reports 2002-II, para 33, and ECtHR (Grand Chamber), *Hirst v The United Kingdom (No 2)*, Reports 2005, para 60, and IACtHR, *Yatama v Nicaragua*, Series C, No 127 (2005), para 218.

[90] ECtHR (Grand Chamber), *Ždanoka v Latvia*, Application No 58278/00 (2006), para 115.

[91] ECtHR (Grand Chamber), *Hirst v The United Kingdom (No 2)*, Reports 2005, para 62.

[92] HRCttee, General Comment No 25 (1996), para 10.

[93] HRCttee, General Comment No 25 (1996), para 11.

[94] HRCttee, *Mátyus v Slovakia*, Communication No 923/2000 (2002).

[95] ECtHR (Grand Chamber), *Matthews v The United Kingdom*, Reports 1999-I. The case concerned the denial of the right to vote in EU elections in Gibraltar, which is a dependent territory of the United Kingdom.

legitimate in a case concerning the right to take part in a referendum on the independence of the French overseas territory of New Caledonia.[96]

In many cases, persons with a criminal record lose their right to vote. It is clear today, that a *general and automatic* disenfranchisement of convicted criminals is incompatible with the right to vote,[97] as does the striking from the electoral register of persons who are in pre-trial detention[98] or under police surveillance because of their alleged membership in a criminal organization.[99] With regard to the continuing widespread practice of depriving persons of voting rights as a criminal sanction, the European Court of Human Rights does not consider it a violation of P 1/ECHR, Article 3 as long as the sanction is imposed case by case in a fair trial.[100]

States have a wider margin of discretion when it comes to determining the conditions governing the right to stand for election, ie *passive electoral rights*.[101] For instance, states are authorized to demand a certain number of signatures in support of a candidacy, a certain duration of residence and a certain command of the official language, as well as to adopt regulations on incompatibility with the exercise of other public offices.[102] The European Court of Human Rights considered for example that the right to vote and stand for election was not violated by the revocation of a person's right to stand for election because of his or her involvement with a political party that had unsuccessfully attempted to overthrow the government.[103] It came to the same conclusion concerning a person who could not become a member of parliament because, contrary to legal requirements, he did not belong to a party that reached at least ten per cent of the people's vote on a national scale.[104] It held, however that striking a member of a minority from the electoral register on account of alleged linguistic inadequacy although the candidate had passed the required language test was unreasonable and hence a violation of his political rights.[105] Finally, it considered that to exclude persons

---

[96] HRCttee, *Gillot et al v France*, Communication No 932/2000 (2002).

[97] ECtHR (Grand Chamber), *Hirst v The United Kingdom (No 2)*, Reports 2005, paras 56–85. In its Concluding Observations to the USA (2006), para 35, the HRCttee emphasized that the general exclusion of convicted criminals even after they have been released is not compatible with the ICCPR.

[98] HRCttee, *Gorji-Dinka v Cameroon*, Communication No 1134/2002 (2005), para 5.6.

[99] ECtHR (Grand Chamber), *Labita v Italy*, Reports 2000-IV.

[100] See for example ECtHR (Grand Chamber), *Ždanoka v Latvia*, Application No 58278/00 (2006), para 105.

[101] ECtHR (Grand Chamber), *Ždanoka v Latvia*, Application No 58278/00 (2006), paras 106 and 115.

[102] HRCttee, *Debreczeny v The Netherlands*, Communication No 500/1992 (1995), paras 9.2 and 9.3; ECtHR, *Gitonas and Others v Greece*, Reports 1997-IV, para 39, *Mathieu-Mohin and Clerfayt v Belgium*, Series A, No 113 (1987), para 52, and *Melnychenko v Ukraine*, Reports 2004-X, paras 53–9.

[103] ECtHR (Grand Chamber), *Ždanoka v Latvia*, Application No 58278/00 (2006), paras 116–31.

[104] ECtHR (Grand Chamber), *Yumak and Sadak v Turkey*, Application No 10226/03 (2008), para 147.

[105] ECtHR, *Podkolzina v Latvia*, Reports 2002-II. Similarly, HRCttee, *Ignatane v Latvia*, Communication No 884/1999 (2001).

with double nationality from the right to stand for parliamentary election is not proportional.[106] The African Commission on Human and Peoples' Rights qualified a constitutional provision to the effect that a person was eligible to run for the office of state president only if both parents were citizens of the country from birth as an inadmissible restriction of political rights.[107]

Issue in focus: The OSCE electoral principles

In 1990, states at the European level agreed on very detailed—albeit not strictly legally binding—general electoral principles in the so-called Copenhagen Document. These principles also constitute the basis for the system of international election observer missions:

(7) To ensure that the will of the people serves as the basis of the authority of government, the participating States will

(7.1) – hold free elections at reasonable intervals, as established by law;

(7.2) – permit all seats in at least one chamber of the national legislature to be freely contested in a popular vote;

(7.3) – guarantee universal and equal suffrage to adult citizens;

(7.4) – ensure that votes are cast by secret ballot or by equivalent free voting procedure, and that they are counted and reported honestly with the official results made public;

(7.5) – respect the right of citizens to seek political or public office, individually or as representatives of political parties or organizations, without discrimination;

(7.6) – respect the right of individuals and groups to establish, in full freedom, their own political parties or other political organizations and provide such political parties and organizations with the necessary legal guarantees to enable them to compete with each other on a basis of equal treatment before the law and by the authorities;

(7.7) – ensure that law and public policy work to permit political campaigning to be conducted in a fair and free atmosphere in which neither administrative action, violence nor intimidation bars the parties and the candidates from freely presenting their views and qualifications, or prevents the voters from learning and discussing them or from casting their vote free of fear of retribution;

(7.8) – provide that no legal or administrative obstacle stands in the way of unimpeded access to the media on a non-discriminatory basis for all political groupings and individuals wishing to participate in the electoral process;

(7.9) – ensure that candidates who obtain the necessary number of votes required by law are duly installed in office and are permitted to remain in office until their term expires or is otherwise brought to an end in a manner that is regulated by law in conformity with democratic parliamentary and constitutional procedures.

---

[106] ECtHR, *Tănase and Chirtoacă v Moldova*, Application No 7/08 (2008).
[107] ACmHPR, *Legal Resources Foundation v Zambia*, Communication No 211/1998 (2001).

(8) – The participating States consider that the presence of observers, both foreign and domestic, can enhance the electoral process for States in which elections are taking place. They therefore invite observers from any other [OSCE] participating States and any appropriate private institutions and organizations who may wish to do so to observe the course of their national election proceedings, to the extent permitted by law.

3. Equal access to public service

Like most regional conventions,[108] the ICCPR embodies in Article 25(c) the right of access, on terms of equality, to public office and public service in the executive, the judiciary and the legislature as further participation in the conduct of public affairs. It is clear from the wording of this provision that the right of equal access to public service does not imply any individual entitlement to accede to a particular office or position; rather, such access, ie the selection of candidates, must be based on terms of equality and, in particular, it must be non-discriminatory.[109]

The right of equal access is not violated by temporary affirmative measures enacted on behalf of genuinely disadvantaged population groups in order to ensure equal access to public service.[110] For instance, civil service positions may, as a general rule, not be reserved for members of a majority ethnic group or religion but temporary affirmative measures on behalf of genuinely disadvantaged population groups are permissible.[111] Thus, in view of the clear under-representation of women in the Belgian judiciary, the Human Rights Committee held that a quota requirement to the effect that an eleven-member advisory body on judicial appointments be composed of at least four persons of each sex was in conformity with this guarantee.[112] The extent to which this provision precludes states from disqualifying members of allegedly extremist parties or radical religious communities from public service employment depends on the specific circumstances of the case.[113]

The principles laid down by ICCPR, Article 25(c) are also applicable to dismissals of public employees and office holders, including judges.[114] The Human Rights Committee requires states parties to enact laws setting out in abstract terms the permissible grounds for dismissal of persons from public service.[115]

---

[108] The ECHR is the exception.
[109] See for example, HRCttee, *Hinostroza Solís v Peru*, Communication No 1016/2001 (2006), para 6.2.
[110] HRCttee, General Comment No 25 (1996), para 23.
[111] HRCttee, General Comment No 25 (1996), para 23.
[112] HRCttee, *Jacobs v Belgium*, Communication No 943/2000 (2004), paras 9.3–9.6.
[113] See, for example, HRCttee, Concluding Observations Germany (2004), para 19.
[114] See, for example, HRCttee, *Kall v Poland*, Communication No 552/1993 (1997), paras 13; and *Busyo et al v The Democratic Republic of the Congo*, Communication No 933/2000 (2003), para 5.2.
[115] HRCttee, General Comment No 25 (1996), paras 16 and 23.

It also demands that decisions to dismiss someone rest on objective and reasonable grounds.[116] These principles are of great practical importance, especially in cases of regime change[117] or where an autocratic regime seeks to divest itself of an inconvenient judiciary.[118]

[116] See, eg, HRCttee, *Jacobs v Belgium*, Communication No 943/2000 (2004), para 9.3, and *Raosavljevic v Bosnia and Herzegovina,* Communication No 1219/2003 (2007), para 7.6.

[117] See, for example, HRCttee, Concluding Observations Germany (1996), para 17: 'The Committee expresses its concern that the criteria used to evaluate for retaining or dismissing former GDR public servants, including judges and teachers, are vague and leave open the possibility for deprivation of employment on the basis of political opinions held or expressed. The Committee therefore suggests that the criteria for dismissing public servants of the former GDR be made more precise so that no public servant will be dismissed on the ground of political opinion held or expressed by him or her.'

[118] HRCttee, *Pastukhov v Belarus*, Communication No 814/1998 (2003), para 7.3, and Concluding Observations Belarus (1997), para 13.

17

Protection During Migration, Forced Displacement, and Flight

Relevant provisions: UDHR, Article 14; ICCPR, Articles 7, 12, 13; CAT, Article 3; CRC, Articles 10 and 22; CRPD, Article 18; ICRMW; GC IV, Article 49; AP I, Article 73; AP II, Article 17; Rome Statute, Article 7; CSR; CSSP; Guiding Principles on Internal Displacement; ACHR, Article 22; P 2/ACHPR, Articles 4, 10, 11; Convention on Territorial Asylum (Caracas) of 28 March 1954; Convention on Diplomatic Asylum (Caracas) of 28 March 1954; ACHPR, Article 12; Convention Governing the Specific Aspects of Refugee Problems in Africa of 10 September 1969; ArCHR, Articles 8, 26 and 28; ECHR, Article 3; P 4/ECHR, Article 2; P 7/ECHR, Article 1.

I. The Problem

Migration, forced displacement and flight have been part of the human experience from the earliest times. From a human rights perspective, migrants, people displaced within their own country (internally displaced persons) and refugees are groups that require special protection because they have been deprived of the security normally enjoyed by people who can remain in their homes.

Movement of persons can be voluntary or coerced and can occur within a person's own country or across international frontiers. Four distinct groups of people in need of human rights protection may be derived from combinations of these elements: (1) those who leave their homes voluntarily for economic, family-related, or other reasons to settle elsewhere within their country; (2) migrants, ie those who move to another country for the same reasons; (3) internally displaced persons (often called 'IDPs'), ie those who are forced to leave their homes to seek refuge in another part of their own country; and (4) refugees, ie those who are forced to seek protection against persecution by fleeing abroad.[1]

---

[1] This is the legal terminology as derived from existing treaty law as well as soft law instruments. Social sciences distinguish between forced and voluntary migration with IDPs and refugees belonging to the first and persons moving inside their country as well as migrants belonging to the second category. To call all these persons 'migrants' risks confusing the profound legal differences between the categories and is therefore not suitable for legal analysis.

While there are no global statistics on voluntary or economically motivated within-country movement of persons, an estimated 191 million people currently fall into the category of migrants living outside their country of origin.[2] Although many of them feel compelled to leave their homes because of poverty, unemployment or unacceptable living conditions, in legal terms their migration is nevertheless deemed 'voluntary' since they still have the option not to migrate.

The coercive nature of displacement and flight differentiates internally displaced persons and refugees from migrants. Whereas refugees accounted for the majority of displacement in the second half of the twentieth century, internally displaced persons are now more numerous. According to the Office of the UN High Commissioner for Refugees (UNHCR), there were a total of 11.4 million refugees and 647,200 asylum-seekers at the end of 2007.[3] In 2007, the number of persons internally displaced by acts of violence and armed conflict stood at about 26 million, ie more than double the number of persons who had fled abroad.[4]

II. Liberty of Movement in One's Own Country

The *right to liberty of movement and freedom to choose a residence in one's own country* is a fundamental component of personal development and is guaranteed by ICCPR, Article 12(1), ACHR, Article 22, ACHPR, Article 12, ArCHR, Article 26(1), and P 4/ECHR, Article 2. People should be able to settle where they find employment or other economic opportunities, where they are being educated or trained, or where they want to raise a family. Freedom to choose a residence includes the right to remain where one is settled and affords protection against forced displacement or relocation.[5] Freedom of movement also includes the *right to leave one's own country* (ICCPR, Article 12(2)) and hence the right to a passport.[6] These rights can be restricted by law where such action is necessary to protect national security, public order, public health or morals, or the rights of others (ICCPR, Article 12(3)). Provided they are based on one of these motives and are proportional, permissible measures include

---

[2] 'International Migration and Development', report of the UN Secretary-General of 18 May 2006, UN Doc A/60/871, para 4.

[3] UNHCR, 2007 *Global Trends: Refugees, Asylum-seekers, Returnees, Internally Displaced and Stateless Persons* (June 2008). This number of refugees does not include the 4.6 million Palestinian refugees.

[4] Global IDP Project, Norwegian Refugee Council, *Internal Displacement, Global Overview of Trends and Developments in 2007* (Châtelaine (Geneva), 2008), 7. Additional dozens of millions were displaced by natural disasters or development projects without proper relocation of those affected.

[5] See below section IV.2.

[6] HRCttee, *Vidal Martins v Uruguay*, Communication No 57/1979 (1982), para 9, and *El Dernawi v the Libyan Arab Jamahiriya*, Communication No 1143/2002 (2007), para 6.2. This right can also be invoked by nationals living abroad: HRCttee, *El Ghar v the Libyan Arab Jamahiriya*, Communication No 1107/2002 (2004).

forced evacuation from disaster areas, the establishment of restricted military zones or the establishment of restricted zones in the event of an epidemic. It is also permissible to prevent persons subject to military service from leaving the country or to deny them a passport.[7] In contrast, such measures were not proportional in a case where an arrest warrant had been pending for seven years and the person concerned continued to be denied a passport due to the pending warrant.[8]

According to Article 12(4) of the ICCPR, nobody may be arbitrarily deprived of the *right to enter his or her own country*. As stressed by the Human Rights Committee,[9] this provision has various facets. It implies the right to remain in one's own country, thus basically prohibiting expulsion or punishment by exile.[10] It guarantees the right to return not only for persons who have travelled abroad but also for those who are visiting their country for the first time because they were born abroad. The right to return is also important for refugees seeking voluntary repatriation after having fled from the danger of persecution. Although these rights are not absolute, the Human Rights Committee has stressed that there are few, if any, circumstances in which the application of a restriction to one's own nationals can be reasonable.[11]

III. Migrants

1. Entry

In principle, states are free to exercise their territorial sovereignty in regulating the entry, residence, and departure of foreigners. However, this freedom of action is limited not only by bilateral treaties and EU provisions concerning the free movement of persons[12] but also in specific cases by human rights such as the prohibition of discrimination[13] or the right to family reunification.[14]

2. Residence

The right to freedom of movement and freedom to choose one's residence under ICCPR, Article 12 is applicable not only to nationals of the country concerned

---

[7] HRCttee, *Peltonen v Finland*, Communication No 492/1992 (1994), para 8.4.
[8] HRCttee, *González del Río v Peru*, Communication No 263/1987 (1992), para 5.3.
[9] HRCttee, General Comment No 27 (1999), para 19.
[10] HRCttee, Concluding Observations Dominican Republic (1993), para 6.
[11] HRCttee, General Comment No 27 (1999), para 21.
[12] EC Treaty, Arts 39–55. See also the agreement on free movement of persons between Switzerland and the EU of 21 June 1999.
[13] CtteeERD, General Recommendation XXX (2004), para 9. See also ECtHR, *Abdulaziz and Others v The United Kingdom*, Series A, No 94 (1985).
[14] See ECtHR, *Gül v Switzerland*, *Reports* 1996-I.

but also to '[e]veryone lawfully within [the] territory' of the state. Foreigners who meet this condition are therefore also protected. However, the right is subject to restriction under paragraph 3 of Article 12. In the *Celepli v Sweden* case, for instance, the Human Rights Committee held that it was permissible to prohibit a refugee suspected of supporting terrorist activities from leaving the municipality where he lived without permission from the authorities.[15]

Regardless of their residence status, foreigners are in principle entitled to invoke all human rights *vis-à-vis* their state of residence.[16] However, only citizens enjoy the right of access to public services and the right to take part in elections and referendums (ICCPR, Article 25). Other rights, such as the right to freedom of political expression,[17] may be subject to more extensive restrictions than are permissible for a country's own nationals. Thus, differentiating between citizens and non-citizens does not *per se* constitute discrimination if differential treatment can be shown to pursue a legitimate aim.[18] Relatively strict limits may be imposed on persons without lawful residence status, especially in terms of rights that are subject to restrictions. Core human rights guarantees, however, such as the right to protection of life and physical integrity, the right to primary schooling and due process guarantees are applicable without restriction, regardless of status.

Special rights for migrants are contained in the International Convention on the Protection of the Rights of All Migrant Workers and Members of Their Families adopted in 1990. The Convention defines the term 'migrant worker' as 'a person who is to be engaged, is engaged or has been engaged in a remunerated activity in a State of which he or she is not a national' (Article 2, paragraph 1). The Convention defines the rights of migrant workers before departure, while in transit, and while working abroad and thus establishes obligations for countries of origin, transit, and employment. Although the Convention creates no entitlement to entry and residence, it sets out the rights of persons falling into the category of migrant workers in great detail, including the rights of those not lawfully resident in the country concerned (undocumented migrants). While, to a large extent, it reflects existing principles established by previous human rights instruments, some of the provisions on migrant workers in an irregular situation arguably go beyond the norms hitherto embodied in general human rights guarantees, and it is largely for this reason that the Convention has found it difficult to secure sufficient backing from states.[19]

---

[15] HRCttee, *Celepli v Sweden*, Communication No 456/1991 (1994), para 9.2.

[16] For a detailed analysis, see IACtHR, Advisory Opinion on the *Juridical Condition and Rights of Undocumented Migrants*, Series A, No 18 (2003), paras 111 ff.

[17] See ECHR, Art 16 allowing contracting states to impose restrictions on the political activity of foreigners.

[18] CtteeERD, General Recommendation XXX (2004), paras 1–4. See also HRCttee, *Karakurt v Austria*, Communication No 965/2000 (2002).

[19] The Convention only entered into force in 2003, ie 13 years after its adoption, and no state with a significant number of migrants has ratified it yet.

3. Expulsion

By virtue of the principle of territorial sovereignty, states are basically free to determine the conditions governing not only the entry but also the departure of foreigners. However, where persons are lawfully resident in the territory of a state,[20] the authorities who wish to expel or extradite them[21] must respect certain procedural guarantees.

Expulsions and deportations are unilateral acts of the state, ordering a person to leave its territory and, if necessary, forcefully removing him or her. The terminology used at the domestic or international level is not uniform but there is a clear tendency to call *expulsion* the legal order to leave the territory of a state, and *deportation* the actual implementation of such an order in cases where the person concerned does not follow it voluntarily. Expulsion and deportation as unilateral acts must be distinguished from *extradition*, ie the surrender of a person accused or convicted of a criminal act from one country to another on the basis of the latter's request.

According to ICCPR, Article 13, ICRMW, Article 22, ArCHR, Article 26[22] and P 7/ECHR, Article 1, expulsions are permissible only where two conditions are met: (1) the decision to expel is reached 'in accordance with the law', ie based upon and compatible with substantive provisions and procedural safeguards as set out by domestic law; and (2) the person concerned is, even if domestic law does not provide such guarantees, allowed to submit the reasons against his or her expulsion, to have the case reviewed by an administrative authority or a court[23] and to be represented in the proceedings; these rights may be withheld, however, where compelling reasons of national security so require. These procedural requirements were breached, for example, when the French lawyer Maître Hammel, who had lived in Madagascar for many years, was driven without warning to his home by the local police, given two hours to pack his belongings and expelled to France on the same day.[24]

These procedural provisions are purely formal and contain no substantive rights against expulsion. Nevertheless, the right to present a defence and to have the case reviewed means that a decision must be rendered in each individual case;

---

[20] Accordingly, protection under ICCPR, Art 13 ceases if a person remains in a state after the expiry of his or her permit (see HRCttee, General Comment No 15 (1986), para 9). However, ICRMW, Art 22 goes beyond this limitation by granting rights to all migrant workers regardless of whether or not their stay is regular according to domestic law.

[21] ICCPR, Art 13 is applicable to all kinds of removal measures, including extradition (see HRCttee, *Kindler v Canada*, Communication No 470/1991 (1993), para 6.6).

[22] ArCHR, Art 26(2) does not grant the right to be represented. ACHR, Art 22(6) embodies a guarantee against being expelled based on a decision that is not in accordance with law, but does not contain the procedural guarantees contained in the ICCPR.

[23] ICCPR, Art 13 and P 7/ECHR, Art 1 confer no right of access to a court, so that the designation of a competent authority is left to domestic legislation.

[24] HRCttee, *Hammel v Madagascar*, Communication No 155/1983 (1987), para 18.2.

it follows that *collective expulsions*, whereby members of a particular group are collectively required to leave a country without an individual examination of each case, are incompatible with human rights law.[25]

Further substantive restrictions can be derived from other human rights. The right to protection of the family is particularly important since it prohibits expulsions in cases where the family cannot be expected to follow its expelled member abroad and where the family's interest in continuing to live together outweighs the public interests served by the removal measure.[26]

The right under ICCPR, Article 12(4) to enter one's own country has also acquired implications for foreigners since the Human Rights Committee extended the scope of this provision. In the *Stewart v Canada* case,[27] the Committee held that the concept 'his own country' is broader than the concept 'country of his nationality' and held that 'it embraces, at the very least, an individual who, because of his special ties to or claims in relation to a given country cannot there be considered to be a mere alien. This would be the case, for example, of nationals of a country who have there been stripped of their nationality in violation of international law and of individuals whose country of nationality has been incorporated into or transferred to another national entity whose nationality is being denied them.'[28] The provision can arguably also afford protection against expulsion to foreigners who, having few ties to the country of their nationality, have lived in a country since early childhood but have not had the opportunity to become a citizen. The case of Stewart who had spent most of his life in Canada demonstrates, however, that this rule does not apply to those who had the opportunity to become citizens but refused to do so.[29] The extended protection against expulsion is particularly important for second or third-generation foreigners

---

[25] See HRCttee, General Comment No 15 (1986), para 10; CtteeERD, General Recommendation XXX (2004), para 26. See also ACHPR, Art 12(5), ArCHR, Art 26(2) and P 4/ECHR, Art 4 which explicitly prohibit the collective expulsion of foreigners, and ACmHPR, *Union Interafricaine des Droits de l'Homme and Others v Angola*, Communication No 159/1996 (1997), paras 14 ff, and *Rencontre Africaine pour la Défense des Droits de l'Homme v Zambia*, Communication No 71/1992 (1996). As a matter of customary law, mass expulsions may be permissible in exceptional cases such as where the security and existence of a state may otherwise be seriously endangered. In any case, they must not be discriminatory or violate other human rights such as the right to life or the right to security.

[26] See Chapter 12, section III.

[27] HRCttee, *Stewart v Canada*, Communication No 538/1993 (1996), paras 12.3–12.5. Confirmed in HRCttee, *Canepa v Canada*, Communication No 558/1993 (1997).

[28] HRCttee, *Stewart v Canada*, Communication No 538/1993 (1996), para 12.4.

[29] Ibid, para 13.5: 'The question in the present case is whether a person who enters a given State under that State's immigration laws, and subject to the conditions of those laws, can regard that State as his own country when he has not acquired its nationality and continues to retain the nationality of his country of origin. The answer could possibly be positive were the country of immigration to place unreasonable impediments on the acquiring of nationality by new immigrants. But when, as in the present case, the country of immigration facilitates acquiring its nationality, and the immigrant refrains from doing so, either by choice or by committing acts that will disqualify him from acquiring that nationality, the country of immigration does not become "his own country" within the meaning of article 12, paragraph 4, of the Covenant.'

in countries where legal or factual impediments to the acquisition of nationality continue to exist even after a very long period. Thus, the protection against
expulsions that would damage family life (found in ICCPR, Article 17 and corresponding provisions in regional conventions) falls within a general protection
against expulsions based on the right to enter one's own country. It is not absolute
but protects against 'arbitrary' expulsions, ie expulsions that are not necessitated
by legitimate and overriding public interests.

Under international humanitarian law, individual or mass forcible transfers of
the civilian population or deportations of protected persons from or to an occupied territory or to any other country is prohibited unless either the security of
the affected population or military reasons so demand.[30]

4. The prohibition of inhuman treatment as an absolute limitation on expulsion, deportation and extradition

Are there restrictions on a state's freedom to decide on a person's expulsion,
deportation or extradition where the individual concerned is threatened with serious violations of human rights in the country of destination? This question arises
not only in connection with the death penalty[31] but also where a threat of torture
or similarly serious human rights violations such as disappearances exists.

Article 3(1) of the CAT answers the question in the affirmative by stating that
'[n]o State Party shall expel, return ("refouler") or extradite a person to another
State where there are substantial grounds for believing that he would be in danger
of being subjected to torture'. Article 16 of the International Convention for the
Protection of All Persons from Enforced Disappearance prohibits return in cases
of danger of disappearances under the same conditions.

The Committee against Torture has stressed that CAT, Article 3 requires
assessing the risk of torture 'on grounds that go beyond mere theory or suspicion. However, the risk does not have to meet the test of being highly probable.
The risk need not be highly probable, but it must be personal and present. In
this regard, ... the Committee has determined that the risk of torture must be
foreseeable, real and personal.'[32] According to Article 3(2), in assessing the risk
of torture 'all relevant considerations including, where applicable, the existence
in the State concerned of a consistent pattern of gross, flagrant or mass violations of human rights' must be taken into account. In this regard the Committee
held that 'the aim of such determination is to establish whether the individual

---

[30] GC IV, Art 49. See also AP I, Art 78 on limitations with respect to the evacuation of children.
According to Art 8(2)(a)(vii) and 8(2)(b)(viii) of the Rome Statute, the unlawful deportation or
transfer of the population of an occupied territory constitute a war crime.

[31] See Chapter 9, section II.2.c.iii.

[32] CtteeAT, *RK et al v Sweden*, Communication No 309/2006 (2008), para 8.3 with reference to its General Comment No 1 (1996), paras 6–7. This has been a standard formula since the
Committee's first case on Article 3: See *Mutombo v Switzerland*, Communication No 13/1993
(1994), para 9.3.

concerned would be personally at risk in the country to which he would return. It follows that the existence of a consistent pattern of gross, flagrant or mass violations of human rights in a country does not as such constitute a sufficient ground for determining that a particular person would be in danger of being subjected to torture upon his or her return to that country; additional grounds must exist to show that the individual concerned would be personally at risk. Similarly, the absence of a consistent pattern of gross violations of human rights does not mean that a person cannot be considered to be in danger of being subjected to torture in his or her specific circumstances.'[33]

Article 3 of the CAT is applicable only where there is a threat of torture within the meaning of Article 1. Hence, torture and severe mistreatment by private actors fall outside the scope of protection of this article.[34] However, in the *Elmi v Australia* case, the Committee against Torture held that the *de facto* authorities in a country where the central government had collapsed (Somalia) came within the scope of the concept of 'public officials or other persons acting in an official capacity' under CAT, Article 1.[35] The same must be true for *de facto* authorities in parts of a country no longer under the authority of the central government.

The drafters of Article 3 of the CAT were inspired by, and have largely codified an approach developed within, the framework of the European Convention on Human Rights. As the act of knowingly surrendering a person to his or her torturers is in itself inhumane, the European Court of Human Rights has long derived from the right to protection against inhuman treatment under ECHR, Article 3 a prohibition on the forcible transfer of a person to a state where he or she is exposed to the risk of being killed, tortured or exposed to similarly serious human rights violations,[36] including, eg, disappearances.

According to the settled jurisprudence of the European Court of Human Rights, expulsion, deportation or extradition[37] to another state are prohibited when *there are substantial grounds to believe that an individual would face a real risk of torture, of inhuman or degrading treatment or punishment*[38] or of being killed.[39]

---

[33] Ibid, para 8.2.

[34] On the limitation of the definition of torture in CAT, Art 1 to *state torture*, see Chapter 10, section II.1.a.

[35] CtteeAT, *Elmi v Australia*, Communication No 120/1998 (1999), para 6.5.

[36] Although the former European Commission of Human Rights had held since the 1960s that such a prohibition of deportation could be derived from ECHR, Art 3 (*Amekrane v The United Kingdom*, Application No 5961/72, *Yearbook* 16 (1973), 357; the United Kingdom agreed to a friendly settlement after the Commission declared the complaint admissible), the Court had its first opportunity to endorse this approach in an extradition case in ECtHR, *Soering v The United Kingdom*, Series A, No 161 (1989).

[37] ECtHR, *Soering v The United Kingdom*, Series A, No 161 (1989) (extradition); *Cruz Varas v Sweden*, Series A, No 201 (1991) (expulsion and deportation) and many other cases.

[38] This is the Court's standard formula. See for example, ECtHR (Grand Chamber), *Chahal v The United Kingdom*, *Reports* 1996-V, para 74.

[39] In the case of *Bahaddar v The Netherlands*, Application No 25894/94 (1995), the ECmHR recognized in its report of 13 September 1996 (published as annex to the Judgment of the Court in

This is a prohibition that can be invoked by everyone, including deserters,[40] criminal offenders[41] and suspected terrorists,[42] as well as asylum-seekers and refugees.[43] The prohibition is applicable not only in cases where the government of the country of destination is involved in torture and ill-treatment but where security forces carry out acts of torture *ultra vires*, ie while manifestly abusing their authority,[44] or where the risk emanates from non-state actors in an internal armed conflict[45] or even from private groups or individuals.[46]

The Court even found that returning a convicted criminal who had served his sentence and was in the final stages of HIV/AIDS to the Caribbean would amount to inhuman treatment as he would be unable to rely on family, social, medical, or financial support and would be likely to spend the final months of his life on the street.[47] Recently, the Court[48] clarified that this was an exceptional case and concluded that ECHR, Article 3 does not, in principle, prohibit deportations even if the state of health and life expectancy of a person would sharply diminish as 'in such cases the alleged future harm would emanate not from the intentional acts or omissions of public authorities or non-State bodies, but instead from a naturally occurring illness and the lack of sufficient resources to deal with it in the receiving country'.[49]

This is not, as highlighted in a dissenting opinion by three judges, a convincing line of reasoning: It is not torture or other forms of state action in the foreign country that are at issue but whether or not it would appear to be inhuman to deport a person in light of what would happen to him or her.

Reports 1998-I) in para 78 that the prohibition of expulsion under ECHR, Art 3 was also applicable in principle where a person's right to life was threatened.

[40] ECtHR, *Said v The Netherlands*, *Reports* 2005-VI.

[41] ECtHR, *Soering v The United Kingdom*, Series A, No 161 (1989); *HLR v France (Grand Chamber)*, *Reports* 1997-III; *D v The United Kingdom*, *Reports* 1997-III.

[42] ECtHR (Grand Chamber), *Chahal v The United Kingdom*, *Reports* 1996-V, and *Saadi v Italy*, Application No 37201/06 (2008).

[43] ECtHR *Cruz Varas v Sweden*, Series A, No 201 (1991) and *Ahmed v Austria* (Grand Chamber), *Reports* 1996-VI and *Ismoilov and Others v Russia*, Application No 2947/06 (2008).

[44] ECtHR (Grand Chamber), *Chahal v The United Kingdom*, *Reports* 1996-V.

[45] ECtHR (Grand Chamber), *Ahmed v Austria*, *Reports* 1996-VI.

[46] ECtHR, *HLR v France* (Grand Chamber), *Reports* 1997-III, *N v Finland*, Application No 38885/02 (2005), para 163, and *Salah Sheekh v The Netherlands*, Application No 1948/04 (2007), paras 139 ff.

[47] ECtHR, *D v The United Kingdom*, *Reports* 1997-III.

[48] ECtHR (Grand Chamber) *N v The United Kingdom*, Application No 26565/05 (2008), paras 42 ff.

[49] Ibid, para 43. Based on these considerations, the Court decided that the deportation of a Ugandan woman suffering from multiple illnesses due to HIV/Aids and whose state of health had been stabilized by therapy in the UK did not violate ECHR, Art 3. The Court admitted that an interruption of the therapy would cause a rapid degradation of her state of health, grievous suffering, and ultimately her death within a few years time. However, the antiviral medication necessary for her therapy was in principle available in Uganda, even if lack of resources meant that only half of the needy could obtain them. The argument that she could not afford the medical treatment and that the medication was not available in the area of the country she came from could not sway the Court's decision (paras 50–51).

In this regard, the Court explained:

Although the establishment of such responsibility involves an assessment of conditions in the [foreign] country against the standards of article 3, there is no question of adjudicating on or establishing the responsibility of the receiving country, whether under general international law, under the Convention or otherwise. In so far as any liability under the Convention is or may be incurred, it is liability incurred by the extraditing Contracting State by reason of its having taken action which has as a direct consequence the exposure of an individual to proscribed ill-treatment . . .[50]

For these reasons, ECHR, Article 3 can be invoked against a state party even if those concerned are to be sent to countries outside of Europe. This reasoning, in essence, rests on the idea that the acts of deportation, extradition or expulsion are inhuman acts in the sense of Article 3 if they return a person to a country where his or her most basic human rights would be seriously violated. The sending state is responsible under the Convention because the return measure constitutes a crucial element in the chain of events leading to the human rights violation in the receiving state. Thus, a violation of human rights in the form of killing or torture by the receiving country will also entail a human rights violation by the sending state for the act of rendering the individual.

The Human Rights Committee follows the same line as the European Court of Human Rights as regards expulsion, deportation, or extradition to a country where the individual concerned would face torture or a violation of the right to life.[51] In its 1992 General Comment No 20 on Article 7, it stated that 'States Parties must not expose individuals to the danger of torture or cruel, inhuman or degrading treatment or punishment upon return to another country by way of their extradition, expulsion, or refoulement'.[52] The Committee has also decided that forcible return might be prohibited if the individual concerned risks a violation of the right to life.[53] This was first recognized in extradition cases[54] and later extended to deportation.[55] The Committee assesses whether the human rights violation in the country of destination would be 'the necessary and foreseeable consequence'

---

[50] ECtHR, *Cruz Varas v Sweden*, Series A, No 201 (1991), para 69.

[51] HRCttee, General Comment No 20 (1992), para 9. HRCttee, *C v Australia*, Communication No 900/1999 (2002), para 8.5. In *Byahuranga v Denmark*, Communication No 1222/2003 (2004), para 11.3, the Human Rights Committee held that not only Byahuranga's earlier activities but also his activities in exile had to be taken into account in assessing the danger.

[52] HRCttee, General Comment No 20 (1992), para 9. Similar: HRCttee, *Ng v Canada*, Communication No 469/1991 (1993), para 14.2. See above, Chapter 9, section II.2.c.iii on extradition to a country where the person concerned would face the death penalty.

[53] HRCttee, *Kindler v Canada*, Communication No 470/1991 (1993), para 13.1.

[54] In the *Ng* case, involving an extradition from Canada to the United States where the individual concerned faced the death penalty, the Human Rights Committee observed: 'If Mr. Ng had been exposed, through extradition from Canada, to a real risk of a violation of article 6, paragraph 2, in the United States, this would have entailed a violation by Canada of its obligations under article 6, paragraph 1'; HRCttee, *Ng v Canada*, Communication No 469/1991 (1993), para 15.3.

[55] HRCttee, *GT v Australia*, Communication No 706/1996 (1997), para 8.2, and *ARJ v Australia*, Communication No 692/1996 (1997), para 6.9.

of the expulsion, deportation or extradition of the person concerned.[56] Similar to the European Court of Human Rights, it stresses that, in such cases, it is not the accountability of the country of destination that is at issue but rather the fact 'that the State party itself may be in violation of the Covenant'.[57]

Issue in focus: Diplomatic assurances in situations of high risk of torture

In the context of actions taken against international terrorism states have repeatedly resorted to extraditing suspected terrorists to countries where there exists a high risk of torture. States have justified such action with the argument that they received diplomatic assurances from the country of destination that its authorities would not resort to torture. Experience shows that such promises are often not kept. This happened, for instance, in the case of two alleged terrorists, Mr Agiza and Mr Alzery, who were handed over by Sweden to Egyptian authorities and subsequently tortured (see cases below).

Such incidences raise the question as to whether international human rights law allows extradition to countries where a serious risk exists if diplomatic assurances are given. Present case law indicates that extradition in such cases is neither automatically permissible nor entirely prohibited; rather, admissibility of such extraditions depends on the quality of the assurances in each specific case and the context in which it was provided. In this sense, the European Court of Human Rights, in a general manner, indicated that diplomatic assurances do not absolve it 'from the obligation to examine whether such assurances provided, in their practical application, a sufficient guarantee that the applicant would be protected against the risk of treatment prohibited by the Convention... The weight to be given to assurances from the receiving State depends, in each case, on the circumstances obtaining at the material time.'[58]

In line with this approach, the Committee against Torture concluded in the case of *Agiza v Sweden* that Sweden had violated CAT, Article 3 because, based on the circumstances of the case and given the lack of effective supervision of the given assurances by the Swedish Embassy in Cairo, a high risk of torture was discernible in advance. The absence of any possibility for an alleged terrorist to contest the decision of deportation in front of an independent authority under Swedish law was also found to be incompatible with the procedural requirements flowing from Article 3.[59]

The other victim, Mr Alzery, turned to the Human Rights Committee which also found a violation, mainly because Sweden had not ensured that the implementation of Egypt's assurances could be effectively supervised.[60] In this regard, it highlighted the following:

11.4 The Committee notes that, in the present case, the State party itself has conceded that there was a risk of ill-treatment that—without more—would have prevented the

---

[56] HRCttee, *GT v Australia*, Communication No 706/1996 (1997), paras 8.1 and 8.6; *ARJ v Australia*, Communication No 692/1996 (1997), paras 6.8, 6.10, 6.12, 6.14.

[57] HRCttee, *GT v Australia*, Communication No 706/1996 (1997), para 8.2, and *ARJ v Australia*, Communication No 692/1996 (1997), para 6.9.

[58] ECtHR (Grand Chamber), *Saadi v Italy*, Application No 37201/06 (2008), para 148.

[59] CtteeAT, *Agiza v Sweden*, Communication No 233/2003 (2005), paras 13.2 ff.

[60] HRCttee, *Alzery v Sweden*, Communication No 1416/2005 (2006).

expulsion of the author consistent with its international human rights obligations (see *supra*, at para 3.6). The State party in fact relied on the diplomatic assurances alone for its belief that the risk of proscribed ill-treatment was sufficiently reduced to avoid breaching the prohibition on refoulement.

11.5 The Committee notes that the assurances procured contained no mechanism for monitoring of their enforcement. Nor were any arrangements made outside the text of the assurances themselves which would have provided for effective implementation. The visits by the State party's ambassador and staff commenced five weeks after the return, neglecting altogether a period of maximum exposure to risk of harm. The mechanics of the visits that did take place, moreover, failed to conform to key aspects of international good practice by not insisting on private access to the detainee and inclusion of appropriate medical and forensic expertise, even after substantial allegations of ill-treatment emerged. In light of these factors, the State party has not shown that the diplomatic assurances procured were in fact sufficient in the present case to eliminate the risk of ill-treatment to a level consistent with the requirements of article 7 of the Covenant. The author's expulsion thus amounted to a violation of article 7 of the Covenant.

The criteria developed by the Human Rights Committee focus on effective supervisory mechanisms and thus impose on the extraditing state a duty to protect continuing for a potentially prolonged period of time after the handover of the individual concerned. In practice, this burden on the sending country is rather heavy, thus creating a high threshold for the admissibility of extradition or deportation based on diplomatic assurances to a country with a generally high risk of torture. Despite certain criticism,[61] a similar approach is taken by the European Court of Human Rights.[62]

The prohibition of expulsion, extradition or deportation to a country where there are substantial grounds to believe that an individual would face a real risk of torture is absolute. This means that it is also applicable to cases in which refugee law[63] would allow sending a person back to his or her country of persecution; thus the protection afforded by ICCPR, Article 7, CAT, Article 3, and ECHR, Article 3 is wider than that provided by the Convention on the Status of Refugees.[64]

[61] Taking into account all the difficulties inherent in diplomatic assurances, UN Special Rapporteur on Torture Manfred Nowak concluded that they 'are not legally binding, undermine existing obligations of States to prohibit torture and are ineffective and unreliable in ensuring the protection of returned persons, and therefore shall not be resorted to by States' (Report of the Special Rapporteur on torture and other cruel, inhuman or degrading treatment or punishment, Manfred Nowak, UN Doc A/61/259 (2006), para 2, referring to his 2006 Report to the Human Rights Commission, UN Doc E/CN.4/2006/6, paras 28–33).

[62] See ECtHR, *Chahal v The United Kingdom* (Grand Chamber), *Reports* 1996-V, para 105, *Saadi v Italy* (Grand Chamber), Application No 37201/06 (2008), paras 147 f, *Ismoilov and Others v Russia*, Application No 2947/06 (2008), para 127, and *Soldatenko v Ukraine*, Application No 2440/07 (2008), para 73.

[63] Art 33(2) of the Convention on the Status of Refugees allows forcible return to the country of persecution in the case of 'a refugee whom there are reasonable grounds for regarding as a danger to the security of the country in which he is, or who, having been convicted by a final judgment of a particularly serious crime, constitutes a danger to the community of that country'.

[64] ECtHR (Grand Chamber), *Chahal v The United Kingdom*, *Reports* 1996-V, para 80, and *Saadi v Italy*, Application No 37201/06 (2008), para 138.

Example: The ECtHR judgment in *Saadi v Italy*[65]

In this case, the European Court of Human Rights had to pronounce on the admissibility of the deportation to Tunisia of a member of a terrorist organization. During the court proceedings, Italy, as well as the United Kingdom, argued that the absolute prohibition enshrined in ECHR, Article 3 should not apply in cases where the issue was not torture carried out by the state against whom the application is brought but by a third state receiving the deported person; particularly in cases of terrorists, the sending state should be entitled to balance its security interests with the interests of the individual concerned. The Court rejected this position with the following arguments:

137. The Court notes first of all that States face immense difficulties in modern times in protecting their communities from terrorist violence... It cannot therefore underestimate the scale of the danger of terrorism today and the threat it presents to the community. That must not, however, call into question the absolute nature of Article 3.

138. Accordingly, the Court cannot accept the argument of the United Kingdom Government, supported by the respondent Government, that a distinction must be drawn under Article 3 between treatment inflicted directly by a signatory State and treatment that might be inflicted by the authorities of another State, and that protection against this latter form of ill-treatment should be weighed against the interests of the community as a whole... Since protection against the treatment prohibited by Article 3 is absolute, that provision imposes an obligation not to extradite or expel any person who, in the receiving country, would run the real risk of being subjected to such treatment. As the Court has repeatedly held, there can be no derogation from that rule... It must therefore reaffirm the principle stated in the Chahal judgment... that it is not possible to weigh the risk of ill-treatment against the reasons put forward for the expulsion in order to determine whether the responsibility of a State is engaged under Article 3, even where such treatment is inflicted by another State. In that connection, the conduct of the person concerned, however undesirable or dangerous, cannot be taken into account, with the consequence that the protection afforded by Article 3 is broader than that provided for in Articles 32 and 33 of the 1951 United Nations Convention relating to the Status of Refugees...

139. The Court considers that the argument based on the balancing of the risk of harm if the person is sent back against the dangerousness he or she represents to the community if not sent back is misconceived. The concepts of 'risk' and 'dangerousness' in this context do not lend themselves to a balancing test because they are notions that can only be assessed independently of each other. Either the evidence adduced before the Court reveals that there is a substantial risk if the person is sent back or it does not. The prospect that he may pose a serious threat to the community if not returned does not reduce in any way the degree of risk of ill treatment that the person may be subject to on return. For that reason it would be incorrect to require a higher standard of proof, as submitted by the intervener, where the person is considered to represent a serious danger to the community, since assessment of the level of risk is independent of such a test.

140. With regard to the second branch of the United Kingdom Government's arguments, to the effect that where an applicant presents a threat to national security, stronger evidence must be adduced to prove that there is a risk of ill-treatment..., the Court observes that such an approach is not compatible with the absolute nature of the protection afforded by Article 3

---

[65] ECtHR (Grand Chamber), *Saadi v Italy*, Application No 37201/06 (2008).

either. It amounts to asserting that, in the absence of evidence meeting a higher standard, protection of national security justifies accepting more readily a risk of ill-treatment for the individual. The Court therefore sees no reason to modify the relevant standard of proof, as suggested by the third-party intervener, by requiring in cases like the present that it be proved that subjection to ill-treatment is 'more likely than not'. On the contrary, it reaffirms that for a planned forcible expulsion to be in breach of the Convention it is necessary—and sufficient—for substantial grounds to have been shown for believing that there is a real risk that the person concerned will be subjected in the receiving country to treatment prohibited by Article 3...

5. Acquisition of nationality and the legal status of stateless persons

In principle, international law neither recognizes a right to acquire a particular nationality nor establishes specific criteria for the granting of citizenship.[66] States are therefore free in principle to take sovereign decisions on who should be recognized as their citizens.

Only ACHR, Article 20 and ArCHR, Article 29 deviate from this principle by enshrining a right to citizenship, a right to be protected against arbitrary deprivation of one's nationality, and a right to change nationalities. In addition, ACHR, Article 20(2) guarantees the right to claim citizenship of the territory on whose soil a person is born on condition that the person has no claim to any other citizenship. The Inter-American Court of Human Rights found the Dominican Republic to have violated the right to citizenship on these grounds. The Court based its ruling on the country's failure to justify its refusal to deliver birth certificates to children of Haitian descent born within its territory notwithstanding its adherence to the principle of *ius soli* and despite national law following this principle. The children consequently remained stateless for several years. The court considered this behaviour both arbitrary and discriminating and concluded that ACHR, Article 20 read in conjunction with the principle of equal protection of the law (ACHR, Article 24), the right to juridical personality (ACHR, Article 3), the right to a name (ACHR, Article 18) and the rights of the child (ACHR, Article 19) had been violated.[67]

States not parties to the ACHR and ArCHR, despite their sovereignty in matters of citizenship, do not possess unfettered discretion over the granting of citizenship and must refrain from *discrimination* when taking such decisions. Thus, CEDAW, Article 9 stipulates that states parties must 'grant women equal rights with men to acquire, change or retain their nationality'. Discrimination occurs, for instance, where women, but not men, lose their nationality when they marry a foreigner, where 'change of nationality by the husband during marriage shall automatically change the nationality of the wife, render her stateless or force upon her the nationality of the husband'[68] or where, conversely, only foreign

---

[66] See HRCttee, *Borzov v Estonia*, Communication No 1136/2002 (2004), para 7.4.
[67] IACtHR, *Case of the Girls Yean and Bosico v Dominican Republic*, Series C, No 130 (2005).
[68] CEDAW, Art 9(1), second sentence.

husbands can acquire the nationality of a particular country through marriage but not foreign wives.[69] Similarly, CERD, Article 5(d)(iii) prohibits distinctions in the area of nationality rights based on race, colour, or national or ethnic origin. Lastly, as the Human Rights Committee has stressed, the principle of equal protection of the law embodied in ICCPR, Article 26 implies the prohibition of the denial of citizenship on arbitrary grounds. The Committee's views deal in particular with stateless persons who can be kept in this position if a state has legitimate grounds to refuse citizenship. For instance, it is not arbitrary for a country that has recently become independent to refuse granting citizenship on grounds of national security to a senior military officer, now stateless, who was a citizen of the country that formerly controlled the territory concerned.[70] Similar to the Human Rights Committee, the African Commission on Human and People's Rights bases a prohibition of arbitrary denial of citizenship on ACHPR, Article 3(2).[71]

Thus, it can be concluded that, regardless of whether or not the text of a particular convention explicitly provides for a right to citizenship, states may exercise a high degree of discretion when deciding whom they should admit as their nationals, but such discretion must be exercised without discrimination or arbitrariness.

Some human rights provisions aim at preventing cases of statelessness. For instance, Article 7 of the Convention on the Rights of the Child requires states to enact legislation securing a child's right from birth to acquire a nationality. The Convention on the Reduction of Statelessness of 30 August 1961 obliges every contracting state to grant its nationality to persons born in its territory and regulates in detail the conditions on which nationality should be granted in other cases.

The rights of stateless persons are set out in the Convention relating to the Status of Stateless Persons,[72] a treaty ratified by a relatively small number of states. The treaty specifies the areas in which stateless persons who are lawfully in the territory of a state must be accorded the same treatment either as foreigners in the same circumstances or as the state's own citizens. For instance, stateless persons must be given access to the labour market under no less favourable conditions than foreigners admitted to employment in the country, and stateless children must be accorded the same treatment as nationals in primary education.[73]

[69] See HRCttee, General Comment No 28 (2000), para 31.

[70] HRCttee, *Borzov v Estonia*, Communication No 1136/2002 (2004), para 7.4. On the prohibition of arbitrary denial of nationality, see also ACmHPR, *Modise v Botswana*, Communication No 97/1993 (2000).

[71] ACmHPR, *Modise v Botswana*, Communication No 97/1993 (2000).

[72] Convention relating to the Status of Stateless Persons of 28 September 1954 (CSSP, 63 states parties as of 22 December 2008). The content and structure of this Convention are based to a large extent on those of the 1951 Convention relating to the Status of Refugees.

[73] CSSP, Arts 17–19, 22 and 24.

IV. Internally Displaced Persons (IDPs)

1. Basic principles

Internally displaced persons (IDPs) are persons who are forced or obliged to flee or leave their homes and places of residence but remain at a (relatively) safe location within their country. Thus, unlike refugees,[74] internally displaced persons remain within their own country and are therefore not in need of international protection replacing the protection of their country of origin. This explains the fundamental legal differences in the way in which the two groups are treated.

While the Refugee Convention[75] creates a wholly separate legal regime for people who have fled to another country, no specific legal norms governing the circumstances of internally displaced persons exist. As citizens or long-term residents of their state, they are entitled in principle to invoke all human rights recognized in the country concerned as well as the applicable norms of international humanitarian law during armed conflicts. However, the fact that they have left their homes involuntarily or even under coercion and are unable to return makes them particularly vulnerable and creates special needs that differentiate them from those who can remain in their homes. Particular needs for displaced persons are shelter while away from their homes and protection against being forcibly returned to danger zones. Internally displaced persons also have to deal with the loss of livelihoods and property and the subsequent difficulties encountered in trying to regain them, the replacement of documents that can only be obtained from the authorities at the place of habitual residence, and the inability to register as voters as this can only be done in the place they have left. Finally, only internally displaced persons face the challenge of finding a durable solution to their being displaced such as return to their homes, integration at their new location, or settlement in another part of the country.

The absence of specific norms addressing the specific protection needs of internally displaced persons prompted the former Representative of the UN Secretary-General for internally displaced persons, Dr Francis Deng, to submit a text drafted by a group of experts to the UN Commission on Human Rights in 1998 listing the rights of internally displaced persons. These Guiding Principles on Internal Displacement[76] (Guiding Principles) reflect, and are based upon, international human rights and humanitarian law and spell out in greater detail relevant guarantees as they are inherent in and can be derived from these bodies of law. Thus, the Guiding Principles, although legally non-binding 'soft law',[77] derive legal authority from their underlying norms. They have been 'recognize[d] . . . as an important

---

[74] See section V.1 below.
[75] Convention relating to the Status of Refugees of 28 July 1951; see section V below.
[76] UN Doc E/CN.4/1998/53/Add.2 (Annex).
[77] On this concept, see Chapter 2, section IV.

international framework for the protection of internally displaced persons' by the Heads of State and Government gathered in New York in September 2005 for the World Summit.[78] They play an important practical role in a number of countries where they have been incorporated into national laws and policies.

The Guiding Principles describe internally displaced persons as persons 'who have been forced or obliged to flee or to leave their homes or places of habitual residence, in particular as a result of or in order to avoid the effects of armed conflict, situations of generalized violence, violations of human rights or natural or human-made disasters, and who have not crossed an internationally recognized State border'. The core components of this definition are: (1) the coercive character of the flight or displacement; and (2) the fact that the internally displaced persons remain in their home country. The coercive element differentiates internally displaced persons from persons who leave their homes for economic and similar reasons based essentially on a voluntary decision. The fact that no border is crossed accounts for the difference between internally displaced persons and refugees.

What rights are enjoyed by internally displaced persons? As already mentioned, internally displaced persons are entitled to invoke all applicable human rights as well as relevant international humanitarian law guarantees during armed conflicts.[79] However, some rights are of key importance for internally displaced persons because of the specific vulnerabilities and needs created by their displacement. Such guarantees are relevant for the stages before, during and after displacement.

2. Protection from displacement

Steps must be taken in the first place to protect people from being displaced. In this sense Principle 6 of the Guiding Principles on Internal Displacement states that everyone has the *right to be protected against being arbitrarily displaced* and provides the following as examples of causes for protection: ethnic cleansing; forced evacuation during armed conflicts that is not necessary for the security of the civilians involved or imperative military reasons; forced resettlement in cases of large-scale infrastructural and development projects that are not justified by compelling and overriding public interests; evacuation in cases of disasters, unless the safety and health of those affected so requires; and displacement as a form of collective punishment. This list indicates that there are cases of displacement that, although forced, are lawful. Such cases include evacuations from danger zones in the event of an armed conflict or a major natural disaster in order to protect people from harm or relocations in accordance with the law and applicable human rights standards as a consequence of development projects such as dams, highways, airports and the like. Even where displacement is not arbitrary,

---

[78] 2005 World Summit Outcome, UN General Assembly Resolution A/Res/60/1 (2005), para 132.
[79] Despite the similarity of the factual circumstances, refugee law, which accords a lower level of protection than that accorded to the citizens of the state of refuge, is not applicable.

those concerned remain internally displaced persons entitled to protection of their rights during and after displacement.

The prohibition of arbitrary displacement is forged from a synthesis of three sets of norms. In the area of human rights, ICCPR, Article 12(1) guarantees every-one not just freedom of movement but also the right 'to choose [one's] residence', which includes the right to remain in the place of one's choice and not be dis-placed.[80] The Inter-American Court of Human Rights also deduces the prohib-ition of forced displacement from the right to freedom of movement in ACHR, Article 22.[81] International humanitarian law contains more specific guarantees. According to Article 17 of Additional Protocol II, in internal armed conflicts '[t]he displacement of the civilian population shall not be ordered for reasons related to the conflict unless the security of the civilians involved or imperative military reasons so demand' (paragraph 1). Article 49(2) of GC IV contains a similar provision concerning occupied territories in international armed con-flicts. These provisions have acquired the status of customary law.[82] Lastly, dis-placement has been declared a criminal act under international criminal law. According to Article 7(1)(d) of the Rome Statute of the International Criminal Court, the systematic or widespread 'deportation or forcible transfer of popula-tion' is a crime against humanity, which is defined as 'forced displacement of the persons concerned by expulsion or other coercive acts from the area in which they are lawfully present, without grounds permitted under international law'.[83] Violations of the prohibitions of displacement under international humanitarian law are prosecuted as war crimes.[84]

Issue in focus: Ethnic cleansing as a crime against humanity

Ethnic cleansing, ie the forced displacement of a particular ethnic group from a given territory in order to create an ethnically homogenous area, is liable to prosecution as a crime against humanity, namely that of 'persecution' on racist, religious, political or other grounds.[85] Based on the Statute of the International Criminal Tribunal for the Former Yugoslavia[86] the crime of persecution was the basis of a conviction for ethnic cleansing in the *Kupreskic* case:[87]

749....On 16 April 1993, in a matter of few hours, some 116 inhabitants, including women and children, of Ahmici, a small village in central Bosnia, were killed and about 24 were

---

[80] Explicitly stated in HRCttee, General Comment No 27 (1999), para 7.
[81] IACtHR, *Case of the Mapiripán Massacre v Colombia*, Series C, No 134 (2005), para 188.
[82] See Jean-Marie Henckaerts and Louise Doswald-Beck, *Customary International Humanitarian Law*, vol I: Rules (Cambridge University Press: Cambridge, 2005), rule 129.
[83] Rome Statute, Art 7(2)(d).   [84] Rome Statute, Art 8(2)(b)(viii) and (e)(viii).
[85] Rome Statute, Art 7(1)(h) includes among crimes against humanity '[p]ersecution against any identifiable group or collectivity on political, racial, national, ethnic, cultural, religious, gender... or other grounds that are universally recognized as impermissible under international law, in connec-tion with any act referred to in this paragraph or any crime within the jurisdiction of the Court'.
[86] Statute of the International Criminal Tribunal for the Former Yugoslavia (SICTY), Art 5(h).
[87] ICTY, *The Prosecutor v Kupreskic et al*, Case No IT-95-16-T (2000).

wounded; 169 houses and two mosques were destroyed. The victims were Muslim civilians. The Trial Chamber is satisfied, on the evidence before it in this case, that this was not a combat operation. Rather, it was a well-planned and well-organised killing of civilian members of an ethnic group, the Muslims, by the military of another ethnic group, the Croats. The primary purpose of the massacre was to expel the Muslims from the village, by killing many of them, by burning their houses and their livestock, and by illegally detaining and deporting the survivors to another area. The ultimate goal of these acts was to spread terror among the population so as to deter the members of that particular ethnic group from ever returning to their homes...

751. Persecution is one of the most vicious of all crimes against humanity. It nourishes its roots in the negation of the principle of the equality of human beings. Persecution is grounded in discrimination. It is based upon the notion that people who share ethnic, racial, or religious bonds different to those of a dominant group are to be treated as inferior to the latter. In the crime of persecution, this discriminatory intent is aggressively achieved by grossly and systematically trampling upon the fundamental human rights of the victim group. Persecution is only one step away from genocide...In the crime of genocide the criminal intent is to destroy the group or its members; in the crime of persecution the criminal intent is instead to forcibly discriminate against a group or members thereof by grossly and systematically violating their fundamental human rights. In the present case...the killing of Muslim civilians was primarily aimed at expelling the group from the village, not at destroying the Muslim group as such. This is therefore a case of persecution, not of genocide.

3. Protection during displacement

Principle 1 of the Guiding Principles reaffirms that people who are displaced but have not left their country enjoy the protection of all the guarantees of human rights and international humanitarian law applicable to the population of the country concerned. In addition to rights that are also vital for non-displaced persons, such as the prohibitions of torture and arbitrary killing, three categories of guarantees are of special importance for internally displaced persons:

(1) *Prohibitions of discrimination*: As experience shows, internally displaced persons are frequently confronted in the areas where they seek refuge with prejudice or downright hostility on the part of authorities and local populations. The risk of discrimination is particularly acute in situations of internal armed conflict if the internally displaced persons belong to, or are suspected of politically supporting, the same ethnic or religious group as the insurgents. Displaced women often suffer multiple discriminations based on displacement as well as gender. In such cases protection is afforded by the general prohibition of discrimination based on race, ethnic origin, religion, political opinion or sex and, in addition, by Guiding Principle 1 stipulating that displaced persons may not be discriminated against 'on the ground that they are internally displaced'.[88] Protection against discrimination is of practical

---

[88] Although the prohibitions of discrimination under human rights treaties (especially ICCPR, Arts 2(1) and 26) do not include displacement among the relevant characteristics, they can be subsumed under the 'other status' characteristic in the treaties concerned.

importance in this context in connection with, for example, the exercise of political rights,[89] since internally displaced persons are often prevented from participating in ballots on the ground that the right to vote and to stand for election may be exercised only in one's place of residence.

(2) *Freedom of movement*: The right to freedom of movement guarantees internally displaced persons the right to flee from danger zones and seek safety in another part of the country; but it also gives them the right to leave the country and seek asylum in another state.[90] Internally displaced persons enjoy protection against forcible return to zones where their life, safety, liberty or health would be at immediate risk.[91] Internally displaced persons living in camps have the right to move freely in and out of their camp.[92] Closed camps are prohibited unless internment is unavoidable on important grounds; and in such cases, internment should not last any longer than is absolutely necessary.[93] As stressed by the Inter-American and European Courts of Human Rights, the right to freedom of movement creates positive obligations for states to ensure the return of displaced persons to their original place of residence as quickly as possible if they had to flee because of acts of violence committed by, or imputable to, the state.[94]

(3) *Protection in respect of special needs*: As internally displaced persons are unable to attend to their own needs during flight or evacuation and while in displacement, they are particularly dependent on humanitarian assistance in order to obtain food, housing, medical care and other necessities. They may therefore invoke the corresponding social rights guaranteeing access to such goods and services.[95] The same is true for the educational needs of the displaced given that they are often excluded from schools while in displacement.[96] Particularly important are measures to address the specific needs of women as well as other vulnerable groups such as children, persons with disabilities, those suffering from HIV/AIDS or older persons.[97]

---

[89] Principle 22(d) of the Guiding Principles on Internal Displacement.

[90] Principle 15(a)–(c) of the Guiding Principles on Internal Displacement. This provision is based, *inter alia*, on ICCPR, Art 12 and UDHR, Art 14.

[91] Principle 15(d) of the Guiding Principles on Internal Displacement. This is based on an analogous application of the jurisprudence under ECHR, Art 3 and under ICCPR, Art 7 and CAT, Art 3 regarding the inhumanity of forcible return where there is a risk of torture or death (see section III.4 above and Chapter 10, section II).

[92] Principle 14(b) of the Guiding Principles on Internal Displacement. This entitlement is derived from the right to freedom of movement under ICCPR, Art 12.

[93] Principle 12(2) of the Guiding Principles on Internal Displacement, which is based, *inter alia*, on ICCPR, Art 9.

[94] IACtHR, *Case of Moiwana Community v Suriname*, Series C, No 124 (2005), para 120, and ECtHR, *Degan and Others v Turkey*, Applications Nos 8803–8811/02 and 8815–8819/02 (2004), para 154.

[95] See Principles 18 and 19 of the Guiding Principles on Internal Displacement.

[96] See Principle 23 of the Guiding Principles on Internal Displacement.

[97] See Principles 4(2), 11, 13, 18(3), 19(2), 20(3), and 23 of the Guiding Principles on Internal Displacement.

(4) *Documentation*: A special problem that often besets internally displaced persons is the fact that they no longer possess official papers such as identity cards, passports, or marriage or birth certificates and cannot obtain new papers as, under the laws of the country concerned, such documents may be issued only at a person's habitual place of residence, to which internally displaced persons are by definition unable to return. The right of every human being under ICCPR, Article 16 to recognition as a person before the law may be interpreted as implying that the *de facto* exercise of this right in the case of internally displaced persons cannot be inhibited by requirements, such as those just mentioned, which they are unable to meet.[98]

4. Protection after the end of displacement

When the causes of flight or displacement have ceased, internally displaced persons have the right either voluntarily to return to their original place of residence, to begin a new life in the area to which they were displaced (local integration) or to settle in another part of the country.[99] This freedom of choice is derived from the right to liberty of movement and freedom to choose one's residence.[100] Return, in particular, is often only possible if safety and security are restored and where conditions are created that, like access to livelihoods and basic services including health and education, allow the resumption of normal life. Of particular importance is the obligation of authorities to assist internally displaced persons in recovering their property or, if this is not possible, obtaining compensation.[101]

V. Refugees

1. Definition of a refugee

Rather than characterizing everyone who has been forced to flee from his or her home as a refugee, international refugee law has established its own narrower definition. According to Article 1(A)(2) of the 1951 Convention relating to the Status of Refugees (CSR), a refugee is any person who 'owing to a well-founded fear of being persecuted for reasons of race, religion, nationality, membership of a particular social group or political opinion, is outside the country of his nationality and is

---

[98] See Principle 20(2) of the Guiding Principles on Internal Displacement.
[99] Principle 28 of the Guiding Principles on Internal Displacement. The right to return has been confirmed by the UN Security Council on occasion. See, for example UN Security Council Resolutions 1795 (2008), para 7 (Cote d'Ivoire); 1770 (2007), para 2(b)(i) (Iraq), and 1756 (2007), para 2(b) (Democratic Republic of Congo). The right to return is also guaranteed in many peace agreements, eg Dayton Peace Agreement for Bosnia and Herzegovina (1995), Annex 7, Art I(1), Comprehensive Peace Accord for Nepal (2006), para 7.3.3.
[100] ICCPR, Art 12.
[101] Principle 29(2) of the Guiding Principles on Internal Displacement.

unable or, owing to such fear, is unwilling to avail himself of the protection of that country'. A core component of the definition of a refugee under international law is the concept of *being persecuted for specific reasons*. The definition comprises three key elements: (1) a stay outside of one's country of origin; (2) the severance of relations between the applicant and the persecuting state; and (3) a well-founded fear of persecution on racial, religious, political or other relevant grounds.

The requirement that the refugee should be abroad does not mean that the person concerned must have fled, ie left his or her home country on account of persecution. A refugee in the legal sense can also be someone who as a tourist, a student or a gainfully employed person was caught unexpectedly while abroad by a change of regime in his or her home country (objective reasons subsequent to flight). The same applies to those who take an active stance against their country's government only after leaving the country and must therefore fear persecution on return (subjective reasons subsequent to flight).[102]

The criterion of *severance of relations with the persecuting state* reflects the belief that refugees need special protection under international law because their home country will neither allow them to enjoy the rights available to the population at large back home nor offer them diplomatic protection abroad if there rights are disregarded in the country of refuge. This is clearly reflected in the wording of CSR Article 1(A)(2), which requires that a refugee should be 'unable, or…unwilling to avail himself of the protection of' his country of origin. Refugees are unable to avail themselves of the protection of their home country if the country of persecution itself, as in the case of withdrawal of citizenship, severs relations with the persecuted person. More frequently, the severance is initiated by the individual, who refuses to return home on account of the risk of persecution. In both cases, the legal status afforded to refugees and the fact that the Office of the High Commissioner for Refugees (UNHCR) is mandated[103] to intervene on their behalf with the authorities of the country of refuge, if necessary, create a certain degree of international protection substituting the protection no longer available from the country of origin.

The subjective will to break off relations is not sufficient for the acquisition of refugee status. Rather, it must be based on objective grounds arising out of previous persecution or the threat of persecution.[104] Thus, the 'well-founded fear of being persecuted' is a core component of the definition of a refugee. This requirement is met under the following (cumulative) circumstances:

(1) The person has already suffered *serious adverse treatment* or has reason to fear such treatment in the future. The term 'serious' denotes, in particular,

---

[102] A number of states do not grant asylum in the second case but respect the prohibition on forcible return.

[103] See CSR, Art 35, requiring the contracting parties to cooperate with the UNHCR in the exercise of its functions and to facilitate its duty of supervising the application of the Convention and UN General Assembly Resolution 428(V) of 14 December 1950, Statute of UNHCR, para 2.

[104] CSR, Art 1(A)(2); see UNHCR, *Handbook on Procedures and Criteria for Determining Refugee Status*, para 100.

killing, torture, inhuman treatment and long-term detention. In contrast, mere discrimination or the violation of economic, social and cultural rights do not reach the threshold of persecution unless a person's physical integrity is thereby endangered, for instance through the denial of basic medical care in a life-threatening situation.

(2) The adverse treatment is *intentionally* inflicted on the person concerned, ie the effect may not be merely fortuitous. Thus, a person who happens to get caught between the fronts in an internal armed conflict is not, for example, considered to be a refugee. However, civilians who are targeted because they are on the 'wrong' side of the conflict or are suspected of supporting the adverse party would qualify as refugees.

(3) The adverse treatment must be inflicted for specific *reasons*, ie because of the race, religion, nationality, membership of a particular social group, or political opinions of the persecuted person. Human rights violations do not qualify as persecution where they are perpetrated for other reasons. Sometimes it is difficult to draw the line between relevant and other motives, eg in the case of women victim of domestic violence. The refusal of the police or the judiciary to intervene on their behalf may amount to persecution if such refusal is based on the assumption that women are second-class citizens not deserving the full protection of the law.[105]

(4) The persecution must either have already occurred and have a *causal* link with a person's flight, or the *fear* of future persecution must be *real* and objectively *well-founded*.[106]

(5) As regards the agent of persecution, relevant persecution is usually inflicted by the state and its authorities. The acts of private perpetrators are relevant if the state condones their activities or is otherwise *unwilling* to protect the victim. The large majority of states also recognize as refugees persons persecuted by private actors where the state of origin is *unable* to protect them. If, however, a person falling victim to private persecution can get protection from state authorities, refugee status will not be granted even if all the other elements of persecution are present.

This definition of a refugee does not cover everyone who is compelled to seek protection abroad. While people fleeing from armed conflict or other situations of generalized violence may also be refugees in the legal sense, many among them may not be individually at risk of persecution but seeking refuge from the general dangers associated with armed conflicts. They are protected by the broader

---

[105] In this sense House of Lords, *Islam (AP) v Secretary of State for the Home Department Regina v Immigration Appeal Tribunal and Another Ex Parte Shah (AP) (Conjoined Appeals)*, 25 March 1999.

[106] Lastly, according to the case law in many states there must be *no internal flight alternative*, ie it must be impossible or at least an unreasonable alternative for the person concerned to obtain effective protection against persecution and acceptable living conditions in another part of his or her home country.

refugee definition found in the Convention Governing the Specific Aspects of Refugee Problems in Africa of 1969,[107] which covers, in addition to refugees as defined by CSR, Article 1(A)(2) victims of external aggression, occupation, foreign domination or events seriously disturbing public order. The same is true for the so-called Cartagena Declaration on Refugees.[108]

Based on CSR, Article 1(F) those who have committed war crimes, crimes against humanity, or serious non-political crimes are excluded from refugee protection even if they are persecuted as defined above.

2. Asylum

There is no human right to asylum. Article 14 of the UDHR guarantees only the right 'to seek and to enjoy in other countries asylum from persecution' but not the right to obtain it.[109] This right, which in treaty law has only been included in ArCHR, Article 28 but arguably enjoys customary law status, is important inasmuch as it gives persecuted persons the right to leave their home country and seek protection abroad. This right is given concrete substance in CSR, Article 31 according to which refugees may not be punished for illegal entry if they come directly from the persecuting state and present themselves without delay to the authorities of the state of refuge.

The granting of asylum is a sovereign right of states. As such, it allows a state to admit refugees at its own discretion without rendering itself culpable of a hostile act or inadmissible interference *vis-à-vis* the state of origin. This right is a necessary precondition for enabling refugees to find a safe haven and remain beyond the reach of their home state.

From a negative perspective, this understanding of asylum as a right of states means that they are free to deny admission to refugees whenever they see fit. This freedom, however, is limited by the principle of non-refoulement, ie the prohibition on forcibly returning refugees to their country of persecution (see below, section 3).

Thus, asylum is the status granted to refugees on the basis of domestic law. Such status normally includes the right to remain in the country of asylum (including protection against expulsion and deportation) as well as specific rights regarding different aspects of life (economic activities, education, access to property) that can go beyond but must not fall below the status rights afforded by the CSR (see below, section 4).

---

[107] Art 1 of the Convention Governing the Specific Aspects of Refugee Problems in Africa of 10 September 1969.

[108] Cartagena Declaration on Refugees of 22 November 1984 (Annual Report of the Inter-American Commission on Human Rights, OAS Doc OEA/Ser.L/V/II.66/doc.10, rev. 1, at 190–93 (1984–85)).

[109] This effectively limits the guarantee to a dubious 'right to flee' (see Otto Kimminich, *Der internationale Rechtsstatus des Flüchtlings* (Heymann: Cologne, 1962), 81).

As a rule, asylum is granted only to refugees meeting the legal definition of applicable instruments. This leaves persons fleeing the dangers of armed conflict who are not individually at risk of persecution without protection, especially in Europe. The EU has therefore established an instrument detailing the minimum standards for giving temporary protection,[110] which provides temporary protection through the granting of admission and support without detailed examination of individual cases for a maximum period of three years in the event of mass influx of persons fleeing the dangers of a particular armed conflict.[111]

Neither the Convention relating to the Status of Refugees nor any other international treaty contains international rules governing asylum procedures.[112] It may, however, be inferred from the right to an effective remedy[113] that persons with a well-founded fear of torture and similar ill-treatment in the state to which they are to be returned have a right to an effective remedy and cannot be deprived of that remedy on the ground of denial of access to the asylum procedure.[114]

3. Non-refoulement

The principle of non-refoulement is the cornerstone of refugee law. Although it does not establish a right to asylum, it lays the basis for an internationally guaranteed *right of refugees to remain beyond the reach of the persecuting state* as long as their fear of persecution remains well-founded. The principle does not preclude states from denying refugees asylum and sending them to another state, provided that third states refrain from sending them to the country of persecution. If no other safe country is prepared to admit the refugees, they must be allowed to stay, even when denied asylum.

The proscription of forcible return is not only embodied in the human rights prohibition of inhuman treatment[115] but also in refugee law. Article 33 of the

---

[110] Council Directive 2001/55/EC of 20 July 2001 on minimum standards for giving temporary protection in the event of a mass influx of displaced persons and on measures promoting a balance of efforts between Member States in receiving such persons and bearing the consequences thereof (OJ L 212/12, 7 August 2001).

[111] Switzerland has a similar provision in Art 4 of the Asylum Act of 26 June 1998 (SR 142.31).

[112] See, however, EU Directive 2005/85/EC of 1 December 2005 on Procedures in Member States for granting and withdrawing refugee status: OJ L 326/13, 13. December 2005. The Grand Chamber of the European Court of Justice annulled Art 29(1) and (2) and Art. 36(3) of this Council Directive (co-decision procedure of the Commission and the Council to in determining the list of secure countries necessary), ECJ (Grand Chamber), Case C-133/06 *European Parliament v Council of the European Union* (2008), para 63–7.

[113] ACHR, Article 25; ACHPR, Article 7(1)(a); ArCHR, Article 9; ECHR, Article 13; ICCPR, Article 2(3).

[114] ECtHR, *Jabari v Turkey*, Reports 2000-VIII. The right to an effective remedy also guarantees the right in appeal proceedings to review of the legal presumption of the safety of a third state to which the refugee is to be returned; however, this right exists only if the objections concerned are sufficiently arguable to justify review by an appellate body (ECtHR, *TI v The United Kingdom*, Reports 2000-III).

[115] See section III.4 above.

CSR, whose content has now acquired customary international law status,[116] prohibits states, as a non-refoulement principle under refugee law, from sending a refugee 'in any manner whatsoever' to a country 'where his life or freedom would be threatened on account of his race, religion, nationality, membership of a particular social group or political opinion'. Whether such a threat exists is determined according to the same standards as whether the existence of persecution is well-founded, ie there need not be irrefutable proof but only evidence of a high probability. This provision can be invoked only by persons who are refugees in the legal sense. Moreover, the protection afforded is not absolute, since CSR, Article 33(2) permits the return of a refugee 'whom there are reasonable grounds for regarding as a danger to the security of the country in which he is, or who, having been convicted by a final judgment of a particularly serious crime, constitutes a danger to the community of that country'. The exception under Article 33(2) CSR is without effect, however, where prohibitions of refoulement under human rights law are applicable, since these provisions take precedence in cases where the Refugee Convention as such would permit refoulement.[117]

Article 33 of the CSR is supplemented in the case of refugees who are lawfully in the territory of a contracting state by Article 32 of the Convention, which guarantees them the same due process rights as those enjoyed by foreigners in general under the human rights treaties[118] and furthermore limits the grounds for expulsion to those of national security and public order.

4. Status rights

Refugees, as foreigners who are often unwelcome in the state of refuge but who must be admitted owing to the prohibition of refoulement and the absence of a welcoming third state, often find themselves in particularly difficult circumstances. This is why the 1951 Convention relating to the Status of Refugees and regional instruments[119] have created a special legal status for refugees. They enjoy specific rights that must be guaranteed by the state of refuge and, as mentioned

---

[116] Explicitly confirmed in the final Declaration of the states parties to the CSR at their fiftieth anniversary meeting, Declaration of States Parties to the 1951 Convention and its 1967 Protocol Relating to the Status of Refugees, 13 December 2001, preambular para 4. See also Elihu Lauterpacht and Daniel Bethlehem, 'The scope and content of the principle of non-refoulement: opinion', in Erika Feller, Volker Türk, and Frances Nicholson (eds), *Refugee Protection in International Law, UNHCR's Global Consultations on International Protection* (Cambridge University Press: Cambridge, 2003), Part 2, 78–177.

[117] See explicitly ECtHR (Grand Chamber), *Chahal v The United Kingdom*, Reports 1996-V, para 80.

[118] See section III.3 above.

[119] For regional instruments with provisions concerning refugee law, see: Convention Governing the Specific Aspects of Refugee Problems in Africa of 10 September 1969; Convention on Territorial Asylum (Caracas) of 28 March 1954; Convention on Diplomatic Asylum (Caracas) of 28 March 1954; Art II-78 of the Treaty establishing a Constitution for Europe (not yet ratified by all EU member states at the time of writing); Arts 61–9 of the European Community Treaty and the various directives of the Council of the European Union relating to asylum (eg directive

above, they benefit from the ability of the UNHCR to intervene on their behalf where these rights, including the right to be protected against refoulement, are violated or where refugee status is denied to them although they fulfil all conditions under the CSR.[120]

The status rights afforded to refugees under the CSR include, for example, the right to protection of property (CSR, Articles 13 and 14), the right of access in principle to wage-earning employment, though subject to certain limitations (CSR, Articles 17–19), the unrestricted right to primary education for refugee children (CSR, Article 22(1)), certain housing and social welfare rights (CSR, Articles 20, 21, 23 and 24), and the right to a travel document (refugee passport, CSR, Article 28).

Refugee status can be withdrawn when the reasons justifying refugee protection have ceased to exist, eg there is a profound change of circumstances in the country of origin that led to the persecution or the person concerned is granted citizenship of the country of refuge or any other third country.[121]

---

on asylum procedures, status directive, admission directive, directive on temporary protection); ACHR, Art 22(7) and (8); ACHPR, Art 12(3).

[120] CSR, Art 35.
[121] For these and other circumstances see the cessation clauses contained in CSR, Art 1(C).

Select Bibliography

A. COMMENTARIES, GENERAL TREATISES

ALFREDSON, GUDMUNDUR AND EIDE, ASBJØRN (eds), *The Universal Declaration of Human Rights, A Common Standard of Achievement* (Brill: The Hague, 1999).

ANKUMAH, EVELYN A, *The African Commission on Human and Peoples' Rights: Practice and Procedures* (Brill: The Hague, 1996).

BADERIN, MASHOOD A AND MCCORQUODALE, ROBERT (eds), *Economic, Social and Cultural Rights in Action* (Oxford University Press: Oxford, 2007).

BAIR, JOHANN, *The International Covenant on Civil and Political Rights and its (First) Optional Protocol: A Short Commentary Based on Views, General Comments and Concluding Observations by the Human Rights Committee* (Peter Lang: Frankfurt am Main, 2005).

BÉLANGER, MICHEL, *Droit international humanitaire* (Gualino Editeur: Paris, 2002).

BERGER, VINCENT, *Jurisprudence de la Cour européenne des droits de l'homme* (10th edn, Paris, 2007).

BOSSUYT, MARC J, *Guide to the 'travaux préparatoires' of the International Covenant on Civil and Political Rights* (Martinus Nijhoff: Dordrecht, 1987).

BOTHE, MICHAEL, PARTSCH, KARL JOSEF, AND SOLF, WALDEMAR A, *New Rules for Victims of Armed Conflicts, Commentary on the Two 1977 Protocols Additional to the Geneva Conventions of 1949* (Martinus Nijhoff: The Hague etc, 1982).

BOUCHET-SAULNIER, FRANÇOISE, *The Practical Guide to Humanitarian Law* (2nd edn, Rowman & Littlefield: Lanham etc, 2007).

BUERGENTHAL, THOMAS AND SHELTON, DINAH, *Protecting Human Rights in the Americas: Cases and Materials* (4th edn, Engel: Kehl, 1995).

——, SHELTON, DINAH AND STEWART, DAVID, *International Human Rights in a Nutshell* (3rd edn, West Publishing Co: St Paul Minnesota, 2002).

CAMERON, IAIN, *An Introduction to the European Convention on Human Rights* (Iustus Förlag: Uppsala, 2002).

CAREY, JOHN, DUNLAP, WILLIAM V, AND PRITCHARD, JOHN R (eds), *International Humanitarian Law: Origins, Challenges, Prospects* (3 vols, Transnational Publishers: Ardsley, 2003).

CARLSON, SCOTT AND GISVOLD, GREGORY, *Practical Guide to the International Covenant on Civil and Political Rights* (Transnational Publishers: Ardsley, 2003).

CASSESE, ANTONIO, *International Criminal Law* (Oxford University Press: Oxford, 2003).

——, GAETA, PAOLA AND JONES, JOHN RWD, *The Rome Statute of the International Criminal Court: A Commentary* (Oxford University Press: Oxford, 2002).

CRAVEN, MATTHEW CR, *The International Covenant on Economic, Social and Cultural Rights—A Perspective on its Development* (Clarendon Press: Oxford, 2002).

DAVID, ERIC, *Principes de droit des conflits armés* (3rd edn, Bruylant, Bruxelles, 2002).

Davidson, Scott, *The Inter-American Human Rights System* (Dartmouth: Aldershot, 1997).

Detter, Ingrid, *The Law of War* (2nd edn, Cambridge University Press: Cambridge, 2000).

Dijk, Pieter van, Hoof, Fried van, Rijn Arjen, van, and Zwaak Leo (eds), *Theory and Practice of the European Convention on Human Rights* (4th edn, Intersentia: Antwerp/Oxford, 2006).

Dutertre, Gille, *Key Case-Law-Extracts, European Court of Human Rights* (Council of Europe: Strasbourg, 2004).

Ehlers, Dirk (ed), *European Fundamental Rights and Freedoms* (Rechtswissenschaften de Gruyter: Berlin, 2007).

Eide, Asbjørn (ed), *The Universal Declaration of Human Rights, A Commentary* (Aschehoug: Oslo, 1992).

——, Krause, Catarina, Rosas, Allan (eds), *Economic, Social and Cultural Rights: A Textbook* (2nd edn, Brill : Dordrecht etc, 2001).

Ergec, Rusen, *Protection européenne et internationale des droits de l'homme* (La Documentation française: Brussels, 2004).

Evans, Malcolm and Murray, Rachel (eds), *Documents of the African Commission on Human and Peoples' Rights 1999–2005* (Hart: Oxford, 2008).

——, *The African Charter on Human and Peoples' Rights: The system in practice 1986–2006* (2nd edn, Cambridge University Press: Cambridge, 2008).

Fleck, Dieter (ed), *The Handbook of Humanitarian Law in Armed Conflicts* (2nd edn, Oxford University Press: Oxford, 2008).

Frowein, Jochen A and Peukert, Wolfgang, *Europäische Menschenrechtskonvention, Kommentar* (2nd edn, Engel: Kehl, 1996).

Gasser, Hans-Peter, *Humanitäres Völkerrecht—Eine Einführung* (Schulthess Juristische Medien: Zurich etc, 2007).

——, 'International Humanitarian Law' in Hans Haug (ed), *Humanity for All, The International Red Cross and Red Crescent Movement* (Henry Dunant Institute: Berne etc, 1993).

Golsong, Heribert, Karl, Wolfram, Miehsler, Herbert et al, *Internationaler Kommentar zur Europäischen Menschenrechtskonvention* (Carl Heymanns Verlag: Köln, 1994).

Gomien, Donna, *Short Guide to the European Convention on Human Rights* (3rd edn, Council of Europe: Strasbourg, 2005).

——, Harris, David and Zwaak Leo, *Law and Practice of the European Convention on Human Rights and the European Social Charter* (Council of Europe: Strasbourg, 1996).

Grabenwarter, Christoph, *Europäische Menschenrechtskonvention* (3rd edn, C. H. Beck, Munich etc, 2007).

Green, Leslie C, *The Contemporary Law of Armed Conflict* (2nd edn, Manchester University Press: Manchester, 2000).

Greer, Steven, *The European Convention on Human Rights—Achievements, Problems and Prospects* (Cambridge University Press: Cambridge, 2006).

Hannum, Hurst (ed), *Guide to International Human Rights Practice* (4th edn, University of Pennsylvania Press: Ardsley, 2004).

Hanski, Raija and Scheinin, Martin, *Leading Cases of the Human Rights Committee* (Åbo Akademi University: Turku, 2003).

HARRIS, DAVID J AND LIVINGSTONE, STEPHEN (eds), *The Inter-American Human Rights System of Human Rights* (Clarendon Press: Oxford, 1998).

——, O'BOYLE, MICHAEL AND WARBRICK, CHRIS, *Law of the European Convention on Human Rights* (Oxford University Press: Oxford, 1995).

—— AND JOSEPH, SARAH (eds), *The International Covenant on Civil and Political Rights and United Kingdom Law* (Clarendon Press: Oxford, 1995).

HENCKAERTS, JEAN-MARIE AND DOSWALD-BECK, LOUISE, *Customary International Humanitarian Law* (3 vols, Cambridge University Press: Cambridge, 2005).

HEYNS, CHRISTOF (ed), *Human Rights Law in Africa*, vol I: International Human Rights Law in Africa, The United Nations and Human Rights in Africa (Brill: Leiden etc, 2004).

JANIS, MARK W, KAY, RICHARD S, AND BRADLEY, ANTHONY, *European Human Rights Law: Text and Materials* (3rd edn, Oxford, 2008).

JOSEPH, SARAH, SCHULTZ, JENNY, AND CASTAN, MELISSA, *The International Covenant on Civil and Political Rights* (2nd edn, Oxford University Press: Oxford, 2004).

KARLSHOVEN, FRITS AND ZEGVELD, LIESBETH, *Constraints on the Waging of War: An Introduction to International Humanitarian Law* (3rd edn, International Committee of the Red Cross: Geneva, 2003).

KOENIG, MATTHIAS, *Menschenrechte* (Campus Verlag: Frankfurt am Main, 2005).

KOLB, ROBERT, *Ius in bello, Le droit international des conflits armés* (Bruylant: Basel etc, 2003).

LANFORD, MALCOLM (ed), *Social Rights Jurisprudence* (Cambridge University Press: Cambridge, 2009).

LEACH, PHILIP, BRATZA, NICOLAS, AND WADHAM, JOHN, *Taking a Case to the European Court of Human Rights* (2nd edn, Oxford University Press: Oxford, 2005).

LECKIE, SCOTT AND GALLAGHER, ANNE (eds), *Economic, Social, And Cultural Rights: A Legal Resource Guide* (University of Pennsylvania Press: Pennsylvania, 2006).

MACDONALD, RONALD, MATSCHER, FRANZ, AND PETZOLD, HERBERT (eds), *The European System for the Protection of Human Rights* (Kluwer Law: Dordrecht etc, 1993).

MARKS, SUSAN AND CLAPHAM, ANDREW, *International Human Rights Lexicon* (Oxford University Press: Oxford, 2005).

McGOLDRICK, DOMINIC, *The Human Rights Committee: Its Role in the Development of the International Covenant on Civil and Political Rights* (Clarendon Press: Oxford, 1994).

MERRILLS, JOHN G AND ROBERTSON, ARTHUR H, *Human Rights in Europe, A Study of the European Convention on Human Rights* (4th edn, Manchester University Press: Manchester, 2001).

MEYER-LADEWIG, JENS, *Europäische Menschenrechtskonvention: Handkommentar* (2nd edn, Baden-Baden, 2006).

MOWBRAY, ALASTAIR, *Cases and Materials on the European Convention of Human Rights* (2nd edn, Oxford University Press: Oxford, 2007).

MUGWANYA, GEORGE WILLIAM, *Human Rights in Africa, Enhancing Human Rights through the African Regional Human Rights System* (Transnational Publishers: Ardsley, 2003).

NMEHIELLE, VINCENT O, *The African Human Rights System, Its Laws, Practice and Institutions* (Brill: The Hague, 2001).

NOWAK, MANFRED, *Introduction to the International Human Rights Regime* (Martinus Nijhoff: Leiden/Boston, 2003).

——, *UN Covenant on Civil and Political Rights, CCPR Commentary* (2nd edn, Engel: Kehl, 2005).

O'FLAHERTY, MICHAEL, *Human Rights and the UN: Practice Before the Treaty Bodies* (2nd edn, Brill: The Hague, 2002).

OUGUERGOUZ, FATSAH, *The African Charter of Human and Peoples' Rights, A Comprehensive Agenda for Human Dignity and Sustainable Democracy in Africa* (Martinus Nijhoff: Leiden etc, 2003).

OVEY, CLARE AND WHITE, ROBIN, *Jacobs & White: European Convention on Human Rights* (4th edn, Oxford University Press: Oxford, 2002).

PALMER, ELLIE, *Judicial Review, Socio-Economic Rights and the Human Rights Act* (Hart: Oxford/Portland, 2007).

PASQUALUCCI, JO M, *The Practice and Procedure of the Inter-American Court of Human Rights* (Cambridge University Press: Cambridge, 2003).

PETTITI, LOUIS-EDMOND, DECAUX, EMMANUEL, AND IMBERT, HENRI (eds), *La Convention européenne des droits de l'homme, commentaire article par article* (2nd edn, Economica: Paris, 1999).

PICTET, JEAN S (ed), *Commentary on the Geneva Conventions of 12 August 1949*: vol I-IV (International Committee of the Red Cross: Geneva, 1952–1959).

PROVOST, RENÉ, *International Human Rights and Humanitarian Law* (Cambridge University Press: Cambridge, 2003).

REID, KAREN, *A Practitioner's Guide to the European Convention on Human Rights* (3rd edn, Sweet & Maxwell: London, 2007).

RONZITTI, NATALINO, *Diritto internazionale dei conflitti armati* (3rd edn, Giappichelli: Torino, 2006).

SAMUEL, LENIA, *Fundamental Social Rights, Case Law of the European Social Charter* (2nd edn, Council of Europe: Strasbourg, 2002).

SANDOZ, YVES, SWINARSKI, CHRISTOPHE, AND ZIMMERMANN, BRUNO (eds), *Commentary on the Additional Protocols of 8 June 1977 to the Geneva Conventions of 12 August 1949* (International Committee of the Red Cross: Geneva, 1987).

SASSÒLI, MARCO AND BOUVIER, ANTOINE A, *How Does Law Protect in War?: Cases, Documents and Teaching Materials on Contemporary Practice in International Humanitarian Law* (2nd edn, International Committee of the Red Cross: Geneva, 2006).

SCHILLING, THEODOR, *Internationaler Menschenrechtsschutz, Universelles und Europäisches Recht* (Mohr Siebeck: Tübingen, 2004).

SHELTON, DINAH, *Regional Protection of Human Rights* (Oxford University Press: Oxford, 2008).

STEINER, HENRY J, ALSTON, PHILIP, AND GOODMAN, RYAN, *International Human Rights in Context: Law, Politics, Morals* (3rd edn, Oxford University Press Oxford, 2008).

SUDRE, FRÉDÉRIC, *Droit européen et international des droits de l'homme* (8th edn, Presses Universitaires de France : Paris, 2006).

SYMONIDES, JANUSZ (ed), *Human Rights: International Protection, Monitoring, Enforcement* (Ashgate: Aldershot, 2003).

—— AND VOLODIN, VLADIMIR (eds), *A Guide to Human Rights Institutions, Standards, Procedures* (UNESCO: Aldershot, 2003).

TOMUSCHAT, CHRISTIAN, *Human Rights between Idealism and Realism* (2nd edn, Oxford University Press: Oxford, 2008).

Umozurike, Oji, *The African Charter on Human and Peoples' Rights* (Brill: The Hague etc, 1997).

Young, Kirsten A, *The Law and Process of the U.N. Human Rights Committee* (Transnational Publishers: Ardsley, 2002).

B. PART I: THE FOUNDATIONS OF INTERNATIONAL
HUMAN RIGHTS LAW (CHAPTERS 1–5)

Alston, Philip (ed), *Peoples' Rights* (Oxford University Press: Oxford, 2001).

——, *Non-State Actors and Human Rights* (Oxford University Press: Oxford, 2005).

An-Na'im Abdullahi A (ed), *Cultural Transformation and Human Rights in Africa* (Zed Books: London, 2002).

—— and Deng Francis (eds), *Human Rights in Africa, Cross Cultural Perspectives* (Brookings Institution Press: Washington DC, 1990).

Baylis, Elena A, 'General Comment 24: Confronting the Problem of Reservations to Human Rights Treaties' (1999) *BJIL* 277 ff.

Becker, Ulrich, 'European Social Charter' (2007) *EPIL*.

Bothe, Michael, 'Die Anwendung der Europäischen Menschenrechtskonvention in bewaffneten Konflikten—eine Überforderung?' (2005) *ZaöRV* 615 ff.

Brems, Eva, *Human Rights: Universality and Diversity* (Martinus Nijhoff: Leiden etc, 2001).

Bugnion, François, 'Law of Geneva and Law of The Hague' (2001) *IRRC* 901 ff.

Burgers, Jan H, 'The Road to San Francisco: The Revival of the Human Rights Idea in the Twentieth Century' (1992) *HRQ* 447 ff.

Cassimatis, Anthony E, 'International Humanitarian Law, International Human Rights Law, and Fragmentation of International Law' (2007) *Int Comp Law Q* 623 ff.

Charlesworth, Hilary, 'Universal Declaration of Human Rights (1948)' (2008) *EPIL*.

Clapham, Andrew, 'Human Rights obligations of non-state actors in conflict situations' (2006) *IRRC* 491 ff.

—— *Human Rights Obligations of Non-State Actors* (Oxford University Press: Oxford, 2006).

Coomans, Fons and Hoof, Fried van (eds), 'The Right to Complain about Economic, Social and Cultural Rights', *SIM Special No 18* (Netherlands Institute of Human Rights: Utrecht, 1995).

—— and Kamminga, Menno (eds), *Extraterritorial Application of Human Rights Treaties* (Intersentia: Antwerp etc, 2004).

Craven, Matthew, 'Legal Differentiation and the Concept of the Human Rights Treaty in International Law' (2000) *EJIL* 489 ff.

Dijk, Pieter van, ' "Positive Obligations" Implied in the European Convention on Human Rights: Are the States Still the "Masters" of the Convention', in Monique Castermans-Holleman, Fried van Hoof, and Jaqueline Smith (eds), *The Role of the Nation-State in the 21st Century—Human Rights, International Organisations and Foreign Policy, Essays in Honour of Peter Baehr* (Brill: The Hague etc, 1998), 17 ff.

EMBERLAND, MARIUS, *Companies before the European Court of Human Rights, Exploring the Structure of ECHR Protection* (Oxford University Press: Oxford, 2006).

FASSBENDER, BARDO, 'Targeted Sanctions Imposed by the UN Security Council and Due Process Rights', in (2006) *International Organizations Law Review* 437 ff.

FERIA, TINTA MÓNICA, 'Justiciability of Economic, Social, and Cultural Rights in the Inter-American System of Protection of Human Rights: Beyond Traditional Paradigms and Notions' (2007) *HRQ* 431 ff.

FRANK, THOMAS J, 'Is Personal Freedom a Western Value?' (1997) *AJIL* 593 ff.

FREEMAN, MICHAEL, 'Human Rights and Real Cultures: Towards a Dialogue on Asian Values' (1998) *NQHR* 25 ff.

—— 'The Problem of Secularism in Human Rights Theory' (2004) *HRQ* 375 ff.

GÖLLER, THOMAS (ed), *Philosophie der Menschenrechte: Methodologie, Geschichte, kultureller Kontext* (Cuvillier: Göttingen, 1999), 150 ff.

GOODHART, MICHAEL, 'Origins and Universality in the Human Rights Debates: Cultural Essentialism and the Challenge of Globalization' (2003) *HRQ* 935 ff.

GOODMAN, RYAN, 'Human Rights Treaties, Invalid Reservations, and State Consent' (2002) *AJIL* 531 ff.

GROSS, AEYAL M, 'Human Proportions: Are Human Rights the Emperor's New Clothes of the International Law of Occupation?' (2007) *EJIL* 1 ff.

HARATSCH, ANDREAS, *Die Geschichte der Menschenrechte* (Universitätsverlag Potsdam: Potsdam, 2002).

HASTRUP, KIRSTEN, *Human Rights on Common Grounds, The Quest for Universality* (Brill: Leiden etc, 2001).

IBHAWOH, BONNY, 'Cultural Relativism and Human Rights: Reconsidering the Africanist Discourse' (2001) *NQHR* 43 ff.

INTERNATIONAL COUNCIL ON HUMAN RIGHTS POLICY, *Beyond Voluntarism, Human Rights and the Developing International Legal Obligations of Companies* (International Council on Human Rights Policy: Versoix, 2002).

KÄLIN, WALTER, 'Menschenrechtsverträge als Gewährleistung einer objektiven Ordnung', (1994) 33 *Berichte der Deutschen Gesellschaft für Völkerrecht*, 9 ff.

KLEIN, ECKHART (ed), *The Duty to Protect and to Ensure Human Rights* (Berlin, 2000).

KNOX, JOHN H, 'Horizontal Human Rights Law' (2008) *AJIL* 1 ff.

KOJI, TERAYA, 'Emerging Hierarchy in International Human Rights and Beyond: From the Perspective of Non-derogable Rights' (2001) *EJIL* 917 ff.

KOLB, ROBERT, 'Human Rights and Humanitarian Law' (2006) *EPIL*.

KORKELIA, KONSTANTIN, 'New Challenges to the Regime of Reservations under the International Covenant on Civil and Political Rights' (2002) *EJIL* 437 ff.

KRETZMER, DAVID, 'Emergency, State of' (2008) *EPIL*.

KÜNZLI, JÖRG, *Zwischen Rigidität und Flexibilität—Der Verpflichtungsgrad internationaler Menschenrechte* (Duncker & Humblot: Berlin, 2001).

LEINO, PÄIVI, 'A European Approach to Human Rights?, Universality Explored' (2002) *Nordic Journal of International Law* 455 ff.

LORENZ, DIRK, *Der territoriale Anwendungsbereich der Grund- und Menschenrechte* (Berliner Wissenschafts-Verlag: Berlin, 2005).

MARKS, STEPHEN P, 'From the "Single Confused Act" to the "Decalogue for Six Billion Persons": The Roots of the Universal Declaration on Human Rights in the French Revolution, (1998) *HRQ* 459 ff.

MÉGRET, FRÉDÉRIC AND HOFFMANN, FLORIAN, 'The UN as a Human Rights Violator? Some Reflections on the United Nations Changing Human Rights Responsibilities' (2003) *HRQ* 314 ff.

MERON, THEODOR, *Human Rights and Humanitarian Norms as Customary Law* (Clarendon Press: Oxford, 1989).

—— *The Humanization of International Law* (Brill: Leiden 2006).

MORSINK, JOHANNES, *The Universal Declaration of Human Rights, Origins, Drafting and Intent* (University of Pennsylvania Press: Philadelphia, 1999).

NEUMAN, GERALD L, 'American Convention on Human Rights (1969)' (2007) *EPIL*.

NORMAND, ROGER AND ZAIDI, SARAH, *Human Rights at the UN: The Political History of Universal Justice* (Indiana University Press: Bloomington, 2007).

NOWAK, MANFRED, 'Limitations on Human Rights in a Democratic Society', *All-European Human Rights Yearbook* 1992, 111 ff.

ORAA, JAIME, *Human Rights in States of Emergencies in Public International Law* (Oxford, 1992).

ORAKHELASHVILI, ALEXANDER, 'Restrictive Interpretation of Human Rights Treaties in the Recent Jurisprudence of the European Court of Human Rights' (2003) *EJIL* 529 ff.

—— 'The Interaction between Human Rights and Humanitarian Law: Fragmentation, Conflict, Parallelism' (2008) *EJIL* 125 ff.

OUGUERGOUZ, FATSAH, 'African Charter on Human and Peoples' Rights (1981)' (2007) *EPIL* (2007).

SAJO, ANDRÀS (ed), *Human Rights with Modesty: The Problem of Universalism* (Brill: Leiden etc, 2004).

SCHNEIDER, JAKOB, *Die Justiziabilität wirtschaftlicher, sozialer und kultureller Menschenrechte* (Deutsches Institut für Menschenrechte: Berlin, 2004).

SEPULVEDA, MAGDALENA, *The Nature of the Obligations under the International Covenant on Economic, Social and Cultural Rights* (Intersentia: Antwerp, 2003).

SIMMA, BRUNO AND ALSTON, PHILIP 'The Sources of Human Rights Law: Custom, Jus Cogens and General Principles', *Australian Year Book of International Law 1992*, 82 ff.

SVENSSON-MCCARTHY, ANNA-LENA, *The International Law of Human Rights and States of Exception* (Brill: The Hague etc, 1998).

TALBOTT, WILLIAM J, *Which Rights Should be Universal?* (Oxford University Press: Oxford, 2005).

TILLEY, JOHN J, 'Moral Arguments for Cultural Relativism' (1999) *NQHR* 31 ff.

TOMUSCHAT, CHRISTIAN, 'International Covenant on Civil and Political Rights (1966)' (2007) *EPIL*.

TONDINI, MATTEO, 'UN peace operations: the last frontier of the extraterritorial application of human rights' (2005) *Studia diplomatica* 75 ff.

WIESBROCK, KATJA, *Internationaler Schutz der Menschenrechte vor Verletzungen Privater* (Berliner Wissenschafts-Verlag: Berlin, 1999).

WILDHABER, LUZIUS, 'The European Convention on Human Rights and International Law' (2007) *Int Comp Law Q* 217 ff.

ZIEMELE, INETA (ed), *Reservations to Human Rights and the Vienna Convention Regime: Conflict, Harmony and Reconciliation* (Martinus Nijhoff: Leiden etc, 2004).

C. PART II: IMPLEMENTATION OF HUMAN RIGHTS (CHAPTERS 6–8)

ABRAHAM, MEGHNA, 'Building the New Human Rights Council—Outcome and analysis of the institution-building year', Friedrich Ebert Stiftung, *Occasional Papers* No 33, August 2007.

ALSTON PHILIP, *The United Nations and Human Rights—A Critical Appraisal* (Clarendon Press: Oxford, 1992).

—— AND CRAWFORD, JAMES (eds), *The Future of UN Human Rights Treaty Monitoring* (Cambridge University Press: Cambridge, 2000).

——, FOSTER, JASON MORGAN, AND ABRESCH, WILLIAM, 'The Competence of the UN Human Rights Council and its Special Procedures in relation to Armed Conflicts: Extrajudicial Executions in the War on Terror' (2008) *EJIL* 183 ff.

ARAMBULO, KITTY, *Strengthening the Supervision of the International Covenant on Economic, Social and Cultural Rights: Theoretical and Procedural Aspects* (Intersentia: Ardsley, 1999).

BAYEFSKY, ANNE F, *How to Complain to the UN Human Rights Treaty System* (Transnational Publishers: The Hague, 2003).

BOEREFIJN, INEKE, 'Human Rights, United Nations High Commissioner for (UNHCHR)' (2008) *EPIL*.

BOVEN, THEODOR, 'Victims' Rights' (2007) *EPIL*.

BYRON, CHRISTINE, 'A Blurring of the Boundaries: The Application of International Humanitarian Law by Human Rights Bodies' (2007) *Virginia Journal of International Law* 839 ff.

CESARE, ROMANO, NOLLKAEMPER, ANDRÉ, AND KLEFFNER, JANN K (eds), *Internationalized Criminal Courts Sierra Leone, East Timor, Kosovo, and Cambodia* (Oxford University Press: Oxford, 2004).

CHURCHILL, ROBIN R AND KHALIQ, URFAN, 'The Collective Complaints System of the European Social Charter: An Effective Mechanism for Ensuring Compliance with Economic and Social Rights?' (2004) *EJIL* 417 ff.

DENNIS, MICHAEL J AND STEWART, DAVID P, 'Justiciability of Economic, Social, and Cultural Rights: Should There Be an International Complaints Mechanism to Adjudicate the Rights to Food, Water, Housing, and Health?' (2004) *AJIL* 462 ff.

FITZPATRICK, JOAN M, *Human Rights Protection for Refugees, Asylum Seekers and Internally Displaced Peoples: A Guide to International Mechanisms and Procedures* (Transnational Publishers: Ardsley, 2002).

GOY, RAYMOND, *La Cour internationale de justice et les Droits de l'homme* (Bruylant: Bruxelles, 2002).

GROSSMAN, CLAUDIO M, 'Inter-American Commission on Human Rights (IACommHR)' (2007) *EPIL*.

GUTTER, JEROEN, *Thematic procedures of the United Nations Commission on Human Rights and International Law: In Search of a Sense of Community* (Intersentia: Antwerp etc, 2006).

HAECK, YVES, HERRERA, CLARA BURBANO, 'Interim Measures in the Case Law of the European Court of Human Rights' (2003) *NQHR* 625 ff.

HANNUM, HURST, 'Human Rights in Conflict Resolution: The Role of the Office of the High Commissioner for Human Rights in UN Peacekeeping and Peacebuilding' (2006) *HRQ* 1 ff.

KOLB, ROBERT, *Droit humanitaire et opérations de paix internationales: les modalités d'application du droit international humanitaire dans les opérations de maintien ou de rétablissement de la paix auxquelles concourt une organisation internationale (en particulier les Nations Unies)* (2nd edn, Bruylant : Brussels, 2006).

LEMPINEN, MIKO, *The United Nations Commission on Human Rights and the Different Treatment of Governments* (Åbo Akademi University: Turku, 2005).

MÜLLER, LARS (ed), *The First 365 Days of the United Nations Human Rights Council* (Baden, 2007).

MURRAY, RACHEL, 'African Commission on Human and Peoples' Rights (ACommHPR)' (2007) *EPIL*.

NEUMAN, GERALD L, 'Inter-American Court of Human Rights (IACtHR)' (2007) *EPIL*.

NIFOSI, INGRID, *The UN Special Procedures in the Field of Human Rights* (Intersentia: Antwerp, 2005).

RAMCHARAN, BERTRAND G (ed), *Judicial Protection of Economic, Social and Cultural Rights, Cases and Materials* (Martinus Nijhoff: Leiden, 2005).

—— *The Security Council and the Protection of Human Rights* (Brill: The Hague etc, 2002).

—— *The United Nations High Commissioner for Human Rights: The Challenges of International Protection* (Brill: The Hague, 2002).

RIEDEL, EIBE, 'Committee on Economic, Social and Cultural Rights (CESCR)' (2007) *EPIL*.

RODLEY, NIGEL, 'United Nations Human Rights Treaty Bodies and Special Procedures of the Commission on Human Rights—Complementarity or Competition?' (2003) *HRQ* 882 ff.

SHELTON, DINAH, 'Human Rights, Individual Communications/Complaints' (2006) *EPIL*.

—— *Remedies in International Human Rights Law* (2nd edn, Oxford University Press: Oxford, 2006).

SMITH, ANNE, 'The Unique Position of National Human Rights Institutions: A Mixed Blessing' (2006) *HRQ* 904 ff.

TIGROUDJA, HÉLÈNE, *La cour interaméricaine des droits de l'homme* (Bruylant: Bruxelles, 2003).

TOMAŠEVSKI, KATARINA, 'Sanctions and Human Rights', in Janusz Symonides (ed), *Human Rights: International Protection, Monitoring, Enforcement* (Aldershot, 2003), 303 ff.

TOMUSCHAT, CHRISTIAN, 'Human Rights Committee' (2007) *EPIL*.

VANDENHOLE, WOUTER, *The Procedures Before the UN Human Rights Treaty Bodies, Divergence or Convergence?* (Intersentia: Antwerp, 2004).

VILJOEN, FRANS, 'Fact-Finding by UN Human Rights Complaints Bodies—Analysis and Suggested Reform', *Max Planck YUNL* 2004, 49 ff.;

—— AND LOUW LIRETTE, 'State compliance with the recommendations of the African Commission on Human and Peoples' Rights, 1994–2004' (2007) *AJIL* 1 ff.

WISEBERG, LAURIE S, 'The Role of Non-Governmental Organizations (NGOs) in the Protection and Enforcement of Human Rights', in Janusz Symonides (ed), *Human Rights: International Protection, Monitoring, Enforcement* (Ashgate: Aldershot, 2003), 347 ff.

D. PART III: SUBSTANTIVE GUARANTEES
(CHAPTERS 9–17)

ABRESCH, WILIAM, 'A Human Rights Law of Internal Armed Conflict: The European Court of Human Rights in Chechnya' (2005) *EJIL* 767 ff.

ALEINIKOFF, THOMAS A (ed), *Migration and International Legal Norms* (Asser Press: The Hague, 2003).

ALFREDSSON, GUDMUNDUR AND FERRER, ERIKA, *Minority Rights: A Guide to the United Nations Procedures and Institutions* (Minority Rights Group: London etc, 1998).

ALSTON, PHILIP (ed), *Labour Rights as Human Rights* (Oxford University Press, Oxford, 2005).

—— '"Core Labour Standards" and the Transformation of the International Labour Rights Regime' (2004) *EJIL* 457 ff.

AMIRTHALINGAM, KUMARALINGAM, 'Women's Rights, International Norms, and Domestic Violence: Asian Perspectives' (2005) *HRQ* 683 ff.

ANAYA, JAMES S, *Indigenous Peoples in International Law* (2nd edn, Oxford University Press: Oxford etc, 2004).

ANDREU-GUZMÁN, FEDERICO, 'The Draft International Convention on the Protection of All Persons from Forced Disappearance', (2001) 62–63 *International Commission of Jurists Review* 73 ff.

ARAT, ZEHRA F, 'Analyzing Child Labor as a Human Rights Issue: Its Causes, Aggravating Policies and Alternative Proposals' (2002) *HRQ* 177 ff.

ARNARDÓTTIR, ODDNÝ MJÖLL, *Equality and non-discrimination under the European Convention on Human Rights* (Brill: The Hague, 2003).

ASKIN, KELLY AND KOENIG, DOREAN, *Women's Human Rights: A Reference Guide* (Transnational Publishers: Ardsley, 1999).

ASSOCIATION POUR LA PRÉVENTION DE LA TORTURE (APT), *Guide to Jurisprudence on Torture and Ill-treatment, Article 3 of the European Convention for the Protection of Human Rights* (Association for the Prevention of Torture: Geneva, 2002).

BAGSHAW, SIMON, *Developing a Normative Framework for the Protection of Internally Displaced Persons* (Transnational Publishers: Ardsley, 2005).

BAYEFSKY, ANNE F (ed), *Human Rights and Refugees, Internally Displaced Persons and Migrant Workers: Essays in Memory of Joan Fitzpatrick and Arthur Helton* (Brill: Leiden etc, 2006).

—— AND FITZPATRICK JOAN (eds), *Human Rights and Forced Displacement* (Martinus Nijhoff: The Hague, 2000).

BEITER, KLAUS DIETER, *The Protection of the Right to Education by International Law: Including a Systematic Analysis of Article 13 of the International Covenant on Economic, Social, and Cultural Rights* (Brill: Leiden etc, 2006).

BENVENISTI, EYAL, 'Water, Right to, International Protection' (2007) *EPIL*.

BERTRAND, MATHIEU, *Europeans and Their Rights: The Right to Life in European Constitutional and Conventional Case Law* (Council of Europe: Strasbourg, 2006).

BOEREFIJN, INEKE (ed), *Temporary Special Measures, Accelerating De Facto Equality of Women Under Article 4(1) UN Convention on the Elimination of All Forms of Discrimination Against Women* (Intersentia: Antwerp etc, 2003).

BOGUSZ, BARBARA ET AL (eds), *Irregular Migration and Human Rights: Theoretical, European and International Perspectives* (Brill: Leiden etc, 2004).

BORGHI, MARCO AND POSTIGLIONE BLOMMESTEIN, LETIZIA (eds), *The Right to Adequate Food and Access to Justice* (Bruylant-Schulthess: Geneva etc, 2006).

BOYLE, KEVIN (ed), *Freedom of Religion and Belief* (Routledge: London etc, 1997).

BREEN, CLAIRE, 'The Right to Education of Persons with Disabilities' (2003) *NQHR* 7 ff.

BREMS, EVA, *A Commentary on the United Nations Convention on the Rights of the Child : Article 14, The Right to Freedom of Thought, Conscience And Religion* (Brill: Leiden etc, 2005).

BUNCH, CHARLOTTE, 'Women's Rights as Human Rights: Towards a Re-Vision of Human Rights' (1990) *HRQ* 486 ff.

CAFLISCH, LUCIUS, 'Family, Right to, International Protection' (2008) *EPIL*.

CERONE, JOHN, 'Human Trafficking' (2007) *EPIL*.

CHETAIL, VINCENT, *Globalization, Migration and Human Rights: International Law under Review*, vols I and II (Bruylant: Bruxelles, 2007).

CHINKIN, CHRISTINE, 'Women, Rights of, International Protection' (2006) *EPIL*.

CHIRWA, DANWOOD MZIKENGE, 'Reclaiming (Wo)Manity: the Merits and Demerits of the African Protocol on Women's Rights' (2006) *NILR* 63 ff.

CHOLEWINSKI, RYSZARD, 'Migrant Workers' (2007) *EPIL*.

CLAPHAM, ANDREW, *Human Rights in the Private Sphere* (Clarendon Press: Oxford, 1993).

CLAYTON, RICHARD AND TOMLINSON HUGH, *Privacy and Freedom of Expression* (Oxford University Press: Oxford, 2001).

ÇOBAN, ALI RIZA, *Protection of Property within the European Convention on Human Rights* (Ashgate: Aldershot, 2004).

COHEN, CYNTHIA PRICE, *Human Rights of Indigenous People* (Transnational Publishers: Ardsley, 1998).

COHEN, ROBERTA AND DENG, FRANCIS, *Masses in Flight: The Global Crisis of Internal Displacement* (Brookings Institution: Washington DC, 1998).

—— AND DENG FRANCIS, *The Forsaken People: Case Studies of the Internally Displaced* (Brookings Institution Washington DC, 1998).

COHEN-JONATHAN, GÉRARD, 'Le droit de l'homme à la non-discrimination racial' (2001) *RTDH* 625 ff.

COUNCIL OF EUROPE (ed), *Mechanisms for the Implementation of Minority Rights* (Council of Europe: Strasbourg, 2005).

—— *The Right to Organize and to Bargain Collectively: Study Drawn on the Basis of the Case Law of the European Social Charter* (2nd edn, Council of Europe: Strasbourg, 2001).

COURTIS, CHRISTIAN, 'The Right to Food as a Justiciable Right: Challenges and Strategies', *Max Planck YUNL* 2007, 317 ff.

CULLET, PHILIPPE, 'Human Rights and Intellectual Property Protection in the TRIPS Era' (2007) *HRQ* 403 ff.

DE JONG, CORNELIS D, *The Freedom of Thought, Conscience and Religion or Belief in the United Nations (1946–1992)* (Intersentia: Antwerp, 2000).

DERCKX, VEELKE, 'Expulsion of Illegal Residents (aliens) with Medical Problems and Article 3 of the European Convention on Human Rights' (2006) *European Journal of Health Law* 313 ff.

DÖRR, OLIVER, 'Detention, Arbitrary' (2007) *EPIL*.

DOSWALD-BECK, LOUISE, 'The Right to Life in Armed Conflict: Does International Humanitarian Law Provide All Answers?' (2006) *IRRC* 881 ff.

—— AND KOLB, ROBERT, *Judicial Process and Human Rights, United Nations, European, American and African Systems, Texts and Summaries of International Case-Law* (Engel: Kehl etc, 2004).

DOWNES, CHRIS, 'Must the Losers of Free Trade Go Hungry?: Reconciling WTO Obligations and the Right to Food' (2007) *Virginia Journal of International Law* 619 ff.

EIDE, ASBJØRN, *Right to Adequate Food as a Human Right* (United Nations Center for Human Rights: New York, 1989).

ERIKSSON, MAJA K, Family Planning in the Spirit of Human Rights, in Gudmundur Alfredsson and Peter Macalister-Smith (eds), *The Living Law of Nations, Essays on Refugees, Minorities, Indigenous Peoples and the Human Rights of Other Vulnerable Groups* (Engel: Kehl etc, 1996), 367 ff.

—— *Reproductive Freedom in the Context of International Human Rights and Humanitarian Law* (Brill: The Hague, 2000).

—— *The Right to Marry and to Found a Family* (Almqvist & Wiksell: Uppsala, 1990).

EVANS, CAROLYN, *Freedom of Religion under the European Convention of Human Rights* (Oxford University Press: Oxford, 2001).

FELICE, WILLIAM F, 'The UN Committee on the Elimination of All Forms of Racial Discrimination: Race, and Economic and Social Human Rights' (2002) *HRQ* 205 ff.

FELLER, ERIKA, TÜRK, VOLKER AND NICHOLSON, FRANCES (eds), *Refugee Protection in International Law, UNHCR's Global Consultations on International Protection* (Cambridge University Press: Cambridge, 2003).

FILMER-WILSON, EMILIE, 'The Human Rights-Based Approach to Development: The Right to Water' (2005) *NQHR* 213 ff.

FRANCONI, FRANCESCO AND SCHEININ, MARTIN (eds), *Cultural Human Rights* (Martinus Nijhoff: Leiden, 2008).

FRASER, ARVONNE S, 'Becoming Human: The Origins and Development of Women's Human Rights' (1999) *HRQ* 853 ff.

FREDMAN, SANDRA (ed), *Discrimination and Human Rights—The Case of Racism* (Oxford University Press: Oxford, 2001).

FROWEIN, JOCHEN ABR, 'Meinungsfreiheit und Demokratie' (2008) *EuGRZ* 117 ff.

GALLAGHER, ANNE, 'Human Rights and the New UN Protocols on Trafficking and Migrant Smuggling: A Preliminary Analysis' (2001) *HRQ* 975 ff.

GHANEA, NAZILA AND XANTHAKI, ALEXANDRA (eds), *Minorities, Peoples and Self-Determination: Essays in Honour of Patrick Thornberry* (Martinus Nijhoff: Leiden etc, 2005).

GOODWIN-GILL, GUY S, *Free and Fair Elections, International Law and Practice* (2nd edn, Inter-Parliamentary Union: Geneva, 2006).

—— AND MCADAM JANE, *The Refugee in International Law* (3rd edn, Oxford University Press: Oxford, 2007).

GROSSMANN, CLAUDIA M, 'Disappearances' (2008) *EPIL*.

GRUSKIN, SOFIA (ed), *Perspectives on Health and Human Rights* (New York, 2005).

HAMMER, LEONARD M, *The International Human Right to Freedom of Conscience: Some Suggestions for its Development and Application* (Dartmouth: Aldershot, 2001).

HASTRUP, KIRSTEN AND ULRICH, GEORGE, *Discrimination and Toleration* (Brill: Leiden etc, 2002).

HATHAWAY, JAMES, *The Rights of Refugees under International Law* (Cambridge University Press: Cambridge, 2005).

HAUGEN, HANS MORTEN, *The Right to Food and the TRIPS Agreement: With a Particular Emphasis on Developing Countries' Measures for Food Production and Distribution* (Brill: Leiden etc, 2007).

HAYNES, DINA FRANCESCA, 'Used, Abused, Arrested and Deported: Extending Immigration Benefits to Protect the Victims of Trafficking and to Secure Prosecution of Traffickers' (2004) *HRQ* 221 ff.

HENRARD, KRISTIN, 'Charting the Gradual Emergence of a More Robust Level of Minority Protection: Minority Specific Instruments and the European Union' (2004) *NQHR* 559 ff.

—— 'Equality of Individuals' (2008) *EPIL*.

HESTERMEYER, HOLGER P, 'Access to Medication as a Human Right', *Max Planck YUNL* 2004, 101 ff.

—— *Human Rights and the WTO, The Case of Patents and Access to Medicines* (Oxford University Press: Oxford, 2007).

HIGGINS, ROSALYN, 'Extradition, the Right to Life, and the Prohibition against Cruel and Inhuman Punishment and Treatment: Similarities and Differences under the ECHR and the ICCPR in Paul Mahoney et al (eds), *Protecting Human Rights, Studies in Memory of Rolv Ryssdal* (Carl Heymanns: Köln, 2000), 605 ff.

HODGSON, DOUGLAS, *The Human Right to Education* (Dartmouth: Aldershot, 1998).

—— 'Education, Right to, International Protection' (2006) *EPIL*.

HODSON, LOVEDAY, 'Family Values, The Recognition of Same-Sex Relationships in International Law' (2004) *NQHR* 33 ff.

HOFMANN, RAINER, 'Menschenrechte und der Schutz nationaler Minderheiten' (2005) *ZaöRV* 587 ff.

—— 'Minorities, European Protection' (2007) *EPIL*.

HOLDER, CINDY L AND CORNTASSEL, JEFF J, 'Indigenous Peoples and Multicultural Citizenship: Bridging Collective and Individual Rights' (2002) *HRQ* 126 ff.

HUDSON, PATRICK, 'Does the Death Row Phenomenon Violate a Prisoner's Human Rights under International Law?' (2000) *EJIL* 833 ff.

HUNT, PAUL AND MESQUITA, JUDITH, 'Mental Disabilities and the Human Right to the Highest Attainable Standard of Health' (2006) *HRQ* 332 ff.

INGELSE, CHRIS, *The UN Committee against Torture—An Assessment* (Kluwer Law: The Hague etc, 2001).

JIA, BING BING, ' "Protected Property" and its Protection in International Humanitarian Law' (2002) *LJIL* 131 ff.

JOVANOVIC, MIODRAG A, 'Recognizing Minority Identities Through Collective Rights' (2005) *HRQ* 625 ff.

KÄLIN, WALTER, 'Aliens, Expulsion and Deportation' (2007) *EPIL*.

—— 'Assimiliation, Forced' (2007) *EPIL*.

—— 'Flight in Times of War' (2001) *IRRC* 629 ff.

—— 'Guiding Principles on Internal Displacement—Annotations, American Society of International Law', *Studies in Transnational Legal Policy* No 38 (2nd edn, American Society of International Law: Washington DC, 2008).

—— 'Temporary Protection in the EC: Refugee Law, Human Rights and the Temptations of Pragmatism' (2002) *GYIL* 202 ff.

KAUFMANN, CHRISTINE, *Globalization and Labor Rights—The Conflict Between Core Labor Rights and International Economic Law* (Hart: Portland, 2008).

KEARNEY, MICHAEL G, *The Prohibition of Propaganda for War in International Law* (Oxford University Press: Oxford, 2007).

KENTRIDGE, SIDNEY, 'Freedom of Speech, Is it the Primary Right?' (2006) *Int Comp Law Q* 253 ff.

KLEIN, ECKART, 'Movement, Freedom of, International Protection' (2007) *EPIL*.

—— *Meinungsäusserungsfreiheit versus Religions- und Glaubensfreiheit* (Berliner Wissenschafts-Verlag: Berlin, 2007).

KNOP, KAREN (ed), *Gender and human rights* (Oxford University Press: Oxford, 2004).

KRESS, CLAUS, 'The International Court of Justice and the Elements of the Crime of Genocide' (2007) *EJIL* 619 ff.

KRETZMER, DAVID 'Torture, Prohibition of' (2007) *EPIL*.

KRUGMANN, MICHAEL, *Das Recht der Minderheiten. Legitimation und Grenzen des Minderheitenschutzes* (Duncker & Humblot: Berlin, 2004).

LECKIE, SCOTT (ed), *Returning Home: Housing and Property Restitution Rights for Refugees and Displaced Persons* (Transnational: Ardsley, 2003).

LENZERINI, FEDERICO, *Reparations for Indigenous Peoples: International and Comparative Perspectives* (Oxford University Press: Oxford, 2008).

LERNER, NATAN, *Group Rights and Discrimination in International Law* (2nd edn, Brill: The Hague etc, 2003).

LEVINSON, SANFORD (ed), *Torture—A Collection* (Oxford University Press: Oxford, 2004).

LIDDY, JANE, European Convention of Human Rights Case Law on the Right to Education, in Jan de Groof (ed), *The Legal Status of Pupils in Europe* (Kluwer Law: New York, 1998), 131 ff.

LINDHOLM, TORE, DURHAM, COLE W, AND TAHYIB-LIE, BAHIA G (eds), *Facilitating Freedom of Religion or Belief: A Deskbook* (Martinus Nijhoff: Leiden, 2004).

LITTLE, DAVID, 'Religious Human Rights under the United Nations', in Johan D van der Vyver and John Witte jr (eds), *Religious Human Rights in Global Perspective: Legal Perspectives* (Brill: The Hague etc, 1996), 45 ff.

LOUCAIDES, LOUKIS G, 'The Protection of the Right to Property in Occupied Territories' (2004) *Int Com Law Q* 677 ff.

MECHLEM, KERSTIN, 'Food, Right to, International Protection' (2008) *EPIL*.

—— 'Harmonizing Trade in Agriculture and Human Rights: Options for the Integration of the Right to Food into the Agreement on Agriculture', *MaxPlanck YBUNL* 2006, 127 ff.

MELZER, NILS, *Targeted Killing in International Law* (Oxford University Press: Oxford, 2008).

MERON, THEODOR, 'The Meaning and Reach of the International Convention on the Elimination of All Forms of Racial Discrimination' (1985) *AJIL* 283 ff.

MERRY, SALLY ENGLE, 'Rights Talk and the Experience of Law: Implementing Women's Human Rights to Protection from Violence' (2003) *HRQ* 343 ff.

MORGAN, ROD AND EVANS MALCOLM D, *Protecting Prisoners: The Standards of the European Committee for the Prevention of Torture in Context* (Oxford University Press: Oxford, 1999).

NEUWIRTH, JESSICA, 'Inequality Before the Law: Holding States Accountable for Sex Discriminatory Laws Under the Convention on the Elimination of All Forms of Discrimination Against Women and Through the Beijing Platform for Action' (2005) *Harvard Human Rights Journal* 19 ff.

NOVITZ, TONIA, *International and European Protection of the Right to Strike* (Oxford University Press: Oxford, 2003).

NOWAK, MANFRED, 'Challenges to the absolute nature of the prohibition of torture and ill-treatment' (2005) *NQHR* 674 ff.

—— 'The Prohibition of Gender-Specific Discrimination under the International Covenant on Civil and Political Rights', in Wolfgang Benedek, Esther M Kisaakye and Gerd Oberleitner, *Human Rights of Women: International Instruments and African Experiences* (Zed Books: London, 2002).

—— 'What Practices Constitute Torture? US and UN Standards' (2006) *HRQ* 809 ff.

—— AND MCARTHUR, ELIZABETH, *The United Nations Convention Against Torture: A Commentary* (Oxford University Press: Oxford, 2008).

NUSSBERGER, ANGELIKA, 'Work, Right to, International Protection' (2007) *EPIL*.

O'HARE, URSULA A, 'Realizing Human Rights for Women' (1999) *HRQ* 364 ff.

O'KEEFE, ROGER, 'Cultural Life, Right to Participate in, International Protection' (2007) *EPIL*.

—— *The Protection of Cultural Property in Armed Conflict* (Cambridge University Press: Cambridge, 2006).

PAGLIONE, GIULIA, 'Domestic Violence and Housing Rights: a Reinterpretation of the Right to Housing' (2006) *HRQ* 120 ff.

PCOUD, ANTOINE, *Migration and Human Rights Law: The United Nations Convention on Migrant Workers' Right* (Routledge: London etc, 2007).

PEJIC, JELENA, 'The Right to Food in Situations of Armed Conflict: The Legal Framework' (2001) *IRRC* 1097 ff.

PENTASSUGLIA, GAETANO, *Minorities in International Law: An Introductory Study* (Council of Europe: Strasbourg, 2002).

—— 'Minority Issues as a Challenge in the European Court of Human Rights. A Comparison with the Case Law of the United Nations Human Rights Committee' (2004) *GYIL* 401 ff.

PETERSEN, NIELS, 'Elections, Right to Participate in, International Protection' (2007) *EPIL*.

—— 'Liberty, Right to, International Protection' (2008) *EPIL*.

—— 'Life, Right to, International Protection' (2007) *EPIL*.

—— 'The Legal Status of the Human Embryo in vitro: General Human Rights Instruments' (2005) *ZaöRV* 447 ff.

PHUONG, CATHERINE, *The International Protection of Internally Displaced Persons* (Cambridge University Press: Cambridge, 2005).

QUANE, HELEN, 'The Rights of Indigenous Peoples and the Development Process' (2005) *HRQ* 652 ff.

RADACIC, IVANA, 'Gender Equality Jurisprudence of the European Court of Human Rights' (2008) *EJIL* 841 ff.

RAMCHARAN, BERTRAND G (ed), *Judicial Protection of Economic, Social and Cultural Rights, Cases and Materials* (Martinus Nijhoff: Leiden, 2005).

REBOUCHÉ, RACHEL, 'Labor, Land, and Women's Rights in Africa: Challenges for the new Protocol on the Rights of Women' (2006) *Harvard Human Rights Journal* 235 ff.

REHMAN, JAVID, *The Weaknesses in the International Protection of Minority Rights* (Brill: The Hague, 2000).

RIEDEL, EIBE, 'Health, Right to, International Protection' (2007) *EPIL*.

—— AND ROTHEN PETER (eds), *The Human Right to Water* (Berliner WissenschaftsVerlag: Berlin, 2006).

RODLEY, NIGEL S, 'The Definition(s) of Torture in International Law' (2002) *Current Legal Problems* 467 ff.

—— *The Treatment of Prisoners under International Law* (2nd edn, Oxford University Press: Oxford, 1999).

RODRIGUEZ-PINERO, LUIS, *Indigenous Peoples, Postcolonialism, and International Law, The ILO Regime (1919–1989)* (Oxford University Press: Oxford, 2006).

RYNGAERT, CEDRIC, 'Universal criminal justice over torture: a state of affairs after 20 years UN Torture Convention' (2005) *NQHR* 571 ff.

SAMUEL, LENIA, *Fundamental Social Rights—Case Law of the European Social Charter* (2nd edn, Council of Europe: Strasbourg, 2002).

SCHABAS, WILLIAM A, 'Genocide' (2007) *EPIL*.

—— *The Abolition of the Death Penalty in International Law* (3rd edn, Cambridge University Press: Cambridge, 2002).

SCHEININ, MARTIN, 'Security, Right to, International Protection' (2007) *EPIL*.

—— AND TOIVANEN REETA (eds), *Rethinking Non-Discrimination and Minority Rights* (Åbo Akademi University: Turku etc, 2004).

SCHÖPP-SCHILLING, HANNA BEATE AND FLINTERMAN, CEES (eds), *The Circle of Empowerment: Twenty-Five Years of the UN Committee on the Elimination of Discrimination Against Women* (The Feminist Press: New York, 2008).

SCOVAZZI, TULLIO AND CITRONI, GABRIELLA, *The Struggle against Enforced Disappearance and the 2007 United Nations Convention* (Brill: Leiden etc, 2007).

SINGH, KISHORE, 'Right to Education and International Law, UNESCO'S Normative Action' (2004) *Indian Journal of International Law* 488 ff.

SKOGLY, SIGRUN I, 'Right to Adequate Food: National Implementation and Extraterritorial Obligations', *Max Planck YUNL* 2007, 339 ff.

SÖLLNER, SVEN, 'The Breakthrough of the Right to Food: The Meaning of General Comment No. 12 and the Voluntary Guidelines for the Interpretation of the Human Right to Food', *Max Planck YUNL* 2007, 391 ff.

SÖTTIAUX, STEFAN 'The Breakthrough of the Right to Food: The Meaning of General Comment No. 12 and the Voluntary Guidelines for the Interpretation of the Human Right to Food', *Max Planck YUNL* 2007, 391 ff.

SOTTIAUX, STEFAN, 'Anti-Democratic Associations: Content and Consequences in Article 11 Adjudication' (2004) *NQHR* 585 ff.

—— AND DE PRINS, DAJO, 'La Cour européenne des droits de l'homme et les organisations antidémocratiques' (2002) *RTDH* 1008 ff.

SUDRE, FRÉDÉRIC, *Le droit au respect de la vie familiale au sens de la Convention européenne des droits de l'homme* (Bruylant : Bruxelles, 2002).

TAHZIB, BAHIYYIH, *Freedom of Religion or Belief: Ensuring Effective International Legal Protection* (Brill: The Hague, 1996).

TAYLER, WILDER, 'Background to the Elaboration of the Draft International Convention on the Protection of All Persons from Forced Disappearance' (2001) 62–63 *International Commission of Jurists Review* 63 ff.

TAYLOR, PAUL M, *Freedom of Religion—UN and European Human Rights Law and Practice* (Cambridge University Press: Cambridge, 2006).

TEMPERMANN, JEROEN, 'Blasphemy, Defamation of Religions and Human Rights Law' (2008), *NQHR* 517 ff.

THIENEL, TOBIAS, 'The Admissibility of Evidence Obtained by Torture under International Law' (2006) *EJIL* 349 ff.

THORGEIRSDÓTTIR, HERDÍS, 'Journalism Worthy of the Name: An Affirmative Reading of Article 10 of the ECHR' (2004) *NQHR* 601 ff.

THORNBERRY, PATRICK AND ESTEBANEZ, MARÍA AMOR, *Minority Rights in Europe* (Council of Europe: Strasbourg, 2004).

THYM, DANIEL, 'Respect for Private and Family Life Under Article 8 ECHR in Immigration Cases: A Human Right to Regularize Illegal Stay' (2008) *Int Comp Law Q* 87 ff.

TOEBES, BRIGIT, *The Right to Health as a Human Right in International Law* (Intersentia: Antwerp, 1999).

—— 'Towards an Improved Understanding of the International Human Right to Health' (1999) *HRQ* 661 ff.

TRECHSEL, STEFAN AND SUMMERS, SARAH, *Human Rights in Criminal Proceedings* (Oxford University Press: Oxford, 2005).

TULLY, STEPHEN, 'A Human Right to Access to Water? A Critique of General Comment' (2005) 15 *NQHR* 35 ff.

TÜRMEN, RIZA, 'Freedom of Conscience and Religion', in Marcelo G Kohen (ed), *Promoting Justice, Human Rights and Conflict Resolution Through international law: Liber Amicorum Lucius Caflisch* (Martinus Nijhoff: Leiden, 2006), 591 ff.

TWISS, SUMNER B, 'Torture, Justification, and Human Rights: Toward an Absolute Proscription' (2007) *HRQ* 346 ff.

ULFSTEIN, GEIR, 'Indigenous Peoples' Right to Land', *Max Planck YUNL* 2004, 1 ff.

UNITED NATIONS HIGH COMMISSIONER FOR REFUGEES, *Handbook on Procedures and Criteria for Determining Refugee Status under the 1951 Convention and the 1967 Protocol relating to the Status of Refugees* (Geneva, 1992).

VAN BANNING, THEO RG, *The Human Right to Property* (Intersentia: Antwerp, 2002).

VAN BOVEN, THEODOR, 'Racial and Religious Discrimination' (2007) *EPIL*.

VAN LEEUWEN, FLEUR, 'A Woman's Right to Decide?—The United Nations Human Rights Committee, Human Rights of Women, and Matters of Human Reproduction' (2007) *NQHR* 97 ff.

VANDENHOLE, WOUTER, *Non-discrimination and equality in the view of the UN human rights treaty bodies* (Intersentia: Antwerp etc, 2005).

VERHEYDE, MIEKE, *The Right to Education* (Brill: Leiden, 2006).

VICKERS, LUCY, 'The Protection of Freedom of Political Opinion in Employment', *European Human Rights Law Review* 2002, 468 ff.

VON POTOBSKY, GERALDO, 'Freedom of Association, The Impact of Convention No 87 and ILO Action', *International Labour Review* 1998, 195 ff.

VON SCHORLEMER, SABINE (ed), *Die Vereinten Nationen und neuere Entwicklungen der Frauenrechte* (Peter Lang: Frankfurt aM, 2007).

WALTER, CHRISTIAN, 'Religion or Belief, Freedom of, International Protection' (2007) *EPIL* (2007).

WEISSBRODT, DAVID S, 'Immigration' (2008) *EPIL*.

—— 'Slavery' (2007) *EPIL*.

—— *The Human Rights of Non-citizens* (Oxford University Press: Oxford, 2008).

—— *The Right to a Fair Trial under the Declaration of Human Rights and the International Covenant on Civil and Political Rights* (Brill: The Hague, 2001).

—— AND WOLFRUM, RÜDIGER (eds), *The Right to a Fair Trial* (Springer: Berlin, 1998).

—— AND COLLINS, CLAY, 'The Human Rights of Stateless Persons' (2006) *HRQ* 245.

WELLER, MARC, *The Rights of Minorities, A Commentary on the European Framework Convention for the Protection of National Minorities* (Oxford University Press: Oxford, 2005).

—— *Universal Minority Rights, A Commentary on the Jurisprudence of International Courts and Treaty Bodies* (Oxford University Press: Oxford, 2007).

WESTENDORP, INGRID, 'Housing Rights and Related Facilities for Female Refugees and Internally Displaced Women' (2001) *NQHR* 403 ff.

WIENER, MICHAEL, *Das Mandat des UN-Sonderberichterstatters über Religions- und Weltanschauungsfreiheit: Institutionelle, prozedurale und materielle Rechtsfragen* (Peter Lang: Frankfurt aM etc, 2007).

WINTEMUTE, ROBERT, 'Strasbourg to the Rescue? Same-Sex Partners and Parents under the European Convention', in Robert Wintemute and Mads Andenas (eds), *Legal recognition of same-sex partnerships: A study of national, european, and international law* (Hart: Oxford, 2001), 713 ff.

XANTHAKI, ALEXANDRA, *Indigenous Rights and United Nations Standards—Self-Determination, Culture and Land* (Cambridge University Press: Cambridge, 2007).

ZIEGLER, JEAN, *Le droit à l'alimentation* (Mille et Une Nuits : Paris, 2003).

ZILLI, LIVIO, 'Decriminalising Consensual Heterosexual Conduct Outside Marriage: The Women's Case under International Human Rights Law' (2002) *NQHR* 299 ff.

Index